A PLACE OF STONES
&
SKY

Deirdre Purcell was born in Dublin in 1945 and was educated there and in County Mayo. She then joined the Civil Service, moved within six months to the Irish national airline, Aer Lingus, and two years later, as a result of appearances on the amateur stage in Dublin, was invited to join the Abbey Theatre as one of its permanent company of actors.

In 1968 she went to the United States, where she remained for five years. She returned to Dublin where she joined RTE, the Irish state broadcasting service, rising to the position of anchor-person on the station's nine o'clock news.

She began writing in 1983 for the *Irish Press* and then spent seven years with the *Sunday Tribune*, with which she won the two most prestigious awards in Irish journalism – the Benson and Hedges Award and the A.T. Cross Award. Now concentrating on her fiction, she continues her association with the *Sunday Tribune*.

Deirdre Purcell lives in Dublin and has two sons.

DEIRDRE PURCELL

A PLACE OF
STONES
&
SKY

PAN BOOKS

A Place of Stones first published 1991 by Macmillan London Ltd
and first published by Pan Books 1992
Sky first published 1995 by Town House & Country House in association with
Macmillan, first published in paperback 1996 by Town House & Country House,
first published in Great Britain 1996 by Macmillan,
first published by Pan Books 1997

This omnibus edition published 2002 by Pan Books
an imprint of Pan Macmillan Ltd
Pan Macmillan, 20 New Wharf Road, London N1 9RR
Basingstoke and Oxford
Associated companies throughout the world
www.panmacmillan.com

ISBN 0 330 41823 8

A PLACE OF STONES

For my mother, Maureen

ACKNOWLEDGEMENTS

The poem 'Tarantella' by Hilaire Belloc is reprinted by permission of the Peters Fraser and Dunlop Group Ltd.

I should like to thank Dr Aidan Nulty, Joe Lennon and Harry Sydner for their meteorological and aviation advice; Pat Brennan and Frank Byrne for reading the manuscript; Michael Legat and Jane Wood for their editorial skills, Vincent Browne and the *Sunday Tribune* for their understanding and encouragement.

I thank my agents, Treasa Coady and Charles Pick, for pushing me into doing this in the first place and the Tyrone Guthrie Centre, Annaghmakerrig, for giving me a room with a view.

Last but most, I should like to thank my family and friends, particularly Kevin, Adrian and Simon, for putting up with me while I wrote.

PART ONE

CHAPTER ONE

The DC3 was loading up. Through the dirty window of the operations room at Midway, her captain, 'Tucker' Thompson, studied her as her newly washed frame and cowlings of her Pratt and Whitney 1830 engines glinted under the metallic Chicago sun. Although it was still early the air in the room was heavy, acrid with the smell of kerosene. The elderly electric fan placed on a filing cabinet gave little relief, barely elevating the red and blue plastic streamers attached to its bent frame; the fan's orbiting hinge needed oiling and its rhythmic creaking was getting on Tucker's nerves. Even the clicking of the teleprinters was bothering him this morning.

Pulling at his shirt collar where it cut into dewlaps of flesh, Tucker watched the relaxed activity on the tarmac around the plane as she was fuelled and provisioned for the long flight ahead. In her captain's sour view, the modifications had turned this good workhorse of a plane into the equivalent of a flying couch. Yet despite the extra tanks fitted behind a false bulkhead when she was modified after the war the DC3's limited range meant they had to make the journey in a series of hops, from Midway to Bangor, Maine, to Goose Bay, to Prince Christian in Greenland, to Reykjavik, to Shannon and then to London. Well, at least the forecast was favourable, he thought gloomily – tailwinds. At a steady 150 knots the trip should not be too demanding.

He looked again at the manifest and it did not improve his mood. These Smiths, like all rich people, toted a huge amount of luggage. Three trunks and seven suitcases, weighing a total of nearly 1200 pounds. All for three adults and a baby! thought Tucker, swatting irritably at a fly which buzzed the streaked window-pane.

Tucker, an ex-ferry pilot, one of the brave, somewhat reckless breed who flew war supplies to Europe on the dangerous transatlantic run, had never married. He was squat and built somewhat like a miniature bison, with a powerful neck supporting a shaggy, jowled head. His face was creased and leathered and he viewed the world through hooded, cynical eyes of faded brown. All through the war, Tucker had made plans for afterwards – his own airline maybe, or even Chief Pilot in someone else's airline. But here it was, 1953, and he was still jobbing at charter work. He sighed and turned his attention towards the briefing table where the dark head of his co-pilot for the trip was bent over the documents. Tucker sighed a second time: the Second Officer had no such worries. He was apple-cheeked, a child . . .

The boy looked up and smiled as his superior joined him at the briefing table but Tucker did not smile back. By long tradition, captains kept their distance from co-pilots and chumminess, at least in front of operations and met. men, was not on.

'Heard anything about these Smiths?' Tucker asked.

''Fraid not, Captain!' The co-pilot's voice was light and eager. 'All I know is that they're in brewing. You know – Smith's Oaken? Smith's Arrow?'

Tucker recognized the brands. They were from a brewery which prided itself on independence and quality of product but he merely grunted and took the clutch of forecast telexes from the meteorologist, who was picking his nails on the other side of the briefing table. He studied the telexes and TAFs – Terminal Area Forecasts – for London and for each stop *en route*. CAVOK everywhere: ceiling and visibility OK. The telexes also showed that along this route they could expect overcast conditions between 020 and 100, between 2000 and 10,000 feet. Since Tucker had planned a cruising altitude of 10,000 that posed no problems.

He lowered his head over the charts with their swirling lines and little triangular symbols denoting warm and cold fronts. There was an anticyclone marked in, about 1000 miles southwest of Ireland and a long cold front was drawn a couple of degrees south of the polar regions, its leading edge shown to be crossing Spitzbergen in the Arctic Ocean. It was moving

12

southwestwards, according to the direction of its wind arrows. Along its length the met. man had cross-hatched a long, scalloped ovoid, around the abbreviations ISOL CB and MOD ICE. The danger of icing was forecast to be 'moderate' and they should encounter only isolated cumulo-nimbus clouds.

Still picking his nails, the meteorologist watched Tucker pay particular attention to the cold front and answered the question before it was asked. 'Slow-moving,' he drawled. 'No problem. Not expected to reach your latitudes until at least this time tomorrow.'

In the wooded suburb of Evanston, north of the city, the Cadillac was already pulled up outside the pillared entrance of Greentrees, the mansion owned by the Smith family. A small pantechnicon was backed up against the front steps, the driver of which, assisted by the Cadillac's chauffeur, was loading into its maw the last of three heavy trunks. Finally the doors were closed and the van sped off, spraying gravel as it turned out through the ornate iron gateway into the cobbled street outside.

Inside the house, Malcolm Smith had almost finished his breakfast. On this warm day, the french windows to the lawn stood open and the morning room was flooded with light reflected from the mirror of Lake Michigan. Malcolm always breakfasted alone and the servants knew not to come near him.

He gazed at the expanse of bright water, which this morning glittered and danced as far as the eye could see. Today, he thought, was going to be a hot one.

'Yes, a hot one!' he said aloud.

When sitting in his chair, a worn museum piece with sheltering wings, Malcolm frequently voiced the tail-ends of his thoughts or finished imaginary conversations. At first when it began to happen and he heard his own voice drop into the morning stillness, he would start in the chair and look round, afraid that someone else might have heard. But that was years ago.

Malcolm was a quiet man on whom the years lay well. An immigrant from Wales who remained grateful to his Maker for

13

the good fortune bestowed on him, he cultivated orderliness in all things – in his household, his brewery and his person. His wife Cordelia was fond of saying that in the unlikely event of a Chicago earthquake Malcolm would be surprised all right but his routine would survive.

On this particular Saturday at the end of April Malcolm had risen as usual at 6.45, but today he had not been the first and already he could hear the sounds of others moving around in the house. As he had padded down the back staircase towards the kitchen he had heard movement from the bedrooms occupied by his son Cal and daughter-in-law Maggie. Cal, he saw, had put one of his suitcases outside his door for collection.

Taking a last satisfying swig of his coffee as he finished his breakfast, Malcolm reached into his breast pocket for his cigar and silver cutter but was interrupted by the arrival in the room of his granddaughter and her nanny.

Susanna, a sunny, placid child, chittered with delight and stretched out her arms when she saw him. The pleasure was mutual. She was almost a year old now and from the moment she was born her grandfather had been besotted by her. He hated the fact that she was going to Europe for a month with her parents.

'It's OK, Rosemary.' He addressed the English nanny but had eyes only for the baby. 'I'll take her.'

The nanny, a pale, fair-haired girl in her early twenties, handed over the child and smiled. 'Mind you don't get her dirty, Mr Smith. She's all dressed up for her holidays!'

'Aren't you the little doll!' Malcolm stroked the baby's blonde head and Susanna giggled.

'Oll!' said Susanna – or so it sounded to her grandfather's enchanted ears.

'Did you hear that?' he exclaimed to the nanny. 'Did you *hear* that, Rosemary? She distinctly said "doll!" I heard her! Did you hear her?' He turned to the baby again. 'Doll! Susanna. Say it again, you little charmer. You're a *doll*!'

But this time the baby just giggled.

The nanny grinned. 'I'll go and find Christian to come and say goodbye.' She left the room, soft-footed in her crêpe-soled shoes.

14

Malcolm took Susanna out on to the lawn on which the hissing sprinklers turned, creating rainbows in the sunshine. Susanna wriggled to be put down and her grandfather, who could deny her nothing, stooped and placed her gently upright on wobbly, plump legs. She clung on to his trousers for a second, then the legs gave way and she plonked onto the grass.

'Oooh, no!' Malcolm picked her up again. 'Grass wet! Mommy wouldn't like you to sit on the grass in your lovely new dress.'

The child allowed herself to be picked up again without demur. She patted her grandfather's cheek and smiled coyly at him. Delighted all over again he chuckled back at her. 'Oh, you little doll!'

In her bedroom, which was in disarray, Maggie sat in front of her dressing-table fastening a string of pearls around her neck. Dressed expensively and plainly in a grey dress, she was of the type who looks as good at sixty as thirty, large but not fleshy, with wide shoulders and high cheekbones. Once again, gazing at herself in the mirror, she tried to infuse herself with courage. She must have been mad to agree to this trip. She dreaded it, dreaded the next half-hour when she would have to say goodbye to Christian. She heard her husband moving around in his own room next door. He was whistling. She looked at her watch. No more dithering.

Maggie went along the corridor to Christian's room but the door was open and his bed was empty. She went downstairs, her feet silent on the thick carpeting of the staircase. There was no one in the morning room but the doors were open and from outside there came the faint sound of laughter. Maggie went across to the french windows, her heels clicking on the parquet. She could see her father-in-law about fifty yards away. He had Susanna in his arms and was picking leaves from a shrub, throwing them in the air so that they fell like confetti around the heads of himself and the baby.

She watched, smiling, for a few seconds and then went

through to the kitchen where the housekeeper was tidying up after Malcolm's breakfast. 'Have you seen Christian, Bridie?'

The housekeeper dried her hands on her apron and, rolling her eyes sympathetically to the ceiling, inclined her head in the direction of the larder.

The small room was dim but Maggie did not turn on the light, pausing inside the door to allow her eyes to adjust. She saw him within a few moments, folded into a corner under a wide shelf which held Bridie's supplies of flour, sugar and salt.

'Christian?' she called softly. 'Come on out, honey. Don't you want to say goodbye?'

There was no sound or movement. He was still as a cat.

Maggie did not move towards him but hunkered down where she stood. 'Sweetheart, come out, please. You don't *have* to come out. But please, I want to talk to you, to say goodbye. I'll be very, very sorry to have to go away without saying goodbye . . . ' She saw the light from the kitchen flash where his eye should be. 'Christian?'

'What?' The voice was sullen.

'Will you come outside with me? I have something very important to tell you.'

No answer, no movement.

'You'll like it – I promise you . . . '

Still no answer.

'Have I ever broken a promise to you? I *promise* you, you will like what I have to tell you.'

She held her breath.

'What?' he said again. The voice was still belligerent but there was a flicker of interest.

'I can't tell you in here, it's too dark. You know how I hate the dark!'

There was a pause. Then he scrambled out from under the shelf. 'What is it?'

She stood up but still she didn't approach him although they were only two feet apart. 'Come on into the morning room and I'll tell you there.' She put out her hand to take his but he darted past her, holding his own arm across his body as if fearful of contamination.

16

When they were in the morning room he stood away from her, eyeing her with something approaching hatred. Maggie's heart nearly broke. So young, only ten and so much he could not understand, could not be told. For a second or two she stared out through the doors. Although it was still so early two sailing-boats tacked across the glistening water and between her and them Malcolm and the baby still played on the grass. No, it was not fair to take the baby and leave Christian behind. She had fought but been defeated by Cal who had pointed out, not unreasonably, that while the baby would be no distraction, being cared for by her nanny, a ten-year-old boy certainly would.

She took a deep breath. 'Now listen, honey, I want you to do me a favour . . . '

He did not answer, but stared at her with his large blue eyes.

She plunged on, improvising. 'You know that old pile of wood in the garage that Grandpa wouldn't let Sam throw out? Well, I want you to get that pile of wood . . . ' she paused for effect, 'and I want you to build a kennel out of it . . . '

She could see the struggle in his face.

'A kennel?' he said, looking away. 'What's the point of a kennel when I've no dog?'

'You can have a dog.'

He abandoned his surliness. 'You mean you're going to let me have a *dog*?'

He had been badgering them for a puppy since he was seven years old but Cal had refused to allow it. Maggie had now decided that she was overruling Cal.

'Oh, Mom, can I pick it out myself?'

'Yes, honey, you can,' she said, 'but don't tell Dad just yet. For now it can be our secret. OK?' She made their sign which they used to one another when they had a special secret, an 'O' formed between finger and thumb and held up in front of the face.

Christian ran his fingers through his hair. The cowlick which defeated all ministrations of comb, brush or barber stood even more untidily at the crown of his head.

Maggie walked across to him and hugged him. He had still not

17

capitulated completely, but he allowed himself to be embraced. 'I'll call the puppy Bluey,' he said.

She laughed and hugged him tighter. 'Well, wait until you get him. He might be yellow, or black or even patched or spotty. You never know . . . '

She held him away from her and stroked his unruly hair. 'Will you help me bring down my bags?' she asked, pressing home her advantage.

He nodded and accompanied her up the stairs, taking them two at a time ahead of her. She watched his sturdy little body, athletic like his father's, and had to swallow hard. I will never, ever, leave this child again! she thought fiercely.

When they got back to the entrance hallway, she saw that a small group had gathered around the Cadillac. Malcolm had brought the baby out and she was being handed in to the nanny who was already sitting in the back seat of the automobile. With his height and erect carriage, thought Maggie fondly, her father-in-law might be taken for a distinguished actor.

He heard her approach and turned round. 'Good morning, Maggie.'

She threw her own arms around his neck. 'I'll miss you, Dad!'

He hugged her back. 'I'll miss you too, Maggie. Now you take care of yourself and come back safely to us.'

'I will,' she promised.

Cal came down the steps then, two at a time. Malcolm seemed about to say something, but turned instead to Christian. 'Everything OK, Chris?'

Christian nodded.

'I wonder would you be interested in a sourball?'

Malcolm rooted around in a rustling pocket, handed over a piece of the tart candy and popped a piece into his own mouth. 'I'd better fetch your grandma.'

Cal was sitting in the front seat of the car but Maggie and Christian stood side by side, watching as Malcolm went back up the steps into the house, calling, 'Delia! Delia! They're leaving now!'

Maggie pulled Christian tightly to her side and he did not

resist. When the time came to say goodbye, they hugged each other without saying the words.

Maggie risked a last look as the car turned out of the driveway. Malcolm and Cordelia each had a hand raised in farewell. Maggie's son was standing between his grandmother and grandfather. Even at the distance of fifty yards, his mother could see the erect cowlick and that his small right hand was held up in front of his face, a jaunty round 'O' formed between the index finger and thumb.

'Let me take your coats,' offered the stewardess as the passengers boarded the DC3. She was petite and dark-eyed and beside her Maggie felt like a big bony horse. Cal, she noticed wryly, did not react to the girl's vitality as once he might have. Maybe he's losing his touch, she thought. Or maybe I am!

For once, she decided as she settled into her seat, Cal had been right to insist that they charter an aircraft instead of taking any of the new scheduled services from BOAC or PanAm. The cabin was luxurious, fitted with thick carpet in olive-green; its eight passenger seats, wide, deeply padded and upholstered in velvet of paler green, reclined fully for sleeping; there was a small lounge area in front of the bulkhead, with two ottomans and a coffee table stacked with newspapers and current copies of *Photoplay*, *Look* and *Life*, all held to the surface of the table with specially designed brass clips.

'Would you like a drink before we take off?' Having put the coats away and helped the nanny to organize the baby, the stewardess opened a cabinet in the lounge area fitted with brass racks of bottles, decanters and crystal glasses. Maggie accepted a vermouth and attempted to relax for the first time that morning. Having poured a bourbon for Cal and a sherry for the baby's nanny, the stewardess then went behind the bulkhead into the cockpit.

'How do you feel?' Cal leaned towards his wife, scanning her face for clues, his own face anxious.

'I'm fine, Cal.' She smiled.

'Looking forward to the trip?'

'Ye-es . . . '

He caught the hesitation. 'But what, Maggie?'

'But nothing, Cal.'

The propellers outside the window turned once and roared into life distracting him and, to Maggie's relief, making any further intimate conversation difficult. She lay back in her seat.

The plane roared down the runway and took off slowly. As the ground fell away Maggie strained to look across her husband and out of the window. From this vantage point she saw that the city was surprisingly full of trees and as they headed out towards the lake the parklands became wider, dotted with the little turquoise eyes of swimming pools. She was able to pick out the curve of Sheridan Road where it fringed the northern suburbs, Evanston, Wilmette, Winnetka, Glenview, Highland Park, Lake Forest. Christian was down there, along the lake. She wondered how he was and what he was doing and then suppressed the speculation. She had to be positive. She took another mouthful of her vermouth.

By the time lunch was served in the cabin, an hour after take-off, the passengers had had several drinks and the atmosphere was easy. Maggie and Cal said little to one another but at least, she thought, the tension seemed to have been defused. When she had finished her own lunch, she took the baby from her nanny and while Cal leafed methodically through the newspapers Maggie spoon-fed Susanna from the supplies of baby-food they had brought with them. The baby had taken happily to flying, spending her time crawling along the wide aisles of the aircraft, pulling herself upright on the seats, playing peek-a-boo with the stewardess who was of Italian extraction and easily taken with babies.

When Susanna had finished feeding and been taken away for a change by the nanny, Maggie slept a little. She came awake with the realization that the plane's engine note had changed in frequency. They were making their descent into Bangor. She looked across at Cal. He was staring at her.

*

While his mother and father were stretching their legs in Bangor, Maine, Christian was on his way to Wrigley Field with his grandpa Malcolm. There was a double-header on today between the Cubs and the Cardinals. Christian was not all that interested in baseball but he loved the excitement, the chaos outside the ground before the game began, the wisecracking of the good-humoured crowd who sat in their shirtsleeves or bare-chested under the warm sun, the distortion of the electric organ through the loudspeakers as everyone sang along with 'Let's Go Out To The Ballgame', the little sandstorms on the bases as the players slid home, the inter-team hand-signals, nose-rubbing, cap-pulling, touching of bootlaces, the cries of the vendors with their trays of goodies, the hotdogs in sweet buns, oozing with 'the works' – ketchup and mustard, chopped onion and piccalilli – the sodas with the fizz warmed out.

The Cadillac was easing its way through the jaywalkers and clogged hooting traffic at Sheridan and Irving Park. Only a few hundred yards to go. Christian, jigging up and down impatiently in the back seat, decided that he could trust his grandpa with the secret. He was sure his mom would not mind.

'Grandpa, can you keep a secret?'

Malcolm nodded. 'Of course I can, Chris!'

'Guess what Mom told me I can have when she gets back from Europe.'

'Let's see now.' Malcolm pretended to consider. 'A new bicycle?'

Christian shook his head.

'A pair of rollerskates?'

'No!'

'I've got it – a duck-billed platypus!'

Christian giggled. 'Grandpa, this is *serious*. A serious secret!'

'Oh dear, well, let's see. A zoot suit?'

'*Grandpa!*'

'All right, Chris, I give up!'

Christian leaned over and mouthed the secret into Malcolm's ear.

'Well, well! And does your dad know?' asked Malcolm, who was aware of the running battle about the puppy.

21

'Of *course* he does, Grandpa! Actually, it was all Dad's idea,' Christian invented. 'He really wanted me to have a puppy ages ago, you see, but Mom thought it would bite the baby.' Christian rarely called Susanna by her name. 'And when Dad said to Mom earlier today that I should have a puppy, he was too busy getting everything organized for Europe to tell me himself so it was Mom who had to tell me. You see?' He nodded his head for emphasis. 'You see, Grandpa?'

Malcolm did. He had observed Christian's defence of Cal – and his jealousy of his sister – many times. Luckily the car was pulling up outside Wrigley Field so he did not have to answer. He tapped the glass between the back-seat compartment and the driver. 'Here we are! You can let us off here.' And as they got out, 'There'll be nothing else today. We'll get a cab home after the game.'

'I'm going to`call the puppy Bluey!' said Christian as they went through the gates of the ballpark. 'And he's going to be mine. *She*'s not allowed to touch him.'

Five thousand miles away on the west coast of Ireland Conor Ó Briain, twelve – two years older than Christian – burned with shame.

It was dinner time at St Kevin's School for Boys and in the refectory the pupils were eating boiled beef, cabbage and potatoes. They ate at uncovered deal tables, twenty to each one, in what was supposed to be silence but was in reality a cacophony of tin on delph as the boys wolfed their food from their plates with cheap cutlery. Outside the refectory the stony Connemara landscape was dark with drizzle and the lights had been switched on, five bare bulbs swinging from the mottled ceiling on flexes frayed with age. The bulbs were opaque with the fine mist of steam which rose from the cabbage on each plate – and also from the boys' breath, visible in the damp air. The smell was strong, a mingling of cabbage, damp and the sweetish, unpleasant scent of imperfectly washed adolescent bodies.

The boys ate under the watchful eye of Brother Patrick, a

sandy-haired giant who patrolled slowly between the tables, his leather belt cutting the bulge of his stomach into half moons under his soutane, his hands, as big as half-hams, behind his back. Brother Patrick, it was said, had been a boxer in his youth.

Conor was a scholarship boy from the Aran island of Inisheer off the Galway coast. Because there were no secondary schools on the island, the government paid automatically for all Aran Island children to attend school on the mainland. Although this was well known among the other boys at St Kevin's, it was not unknown for the scholarship boys to be the butt of teasing and Conor hated his status – more so than ever today.

He was not eating with the others but was kneeling on the platform at the top of the long room facing his schoolmates. He was big for his age, loose-jointed with large hands and feet, and his black hair had been cut in the pudding-bowl manner, so that seen from the front it came only half-way down his ears and made his long face seem longer still. But he had extraordinary eyes, fringed with thick, girlish lashes. The eyes were large, deepset but wide open, of a gradated blue. Around the pupil the irises were pale but the blue grew darker towards the outside until the rims were deep grey, almost black. The eyes were wide now, staring but entirely expressionless, fixed somewhere above the heads of the boys. Most of these, out of a sense of collegial decency – or at least the knowledge that tomorrow it could be one of them – kept their own eyes averted. But a few, the bullies and those who gained savage satisfaction from the misfortunes of others, stared openly and, when they were sure they were unobserved by Brother Patrick, elbowed each other in the ribs and sniggered. Among these was Conor's brother Brendan, two years older than Conor, whose seat was quite close to the platform. Brendan nudged the boy next to him, currying favour, anxious to be one of the gang. He was slighter than his younger brother although of the same height. Because of untreated adenoids his mouth hung almost permanently open, giving him a vacant look.

The sequence which led to this humiliation had begun the previous evening. Conor had been eating his tea when the

23

Brother on duty had handed him a letter from home, as usual already open and pre-read. The news from his mother appalled him. His baby sister Molly had pneumonia: a cold caught in the wet depths of February had persisted and now she was critically ill with a high fever. Conor looked across the refectory and saw that Brendan, too, had received a letter but Brendan had just read his as though there were nothing untoward in it. Perhaps there was not. Although Conor's family was small by island standards it was divided. Conor was close to his mother and baby sister while Brendan had, since an early age, aligned himself with their father, Micheál. The brothers, thrown together for companionship while they were younger, had fallen with relief into separate circles as soon as Brendan went away to school and now, except when actually in the cottage together on Inisheer, had little to do with one another. Where Conor was thoughtful Brendan was watchful. Conor was aware that his brother was jealous of him, feeling Conor got favourable treatment from their mother. And if Conor was honest he had to admit there was some basis for his brother's feelings.

After he had read his mother's letter, he had folded it carefully and put it in his pocket, his hands shaking. Saying he was not hungry he had passed the bread off his own plate to that of his neighbour, a bespectacled, fat child named Sean Lyons who was adept at wriggling out of trouble by bringing on one of his asthma attacks. Places at table and in the dormitory were allocated by the Brothers on the first day of school and Sean and Conor had struck up a sort of friendship, in which proximity took a larger role than liking.

At recreation that evening, while some of his class squabbled over the use of the pitted table-tennis table in the recreation hall and others listened to ceilidhe music on the radio, Conor stole away to the chapel which was the only place in the school where, during recreation, a boy was permitted to go without permission. The only other person in the chapel was Brother Jarlath, white-haired and feeble who, long-retired from teaching, spent his days either sitting here at his *prie-dieu*, answering the back door to tradesmen and tinkers or feeding the fowl in the small hen-run beside the stream at the boundary of the school property. The boys liked him.

The chapel was dim and very quiet, lit only by the sanctuary lamp and a single, shaded wall-lamp above Jarlath's *prie-dieu*. The studs gleamed in the fat Easter candle on the altar. A radiator rumbled and there was a rustling behind it, probably made by a mouse.

Conor fixed his eyes on a sliver of the tabernacle which shone through a gap in the white satin curtain covering it but he could not pray. He took the letter out of his pocket and read it again, seeing his mother in the kitchen as she wrote it, the oil lamp turned up to its fullest. In his imagination he saw her crying. The letter rustled and Brother Jarlath looked round, his eyes trying to focus over the tops of his glasses. Conor lowered his head in an attitude of prayerful meditation, stuffing his fingers into the inner corners of his eyes to stem the wetness.

When he had composed himself he stood up, genuflected in the aisle and left the chapel. He got back to the recreation hall just before the bell and filed with the others into the study hall. But while all around him nibs scratched and pages turned, he could not concentrate on his geometry theorems. The lines kept blurring.

Later in bed he could not sleep. Molly would not die. She could not die. God would not allow it. Fiercely, daring God, he tossed himself over on to his stomach and the bedsprings groaned loudly.

'Who's that?' called out Brother Patrick, from his cubicle in the corner.

Conor's heart contracted. 'It's me, Brother.'

'Who's me – the cat?' Some of the boys stifled giggles at the sarcasm.

'It's Conor Ó Briain, Brother.'

'What are you at, Ó Briain?'

'Nothing, Brother.'

'I'll give you nothing! Are you out of your bed?'

'No, Brother.'

'Well, stop disturbing others and go to sleep or you'll taste something you won't forget in a hurry!'

25

Conor lay rigid for a long time but eventually he drifted into sleep.

In the morning when Brother Patrick rang the bell at ten past seven he sprang out of bed – there were fines and penalties for being late for Mass. The cold air hit him around the legs more keenly than usual. On examination he discovered, to his horror, that his pyjamas were wet and so was his bottom sheet. He had wet his bed. It could not have happened on a worse day because on Saturday mornings there was dormitory inspection after breakfast. On any normal day, the boys had to strip and remake their beds before going down to Mass but on Saturdays they left them stripped for airing. Conor ripped off the stained sheet and placed his counterpane on top of it over his chair. He was afraid he would burst into tears like a cry-baby.

At Mass, while the others around him shuffled and coughed, fiddled with their missals or, their heads resting comfortably in their hands, caught forty winks while pretending to be meditating, Conor prayed as he had never prayed before, despairing, desperate adolescent prayers. He assaulted heaven. His eyes bored through the chasubled back of the priest, through the ornate door of the tabernacle and right inside it as though he would force its Occupant to accede. He divided his prayers between his two intentions, each as urgent as the other.

O Jesus, please, please, please, don't let them find out.

Please, Jesus, I promise you that I'll be a priest. I'll help Brendan with his schoolwork. I'll never talk back to my father again . . .

And please, Jesus, help Mam and Molly. Please make Molly well again. Please, Jesus, don't let her die.

But please, Jesus, O Sacred Heart, Immaculate Mother, St Ciarán, please, please, don't let them find out . . .

After Holy Communion, he battered Jesus with wild promises. He had no money to light candles or to make offerings but he promised that for the rest of the term he would keep silence until lunch-time every day. That was allowed, except in class, if you explained that it was for a special intention. And he promised that during the school holidays he would make a visit to the Blessed Sacrament on the island church twice a day . . .

During breakfast, not wanting to draw on himself a scintilla of attention, he spooned up every last trace of the porridge on his plate despite the sick, tight feeling in his stomach. He prayed all the way up to the dormitory afterwards.

But they were all in vain, all the prayers and the promises. Because despite his efforts to hide them Brother Patrick noticed the yellow stains, still damp.

'What's this?' He picked up the sheet with the tips of his spatulate, tobacco-stained fingers, exaggeratedly fastidious. 'What's this, Ó Briain?' He held up the sheet to the weak light from the window of the dormitory. The other boys suspended operations around their own beds and watched, half fascinated, half horror-struck. Conor, mortified, could not speak.

'Take it!' The Brother flung the sheet at Conor, then caught hold of his ear and paraded him, bent double, to the bathroom where he stood over him while Conor held the stained part under a running tap. Then the Brother took the ear again – so hard that Conor yelped – and led him back down the dormitory towards the window, the dripping sheet leaving a trail of water on the varnished floorboards.

'This boy is a bed-wetter,' announced Brother Patrick loudly as they reached the window. 'We'll have to make a man out of this baby, won't we, boys?' Then, when there was no answer, '*Won't we, boys?*' over his shoulder at the round-eyed juniors.

'Yes, Brother,' they answered in ragged chorus, some so frightened that their voices were barely audible.

'Right, boys!' said Brother Patrick. He pushed up the sashed window, indicating to Conor that the sheet should be hung out to dry on the windowsill.

Conor pushed the dripping sheet out through the opening. Too fast. He failed to hold on to a corner of it as he let it out. The wind caught the fabric, filled it like a sail and it went ballooning across the grass in front of the school, flapping and turning, until it sank to rest about a hundred yards into a field snagged against a thorn bush.

Brother Patrick's thick neck reddened with rage. 'Now look what you've done, you stupid, asinine cretin! Stupid, stupid cretin!'

He knuckled Conor hard, right on the poll of the boy's head. Instinctively Conor ducked, raising his arms to protect himself. This enraged the Brother even more and, not pausing to unbuckle his leather strap from where it hung on his belt, with one hand he caught hold of Conor's thick hair and with the other swung at him indiscriminately with the short length of the strap which hung free. Because it was still attached to his belt, he could get no purchase and the strap did little damage but the energy and sound of the assault were terrifying.

One of the other boys began to snivel. Brother Patrick swung around on him. 'And what's wrong with *you*, me bucko? You shut up or you'll get some of the same!' He turned back to the cowering Conor, a handful of whose hair he still grasped, and swiped at him again. Then he let go and straightened up, panting. 'Now, you, go and get that sheet and bring it down to the line in the orchard. You'll pay for this at dinner.'

Conor did not obey at once but stood holding his head where the Brother's hand had been entangled in his hair. His left ear, the target of many of the blows from the strap, glowed crimson.

As he hesitated, the Brother's rage erupted again. *'Did you hear me, you idiotic, oversized sheep? Get out of my sight!'*

Conor fled, his heavy shoes skidding on the wet floor.

Later, at the beginning of dinner and as the boys stood for grace before meals Conor did not take his place but walked in front of Brother Patrick to the platform. He did not look right or left and knelt without being told to do so.

He had now been kneeling for about twenty minutes and his knees were beginning to hurt. But he saw that his ordeal was nearly over. The boys were queuing in order of class seniority at the big serving table near the door where, from stainless steel vats, two prefects were doling out dollops of runny stewed apple and watery custard.

After the meal the boys filed out of the refectory in a decorous double line but as they were released through the door the lines broke up and they thundered along the stone-floored corridor towards the cloakroom where their outdoor boots were stored in rows of numbered cubbyholes. Saturday was a half-day with only the morning spent in classes and after dinner they were all required to play games – Gaelic football or hurling, basketball or handball. Still, Conor did not dare to move until formally released.

When the last boy had left, Brother Patrick walked back up the room. The platform was only two feet high and his eyes were level with Conor's. This time Conor did not flinch. He stared at the Brother's mouth, at the thick lips, noticing that in both corners there were tiny encrustations of yellowish flakelets. Brother Patrick smoked Sweet Afton.

As Conor stared at him without moving, for once Patrick appeared nonplussed. 'Get down off there,' he said gruffly, after a few seconds. 'Go into the kitchen and get your dinner.' He turned and swept towards the door, snapping off all the light switches on a wall panel before disappearing from Conor's view with a swish of his soutane.

Conor stood and rubbed his aching knees. Stiffly he walked down the echoing room and into the adjoining kitchen. Two local girls laboured over the dinner dishes in the sinks full of greasy water. On a draining-board beside one of the sinks was a plate of congealed potatoes and cabbage on which were heaped ragged scraps of greyish meat. He took the plate and brought it out into the empty refectory. He sat in his allocated place at one of the tables but when he began to eat the unappetizing food he found he could not stomach more than a few mouthfuls, even though he had thought himself hungry.

It was during the DC3's fourth stop, at Reykjavik when the trip was more than half-way over, that Tucker Thompson became worried. He could not say why. The aircraft had behaved impeccably throughout the journey so far and although the wind had come up slightly during the hours of darkness, the sky was still clear. Yet some sixth sense warned him to be careful. All good flyers trusted their hunches – all flyers trusted their hunches – and Tucker was well aware that the difference between being successful and unsuccessful as a captain depended not only on skill but on separating hunches from emotions.

While Cal dozed in a chair and Maggie walked up and down in the spartan waiting room soothing the baby made fretful by rude awakening, Tucker stood back a little from the plane on the tarmac looking critically at its silvery outline etched huge against the stars. Was there something he was missing? Like a horse he raised his head and sniffed the cold breeze. He got a torch and prowled around the fuselage, checking rivets on the wings, examining the undercarriage and the radio aerials. He ran the light carefully along each of the propeller blades, moving them slightly, watching for minute fractures or cracks, but they seemed sound. He took a ladder, mounted it, swung the rudder back and forth and peered closely at the ailerons and flaps. He went inside the cabin and checked the fuel tanks behind the false bulkhead. No leaks. No untoward smells.

In the ops room, the weather forecast for their route showed little development from what they had been given at their last stop in Greenland, yet he was still uneasy. He rechecked the telexes. Everything looked fine. So what was this niggle? He concentrated on the large area map. The anticyclone was still stationary about a thousand miles southwest of Ireland. Tucker traced his finger along the length of the cold front, which had moved, but not significantly, since he saw it first at Midway. Its present position now stretched, northwest to southeast, from just south of the thirty-five-miles-long volcanic island of Jan Mayen in the Arctic Ocean, southwestwards into the centre of Norway.

'Are you absolutely sure about the speed of this thing?' he asked the duty meteorological officer. 'Any chance of a push from polar air?'

Not often, but frequently enough to give cause for worry, a sudden influx of freezing gales from inside the Arctic Circle collided with the rear of a cold front causing it to accelerate rapidly and – because of the relatively warm and humid air the front was pushing ahead of it – churning it up internally.

The met. man shook his head. 'Not so far as we know,' he said, 'although, as you know, we can't be a hundred per cent certain . . . ' He suppressed a sigh. As this captain well knew there was always a paucity of hard information from the polar regions. What more did the fellow want?

Tucker weighed up the possibilities. Many of the problems faced by pilots over the Atlantic where they were out of contact with Air Traffic Control involved icing of the engine, airframe or propellors. Because of this ever-present danger the leading edges of the wing and tail sections of the DC3 – the most vulnerable part of the airframe – were covered with rubber boots. If the pilot suspected icing he could, by means of a timer-controlled pump, force a large volume of air into these boots through a valve; when they swelled, the accretions of ice broke off harmlessly. Tucker had paid particular attention to these boots during his visual inspection, but they were sound and unpunctured.

He also knew that his alcohol carburettor de-icing equipment was working perfectly and decided he was being over-fussy. He thanked the duty officer and headed back to his plane from which the refuelling nozzle was just being removed. He went on to the flight deck to go through his pre-flight check procedures for the fifth time that day.

While everyone else slept Conor Ó Briain lay awake, fully clothed under his pyjamas. He was planning to run away. He had no money at all and the school was a long way from Galway and the ferry to Inisheer. But there was late rising – eight o'clock – on a Sunday and he had figured out that if he managed to slip out in the very early morning just before dawn he could make it to the main Galway road and maybe get a lift towards the city from someone going the road to a creamery or to early Mass before anyone missed him. Then when he got to the ferry dock he was sure to meet one or more of his Inisheer neighbours who would lend him the fare.

He had planned his escape the previous afternoon while he was kneeling on the platform during his punishment and had later made rudimentary preparations. Unseen during the activity on the playing pitch in the afternoon he had hidden his outdoor boots under a bush by the main gates. And during supper, on the pretext of going to the lavatory, he had managed to smuggle six thick slices of bread out of the refectory, hiding them under his jumper. His heart in his mouth, he had raced up to the dormitory – to which access was forbidden during the day – and had hidden the bread behind the sponge bag in his bedside locker, getting back to the refectory just as the bell was rung for grace after meals.

The bread now lay at his feet, ready wrapped in his spare shirt, just under the edge of the mattress. He kept his knees bent in the bed so the bread would not be too squashed.

He had taken Sean Lyons into the plot. Round-eyed with the importance of the task entrusted to him and the daring of it all, Sean had agreed to have one of his asthma attacks after Mass just before breakfast. The plan was that the Brother on duty would be distracted into looking after him and bringing him to the infirmary and in the confusion Conor's absence from the refectory during breakfast might not be noticed. Even if it was, the prefects would probably assume that he had gone to the infirmary with his friend.

He craned his neck to see the big clock above the window at the end of the dormitory. It must be close to three o'clock. The glass on the clock face reflected the blue glow cast by a votive lamp in front of the statue of Our Lady on the windowsill but Conor could not see the hands. He was terrified he might fall asleep and, moving as slowly and quietly as possible, retrieved one of his slippers from under his bed and eased it under the small of his back. If he nodded off the discomfort should wake him up again.

On the flight deck of the DC3 the pilot and Second Officer drank black coffee. The night was moonless and, as they flew on, that special womb-like peace of night-flying enveloped the dimly lit cockpit. The instruments glowed in front of them, the sensitive needles moving slightly, the half-circle of the artificial horizon quite stable. They seemed to float in the blue-blackness, suspended between the quilt of stars and the luminous floor of cloud which stretched beneath them like an undulating carpet of softest white wool. Reacting, they lowered their voices.

When they were about three and a half hours out of Reykjavik, Tucker handed control of the aircraft to the younger man so he could snatch forty winks. The aircraft was rock steady and with the friendly tailwinds they were ahead of schedule. Before he closed his eyes he glanced at the log. If this kept up they would be landing at Shannon in less than two hours.

In the passenger cabin the nanny was sound asleep and Cal and Maggie continued to converse quietly over the head of the sleeping Susanna, whose bassinet Maggie had placed on the floor in front of them. They had each slept a little but were now wakeful. Lulled by the steady, unvarying drone of the engines outside the windows they were in a rare state of peace with one another. They had been talking of the trip to come and of its implications.

'Maggie,' said Cal, 'all I can ask of you is to trust me just one last time. Give us this chance, please, for all our sakes. I promise you won't regret it.'

'I wouldn't have come at all if I didn't think it was worth one more try.' Soothed, somnolent, Maggie felt no rancour or urgency. She really was going to put the past away and make an effort. She and Cal had not made love, nor even slept in the same bed, for nearly fifteen months now. Almost as if it were not herself involved she wondered what it would be like to make love in London, Paris and Rome.

'I promise you won't regret it,' said Cal again and Maggie allowed him to take her hand.

Susanna stirred in her sleep and then whimpered, about to wake. Maggie looked behind her and seeing that the nanny was still fast asleep decided not to wake the girl. She leaned forward, picked up the baby and rooted around in her carry-all to find a bottle of baby formula. Susanna, her face rosy and eyes wide in the dimmed lights, nuzzled into her mother's shoulder, snuffling.

Maggie cradled her, then offered her the milk. Susanna fastened on to the bottle with both hands and clamped her mouth round the teat, sucking contentedly. After a while one

33

of her hands moved to Maggie's face and she kept it there while she sucked.

The aircraft bumped slightly.

In the cockpit Tucker jolted awake, instantly alert. The motion of the plane had not altered appreciably but he felt rather than heard his co-pilot's gasp. He looked out of the window ahead of him and saw what the co-pilot had just seen. Towering ahead at about four kilometres and stretching from left to right as far as the eye could see rose an ominous wall of cloud, soaring like a skyscraper out of sight and blocking out all the stars. Tucker envisioned its head stretched like an anvil in the jet-stream.

'Damn!' he said. This was a biggie, he knew. Some of these cumulo-nimbus systems extended for hundreds of miles, with a depth of up to fifty. And he knew that inside that baby, rapidly coming closer, were huge storm systems of freezing rain, hail, ice and God knew what else.

Tucker had no doubts about his or his plane's ability to handle the storms but he had the passengers to think about. Telling the Second Officer to plot another course, triangular, which should take them on a south-southwesterly backtrack followed by due east heading and then, when the danger was over, one which would take them north-northeast, he took over the controls and bringing her nose down slightly hauled the plane round. Their ETA would be delayed but that could not be helped. He had plenty of fuel. He checked the gauges. One of the tanks was showing almost empty. He switched to a full one, snapped on the PA and asked his passengers to fasten their seat belts.

In the cabin, the sound of the PA shattered the calm. Susanna dropped her bottle and began to cry and the stewardess came down the aisle and took her on her own lap while the others struggled to get their seats upright and their seat belts fastened. The baby twisted round and stretched her arms to her mother but before Maggie could take her back they were caught in the storm and were bucketing around, making the transfer impossible.

Up front Tucker's mind had clicked into overdrive. 'Tighten

34

your harness,' he barked at his junior officer, 'and lower your seat as far as it will go.'

'Why?'

'You'll see.'

The co-pilot obeyed until his seat rested almost on the floor.

Tucker turned his cockpit lights up to full power to counter the flash-blindness which occurs after lightning. Then, eyes moving swiftly over his controls, he made sure his de-icing systems were on and synchronized the direction indicator with the magnetic compass. The turn-and-run manoeuvre had failed. The front was on them. No choice. Too late. Nothing for it now but to ride this one.

Almost as a reflex, he turned on his landing lights and immediately wished he hadn't. Twin spears, they bounced against a monstrous acropolis of *son et lumière*, twisting yellow pillars of vapour illuminated from within by flashing displays of dirty light. He turned off his lights again.

Thunder experienced at such close quarters feels as if it is exploding right inside your head. It is abrupt and shocking, with no cushioning echo.

The co-pilot soon found out why he had been ordered to lower his seat to below the eye-level of the windscreen – the position afforded the illusion of some sort of security, so that even though the indicators were swinging wildly, if he kept his eyes fixed on them and not on what was happening outside, there was some semblance of normality.

But then he looked with horror at the altimeter. The captain had his hands welded to the stick, pushing it forward with all his might to keep the plane's nose down and yet the altimeter showed that the plane was rising like a cork on a geyser. Then when it reached the apex of the upward current it began to plunge downwards. The reverse was also true. While the captain fought to bring the plane's nose up, they went down again as if over the face of a waterfall.

The co-pilot held on to his own controls, adding his own strength, mimicking what Tucker did, seeing that his captain's aim was to keep the line on his artificial horizon as straight as

35

possible, allowing the storm itself to dictate the altitude. At one point as the plane again began its stomach-churning descent he almost panicked, jamming his feet on the rudder which caused a wild slewing.

'Get your feet off that!' yelled Thompson. 'Do you want to break us up?'

'Sorry!' he yelled back, remembering too late that the books said more aircraft disintegrated inside a system like this through pilot-panic and over-correction – which put intolerable stress on the airframe – than from any other cause. Tucker's aim, the co-pilot saw, was to make any corrections as small and smooth as possible.

The sweat was pouring down the captain's face getting into his eyes and he kept trying to blink it away while keeping his hands glued to the controls. 'Get on the radio – try to see if there's anything out there!' he shouted.

The co-pilot nodded and holding his right forearm steady with his left hand he operated the high-frequency radio, which had a range of 1000 miles, attempting to call in any other aircraft or ships in the area. The attempt was futile. All he heard in his headset was a deafening torrent of static and crackling. He persisted for about five minutes. 'Nothing, Captain,' he shouted over the din.

Tucker nodded. It was a long-shot anyway. They were on their own.

There was chaos in the passenger cabin as Susanna continued to scream. Maggie tried to leave her seat to take her from the stewardess but, as she unbuckled her belt, the aircraft jolted wildly and she was bowled sideways, right across the aircraft to the other wall. She was slammed hard into it, hurting her shoulder.

Seeing her mother slewing across the floor the baby doubled the volume of her screams.

Maggie crawled with difficulty back to her seat, holding her arm at an awkward angle hoping she hadn't done it any great damage. She was frightened but had always had the ability to postpone the full extent of her panic until the crisis was over.

One-armed, she buckled herself back into her seat and hoped that she would still be able to help the others.

In the radar room of Shannon airport, slumped wearily in front of his flickering screen, the operator on the evening shift rubbed his eyes and then, for the umpteenth time that night, looked at his watch. It was coming up to midnight and knocking-off time, thank God. It had been an exceptionally boring shift and he had just logged the latest arrival on his screen which was, he reckoned, about 180 miles out. He consulted the file of active flight plans. Like all flights he had logged that evening, she was early.

He updated his logs, ready to hand them over to the man who was to succeed him but when he looked again the blip, which should have moved further in, had moved back outwards towards the perimeter of his screen and instead of progressing southeasterly now seemed to be on a southwesterly course. If they continued that way, he thought, he'd lose them off his screen altogether as his range was only 200 miles. He picked up the flight plan again. They were off course – or had changed course. Poor buggers, he thought. Probably caught in the storm which had passed overhead about forty minutes earlier ...

He logged the changed direction and, sure enough, when he raised his eyes again to the flickering green screen the blip had disappeared. He noted that too, then, yawning, he glanced at the door. This night man, he thought irritably, would be late for his own funeral.

The blip had not reappeared by the time the night man, a weedy individual with a cadaverous face, pushed open the door. He was briefed by his younger colleague as he was still removing his woollen coat and the bicycle clips from around his ankles. When the door slammed behind the other man, he placed the clips on the scarred top of a wooden cupboard beside his paper-wrapped sandwiches and lemonade bottle filled with milk. Keeping an eye on the screen, he moved the one-bar electric fire as close to the desk as its flex would allow, aiming its puny heat at his shins. Then he sat down, the logs in front of him. Still no sign of that Dak . . .

The baby continued to cry, screams reaching a climax as, despite the stewardess's iron grip, her head cracked against the rim of the window beside the seat. The rest of the passengers were coping well enough up to the moment when the nanny, who had had her eyes closed, risked a look out of her porthole. To her horror she saw, in the blackness, a jagged blue halo of flame dancing around the port engine like an ethereal catherine wheel. She opened her mouth and she too began to scream, terrifying the baby even more.

The turbulence was so severe that the stewardess was powerless to do anything except to stay locked in her seat. In vain she tried to make her voice heard, yelling that the phenomenon was harmless. 'It's only St Elmo's Fire,' she shouted, again and again – but to no avail.

Worse was to come. As they shot upwards on one of their dizzy ascents, they seemed to cannon through a solid wall which disintegrated around them in a fusillade of what sounded like machine-gun fire. The wall they had hit was one of hail.

Cal began to retch, the vomit skewing around him. Maggie, who gripped the armrests of her seat, continued to tell herself that there was nothing she could do for anyone else so she concentrated on *not* being sick so that she would not add to the general mayhem and would be fit, when they got out of this, to help the others in distress.

But the conditions were so bad up front Tucker had failed to notice that the aircraft was not responding to his handling as she should. He became alert to it only when he realized that for the second time in five minutes he had had to open the throttle to maintain engine revs. She was using far too much fuel. His brain flicked along a checklist. Rudder? Seemed OK. Carburettor? No, the engine revs were steady and there was no roughness – as far as he could tell in this turbulence. Icing? His de-icing systems were on. He risked opening a side window for an instant to look back at the wing. Water and hail poured into the cockpit, blinding and drenching him, but he held his nerve for a few seconds and managed to see that the shape of the nacelle was regular and the wing was clean, or so it seemed, no tell-tale bulge on the leading edge. He crossed off his mental list the problem of opaque rime ice, which grows fast into an ungainly bulge and wreaks havoc with the aerodynamics.

The other possibility was rain ice. On such a short visual inspection in these conditions there was no way of knowing for sure, as this invisible, insidious substance flows and freezes and flows again glacier-like along vulnerable surfaces, rendering impotent the de-icing boots which inflate and deflate uselessly inside it.

Tucker looked at his controls again. No help there, but watching his airspeed indicator dropping alarmingly near stalling speed and having to open his throttle further his hunch was that the problem was, indeed, rain ice.

Somehow they had to get below the altitude where the rain ice was forming. Tucker gripped the stick with all his strength and gritted his teeth . . .

There was a tremendous crash from the galley, followed by a second one which temporarily eclipsed the rattling and banging that was going on inside the fitted bar. The doors of the washroom and the storage closet were swinging open and shut in counterpoint. Even the walls of the cabin were creaking and straining. Maggie continued to grip the armrests of her seat, wishing that she was near enough to the nanny to slap her as the girl continued to scream on a long, sustained note, broken only when she paused to draw breath. She exchanged a glance with the stewardess, who managed to smile professionally although Maggie could see that, like herself, there was little she could do, strapped in as she was and restraining the struggling, hysterical baby. Maggie reached over to touch Cal who sat, almost catatonic, streaked in his own vomit. He was rigid

39

with fright, his face grey and his hair plastered to his head with perspiration. He did not respond to her touch and then she was jolted sideways again away from him and had to look to her own equilibrium.

Tucker, aided by the co-pilot, had managed to get down to a median level of about 4000 feet. Not long now, he thought, feeling gratefully, from the way she was handling, that the plane was lightening. Either the de-icing system was now working again or the ice was coming off under the flood of rain which obscured his windscreen and was so heavy that it leaked a little through the seals of the side windows. His fingers felt as though they would never again unclasp from the stick as he fought to control the aircraft which still bounced around like a paper cup tossed into a torrent of white water.

Then, just as suddenly as it had begun, it was over, and after a few minor bumps they were into relatively clear air. Tucker looked across at his co-pilot. The younger man was pale but had borne up well.

'You OK, kid?' asked the captain.

'Yeah, I'm fine. Hope they're all right down the back. That one was really a doozy.'

'You take over, will you? I'm going down to see how things are.' But he had to peel his fingers off the stick one by one with his free hand before he could stand up and he had difficulty unstrapping his harness.

'Want me to get our bearings?' asked the co-pilot, who did not have the presumption to ask if his captain needed any help.

'Yeah,' said Tucker, who, to his shame, felt that his knees were weak.

The night man at Shannon was not yet seriously worried. According to the flightplan she had filed the DC3 was only now due within range. He accepted that his predecessor's theory was probably correct – that they had changed course to avoid the storm. In that case, they should be due on his screen within five minutes. Although it was still early on his shift he weakened as he did every night and extracted a tomato sandwich from the greasy brown paper bag he had brought in with him. He promised himself he would eat only one. As he munched the limp sandwich, soggy with tomato juice, he tracked the overflight of two US military aircraft and watched for the DC3. Then he reached for a second sandwich.

Tucker Thompson had calmed down his passengers as best he could. The English girl was in a really bad state. She had stopped screaming but had wrapped herself completely in her blanket and the tears coursed down her white face as she shivered uncontrollably in her seat.

He got no sense from the man and left him to the ministrations of the stewardess but he saw that the mother had come through well enough. At present she was engaged in soothing the hiccuping baby. Aiming his words at her he reassured them all that there should be no further problems although they would now be late arriving at Shannon since they were flying not with friendly tailwinds but against quite a heavy headwind which had followed the storms.

As the captain walked back into the cockpit Cal, white-faced, who had not seemed to listen to a word the man had uttered, asked the stewardess, who was cleaning him up with soda water and tissue, if he could have some brandy.

Maggie dandled Susanna who settled down seeming none the worse for wear although she hid her face in Maggie's neck when the stewardess approached with the brandy for Cal and the nanny. Maggie, too, accepted a drink, juggling it, humming quietly in Susanna's ear and soon the baby pillowed her head on her mother's shoulder and dropped off again to sleep. The DC3 ploughed on as though nothing had happened.

But something had.

In the cockpit, Tucker's disbelieving eyes checked and double checked his fuel gauges. He had been so busy fighting the storm

41

that he had not realized the extent of the icing and the aircraft, carrying perhaps more than an extra ton and a half of weight, had gobbled the fuel.

'Have you figured out where we are yet?' He spoke gruffly.

'Just about,' answered the co-pilot who, now that the sky was clear again, had been able to use the directional gyro aimed at Sirius.

The news was not good. They were eighty miles south and seventy west off their planned course.

Tucker checked his fuel gauges again and made calculations. With the throttles full open, the Dak could make speed of only 130 knots in this headwind. Even by the most optimistic forecasts, they did not have enough fuel to make Shannon.

He thought swiftly. There was no cargo, nothing on board he could dump to lighten the load except, he remembered, the passengers' luggage. Twelve hundred pounds. It would have to go. He told the co-pilot to bring the plane slowly down to 2000 feet and went back into the passenger cabin.

The appearance of the cabin was returning to normal as the stewardess tidied up but two of the glasses had smashed and hundreds of crystal fragments crunched under the soles of Tucker's ankle boots as he entered the compartment. He sat in one of the seats opposite the couple and on instinct decided to address Maggie. Keeping his eyes on her he explained the situation as calmly and encouragingly as he could.

The husband began to bluster. 'I refuse to allow this! There are thousands and thousands of dollars' worth of clothes and equipment in that luggage . . . ' Tucker ignored him, keeping his eyes fixed on the woman. She held his eyes with her own, quite steady.

'How bad is it?' she asked, finally.

Tucker thought fast. There really wasn't much point in fudging. 'Put it this way, Mrs Smith,' he said, 'if we lighten the load sufficiently we have a fighting chance. If we don't we will run out of fuel. It's as simple as that.'

The grey eyes flickered but she made no other movement.

'We are still making calculations,' he went on, 'and you can be sure we're not alone in this part of the Atlantic. There are ships around and we are already mobilizing Shackletons from the RAF as escorts. We'll be OK—'

Cal butted in again. 'This is preposterous—' he began.

Tucker cut him off. 'I don't want to frighten you,' he said, still addressing Maggie, 'but every second we carry that extra weight is a second extra of fuel burned. Your luggage is replaceable, I'm sure . . .' He emphasized the word 'luggage' and let the implication sink in. To her credit, he thought, the woman still did not blink.

'Can I get a few things out of one of the trunks?' she asked finally. The only hint of distress was a small quiver in her voice.

'I'm afraid there isn't time,' said Tucker. And with that he stood up and made his way back to the cockpit. He took over the controls and sent the co-pilot to do the job.

Tucker knew from his controls what was happening. With each dislodgement of luggage the plane jumped slightly. And with each jump the airspeed indicator crept up a few knots. He decided to keep her low, at 2000, because the winds at this level would not be so strong and their chances of a visual sighting of a ship or large fishing trawler were better. When the co-pilot came back he ordered him to plot the most direct route to Shannon and to search on his high-frequency radio for contacts.

But no matter how the sums were done they came out the same. Ireland was still just under two hours' flying time away. At best estimates they had fuel for one hour and forty-five minutes. He began to call on his radio.

A pilot's priority during an emergency is to deal with it as expeditiously as possible. It is only when he has done all he can to safeguard his aircraft and load that he will call for assistance. The acronym in that case is PACER – he radios Position, Altitude, Conditions, Estimate of next contact and a Request for whatever it is he needs.

Over and over again, Tucker's junior colleague called these out – but there was no response.

At last! Fifteen minutes later the night man at Shannon caught the blip on the side of his screen. He had become concerned at the non-appearance of the DC3 but there it was, about 190 miles out.

He checked the log. The time they had left Reykjavik indicated that they should have been landing at Shannon within the next half-hour but at their present rate they could not make it for at least seventy minutes. He took a gulp of his dark brown tea and wondered if he should make a few enquiries.

Better be safe than sorry, that was his motto. He lifted the telephone and contacted Shannon air-sea rescue centre, asking for the duty officer. 'Hello, Seamus,' he said when the officer came on. 'Listen, it may be nothing to worry about but have you had any calls about a DC3? She's behind time – the storm, I think – and I was wondering if anyone had picked up anything.'

He listened for a minute and nodded. 'Well, I'm just wondering about her endurance. Six people on board . . . ' He nodded again. 'OK. Well, I'll keep you posted.'

He replaced the receiver, took a wodge of fruit cake out of his paper bag and chewed it thoughtfully as he watched the screen in front of him.

The co-pilot was still calling on the radio, moving his frequencies. Miraculously there was an answer at last from Shannon air-sea rescue. Quickly he gave his location, altitude, course and estimated flying time left on the fuel. Forty-five minutes – at most fifty.

'Roger,' said the faint voice in his earpiece. 'We have you on radar at Shannon. Don't worry. Keep in contact. We'll get in touch with the RAF to intercept and escort.'

Tucker set his propellers at low revs – said by engineers to conserve fuel, although he had his doubts about it – and had his co-pilot plot a slightly new course which would take them more broadside than head-on into the wind. He was going to try to outmanoeuvre the wind and conserve his fuel searching for a friendlier airstream.

The co-pilot called in the new course to Shannon.

'Roger,' said the voice at the other end. 'Got that. We're sending the troops. Keep in touch.'

Tucker looked at his hands for a long minute, then made up his mind. 'Take over,' he said to his colleague. 'Time to tell the truth.' Then he opened the door into the passenger cabin and beckoned to the stewardess to join him.

Maggie watched the stewardess and the captain coming towards her. The hefty measure of brandy had calmed her nerves and the warm weight of the baby lying cradled in her arms was additionally soothing. But the set expression on Tucker's face shot alarm into the back of her throat. 'What is it?' she asked quietly, before he could say anything.

Cal, who had been dozing, sat up.

'We've a major problem, ma'am,' said Tucker.

'What! What now?' Cal's voice was high.

'Stop it, Cal!' said Maggie sharply. 'Go on, Mr Thompson.'

'The simple fact is that we haven't got enough fuel on board to reach our destination. Or any land,' he added.

Cards all on the table, face up.

His words did not wholly sink into Maggie's brain. They seemed outlandish, indecipherable. The cabin of this plane was their bounded world. It had kept them safe through storm and wind and hail and lightning. It was cosy and quiet, a secure moonlet moving quietly under the stars. And they had already made their sacrifice to safety. She began to stroke Susanna's sleeping head. 'What are you saying, Mr Thompson?'

'What I'm saying, Mrs Smith, is that there is every possibility that we may have to set the aircraft down on the sea.' Tucker hoped his own voice matched hers. For obvious reasons, there was no live training for ditching, it was all done with models and tanks. Pilots learned the theory but very few lived to talk about the actual test, which was entirely unpredictable. And the only thing consistent about ditching in the open sea was that the results were inconsistent.

'I see.' She was still stroking the baby's head.

'Now look here, Thompson—' Cal's voice had risen in pitch.

'*Shut up*, Cal!' The violence of her response startled even herself. She turned to the captain again. 'How much longer – I mean, how soon . . . '

'At our present speed and heading, I would say about forty-five minutes,' said Tucker. 'But may I point out that it is not all bad news. We have been in touch with Shannon air-sea rescue centre and they have, in turn, been in touch with the RAF. There is already a Shackleton reconnaisance aircraft in the air, on its way to intercept us.'

Privately, he hoped there was. He waited as she thought for a moment. 'How will they find us in the dark?'

'We have flares and rockets and we will be in constant touch by radio.'

Again Tucker waited. The husband seemed about to open his mouth again but she put a restraining hand on his arm. 'Right, captain. You just tell us what to do and we'll do it.'

'Well, when the time comes, about ten minutes beforehand I'll tell the stewardess here and she will tell you what to do. That should be' he looked at his watch 'in about thirty minutes from now.'

She nodded and he stood up. He stood in front of her for a second in admiration, not knowing what to say. This was some lady. He saw her rubbing her shoulder across the body of the sleeping baby. 'Is your arm OK?' he asked.

'Fine, fine,' said Maggie. 'I just gave it a knock. It's absolutely fine.'

In a strange way, thought Maggie, watching the retreat of his wide back, she was not afraid. She felt detached. She looked down at the peaceful baby and then across at Cal who was again rigid, jaws working. She decided there and then that if they survived this she would divorce him. Her brain felt like an abacus clicking away, simple and crystal-clear. Her priorities were Susanna and Christian and finally herself. She had been floundering around trying to please too many people. It was now her responsibility to get them all safely through the next few hours. She had a baby to look after and a small child to get back to.

'Take the baby.' Without meeting his eyes she handed Susanna to Cal who, responding to the note of quiet authority in her voice, took his daughter without saying a word. Then Maggie went over to the sleeping nanny, shaking her awake. The girl's eyes fluttered open, bloodshot and red-rimmed from her earlier tears. 'Yes, Mrs Smith?' She struggled upright. Keeping her voice as calm as she could Maggie briefly explained the situation.

The nanny's eyes widened but Maggie put both hands on her shoulders, willing her to be quiet. 'We will be rescued, Rosemary,' she said, every word firm and emphatic. 'We will be rescued, by the Royal Air Force. They are already on the way.'

The girl's eyes filled with tears and she clapped her hand over her mouth. 'Oh, Mrs Smith—'

The last thing Maggie wanted or needed, was another bout of hysterics. 'Now, Rosemary, pull yourself together,' she said. 'It's only by being calm that we will all survive this thing. I'm sure everything is going to turn out OK. We will all have specific tasks. I want you to take charge of Susanna. We have about half an hour before things start to get busy around here. 'Here is a lifejacket,' she went on, slowly and calmly, handing over the Mae West she had taken from the stewardess. 'Now I want you to wrap Susanna in a blanket and then tie this on over it,' she said. 'Be very careful with the straps. Tie it around her with her arms inside it, so she can't struggle. OK? If you have any difficulty, call me. She can have her pacifier in her mouth, that should help.'

The nanny gave a little sob but nodded. She grasped the lifejacket, went over to Cal and took the baby from him.

Maggie went to the galley. 'Now tell me,' she said to the stewardess, 'what *exactly* is going to happen . . .'

For the next twenty minutes, Maggie refused to let herself think of anything but how to deal with this situation. She was kind to Cal, patting his shaking hand.

'Oh, Maggie, if only we had it all to live over again—' he started, but she cut him short, like a kindly nurse. 'Now, Cal, there's no time for that.'

47

He asked then for another brandy but she refused to let him have it. 'We're all going to have to have our wits about us.'

Before binding on the Mae West the nanny had followed Maggie's instructions and swaddled the baby tightly in her blanket. Susanna, like a strange little orange larva, responded to the air of calm and purpose and made no sound but sucked quietly at her pacifier while the nanny rocked her. Maggie sat upright in her own seat, every nerve alert.

All too soon, the stewardess was in front of her with a Mae West. 'Don't inflate it inside the aircraft,' she instructed. She gave two other lifejackets to Cal and the nanny, then pulled an orange life raft from its bin and placed it in readiness near the door. She explained how they should brace themselves for the impact, bent double in their seats, one arm behind the neck, the other across the chest.

Her voice was crisp. 'After we ditch there will only be a matter of a minute or two for us all to get out of the aircraft.' She turned to the nanny. 'I want you to go first,' looking across at Maggie, 'then you, Mrs Smith. I will hand the baby to you when you are safely in the raft. Make sure that you pull the string to inflate the baby's lifejacket the moment she gets to you. And don't forget your own. You go next, Mr Smith,' she continued. 'The captain and co-pilot and I will follow you.'

In the cockpit, while his co-pilot continued to broadcast their coordinates, Tucker was watching the altimeter, bringing the aircraft gently up to 6000 feet. His plan was not to wait until the fuel had entirely run out but to have some left to assist the ditching. The theory was that the plane should be brought down, nose kept as high as possible, on the upward face of a large swell. But, as far as he had been able to in the darkness, he had seen that the sea was choppy with large swells and whitecaps and secondary waves and cross-wavelets which broke the symmetry of the surface. This was not going to be easy and he wanted enough fuel left to rise again on full power if his first, second, or even third attempt to ditch proved too dangerous.

He looked at his gauges. About enough for ten minutes. Right, this was it. He told the co-pilot to give the order to brace over the passenger PA, then turned on his landing lights and brought the DC3 in a long slow descent towards the heaving black water.

At fifty feet, he eased back the throttle and the plane began to sink but in the split second before he hit a curling whitecap rose, rearing upwards against the twin beams of his light. Tucker's automatic reaction was to pull on the stick and open the throttle fully. The plane shuddered and jerked and some of the water splashed up over the nose but, like the Trojan she was, she gathered herself and surged at an angle of 45 degrees, roaring into the sky. Tucker's mouth was dry and his heart was thudding painfully against his ribs. He looked at his instruments and gauges again. Three thousand feet and still climbing, only two minutes left in the tanks. The next attempt had to succeed.

He forced himself to think calmly. Even as he set the plane again into a shallow dive he re-created the moments he had almost come in contact with the water. He had registered that although the waves were not tremendously high they were choppy with no discernible pattern. It would be a matter of luck.

The last seconds ticked away. First the port, then the starboard engine, sputtered and died. Then there was silence, eerie after the hours of droning, broken only by the rushing wind outside and the sound of the co-pilot's voice still calling continuous Mayday into the radio, repeating it like a mantra. 'November-Two-Three, Mayday, Mayday, November-Two-Three we are ditching, Mayday, we are ditching, November-Two-Three, Mayday . . .' Each time he gave his latitude and longitude, about sixty-five miles off the west coast of Ireland.

In the last few precious seconds Tucker flattened out, searching ahead for a friendly wave. No more time. His height was zero.

In the cabin the sound of the impact was like a small explosion and despite herself Maggie cried out.

There was a skidding, tearing, ten-second interval while the fuselage juddered along the wavetops until finally, like an ungainly powerboat whose engine has been suddenly cut, the aircraft skidded to a violent halt. Miraculously she stayed afloat and the lights stayed on.

The moment she stopped the stewardess unstrapped herself and pushed open the door. Water began to pour into the cabin. Within seconds it was a foot deep. Maggie unstrapped her own belt and waded over to the door, helping the stewardess to shove the folded orange raft out into the darkness, keeping tight hold on its rope. They saw it expand to its full size as soon as it hit the water outside. The stewardess grabbed the baby's bassinet and wedged it in the opening to act as a temporary if inefficient barrier against the water, which poured in a new flood each time the aircraft lurched sideways as it rose and fell on the waves.

'Cal! Rosemary!' screamed Maggie at the other two.

Both appeared to be riveted to their seats. Both were still bent double – the nanny's head was pillowed on the baby in her lap – and neither answered.

So far they had been in the water for seventeen seconds.

The bulkhead door opened and Tucker and his co-pilot came through.

'Help them!' screamed Maggie indicating the two still in the seats as she saw the pilots appear. The water continued to wash in. It was very cold. The wind outside howled.

The stewardess continued to hang on to the raft's mooring rope, while she struggled to keep the bassinet wedged against the door.

Tucker extricated the baby from the nanny and passed her, whimpering but still sucking the pacifier, to her mother. Then he unsnapped the nanny's seat belt and pulled her to her feet, manhandling her through the rising water towards the door.

Meanwhile, the co-pilot, having undone Cal's seat belt, was pulling with all his might at the man's shoulders, trying to dislodge him. But Cal was strong and determined and wouldn't budge, his face like rock. The young pilot slapped his face over and over again but it was useless. The older man did not try to avoid the blows, just closed his eyes.

They had been in the water for thirty seconds. They had a maximum of a minute to go before they sank.

Maybe less, for at that moment, the plane lurched to starboard and the water washed the bassinet back into the cabin in a great flood.

'Leave him!' screamed Maggie as the co-pilot continued to harry Cal. She waded towards the nanny and helped the captain push her towards the door.

The water was now above their knees.

The stewardess had managed to keep hold of the tethering rope to the raft. With her free hand, she helped Maggie bundle the nanny out of the door and tumbled her into the raft, which rocked dangerously but stayed upright.

The tail of the DC3 was caught by a wave and the aircraft swung round about 30 degrees. The stewardess fell backwards almost losing her grip on the rope but was steadied by Maggie.

The water was now up to their thighs and they were plunged into darkness as all the lights went out. The aircraft was rocking and being buffeted in the swell and it was difficult to keep their footing.

Maggie groped for Susanna, found her in Tucker's arms and took her from him. While the stewardess strained on the rope to bring the raft back to the door of the aircraft, Maggie managed to pass the baby out to the nanny.

Another inrush of water beat all three of them back from the door, now half-submerged. This time it was Maggie who lost her footing and fell backwards. She disappeared under the water, cracking her head hard against the corner of the brassbound bar. A tide of green and black rose before her eyes and her head was bleeding badly when she was fished out by Tucker but although she was dizzy she assisted him as much as she could as he half-carried her towards the door. The stewardess helped her through the opening and then pushed her so she tumbled head first into the raft, landing on top of the nanny and the baby.

The stewardess hesitated at the door. They had maybe fifteen seconds left.

Tucker knew that she was thinking of her duty to her other passenger. The water was up to their armpits and they could feel the suction as the sea pulled at them.

'Forget him, that's an order!' snapped Tucker. *'Now get into that raft!'*

She obeyed, passing the rope to the captain and half-swam, half-climbed through the door. From the raft outside Maggie could see her head and then her arms thrashing strongly in the water.

The DC3 was going down fast. All that remained above water now was the fin and starboard wing.

The stewardess made it to the raft and Maggie pulled her in. Then, as the three women in the raft looked on in horror, the water surged and the plane slipped under the waves. Even in the darkness Maggie could see the wide circle of swirling white which its plunge left on the dark surface.

The raft, already rising and falling alarmingly on the waves which came from all sides, reared upwards then spun crazily over the swell.

Against the white water an arm appeared and then a head. It was Cal. He was not wearing a lifejacket but somehow, in the last moments, he had swum or been washed out of the fuselage. The stewardess threw him a rope and he caught it but, as if he were a participant in a horrific slow-motion water ballet, he was rolled across the surface then pulled under by the suction created by the DC3 as she sank.

He did not let go of the rope and the raft, weighted by him, teetered dangerously, one side clear out of the water. A large swell rose under the raised side and pushed the whole vessel over, heeling its human cargo into the sea.

Maggie struggled under the surface. The freezing temperature shocked her into full consciousness. Her lifejacket was only partially inflated but she kicked strongly and with the help of its buoyancy managed to break the surface.

Something brushed her feet and then surfaced beside her. It was the small figure of Susanna, a compact orange bundle. The baby's eyes were closed and her mouth was slack. Maggie grabbed on to her and struggled to keep them both afloat.

A short distance away, maybe thirty feet, the raft had righted itself.

Maggie, despite shock and her head wound, was strong and

healthy and a good swimmer. Keeping one arm tightly wrapped around the baby she struck out with the other to where she saw the raft appear and disappear intermittently between the waves which rose all around her.

Several times she and the baby were swamped and her mouth filled with water but each time, with grim strength, she spat and surfaced and continued her one-armed progress until she reached the side of the raft. It was rising and falling with the waves but still listing hard to one side, one edge almost under the water. Cal was obviously still attached to the rope.

It was his last service to his family because Maggie was exhausted now and would have found it very difficult to get the baby and herself on board if the raft had been riding high. With a huge effort, she heaved Susanna ahead of her – the baby had not made a sound nor moved – and dragged herself on board after her. She lay beside her daughter, panting and spluttering on the listing floor as the waves washed over the sunken edge. Then she hauled herself to her knees and forced her numb fingers into action. She took one of the straps which trailed free from the baby's lifejacket and tied it to the rope which ran around the inside of the raft. She did not know whether her daughter was alive or dead.

She started to untie the rope to let her husband go. But she miscalculated. The knot opened faster than she bargained for and the raft, relieved of Cal's weight, bounced level as she was still leaning forward and off-balance. She fell forward from her knees and instinctively thrust out her hands. The momentum carried her over the edge and she fell back into the sea. This time, she did not struggle.

The raft was light now, buoyant and free, with only the baby on board. Maggie watched, almost dreamily, as it drifted fast away from her. Her head hurt but the water did not seem so cold. It was soft, in fact. Soft kind water. Underneath the waves there was peace. No sound after the din. Even the pain was quietened. Quiet soft water. Blessed quiet dark water. Soft black cradle.

The raft was now several hundred yards away, tipping briskly along on the restless lacy surface.

CHAPTER TWO

It was nearly time. Conor's bed was second last in a long double row in the dormitory. He lay awake, barely daring to breathe, as the sky outside the window at the far end of the room turned gradually from black to pearl. When it was possible to pick out detail in the frame around the window, the butterflies in his stomach began to flutter hard. He had not wanted to make his move until there was some light for fear of waking someone by stumbling or bumping into something; he knew it would have been impossible to explain why he was creeping around the school at dawn with his pyjamas on over his clothes.

When there was enough light to differentiate solid objects from shadows he could wait no longer. Inch by inch, his heart thumping, he stole out of his bed, timing his movements to the rhythmic snores of Sean Lyons in the bed beside him. He eased the shirt-wrapped bread out from under the mattress then, one agonizing step after the other, he crept out of the dormitory avoiding the boards he knew were the creakers. On the small landing outside the door he paused for a moment and exhaled, realizing that his chest hurt from holding his breath for so long. He had a strong urge to go to the toilet but did not dare. Instead he started to move carefully down the worn stone steps which opened on to the front corridor.

Once there his progress was easier. Although the corridor was a long one, lit only by a window at each end, there were religious statues in niches all along the walls facing the classrooms and in front of each burned a votive lamp, little lighthouses of red and blue in the passage towards the door. As he crept along he was conscious of an overwhelming smell of floor polish.

Down a further flight of steps, along another corridor and he was into the front hall tiled with squares of marble. His

54

stomach jumped with relief. There was a key in the iron lock of the front door – it was the one thing he had not been able to check in advance. He turned it and, well oiled, it gave easily. Then he took a deep breath and unlatched the door itself. The click resounded so loudly that he froze. He waited for a full minute straining his ears but the only sounds were his own fast breathing and the thudding of his heart as it banged against his ribcage. He slipped outside into the semi-darkness not daring to pull the door shut after him. He knew that when it was discovered to be open there would be a hue and cry but he could not help that. It was heavy, made of oak, and impossible to close without making a substantial thump.

Keeping close to the walls of the house, his breath misting, he moved like a shadow along the damp grass which was cold and slippery under his bare feet. At least it was not raining but to his dismay he saw that his bare feet left clear imprints in the dew. It could not be helped now. During the violent storm which had passed over the school at around midnight he had thought seriously about aborting his escape but now there was no going back. Bending low he crossed the gravelled driveway in front of the school, ignoring the discomfort as the stones cut into the soles of his feet. When he reached the playing fields he felt very exposed and remained doubled over, making himself as small as possible. The Brothers allowed a local farmer to graze sheep on the pitches to keep the grass down. The flock was resting, woolly bodies seeming to float above the drifting ground fog. As Conor's humped shape approached, the nearest ewe struggled up on dainty hooves and trotted away from him, followed by her two lambs. One of the lambs bleated shrilly and Conor froze again in his tracks, risking a look over his shoulder at the grey bulk of the school building. Some of the windows on the upper storeys glowed faintly, lit by votive lamps or nightlights, but none was fully lit and although he watched for a few moments no lights snapped on. So far so good.

He reached the big iron gates and finding his boots where he had left them sat on the grass to lace them on, first putting on the socks which he had carried with him in the breast pocket of his pyjama jacket. In his panic he had forgotten to take off his pyjama bottoms before putting on the boots so, again glancing over his shoulder, he forced the garment over the boots, ripping the worn cotton along the seams. Then, rolling the pyjamas into a little ball, he shoved them into the hollow under the bush where he had previously hidden the footwear. Taking one last look behind him he set off along the little laneway towards the main road. He was coatless and knew that he was very conspicuous in his school uniform but he had a story ready for any carter or farmer who might pick him up. He was a prefect, he would say, and had been sent by the Superior, Brother Camillus, into Galway on an errand.

As he trotted along between the furze hedges and lichen-covered walls bordering the laneway, the cool air of the May morning felt sharp and clean against his cheek and he began to feel almost lighthearted. He rehearsed his arrival at Inisheer: his mother would be surprised to see him – and afraid for him – but he knew she would be glad. His place was at home at a time like this and he would deal with the consequences later.

He stopped for a few seconds to catch his breath leaning on a five-barred gate, his boots sinking into the quagmire churned up around its base by livestock. Conor had always been intensely aware of the busy lives led by animal, insect and bird in the countryside and now, in spite of his hurry, he could not resist the waking landscape of dawn. Two heifers huffed loudly as they tore rhythmically at the new growth between clumps of sedge and reeds in the marshy field on the other side of the gate. An old sway-backed donkey trotted across to greet him and shoved its soft nose through the bars for a caress. The crows were stirring in the branches of a pair of intertwined horse-chestnut trees beyond the hedge and, somewhere hidden, a blackbird tested his throat. Water gurgled in the ditch beneath the hawthorn hedge on either side of the gate and he was sure that if he had time he could root out thriving colonies of voles, shrews and field-mice just yards from where he stood. Far off across the bog he heard a curlew.

He must not dawdle. He gave the donkey a final pat and looked towards the main road. From where he stood, he could see the coppice of rowans planted by the Brothers around the

Lourdes grotto at the junction of the main road and the laneway to the school. He scraped his boots on the lowest rung of the gate and set off again.

While, on the mainland, his son hurried towards the Galway road, Micheál Ó Briain lifted his tired body from where he had sat most of the night. The chair legs scraped on the stone floor of the hearth as he stood up. He dragged his feet a few steps to the window of his kitchen to look out across the stone landscape of the island. It was a clear dawn. His bones ached with the stiffness of the long night but he must have dozed for a small while at least because, looking back, he noticed that the fire was nearly out. He took four sods of turf from the creel in the chimney corner and threw them onto the heap of white ashes, raising a shower of sparks.

He leaned against the chimney breast and looked across at the other side of the hearth where his wife Sorcha was still rocking the child. Her head was low and resting on the child's fair, lifeless head. Molly had died two hours before and Micheál mourned her but right now he was angry more than sorrowful. Frustration with his way of life had, in middle age, turned to bitterness and Micheál was not really surprised that his only daughter was dead.

Sometimes he wondered what he had done to deserve such a grubbing, mean life. It was no consolation that nearly every family on the island was in a similar position to his own, scratching a living from the rocks and getting a few shillings from the government, watching the post for the money-bearing letters from the relatives in Boston or Birmingham or Coventry. Micheál and his brother shared a currach and a few lobster pots, which they set each night but the money they got from the mainland for the lobsters paid only for a few basic groceries.

He watched as the sods of turf caught. The cottage was very quiet. There was only the small, rhythmic sound as one of the legs of the chair on which Sorcha rocked their daughter tapped against an uneven part of the flags.

Micheál was not an imaginative man but stealing another

look at his wife his thoughts ranged backwards to the time he had got married.

He had met Sorcha Ni Choirreain, a gentle girl from a village on Inishmaan, a sister island of his own, at a ceilidhe in the Inishmaan hall. It was not the first time he had noticed her but on the other occasions he had been wary of asking her to dance seeing that she was proficient and knowing that he, on the contrary, was a clodhopper. On this particular night, however, emboldened by porter, he cut in as she paraded gravely around the hall with her sister in the Stack of Barley.

' 'Tis not right for two girls to be dancing together.'

'Is it not now?' The sister was pert. Sorcha said nothing but was standing with her eyes cast down.

He addressed her directly, offering his arm. 'Will we go, so?'

'All right.' She took the arm and they carried on around the room leaving the sister to drag another young fellow on to the floor.

Afterwards Micheál had asked Sorcha if he could walk her home across the unlit island but she had refused. 'I'll be going with my sisters.'

'Will you be coming to the pattern on Inisheer?'

'I might.'

'Will I see you there?'

'You might.'

'Will you come, so?'

'I told you, I might.'

And with that he had to be content.

She did come to the pattern and they began a long slow courtship. In his favour, she felt he was tall, good-looking and did not drink too much (and in those days he had his temper well under control). He also had a priceless asset. Since he was the eldest son of his family and both his parents were dead, he had a house and a couple of perches of land – and what's more, the house was free of a mother-in-law.

In his eyes, she was warm-hearted, clever and acquiescent. She could cook. She was modest but attractive too and on summer evenings he preened as the other boys envied him his stewardship of her on her pier or on the launching points on Inisheer as one or other of them embarked for home across the one-and-a-half-mile stretch of water between their islands, appropriately named Bealach Na Fearbhach, or Foul Sound.

But that courtship had proven to be the high point of their lives together. After marriage he found her fearful and prudish in bed and knew to his chagrin that she found him coarse and brutal. But, as was the way, they never discussed such things so her fear and his resentment blossomed between them like weeds, so voracious they could no longer be contained by darkness but were spread across the daylight.

He looked across to where she still cradled their dead daughter. He thought it odd that he was thinking such thoughts at a time like this, but it was as if his weary brain was unwilling to deal with more immediate problems. Sorcha rocked and rocked, the child's hand covered in her own, the blank face held into her shoulder. The quietness of the kitchen pressed in all around him and he felt his anger grow.

But looking at his wife's worn face, Micheál realized with unaccustomed clarity that if he was disappointed Sorcha was too, and he hated himself for that. It was not that he meant to be violent but sometimes a red tide rose before his eyes. Sorcha's long-suffering silence did not help. If she would retaliate sometimes . . .

He struggled with the thought, blaming her for his own rage.

The worst of all was that she was afraid of him and so were his children. Their fear merely increased his rage. He threw another sod on the fire. If they could talk together, even over the head of their dead child . . . But he could see no opening in the walls around their separate hearts and had had no practice in making one. The chair leg still tapped. He could stand the oppressive kitchen no longer. '*Taím a' dul amach*,' he said gruffly, immediately – as good as his word – stamping towards the door in his heavy boots. Sorcha made no answer and he looked at her with something approaching hatred. She was so meek and mild and accepting – a living reproach to him. Almost tearing the latch off its screws Micheál lifted it savagely and went outside, slamming the door shut behind him.

The family's small collie dog, black and white, emerged from the lean-to turf-shed as he came out. She stretched, yawned, shook herself and came warily towards him, wagging her scraggly tail. Micheál aimed a kick at her but she was agile and well used to avoiding his boot. There was a small can of milk covered with a saucer on the windowsill of the cottage. He picked up the can. Yet another offering for the child from a neighbour, placed there after darkness to avoid offence. Much good it would do her now. He swung the can around his head and threw it with all his strength down the hill. It sailed high over the limestone releasing an arc of milk, then clattered thinly against the stones of a wall.

The Ó Briains' cottage was high on the island, about half a mile above the shore. The air was fresh and cool after the stuffiness of the kitchen. It was that still period before the day when the wind has all but died and Micheál could hear the sea below, still restless after the storm. It was black to the west, where the next landfall was America, but across on the mainland, about nine miles to the east, the sun had raised tentative fingers of pink and gold above the horizon, lightening Inisheer and giving it texture. The whole island was a single fissured rock, flat limestone, grey on grey, crisscrossed by a latticework of low walls and pocked with minute fields of forced grass.

Micheál looked back at his house, which had been his father's, where he brought a wife, where his children were born – and died – and where he too would die. Three rooms and an outside privy. A few sticks of furniture and a bit of delph Sorcha had brought with her when they got married. That was the sum total of a lifetime's work. His fury of a few minutes before ebbed away and was replaced by deep depression. Why him? Why them? The death of an infant was not all that unusual on the island but Sorcha had been a good mother and he had worked his fingers to the bone. He saw that the thatch on the roof needed patching after the storm. He would do it after the funeral. He decided to walk down to the shore.

60

The ache in his joints eased as he clumped down the boreen between the walls. He and the dog were the only moving creatures on the island as far as he could see. Two donkeys slept nose to tail in the lee of a wall. Marcus Ó Braonáin's bony cow sat dozing in her tiny field, painstakingly created around the cracks of limestone by three generations of Ó Braonáins. They had cleared the loosest of the rocks, using them to build the walls, and then hauled huge loads of seaweed and sand from the seashore, spreading the material across the rock and adding it to the precious filaments of soil which they dug out of the crevices in the limestone. As a result of this back-breaking labour, they had been able to plant enough grass to graze a cow.

Micheál stopped at the wall to look at the cow and his heart leapt with jealousy. Her head was curled on to her hind legs and he could hear the rasping of her breath. He would never own a cow. His own handkerchief of land supported enough soil for two short drills of potatoes and that was all. If he had had a cow maybe his daughter would not have died. Even if he had been born not on Inisheer but on Inishmore, the biggest of the three islands where the land was warmer, he might have had a chance. Molly might have had a chance.

He left the cow and was coming close to the white beach when he stopped again, for there, in the small bay bobbing across the breakers, was a little rubber boat of bright orange, luminous against the dark grey water.

It was not unusual on the morning after a storm that sea debris should be washed up on Inisheer. They got oars and lobster pots and planks of wood, cork lifebelts – even barrels of porter and preserved fish. Once, he himself had picked up three shoe boxes tied together with string. The fragile high-heeled shoes inside would have been entirely unsuitable for any island woman since the heels would have broken off within minutes on the rough, uneven boreens and pavements. But Sorcha had dried them out, polished them and taken them on one of her trips to the mainland where she had managed to sell them in the market. Several times in his memory the island had drawn in an empty boat and although he had never seen one himself he had heard tell of boats like this which had been washed

61

up on the shores of the mainland. They contained serviceable and useful goods: torches and whistles, even wirelesses – and sometimes food. And the rubber was good for patching, or for covering the winter ricks of turf.

He hurried the last few hundred yards down to the beach and across the soft sand to the edge of the sea. The tide was coming in and each wave brought the little orange boat closer. It was a peculiar shape. Square. He waited patiently. The collie stood beside him, watching his face so she could be ready for the next move.

Five minutes later the boat was almost on the beach. Micheál waited for a receding wave and as it was bobbing away from him again, he reached out and grasped its edge, hauling it behind him up above the water line. He heard an odd noise distinct from the sound of the sea and looked round. He heard the sound again, like the mewing of a kitten. It was coming from a bundle in the raft which, it being the same colour, he had not noticed earlier. The bundle was a lifejacket and it was moving. But it was not a kitten. There were small bare feet protruding from one end and from the other the back of a small blonde head. To Micheál's astonishment the lifejacket, tied to the side of the raft, contained a baby and the baby was alive. As he stood transfixed, the baby continued to whimper weakly.

Carefully he untied the string which bound the lifejacket to the side of the raft and then undid the lifejacket. Underneath was a wool blanket, damp but warm to the touch. Micheál, like all the island fishermen and their wives, knew that wool, even when wet, is a good insulator. It was probably the blanket that had saved this child from dying of exposure. It was a girl he saw because she was wearing a pink smocked dress. He strained his eyes looking out to sea. There was no other flotsam to be seen.

He looked down at her again, surprising himself by speaking aloud. '*Céard as tú*?'

She opened her eyes and looked straight up into his own and for a second or two they appraised one another. Her eyes were wide and of a clear blue and he noticed that although her hair was very fair the lashes and brows were darker. He picked her up and she lay very still in his arms while she scrutinized him. Then she started to whimper again but dry-eyed and exhausted as though she had no more tears.

As he stood holding her he conceived a terrible idea. Except for the eyes – Molly's eyes had not been so blue – the baby was approximately the same colouring and weight as his daughter, so recently dead. Very few people had seen Molly in the last two months of her illness, not even her brothers away at school on the mainland. At the present moment, no one except himself and Sorcha knew she had died in the night.

While the baby continued to whimper, Micheál argued the case to and fro in his mind. She obviously came from a ship or an aeroplane somewhere far away. Someone may even have set her adrift deliberately. For once, thought Micheál, God might be on my side. If anyone on the island did suspect anything – if there was any malicious gossip about changelings – like everything else it would be a nine days' wonder until something newer came along. They could just ignore it, he and his family. The belief about changelings persisted in the islands, particularly amongst the older people who said that the fairies often stole children and replaced them with their own. And who was to gainsay them? thought Micheál as, addled by lack of sleep and grief, he looked down at this child.

But they must be careful. Someone would be looking for her. His brain raced. If there was any gossip it would lead to nothing. Certainly nothing outside the island. The island people kept their own business to themselves. He looked out to sea again. Definitely nothing else, only the small orange raft. When that was found it would be assumed that all aboard had been lost.

The child had closed her eyes and appeared to be sleeping. Her peaceful baby face stirred a tenderness in him he had thought long gone and he felt the prick of tears for his own lost daughter. He knew that Sorcha was very lonely. This child might please Sorcha.

He took a final careful look behind and all around him. Still nobody in sight. Then, quickly, he wrapped the baby again in the blanket. The collie, sensing excitement, began to make little yipping noises and ran ahead of her master, who hurried along the strand towards the rocks which bordered it at the far end. He went as close to the edge of the water as he dared and, first looking round to make sure that he was still unobserved, he threw the lifejacket as far as he could with one arm out to sea. Then, preceded importantly by the collie, he turned and loped back up the hill through the vacant landscape towards his house. Behind him the empty raft bobbed in the surf on the shoreline.

Christian could not get to sleep. There was a lot of to-ing and fro-ing downstairs, with telephones ringing and cars scrunching in and out of the driveway. He raised himself in the bed and clicked on the bedside lamp, throwing soft light in a pool across the floor and illuminating the colourful, ordered chaos of his own small world. Christian was a hoarder and did not allow anyone to throw out any of his outgrown possessions. Neatly ranged on a shelf were teddy bears and stuffed animals from his babyhood and some of the carpeted floor was taken up with a Hornby train set imported from England, still laid out but unused for a number of years. In one corner a junior trampoline shared space with a handmade rocking-horse from Marshall Field's with mane and tail of real hair, in another stood a half-sized pool table. His Davy Crockett hat, Indian headdresses and stetsons decorated the length of one entire wall and the lid on his custom-made toybox was so full it did not close properly.

Above his homework desk specially fitted shelves held his collection of exotic seashells and Christian's bookcase, a bright wooden one painted in bold shades of primary red and blue, held leather-bound sets of children's classics, fairy-tales and encyclopaedias, clearly little used – but there was one small section where books and Marvel comics were dog-eared and piled in untidy heaps, spilling from the shelves on to the floor. It was for this section that he headed. On top was an illustrated version of *Huckleberry Finn*, so often read that it was falling apart, and an even tattier book underneath, in Christian's opinion the best book of all, Anna Sewell's *Black Beauty*. He retrieved it carefully, trotted back to bed and snuggled down again under his striped counterpane.

The book fell open naturally at the passage where the old war-horse, Captain, tells Beauty of his experiences in the Crimean War. '"I, with my noble master, went into many actions together without a wound; and though I saw horses shot down with bullets, pierced through with lances and gashed with fearful sabre-cuts; though we left them dead on the field, or dying in the agony of their wounds, I don't think I feared for myself."'

It was Christian's favourite passage of literature. His mind took off from there. He rode his own charger into mighty battles and although in the Crimea Captain had no canine companion, in Christian's scenario there was always a hound, called Shep or Blue or Rusty, running faithfully by his side. Christian travelled in his mind from the Crimea to other exotic places with names which resounded in his ears: Afghanistan, India, Timbuktu, Mexico, the Congo. He and his animal companions fought battles in China and Mongolia and Spain. They charged up the slopes of Mount Everest and fought for their lives in the flash floods of the Amazon.

His grandpa had told him many stories about his childhood in the villages and coal pits of Wales and how, tragically, his grandpa's dad and two brothers had been killed underground in a big explosion. Christian was relieved that, unlike most Welsh boys, he did not have to go into any coal pits when he was fourteen but generously he included Wales in his tour of knightly valour. On hearing an explosion, or maybe two, Rusty or Shep or Blue would run ahead, digging through the rubble while Christian and his charger would perform mighty deeds of bravery, dragging huge rocks from the collapsed mouths of pits and rescuing black-faced, battered miners.

Downstairs, he heard the doorbell ring for the umpteenth time that night. His grandma and grandpa must be having a party, he decided, although it was strange he had not heard any music or laughter. He was tempted to get out of bed again to investigate but he was tired. He turned out his lamp. Christian's last waking thought was of his puppy and whether it should be a big brave one able to do battle or a small floppy one he could take round with him in a special carrier on his bicycle.

He was asleep half an hour later when his bedroom door opened and his grandparents stood framed in the light from the landing outside.

'Let him sleep,' said Cordelia Smith to Malcolm. 'He's only a baby. He'll know soon enough . . . '

She crossed the room and picked up from the floor beside the bed an ancient stuffed rabbit, barely recognizable as such because it was earless, one-eyed and bald. Carefully, she placed it on the pillow beside Christian's sleeping blond head.

The sun was now fully risen, shafting through the ragged clouds which raced across the sky after the storm. The Inisheer landscape was still empty although once Micheál, checking fearfully behind him, thought he saw a currach put out in the surf. It was his imagination: there was nothing there.

He worked quickly and competently, his spade moving easily through the damp sandy soil, so much worked that its texture was like coarse sugar laced with minute fronds of seaweed not yet fully rotted. As he worked he removed the small potatoes he unearthed, still not much more than seed, setting them tidily to one side in a row. The hole he dug was neat, not quite rectangular, an ovoid. He dug it very deep, deeper than the potatoes would be planted, right down until he hit the rock.

Sorcha stood to one side, her back to the sagging turf rick. The longish skirt she wore whipped round her legs in the fitful wind and she shook violently, shivering from tiredness, cold and tension. She did not look at all at the small, sheet-wrapped burden in her arms but kept her eyes fixed on a point in the landscape over Micheál's shoulder. And although she made no sound the tears ran unchecked down her white, worn face, joining like a river over her mouth. From time to time she licked them away.

Within minutes the hole was ready and Micheál approached his wife, holding out his hands to take the bundle from her.

But Sorcha would not give her. Instead, head bent, she walked the few steps to the grave and knelt. In one movement, she placed her baby's body in the earth and stood up.

Micheál moved forward with his spade but Sorcha, uncharacteristically violent, pushed him aside. She knelt beside the hole and took the little body out again. Carefully, concentrating, she unwrapped the sheet while Micheál bowed his head low over the handle of his spade. The baby's face became visible. The eyes were open, like clouded marble. Sorcha kissed her daughter on the mouth and held the face once more to her breast. Then she wrapped her up again and placed her back in the grave. She got up and walked away, not waiting for Micheál to fill in the earth.

From inside the cottage came the thin high wail of the other child.

Micheál shovelled in some of the soil then replanted his small potatoes.

Four hours later, while two RAF Shackletons flew wide co-ordinated sweeps over the area of sea from which the DC3 had made its last radio call, Christian Smith slept on and dreamed of brave horses and fleet, valorous dogs. But on the dockside in Galway city, Conor Ó Briain stood dejected while the wind blew off the Claddagh and rocked the hookers and fishing boats tied up alongside the jetties. He had achieved his objective but he had forgotten that on Sundays the ferry service did not run to the Aran Islands.

There was no point in hanging around and he was cold. Behind him, the city rang with church bells. He decided to go to Mass. It would be warm, it would give him time. He followed the sounds of the bells, across the bridge over the fast-flowing Corrib, hurrying along behind other churchgoers, decked out in their Sunday best. The men looked uncomfortably compressed in suits and ties; the women clicked along on high heels, wearing hats or headscarves or carrying mantillas; the boys' knees were red from scrubbing and their hair was flattened with water or Brylcreem; the girls, on the other hand, wore smug expressions and ribbons in their ringlets. Conor, afraid that the unusual bundle he carried might attract attention, shoved his shirt-wrapped bread under his navy school jumper and held his hands in front of the bulge in an effort to hide it. As he walked, he made efforts to shine first one shoe, then the other, on the back of his school trousers.

When he reached it the church was tall and echoing with long stained-glass windows depicting the tortures and triumphs of various saints and martyrs. Big sprays of lilies stood on the altar and the priest had already begun the *Confiteor*. Conor sat at the back of the church and joined in the familiar responses when the priest turned around to face the congregation.

'*Dominus vobiscum.*'

'*Et cum spiritu tuo . . .*'

When the time came he did not dare take Communion, feeling that he would draw attention on himself in his shabby uniform. But when everyone else had gone up, snaking along the aisles in two long lines, he felt even more conspicuous alone in his pew and fancied that everyone was looking at him, wondering if he had broken his fast or what heinous crime he had committed. He buried his head in his hands, trying to look exceptionally holy as if this were not his first Mass today and he had already received.

When the Mass ended and the congregation spilled out into the fresh air he left the church with them but once outside had no idea what to do next. So he hung around, first looking expectantly into the distance as if waiting for someone, then turning to study the church notices in the porch. The congregation for the next Mass was already gathering. When the church was nearly full Conor slipped inside again.

He attended three Masses and a baptism. During the baptism he stayed well at the back. Throughout the ceremony the baby cried, a lusty, full-blown shriek. Conor hated the sound. Inevitably the crying reminded him of his baby sister, increasing the feeling of helplessness and frustration in his own heart. He had a more urgent problem, however: he was ravenously hungry and his stomach rumbled so loudly that he was sure the baptism party would hear it.

When the baptism was over, the congratulations made and all the snaps taken, the sacristan snuffed out the altar candles. Besides himself the only other person in the church, suddenly so dusky and quiet, was an old lady dressed all in black, walking and genuflecting her way around the Stations of the Cross. Conor, still pretending to pray, was afraid to leave this bolt-hole but his stomach was now not only rumbling but actually in pain. At about this time, he remembered with longing, the boys in St Kevin's were sitting down to dinner. Sundays meant bacon and marrowfat peas and extra potatoes. His fear struggled with his hunger and hunger won easily so he went outside and round to the back of the church where there were no overlooking houses. Leaning on a set of railings he unwrapped his bread and devoured all six slices, one after the other. He badly wanted to urinate, so feeling thoroughly ashamed he squeezed himself into a corner made by the church building and a wall where there was a downpipe emptying into a shore. Then he went back into the church again – it seemed the only option. By now he would certainly have been missed from the school.

The curate, Father Tom Hartigan, a little man whose most obvious feature was a large hooked nose, found him at about six o'clock curled up on a bench in a side chapel dedicated to Our Lady. It was quite dark in the peaceful alcove but the guttering bank of small candles in front of the Virgin's statue illuminated the sleeping face with its twin crescents of dark lashes. The head with the pudding-bowl haircut was pillowed on the hands. The uniform was a little too small and the bony wrists stuck out of the sleeves.

The priest shook him gently. 'Son, son, wake up. You shouldn't be here.'

Conor sat up, instantly awake, heart thumping. 'Sorry, Father.'

The curate removed his glasses and cocked his head to one side. 'What are you doing here, son? What's your name?'

Conor hung his head.

'Come on now, son, I'm a priest. You know you can tell anything to a priest. Even your name . . . ' He chuckled making a strange noise, half snuffle, half snort, through his huge nose.

'Conor Ó Briain,' said Conor. Despite his discomfort he could not help smiling at the extraordinary sound.

The priest did not catch the mumbled answer but he understood the situation. This boy was not the first runaway he had encountered. 'If you tell me your name I'll bring you over to the house and we can have a bite to eat and a bit of a chat . . . '

Conor was as ravenous as ever and the offer was very tempting. But he was alarmed. Anyone in a soutane was suspect. 'I don't know, Father, but thanks anyway. I'd best be getting home.'

The priest was not deceived. 'Come on now. I've a housekeeper over there makes the best apple tart in the county.'

That was more than flesh could bear. 'All right, Father.'

'So what's your name?' the priest asked again as they crossed the church grounds towards the two-storey presbytery.

'Conor Ó Briain.'

'Where from?'

'Inisheer.'

'And what are you doing here?'

Conor struggled to answer but the words would not come. The priest's kindness broke through the last reserves of his composure and self-control and at last he gave way to all the emotions of the past thirty-six hours.

'Don't worry, son,' said the curate, patting his shoulder. 'Whatever it is, we'll sort it out. You'll feel better after a bite to eat and a cup of tea and then I'll help you sort it out.'

Before they sat down to eat Conor went to the bathroom to wash his face and hands but when he buried his face in one of the priest's soft towels the enormity of his predicament hit him fully. What was he going to do? Authority in the shape of a priest waited downstairs. He had no money to run any farther, no way to get to Inisheer. He did not dare contemplate the scene which faced him if he made his way back to St Kevin's.

Father Hartigan was sitting in a chintz-covered fireside chair in the little parlour off the kitchen. A coal fire burned in the grate and a murmur of voices came from the Bakelite radio on a two-tiered trolley in the corner. Right in front of the fireplace a small table had been laid with the promised apple tart and the tea things.

'There you are,' said the priest as Conor, pink from washing, recent tears and embarrassment, came shyly into the room. 'Sit down there now, till I get the tea,' he continued, 'it's already wet and drawing. How do you like it? Strong or weak?'

'A-any way at all, Father . . .' Conor stammered, entirely unused to being consulted about how he liked his tea.

'Right. It should be ready by now,' said the priest getting up and going into the kitchen. 'Inisheer. Is that where you said you were from?' he called.

Conor, who was sitting in the second fireside chair, tensed even more than he had already. 'Yes, Father.'

'I know Inisheer quite well. Which part are you from?'

This was dangerous. There were fewer than four hundred inhabitants on Inisheer on only 1400 acres. Why did the priest want to pin him down?

Father Hartigan was back. 'Which part did you say?'

'Near Cashel, Father.'

'Ó Briain, Ó Briain,' mused the priest as he poured the tea. 'I'm afraid I've never come across any Ó Briains in those parts.'

He could see the relief on the boy's face. What was he trying to hide? 'My name is Father Hartigan, by the way,' he said conversationally as he cut up the apple tart. 'I'm not from around here at all. I'm from Dublin. Have you ever been to Dublin?'

'No, Father.'

Conor's eyes were on the viscous juice which bubbled out of the pastry case as the priest wielded the knife. His teeth were watering.

'Dublin's a great city. A great place for a boy to grow up in. I like Galway too, of course, but where a man grows up is always the place he wants to live – wouldn't you say?'

'Yes, Father.'

Conor did not care where the priest wanted to live or didn't want to live. If he had been alone Conor would have stuffed the entire apple tart, there and then, into his mouth. Father Hartigan served him a large slice, about a third of the whole, and helped himself to a sliver. He waited until the boy had consumed the last mouthful of the first slice then placed another huge slice on his plate. 'Now, Conor,' he said, 'why don't you tell me what brings you here?'

Conor swallowed. 'I – I'm trying to get home, Father.'

The priest had recognized the St Kevin's uniform. 'Did something happen to you in school? Is that why you're going home?'

But Conor did not trust anyone in a black soutane. 'No, Father, school is fine . . . ' He hesitated. 'It's just – it's just that my little sister is sick, very sick, and I want to see her before— ' His voice wobbled and again he swallowed.

Father Hartigan poured some more tea, putting three spoonfuls of sugar into the boy's cup. 'Are you afraid she is going to die?' he asked gently.

'Yes, Father . . . ' and to his chagrin, Conor's tears began to flow again.

'Drink your tea, son, and we'll see what we can do for you.'

They ate in silence. Although the tears continued to run down his face making the apple tart taste salty, Conor finished everything on his plate. When he had swallowed the last of his tea Father Hartigan spoke again. 'Listen, Conor, the first thing we have to do is to let the Brothers know you're all right. They probably have the Guards out for you at this stage.' He saw the boy turn white and leaned forward, gripping his wrist. 'It's all right, son, it'll be all right. I know Brother Camillus. I'll ring him up and tell him you're with me. You can stay here tonight and then in the morning we'll organize a boat for you to Inisheer. All right?'

Conor seemed not to be convinced. The priest could feel his whole body vibrate with terror through the wrist he continued to grip. 'What is it? You can tell me what you're afraid of. I promise, I swear by the Lamb of God, that I won't tell anyone what you tell me.'

'Nothing, Father.'

'Son, I know it's something. You can tell me. Honestly.'

72

Conor risked one direct look into the priest's eyes. 'Brother Patrick, Father,' he whispered. 'He'll kill me.'

Father Hartigan took the boy's chin with his free hand. 'Look at me now, Conor. No one, Brother Patrick or *no one*, is going to kill you. I promise. I'll bring you back to the school myself when you get back from Inisheer and I'll make sure that nothing happens to you.'

Conor closed his eyes.

'Do you not believe me, son?'

Conor nodded slowly then and the priest released him. 'All right, so. Now, I'd better get on the telephone before the Guards arrest me for kidnapping!' The joke raised no answering smile and after a moment or two Father Hartigan left the room and went into the hall from where Conor heard him dialling a number.

Christian was confused. Sunday mornings were predictable in his house – early morning bustle, big breakfast – but this morning he woke up by himself. He saw by the clock on the wall above his bookshelf that it was after nine o'clock. Not only had he not been woken up for his breakfast but there was hardly any noise in the house. He looked out of the window. The driveway was empty – it should have the car there by now to take them to church.

He put on his dressing-gown and slippers and went downstairs. No one was in any of the rooms, not even a maid. He found Bridie in the kitchen but there was no smell of food, no roast in the oven. Bridie was sitting at the big table. Her eyes were red and she was crying, wiping away the tears with her apron. He became seriously alarmed.

'What's wrong, Bridie? Where's everyone? Where's Grandma and Grandpa?' he asked.

Bridie did not answer him. She let out a great sob and went to the Frigidaire to get the milk for his cereal.

'Bridie, what's wrong?' Christian's heart began to hammer.

The housekeeper waved her hands in the air but still did not say anything. Bridie was well known in the house for crying easily about everything, Christian reassured himself. She even cried at *The Mouseketeers* on television, saying they were lovely ('Such little lambs!'). But this crying seemed different.

'Is someone sick, Bridie?' he asked again helplessly, this time addressing Bridie's ample back which still shook with sobs as she stirred the milk in a pot on the big gas stove. He felt his own tears starting in sympathy with Bridie but he tried not to let them out. 'Will I get Grandma, Bridie?' he asked. 'Where's Grandma?' He really wished his mom was not away – she always knew how to deal with Bridie.

'Your grandma and grandpa had to go out early,' Bridie managed to gasp before the next onslaught of tears.

Christian now felt embarrassed and could not wait to get out of the kitchen. 'Bridie, I'm not very hungry this morning,' he said. 'I think I'll skip breakfast,' and before she could turn round he had fled from the kitchen.

He sat on his bed in his room and tried to puzzle things out. There was definitely something wrong in the house – it felt wrong. He picked up *Black Beauty* from the floor where it had fallen when he had gone to sleep the night before but for once the words failed to hold his interest.

He decided to get dressed. He was still worried but his mom always said that work and activity were always the best things to fight worry. He would make a start on building his kennel.

Forty-five minutes later Christian was absorbed in his task. He had joined together two sides of the kennel, using two small angle-irons he found in the gardener's tool-box, when he sensed that someone else was in the garage.

He looked around. The chauffeur was standing behind him. 'Hello, Jim,' he chirped. 'I'm just building a kennel here – see? Mom said I could have a puppy when she gets back from Europe and I want everything to be ready for him when I get him.'

Then something about the chauffeur struck him as odd: he was not dressed in his uniform but in a suit. The only other time Christian had seen Jim Maskowski in a suit was when he and his grandpa had met him by chance on the sidewalk when they were paying a visit to his grandpa's Auntie Mamie on the southside.

74

But before he could ask Jim about this, the chauffeur spoke. 'I know all about the puppy, Christian – your grandpa told me.'

Christian was flabbergasted. 'He wasn't supposed to tell *anyone*! It was a *secret*!'

'Yes, but he told me because he wants to get you the puppy now.'

'Now? Today?'

'Yes, Christian.' The chauffeur's voice was level. 'He wants me to drive you to Orphans of the Storm where we can pick out whatever puppy you like. That's by far the best place to get a puppy, you know, because all the puppies there have been abandoned and have no homes. So you can do a good deed, save one and give it a nice home here.'

Malcolm had discussed with the chauffeur the availability of puppies on a Sunday and they had concluded that Orphans of the Storm, being a charitable institution, was the only likely source.

Christian looked doubtful. 'Are you sure, Jim? Mom said she would come with me when they got home from Europe. Are you sure she won't mind?'

'Yes, Christian, I'm absolutely sure she won't mind. Your grandpa's sure she won't mind.' The chauffeur rubbed at something in his eye.

Christian ran into the house to fetch his jacket and when he came out again, bounding down the entrance steps three at a time, he hopped into the front of the Cadillac. 'This is terrific, Jim. Do we need money? How much do we need? Should I go back and get my savings box?'

'It's OK, Christian,' said the chauffeur responding, despite his feelings, to the boy's excitement. 'I have all we need. Your grandpa gave me money.'

All the way to Riverwoods, Christian bubbled over with plans for his puppy. As they travelled through the suburb of Deerfield, he spotted a woman being hauled along the sidewalk by a St Bernard. 'I wonder if I'll get a big one?' he asked the chauffeur. 'What do you think, Jim?'

'Well, it's up to you, of course, Christian, but I think one that size would be a bit difficult. How big is your kennel going to be?'

Christian nodded sagely. 'You're probably right. Maybe one not so big . . . ' Then, 'Do you think the puppy will love me right away? How will I know which one to pick? Oh, I hope I'll be able to find one that'll love me right away . . . '

As it was still morning there were very few potential pet-rescuers at Orphans of the Storm. The girl tending the reception desk took them out to the yards where Christian's eyes widened with pity. The cats were in rows of raised hutches about three feet square. Most of them ignored all efforts to attract their attention, but one or two mewed loudly and stuck a front paw through the wire grille on their cages in an effort to make contact with humans. Christian wished he could take them all home.

The dogs, who had wired-in runs, had a different attitude. They were wildly hopeful and as soon as he approached started to bark and whine with excitement, rushing up and down their runs, pressing up against the wire gates, climbing over one another. 'Take me home, take me home! Me, me!' each one seemed to plead with Christian and he became quite upset at the thought that he could only rescue one.

He couldn't make up his mind between an excited young yellow labrador, which bounced around trying desperately to lick him through the bars, or a very sad black and white mongrel, which hung back at the rear of its run as if it knew there was no point in asking any favours in such glamorous company. It sat, a resigned expression on its intelligent face, looking away from Christian but darting occasional glances of query at him while he dithered. After a while it flopped down, put its head on its feathery paws and seemed to give up.

Christian could not resist such sorrow. 'I'll take that one,' he said to the chauffeur pointing at the mongrel, which seemed to sense the decision because it sat up on its forepaws and wagged its tail – but only the very tip of its tail as though not wanting to count any chickens until it had supervised them all safely out of their shells.

The formalities were easy. Christian and the chauffeur selected a collar, leash and two bowls, one for feeding and one for water. Then the girl went to get the dog.

When it was brought out it was transformed, wagging its tail until its whole body was in motion, ears pricked, panting happily. It jumped up at Christian licking his face and then his hands, licking the chauffeur too as if to thank both of them. The chauffeur made his donation and they went back to the car. The dog had no hesitation in leaping through the open door on to the back seat.

'Where'll we keep him?' worried Christian. 'I don't have his kennel ready yet.'

'Don't worry about it,' said the chauffeur. 'Your grandpa will probably let you keep him in your room for a little while until you have the kennel ready.'

The kennel was never completed. The dog, which Christian named Flash because it had a white streak on its black muzzle, moved into Christian's room that night and slept there until it died six years later.

His grandparents were waiting for him when he got back from his first walk with Flash. Cordelia met him in the hall and he saw immediately that something was seriously wrong because her face was puffy. She had definitely been crying. His heart began to hammer again. 'What's wrong, Grandma?' he asked, alarmed as he had been in the kitchen earlier that day.

'Christian, darling,' said his grandmother, 'will you come into the morning room?' She took his hand. 'Your grandpa and I have something very sad to tell you.'

Malcolm was sitting in his wing chair but it was turned away from the lake and facing the door. His face looked all funny as well. Christian realized that his grandpa, too, had been crying. His heart seemed to shrink in his chest.

His grandpa held out his arms to Christian who still had Flash on the leash. The dog pulled back, paws splayed, fearful of the feel of the polished parquet, but Christian dragged him forward and, still holding him tightly, went reluctantly across to Malcolm. He was afraid to look at his grandpa's face and resisted his embrace, standing a little way away.

Malcolm did not insist on the contact. 'Christian,' he said, 'I don't know how to tell you this, but there's been an air crash . . .'

Christian said nothing but kept his eyes fixed on Flash who, tail between his legs, was facing away from him and straining towards the door.

'Do you understand, Christian?' Malcolm repeated. 'Your mom and dad and Susanna have been in an air crash.'

The world stopped for Christian. He felt himself growing smaller and smaller until he was a little dot. The only real thing in the room was Flash. 'How do you know it was the right plane?' he asked eventually. His voice sounded as small as himself.

Malcolm raised his hands as if he was making a sort of an appeal. 'Honey, we've checked and checked. We were up all night. We've been to the police station. There's no mistake.'

Christian kept his eyes on Flash. He saw that one of the dog's ears was higher than the other. 'How do you know they crashed? Dad said they were flying over Greenland, he showed it to me on the atlas. They could've just landed in Greenland and nobody's found them yet.'

'Christian, that would be impossible because they took off from Iceland in the plane all right but they never reached Ireland. And a life raft from the plane was found washed up on some island off Ireland's west coast. Christian, it was empty.'

Christian concentrated on the dot that was himself. He was afraid it would disappear altogether.

Malcolm put his head in his hands. Christian saw that his strong, humorous grandpa looked like a frail old man. But he had to keep holding tightly on to his still shrinking self. He glanced at Cordelia but she too had her hands up to her face so that only her eyes were visible, brimming over with tears. He noticed the tears running down the backs of her splayed hands, watching the way they ran through the big freckles on them like little streams through brown rocks. 'Can I go now?' he asked conversationally.

His grandfather nodded without looking at him.

'I'll come up in a minute, Christian,' said Cordelia, in a funny, muffled way.

Christian walked quietly out of the room, his dog trotting alongside him. When he got to the foot of the stairs he looked back through the open door into the morning room. His grandpa was still sitting in his chair and he could see just the tip of his grandma's foot. The sun blazed in from the lake. Christian thought the scene looked like a painting.

Conor woke early. For the first few moments he did not know where he was. The bed was softer than he was used to and he was in a room by himself. He crept out of bed and looked out of the window. It was a beautiful morning: the sun, not long risen, danced along the empty street beyond the churchyard and lit the white lilac in the garden of the house on the other side. The birds were going crazy; blackbirds and crows, starlings and sparrows created a ruckus which would have woken him if the bell had not. He longed to be on Inisheer – the air, the birds calling, the translucent sea. His heart sank. Who knew what faced him over there? How was Molly? Was she already dead? How would he cope?

He went back to bed to try to sleep some more until he was called by someone in authority.

At seven thirty he was called by the priest's housekeeper. She fussed over him, delighted with him, serving him rashers and eggs and thick fried bread for his breakfast. Conor, starving as usual, wolfed the food and had finished before Father Hartigan joined him having celebrated early Mass in the church.

The time ticked past in slow motion. While he ate his own breakfast Father Hartigan tried to distract his guest by asking him about his studies, eliciting the information that Conor's favourite subject in school was geography.

'Why do you like geography?'

'I don't know, Father.'

'Come on now, if it's your favourite subject you must know why you like it.'

Just as he was unused to being consulted about his likes and dislikes, Conor was totally unused to conversation on an equal footing with an adult. And here was someone, a priest at that, actually interested in what he felt. Hesitantly he tried to tell the priest what attracted him to geography. 'I don't really know, Father. I like to imagine what it must be like in other countries. Hot countries,' he added.

'What hot countries have you imagined?'

'Places like Africa or Mexico or India. There are great animals in those places and huge plants – because of the heat, Father – and you can grow anything you like. They have bananas growing there and fruit and they don't have to wear a lot of clothes and there must be great freedom.'

The priest saw the animation in the boy's extraordinary eyes. It was the first time he had dropped his careful guard.

'And what do you mean by freedom, Conor?' he asked, helping himself to a slice of toast.

The light dimmed. 'I don't know, Father,' answered Conor. He had obviously sensed a threat in the question.

'You must know what you mean when you use the word "freedom",' Father Hartigan persisted. 'Don't be afraid to tell me. It's not a trick question – I'm just interested. I have a definition of freedom that you might not have. Everyone has his own. Maybe you can give me yours and then I'll give you mine and we can learn from each other.'

Conor considered. 'I think,' he said slowly, 'that in other countries they have different customs and different religions and they don't all believe the same thing. But they don't get punished for not behaving the same as everyone else. That's being free. Freer than here,' he amended.

Before the priest could organize a satisfactory answer the telephone rang and he went to answer it.

The call was from Brother Camillus. Conor heard only one side of the conversation and the priest said very little. But after the call had been terminated Father Hartigan bounced back into the kitchen making that amazing snuffling noise which passed for a chuckle. It would not now be necessary to hire the boat. Apparently, after his call to the school the previous evening, Camillus had telephoned the big island, Inishmore. A radio call had been placed from there to Inisheer, enquiring as to the latest news of the Ó Briain family. The reply had been received this morning and the news was good.

'It seems you were worrying for nothing, son,' said the priest. 'Your little sister took a turn for the better during the night and she's on the mend. She'll still have to be nursed for a while more but everything's going to be all right.'

Conor felt giddy with relief and then half disappointed that he would not now be going out to the island. His disappointment hardened into alarm. He would have to go back to the school . . .

The priest watched the play of different emotions. He had anticipated at least the alarm. 'I'm going to drive you back out to St Kevin's in the car,' he said, putting a hand on Conor's shoulder. 'You're not to worry. Nobody, I mean *nobody*, is going to harm you. I promise.'

He looked at the boy, whom he saw was not convinced. 'If there ever is any problem,' he went on impulsively, 'you can rely on me. And if you like I'll come to visit you from time to time. Not every visiting day, mind, but sometimes. That'll keep Brother Patrick in line if he knows you have a friend who's a priest. Even the Brothers are afraid of the priests!'

This time Conor smiled. It was the first time he had done so since they met and Father Hartigan marvelled at the change in the boy's face. Conor's smile lit up his long face, overcoming the ugly haircut and the pasty, boarding-school complexion. This one was going to be a charmer, thought Tom Hartigan who, looking at this open, dazzling smile, felt helpless. What do we do to our children? he wondered, finishing his second cup of tea. This child should be romping in the sun.

He was one to talk, he thought then, locked greyly into his own celibate loneliness, shut off from human affection. His parents were dead and he was an only child so, unlike many of his clerical friends who held 'favourite-uncle' status, he did not even have nephews or nieces to take out or to whom he could send birthday cards. He rubbed the side of his huge nose and smiled back at Conor, still looking at him with such conspiratorial hope. He rose from the table and the boy rose reflexively with him.

Maybe they could help one another, thought Father Hartigan. The Lord moved in mysterious ways.

The trip out to the school was uneventful. The priest did his best to keep his young companion's spirits up but he noticed that the nearer they came to the school the more tense Conor became.

Father Hartigan pulled off the road on the pretence that he had to make a call on someone he knew in a local smallholding. 'Come on with me,' he invited, when he had driven into the deserted farmyard and turned off the ignition.

Conor got out of the car and the two walked up to the farmhouse, the door of which was ajar.

A scrawny greyhound bitch, obviously nursing, ran out of the house to meet them, fawning and smiling. Conor bent and tickled the animal under the chin and she rolled over on her back, bicycling ecstatic paws in the air.

'Anyone home?' called the priest through the open door. There was no reply. 'He must be down the fields,' said Father Hartigan. 'I'll call again on the way back.'

Conor was very glad to get back out to the open air.

'Tell you what,' said Father Hartigan as if he had just had a great idea, 'I feel the need of a bit of a walk. Let's stretch our legs – OK?'

'Yes, Father.' Conor was surprised. He did not know what to expect next from this unpredictable cleric. Up to now his personal experience with men of the cloth had been almost entirely negative.

'Are you sure you want to come?' The priest's eyes were mischievous. 'Maybe you're in a desperate hurry to get back to Brother Patrick?'

Conor smiled again, that dazzling, lighting-up smile, and Father Hartigan could see his whole body unclench.

They walked across the fields and the priest saw immediately the change undergone by his young companion. Conor's walk

82

loosened. He seemed to grow and straighten. Out here in the open, thought Father Hartigan, no man is this boy's master. 'Tell me about Brother Patrick,' he said casually.

Conor shot him a look but the priest was intent on examining a piece of fungus on the rotten bark of a dead ash tree.

'What do you want to know, Father?'

'Well, maybe I shouldn't tell you this, but I know a lot about the Brother. He and I go back a long way. We're the same age, you know, and we studied in the junior seminary together. I don't think anything you tell me would surprise me.'

Conor told him then. He was scarlet with embarrassment but the words came flooding out.

'I see,' said the priest when the story was finished. His tone was casual – after all, he had to show some sort of solidarity with the boy's authority figures – but his heart beat with savage anger. They had taken a route which led them in a wide circle back towards the car and were crossing a drain between two of the absent farmer's stony fields. 'Listen to me now, Conor,' he said, 'do you remember the promise I made you back at the presbytery? That you would have nothing to fear from Brother Patrick?'

Conor nodded. The remnants of his embarrassment still showed in two bright spots of red high on his cheekbones.

'Well, I think I can guarantee that from today you will never have to suffer at his hands like that again.'

'How are you going to do that, Father?'

The priest hated to hear the timidity in his voice. 'That's for me to know, Conor. But I give you my personal word. All right?'

'All right, so.'

They smiled at one another then. Father Hartigan extended his hand and Conor shook it. The priest realized for the first time that he was smaller than the boy.

They encountered no one on the long driveway into the school and when they pulled up in front of the grey façade it was as lifeless as if this Monday morning fell in the middle of the school holidays. When they got out of the car, however, they could hear the sound of voices, some in unison, through the open windows of the various classrooms.

Father Hartigan squeezed Conor's arm to give him courage.

The door was answered by the school principal – Brother Camillus himself. 'Thought it would be you!' he said cheerfully. He was bespectacled, rotund and permanently harassed but the boys in St Kevin's, while treating him with the wary respect due to his status, acknowledged amongst themselves that he was not the worst of them. 'Come on in,' he said taking the priest's hand. 'How're you keeping, Tom?' He closed the big door behind them. 'This man here gave us a fright. Just as well it was yourself that found him, Tom.' He talked about Conor as though he were a package gone astray in a railway station.

The three of them stood an awkward second. Conor was again aware of the overpowering smell of floor polish, at this time of day overlain with the aroma of cooking cabbage.

'I'd like a word with you in private, Aidan,' said Father Hartigan, breaking the awkwardness, and this was the first Conor knew that Brother Camillus had any other name than the one he had been given in religion.

'Sure thing, sure thing, sure thing!' said the Brother, relieved to be in action again and flinging open the door to the parlour. 'Wait you out here, Ó Briain,' he said over his shoulder to Conor. In times of particular harassment, Brother Camillus's Kerry origins showed in his speech. He cantered into the room ahead of the priest.

Before Father Hartigan closed the parlour door he aimed a huge wink at Conor.

Conor strained to discern individual words in the murmur of voices that came through the heavy parlour door but could not distinguish anything and lacked the courage to go closer to the door. He whiled away the time by counting the black and white squares in the floor tiles but was too nervous to concentrate and kept losing count. He was examining the two pictures in the hall – one, a gloomy, fly-specked portrait of the Brothers' founder, the other a garish photograph of Pius XII – when he heard the door of the parlour open.

Father Hartigan came out first. He walked right across the hall and took Conor's arm. 'Right,' he said. 'Come on! Walk me to my car.'

Conor looked for permission at the Head Brother, who was rocking on the balls of his feet and fidgeting with something in his cassock pocket, making a continuous crackling sound. He could not interpret the Brother's expression but Camillus waved him out of the door. 'Go on, go on, go on, go on!'

They walked down the steps to the car. Father Hartigan opened the door and then turned to the boy. His face was deadly serious. 'Now listen, Conor. If you mind your Ps and Qs and do your work you'll have no more trouble in this school.'

'What – what did you say to him?' Conor stammered.

'What I said is neither here nor there. I told you before that Brother Patrick and I go back a long way – and I know Camillus well enough too. That's all you need to know . . . except this.'

Taking a crumpled envelope out of his pocket he rummaged around in the glove compartment of the car, extracting a half-bitten ballpoint pen. He scribbled something on the envelope. 'That's my telephone number. If you need me for anything – I mean *anything* – you telephone me. All right? I've told Brother Camillus that I'm giving you this permission and he will arrange that you get to the telephone.'

Conor looked at him in stupefaction.

'Take that look off your face!' The priest gave him a friendly thump on the biceps. 'Now I don't expect you to ring me when you fancy the need for a bar of chocolate! But do ring me if you need to talk. All right?'

Conor nodded, still dumb.

The priest hopped into the car and, starting the engine, roared off down the driveway.

It was not until that night in the dormitory that Conor, while transferring the telephone number from the back of the envelope to his writing case, found that the envelope contained a five-pound note. He was putting the writing case away in his locker when he heard Brother Patrick's heavy tread on the boards of the dormitory floor. The curtains of his cubicle swished open and the Brother stood framed huge in the opening. Conor's immediate instinct was to cower but instead he got out of bed and stood as tall as he could. Brother Patrick and he stared at one another. In the semi-darkness, he could see that the Brother's fists were bunched at his side.

'The big fella!' said the Brother. 'Look at the big fella!' He was so enraged that a gob of spittle shot out of his mouth and landed on his chin.

The priest had been as good as his word. Conor's day-to-day life at St Kevin's became much calmer and stayed calm until the day he left.

A week after Conor's return to school, his uncle, Seán Ó Briain, was stranded by weather on Inishmaan, the middle island. He was not the only one from Inisheer: the second man in Seán's own currach and two from another were stranded too with two fishermen from Inishmore. There was a stranger in the pub that night, an anthropologist from Norway, the latest in a long line to come to study the islanders' way of life. This one was sturdier than most: having arrived the previous June, he stayed the winter.

The drink in the pub that night was recently landed and in great condition so the bar was full and raucous and the Norwegian anthropologist, part of the furniture as far as the men were concerned, sat quietly on his own in a corner. He still did not understand more than a fraction of what he heard. The language, spoken so rapidly, bore little relation to his dictionaries and grammars. And he had the strong impression that when he was around even the words he might have understood were slurred or glossed to keep them private.

Having acquired a taste for stout he had battled his way through the weather and was sucking his pint, bothering no one, when suddenly he heard an explosion of talk more furious than the rest. There was a loud crack, a tinkle of glass and then silence as all the talk ebbed away.

He looked around. The Inisheer men were on their feet. One held a broken bottle, jagged edge pointed at one of the men from Inishmaan. The other three from Inisheer moved slowly and stood tightly beside him until the four of them were packed together, the one who held the broken bottle in front. Like stalking dogs, they stretched out their necks. The other men in the pub moved around the threatened man from Inishmaan until the anthropologist and the two men from Inishmore were the only people in the pub still seated.

There was no sound from any in the two groups and the anthropologist saw that the Inisheer men were outnumbered vastly, four to one. The woman behind the counter banged it loudly with the base of a pint glass and called something that the anthropologist, to his deep frustration, did not understand. Both groups of men ignored her.

For thirty seconds the men faced each other unmoving. Then slowly the men from Inisheer, stiff-legged, backed slowly out of the door. The man who held the broken bottle stopped at a table beside the door and slowly placed the bottle on it, broken edge facing the men from Inishmaan.

When they were gone the Norwegian anthropologist asked the woman behind the bar what had happened but she said she did not know. He did not find out until half an hour later when, in conversation with the men from Inishmore, he learned that a man from Inishmaan had said there was talk of strange goings-on, of changelings even, on Inisheer.

The anthropologist, who knew the legend, was excited. But try as he might for the rest of the winter he could not secure a single detail. Even on Inisheer.

CHAPTER THREE

Molly's day-to-day life on Inisheer was that of any little girl, learning to fasten her petticoats, helping her mother with the chores as soon as she was big enough, playing with the collie, which she had named Beauty, outside the house on fine days, going to school, learning her prayers, her numbers and letters on the kitchen table with her mam when it was too cold or wet to go out.

But today, 26 May, was going to be a big day, maybe the biggest in Molly's life, she thought when she woke up. She would be exactly five years, three months and twenty-six days old and she was going to the mainland for the very first time.

It was always easy to know how old she was exactly because her mam had taught her the calendar and she could count from her birthday on 1 February – Lá'le Bhríde, the feast of St Brigid patron saint of Ireland. It was a good day to have your birthday, her mam always said, because it was the first day of spring. Molly was a bit doubtful about that at first because each year when she looked out of the window on her birthday it was usually very cold and wet and stormy. But her mam had told her that on this day under the ground all the plants started to uncurl their leaves, getting ready to push them up into the fresh air. Molly felt privileged then. And she pitied anyone who had a birthday on any old ordinary day.

She woke early with a fluttery feeling all over. For weeks she had been counting off the days, marking them in pencil on the calendar on the kitchen wall. She had been too young to go to the mainland before but now that she was nearly five and a half her mam said she was old enough not to get lost.

She looked up and there, on a hanger on the big nail in the wall over her bed, was the confirmation: the blue silk frock.

Molly knelt up on the bed and touched it. It swung a little. It must be just about the most beautiful frock in the whole world, Molly thought. It had yellow teddy bears chasing each other all round the hem and a yellow sash which tied in a big bow at the back. When she had tried it on it felt cool and sort of slippy against her bare legs and made a soft rustling noise when she moved. There was a real foreign smell off it, which wasn't surprising because it had come in a parcel from America. The frock did not belong to her but to Aine Kett up the road. The parcel came for the Ketts from their auntie in Boston but Aine was still too small to wear it so her mother had loaned it to Molly's mam so that Molly could look respectable when she went to Galway.

She hopped out of bed and went to the window. The sun was shining already but there was nobody else up. She wondered if it was too early to get dressed. She strained her ears, listening for the first signs that her mam might be stirring. Molly knew not to go into her mam's bedroom to wake her up. Her dadda would be annoyed and would shout. There were only the three of them in the house now. Conor was still at school in Galway and Brendan was away in Birmingham, working at a job which meant he could send home money. Her mam kept the money in a big jar on the mantelpiece and used it to buy things she had never before had money for, like jam and a cloth for the table and wool for knitting and new shoes for Molly. They even had curtains at the kitchen window.

She listened hard at her door but could hear no sounds in the rest of the house so she climbed back into bed and amused herself by watching a line of sunshine crawling along her wall. It started with a shape like a pencil right beside her window. Then slowly the top of the shape stretched out and stretched out, pulling the rest with it until there was another window on her wall, bright yellow, just as yellow as the teddy bears on the dress.

At last she heard the door of her mam's room opening and from the kitchen the sounds of water being ladled from the can into the kettle. She jumped out of bed.

Her mam was raking the fire. 'Molly! You'll catch your death! Put something on.'

Molly went back into her bedroom and pulled a jumper over her nightdress. Then she took her porridge bowl from the dresser and, setting it on the table, sat in her place swinging her legs. She was disappointed that her mam was not yet dressed in her good clothes, just in her house skirt and shawl.

'*Cathain a bhfuil muid ag imeacht?*' she asked, while her mam stirred the porridge in the skillet over the fire. She couldn't help herself – the words just burst out although she knew better than to start annoying her mam right away about how long more it would be until they would be going.

Her mam did not answer, just rolled her eyes to heaven.

The hours felt endless until Molly was allowed to put on the frock. First she had to endure being washed. She hated being washed with all her heart. On Saturday nights, when her mam took out the galvanized bath and set the kettles to boil the water, she always got a sick feeling in her tummy and although she trusted her mam and knew it had to be done sometimes she could not help crying, especially when her mam washed her hair. At least there was no bath today, just an ordinary wash with the face cloth. She screwed up her eyes and tried not to wriggle.

Her mam combed her hair carefully and helped her into the frock and tied the sash. Molly did a twirl and her mam told her she looked like a little princess. She twirled again. She certainly felt like a little princess.

She picked up her new patent leather shoes with the strap across the instep – each shoe stuffed with a new white sock. She was not allowed to wear them yet but had to carry them down to the strand so she would not scuff them or get them wet. She fetched her new white plastic handbag. It bulged and the gilt clasp kept springing open because there was too much in it. Her mam had made sandwiches for the journey, chunks of brown bread spread with butter and thick 'shop' orange marmalade which Molly had packed in the handbag with a clean handkerchief and two carefully folded paper bags. Molly was going to do her own shopping on the mainland. She had a whole pound she had been saving since Christmas.

When she was ready to go she went outside into the sunshine

to wait. They were going to make a real outing of it and stay in a lodging house for the night.

The *Naomh Éanna* was already at anchor in the deep water out in the bay, her cranes busy. Molly hopped up and down, afraid that if her mam didn't hurry they'd miss the sailing. But at last she came out, carrying her shopping bag and, in a lobster pot, two old hens whose legs she had tied and which Molly knew she was hoping to sell in the market around the Spanish Church. Molly had never been to a market and the only church she had ever seen was the little chapel on the island. It all sounded very exotic and exciting. But she did feel a bit sorry for the hens who were bundled so close together in the lobster pot that they looked like one big hen with two heads.

Beauty trotted in front of them as they walked down the hill from their house. Molly had seen the *Naomh Éanna* lots of times before but this time, of course, it was different and she was a bit nervous. It was different because she knew she was actually going to get on to the ship. The steamer looked huge, as big as a castle, especially beside the currachs which were moving in the water all around her taking her cargo.

She watched as the men on the ship unloaded a cow and two heifers. They fastened the animals into special slings attached to the cranes on the ship and swung them high, out over the water and down into the sea where other men in the currachs caught them by their ropes. One of these men was Molly's second cousin, Seán Bán Nóra, who caught the cow's harness as she came within reach and helped guide her into the sea. Then he kept hold of the cow's neck rope as she swam behind his currach to the shore. Several small boys dashed into the waves and helped Seán to hoosh the cow on to dry land but Molly didn't, of course, because she had to keep herself tidy. The cow came out with the water running off her back like rivers; she gave a little kick and swished her tail when she reached dry land.

It was nearly time now because the last loads were coming ashore, cartons of tinned groceries, dusty bags of cement, planks of wood and barrels of porter, fresh bread, eggs, a side of bacon to be cut into rashers, a big piece of beef, tomatoes, newspapers and mail. There were two chimney pots for a house being built by Marcus Ó Briain, another of Molly's cousins, and a second-hand bicycle for a distant relative of her mother's, an eiderdown for a double bed, several neat coils of shiny new rope, a gross of scholars' copybooks and, handled very carefully, a box of tungsten light bulbs for the island houses which had the electric light. Any other time Molly would have been rooting around with the other children checking on everything but she couldn't care less what the ship brought in today.

Eventually, Molly was able to climb into one of the empty currachs to be rowed out. She held tightly to her mam's hand: the sea, getting so deep, frightened her. It moved and heaved and she could imagine what it must be like to fall in, how cold it would be and how dark.

When they got to the side of the steamer, the deck seemed so high as to be on top of a mountain but she was helped on to the boarding ladder by one of the men. Another man took her hand as she climbed on to the deck. The sea was not so frightening from up here although she kept her distance from the rail when they got under way. There was an exciting feeling in the soles of her feet from the steamer's engines as the ship rolled from side to side. She sat beside her mam and enjoyed the wind and the sound of the gulls which spread above the steamer's smokestack looking, she thought, like a holey umbrella. She watched over the stern as Inisheer got smaller and smaller until she couldn't even see her house.

She backed against her mother when they docked in Galway, shocked by the noise and bustle and the crowds and crowds of people. More people than Molly could ever have imagined there were in the whole world. And she held tight to her mam's tweed skirt as they came down the gangway, looking in awe at the paved streets and tall houses – all crammed together side by side – all the shops and horses and motor cars and money changing hands in a language she understood just a little and which she knew was English.

They went to the market right away and her mam's hens were haggled for and bought by a tinker woman with long straggling hair and two missing teeth. Molly was disappointed with the Spanish Church. It was huge, all right, but made only of ordinary grey stone and not some sort of red Spanish stuff like she had imagined. They sat in the sun in Eyre Square and ate their sandwiches, washing them down with a bottle of milk her mam bought from a shop. Then they set off all round the town. Soon her mam's shopping bag was nearly filled with treasure – string and candles and paraffin wicks, matches, white bandages, cough linctus, baking powder, treats like sweet cake, apples, marmalade, Cadbury's chocolate, new wellingtons for Molly's father, a ribbon for her hair . . .

After a couple of hours, Molly's new shoes hurt but she still had not spent her pound and she forgot the soreness when her mam took her into a very special shop. Molly's eyes were out on stalks. The shop was huge and packed with treasure: tons and tons of sweets, little bottles and brushes and pencils and tubes, which her mam said were for colouring ladies' faces, birthday cards and writing paper and big rolls of brown wrapping paper; there were sparkling necklaces with diamonds and books and comic-cuts. There was even a place at the back of the shop lined with rows and rows of toys. And everything was laid out on little platforms so you didn't have to ask the shop girl to show you anything but could pick it up yourself. There was so much to buy that Molly had a terrible time deciding.

But after changing her mind a dozen times and nearly buying a kite, she finally settled for a lovely doll in a lace dress, with blue eyes like her own and blonde hair. She still had more than ten shillings left. So she bought a book in English called *Dancing Star* because she liked the picture of the lady in it. Her mam picked out the words for her at the front of the book. The lady's name was Anna Pavlova and she was Russian. Her mam said she would read a bit of it to her that night in bed and explain the English words Molly did not understand.

Then Molly bought her dadda a pair of shoelaces and a lovely goldy tie-pin for Conor. She bought a toy watch for Aine Kett to thank her for the frock and then because she couldn't decide what to buy for Brendan went back and bought him a pair of shoelaces too. But she still had loads of money. So, while her mam was busy looking at something else, Molly sneaked up to where the jewellery was and picked out a bracelet studded with huge glittering diamonds, white and blue and green.

She gave it to her mam right away and her mam was absolutely thrilled, tearing open the bag and putting on the bracelet right then and there. She allowed Molly to spend the rest of her money on sweets, which the girl shovelled into a big paper bag.

When they had finished Molly's shopping they went to a photographer's studio. Molly was very frightened by the bright light and the man's brusque manner and the loud popping sound made by the flashbulb when it went off as he was photographing her mam. She sat on the floor beside her mam, again holding on to her skirt, dreading her own turn. And when it came she couldn't help crying even though her mam told her over and over again there was nothing to be afraid of. But the photographer had red hair and his face was all red too and he got an expression on his face which made him look just like her dadda when he was getting angry so Molly got even more upset. Eventually her mam lifted her off the velvet chair and said it was all right, that she didn't have to have her picture taken if she didn't want to.

She was a bit disappointed when they got to the lodging house because she had expected a sort of palace. When she and her mam got into their room it was very small, even smaller than her own bedroom at home. And the walls were a horrible colour, brown, with dark stains along the top, and the bed was lumpy and there was a funny smell off the blankets. But she loved the cosy feeling she got, snug in the bed, watching her mam brushing out her hair, long like her own but usually fastened in a knot at the back of her mam's head. The hairbrush made a soft, shushing sound, making Molly feel very peaceful. When she was a little girl the hair used to be the same colour as Molly's, her mam told her once, but now it was sort of faded, like old hay. Molly wondered would her hair fade too, when she had her own children . . .

Then after her mam said her prayers she got into the narrow bed beside Molly and Molly snuggled in beside her, feeling warm and safe despite the noise outside. They were too tired to read a bit of *Dancing Star* but in her arms Molly had her new doll, now called Peggy.

Such a day! She was really happy. But before she fell asleep, she got a bit sorry that she hadn't had her photograph taken, because she had to give the blue frock back and she was afraid she probably would never look like a little princess again.

Conor was due home from school about ten days after Molly's trip to the mainland. On the day he was to arrive Molly, escorted by Beauty, left the house very early in the morning to go down to the beach to watch for the *Naomh Éanna*, even though her mam had told her it would be hours yet.

As soon as she stepped outside the door, the sun warmed her face. The sky was cloudless and there was no wind, just a little breeze which puffed along the flat surface of the sea making patterns. Molly sat on the rock pavement outside her front door and took off her pampooties – she liked the feel of the warm stone under her bare feet. She put the pampooties on the windowsill and stood up again, straining her eyes looking out to sea. As often happened when Inisheer baked like this it was raining on the mainland only nine miles away. Molly could see the rain, grey and slanting down from the sky to the ground. It was so dark that she could barely see the peaks of the Twelve Bens.

She walked down to the beach, stepping carefully along the centre strand of grass which marked the middle of the boreen so she would not cut her feet on the stones, stopping now and then to pick celandines or a few dandelions from the tufts which pushed out between and under the stones of the boundary walls. It was so still and silent she could hear the stalks snapping when she pulled them. A sparrow landed on a wall near where she studied the shape of one of her flowers and when he took off again the whirring of his wings startled her. Even the larks who flooded the sky with song seemed higher up than usual today.

She searched the horizon when she got to the beach but there was still no sign: the sea glittered, empty and flat. She passed the time by riffling through the sand with her fingers, searching for the shells of sea-snail and little pink cowries.

When she tired of this she wandered down on to the harder sand over which the tide would travel soon, stopping now and then to jump on it with all her strength, making sure to come down hard on her heels, then stepping aside to watch the water well up into her footprints.

In Galway the *Naomh Éanna* had not yet even cast off. Conor was being seen off at the dockside by Father Hartigan. The two of them, collars up, stood beside Father Hartigan's battered old Volkswagen under the priest's black umbrella. Absorbed in watching the loading of the steamer they did not speak. The rain drummed on the stretched fabric and Father Hartigan dragged deeply on a Craven A, holding it – lethal and untipped – cupped in his hand so the glowing tip was millimetres from his palm. Suddenly he bent double in paroxysm, coughing as though he would turn his gut inside out.

'Listen, Father,' said Conor when the spasm had abated, 'if you don't give up those coffin nails you're going to die on me!'

'I know, I know,' gasped the priest, tears running down his face. 'But a man has to have some vices. Do you want me to start running with loose women?'

Conor smiled. Although still only sixteen, he was a good twelve inches taller than the little priest now. Their relationship had progressed through the years since Father Hartigan had first found him curled up in the church to the point where now he took his clerical friend almost for granted and their conversations and discussions, frequently heated, were conducted as though they were equals. Because of Father Hartigan Conor had gained immeasurably in self-confidence and no one in the school, boy or Brother, could dent it.

'Do you think you might come out, so, Father?' he asked as the steamer's crane boom swung out yet again, taking on a pallet. Although Father Hartigan continued to nag him, the one intimacy he could not adopt was to drop the 'Father' and to call his older friend 'Tom'.

'I will if I can get away, Conor,' the priest answered. 'I'm sure I will, actually. There's a conference I have to go to in Maynooth but other than that and a few weddings the summer is fairly clear.'

Conor was looking forward to the visit. The previous summer they had spent almost a week together on Inisheer. Father Hartigan stayed with the local curate, but since he was on holiday he had no pastoral duties and the two of them spent most of their time walking the island, fishing for mackerel or swimming in the clean cold sea. Father Hartigan did not object when Molly tagged along as she frequently did and she was easy with him.

Conor had enjoyed displaying his knowledge of the local flora and fauna. He was aware of a certain amount of sniggering and muttered comments about them as they walked the roads together or bent to examine a gentian or picked dog-roses or pulled handfuls of wild garlic to bring home with them. But the sidelong glances and half mocking salutes of the small groups of lounging men they encountered at various crossroads and meeting spots on the island did not bother Conor a whit and he put them down to jealousy.

His mam and dadda could not understand the friendship, he knew that. But he got the feeling, from a few things his mam said especially, that she was secretly proud that a priest would take such interest in her son.

It was nearly time to board. 'I'll write to let you know what my plans are, never fear,' said Father Hartigan.

'All right, so, Father,' said Conor.

'Have you got the books?' asked the priest.

'Yes, safe in the bag,' replied Conor, patting his battered suitcase. In the past year, Father Hartigan had taken out a postal subscription to *National Geographic* and after reading them himself passed them on, usually three or four at a time.

'Don't forget to write to Brother Patrick now.'

Conor did not answer but grinned ironically.

Father Hartigan patted him on the shoulder and said goodbye and Conor walked up the gangway into the steamer. Ignoring the rain, which streamed off his hair and down under his collar, he leaned on the rail. Father Hartigan was already getting into his Beetle. He slammed the door without looking back and the engine roared into life. Conor watched until the car had gone out of sight around a corner of a building. A faint cloud of blue smoke hung in the air where it had turned.

The weather cleared up when they were about a mile off the Galway coast and the journey was pleasant, over a brisk, choppy sea which half-way across the sound flattened out and became completely calm.

Conor identified Molly on the beach long before the *Naomh Éanna* was within shouting distance. Her tiny figure, distinctive with its blonde head, jumped up and down waving frantically with both arms. He waved back although he doubted if at that distance she could pick him out on the deck.

It was half an hour before the vessel anchored and the currachs left the shore to come out. By that time Sorcha had joined Molly on the beach. She did not often wear the Aran shawl but she had it on now, Conor saw, crisscrossed on her breast in honour of his homecoming. He was the first to disembark. When the currach he was in got within six feet of the shore, he jumped overboard into the thigh-deep water, not caring that his school shoes and trousers got wet, and humping his suitcase on his back splashed on to the beach holding out his free arm to his little sister.

Molly, squealing with joy, danced on the sand just in front of the breaking wavelets, holding out both her arms. When he got to her Conor flung the suitcase up the beach and swept her off her feet, whirling her around and around in the air. '*Mo chailín, mo chailín! Féach chomh fásta 's atá tú!*' She had definitely grown. Such a big girl now and so lovely. Boys were not supposed to cry so Conor squeezed his eyes shut and held Molly in the crook of one arm while he hugged his mother with the other. The collie skittered around their heels.

Then the three of them set out for the house.

Micheál Ó Briain was not in when they got home. He was out collecting the lobster pots and Conor was just as glad. He threw his suitcase behind the settle in the kitchen and took a set of his home clothes, thick tweed trousers and a báinín jumper, from the nail on the wall over it. He ripped off his school uniform and changed into the clothes he would wear all summer, loving the freedom of the old worn cloth.

Sorcha laughed when she saw him. 'I'll have to let out those trousers – again!' she said. She bent and examined the wide hems, out of which Conor's ankles stuck like the boles of young trees. She straightened up. 'No letting down left.'

'Doesn't matter, Mam!' Conor could not have cared less about his appearance. 'These are fine.'

Molly stood before him her hands shyly behind her back.

'What's wrong, *a stóirín*?' he asked, squatting in front of her. She brought her hand out, offering the cheap gilt tie-pin.

'Ohhh! Look at this. Real gold!' Conor was moved all over again.

She nodded. 'I got it in Galway when Mam and me went to the mainland.'

Conor fastened the tie-pin into the collar of his shirt. 'Now I'll have to get a real tie, Molly. When I leave school, I'll bring you to the mainland and you can help me buy a proper tie to go with this . . .'

She nodded again, gravely, full of grown-up importance. It was the first present she had ever given him bought with her own money. He gave her a hug and sat at the table where Sorcha had set a meal for him – good bacon and sweet little potatoes with plenty of milk to drink. Molly climbed into her chair at one end of the table and sat watching him eat, her chin in her hands.

When he had finished eating, he swung her onto his shoulders and they were off on their travels around the island.

Molly held tight to her brother's head, burying her fists in his thick hair. First he brought her to the puffing hole beside the cliff. He had brought her there once before when the sea was running and she had been scared and excited all at once each time the white spout of water spumed high into the air through the hole. But it was quiet today, so quiet that Conor let her lie on her belly, holding her feet so she could look straight down into it to where the green sea heaved like liquid glass far below.

In another place, he found primroses for her in little crevices in the rocks, still blooming, hidden from the burning light of the sun and he showed her where, in a few weeks' time, she would be able to pick harebells. They listened for the cuckoo and scanned the high sky for a peregrine falcon, one of a pair they had seen last summer, but the falcon, if she was still around, was not hunting today.

And finally when she was tired he found a little hollow, sheltered under the rim of a cliff, where they could rest. The hollow was soft with couch grass and she curled up beside him. His side was warm against her cheek but not as soft as her mam's. He told her he was going to recite a poem for her, one he had learned this term in school. 'It's a poem about a place far away from here, Molly, a lovely place, where there are high mountains and there is snow in winter and where the cows wear bells around their necks so that even from the cities, the mountains sound like a faraway piano.'

The piano in Molly's school had five notes missing and did not sound at all like tinkling bells but she wrinkled up her forehead and imagined what faraway mountains would sound like, ringing with little bells.

'I'll take you there someday,' continued Conor, throwing back his head to look up at the drifting sky. 'We'll go there together. The poem is in English, Molly, so pay attention. Don't worry if you don't understand. Just listen to the sounds.'

And he began to recite, emphasizing the consonants.

'Do you remember an Inn,
Miranda?
Do you remember an Inn?
And the tedding and the spreading
Of the straw for a bedding,
And the fleas that tease in the high Pyrenees
And the wine that tasted of the tar?
And the cheers and the jeers of the young muleteers
(Under the vine of the dark verandah)?

Do you remember an Inn, Miranda,
Do you remember an Inn?
And the cheers and the jeers of the young muleteers
Who hadn't got a penny,
And who weren't paying any,
And the hammer at the doors and the Din?
And the Hip! Hop! Hap!
Of the clap
Of the hands to the twirl and the swirl
Of the girl gone chancing,
Glancing,
Dancing,
Backing and advancing,
Snapping of a clapper to the spin
Out and in –
And the Ting, Tong, Tang of the Guitar
Do you remember an Inn,
Miranda?
Do you remember an Inn?'

He did not finish the poem, his attention caught by a pair of gulls which wheeled lazily above him, screaming on the wind.

Molly was disappointed when he stopped. She had listened intently and although she understood very few of the words she responded to their rhythm. She had recognized one line in its entirety and pulled at his sleeve. 'I haven't got a penny either,' she said.

He turned on his side and got up on one elbow. 'Molly! You understood! How clever you are! You're going to be the scholar of the family.'

He tried to tickle her but she was too fast for him, getting away before he could catch her. He flopped on his back again to watch the sky and she crept in once more beside him.

She thought her brother was definitely the most wonderful person in the whole world but then she felt disloyal to her mam. Her mam was the most wonderful person in the world too. She couldn't sort out who she loved the most, Conor or her mam.

Christian, long-legged in his tennis whites, took the front stairs two at a time, Flash bounding by his side. The sudden noise was an island of life in the dead house and Christian was very conscious of the disturbance but he did not care. He was sick to the teeth of living in this mausoleum.

It was a Saturday and he was going over to Dick's house.

He flung open the door of his room and stood on the threshold: he had to acknowledge that his grandfather was right, it was a mess. Although she vacuumed and dusted, the housemaid, as a matter of principle, was under orders not to tidy his room and Christian's allowance was dependent on his keeping it straight himself. Today was allowance day.

Flash stood beside him, panting happily, waiting for action, then as soon as Christian moved responded to his frantic pace, hindering the clean-up by rushing in circles around his master, barking, picking up and worrying dirty socks. Christian had to fight him for a T-shirt.

Despite Flash's cavorting, Christian managed to sort out the jumble of clothing on the floor, opening all the doors of his closets and flinging the clothes higgledy-piggledy onto hangers. Those which were dirty – and some which were clean – he shoved into the laundry chute in his bathroom. He did a quick sortie round his bookshelves, jamming in the books which had been strewn on the floor around his bed and then, grunting a little, replaced the heavy television set in its place on a table. It too had been moved to the floor beside his bed.

He surveyed the room while he took a breather: everything seemed to be in order. Christian had refused to allow anything from his childhood to be thrown out and his possessions, augmented yearly as he moved from childhood to adolescence, overwhelmed the room, large as it was. It was now a cross between Aladdin's cave and a crammed five-and-dime, but he was happy with it now and all that was left to be done was the bed itself. Not bothering to straighten the bottom sheet, he untangled the top one from the blankets and pulled the lot up until the bed looked reasonable.

He looked around for the dog, suddenly so quiet. Flash had helped himself to something from one of the shelves and was chewing on it in a corner of the room. He went over to investigate: what Flash had in his mouth was Christian's old stuffed rabbit.

'Give, Flash!' he commanded.

The dog suspended his chewing, rolling his eyes upwards to his master's face, but did not relinquish the rabbit.

'Flash, *give*!' Christian's voice had begun to break. When he raised it, it cracked. His hand flew to his throat. He bent and took hold of the rabbit and there followed a short tussle for possession. Christian did not want to damage the toy beyond repair but eventually, in exasperation, he pulled it violently from Flash's teeth. The threadbare covering ripped and some of the kapok spilled out on the floor.

'Now look what you've done!' Christian's voice wobbled dangerously again. He was close to tears. He picked up some of the kapok and stuffed it back inside the shell but the rabbit, a limp and mangled sausage, drooped in his hands.

He sat on the floor and cried. The dog crept forward and lay beside him but Christian pushed him away.

'Call Christian, will you, Bridie?'

Cordelia presided at the small lunch table in the bay window of the big dining room. The massive hunting table which ran down the centre of the room had not been used for years.

Malcolm was dressed for summer in blazer and slacks. He stole a surreptitious glance at that morning's *Tribune* while they waited for Christian. He heard the housekeeper's heavy tread on the stairs as she went to call his grandson and it struck him that he should offer Bridie Loftus the opportunity of retirement. She had been with the family for more than thirty years.

Eventually Christian arrived in the room, sat at the table without greeting his grandparents and helped himself to a bread roll.

Malcolm folded his newspaper. 'I see Lew Hoad won Wimbledon again, Chris.'

'Uh-unh!' said Christian, his mouth full of bread.

Malcolm looked at Cordelia. She nodded. 'Would you like to come to the ball game this afternoon?' Malcolm already had the tickets.

'No, thank you, Grandpa,' said Christian, not looking up from his plate and reaching for another bread roll. His voice was polite but distant.

Malcolm tried again. 'It's the Cubs and the Pirates. Should be a good one.'

'No thank you. I have other plans.'

'What are you doing this afternoon?' Cordelia took up the running.

'Going to Dick's.'

He continued to spread butter on his bread roll.

Bridie served their soup and the only sound in the room was the clattering of the ladle on the plates.

When she was gone, it was Cordelia's turn to try again. 'Maybe Dick could go with you and Grandpa to the ball game?' She looked at her husband. 'That'd be OK with you, wouldn't it, Malcolm?'

He nodded. 'Of course. Why don't you call him, Christian? Invite him over . . . '

'No, thank you, Grandpa, that's all right. We might watch the ball game on TV but we're going to play tennis in the park.' He scooped the soup into his mouth.

The three of them continued with their lunch, trying instinctively not to offend the silence, to minimize the clinking made by the cutlery on their plates. Malcolm and Cordelia exchanged another look. For some time now they had been worried about Christian's increasing isolation from them and were at a loss to know how to break through the wall their grandson had built around himself.

Bridie took away the soup plates and served roast beef. Conscious of the atmosphere at the table she moved almost on tiptoe, placing the plates in front of them as though they were Meissen and not the everyday china.

'Any news from school, Chris?' Malcolm broke the silence when Bridie had again left the room.

'Uh-uh . . .' Christian shook his head.

Malcolm sighed. He wondered if he should cease insisting that they eat together like this at weekends. He tried to engage Christian in a subject he knew interested him. 'How's the track going?' His grandson was well on the way to becoming a star in his high school athletics team.

'Fine!' Christian applied himself energetically to cutting his roast beef.

Malcolm sighed again and shrugged his shoulders at Cordelia, defeated. For the rest of the meal he pushed the food around on his plate.

Covertly he watched his grandson. Although still far off his adult height he was beautiful with an athletic, wide-shouldered body and clear, healthy eyes. His blond hair was neatly combed and his nails were clean and clipped. He presented a picture of the perfect all-American privileged kid. But there was an angularity about the set of the jaw and a tightness about the lips. Christian seemed permanently to be angry. It was one of the reasons, Malcolm supposed, that he was so good at athletics – in competitive sport he could release some of the aggression he felt.

'Could I be excused?' Christian asked as soon as his plate was clean. His voice had that edge of exaggerated politeness which was impossible to answer so Malcolm simply nodded and the boy got up and left the room without a backward glance. They heard a door slam and then Christian's voice outside calling for Flash.

Malcolm looked after him. 'Maybe I was too hard on him about his room,' he said doubtfully.

'Don't worry too much, Malcolm,' said Cordelia, 'it's probably just a phase he's going through. He'll grow out of it.'

'It's been a long phase. I still think we should take him for some sort of counselling.'

'Leave him be for the moment. I'll have a word with someone down at the St Joe's.' Cordelia spent a lot of her time doing volunteer work at a Chicago hospital.

They heard Christian thundering down the stairs again and Flash galloped into the dining room ahead of him. 'Could I have my allowance, please?' It was the first time Christian had spoken without being addressed first.

Malcolm took out his wallet, extracted a five-dollar bill and handed it over. Christian took it, said, 'Thank you,' and left the room with his dog. Malcolm looked after him. He was only fifty-seven years old but felt as though he were ninety. He told Cordelia he was going for a walk, leaned over to kiss her on the cheek and left the table.

It was a high summer day, hot, overcast and very humid and before he had walked very far along the lake shore, Malcolm's shirt was sticking unpleasantly to his back. He took off his jacket and laid it neatly on the grass at the boundary of his property to be collected on his way back. He looked out over the lake, which lay still and flat as though it too was weary in the heat. There were several motor boats chugging slowly along a few hundred yards offshore but they were travelling so slowly that their wakes caused little disturbance.

Malcolm was physically as well as mentally tired. Lately he had not been sleeping well and as he lay awake he was troubled by a return of the awful visions which first visited him shortly after the air crash four years before. Had Cal and Maggie suffered? How much had they suffered? He was tortured with the vision of his son clinging to a piece of wreckage in the cold Atlantic until his frozen fingers lifted off one by one. He saw the baby screaming and the water pouring in through her open mouth.

Cordelia had an appointment downtown and the empty afternoon stretched ahead until supper. He wondered if he should visit Mamie.

Alan Morgan, the Chicago uncle to whom he had come when he was sixteen, after his father and brothers had been killed, was long dead, but his wife Mamie lived in a retirement home · in Cicero on the west side. Malcolm adored Mamie and time and again had urged her to come and live with him in Evanston but she would not. He had helped her move to the best retirement home he could find, not the most expensive but by far the most cheerful with bright sunny rooms and big gardens. It was non-denominational but run by Catholics. Mamie, who wore dresses of violent green and purple and unsuitable shoes, was frequently taken to the cinema, which had become her greatest passion, and was allowed, within reason, to drink gin, often using it to wash down her tablets before going to bed. At eighty-nine Mamie was having such a good time in the home she was thinking of becoming a Catholic.

Malcolm saw that he had walked as far as he could without crossing into another private property so he turned back. He picked up his jacket and decided to visit Mamie.

On his way to collect the car he called in to the kitchen to ask the housekeeper if she wanted him to deliver any message to Mamie on her behalf. She too had taken instantly to the old lady and although she did not see much of her these days stayed in touch by mail.

He was wearing soft-soled shoes and Bridie did not hear his approach. The coffee-pot perked on the stove but she was sitting at the scrubbed table, her chin in her hands, staring into space. Her lack of movement emphasized the emptiness and redundancy of the big kitchen, Malcolm thought. With its humming iceboxes, rows of copper pots, vegetable racks, pickling jars and neat storage shelves, it was spotless and tidy as always, fragrant with coffee, with garlands of garlic, onions and herbs hung from a wooden trellis under the ceiling. But it needed some young life. The whole house needed an injection, he thought. This sunny room, which used to bubble on Saturdays with people coming and going, taking snacks, heating drinks, chatting and planning, now lay listlessly all around Bridie as if asking 'Where has everyone gone?'

He spoke softly so as not to startle her. 'Bridie!'

She was caught off guard and when she turned round he saw how old and tired she looked. 'I'm going out, Bridie,' he said, 'and so is Mrs Smith. We'll be back for supper.'

'What about Christian?' The housekeeper was flustered at being found sitting doing nothing.

'Don't worry about him. He's over at Dick's house for the afternoon and he didn't say what time he would be back. If he needs anything later, he is perfectly capable of making himself a sandwich. I'm going to see Mamie, actually – any message?'

107

'Oh yes, Mr Smith. Do give her my best love and say that I'll be dropping her a line this weekend.'

He nodded. 'See you later, then, Bridie.'

'All right, Mr Smith.' She had recovered her composure. 'I'll be roasting a chicken for tomorrow and leaving it with a salad in the icebox. And I've made a fruit cake for afters. Will that be enough, do you think?'

'Bridie, it's more than enough. I'm sorry . . . ' But he could not say what he was sorry for. He was sorry for himself and Cordelia, for Christian, for her, for sending his family out to their deaths in an aeroplane.

Christian parked his bicycle against the porch of Dick's home, one in a row of almost identical brick and clapboard houses built alongside the railroad tracks in what his friend's father cheerfully called the low-rent area of Evanston. He had brought over a new Elvis record, wrapped carefully in a T-shirt and as he unfastened the fragile 78 disc from the carrier of his bike his spirits rose. The front door of the house stood open behind the screen and already Christian could hear the hubbub from inside.

There seemed always to be at least two people talking together in Dick's house, competing loudly for ear-space with the radio and the family's recently acquired television. The decibel level was one of the things which attracted him to the place and why, by choice, he would have spent all his time here rather than in the elegant but dismal spaciousness of his own home.

Christian could never see Greentrees through Dick's eyes. Whenever Dick, impressed by the grandeur of his rich friend's home, made any favourable comment about it, Christian dismissed the compliment with contempt. To Christian his grandfather's house was as oppressive as a cemetery and just as much fun. After his parents' death he spent as little time as possible anywhere in it, except in the sanctuary of his own room, and took to spending more and more of his free time at Dick's.

He pulled out the screen door. 'Hi!' he said to the room in general.

Two of Dick's little brothers were rolling around on the floor wrestling with one another while one of his sisters, six years old and therefore in a position of authority over the boys who were three and four, stood over them, hands on hips, ordering them bossily to 'Stop it! Stop it this instant!' They took no notice of her whatsoever, nor of Christian's arrival on the scene of battle.

Another sister, eleven years old, was feeding a baby in her arms while she tried to concentrate on the flickering black and white images of an old Fred Astaire movie. She looked over her shoulder when she heard the screen door banging shut behind her eldest brother's friend. 'Hi, Christian,' she said and pulling the bottle out of the baby's mouth so that the little one squawked with indignation, leaned over to turn up the volume.

Christian walked through to the kitchen. Two kittens were chasing one another around the floor and he stooped to stroke one of them. 'Hi, Mrs Spielberg,' he said to Dick's mother who was concocting something in a mixing bowl at the sink, a dreamy look in her eye.

'Oh, hello, Christian,' she answered, coming out of her daydream. 'How nice of you to come over.'

Christian had expected her to say that – it was what she always said, although she might have seen him only the previous night or even within the previous few hours.

He found a clear space on one of the kitchen chairs and put down the record he was carrying, picked up the kitten and from habit walked to the Frigidaire and opened it, surveying its contents. It was packed with food, some of it decaying but mostly still edible. There were bowls and pots of leftovers – Mrs Spielberg was a good if erratic cook – half-filled jars of peanut butter, jelly, opened packets of bologna, liverwurst, snack crackers, bowls of Jell-o, containers of baby formula. Dick was the eldest of seven, supported by their father's salary as a desk sergeant in the Evanston police department.

Christian selected the larger of two half-eaten hot dogs and closed the door of the fridge. The kitten made a snatch at the food but he held it away from her.

'Why don't you make yourself a sandwich, Christian?' Mrs Spielberg had turned back to her mixing bowl.

'Naw, that's OK, Mrs Spielberg,' he said. 'I just ate. Where's Dick?'

'In the basement, I think.' Dick's mother leaned sideways and with her hand, which was smeared with white goo, turned on the radio which jostled for counter space with the dishes left from the family's brunch.

Still carrying the kitten, Christian stepped over a bundle of magazines at the top of the stairs down to the basement. The greenish light which came from the single half-window near the ceiling made the room seem cooler than the rooms upstairs. He threaded his way through the obstacle course of broken furniture, suitcases, cases of soda pop and heaps of laundry to be washed. Dick, also wearing tennis whites, was sitting on an old car seat absorbed in a *Spiderman* comic. 'Hi!' he said, without lifting his eyes from the page. 'Wanna watch the ball game?'

'I don't mind,' answered Christian, putting the kitten down and sitting on the companion piece of the car seat. 'I brought "All Shook Up".'

'Seventy-eight or EP?'

'Seventy-eight. It's upstairs. Wanna hear it?'

'Later,' said Dick, turning a page, but Christian knew his friend was impressed. 'All Shook Up' was the new number one.

He too picked up a comic and began to read. They were an oddly matched pair, Dick's dark hair and small round frame, already inclining to fat, contrasting with Christian's patrician good looks. The ceiling creaked and pounded above their heads but the two of them read quietly for about an hour, insulated from the din.

Christian's grandfather drove along Sheridan Road towards Lake Shore Drive. He drove unhurriedly allowing others to pass, giving himself the best part of an hour to reach Mamie's retirement home. He was always soothed by driving in this

110

manner. The car was the one place where no one could disturb him.

In Rogers Park he stopped the car on a red light beside an Illinois Trust premises shuttered for the weekend. It brought back bitter memories of his son.

Cal, whose ambitions to become an actor had foundered, was still drifting from job to job eighteen months before the air crash. The Smith Brewery, engaged in diversification, had just acquired a small Midwest cinema chain and Malcolm had placed his son in charge of the subsidiary hoping that, since it had tenuous connections with show business, Cal might enjoy the work and settle down. At first that seemed to be the case: in his first year Cal persuaded the parent company to expand the chain, building three brand-new houses, all of which opened in the autumn of 1952 within two months of each other.

But after Cal's death when a new man was placed in charge of the chain he discovered within six weeks that the accounts were shambolic and that the chain itself was almost bankrupt, with letters and demands from creditors including contractors and building firms bundled away in the back of a drawer in a filing cabinet. With the unwitting help of a friend in a local branch of Illinois Trust, who had fallen for his charm, Cal had apparently manipulated the money at his disposal and borrowed more, paying staff but not creditors, getting deeper and deeper into trouble.

Malcolm had not discovered any of this until three months after his son's death when the new man, trying to unscramble the mess, was visited by a representative of a gambling syndicate downtown. The representative held promissory notes which showed that Cal had tried to bet and borrow his way out of trouble.

The car had reached Cermak Avenue and Malcolm swung right, travelling now through an area of warehouses and used-car lots leaving behind the ritzier area along the Outer Drive. At the junction with Western Avenue a group of kids had opened a fire hydrant and were running, half-naked and screaming, in and out of the gush of water. A woman, obviously the mother of one of them, unleashed a tirade of abuse at them from the other side of the street while trying to control a perambulator and a toddler bent on running across the busy junction to join in the fun. Malcolm watched the little scene, full of rambunctious life, while he waited for his light to change. He thought of his own still, quiet household and his heart almost broke for his motherless, sullen grandson.

It took another ten minutes to reach the retirement home, set back a little from the street. He pulled the car into the small parking lot, planted with a border of gay red and yellow dahlias. The Cadillac was air-conditioned and when he stepped out of it the blast of heat, thick with the smell of asphalt, beat at his face. Before he went in, surreptitious as a thief, he picked a yellow dahlia from the flower-bed to take in to his aunt.

She was in the conservatory, sitting in her wheelchair with her back to him leaning towards an open window and holding back the fronds of a wilting potted palm while conversing round it with a woman who stood outside in the garden.

He walked up to her and touched her gently on the shoulder. 'Hello, Mamie.'

'Malcolm!' Her wrinkled face suffused with delighted surprise. She let the palm drop back across the window. 'You came to see me.'

'Why wouldn't I come to see you?'

She called goodbye to the woman outside the window and he turned the wheelchair away from the window, settling himself in a chair beside her.

'Here's a dahlia. You'd maybe better hide it – it's from outside the door.'

Mamie chuckled. 'Heavens to Betsy! My nephew, The Rustler.' She placed the dahlia in the V of her hot-pink T-shirt and Malcolm crossed his legs comfortably in his chair. 'Bridie sends you her love. She says she's writing this weekend.'

'Oh, thank you, Malcolm. How good she is. Maybe you'd like a little drink?' She picked up her handbag and rooted around in its capacious interior.

He put a hand up, smiling. 'No thanks, Mamie, nothing to drink. But you go ahead.' She pulled out the silver flask he had given her and unscrewed the lid, which doubled as a little cup. Mamie drank her gin neat. He watched as she poured the liquor into the cup and took a small sip. Mamie's outfit – she was dressed in a floral skirt under the pink T-shirt – was poignantly unsuitable for an eighty-nine-year-old woman, he thought. She seemed to have shrunk since last he saw her, which was only six weeks ago. The wrinkled folds of skin hung loose from her upper arms and trembled when she raised the cup to her lips. Her withered arthritic legs were skeletal but her thin hair was curled and neat, sitting on her head like a small white fleece. Her eyes were bright, the lids painted with blue eyeshadow. She wore red lipstick and her cheeks were stained with powdery rouge.

'Now,' she said, when she had taken her drink. 'Tell me how you've been.'

'I came to see you, Mamie,' he said. 'You tell me how *you*'ve been!'

'Oh, pooh!' she said. 'Nothing ever happens around here – ooh, there's Mr Wilson . . . ' as she spotted an elderly black man passing the door on a walking frame. 'Hello, Mr Wilson,' she called. 'Come and meet my nephew.' Malcolm knew that the residents of the home traded in the status of relatives and that Mamie could not let the opportunity to show him off pass her by. He stood to say hello to the man who made his slow progress across the tiled floor of the conservatory.

Mamie preened. 'Malcolm, this is Mr Wilson,' she said in her 'refined' voice, waving a gracious hand. 'You should hear this man sing! He's as good as Paul Robeson ever was.'

'Oh now, Mizz Morgan . . . ' The man laughed. He did indeed have a pealing, sonorous voice. 'I think you exaggerate.'

'My nephew, as you know, is *the* Smith of Smith's Brewery.'

'I do know that, Mizz Morgan. Pleased to meet you, Mr Smith,' said the man, 'and if ever you have a surplus of your product, Mr Smith, you know where to send it. That right, Mizz Morgan?'

'Too right, Mr Wilson,' said Mamie.

'I'll be pleased to send you some beer.' Malcolm was kicking himself that he had not thought of doing so before.

When the old man had gone, Mamie leaned forward in her

113

chair. 'That poor man!' she hissed. 'He has a son who's a doctor and the doctor has just divorced his poor wife and has gone off with his secretary, a little flibbertigibbet half his age.'

'Do you know her?' Malcolm was amused. He should come and see Mamie more often.

'Of course I don't!' Mamie took another dainty mouthful from her silver cup. 'He wouldn't dare bring her *here*!'

'Then how do you know the secretary's a flibbertigibbet?' He said the word with relish. It had always been part of Mamie's vocabulary. 'Maybe it's the wife who's the flibbertigibbet.'

'One can read between the lines.' Mamie pursed her red lips.

There was a companionable pause between them. 'How's Christian doing?' she asked after a bit.

'Mamie, truthfully, I don't know,' he said, 'I can't seem to get through to him. He seems dreadfully angry all the time.'

'Why wouldn't he be angry, poor little mite? Losing his whole family like that. I still can't believe it, you know, history repeating itself like that. You losing all your family twice.' Mamie was old enough to talk without embarrassment about tragedy and death. 'I'll never forget that first time when poor Alan brought you home, with your pinched white face and your big eyes . . . '

'I don't forget it either, the warm house and all that food the first night.' Mamie's motto in dealing with young people had always been 'If in doubt, feed'.

She put down her little cup and took his hand in her own. 'Is it still very dreadful, Malcolm?'

He nodded miserably.

'I don't know what to say, my dear. All you can do is to hang onto the knowledge that you got a lot of years with your lovely family. Use those memories, Malcolm.' Her kind old voice wavered and she rooted again in the handbag, this time to find a tissue. Malcolm watched as she blew her nose. It was she who at the age of eighty-five had travelled to Bangor, Maine, with him and Cordelia to mourn their lost family. On a tiny, rocky beach she had sat in her wheelchair beside the two of them at the edge of the Atlantic as they held each other and

114

cried together before they threw flowers into the waves. She had not cried but sat stoically, a rug round her knees, a black hat hatpinned firmly on her fleece of thin white curls. When their roses were blown back on to the shore by the stiff breeze it was she who had propelled her wheelchair through the shingle to pick them up and throw them back in the water.

'When you're as old as I am, Malcolm,' continued Mamie at last, 'a funny thing happens. The good memories become part of your day-to-day life so much so that it's hard to see the dividing line between how you live now and the way you did then. Sometimes I think Alan and I had our silver wedding only last week.'

'I'm having trouble sleeping, Mamie,' he said. The words came out in a rush. 'And in the middle of the night I think I see that air crash, over and over again.'

Mamie sighed. 'That pain will never go away completely, my dear, but it will fade a little until it's just a crust. And under the crust is all the sweetness of the good times that you can get at any time you want. But you have to help Christian. It's his turn now.'

'I know, but he doesn't want to have anything to do with me. I think he blames me and his grandmother for what happened.'

'He probably does, Malcolm. But put yourself in his shoes. The poor kid has to have someone to blame.' She took his hand. 'Remember, you can never love a child too much.'

'One of the things that worries me – and I don't discuss this even with Delia – is that because I can't seem to get through to him he might turn out to be a drifter like his father . . . and that it will be my fault.'

'So what if he does, Malcolm? There are worse states in life than being a drifter, you know. We're not all cut out to be moguls. God needs people to smell the flowers too.' Malcolm loved Mamie's incipient Catholicism. He looked at her kind, wise face, splotched with the artificial colour.

'You're a wonderful woman!' he said, squeezing her hand.

'Fiddlesticks!' replied Mamie. 'I'm old and have lived longer than you, that's all. I've seen more.'

He stayed with her for nearly an hour. The conservatory was

very quiet. Its pots and hanging baskets, filled with lobelia and nasturtiums and different species of ivy, hung lifeless in the heavy heat and Malcolm coasted on the peace. Mamie had a little more of her gin and chatted on but he saw the blue eyelids fall once or twice. She was getting tired.

'I'd best be going, Mamie,' he said when her head jerked on to her chest.

She roused herself. 'Don't go unless you have to, Malcolm.'

But Malcolm saw that she needed a nap. He kissed her papery cheek. She smelt sweet but slightly musty, of baby powder. 'Goodbye, Mamie. I do wish you would come out to Evanston for a visit.'

'Maybe I will, Malcolm, but I'm very busy here.'

He smiled and kissed her a second time. 'Goodbye, now. I'll see you very soon again.'

She smiled back at him but he could see she was on the very edge of sleep. He looked back from the door but her head had already fallen forwards.

Molly was having a great summer. One of the best days was the day she and her mam and Conor went to the ceilidhe on Inishmaan. From start to finish it was a day of magic.

Brendan was home on holidays from his job in Birmingham but he didn't go. Molly was not surprised. He had always been cranky but he seemed to be even more cranky since he had left home. Because he was a man now, and earning, he was given Molly's room while he was there and she had to sleep on the settle bed in the kitchen while Conor slept on the other bed beside the fire. Brendan never emerged from the room until nearly dinner time. Conor and Molly stayed out of his way as much as they could, although their mam tried all the time to coax him into a better humour. He seemed to enjoy only their dadda's company, frequently going out with him and their uncle in the currach to set the pots and going with them afterwards to the public house.

Sorcha was longing to see her sisters on Inishmaan and the ceilidhe was a great opportunity for there would be many boats going from Inisheer. She asked Conor would he go with her as she would not have gone on her own and Micheál would never have dreamt of taking her.

'I'll go,' Conor had replied, swinging Molly off her feet and above his head, 'if I can take my girlfriend with me!'

Molly's heart had nearly burst.

It was settled that Micheál's brother Seán would take the three of them in his currach.

Ceilidhes on Inishmaan never got under way properly until nearly midnight and they would have to stay overnight so for a whole day beforehand Molly had to help her mam get ready. The blue silk frock was borrowed again from the Ketts and ironed and folded carefully. Sorcha took her own good dress out of its tissue paper and washed it, hanging it out to dry in the fresh wind. Then, late in the evening, helped by Molly, she cooked bacon and made soda bread making sure there was enough food to feed Brendan and Micheál while they were away.

The next morning, the three of them and Seán set off in his currach, which had a small outboard engine. Sorcha sat in the bow surrounded by her bundles and parcels and Molly sat proudly beside Conor on the plank seat in the centre of the boat while their uncle held the tiller in the stern. The sea was bottle-green and choppy and as they bounced along, the spray raised by the currach wet their faces. Molly, whose uneasiness about the sea had abated only a little as a result of her trip to the mainland, held tight to Conor and licked the spray off her mouth; it was cold and salty.

The magic began when they were half-way across Foul Sound. They were joined by a school of dolphins. Molly had seen dolphins and porpoises, even small whales, from the shore – they were common in the waters around Aran – but this was her first experience of the animals up close. When the first one rose she got a terrible fright and gave a little scream but Conor tightened his arm around her shoulder so that Molly felt safe and at the same time thrilled.

Even their uncle, who was well used to dolphins, slowed the engine and got caught up in the excitement as the school churned up the surface of the sea all around their little craft, leaping clear of the water in ones and twos and sometimes threes, gazing across at the occupants of the boat each time they leaped. Molly thought their mouths were laughing. She clapped her hands and saw that in the bow Sorcha clapped her hands too and laughed with exhilaration. The headscarf her mother was wearing had slipped down the back of her head and her hair, caught by the strong sea breeze, had come loose from the knot in which she had wound it.

One of the dolphins, more curious than the rest, kept pace right alongside the currach only about ten feet away. Each time he surfaced, dark and shiny with water pouring off his back, he smiled directly at Molly, one large eye looking straight into her own. And each time he splashed back into the water she saw hundreds of little rainbows caught in the droplets which fell after him.

The school stayed with them for about five minutes before moving off still leaping. Just before they disappeared from view one broke the surface again. Closely followed by a second he threw himself upright, clear of the water, dancing on his tail for a second or two. The other did the same. Then, one after the other, both flopped back into the water raising walls of spray.

After that the rest of the journey was tame. Sorcha's sisters met the boat at the Inishmaan pier and took them to the house of the sister who had the biggest cottage where they all ate a big meal of fish and bacon with Bird's jelly and custard for sweet. All the sisters were there with their husbands and children, everyone packed around the kitchen table, adults sitting, children standing. The children were sent out to play then so the men could smoke and the women could gossip over cups of tea.

Molly was shy with her cousins, although she had met them before, and hung back from the games of hopscotch and skipping but Conor was involved in discussions with the boys and if she was not to be alone she had no choice but to join in.

As the dusk stole in from the sea, they all started titivating in preparation for the ceilidhe. Molly and her mam were squeezed into a bedroom with two of the children of the house. They would be sleeping in the bed while the others had been put on a mattress on the floor. It was difficult to move around in the tiny room but eventually, they were all ready. Everyone admired Molly in her princess frock and all the adults remarked on what a big girl she was for her age and on her lovely silky blonde hair.

Together, a party of twenty, they all set out for the hall where the ceilidhe was being held. The building was on a height and when she was still some distance away Molly could see the light streaming from the open door and could hear, drifting across the tiny fields and stone walls, the faint sounds of music. She wondered if this was how it sounded when the mountains in the high Pyrenees rang with bells but was afraid to walk up to Conor to ask. He was walking ahead with the boy cousins, three lads older than himself and two younger, absorbed in a masculine world she knew she could not enter.

Although it was nearly midnight it was not quite dark yet and far out to sea, to the west of the island, there was still a streak of pale blue above the horizon. But as she walked between her mother and one of her aunts Molly could see pinpricks of light bobbing like groups of fireflies on the web of boreens all round her. The little lights were cast by scores of torches carried by the dancers as they moved steadily towards the hall.

At last they were there. Molly was dazzled by the light inside and stunned by the level of noise. A great wall of conversation rose over the music being played by seven musicians on the platform, five local men and two stars specially brought in from the big island – a melodeon player and a man who played the flute. She wrinkled her nose at the smell of drink as they had to push their way into the hall through a crowd of men and boys packed three-deep around the door.

The women already in the hall greeted her mam; twinsetted and wearing Sunday skirts they sat in a beaming row on chairs set against one wall. Sorcha brought Molly along with her and set her on her lap. The women made a great fuss of her and one of them went to fetch her a glass of lemonade. While she sipped her drink Molly listened to the talk which was all about days and dances long ago. She watched the dancers on the floor, who stamped loudly with one foot or both and twirled and swung, all ages from three to eighty.

Conor came and lifted her out. She did not know how to dance but he whirled her round and round anyway and then another boy came and took her away from Conor and whirled her again so hard that her feet swung off the floor. When the set ended Conor brought her back to her mam, but her mam was already getting out of the chair, asked up to dance by an old man whose back was humped. When the man got out the hump did not hinder him and he was as light on his feet as a fairy. Her mother's face was light, too, and laughing – and Molly thought she looked beautiful, just like she did when she was laughing at the dolphins in the boat. When the old man brought her back to Molly he bowed and stamped his two feet and let out a big 'hurrooo!' and said to Molly he hoped she knew that her mother was the best dancer in Ireland.

The night wore on and Molly got very sleepy. She had never, except when she was sick, been awake so late. Conor made a little nest for her out of a bundle of coats so she could sleep in a corner of the hall. Other children were sleeping there already – two little boys and another girl, not more than about two, Molly thought. As she drifted off to the strains of an old-time waltz her mother passed her by, dancing with one of her sisters. Molly thought how lucky she was to be the daughter of the best dancer in Ireland.

She did not remember being brought back to her aunt's cottage and when she woke up her mam was already getting ready for the trip back to Inisheer. They were leaving early so Sorcha could be home in time to make the dinner for Micheál and Brendan.

The trip across Foul Sound was uneventful this time – no dolphins came to ride with them on the calm sea, only a single gull, floating lazily, very white against the slaty grey of the sky, so grey that their uncle Seán said it looked like rain. They were very tired, all four of them. Molly could hardly keep her eyes open.

There was no one on the beach to meet them but Conor jumped out and dragged the currach up on the beach so Molly and Sorcha did not have to get wet. Then he and Seán turned it over and carried it, a four-legged beetle with a black shell, to where it would be safe above the waterline. They all said goodbye to Seán and trekked up the hill to the house.

Brendan was nowhere to be seen but Molly's dadda was sitting by the fireplace. The fire was out. 'Ye took ye're time,' he said as they came in the door. He stomped out and away down the road.

Conor glowered after him but Sorcha merely sighed and sent Molly out to fetch some turf while she raked the ashes and set a bit of kindling to start the fire again. Then she sent Conor to the well for water as the creamery can they used to store it was nearly empty.

The four of them took their dinner in silence. Micheál came back and sat in his place stabbing at the food with his fork, never raising his eyes. There was no meat today but Sorcha had cooked a few salted herrings her sister had given her as a gift. Like most of their neighbours they ate very little fish but neither Molly nor Conor made any comment today as they chewed the tough, stringy flesh. Brendan was still nowhere in sight but such was Micheál's mood that none of them dared ask about him.

It was a relief when the meal was over. Micheál pushed back his chair from the table without a word, went to the mantelpiece and took some money out of the jar. The rain had started while they were eating and he took his oilskin from its hook behind the door, shrugged himself into it and went out. The other three relaxed. Molly helped her mam clear the plates and mugs off the table and cleaned down the scrubbed surface. Conor took a book out of the bag behind his bed and carried a chair to the window so he could read.

The rain cleared up about tea time and Sorcha sent Molly outside to sit on the wall and report to her when she saw Micheál and Brendan coming home. It was seven o'clock by the time she saw them walking up the hill. Brendan was staggering. Micheál was not so bad but there was an unsteadiness in his gait and a belligerent thrust to his chin.

The table was already laid for their tea, for just the two of them. The other three had already eaten.

'Let you go away out, Conor,' begged Sorcha urgently. 'Slip out and up by the chapel till I get them settled. They'll be better when they've had their tea.'

'Mam,' said Conor quietly, 'I'll go nowhere. I'm doing no harm here and neither is anyone else. We'll all just rest easy.'

Molly heard and understood this exchange. Because when Micheál had drink on him there was usually a row. She wished Conor would go and she would go with him but when he took up his book again by the window she crept into a corner of the kitchen and sat as quietly as she could.

The two men came through the door. Brendan swayed against the wall and would have fallen if Micheál had not caught him under the arm. Sorcha moved to the table. 'The tea's ready, Micheál,' she said.

He helped Brendan to the table and the two of them sat down. Sorcha poured the tea and made sure the bread was within their reach. Brendan was too far gone to eat but sat, his head bobbing unsteadily on his neck, reaching out to the food and then changing his mind and letting his hands drop again.

Micheál ate and drank fast, slurping great draughts of tea and stuffing bread into his mouth. After a bit, looking up as he reached for the butter, he caught Conor's eye. 'What are *you* looking at?' he bellowed, so loudly that small pieces of half-chewed bread sputtered out of his mouth. One piece stuck to his stubbled chin.

Before he could smother it a nervous laugh escaped Conor. This enraged Micheál who sprang to his feet so that his chair clattered on the stone-flagged floor. 'You young pup! I'll teach you to laugh at your father— ' and he made a lunge across the kitchen.

Sorcha ran to intervene, trying to place herself in front of Conor, but Micheál pushed her violently aside. She lost her balance and fell against the dresser.

'Dadda!' screamed Molly from her corner. 'Please, Dadda, don't!'

Conor screamed too. 'Dadda, I'm sorry – please – please, Dadda, I'm sorry!'

But Micheál was too far gone. Maddened he swung at his

son, open-palmed, but Conor ducked and the impetus of his swing carried Micheál onwards so that he crashed into the wall of the kitchen. He clutched his shoulder as if he had hurt it.

He came at Conor again, lunging. Conor was attempting to open the door to escape but it opened inwards and Micheál managed to grab him from behind. The two of them fell struggling to the ground. Conor was big and strong but no match for his much heavier and stronger father. Nevertheless he fought wildly, using his knees and fists.

Molly was so terrified she could not even scream. She flattened herself against the wall as her father and brother rolled around the floor, upsetting the other chairs and crashing into the legs of the table. Sorcha had picked herself up and was attempting to claw at Micheál's back but he brushed her off. She stumbled and fell again on one knee. All the time, Micheál was roaring and cursing in Irish and English, swear words, words Molly had never heard before. 'You fucking little bastard—'

He managed to get a lock on Conor, pinning one of his son's arms to his side, and rising, pulled him up after him still swearing. He dragged him across the floor and into Molly's room, temporarily Brendan's, and slammed the door.

The sounds of the struggle continued with Conor's voice now piteously raised. 'Please, Dadda, I'm sorry, please, please— Please don't! I'm sorry, Dadda, I'm sorry—'

Brendan continued to sit at the table, his mouth slack, barely aware of what was going on. Sorcha could bear no more. Sobbing she took her shawl from the hook and ran out of the door. Molly ran after her but her mother's flight was too fast and Sorcha was fifty yards up the hill before Molly rounded the corner of the house. Molly could hear her sobs, carried across the walls, while from the house the sounds of Conor's screaming continued. Two men going the road stopped and looked after Sorcha and then at each other. Molly nearly died with fright and sorrow. And shame.

She ran under the lean-to roof over the turf rick where the collie usually slept on a bed of dried seaweed. She crept in beside the little dog and buried her head in her warm fur, covering her ears to the sounds still coming from the house, listening fiercely to the beating of the collie's heart. The collie was afraid too – she trembled and licked Molly's bare elbow where it rested.

After a little while, she did not know how long, Molly uncovered her ears. There was peace, no screaming, no crying, no shouting.

Slowly, terrified, she walked back round the corner of the house. She would have looked in at the window but it was still too high for her. So she tiptoed towards the open door. The kitchen was empty. All the chairs were upset and lying around the overturned table. The shards of a bowl lay on the floor in front of the dresser, there were broken eggshells everywhere and the whites and yolks of the eggs had spread in a glutinous slick over a wide area.

She stepped carefully around the mess and opened the door of her room. This room, too, bore signs of the struggle. The blankets were mostly off the bed and an alarm clock, brought home from Birmingham by Brendan, lay on the floor, the glass on its face broken. The clock still ticked.

Conor was lying on the bed, his back to her. He was semi-naked. His trousers were down around his ankles and his shirt was ripped to shreds. Bruises already showed all over his body, particularly on his buttocks and back, and long red weals where his father had thrashed him with something, probably a belt. There were welts on his arms as well because his hands were tied behind his back with baler twine.

Molly ran to the dresser in the kitchen and opened one of the drawers. She took out the big knife her mother used when she was preparing fowl and ran back into the bedroom. She found it difficult to cut the twine and sawed at it ineffectually, for ages it seemed, but although Conor was whimpering he assisted her by flexing his hands and putting pressure on the twine, holding his wrists as far apart as he could to give Molly space.

When the twine parted and he was free he pulled up his trousers to hide his nakedness. Then he looked at Molly, an expression in his eyes that she had never seen before. She was afraid all over again. But the expression went away and Conor's eyes filled with tears. He held out his arms to her and she climbed up beside him on the bed, curling in against his chest like a little kitten. His skin smelt sour. He tightened his arms around her. '*Lá amháin*!' he whispered into her hair. 'One day, Molly. One day I'll get him. One day . . .'

CHAPTER FOUR

The whispering in the dormitory rose until some of the girls became careless and did not bother to whisper at all but talked in low murmurs. Tomorrow was the summer holidays.

Molly's bed was beside the window so one side of her cubicle was not curtained but faced out over the lawn in front of the school towards the lake. The window was a doubtful privilege in winter when the rain battered against it and the wind sent fingers of ice across her cheek through cracks in the putty but on summer nights like this the penances of winter paid off. It was nearly ten o'clock and from the grandstand of her pillow propped up with her dressing-gown Molly watched the sun sink over the lake until it disappeared behind the mountain, which looked to be only a mile away but was nearer to five.

The curtain dividing her bed from the one occupied by her friend, Kathleen Agnes Dwyer, twitched, was pulled aside and Kathleen Agnes's curly head appeared round the edge. 'Molly!' she hissed.

Molly left her sunset and, twisting her body sideways out of bed, leaned her hand on the floor straining to hear what her friend wanted. The nuns had separated them earlier in the year but allowed them back together again when Kathleen Agnes, flashing her dimples, had persuaded Mother Regis that Molly *needed* her and because she was so shy would find it very difficult to make another friend.

Molly found now that Kathleen Agnes had nothing in particular she wanted to say and that she just wanted to repeat some of the arrangements they had made to meet later in the summer. They planned to visit one another in August. Kathleen Agnes's father was a farmer, with a hundred and fifty acres of fat land in Limerick.

When Kathleen Agnes had first mooted the plans, Molly had been reluctant. While she would love to make the trip to Limerick she worried about how her friend would react to the reciprocal visit to her own tiny cottage, which was so primitive by comparison to Kathleen Agnes's luxurious abode. But she had resolved her dilemma by arranging that Kathleen Agnes's week on Inisheer would coincide with Conor's holiday visit in the middle of August. She was banking on Kathleen Agnes's romantic heart being smitten by Conor and that it would not matter about her dadda's moods.

Mother Regis swished into the dormitory to restore order and Molly pushed herself back into bed and answered the rosary with all the others. 'Goodnight, girls!' called the nun when the rosary finished. 'Straight to sleep now! No more messing.' Even Mother Regis was infected with the holiday mood, thought Molly. Her voice sounded young, like a real person's.

'Goodnight, Mother!' she chorused with the rest of the girls.

'Don't let the fleas bite!' A lone voice from the other side of the big room cracked up at its own daring.

Molly snuggled into her bed and closed her eyes. She didn't mind school, in fact she liked it quite well, but she was looking forward to going home. She was sixteen years, four months and seven days old.

When she woke next morning there was already a subdued buzz of activity up and down the dormitory. No one was talking but the girls were ignoring the rule which decreed they should not get up before the bell and were moving in and out of the bathrooms. Locker doors opened and shut and she could hear suitcases being dragged along the floor.

The arrangement for her was that she would be driven into Galway with the others, who were to catch trains and buses, but she was to be in the charge of a lay sister in case the weather was bad and the *Naomh Éanna* delayed or cancelled. In that case the lay sister would bring her back to school. Looking at the sky, she had no worries. The sun was high, it was going to be a fine day.

She hopped out of bed, washed herself, gasping at the coldness of the water against her warm cheeks, and then took her basin into the bathroom to empty the slops down one of the sinks. She was back beside her bed squeezing her sponge bag into her suitcase when the bell rang.

Breakfast was a gala affair, cornflakes instead of porridge. There were no classes, of course – even the Inter and Leaving Cert girls were engaged purely in supervised revision – so after breakfast she and Kathleen Agnes, whose father was driving from Limerick to collect her, strolled down to the shores of the lake across the lawn starred with daisies. Molly's wrists stuck out of her blouse and as she walked she pulled ineffectually at her brown gym slip as if by doing so she could lengthen it. Its hem was way above her knees and she felt exposed. She had grown rapidly during the school year and in her own opinion she looked absolutely awful.

'I look drastic!' she said mournfully to the petite, compact Kathleen Agnes as she had to stoop under a trailing bramble beneath which her friend passed with ease. 'I just hate being tall!'

'For goodness' sake stop moaning!' Kathleen Agnes was never one to mince her words. 'Mother Josephine told me she thought that with your looks you could be a model or a film star.'

Kathleen Agnes was embroidering. What the nun had actually said about her friend was that she'd never before seen such a tall Aran woman. But Kathleen Agnes swung all the time between irritation that Molly should be so gorgeous and not know it – or worse, not care – and her natural inclination to bolster her friend's confidence. 'If I had your looks and your height,' she continued, 'there is no way in the world I'd come back to this kip next year just to do my stupid Leaving Cert. I'd be off to London.'

'Kathleen Agnes, you're *beautiful*! And the Leaving Cert is all about choices later in life,' Molly added primly, echoing the nuns.

'I couldn't give a shit about choices.' Kathleen Agnes tossed her curls. To Molly one of the revelations of boarding-school had been the colourful language of the inmates. 'I'm going to marry a rich man,' Kathleen Agnes continued, '*not* a farmer.

128

I'm going to have only two children – and I'm going to have the time of my life!' She picked up a stone and flung it for emphasis into the clear water of the lake.

Molly was used to Kathleen Agnes's definite opinions and plans. She felt, as usual, inadequate. She had not the faintest idea what she wanted to do after she left school. Imbued with the religious ambience of the convent, she thought vaguely that she might become a nun.

When the time came to leave, she and Kathleen Agnes said goodbye to one another on the untidy gravel outside the front door of the school. 'Write *immediately*!' ordered Kathleen Agnes as she slammed the door of the nuns' minibus which Molly shared with seven other girls, the driver and the lay sister.

'I will!' promised Molly. Kathleen Agnes then passed something to her, a folded piece of paper, through the open window of the vehicle. As they moved down the driveway Molly opened it. It was a holy picture, folded in four. The picture, brown and white, was of St Maria Goretti, the young girl canonized for choosing to be stabbed to death rather than give in to the sexual demands of a man.

Molly turned the picture over: Better be safe than sorry! her friend had written in her distinctive flamboyant hand. Molly suppressed a giggle and darted a glance at the lay sister beside her but the nun had not noticed anything. She was engaged in conversation with the girl on her other side.

The *Naomh Éanna* was crowded as the tourists had already started to travel. Molly stood in the bow of the steamer, which today was calling first at Kilronan on the big island before going on to Inisheer and then Inishmaan. Hefting her suitcase and still pulling at the hem of her gym slip with her free hand, Molly found a spot sheltered from the sea breeze near the vessel's smoke stack.

'It's going to be a fine summer, please God.' The voice belonged to a priest. She had not noticed him. He was sitting on a small case, puffing at a pipe.

'Yes, Father,' she said shyly. Molly's social experience with priests was not wide. At home her house was not one that was frequented by the clergy; at school, the chaplain kept a pair

129

of springer spaniels and liked to hunt with them and Molly, influenced by Conor to respect and love all living things, disapproved passionately of hunting.

She did not know what to say next and tugging at her gym slip pretended to be fascinated by what was happening out on the dockside. He spoke again. 'I don't know you, do I? Are you going to Kilronan?'

'No, Father. I'm for Inisheer.'

'That's where I'm going too,' he said easily. 'It's only my second trip there. Father Naughton is going on holiday and I'm filling in for two weeks. I'm sure we'll see each other.'

She nodded, tongue-tied, and he stuck out his hand. 'I'm Pat Morahan.'

'How do you do, Father? My name is Molly Ní Bhriain.'

'It's breezy enough up here, Molly. Maybe we should go back a bit.'

'All right, Father.' She was nonplussed at being included in his plans.

He found another spot near the stern, which was sheltered by the steamer's infrastructure. Molly searched desperately for something to say but as he seemed not to be paying much attention to her she turned away from him again to look out over the docks. The steamer blasted its horn and she had legitimate cover for her silence while they pulled away from the city.

'You're not doing the Leaving?' he asked when they were about five minutes out into the bay.

'No, Father, next year.'

'And what then?'

He seemed nice enough. 'I don't know, Father. I might go into nursing.' Half the class thought they might be nurses. Molly had not told anyone that she harboured thoughts of entering the convent.

'That's wonderful, Molly. Nursing is a great profession. I thought once I might like to be a doctor.'

'Did you, Father?' She was feeling a little easier with him and, always curious about other people's lives, she was genuinely interested.

'Yes, but unfortunately it didn't work out.'

'Why not, Father?'

'Well, in those days, people like me didn't become doctors. That was for the gentry and the sons of big farmers.'

'So how did you become a priest?' She regretted the stupid question as soon as it was out of her mouth because he looked at her with a strange expression on his face.

'Are you really interested?'

'Sure, Father!'

They were having to shout to make themselves heard above the noise of the steamer's engines and the swishing sea. Molly listened intently as he told her about the poor farm he was brought up on in County Mayo, about his mother's scrimping so he could go to secondary school and about the glamorous missionary who had come around in fifth year asking for volunteers to go on the African missions as soldiers for Christ. 'It seemed like a great escape from the bogs and the slavery on the farm,' he said. 'And the missionary order was going to pay for everything so my mother wouldn't have to worry about university fees or anything like that.'

Molly was so astonished that she forgot her shyness. She had always thought that priests' vocations came to them with blinding suddenness, that out of the blue they heard God calling them. In her imagination she saw shafts of light hitting them in the middle of the night while they lay terrified in their beds. 'And did you go to Africa, Father?' she asked eagerly. 'Was it very exciting and strange?'

'Well, no,' he said, 'I never got to Africa. Actually, I didn't stay with the missionaries.'

She nearly asked why not, but remembered her manners.

'I had two years of theology done so I was accepted in Maynooth for the diocese,' he went on. 'That's how it happened.' He seemed about to say more but instead took a box of matches out of his pocket and concentrated on relighting his pipe, making a little cup from his hands to shelter the match flame from the wind.

He changed the subject then. 'Inisheer is a lovely place, Molly, you're lucky to live there. My own village where I grew up is like

131

a ghost town now. We used to have a cobbler and a blacksmith working in two workshops side by side when I was a boy. All closed up, Molly, all gone. We have no butcher now, no chemist, no dispensary, no doctor – only the public nurse who comes around in her little car. It's very sad.' He puffed on his pipe.

She liked him, she decided, overcoming her shyness. He was easy to talk to. She told him about Kathleen Agnes, whom she hoped to visit in the summer. 'Her father's really rich. They have a motor car and horses and their own telephone and Kathleen Agnes says she will teach me how to ride.'

'That'll be nice.'

'And they have *two* televisions!'

He laughed. 'Do you watch much television?'

'Only saw it once in my life, Father. That was in a shop in Galway. The nuns were taking me to the dentist.'

He laughed again and she smiled back. Then he did a strange thing. He dropped his eyes and turned away. 'I think I'll take a turn around the deck.'

He came back to her side when they were coming in to Kilronan pier on Inishmore. They did not talk much during the disembarking and unloading. The steamer took on very little, just a few crates of fish, and then they were on their way to Inisheer. They could see the island ahead of them, a compact mound in the sea a few miles away with the unmistakable landmark of the Plassy, the steamship wrecked in March 1960 and now aground above the waterline.

Strange things were happening to Father Morahan as he stood beside Molly on the *Naomh Éanna*. His pulse raced and he could not get out of his head the vision she had presented to him of herself astride one of Kathleen Agnes's horses. All his priestly life he had managed to steer a shaky but faithfully celibate path through the obstacle course strewn in his path by his sexual attraction to women. But this girl was different. She was making smithereens of his carefully constructed and maintained defences. He found he was trying to interest her, heard his own voice adopt an unusually vivacious tone. To his

132

horror Father Morahan heard himself flirting. He was appalled. She could not be more than sixteen or seventeen and he was over fifty. He felt as though he was twelve.

He hung back when the steamer anchored, letting her go ahead of him in a different currach to his own. A woman, her mother no doubt, met her on the strand. She turned and waved as she walked with the woman up the hill.

'There's no harm done,' he told himself that night as he knelt beside his bed in the curate's house to say his prayers. 'Yet!' answered his treacherous heart. It was nearly dawn when he got to sleep.

He saw her next morning at Mass in the queue for Holy Communion long before she got to him and he had to swallow hard. Her eyes were closed as she put out her tongue and he hoped that no one could see that the hand which placed the Host on it was shaking.

As he disrobed in the sacristy after Mass he fought the urge to flee, to pretend he was sick and to get a boat and go back home. But he already knew he would not do anything of the sort. He ricocheted between three desires: his desire not to alarm her, his desire to be true to his vows and his overwhelming desire to see her.

That evening and the following day he tramped around the island on long walks, hoping he could fool himself into believing that he was walking for the good of his health – but his heart was not fooled. Inisheer was such a small island, only two miles square, that unless she stayed in her house all the time he was bound to run into her sooner or later.

On the second day he saw her long before she saw him. He had found out where she lived, not difficult in so small a place, and had perched himself on a wall which bordered a road above and behind her house. He looked out to sea all the time and his breviary rested on the wall beside him. A half-hour passed as he waited. He knew he was behaving like a moonstruck schoolboy but it seemed he had lost the power to direct his own actions.

When she came out of the house Father Morahan's heart began to thump and his breath ran short for a few seconds. But he pulled himself together and slipped off the wall. She was coming up the hill towards him. He strolled at a casual pace up the boreen away from her, stopping after a minute or two to examine the fossils on the surface of the limestone pavement, manipulating the situation so that it was she who caught up with him and not the other way round.

'Hello, Father!' She was wearing a longish skirt of red wool and a báinín sweater, the rough texture emphasizing the pearliness of her skin. Her blonde hair was blowing loose in the breeze. Father Morahan felt almost physically ill with desire.

But he schooled his face and voice as best he could. 'Why, hello, Molly!' he said, hoping he sounded surprised. 'I'm just out for a walk.'

To cover his confusion he squatted on the pavement. 'See what I've found,' pointing to the fossils, delicately coiled in the limestone. 'I wonder what these are, now.'

She hunkered down beside him. She smelt of soap.

'They're crinoids, Father,' she said. 'The other name for them is sea lilies. Conor – that's my brother – has made a study of all the island. He knows every stone on it.'

They both stood up. 'Really?' asked the priest, then, 'Do you see that big boulder over there in the middle of the field – the pinkish-coloured one? Do you know what kind of rock it is?' He could have kicked himself for his fatuousness.

'Oh, yes, Father.' She fell in step beside him as the two of them walked up the hill. 'The rock is granite, it was carried here by the glaciers of the ice age but if you go close to it you'll see that the rock is really grey. It's the crystals of feldspar that make it look pink. Do you know what that is?'

His heart hammered. He remembered something learned in his geography classes in primary school. He pretended he was reciting. 'Feldspar-is-a-mineral-deposit-containing-aluminium -and-other-silicates.'

She smiled again and applauded and ludicrously he felt like shouting high into the sky. Instead he said, 'That's brilliant. You know so much about the island, Molly. Any chance you'd have a bit of spare time to show me more? Might as well use my time here constructively.' And then he laughed. To him, the laugh sounded crazed – high-pitched, false and crazed. He felt the nervous sweat begin to gather on his palms and under his armpits.

But she didn't seem to notice anything amiss. 'Certainly, Father,' she said. 'It's just a pity that Conor isn't here yet, he's coming in the middle of August. He would be much better than me to show you around. But I'll be happy to.'

He pushed his luck. 'Were you going somewhere just now or could we start right away?'

'I was just going up to the chapel for a visit.'

'That's fine, Molly. We'll make a visit together and then we'll set off.'

They knelt beside one another in the plain, white-painted chapel. Father Morahan bent his head but could not pray. He was the first to leave. She joined him a minute later and they set off around the island. He tried to concentrate on the little lectures she gave him, about the fact that while there were no rivers on this or on any of the other two islands there were good springs. 'And many centuries ago, Father,' she said, pointing at a couple of dwarf hazels which struggled to survive, 'Aran was covered in trees and was fertile enough. But our ancestors overgrazed and overcultivated the land and cut down the trees and this was the result.' Unconsciously she was speaking like a schoolteacher.

They were standing on the highest point of the island and the rock fell away from them towards the sea, emerald-coloured in the sunshine.

'I wish I was able to paint,' the priest said, overcoming his obsession with her for a few moments and marvelling at the clearness of the light which seemed to be reflected off the rocks back at the sky.

But then she unmanned him again as her smile shot through him. 'Sure, why don't you have a go, Father? You never know till you try!' He forgot about sea and sky and light and longed to take her in his arms there and then. He walked away from her, staying a little way in front until they got to a crossroads.

He thanked her then and was sufficiently composed before they shook hands to suggest they make arrangements to meet again the following day for further exploration. She agreed.

On the way back to the curate's house, Father Morahan felt like Gene Kelly in *Singin' In The Rain*.

That night in Father Naughton's bedroom he pulled the curtains over the window and stripped himself naked. He took the curate's speckled shaving mirror and propped it on the chest of drawers and backed across the room until he could see most of his body reflected in it. He had not looked at himself like this since he was fifteen years of age and terrified that he was not developing normally.

Whoever implied that to be in love was joyful?

He remembered the smooth cool feel of her skin when they shook hands to say goodbye.

He looked at his ageing body, headless and footless in the oval shaving mirror. He knew that what he was doing was mad.

Molly took Father Morahan out again on the following day. This time they visited the ruins of Cill na Seacht n-Inion, the Church of the Seven Daughters, built during monastic times on the site of a much older stone fort. They went to the ruins of the tenth-century church of St Cavan, the brother of St Kevin of Glendalough. She told him how the little church fights bravely against the marauding sandhill which frequently all but covers it and how it is kept in sight only by frequent excavation.

Father Morahan already seemed to know of the islanders' devotion to St Cavan and of their belief in the saint's miraculous intercessions. He certainly knew all about the pattern to be held at his church on St Cavan's feast day in a few days' time.

'Do you believe in miracles, Molly?' he asked as they walked away from the tiny church along the beach.

'I suppose I do, Father,' she said slowly. She didn't really believe in miracles, despite the gospels and all the rest of it. She couldn't have said why not – everyone else believed in them, Kathleen Agnes and everyone – but she could not confess her doubts to a priest.

Then he said a funny thing. 'I think I do too!'

136

She thought that very odd. Priests were supposed to believe completely in miracles. They preached about miracles.

They climbed the island and she found alpine flora for him, sea pinks, saxifrage and ferns, and discovered an old wren's nest in one of the fissures in the limestone pavement. 'Did you know wrens can swim, Father?'

'I certainly did *not* know that!'

'Well, they can. Conor says they can.'

They walked along the clifftops and she explained that the cliffs were mainly too sheer and smooth to provide good nesting for sea birds but they spotted three puffins and, out on the water, a pair of black-throated divers. Since she had got to know him better she was beginning to think that he was definitely a little odd. For instance, he laughed at things she said when they weren't funny. And twice he stopped to look out to sea, pointing in wonder to ask about perfectly ordinary things the identity of which she suspected he must already know. Once it was a mallard drake and once it was just two currachs pulling along beside each other, heading into the island.

After two hours or so they had covered almost everything she could think of. The good weather of the past few days was threatening to break. Clouds were piling up to the west and the air, so warm the day before, had turned cold.

She shivered. 'I'd better go home now, Father,' she said, 'I have to help my mam with the tea.'

'You've been very good to me, Molly.'

'Not at all, Father. I enjoyed it. Maybe we'll do it again – although I think I've shown you every single thing there is to be seen here.' She laughed.

'So! We'll run into each other again.'

Her quick ear picked up again that strange heartiness in his voice when he responded. 'Oh, I'm sure we will, Father,' she said, anxious to be off.

'Sure, I'm not leaving for a week or so yet.' He continued to stand there and for a moment she thought he was going to come with her down to her house.

'No, you're not, Father. Of course we'll see each other.'

He hit the side of his head with his open palm. 'And there's the pattern, of course. You'll be there?'

She nodded. 'The whole island'll be there that day, Father.' She waited but still he did not move.

'And sure we'll see each other later on in the summer.'

'When will you be over again?' she asked politely, taking a few steps backwards down her own road.

'I don't know, probably in August.'

'Oh, I hope you're here when Conor is here. He's much better than me at telling all about the island. You'd really like him.'

They shook hands.

Yes, he was a nice man, she thought as she hurried home, but definitely a little odd. Probably to do with him being a priest.

Nearly two months later, on the day Conor was expected, Molly went down to the beach as usual to watch for the steamer. He did not bound through the waves to swing her off her feet as he used to when she was small but came decorously ashore with the other passengers and tourists.

He threw his bag down, however, and hugged her when he reached her on the strand. 'My God!' he said, holding her away from him. 'You've changed so much! You're not my little sister any more, you're my huge *big* sister!'

'Shut up, Conor,' she said, hating to have her height referred to although she was much more comfortable in her everyday clothes than in the too-small uniform.

She broached the subject of Kathleen Agnes to him as they walked up to the house. 'Listen, Conor, my friend, Kathleen Agnes Dwyer – you know my friend?'

He nodded.

'Well, she's coming to visit next week for the entire week and then I'm going back to Limerick for a holiday at her house when she leaves here. Now, the reason I'm telling you this is that I'm a bit worried that there'll be nothing much for her to do here. She's used to telephones and cars and *television*. So will you be nice to her, Conor? Will you show her around and bring her places and be *nice* to her?'

138

'Whoa!' he said. 'Not so fast. I'm here on *my* holidays! I'm not here to entertain your friends, you know!'

She stopped dead. '*Please*, Conor.'

'For goodness sake, I'm only joking! Of course I'll be nice to your friend.' She linked her arm in his and the two of them continued up the boreen to the house. She was very proud of him. He was twenty-seven years old now and working as a junior lecturer at the National Botanic Gardens in Dublin. He had won a scholarship to train at the gardens but his career had a lot to do with Sorcha who, despite Micheál's frequent raids on the jar on the mantelpiece, had managed to squirrel away enough money to pay for his keep in Dublin during his studies.

The first few days he was home Molly and her brother could not get out much. The weather was stormy, windy and wet, and Conor spent a lot of time reading, keeping well out of Micheál's way. Worried, thinking ahead to Kathleen Agnes's visit, Molly watched the silent sparring between the two of them. Part of the difficulty was that Micheál, whose bad humour had become permanent over the years, thought Conor's job not a proper job at all.

To avoid trouble Conor tried, with Sorcha's collusion, to eat at different times from his father but sometimes this was impossible and those times, when they were forced to sit captive within feet of one another, were the worst for the household. Conor did not rise to Micheál's muttered goading, however, and the fragile peace between them was maintained for a time.

Towards the end of the week, the weather improved at last and Molly set out to walk with her brother around their old haunts. They stopped for a rest, flopping in a little hollow. 'Do you remember the first time I brought you here?' he asked after they had been sitting in companionable silence for a few minutes.

'I do,' answered Molly happily and began to recite the Belloc poem she now knew herself.

> 'Do you remember an Inn,
> Miranda?

139

Do you remember an Inn?
And the tedding and the spreading
Of the straw for a bedding,
And the fleas that tease in high Pyrenees . . . '

'Uh-oh,' said Conor. 'Mistake!'

'What mistake?' She was surprised.

'It's not "In high Pyrenees", it's "In *the* high Pyrenees".'

'It is not. It's "In high Pyrenees". That's the way *we* learned it.'

'Well, you learned wrong!'

'We did not!'

'You did, so!'

'We did not, Conor Ó Briain. It was your rotten school that taught *you* wrong!'

'What did you say, Miss Molly Ní Bhriain? Rotten school? I'll show you rotten!'

He reached out as though to pull her hair. But she was up and away, too fast for him. He got to his feet and chased her round the soft grass. They were both laughing as she danced away from him, always a little out of his reach.

'Come here to me!' he yelled. 'I'll spiflicate you!'

'You'll have to catch me first!' she yelled back, dodging and twisting.

He caught her and, although she struggled and fought, managed to drag her as far as a nearby rock on which he sat and tried to pull her down across his knee. 'I'll teach you how to recite poetry!' he said.

She kicked her legs but he was too strong for her and she felt the breeze as he raised her skirt and started to spank her. She squealed and protested although the spanking did not really hurt but suddenly, after he had given her half a dozen rapid smacks, he stopped, tumbling her off his lap onto the grass. She looked up at him in astonishment.

He stood up. 'That'll do,' he said gruffly.

She picked herself up. Her buttocks tingled where he had spanked her but not unpleasantly and she felt the tingling spread to her blood.

He was standing with his back to her.

'Conor?' she said uncertainly.

'I'm sorry I smacked you,' he said in that strange, gruff voice.

'That's all right, you didn't hurt me.'

'Let's go home. It's getting late.'

She mulled it over in her head as they walked back to the house together. They were walking as far apart as the narrow boreen would allow. She stole a sideways glance at him as he loped along, his head sunk and his face inscrutable. Something new had happened.

For the first time she saw that he was not only her ally, her lovely, gentle brother, he was a man. She was more aware than ever of the tingling sensations on her bottom. The truth was that she had liked being spanked. And she was aware that in some way it was forbidden, which made it all the more exciting.

'Conor?' she said.

'Yes?' For the first time since he had taken her across his knee he looked at her directly. She was relieved but could not fathom the look in his eyes.

'I'm sorry I said your school was rotten.' She knew it was weak.

'It's all right, Molly, you were quite right. It was a rotten school.'

She kept quiet then. A little later, still wreathed in silence, she saw that the steamer had anchored in the little bay and the currachs were bobbing around her. Her arrival three times a week was the main event in the life of the island and knots of people were clustered on the shore. Two tractors with trailers waited for the loads.

'Let's go down to the beach, Conor.' Molly was very anxious to put right whatever had gone wrong between them. He nodded and her spirits lifted. She would give it a little time. It was how she humoured Micheál – and Brendan before he went off to work in England.

The first currach had already deposited four people on the sand by the time they got there. Molly saw that one of them was Pat Morahan.

141

'Oh look, Conor,' she said, 'it's Father Morahan, the priest I was telling you about. Oh, I'm so glad he's come, you'll be able to show him so much more than I did. Come on and meet him.'

The priest was walking up the beach with a small suitcase in his hand.

Father Morahan had spotted her distinctive blonde head as his currach was being rowed ashore and his heart started to thump again so sickeningly that he had to breathe fast in order to breathe at all. She was even more beautiful than he remembered, although he had thought of little else for weeks.

He had never in his life kissed a woman.

He had no sisters and his mother had been a silent woman. At the age of twelve, Pat Morahan had gone from primary school into a single-sex secondary school, which was also a preparatory seminary, and from there he had gone straight into his six years' study for the priesthood.

In his summer holidays from the seminary and down all the years since ordination Father Morahan had sustained mild, secret crushes on various girls and women who came within his ambit but, well warned and well trained, he had always managed, like most of his confrères, to recognize them as unavoidable aberrations in his vocation to celibacy. He avoided 'occasions of sin' by ensuring that he was never alone with one of these aberrations. A relationship between a man and a woman had been up to now, in Pat Morahan's imagination, always in soft focus like a film, an affair of utter rapture filled with soft delights – he looked up at Molly, hurrying to meet him – not this urgent, tearing passion full of pain . . .

He saw a man with her. The man, tall and dark-haired – who bore, he saw, little resemblance to her – must be the brother. He had his face schooled by the time the three of them met but she was shy all over again. 'Hello, Father. This is my brother Conor. You know, the botanist? Do you remember I told you he knows every plant and bird on the island?'

'I do indeed. How do you do?'

The two men shook hands. The priest turned to her. 'And how are you, Molly?'

'Oh, I'm fine, Father. Looking forward to going on my own holidays. Do you remember I told you about going to visit my friend Kathleen Agnes?'

Father Morahan did. The one with the horses. Molly astride . . .

Conor took the priest's bag and she walked between the two of them along the boreen, which was just wide enough to accommodate them walking abreast. She was so near that he imagined he could feel the heat coming from her body.

But super-sensitized as he was he recognized tension in the brother, some of it, he was sure, directed towards himself. Molly seemed to sense it too. She was chattering on about her plans for Kathleen Agnes in a tone he had never heard before.

'Are you home for long, Conor?' he asked, when Molly seemed to run out of steam.

'Another few days.'

'I see.'

He felt a huge surge of something that, to his despair, he recognized as jealousy. This brother was taking up her time, could come and go in her house, could touch her if he wanted to . . . Nevertheless the silence as they walked along became very difficult for him and he was almost relieved when they got as far as her home and the two of them went inside, leaving him to walk alone as far as the house where he was to stay.

To Molly's surprise, Micheál was sitting by the fire when she got inside the house. He looked up when she came in. '*Cá raibh tusa?*' Molly was used to being asked to account for her movements but, adept at interpreting the intonations of his voice, heard that he was quite mellow.

'*Thánaig an Naomh Éanna, Dadda.*' She told him Father Morahan had arrived on the steamer, this time not as locum, but for a holiday. '*Cupán tae, Dadda?*' she asked then and, when he nodded that he would indeed like a cup of tea, she busied herself with the kettle and the teapot. As he took the cup and saucer from her he hesitated as if he wanted to say something. But he merely nodded again at her and

143

drank the tea, pouring it into the saucer and sucking at it.

He was so rarely present in the middle of the afternoon that Molly wondered if he was ill. She was also at a loss as to how to deal with him on her own, particularly in his present quiescent state. She was seldom alone with him since Sorcha left the house only to go to the chapel or for short periods to visit a neighbour. When Micheál was present in the house she was accustomed to being watchful and placatory and to find him sitting solitary and quiet like this was unnerving.

He was always silent but this afternoon, she thought, his silence was sort of different. She had the vivid impression that her father was somehow imprisoned behind a sheet of glass and was trying to break out. She moved nervously around him, ready to refill his teacup, trying to bridge the gap between them. Many, many nights, particularly if he had been sharp with her or after one of the vicious rows between himself and Conor, she had lain in her bed beating into her pillow that she hated him, hated him. But today, as she watched him sucking his tea, she felt an odd tenderness. She saw acutely that he had become old. If they had had a different relationship she might have hugged him. But reticence and wariness in Micheál's presence were habits of a lifetime.

Molly had divined correctly that Micheál wanted to say something to her but did not know how. When she had come in from outside, darkening the sun in the door, he was caught unawares by her entrance. Sorcha had gone up the road to visit the Ketts and for once Micheál had not wanted the company in the pub. Always introspective, today, for some reason, he was in a rare mood of self-analysis. Sitting by the hearth he had been thinking about his life in a way he seldom did, examining his lifetime list of disappointments.

First among them, of course, was his marriage. Although he had provided for them all he knew that he and Sorcha would as happily live apart as together. Perhaps, he thought, she might be better off, she who had loved dancing and beautiful things and good company and who was now worn down by work and weather and harsh conditions until she was

– like most of the other island women of her generation –
beaten.

And, he thought, the worst part was his own role in her
decline. He caught her looking at him sometimes with a puzzled
look, as if she did not know him. That look enraged him. He
had loved her, still loved her, but for many, many years he had
not been able to say or do anything which would demonstrate
to her that he cared.

If they had not been islanders, he thought, they might have
had a chance. He knew that he was not unintelligent and railed
inwardly at the fate that had caused him to be born and trapped
on this small piece of rock, lashed to the seabed of the North
Atlantic.

On the other hand, he accepted that while others had escaped
to the factories, building sites and subways of England or
America, such a life would not have been for him. His thoughts
were as unclear as his speech was inarticulate but he recognized
that the clear air and seas of Aran were essential to him in some
way he could not specify.

Sucking his tea while Molly sat, still as a mouse, on the other
side of the hearth, Micheál kept his eyes fixed on his saucer and
tried to remember the last time he felt happy or fulfilled – or
even peaceful. He stole a glance at his daughter. Maybe when
she was sleeping one night soon after she came to them – and
he and Sorcha had stood by her cradle in the kitchen and he had
put his arms round his wife. Maybe then. That was probably
the last time either of them knew with certainty what the other
was thinking – of the other Molly, the little body buried at the
back of the house. There was a closeness in the shared thought.
Sometimes he wondered alone what that other Molly might have
been like. Would she have grown in beauty like this one who had
bloomed like a flower in this arid house? He wished with all his
heart he had the courage to talk to her, to tell her he was sorry
for the hurt and the violence and the disappointments he had
brought her in her short life. He risked another glance at her
and the words beat at the back of his tongue. But they would
not come to the front. The reticence and the silence of a lifetime
were insuperable and the moment passed.

He finished his tea, took his cap off the hook, said goodbye to her and went outside.

Through the window Molly watched him trudge away towards the public house. She too wished she could have said something. She saw that her father's strong shoulders had become rounded and stooped.

By teatime the August heat had conquered the island and the midges swarmed densely outside the cottage. In contrast to his earlier mood Micheál came home from the pub in truculent form. He sat at the head of the table drumming his fingers irritably while Sorcha hovered around the new bottled gas cooker waiting anxiously for the bread she had baked to be ready. Conor sat at the other end, very still. Every ticking second was like a quarter of an hour in the stifling kitchen.

At last Sorcha picked up the loaf in a tea-towel and carried it towards the dresser to cut it on the bread-board but Molly, in her haste to serve it, intercepted her mother and took the loaf from her. The tea-towel slipped as she took it and the crust of the loaf, still hot from the hob, burned her hand. She dropped the loaf on the floor.

'*Mhuire's trua*! You stupid bitch!' Micheál banged the table making the crockery jump.

'You leave her alone!' Conor's voice was like a whiplash. His face was white and his hands, in front of him on the table, were balled into fists. Molly looked at him fearfully: she had never seen such rage and frustration on his face before.

'What did you say?' Micheál's voice matched his son's.

'I said, you . . . leave . . . her . . . alone . . .'

'Who'll make me?' Micheál tucked in his chin and looked at his son from under his eyebrows. He held his head forward on his neck like a bull about to charge.

'If necessary, I will,' said Conor, his own head forward now, his voice dangerously soft. 'I hope it won't be necessary.'

'Micheál, Micheál, he doesn't mean it *a stór*. You don't mean it, sure you don't, Conor?' Sorcha moved forward automatically but Micheál jumped up and, as he had so often before, pushed her out of the way. He tore off his jacket. 'By God we'll settle this once and for all . . .'

'If you say so, Dadda.' Conor was still cool but his eyes glittered. He too stood up. 'Where would you like it to be, Dadda? Here? Would you like to wreck the furniture again?' The volume rose throughout this speech but he was still in control. Micheál stared at him, temporarily stupefied.

'What's keeping you, Dadda? Perhaps you need time to fetch your twine?' Conor's voice dripped with hatred.

Micheál exploded and lunged at him. 'You fuckin' shite! Speaking to your father like that! I'll kill you!'

Conor stepped aside, too quick for him. 'Oh, no, you won't. I won't let you. But I'm going to beat the shite out of you for all the shite you beat out of me.'

He stepped light-footed outside into the heat. Micheál followed him at a lumbering run.

Molly and Sorcha ran into the back room and shut the door. Molly flung herself face down on the bed and covered her ears. Sorcha lay beside her. She held Molly and both of their bodies shook with fear and weeping and shame that their fighting was to be seen by neighbours who, they knew, would not be long in gathering to watch the sport.

Despite the closed door they could faintly hear, through their distress, the sound of the struggle outside. It went on, augmented by shouts from the small crowd which had gathered, for a good five minutes. Abruptly the roaring stopped. Sorcha sat up on the bed and Molly uncovered her ears. 'What is it, Mam?'

'I don't know, child. Something's happened.' Neither of them moved. They hardly dared breathe.

There was a clatter in the kitchen and the door of the bedroom crashed open. It was Conor, bloody, with a torn shirt. The blood poured from both his eyebrows, his nose and a split lip.

He seemed dazed and held on to the door for support. 'Mam, Mam. Come quick.' His voice was bewildered. 'Dadda's fallen and I think he's hurt.'

Sorcha pulled herself up from the bed and walked outside. Molly followed.

The little group of neighbours who were clustered around

the door parted respectfully as Sorcha emerged. The men took off their caps. One of the old women blessed herself. After the shouting, the quiet was eerie.

Everything was very clear and slow. Micheál lay on the grey pavement. One of his fists was still bunched, the knuckles grazed and purpling. But the other hand lay open-palmed, like a baby's, and Molly noticed the scarring and deep lines which scored it. Her feet were bare and she felt how warm the pavement was under the soles. She saw that Micheál's sightless eyes were open and that there was a trickle of blood out of the corner of one of them. As she watched, more blood came. It came sluggishly from his mouth.

Micheál was dead.

Conor came out of the house and stood at the back of the crowd. Still there was silence. The day was overcast and humid and the earlier brightness of the afternoon had turned to green. More and more neighbours were gathering around the body. A boy had been sent for the priest and Father Morahan came running down from the priest's house, his stole flapping. They all knelt down in a ragged little circle around Micheál while the last rites were administered.

Conor continued to stand at the back but no one paid him any attention. He fixed his gaze on his father's face. He noticed that two flies were buzzing around the blood congealing on the forehead.

The crowd began to recite the rosary and Conor backed slowly into the house and then, moving quietly, packed the few clothes he could lay his hands on into his bag.

The crowd was still on the fourth Mystery when he came back out into the heat. They looked at him as he walked away towards the beach, but no one attempted to stop him and they did not interrupt the rhythm of the prayer.

He looked back from the beach. He could see the crowd, many of them, standing silently watching his departure. Irrelevantly the thought struck him that the rosary must have finished. He turned and continued to walk towards the water but looked back once more and his resolve to flee almost faltered. Molly had come to watch him too. He could pick out her distinctive blonde head, a little apart from the rest of the crowd. She held one arm peculiarly, above her head, forearm resting on the crown.

As he hesitated, he saw Sorcha come to stand beside her.

He must not cause them any more trouble.

Turning his back, he took his uncle's currach. It was awkward to handle for one man but he managed successfully to launch it in the calm sea. He threw in his bag, climbed in after it and began to row.

Even out here on the sea, the August silence was profound and the plashing of the oars loud. The crowd watched him from the front of his house and in return he watched them until he could no longer pick them out as individuals. He strained his eyes, keeping them fixed on Molly and his mother until the heat haze caused them to waver and finally to disappear.

Half-way across to Doolin, the temptation was strong to curl up on the floor of the boat, to let the currents take him where they may. He felt his strength nearly gone. Every bone in his body ached and his hands were badly blistered. He had never rowed so far alone. Inisheer lay low to his face but when he turned round the mainland was still miles away.

He shipped his oars and let the currach drift. He closed his eyes and slumped in defeat on his seat. The boat rocked on the gentle swell. A pair of seagulls, which had been following in the hope of scraps, settled in the water twenty yards away and watched him with their bright, knowing eyes.

After five minutes or so he became aware of the faint throb of diesels from somewhere across the water and, alarmed, he opened his eyes again. It was a small trawler half a mile from him. She was moving briskly northwestwards, too far away for him to read her name but he assumed from her course and her attendant gulls and seabirds that she was motoring homewards to Inishmore with her catch. He could not see if anyone on board had noticed him but if they had the trawler did not change course.

The sight of the trawler galvanized him. He realized the cuts

149

on his face were stinging as badly as the blisters on his hands and he ripped off his torn and bloody shirt. He bathed his hands in the sea and then, taking care not to overbalance the boat, scooped the cooling water over his head and face. Again and again he cleansed himself. The cold water ran down over his chest and back and the shock of its coldness gave him courage. He began to row again.

The sun was setting as he neared the shore and he was so exhausted that he could barely manage to beach the currach at Doolin. The only person about was an old man mending nets about a hundred yards away.

Conor turned the boat, took his bag and his torn shirt and sat on the shingle beach. His legs were trembling and his whole body felt as though it had been put through a mincer. All he wanted to do now was to crawl into the soft grass behind him to sleep but he knew he had to keep moving. The moving was everything.

He looked over his shoulder to see if the old net-mender was watching him; as far as he could tell he was not. He opened the bag, took out a clean shirt and put it on. For the first time he noticed that Micheál's blood, or perhaps his own, had stained his trousers as well as his shirt. He eased them off and replaced them with a clean pair. He bundled up the discarded clothing, placed it in the bag, then pulled himself to his feet.

He had to find a telephone.

Molly stood away from the neighbours and watched the currach pull away on the flat sea until it was almost impossible to see it any more. Her heart felt like lead. She could not cry although she knew she probably should. Behind her she heard some of the neighbours carry Micheál inside and begin the rituals of death, so familiar to all of them.

When she could no longer distinguish the figure in the currach she turned away from the sea and went quietly into the kitchen of the house where she found that the neighbours already had events under control. She sat beside Sorcha and accepted a cup of tea while the women washed Micheál, dressed him in his Sunday suit and put clean sheets on his bed. One neighbour slipped away and brought back two beeswax candles to put on each side of the bedhead. Another lent a white candlewick bedspread. Mrs Kett supplied a linen pillowcase to cover the pillow.

It was only when he was properly laid out and decent, the candles lit and another decade of the rosary said, that it was decided to send word to the doctor on the big island to get the death certificate.

There was an argument then about whether the police should be fetched as well as the doctor, with many of the men objecting, saying that this was the doctor's business if he saw fit and nothing to do with them. But others objected to that and these others prevailed, some thinking privately that Conor was a man who had got above his station.

It was after dark when the doctor and the sergeant arrived. The sergeant spoke to everyone in the house but no one, not even those who thought that Conor had got above his station, could throw light on what had happened to Micheál. No one had seen it. They were polite and helpful. 'Would he have fallen, d'you think?' asked Marcus Ó Braonáin.

'He might have tripped on the pavement, 'tis treacherous out there with the cracks,' offered Seán Bán Nóra, Molly's second cousin.

The sergeant wrote everything down and examined the body with the doctor.

'There's one son in Birmingham. Where's the other son – Conor, is it?' he asked when he came out of the bedroom.

Seán Bán Nóra said the last he saw of Conor was when he went to the beach for a walk. He might be back shortly, he said.

The sergeant spoke to Sorcha, doffing his cap out of respect for her bereavement. 'Sorry for your trouble, ma'am. Is that the truth, ma'am? Did your son go to the beach for a walk?'

Sorcha nodded and several of the neighbours said they had seen Conor go to the beach.

'Well, if he went for a walk, it's a long walk. Where is he now?'

151

'Maybe he's gone to the big island?' suggested a man from the other side of the island.

Another man agreed with him, saying that he heard that Conor had plans to go to Inishmore.

'Something to do with a trawler, maybe,' said a third, cracking his knuckles and then taking a slug from his cup of tea.

'A trawler?' said the sergeant.

'A trawler, aye,' agreed a chorus of the men.

'He has a lot of money, now d'you see, from Dublin,' said the man who was first to say he had heard Conor might be gone to Inishmore.

Molly felt nothing at all as she sat beside her mother. It was as if she was not present in the scene. But in her detachment various pieces of detail engaged her attention. For instance, as he spoke to her mother she noticed the way the oil lamp shone on the sergeant's silver buttons turning them to gold.

The policeman was standing in front of her. 'And what about you, miss? Did you see anything?'

She shook her head.

'I see.' The sergeant snapped his notebook shut and looked around. 'Nobody here saw nothing. Is that the case?'

The men murmured.

'Well, ye'll all be called for the inquest. And if Conor Ó Briain comes back from his *walk* or from his *trawler* any time in the near future be sure to let us know. We'd like to have a word.'

He put his cap back on and stooped through the door.

The wind whistled through the broken glass in the telephone box but Conor, oblivious to the discomfort, gripped the handset. The telephone at the other end rang and rang and he was just about to hang up in despair when there was a click and Tom Hartigan answered. 'Hello?' The voice sounded frail.

The operator came on the line. 'One shilling and eightpence please.'

There was an agonizing delay while he pressed the coins into the slot one by one. He pressed button A and finally he was through. 'Hello, Father?'

'Conor!' The priest sounded pleased. 'Is that you?'

'Yes, Father. Listen, I've no time to explain now, I'll be cut off and I've no more change. But I have a huge favour to ask of you.'

'What is it, Conor?'

'I'm telephoning you from just outside Doolin. I know this is a terrible imposition and I wouldn't ask you except there's no one else I can turn to but is there any chance you would come down here and pick me up? There's no transport out of here at this time of the evening and I don't want to hitch. I could wait for you in Lahinch.'

'Sure, Conor.' The priest didn't hesitate. 'I've nothing on this evening anyway. Be glad to.'

'And could I stay with you tonight?'

'You know you're always welcome here.'

'Thanks, Father. I know it's a tall order, but I'll explain on the way.'

'No problem,' said Father Hartigan. 'Where'll we meet?'

'I'll wait in the Sheaf,' said Conor, mentioning a pub in the town.

They hung up.

Conor welcomed the walk into Lahinch through the deepening twilight as a chance to clear his thoughts. The mugginess of the day had released the scents of the hedgerows and despite his distress and confusion he was conscious of the smell of honeysuckle and wild thyme. It was a fine evening and a lot of people were around, young people on bicycles with packs on their backs, local families out taking the air. Not wanting to appear strange, he returned their greetings.

He tried to sort out his feelings. When his father fell he had waited for a second or two for him to get up, rage and the heat of battle still flushing through his blood. But Micheál had not moved and it was one of the neighbours who had moved forward and checked for a pulse. Conor's first reaction had been one of bewilderment. He had looked stupidly at the body and then at the little crowd of neighbours who were silent. Then he had rushed in to fetch his mother. She had been lying on the bed with Molly.

The memory of Molly earlier in the afternoon, the surge of lust for her as her long legs kicked and he cracked his palm on her bottom washed over him like a wave, competing with the image of his dead father. He had been staggered when it happened and was staggered now. Whatever happened from this day, nothing could ever be the same again between himself and Molly.

Conor, never one for self-pity, decided then that given all the circumstances it would be better for all concerned if he disappeared.

It was almost dark when he dragged his aching legs into the town of Lahinch. His travel bag, so light when he arrived at Inisheer so few days before, felt as though it had tripled in weight.

The sea shushed quietly and the promenade along the beach was still populated with strollers but he made straight for the pub. It was crowded with people, holidaymakers mostly, but to his relief, there was no one he recognized among the men, whom he knew, from their clothing and demeanour, must be locals. He ordered a pint and sat at a table, pretending to watch two young men playing a fiercely contested game of bar billiards.

The priest arrived in the pub less than an hour later when Conor was half-way through his second pint. He stood up from his table. 'I'd offer you a drink, Father, but I'm anxious to get going out of here.'

They went out to the car. Father Hartigan had long ago disposed of his battered Beetle and now drove a Ford Escort, already almost as battered.

It was only when they were approaching Ballyvaughan that he turned to his silent companion. 'Suppose you tell me what happened?'

Two days later after Micheál was buried Father Morahan was the last to leave the house following the customary meal. It had been a terrible day for him emotionally, conducting her father's funeral, seeing her remote, beautiful face at every hand's turn. He found it difficult to behave as a priest should during the obsequies although the rubrics led him along familiar pathways not requiring too much concentration.

He had not, of course, referred at all to the manner of Micheál's death. No one had. It was as if a great silence had descended on all the island. The familiar phrases were passed around the mourners outside the church and in the graveyard.

'He was a fine man.'

'A fine fisherman.'

'He had it hard.'

'He was a good man, he was.'

To an outsider, Micheál Ó Briain might have died in his bed. And no one mentioned Conor. At least not in the priest's hearing.

The most difficult part of the day was the meal in the dead man's house after he was buried. She had served Father Morahan his food and drink, moving around him in the crowded kitchen so close that sometimes he could have touched her merely by shifting his position in his chair.

At last it was over and he could leave. He saw he was the last. He stood up and automatically the other brother, Brendan, stood up too. From time to time throughout the day Father Morahan had noticed Brendan, home for the funeral from Birmingham. He was large and strong, like Conor, but there was a subtle difference. Brendan held himself slightly crooked as if always waiting for someone to hit him.

Father Morahan walked the few steps across the kitchen and shook hands with the man, who would not meet his eyes, and had a final word with Sorcha, who was sitting with her four sisters at the kitchen table. All the time he was conscious that Molly was watching him from her seat at the cold hearth.

He turned to say goodbye to her and she got up to see him to the door. She stepped outside with him into the blue evening.

Before he could stop himself the words were out and he had asked her to take a turn around the island. She hesitated and looked back into the house. She was going to refuse and he was almost relieved.

'I don't know if I should leave Mam and Brendan.'

'Of course, of course,' he said. 'I'll see you some other time.'

155

But to his amazement she looked out over the sea and said, 'The aunties are all there, she'll be all right for a while. I think I would like a walk.'

The day, like previous days, had been overcast but hot and humid and the evening was soft with the lingering warmth. There was no wind and by consent they walked down towards the shore where they would get the coolest air. Neither spoke as they walked slowly along and the priest did not want to break the spell. He did not want to shock or frighten her. He was tongue-tied and delirious at being alone with her.

On the other hand he could not understand why she did not feel the danger and run from him as fast as she could. Every sense was sharp as though newly born. He could smell her cleanness and hear each step of her foot. He had not planned this walk, he told himself in expiation. If she had refused to come as she seemed about to do he would have walked away. But her compliance seemed to him an omen.

They got to the beach and walked along it, their feet scrunching the shells concealed in the sand. She bent and picked up a piece of dried bladderwrack, popping one of its bubbles as children do for entertainment. The sound seemed loud and he saw those delicate fingers playing not with seaweed but with himself and he was maddened with desire. He walked a little ahead, trying to maintain the vestiges of his self-control. But he was aware of her exact physical position relative to his own.

They came to the end of the beach and continued out of the sand into the dunes. The sea washed gently against the rocks beside them. They came to a little hill of grass. It was nearly dark.

'Let's sit down awhile, Molly, it's peaceful here.' To himself his voice sounded strangled.

It appeared she did not notice anything amiss because she sat down against the hill and spread one hand on the marram grass which pushed up through the sand, combing the rough blades between her fingers. He sat down beside her. '*This is madness,*' he told himself. But he could not have stood away from her if his life depended on it.

She spoke then, for the first time. 'Thank you, Father . . .'

'For what?' He was hoarse.

'For being so good to us.'

He took her hands in his. 'Oh, Molly, darling, darling Molly . . .'

She seemed taken aback but not excessively. The words were out before he could stop them. 'Can I kiss you?'

She continued to look at him and he could almost see her thoughts. He was a priest, after all, a pillar of celibacy and respectability.

'I – I don't know, Father.' She sounded puzzled, but still not alarmed.

He threw caution and self-control to the winds. He pulled her to him strongly, feeling against his chest the round young breasts. He kissed her hungrily, pinioning her body with urgent hands while he covered her face and throat with his inexperienced mouth and tongue. She slid easily under him with the pressure of his weight and they were lying together.

She was not struggling and he pulled back from her, searching her face for signals. It was blank and beautiful, staring up at him still with large surprised eyes. He kissed her again and heard his own throat make little moaning sounds. He unbuttoned the blouse she wore and lifted her breasts to his lips, worshipping. They were smooth, ineffably smooth and pliant. Her skirt had buttons too but before he undid the first one, he looked at her face again.

Her eyes were closed. She had slipped from the little hillock against which they lay and her hair spread out behind her, a pale halo paler than the sand.

The buttons slipped through his fingers, the skirt fell away on either side and her long legs and belly were exposed to him. To his eyes her body seemed to shine in the deepening darkness. He almost wept.

When he went to pull down her pants she gave a little cry but he soothed her with soft kisses on her stomach which under his lips had the feel of warm downy silk. His Molly, his beautiful young Molly. His lovely, long-limbed, scented Molly . . .

But out of the blue he was struck with panic. He was fumbling desperately at the zipper of his fly when the voice of some long-forgotten mentor boomed in his brain, some canon in a country pulpit or a Redemptorist missionary raining perdition and brimstone on a congregation of terrified parishioners.

Pictures swirled: his mother's grave; his own body prostrate on the ground at his ordination.

Frightening, gory pictures from his childhood: St Sebastian pierced with arrows. Hellfire. An avenging, terrible God with flaring white beard and thunderbolts for fingers . . .

He looked at this luminous, unquestioning creature spread beneath him and, luridly, she too seemed like a picture from his childhood, an angel, an unblemished martyr, St Maria Goretti, the sixteen-year-old Virgin at the Annunciation; the Little Flower . . .

He pulled himself off her and ran away, stumbling and tripping in the soft sand of the dunes, until he got as far as the sea. Fully dressed he plunged into the water, surging forward until it reached his waist. He beat the water with his hands and bathed his face with it as though its coldness could wash away his sin and his lust.

When he got back to where she lay he was prepared for her not to be there or, if she was, for her contempt. But she was there in the same place. She had not attempted to replace her clothes and lay unmoving on her side, her knees curled up and her arms covering her breasts. The pale hair had fallen over her face.

In the hollow of the sand she looked as delicate and perfect as if newly hatched from the shell of her clothes strewn around her. 'Molly,' he said gently, so gently she did not hear him and he had to repeat her name.

She sat up then and, keeping her eyes averted, dressed herself quickly.

'Molly,' he said again, when she was ready.

'Yes, Father?' She was calm. Too calm.

'Darling Molly, I'm very very sorry . . . but in another way I'm not sorry, can you understand that?'

'Father, you're all wet. What happened?'

He tried again. 'Molly, priests are human beings as well as

158

priests and they fall in love just like other men . . . ' He had a vision of himself, ridiculous and middle-aged, spouting about love in his ruined, dripping, clerical outfit. He did not know whether to laugh or to cry.

'That's all right, Father,' she said. He had to make it all right for her. 'Molly, my dear – it's not your responsibility or your fault – really . . . Please believe me, Molly . . . The fault and the responsibility are all mine . . . '

She gave a little sigh and looked out over the dunes towards the sea. The distance between them became impenetrable. He felt totally helpless and lost. He too looked out to sea.

Then he walked away from her, back down the beach, water squelching in his shoes.

Molly had never been kissed before by anyone. The event had temporarily eclipsed even the horror of her dadda's death.

She had not yet come to terms with all the events which had thundered in on her over the previous few days. She undressed slowly in her bedroom, closing her eyes, trying to recreate the kiss. She regretted that because of her dadda's death, she had had to cancel Kathleen Agnes's visit and wished she were here so she could tell her what had happened. Molly had found that events only become real when you discuss them with someone else.

But a second after she had thought of discussing it she knew that she would never reveal the events in the dunes to her friend or to anyone. Not even to Conor, who was gone – where?

She sat on the side of her bed as the picture of Conor's dark, dishevelled figure, pulling strongly on the oars of the currach, came into vision. Was her brother lost to her? She would not believe it. She made an act of faith. He would come back – he had to. More than her dadda, more than what happened with the priest, Conor pulling away in the currach was the most awful thing that had happened.

The priest had touched her breasts. Before she put on her nightdress she took her breasts, one in each hand, and tried to imagine what they must have felt like in Father Morahan's hands, then, shamed, in Conor's hands . . .

The strangest thing was she had not been at all embarrassed when her breasts had been touched. She certainly would have been if it had been Conor . . . She wondered if that was because she would have *wanted* it. That would have been the embarrassing bit. The feeling was very new . . . Now he was gone and he never would – but of course he never could, anyway. He was her *brother*. It was all very confusing.

But the scene with the priest had been different, simpler . . . It seemed part of a ritual, connected in some way with her father's death. He was a priest. No harm could ever come to her from a priest. When she was with him in the dunes her feelings, which had not been altogether unpleasant, were not an issue and did not seem somehow to belong to her at all.

Anyway, she thought, sliding into her narrow bed – quietly because she heard Brendan moving about in the kitchen – the priest was quite nice. He was old, all right, but not ugly and he had been quite gentle.

She gazed at the ceiling and ran the scene again in her head. She could remember it in every detail, not only what he felt like but how they both looked because even while it was happening her mind was somewhere above the sand looking down on the two of them as if from a great height.

But the most interesting part of the episode was that as he caressed her she had found that his physical mastery of her reawakened sensations she had felt with Conor, those tingling racing feelings in her blood and on her skin. Half-ashamed of the action she cupped her breasts in her hands and once again imagined the hands were now Conor's.

She supposed now she could not be a nun.

Molly turned on her side and tried to go to sleep. But the picture of Conor pulling away in the currach kept coming into her brain.

For the first time since Micheál's death, she wept. She could not separate all the reasons for her tears. She wept for her dadda's death, her mother's sorrow and Brendan's white, anxious face. She wept because Conor was gone. She wept

160

because the priest was in love with her. She wept because she had to grow up now.

When she woke next morning, it was broad daylight and Brendan was standing at the foot of her bed.

'I'll be going, Molly,' he said awkwardly.

She sat up, her head very clear. 'Where are you going, Brendan?'

'I think I'll be going back to Birmingham.'

'So soon, Brendan?'

He shuffled his feet.

'But it's still very early, Brendan! The steamer won't be here until this afternoon.'

'I know! Seán Bán said he'd take me to Inishmore.' He looked at her with what she could see was an appeal. She understood. Brendan had to get away from this house of mourning and of women.

Suddenly her own way became clear. She would have to go too.

She told him to wait a few minutes and when he left the room, unquestioning, got dressed. She took her suitcase down from the top of her wardrobe and put her everyday clothes into it and her sponge bag – the whole lot came to only half-way up the inside of the case. Then she took her money from the drawer of her dresser. She had about eighteen pounds. She always saved her birthday and Christmas money from Brendan and Conor because on Inisheer there was hardly anything to spend it on.

Her writing case was in a drawer in the dresser. She took it and wrote a note to Father Morahan. She wrote it quickly, before she could think about the words.

Dear Father Morahan,
I am very sorry but it won't be possible to show you around the island any more this summer. Something came up and I had to go to Dublin. Thank you for all you did for me and my family. Everything is fine now.

She hesitated before she signed it. She always signed her letters 'lots of love, Molly' but it did not seem right on this occasion.

But neither did 'yours faithfully' or 'yours sincerely' so she simply signed it 'Love, Molly'. She scribbled the 'love' to make it look casual.

Brendan was sitting by the fireplace, staring into its clean depths. 'Won't be a minute, Brendan,' she called. She folded the letter into an envelope, sealed and addressed it and put it aside.

The letter to her mother was more difficult.

> Dear Mam [she wrote],
> I hope you'll understand this, but I have to leave the island and go to Dublin for a while.

She chewed the end of her pen then continued.

> I hope you will be all right and that aintin Mona and aintin Moya will be able to stay with you a little while longer so you won't be too lonely. I'm only going for a week or two and I'll be home before the end of the summer, so don't worry.

She thought again.

> I will be fine in Dublin. I have the telephone numbers of the two girls in my class who live in Dublin and they have invited me to stay with them any time. So I'll ring them just as soon as I arrive.

This was a lie thought up for the letter but the more she thought of it the more Molly, who did have the telephone numbers, thought it a realistic idea. It increased her determination and her courage:

> Again, I hope you won't be too lonely but don't forget I'll be home soon. And I'll write just as soon as I arrive.
> Lots and lots of love,
> Molly.

She put this note into a second envelope and addressed it.

'Nearly ready, Brendan,' she said, propping both letters against a milk jug on the dresser.

She put on her school gaberdine, too small for her but the only coat she owned.

Brendan took her suitcase as well as his own and it occurred to her that he had not once asked her where she was going or why or what their mother would say. She supposed that if she lived to be a hundred she would never fully understand this brother, so different from Conor.

They walked down towards the beach in silence, greeting neighbours they met along the way. There was no sign yet of Seán Bán Nóra. Molly had no idea what her brother's plans were but she intended to take the *Naomh Éanna*, which was not due to call at Inisheer today, from Inishmore.

She sat on her suitcase on the beach and looked out to sea. Brendan paced up and down the sand, scanning the roads of the island for first sight of Seán Bán.

'I wonder should I go to his house?' he asked Molly after a few minutes, wrinkling his forehead.

'Give him another little while,' she said. 'It's still early.' She looked over her shoulder to see if there was any sign of him.

Sorcha was running down the road towards the beach and Molly stood up. The sight of her mother running pierced her detachment.

Sorcha's hair was loose and her feet were bare. She stopped a few feet from her daughter.

'Hello, Mam,' said Molly.

One of her mother's hands was at her throat. 'Molly . . . '

Molly saw that in her other hand her mother carried her letter and another envelope, so old that the paper along the folds was opaque, like old cotton.

Sorcha took a few steps until she was within reach and held out the old envelope. Molly hesitated but took it. It was thick and she knew it contained money.

'Oh, Mam!' she said.

The two faced each other while Brendan stood a little way off. He turned his back.

'What time are you going?' Sorcha asked, her hand still at her throat.

'Seán Bán Nóra is taking us to Inishmore. He'll be here any minute.'

Sorcha nodded.

Molly could see she was trying to look businesslike.

'Don't forget to write,' she said.

'I won't, Mam.'

'And if you see Conor . . . ' Her mother looked away and tightened the hand on her throat. 'Here's Seán Bán now,' she said. 'God bless.' She muttered goodbye to Brendan, then turned and walked back up the beach.

As the two men launched the currach Molly opened the envelope. There was eighty pounds in it. She knew that it must be the money for Sorcha's funeral. All the women on the island put small sums of money aside throughout their lifetimes to pay for the boards for their coffins and supplies for the wake.

CHAPTER FIVE

'You're welcome, I'm sure!'

Christian replaced the receiver and removed his reading glasses, rubbing his weary eyes. He was doubling up, looking after his own copy and also helping out with the phones on the city desk which had been hopping all night. Very few of the calls had been productive from the *Chicago Sentinel*'s point of view: concerned citizens from the 'burbs mainly, wanting to know if it would be safe for their little darlings to go downtown, and if it wasn't these it was out-of-town reporters looking for briefings and updates.

He got back to his profile of Tom Hayden, studying transcripts of the most recent speeches made by the leader of the New Left. They were all in town, a coalition of oddballs and radicals – Hayden and Abbie Hoffman, the Yippie Jerry Rubin, the poet Allen Ginsberg, even the French playwright Jean Genet and the Reverend Ralph Abernathy was expected with his mule train and his Poor People. But in Christian's view the convention in the amphitheatre and in the boiling streets and parks came down to a single contest: Mayor Daley versus The Rest.

He fiddled around with his opening paragraph, trying to frame the words so that they were trenchant but not opinionated. This was difficult given his very strong views on the way Mayor Daley ran Chicago. It might well have been the Middle Ages and not 1968, thought Christian, with Richard Daley behaving as though the city were his own personal fiefdom. Tear gas, mace and head-bashing outside, ructions amongst the delegates inside, but overall, astride Chicago and the Democratic Party, the Mayor had a single clear vision: Things His Way. But Things were not going all his way and there were rumours all around town that Daley would call out the National Guard.

Christian had a large amount of sympathy for the radicals. He himself had escaped the draft and Vietnam only because, absurdly, he had been discovered to have flat feet and defective vision in one eye. As the war dragged on and on, the more useless and wasteful it appeared to him, but professionally he was required to be neutral. The owners of the newspaper were Republican but the *Sentinel*'s editorial line was firmly non-partisan about the war – although, along with all the other newspapers in the city, it had called on the Mayor to grant permits for the demonstrators. It was more than Christian's job was worth to betray his personal opinions in his pieces. He was not all that interested in national politics in any event, more in the 'wider picture'. He had applied for a transfer to the foreign desk but so far there was nothing doing. The telephone rang again. He bent his head over a flurry of typing and ignored it.

'Nearly finished?'

He looked up. Dick, festooned with cameras and laminated passes, was standing in front of him.

'Yeah, another ten minutes.'

'I think I've one or two good shots of Hayden in tonight's stuff,' said Dick. 'I'm going in to dev them now. Want to see them when I'm done?'

'Sure.'

'It's murder out there. You should go and see for yourself.'

'Yeah, maybe tomorrow night.'

The telephone rang again and this time he picked it up. It was a reporter from England, wanting to know if he could use the newspaper's cuttings library.

Christian knew that at present the librarian was run off his feet with requests for clippings from the newspaper's own staff but his sympathy was with the reporter. He had often been in such a position himself – strange city, knowing no one, needing information fast. 'Yeah, that's OK,' he said. 'Just come along to the front desk.'

'How long will you be until you're clear?' he asked Dick as he replaced the receiver.

'About an hour,' answered his friend, who was already moving towards the darkroom.

'Want one?'

Dick hesitated, then, 'OK. See you in the Shamrock.'

Christian, distracted from his copy, watched his best friend's progress through the newsroom. Dick was senior to him in the hierarchy of the newspaper, having joined two years before him, but he hoped that if he did get his transfer Dick would come with him on some of his assignments. Dick was a rock in his life.

But he had noticed Dick's hesitation about joining him in the Shamrock Bar. He was aware that Dick thought he drank too much but in his own view that was his business, not Dick's.

Dublin was bedlam. When she got off the Galway train at Kingsbridge, Molly stood on the platform, her suitcase at her feet, trying to get her bearings. She could not understand the announcements being boomed over the loudspeaker and echoing through the iron struts of the roof and, beside her, the sound of the diesel locomotive which had pulled her train was amplified many times by the marble and metal all over the station. She was very frightened.

'Excuse me, excuse me . . . ' The stream of passengers flowed around her where she stood. The train had been packed.

As the stony Connacht landscape gave way to the green pastures of the midlands, Molly had decided that for the first night at least she could afford to stay in a hotel. She would be safe and it would give her breathing space to think. From the hotel she would telephone one or perhaps both of her classmates. She had bought the *Irish Independent* at the station in Galway and there was a feature in it about the Dublin Horse Show. Her plan was to pretend to her classmates that she was in Dublin to go to the show.

Having made at least one decision about her future had made her feel better. But now that she was actually here the impulse to turn right round and take the next train back to Galway was very strong. She was afraid also that she was an object of curiosity with her too-short school gaberdine. She would have to buy a decent coat.

Yet looking at all the people rushing past her towards the

167

barrier behind which their friends who were meeting them jostled and pushed to get a better vantage point, she realized that not one of them was giving her a second glance. Everyone except herself seemed to have a purpose, to know exactly where to go.

She was truly alone.

The only place names in Dublin with which she was familiar were O'Connell Street and the GPO – the general post office, which had been the scene of the Easter Rising in 1916. She had the notion that if she could get to the GPO it would be somewhere to start from.

She picked up her suitcase and moved along with the stream of people towards the entrance to the station. But when she got outside, she had no idea whether to turn right or left. 'Excuse me,' she said to a man who wore a peaked cap, 'could you tell me how to get to the GPO?'

The man gave her directions but looked doubtfully at her suitcase. 'Are you walking?'

'Yes.'

'Well, it's a goodish walk. You'd be better off with the bus.'

He told her where to get the bus and which number but when she got to the bus stop she had forgotten which bus he had mentioned. Remembering his directions she looked up the quays, jam-packed with hooting, honking traffic, towards the city centre. It did not look all that far . . .

But the walk along the quays proved miserable and again her courage almost failed her. It was drizzling; a pungent, sweetish smell came from the oily Liffey which was at low tide; buses and lorries belched black smoke; sodden litter lay in the gutters alongside the footpath and once, she tripped and almost fell on a broken paving stone.

Also, she seemed to be walking for ever. After ten minutes, the suitcase dragged out of her shoulder and she had to put it down to rest. She looked again towards O'Connell Street. It seemed no nearer . . .

But just ahead of her there was a set of flags drooping on flagpoles from the façade of a grey building and she saw it was a hotel. Molly decided that she could not walk any further. Whatever this hotel was, however much it cost, she would book a room. She picked up the suitcase again, walked the remaining few yards and entered the lobby of the Clarence. It was warm and quiet. A girl stood behind a small counter.

Molly felt obscurely guilty when she asked her for a room – as though she was not entitled to it – but the receptionist did not seem to think anything of the sort and pushed a registration form and pen across the desk. Molly hesitated but decided to act as though she was used to doing this kind of thing. When she examined it the form was simple – it asked only for her name, address and car registration number.

'Do I have to have a car?' she asked in alarm.

This did cause a flicker in the receptionist's eyes but her mouth twitched as she answered, 'No.'

Molly felt utterly stupid.

She completed the form and paid one night in advance, thirty shillings which, the receptionist told her, included breakfast. Then she indicated that Molly should give her suitcase to a porter who had been standing patiently behind her while she registered.

The porter walked ahead of her up the stairs and down a short corridor lined with doors. He stopped in front of one of them and inserted a key in the lock.

Molly's only other experience of hotels had been the one night in the lodging house with her mam in Galway when she was five and she did not know that she was supposed to tip. The porter, a middle-aged man, having opened her door placed her suitcase inside the room. 'Will there by anything else?' he asked. He seemed to be waiting for something.

'No, thank you,' said Molly. 'Thank you very much for carrying my case.'

The porter hesitated but then smiled at her and left. When the door clicked shut behind her, Molly looked around the room. No one cared what she did now. There were no nuns, no Sorcha, to tell her what to do . . .

She concentrated on the fact that she was very hungry. She would have something to eat. She took out her money and counted it – still more than ninety pounds left. It was a fortune but she would have to be careful. This money might have to last her a very long time.

She left the room and went downstairs. A heavy smell of roast beef and cabbage issued from the dining room and for a few seconds she was tempted to follow it but was too shy and unsure as to how she should behave in a hotel restaurant. So she passed it and left the hotel, stepping out again onto the quays outside. The drizzle had stopped but there was a keen wind coming off the river. She headed for O'Connell Street again.

Unencumbered this time, she walked swiftly and began to feel almost exhilarated. She was still frightened but now that she had a base, a temporary home, Molly felt adventurous. She was embarked on – who knew?

When she crossed O'Connell Bridge, she walked up one side of the street and down the other, fascinated by the garish bustle. Everyone seemed to have somewhere to go. People got on and off buses and greeted each other and strolled arm in arm in pairs or in bigger groups. Queues of couples waited outside the cinemas. She found the GPO, recognizing it because of the posting slots and stamp machines. Sheltering under its stone portico, dozens of people stood singly, all dressed up. They had obviously made appointments to meet other people. She wondered how long it would be before she too had an appointment at the GPO.

She crossed the street. The windows of a shop called Clery's were plastered with red signs saying 'SALE' and crammed with goods – bed linen and tea-towels, women's bathing togs, boys' blazers, luggage and teasets, hurleys and tennis rackets, clocks, watches, kettles and cutlery. She had never seen so many things in her life. Sorcha would have loved it, she thought.

Further down the street was a Cafolla's restaurant. There were pictures in the window of plates of food, plump sausages and big chips, bright yellow eggs and massive, pastel ice-cream sundaes. Her teeth watered and she went in.

The meal was not as good as the pictures outside but she felt warm and fed after it and lingered over a cup of tea. She was pleased to see she was not the only one eating on her own. Plenty of the tables had only one person sitting at them.

The streetlights were on when she went back out into O'Connell Street. She wandered past Clery's again, then turned right, walking down North Earl Street and crossing into Talbot Street. At the end of that street there was another railway station – at least she assumed it was another railway station as a bridge ran across the street in front of it. Two railway stations! Although she had often imagined how big Dublin must be, now that she was actually here its size astounded her.

She was standing at the corner of Talbot Place, looking at the railway station, when she noticed, in the window of a pub on the corner, a small piece of paper. 'Help Wanted', it said. Before she could second-guess herself, Molly went inside.

John Pius McCarthy, a middle-aged bachelor who lived with his mother in a flat over his pub, looked up from the row of pints he was pulling. The bar was packed and noisy and a blue fug of cigarette smoke hung in the air.

In front of him stood a girl with a flaming red face, in a brown school coat too small for her – but with such obvious class that John Pius gulped. The girl was saying something but he could not catch it. He leaned forward. 'Did you want something, miss?'

'C-could I talk to the m-manager, please?' she stuttered. Her accent was country soft.

'I'm the manager.' He waited but she seemed to have run out of words. He wiped his hands on an old tea-towel and brought her in through the connecting door from the pub to the lounge, which was also full but not half so noisy. He turned to her. 'Now we can understand each other.'

'It's – it's about the notice in the window . . .'

To give himself time, he plugged in the kettle on the counter behind the bar. 'I see. Do you mind me asking how old you are?'

'Sixteen – nearly seventeen, sir.'

That's what he had thought. 'Would you like a cup of coffee?' he asked.

She nodded. His experienced eye told him that she had

171

probably never been in a pub in her life, much less worked in one. But she seemed to take his silence for encouragement.

'I'll do anything, sir,' she said. 'What kind of work is it you want?'

'Sit down,' said John Pius, indicating that she should sit on a high stool in front of the bar. John Pius, who was shy, always felt himself at a disadvantage with women. He kept the counter safely between them while he busied himself removing glasses from the counter-top to the under-counter by the sink. He ran water noisily and splashed it around as his barman moved swiftly up and down the bar, filling orders from the lounge boy. But as he slopped around John Pius was thinking hard and watching Molly covertly. He was afraid that if he did not hire her, someone else would take advantage of her naïveté and innocence. John Pius, Molly was to learn, had a heart as soft as butter.

He turned off the water. 'Do you have any references?'

She shook her head. 'It's my first job, sir.'

'Well, that's a bit of a problem.'

She looked stricken and he thought she was going to cry. 'I'll tell you what,' he said hastily, 'come back tomorrow evening about nine. I'll need help in the lounge. Would you be willing to stay late?' He had just created a job superfluous to his needs and, since he was giving status to illicit after-hours drinking, entirely illegal.

Her eyes flew wide. Even in the dim light of the lounge he noticed how blue they were. She was really beautiful.

'Of course I would, sir. As late as you like.'

John Pius sighed. 'What's your name, by the way?' he asked.

'Molly. Molly Ní Bhriain.'

'That's it, then,' he said. 'I'm sorry but I have to get back to the bar. Mick the barman'll crucify me!' And to Molly's astonishment John Pius giggled. His ruddy face shrank into his collar like a turtle retracting into its carapace and his whole body shook with noiseless amusement. The effect was irresistible. 'My name's John Pius McCarthy, by the way,' he managed, through his giggles, 'but everyone calls me JP!'

'Thank you very much, Mr McCarthy.'

They shook hands.

'Right-oh,' said JP. 'See you tomorrow night.'

Molly went back out into the street, light-headed with elation. Only four hours in Dublin and already she had a job! She had not planned to get a job, she had genuinely planned to get in touch with her classmates, but now that events had overtaken her she would not fly in the face of them. She had forgotten to ask about money but she knew that even if she had remembered she would not have had the courage. It did not matter. She had a *job* – and instinctively she trusted John Pius McCarthy.

The distance back to the Clarence seemed to be half what it had been when she had left it. When she got into the lobby, a different girl was on duty behind the counter but Molly told her anyway that she would be staying on for two more nights.

She spent the next day window-shopping in the city and went back to the same Cafolla's to eat her dinner.

She was at the pub shortly after eight o'clock, wearing her good skirt and báinín jumper. John Pius was nowhere to be seen and no one seemed to be expecting her. But the barman in the lounge recognized her and allowed her to sit at the counter, giving her a Britvic Orange.

JP arrived in the lounge at a quarter to nine. 'Punctual too!' he said when he saw her.

He made her another cup of coffee and explained what her duties were. They were light: to assist the lounge boy if there was a crowd, to help with the cleaning up after closing time. He explained that not every night but most nights the pub played host to a small circle of special clients – actors, theatre people, writers, artists – who stayed on after closing time. Part of Molly's job would be to serve them and to clean up after them. 'But don't worry if it goes too late. We'll always arrange a lift home for you. Where do you live by the way?'

When she told him her address was the Clarence Hotel, he was scandalized. 'Living in a hotel? It must be costing you a fortune!'

Molly managed her work quite well that first night and since no one came to stay after closing time John Pius drove her home to the Clarence and she was in bed before one o'clock. The next afternoon John Pius arrived unexpectedly, clutching a newspaper. He had found her a flat – a single room above a shop in Dame Street. He had come to show it to her to see if she liked it.

Molly did. It was tiny and heated only with a single-bar electric fire but it was clean and newly decorated and had everything she would need. They went back to the Clarence and checked Molly out.

Then, while Molly was unpacking in the flat, John Pius vanished for a few minutes and when he came back, pink and giggling, he handed her a large paper bag.

'House-warming!' he said.

The bag contained a colourful wall-calendar and a small table lamp with a pretty floral shade.

Molly was speechless at his kindness.

'And here's a plug,' he said, pulling it out of his pocket with a flourish. He taught her then how to wire a plug, using the blade of a knife he found in the cutlery drawer in the minute curtained-off alcove which served as a kitchenette. They plugged in the lamp and switched it on so that the little place, which was dark because its small single window faced north, glowed with warmth.

'Now the party!' said John Pius and he pulled a snipe of champagne out of his other pocket.

Molly, recognizing that John Pius was even shyer than she was, was more at ease with him by the minute. She had never drunk champagne – nor any alcohol – and she was fascinated by the way it fizzed into the chipped glasses John Pius found in her new kitchenette. When she took a sip it prickled on her tongue.

The actors came to the pub that night. They arrived at about 11.00 p.m. and John Pius herded them into a corner until the rest of the patrons had left. Then he stoked the log fire, turned the lights low and brought bottles of wine from his cellar. While Molly cleaned up the counter area and made sure the actors had glasses, John Pius put Bach's Double Violin Concerto to play on his soft-toned hi-fi and then introduced

174

her to everyone individually. She was sure she would never remember the names.

John Pius went upstairs then to cut tuna-fish sandwiches for them in his own kitchen and Molly was left in charge of the lounge. She moved around as unobtrusively as possible. Following John Pius's instructions, she made sure the log fire was replenished and that she was always on hand to give out the drinks. Most of them were drinking wine so it was quite easy.

For long periods that night she had little to do and hung back in the gloom of the lounge beyond the circle of light around the fire. But they called her forward to join them. She sat silently and in awe while these vivacious, glamorous people, keeping their resonant voices under control for fear of a raid by the Guards, drank quietly and reminisced and told stories. Molly was enchanted.

Two of the actors were Macartan O'Toole and Dessie Byrne. On the fourth night he was there Dessie made a point of talking to Molly. He was quick-witted, good looking and very charming. Molly had never met anyone like him before but to her surprise she found it quite easy to talk to him. Dessie Byrne made an art of listening.

Macartan joined them and both men quizzed her gently, eliciting her life history. Not all of it – Molly told them only the bare bones. She told them nothing about Conor or her dadda's death. And when they asked her why she had left school and come to Dublin so young she felt bold enough to say, 'To seek my fortune!'

That gave Dessie and Macartan an idea. There were auditions the following morning at the Abbey, only for extras for crowd scenes in *The Plough and the Stars*, but it would be a start, said Macartan.

John Pius, listening in on the conversation, encouraged Molly to say yes.

'Give it a lash, Molly, why not?' said John Pius.

'There's nothing to it,' said Dessie. 'Honestly, Molly. Piece of cake!'

'I know you're shy, Molly,' said Macartan. 'We're all shy, honestly.' And he did a mock pirouette in front of the fireplace.

175

'Shy, my arse!' said Dessie. 'The day you're shy, Macartan O'Toole, will be the day pigs fly! Seriously, though, Molly,' he said, turning to her, 'actors *are* shy. You know what they say, acting is the shy person's revenge.'

Molly had not heard that saying before. She was very tempted. She was also flattered at all the attention and by them thinking that she could actually walk-on in a show on a real, grown-up, professional stage.

She had been on stage before in school and the nun who taught elocution had encouraged her greatly. Being so tall she had always played men's parts but despite her inhibitions she had been amazed to find that she had loved the experience of being on stage. And although at the time she had thought she was indulging in the sin of pride, she sensed from the reaction of others that she was good. She received no special privileges but subtly it was recognized throughout the school that, for instance, if this year's play was to be *Hamlet*, Molly would automatically play the Dane. The elocution teacher entered her in the local *feiseanna*, glorified talent competitions, and Molly's collection of silver cups and certificates for verse-speaking was proudly displayed in the school's gloomy entrance hall. Rehearsals were fun – and a great, officially sanctioned, excuse to miss schoolwork – but the nights of actual performance were always the best. The ancient, musty stage curtain in the school hall was moth-eaten and, although patched, full of holes and gaps. Against all the rules Molly, tummy fluttering, always peeked through it at the gathering audience. The parents and friends of the pupils who lived locally or within reasonable travelling distance were ranged on the rows of wooden chairs, chatting among themselves in the centre section, while behind them on the refectory forms sat the girls who were not involved in the play.

The front two rows stayed empty until the very last moment when all the nuns, led by Reverend Mother, filed in. They remained standing until, last to arrive, Mother Provincial sat in the very centre of the nuns' row on her symbolic throne – the only chair with arms.

After the performance started Molly always felt a heightened sense of awareness of herself. She loved the way the lights blotted out all faces beyond the edge of the stage and warmed her own, creating a self-contained little world around her as her character moved and spoke through her. On performance nights Molly felt as secure as an oyster in its shell.

Molly looked at the circle of encouraging faces in JP's lounge.

'Well, what about it, Molly?' demanded Dessie.

'Sure, why not?' she said.

She arrived ten minutes before the appointed time, which was ten in the morning. The theatre, which was not far from the pub, was dark and empty but two other girls and a boy were in the auditorium waiting for the audition. They all seemed to know each other and did not address her but from their conversation Molly deduced they had all had some training. Feeling she had no chance she nearly left the theatre. But then a man came in and clapped his hands and called the four of them up to the front of the auditorium.

All she had to do for him was to stand in the middle of the stage cheering loudly as if she were watching a football match and then to walk on and off a few times, using different entrances and exits.

They were all hired, all four of them. Molly rushed back to the pub with the good news and of course John Pius was thrilled for her. He told her that during the run of the play she didn't have to come to work until after the final curtain each night. He took her out to lunch in the Gresham hotel to celebrate and told her she would be a star.

Conor watched a little Arab girl chase the pigeons in Trafalgar Square. Again and again she rushed at them, flapping her own small arms like wings but the pigeons, world-weary, were experienced enough to stay a few inches ahead off her no matter how fast she moved or in what direction. As her veiled mother watched dotingly her father, Nikon motordrive whirring, took photograph after photograph of her.

The little girl, hair tumbling around her face, was dressed in a child's version of a Spanish flamenco dress, red with white spots, complete with multilayered petticoats and fringed shawl, but her legs were encased in leggings.

Conor could not take his eyes off her. Although there was nothing in the child's appearance which even vaguely resembled his sister, something about her laughing and running reminded him of his carefree ramblings with Molly on Inisheer so many years before. Resolutely he turned his attention away from the little scene and, hands in his pockets, watched the other tourists. He had been to London on a few occasions but those times it had been for pleasure – a football match or a weekend holiday. Now it was different. Instead of the joy of discovery and carefree exploration he tramped the London streets ridden by fear and a feeling of loss. He had arrived in the city more than two weeks ago and spent his first night in a sleazy hotel in King's Cross. He had better accommodation at the moment in a small private hotel in Bayswater.

He lived in fear of running into someone from home since the first question was always, 'What county are you from?' and this would lead to others. Therefore he avoided pubs. It was not only the clientele who might be Irish, many of the people behind the bar were too, so for the two weeks he had been in London he had haunted free museums and art galleries, eaten cheaply in fish-and-chippers or in Chinatown, attended movies in the afternoon.

The evenings were the worst since he had nothing to do except go back to his room.

He was running out of money fast. He had to get a job. The thought was daunting. He had to avoid anything in his area of expertise – botany, even gardening – since he supposed that these were the areas the police would check first.

He pulled out his address book. He had not yet telephoned the priest whose name Father Hartigan had given him as a contact in case he needed help. This priest was discreet, his friend had assured him, and Father Hartigan had promised to write immediately to him on Conor's behalf. He seemed to be hiding a lot under the skirts of the clergy, thought Conor grimly as he found the priest's number, but he had created a trap for himself with no other option.

The priest, whose name was Frank O'Hare, made it easy for him when he rang. 'Oh, yes!' he said cheerfully. 'Tom Hartigan's friend. I was expecting you to ring. Now where'll we meet? I don't suppose you want to come all the way out here . . . ' He lived in Willesden.

'I'll come anywhere you say, Father.'

'Frank, please! None of this "Father" stuff over here, not on my beat. I'd drop dead if any of my clients called me Father!' Father Hartigan had told him that Father O'Hare operated in some of the toughest parts of London.

'All right, Frank.' But Conor found it difficult. The Irish deference for the clergy was very deeply ingrained.

'Now, what time is it?' continued the priest, then answered himself, 'Just after two. Do you like fish? There's a lovely fish restaurant just off Leicester Square. Manzi's. Do you know it?'

Conor did not. 'I'm sure I could find it, Father – Frank.'

'All right. I could do with a good bit of fish. Once a month I treat myself. Suppose we meet at Manzi's at about seven?'

'All right, Frank, see you then. And thank you very, very much.'

'Don't thank me yet, I haven't done anything for you. But I've been having a think since I got Tom's letter and maybe we'll be able to get you fixed up. I suppose you don't object to manual labour?'

'No, Father – Frank. I don't object to anything at all. Anyway, I'm hardly in a position to object.'

'Don't talk like that. Where there's life there's hope. All right?'

'All right. Thanks again.'

'Until tonight, then . . . '

'Goodbye, Frank.'

Conor, expending his nervous energy, walked all the way to Cromwell Road and spent the afternoon at the Victoria and Albert Museum.

That evening he found Manzi's easily and went inside. He

was too early, it was only a quarter to seven, but the restaurant was very busy and they could not guarantee him a table for at least an hour.

'Perhaps we can accommodate you at the counter, sir?'

Conor nodded, intimidated. He was virtually a stranger to good restaurants. There were a few in Dublin but not frequented by any in his circle of friends, who tended to congregate in pubs or to eat celebratory meals in each other's houses.

'What's your name?' The man held a silver pen over the reservations book.

'Molloy,' said Conor, using the name under which he had registered at his hotel.

'Sean Molloy.'

If it were not for the tension in the air, sharp as the blade of a knife, Christian might even have been bored. It was dark and nothing had actually happened for what seemed like hours. The demonstrators, nearly all kids as far as he could tell, were determined not to be moved away from this patch of grassy land in Lincoln Park between North Clark and La Salle Drive. The police, he knew, were determined to move them. The impending trouble laced the air between the two sides like a bad smell.

He and Dick hung around with other reporters in a little wooded area, watching as some of the demonstrators built a barricade with benches, tables, branches of trees, garbage, even twigs, anything they could find. Most of the kids milled around ineffectually or sat on the grass talking in low, urgent voices, planning how to behave when the police came.

The pandas prowled quietly nearby, not making much of a fuss. A few of them were revolving their blue and white roof lights but were not operating sirens and the lights on their own gave the scene a surreal aspect. From here and there Christian could hear at low volume the chattering of the police radios. Several of the cops muttered into walkie-talkies.

He had done all the interviews he needed for his piece. He had quotes from Genet and the American writer William Burroughs and acres of crazy, idealistic prose from the kids. But he could not leave until after the trouble. All the other reporters waited too. No one wanted anyone else to have exclusive action. None of them, however, discussed the situation at hand – they talked about expenses.

A girl who was part of a group near Christian was handing out jars of Vaseline from an embroidered Indian bag and the group began to smear the jelly all over their faces and hands. Christian strolled over. 'Excuse me,' he said, 'I'm from the *Chicago Sentinel*. Could you tell me what you're doing?'

The girl, he saw, could not have been more than seventeen, with a fragile, gentle face. 'It's to protect our skin from the mace,' she said. 'That stuff really burns, you know, and if they get your eyes, you're in deep shit.' Her voice shook. She continued to smear Vaseline on her skin. Christian, in the interest of 'colour' for his story, watched her, noting mentally that some of her long fine hair was sticking to her cheek.

Then all hell broke loose.

It started when a police car drove at speed towards the barricade and smashed it. After the calm, the tearing, grinding and gunning of the engine was shocking. For a split second the girl sat, frozen, with the open jar of Vaseline in her hand. Then she leaped to her feet. 'Pig! Fascist pig!' she screamed, her face contorted with hate. She threw the tiny jar in the direction of the police car but it landed just twenty or thirty feet away from her.

Christian retreated to the wooded area and the safety of the phalanx of reporters and newsmen. But the television crews, big burly men, walked towards the action so he walked back with them. The police were swinging their clubs at the youngsters, cracking heads. Christian was shocked but his adrenalin was pumping. He tried to keep calm, talking the description of the action into his tape recorder. He had temporarily lost sight of Dick.

The wooded part of the park was behind him so he heard rather than saw when a band of police, badges and name-plates removed, came surging out, swinging at the photographers and snatching at their cameras. He wheeled round to face them and spotted Dick who, intent on his work, was not watching what was going on behind him. He was kneeling on the grass, photographing a boy in a poncho who seemed to be unconscious, blood pouring out of a wound high on his cheekbone.

'Dick! Dick!' screamed Christian.

But all around the park the youngsters were screaming too and his voice was lost.

Sinister in his helmet, one of the policemen, stick in the air, was bearing down fast on his friend. Before he could think Christian reacted. He sprinted to intercept the cop, who was intent on his target and did not notice Christian coming in from the side. Christian got to him, outstretched hands knocking the man over just a split second before the baton arced at Dick's unprotected head. Prepared for the impact, Christian was poised and quick on his feet so did not fall. But the policeman, carried by his own momentum, cannoned over Dick as though Dick were a vaulting horse. His stick was now a handicap as he put out his hand to save himself. He landed on top of the boy in the poncho. The boy did not move.

Christian bent down to help Dick get up but something exploded in his head, accompanied by bright lights, colours and shocking pain. He passed out.

He woke in Henrotin Hospital, his head pounding. Dick was sitting beside him and so was one of the night editors from the newspaper.

'How are you feeling?' asked the editor.

'What happened?' The muscles in Christian's face hurt when he moved his mouth to speak.

'You were clubbed,' said Dick, 'but don't feel bad. You weren't the only one. Seventeen newsmen! Even the networks!'

Christian closed his eyes. He felt giddy.

'Sorry to have to ask you this,' said the editor after a pause, 'but I don't suppose you know where your notes are?'

Christian shook his head, or tried to. 'Tape recorder?' he managed faintly.

'They took the cassette,' said Dick, 'and my film. All of it.'

Despite the pain Christian felt the rage well up from his toes. 'Don't need notes,' he said. 'My clothes . . . '

'You can't leave here. You've had a bad concussion.' But the editor's voice lacked conviction. They had already missed the first edition and they weren't covered.

Fuelled by his fury, Christian was feeling stronger. 'Dick,' he said, 'get me out of here.'

'Are you sure?'

'I'm sure.'

Against the doctors' explicit advice, Christian signed himself out of Henrotin. He felt groggy and the pain still split his skull but his rage was stronger than the pain. He was going to get the bastards, he told himself. When he had the story written he could have days of sleep.

The newsroom was frantic with telephones. Christian sat at his typewriter and took a deep breath, trying consciously to bite back his fury so he would use nothing but the facts. He started to type, forcing himself to write only exactly what he had seen, but even as the words flowed he knew exultantly that this would be the best thing he had ever done. The story poured like molten steel, hardening precisely on the pages.

It took only forty minutes to write and the night editor, who stood by Christian's desk and took the pages one by one as they were finished, changed not a single comma. When the last page was off his desk Dick drove Christian home to his apartment in Old Town. He took a large whiskey and fell into bed.

The next day he woke around noon and still felt diseased. But at least, he thought flexing his arms and legs, he no longer felt he was going to die. In his bathroom he shook four aspirin into his hand, gulped them down with a glass of water, then padded into his kitchen and made himself a cup of strong black coffee into which he poured a tot of whiskey. He lay down on his bed again but within half an hour he was feeling a little better and put a call through to the newsdesk from the telephone on his night table.

'There's a message for you – by the way, congratulations on your story – Morton wants to see you,' said the news-editor. Morton was the newspaper's editor-in-chief.

'What's it about?'

'Haven't a goony's,' said the news-editor. 'Why don't you call him?'

'OK,' said Christian. He dialled the newspaper again and was put through to the editor's office straight away.

'That was a fine story from the park, Smith,' said the editor, who called all his staff by their surnames.

'Thank you, sir.'

'The wires picked it up and I believe you were quoted on BBC Television news in London.'

'That's great, sir.'

'Yes, well, it's probably not the time to talk about it now but I believe you're looking for a transfer to the foreign desk?'

'Yes, sir.' Christian's heart began to pound.

'I don't see any problem with that, Smith. We've no actual vacancy at the moment, as you know, but we had been talking here on the top floor of expanding our international input. I was thinking this morning that one of the things we could do is put you on a sort of roving brief. You wouldn't have much political analysis to do, we'd leave that to the desk, but you could be the guy to send to events, you know, earthquakes, that sort of thing. Your colour stuff and description of last night was first class. I think it's probably your strength and the paper could use it. What do you think?'

It was beyond Christian's wildest hopes and was exactly the type of coverage he knew he could do well.

'That would be absolutely fine, sir,' he answered, shakily.

'OK, then. Call in and we'll fix up the details. I'll put you back to my secretary and she can make an appointment. By the way, how's your head?'

'Getting better, sir. No lasting damage.'

'Bastards!' said the editor-in-chief before he broke the connection.

Molly fell excitedly into her new life. She wrote to her mother and to Kathleen Agnes, who was already back at school, telling them about her good fortune and asking her mam's permission not to go back to school at all:

If this doesn't work out, Mam, I can always go back and do my Leaving Cert again. Honestly. And I honestly will, you can be sure of that. I'm not being stupid. John Pius and all the people in the theatre are being very kind to me and they all think that maybe I can have a career in the theatre. It's much, much different to acting in school, I can't really explain it – it's just that everyone around you is so good and works so hard. It's sort of half fun, half the most serious thing in the world. Oh, I'm making a mess of this. I can't really describe it. You'll have to see it for yourself.

That's a great idea. Maybe you and Brendan or one of the aunties could come up to see me on the stage? I'd love to have you see me (although I don't have all that much to do, no lines or anything, but all the actors say I'm quite good) and anyway I'd really like to see you.

I hope you're not too lonely. Maybe you'd come up to Dublin soon and you can stay in my flat? It's real nice, Mam, in the middle of Dublin so that I can walk everywhere. I pass Trinity College, where the Book of Kells is, on my way to work every day. Think about it. Apart altogether from coming to see *me*, I could take you to a cinema – there are great pictures on in Dublin and they are on all afternoon, every day.

Dublin is very exciting. Must close now as it's time to go to rehearsal.

REHEARSAL! Doesn't that sound great?

Love to yourself and all the aunties. Have you heard from Brendan? I'll be home soon, don't worry. The only thing I worry about is where Conor is. But knowing him, he will be fine.

Before sealing it, Molly reread the letter. Where was Conor? Hardly a day went by that she did not worry about her brother. In her imagination Conor sometimes lived exotically, a nomad in the deserts of Arabia, sometimes mundanely on the building sites of Birmingham of which she knew a little from Brendan.

She never for a second, however, doubted that he was alive and surviving.

He had written to her just once, a short note forwarded to her via her mother by his friend the priest, Father Hartigan. In the letter, he told her not to worry about him and finished by saying that, God willing, he would see her as soon as he could even if it proved to be a long time. She missed him dreadfully but every time she thought about him that last appalling scene of her father's death was superimposed on his face. No matter how tired she was that image haunted her every night as she lay in her narrow bed.

Resolutely she put away the image now, placed a five-pound note in the envelope addressed to her mother and sealed it.

John Pius came to her opening night, of course, and at ten past one the following morning, while the Galway mail-train moved slowly along the tracks behind the pub, he opened a bottle of champagne in honour of Molly's début.

Molly continued to work for John Pius and went as an extra from show to show in the Abbey, which operated in two venues – the Abbey itself and the smaller Peacock Theatre in the basement. In October she was offered a slot as a full-time assistant stage manager. She was quick and willing and already very popular.

The routine at the Abbey was morning rehearsal, afternoon free, performance in the evening. Molly took full advantage of the afternoons, becoming an avid cinema-goer. Sometimes when the days were too fine to incarcerate herself at the pictures she explored the city, riding the buses out to their farthest stops in Tallaght and Stillorgan, Ballymun, Ballyfermot, Clontarf, Sutton, Finglas, Howth and even Bray, just for the pleasure of the rides.

She loved Henry Street and the fruit vendors in Moore Street. Sometimes she bought a bag of apples so she could hear the Dublin accent, so different from her own. She practised the accent, which at night she heard regularly in some of the plays she worked on, and tried it out on John Pius. Giggling he told her that for a country girl she was doing fine . . .

All the time there was the enchantment of her new job.

186

Molly was amused but still fascinated at the bitchy, witty talk of theatre people even though she was now accustomed to it. She had come to the Abbey in a state of nervous anticipation, expecting a group of very special, dramatic and high-octane personalities. She expected uplifting discussions about Art and that she would learn her trade at the feet of serious Artists on intimate terms with the language of Seán O'Casey and John Millington Synge . . .

What she found was a group of people who complained all the time about the cold, about draughts, about the length of their lunch hours, about the miserable effin' management who wouldn't give them the time of day; actors who read newspapers during rehearsals if not actually on stage – and sometimes when they were – who knitted, wore woolly hats and mufflers while rehearsing love scenes and who drank endless cups of tea. She never ceased to be amazed each night when from her prompter's corner she saw this crowd of moaning caterpillars transmogrify themselves into elegant butterflies.

Her favourite time of day was at around six o'clock in the evening when the box-office and day staff had left and the night staff had not yet come in. She was frequently alone in the theatre at that time and although the building was a new one, on the outside an uninspired concrete pillbox, Molly's vivid imagination clothed its bowels with history and fantasy and peopled its vast open stage with traditional spirits.

She wandered about, loving the odd smells of venerable costumes, of flats repainted a hundred times, of sized wood and canvas; she walked softly across the darkened stage and listened for old whispers; she peered out into the tiers of empty seats which spread across the auditorium like a wide feathered fan of blue.

One evening, when she was absolutely sure she was alone, Molly stood very still stage centre. She closed her eyes and imagined that she was an actress – a real actress, the lead in one of the Abbey plays, Nora Clitheroe in *The Plough and the Stars* or Deirdre in Synge's *Deirdre of the Sorrows* . . . In her imagination, the performance had been a triumph and she was taking her curtain calls while wave after wave of applause and

187

cheering swept over her. 'Well done, Molly!' said her co-stars to her as they held a hand on each side of her and took their bows at her side . . .

The sound of a door closing in the distance caused Molly's eyes to fly open in fright. Feeling foolish, shading her eyes against the single worklight, she peered into the auditorium, ready with an excuse – but no one was there. She went over and sat in her prompt corner and, turning the pages of her production book, mentally rehearsed her sound and light cues so that she would not miss a single one. Molly felt truly at home in the theatre but never more so than when she was alone.

At night, she was accepted into the pub circle, not only in John Pius's pub but in the bars and lounges the actors went to immediately after the performances. She listened to the outrageous character assassinations and watched, with some fascination, the shifting romantic attachments.

It rarely occurred to Molly that she herself could be the object of male fantasy. Although, instinctively, she comprehended something of what Father Morahan had felt for her, the memory of the episode in the dunes was like vapour, passing across her mind occasionally but leaving no impression. On the other hand, she found her memories of Conor to be vivid and sensual. They seemed in a way fulfilling and complete in themselves. Molly found she was constantly comparing her new friends to her brother – and always finding the friends wanting.

But one night in the pub across the road from the theatre she was approached by a young man. 'Hello,' he said boldly. 'I've been watching you!'

Molly was temporarily alone: Macartan, with whom she had been having a drink, had gone to the gents. 'Hello,' she replied, startled.

'Is he your boyfriend?' asked the young man who, Molly noticed, had eyes of the clear, bright blue not often seen in Ireland.

'I beg your pardon?' she said, although she knew perfectly well what his question had been.

'Is he your boyfriend? The man you're with?' He indicated the gents.

Molly shook her head. 'He's a colleague.'

'Oh, good!' said the young man. 'I'll join you, may I?'

His breezy assertiveness was outside Molly's experience and, despite her keen ear, so was his accent. Helplessly she watched as he removed a folded gaberdine coat from a bar stool and placed it on the floor. He pulled the stool up beside Molly's and sat facing her, smiling. It seemed as if he was quite comfortable and could wait all night for her to say something. His gaze unnerved her. 'Are you Irish?' she asked, making conversation, hoping against hope that Macartan would return soon. Over the man's shoulder, she saw him come out of the gents but he was intercepted by two women who had obviously been at the performance that evening. The women were producing programmes, which Macartan was proceeding to sign.

'I'm Swedish, actually,' said the man. 'I have been touring Great Britain and Ireland.' Then, when Molly did not answer, 'I know Ireland. I come here very often. I did my doctorate on William Butler Yeats.'

'That's nice,' said Molly and took such a huge sip of her drink that she almost choked. 'William Butler Yeats,' she repeated, when she had recovered. 'You'll be going to Sligo, then?'

'I have been many times to Sligo,' he said, waving his hand dismissively. 'But let us talk about you. You are an actress?' He pronounced it 'ektress'.

'Well, sort of,' said Molly. 'Well, I hope to be, actually. I've just started, I was in tonight's play, as a matter of fact. Only a walk-on!' she added hastily, in case he had been at the show.

'Per Keller,' said the man, putting out his hand.

Molly shook it. 'Molly Ní Bhriain.'

'Ahh, Gaelic.' He smiled at her and she noticed that he had almost perfect teeth. Molly was in the habit of making instant decisions about people. She decided she liked him. 'How long are you going to be here, Per?'

'That depends. I don't know how much Ireland has to offer – especially Gaelic Ireland.'

The implication was clear. Molly, inexperienced as she was, could not have missed it. She took another gulp from her glass

189

of orange juice although it contained less than half an inch of liquid.

'May I buy you another one?' asked the Swede, clearly amused. 'Another juice?'

'Thank you,' said Molly, looking desperately towards Macartan who was still deep in conversation with the two theatre-goers.

The Swede caught the barman's attention. At that time of night the pace behind the bar was furious but this man, Molly saw, had the knack of attracting instant attention. He ordered a juice for Molly and a half-pint of Guinness for himself but before the barman brought the drink Macartan had rejoined them.

'Macartan,' said Molly, 'this is Per . . . I'm sorry,' she said, turning to the Swede, 'I've forgotten your second name.'

'Keller,' he said, shaking hands with Macartan who introduced himself.

'Per has studied William Butler Yeats,' said Molly.

'I see,' said Macartan. 'Been to Sligo, have you?'

'Many times,' said the Swede patiently. 'Would you like a drink, Macartan?' He had no difficulty with the name.

'Sure thing, Per.' Macartan never refused a drink.

Safe in Macartan's protection Molly relaxed. She watched the other man deal with the barman and found to her surprise that she was admiring the cut of his jaw.

He came with Macartan and herself to a party that night in a flat in Rathmines Road. The three of them went by taxi, stopping at an off-licence on the way to buy supplies. When the taxi pulled up outside the shop the Swede offered to go inside.

'Right, right, Per!' said Macartan. 'Two six-packs should be enough. We won't stay long.'

'We should give him some money,' protested Molly to Macartan when the Swede had got out of the car.

'Nonsense,' said Macartan. 'He thinks this is great. Two Abbey actors. A party. Drink! This is really *living* for a Swede.'

'That's rubbish, Macartan, and you know it,' but Molly was laughing.

'Have you ever been to Sweden? Shut up, Molly, here he is, back . . . Hello, Per . . . Good man, good man . . .'

190

And Per paid for the taxi when they got to the house where the party was being held. It was an impromptu party, celebrating nothing in particular. The tiny flat was packed with groups and couples sitting and standing on chairs and arms of chairs, on each other's laps and on the floor. One group ranged on two sides of a corner made room for the newcomers and Molly settled herself with her back to a wall between Per and Macartan. She was wearing a miniskirt and took care to arrange her legs modestly to one side of her but noticed that Per was looking at them. One part of her liked it, the other wished she had worn her jeans.

For atmosphere the host, another actor, had turned out all the lights and set dozens of lighted candles in milk bottles and jam jars on the mantelpiece over the blocked-up fireplace. The candles threw long dancing shadows and their waxy smell combined in the room with the cloying aroma from joss sticks. The Beatles' *Sergeant Pepper* album played softly on the record player, almost completely overwhelmed by the tidal wave of talk. Molly noticed that the stacking arm was out, meaning that *Sergeant Pepper* was the only record they would get to hear that night. She was conscious of the Swede's open stare but, confused and uncertain as to how to handle him, she plastered a smile on her face and leaned towards Macartan.

Macartan showed Per how to open a bottle of beer with his teeth. The Swede laughed. 'That's very good, my friend. But I think I will not try it tonight.' He turned to Molly. 'Shall I find us a bottle-opener, Molly?'

'That's OK, Per,' said Macartan. 'I'll open one for her too. There you go, darling.' He handed Molly the open bottle.

Molly hated beer but, not wanting to offend Macartan, took a tiny sip out of the bottle. The Swede was still watching her. 'How old are you, Molly?' he asked suddenly.

'Eighteen,' she lied. It was the first time she had ever done so and she was astonished. Immediately he slipped an arm around her waist. 'You are very lovely,' he said softly. Not knowing what to do, she sat rigid. 'What's the matter?' he asked.

On her other side Macartan had felt her stiffen. He leaned

forward. 'Is everything all right, Molly?' he asked her, but looked at the Swede.

'Everything's fine,' said Molly.

'Are you sure?' asked Macartan.

'She's fine, Macartan,' said the Swede, who did not remove his arm.

After a while Molly found that the embrace was not unpleasant. The Swede was putting no pressure on her but continued to chat easily about his university career in Uppsala, about previous travels in Ireland. Macartan was absorbed in a passionate argument about the film *The Lion in Winter*, which was all the rage among the actors at that time, and Molly was left to her own devices as skilfully the Swede created an exclusion zone around the pair of them. Bit by bit he drew her out, encouraging her to tell him about her childhood on Inisheer – it never ceased to amaze Molly how interesting people found Inisheer. He told her he had visited the island on one of his previous trips to Ireland.

He finished his beer, put the bottle on the floor beside him and casually took Molly's hand in his so that she was completely encircled. 'Are you a virgin, Molly?'

Macartan, still on Molly's other side, again felt her fright. He stopped in mid-argument and turned round. 'What was that, Per?'

'I beg your pardon?' The Swede did not let go of Molly's hand or remove his arm from around her waist.

'What was that you asked Molly?' Macartan's tone was polite but frigid.

'I'm sorry but I don't think this is any of your business . . . '

'Oh, but it is. Did you know this girl is only seventeen?'

'She told me she was eighteen but again I don't see what this has—'

'Molly.' Macartan addressed her directly. 'What did he ask you?'

Molly felt exquisitely embarrassed.

'Look,' said the Swede, cutting across her and looking into her eyes, 'it is no big affair. It is of no consequence. And it is certainly not a problem from which to make an international incident.'

192

'Sorry, Per,' Macartan's voice was rising, 'but I'm not making an incident of this. I'm merely asking you what it is you asked this girl.'

'Please, Macartan, it's all right,' said Molly faintly. Her hand felt as though it were burning in the palm of the Swede's but she did not have the confidence to withdraw it.

'I think we should go,' said Macartan decisively, standing up in one lithe movement. He leaned forward and crooked a hand under Molly's arm. 'Come on, darling, let's go.'

'Just a moment,' said the Swede. 'I think we should let Molly decide whether she thinks it is time to go or not. We were having a pleasant conversation. I think perhaps it is up to her whether she wishes it to continue—'

'Well, Molly?' demanded Macartan, still with his hand under her arm. .

Held between the two of them Molly felt like a bird impaled on the spikes of a public railing. 'Yes, y-yes,' she stuttered, feeling as though everyone in the entire room was staring at her, 'it's – it's getting a bit late . . .'

The Swede instantly withdrew both his arms and held them up in a gesture of surrender. Macartan helped Molly to her feet and stood close beside her while, feeling like a fool, she extended her hand to the Swede. 'Well, goodbye, Per, it was nice meeting you.'

The Swede took her hand and shook it briefly. The expression on his face was bland and cheerful. 'Goodbye, Molly. Perhaps we meet again when you are a little older and without your guard dog!'

'Come on, Molly.' Macartan did not give the Swede another glance. He ushered her through the sprawling bodies towards the door of the flat, pausing briefly to say goodbye to their hosts. Molly looked back from the door. The Swede was still sitting, quite comfortably, apparently unabashed. He was attempting to open another bottle of beer with his teeth.

Out on the Rathmines Road, they had to walk for ten minutes, watching ahead and over their shoulders before they spotted a taxi. Macartan marched along and Molly walked beside him, not knowing what on earth to say.

They got into the taxi, still without a word. Then, when they were travelling down Camden Street, abruptly Macartan took her in his arms and kissed her soundly on the lips. She was too surprised to resist.

He kissed her a second time, more gently, and then released her, sitting well back into his own corner. 'Now, Molly, don't get the wrong impression. I think you are the most stunningly beautiful kid I've met for a long time and I've wanted to kiss you since I met you. But you've got to be careful. There are millions of piranhas in this here fish bowl.'

'What's a piranha?' It was all Molly could think of to say.

He took her hand. 'A piranha is a beautiful shining fish that will gobble you up and strip your bones before you even see him coming.'

'I see.'

'I don't think you do. But people like Dessie and me, we're opportunists all right, but we're not piranhas. Stick with us, kid. We'll see you right.'

Molly smiled. She felt warm and grateful. 'Thanks, Macartan.'

'Thank me for nothing,' he said softly. 'I could be a piranha too with you, given half a chance. You'll go far, Molly, further than me and Dessie, further, I think, than anyone in the bloody Abbey. But you've got to be careful. I wish I could go with you but you're going to be too good for me . . . I just know it.' He dropped her hand.

'Now,' he continued more briskly as the cab turned from George's Street into Dame Street, 'you're nearly home. One more kiss, OK?'

'OK!' and Molly offered her face. He took it between both his hands. 'You're lovely, Molly, you really are. Here's one for the road . . . ' He kissed her on the mouth but did not linger. The taxi pulled up in front of the door of her flat and she got out.

'Good night, Macartan.'

'Good night, darling – and remember your uncle Mac in your dreams!'

'I will!' She shut the taxi door and waved as it pulled away.

One morning in late November rehearsals were in progress for an avant-garde production of Shakespeare's *A Midsummer Night's Dream* to be staged in the Peacock. The theatre's management had imported an English director for the event, a man with a formidable reputation named John Chalmers. One of the actresses was ill and missing from the rehearsal and, as was customary, Chalmers asked Molly as the ASM to read the missing actress's lines holding the book.

With no pressure on her to perform Molly moved about the stage quite naturally, taking cues, reading the lines without 'acting', never raising her eyes from the prompt book in her hand.

When they broke for a cup of tea, Chalmers called her over. 'Had much experience on stage, Molly?'

'Well, I was an extra in a few plays upstairs in the Abbey.'

'Are you going to be a stage manager?'

'I haven't thought much about it, Mr Chalmers. It's all so new.'

'Ever thought about being an actress?'

PART TWO

PART TWO

CHAPTER SIX

When the ferry docked in Harwich Conor, like most of the other passengers, followed the signs for the train to London. Unusually, because he was careful now by habit, he had struck up an acquaintance with an American backpacker, a girl from Lubbock, Texas, with Texan teeth and broad Texan hips. She was 'doing Europe'.

'Irish, eh? How 'bout that? Y'all are certainly the first Irish guy I've met in Europe!' She pronounced it 'Yerp'.

Her name was Kirsty and Conor already knew she had spent Easter in Paris, had loved Amsterdam, hated Rome, was dubious about Berlin. She had questioned him closely about Dublin, which was her last stop on her trip – what to see, where the guys were, how safe were the streets. Assuming he would never see her again some streak of recklessness, or perhaps loneliness, prompted Conor to direct her to the National Botanic Gardens and to say to any of the gardeners there that she had met Conor Ó Briain. He regretted it immediately, because naturally, she made an issue of it:

' "Conor", what a cute name! Is that with a C or a K?' extracting her journal and waterproof pencil from one of the pockets of her backpack and writing down his name.

'With a C,' he said faintly. What had possessed him? She would undoubtedly head straight for the gardens. He consoled himself that after six years the personnel would probably have changed. But he realized he had created a worse problem for himself when they docked because she would undoubtedly stick to him like glue through the formalities of Customs and Immigration. His passport, in the name of Sean Molloy, felt heavy in his wallet pocket. When the time came, however, he managed to join a separate passport queue and got through without incident, but he was sweating as he joined her again to board the train.

The episode was a warning to him. 'Sean Molloy', the itinerant labourer who had worked on building sites in London, in canning plants in Holland, in Volkswagen assemblage in Germany, was second nature to him now – or so he had thought. It had been years since he had made such a slip.

Kirsty stowed her voluminous backpack inside the door of the train and joined him in his seat. Conor forestalled more questions. 'Would you mind if I tried to have a little sleep, Kirsty?' he asked.

'Of course not, Conor. You go right ahead.'

The clacking of the train was soporific and Conor, who had taught himself to nap anywhere since he had begun his new life as Sean Molloy, was soon asleep. When he woke up Kirsty was, in her turn, asleep, her cheek flattened against the train window. She did not wake until they pulled into Liverpool Street.

He ignored her broad hints that they should get together while she was in London but before they separated accepted her address in Lubbock, 'in case you're passing through', an event of as much likelihood, he thought as he walked towards the entrance to the Tube, as his passing the moon on the way to Mars.

He stopped at the bank of telephones to put in a call to Frank O'Hare. The priest was the only person in London with whom he maintained contact. It had been Frank who had told him of Tom Hartigan's death from lung cancer six months after Conor had first arrived in London.

In his letters to Conor, sent *poste restante*, his old friend gave no hint that he was so seriously ill. His last communication, the Christmas before he died, was cheerful, optimistic and kind as always. By mid-January he was dead.

Apart from the immediate aftermath of his flight, the days following that news were the worst of the six years since he had left Inisheer. Conor had felt appallingly alone, cut loose and adrift. He even contemplated turning himself in to the police and facing the consequences but an innate, island-bred distrust of the law stopped him from doing so.

The London priest had been kind and concerned but he was run off his feet with his duties and in any case Conor, fearing that he was simply transferring emotional dependency from the apron strings of one cleric to another, was angry with himself for his weakness and rejected the option. So although he kept in touch – and although the priest helped him with accommodation and jobs whenever he was in town – the two never became close.

Father O'Hare's telephone now rang unanswered. Conor looked at his watch. It was still not eight in the morning. The priest was probably out at early Mass. He would try his office in Camden Town later on.

The morning rush hour was in full swing in the Underground and Conor hesitated as the commuters flowed around him in a dark-suited tide. He needed a place to dump his bag until he found a flat. The last flat he had had was in a sidestreet off Pentonville Road but it was an area he did not like. He decided to take the Tube to Earl's Court.

The amplified wail of a busker's violin rose through the crowds as he descended to the trains. The busker was young – about twenty, Conor judged – and, to his own untrained ear, highly accomplished. He felt around in his pocket until he found some coins but as his step on the escalator was about to level out at the busker's feet, Conor's eye was caught by a poster on the wall of the 'up' side. It advertised a West End play, a revival of Noël Coward's *Blithe Spirit*. Conor was not a theatre-goer. What riveted his attention were the pictures of the three stars, a man and two women. One of the women, the younger, was his sister. He was sure of it.

He came off the escalator and joined the stream of commuters going up to the street. There was a number of the posters, spaced apart from bottom to top so that he could read everything on it. None of the names was his sister's but the name under the younger woman's face was 'Margo Bryan'. There was no doubt about it. She was Molly.

*

Molly, as usual three hours early for the performance, passed under the marquee of Wyndham's. And as usual she could not resist glancing at the playbills on the front of the theatre:

Annabel Critchley

in

BLITHE SPIRIT

by

Noël Coward

with *Margo Bryan* and *Jeremy Forsythe*

Six months into the run Molly still could not fully believe that the huge lettering referred to herself. She paused for a second to say hello to the doorman.

'Lovely day today, Peter.'

'Lovely, Miss Bryan. Great news about Princess Anne, eh?'

Molly smiled. On her way to the theatre she had seen the 'Anne To Wed Mark!' billboards on the news-stands. 'Yes, Peter, hope it stays fine for them!'

'Let's hope so!' The doorman seemed set for a natter but she smiled and passed round into the alleyway beside the theatre towards the stage door.

Although she still had to pinch herself to ensure that she and not someone else was actually one of the stars of this show she was, however, getting used to her new name. She saw herself now as two selves. Molly was the girl who had a history in Ireland and whose life was bound up in her childhood. Margo was an actress who happened to be Irish.

She went in through the stage door, bidding another cheerful hello, this time to the stage-doorman, climbed the stairs and went along a corridor, stopping in front of the small, scuffed door to her dressing room. She turned the key and pushed open the door. The room was dark, lit only by a single shaft of grey light from the barred window which faced over the alleyway behind the theatre.

She closed the door behind her and switched on the lights. Naturally Annabel Critchley, who was playing Madame Arcati, had the number one dressing room and Margo's little hutch was tiny and dingy. It was in dire need of a coat of paint and the spaces between the floorboards were packed with dust probably dating back to the last century which had congealed over the years to a substance resembling black mortar – but for the moment it was her own little domain and, looking around it, Molly sighed with pleasure. She was usually the first of the cast to arrive and this period before the other players came in was always her favourite part of the day, when the bustle and traffic outside seemed very far away and when the theatre all around her was hushed and waiting, the smells and rustles of the past undisturbed by the present. The bulbs around her mirror shone soft and golden and welcomed her like old friends.

There were several letters and messages for her on her table and she picked them up. The one on top was from Dolly, reminding her that an interview had been set up for her with a talk show on ITV. Her name change had been on Dolly's insistence. Dolly Mencken was Margo's agent, introduced to her by John Chalmers during the run of the first experimental production they did together. It was Chalmers who had originally brought her to London to play in one of his workshop productions and who, in the beginning, had deftly guided her through the maze of theatrical life in London, so different from the cosy little world she had left in Dublin.

She was still so young that she came to think of John Chalmers almost as a father or an uncle and he seemed to encourage this. When he told her that it was quite a coup to have someone of Dolly Mencken's status and influence interested in her she was impressed.

Dolly, on Chalmers's invitation, had come to see Molly perform in the workshop production and the next day the three of them met for lunch in a wine bar in Soho. Molly was very unsure of her at first although Dolly was loud in her praise of Molly's talent. What Molly saw was an overdressed, over-talkative little woman who wore a lot of jewellery and was far too bossy.

203

'Come on, darling,' Dolly had urged over that first lunch. 'Your name is nowhere. Old-fashioned. Not zingy enough. What did Shakespeare say? "What's in a name?" Was it Shakespeare who said that, darling? Do you know who said that, John?'

Before either of the other two could answer, she had waved a fat, much-ringed hand. 'What does it matter, darling? What does it matter whether your name is Hopalong Cassidy so long as they can *pronounce* it and *remember* it and it has *zing*? It's *essential*, darling, that it has zing! "Molly" is at home sitting by the fire knitting socks.' She took a mouthful of her wine. 'You go home, darling, and have a little think and decide what you could be called that's easy and that you like and that they can *pronounce* and *remember* and that has *zing*.'

She paused for breath. 'Now I think two-syllable—one-syllable names are nice,' she continued. 'Jud-i *Dench*! Dor-is *Day*! Get it? Got a nice strong ring to them, haven't they, darling? You certainly remember Doris *Day*!'

Molly, dazed before the gusty onslaught of Dolly's personality, felt bludgeoned. That night after the show she and John cobbled Margo Bryan out of Molly's real name. Next day she telephoned Dolly to suggest it. Dolly was thrilled. 'Now that's a *good* name, darling. Good and strong. Ten letters, five each one. Symmetrical. Will look good on credits.'

Their next meeting was at a party in Dolly's Chelsea home, which Dolly threw to introduce her new client to casting directors and producers. An hour into the party the new Margo was dizzy from introductions. She also disliked most of the people to whom she was being introduced. She told Dolly she wanted to go home but Dolly, smiling brightly, took her firmly by the arm and marched her round, making up for her client's conversational deficiencies with torrents of words of her own.

That party led to a small part in a BBC television play, which in turn led to a bigger one in a play for Granada. Dolly then put her up for audition for the role of the bewildered daughter of a forceful Scottish divorcée in *Without Dad*, a new prime-time sitcom. Molly's nerve almost failed on the day of her audition – her principal worry being that she would not manage the

204

Scottish-English accent. But her quick ear for accents did not fail her, the director liked her and, much to her own surprise, she got the part.

The power of television was evident within weeks of transmission of the first episode. The show proved instantly popular and it was still a shock to her that she was often recognized by the public. Dolly, naturally, seized on the opportunity, feeding the tabloids with selective, non-salacious titbits about her, and quite soon popular magazines like *Woman* and *Cosmopolitan* started to run features on her.

Dolly even stage-managed her client's social life: Molly found that she was being photographed at various functions and that the photographs were appearing regularly in the press. But even so eyebrows had been raised cynically – and jealously – when she had been cast as Elvira in this revival of *Blithe Spirit*. Elvira, created originally by the incomparable Kay Hammond, was such an *English* part, said the *cognoscenti*. But Dolly had once again chosen shrewdly and the production was sold out for the remainder of its run. Margo Bryan, whose notices had been unanimously favourable, was now, if not a fully fledged star, already well in the ascendant.

And within a short while Molly had come to see that beneath Dolly's bombast and shrewdness her agent was soft-hearted and kind. Dolly became a friend, a surrogate aunt. She helped Molly find a small terraced house near Bayswater and since her client's bank account was very new Dolly stood guarantor for a mortgage, waving away all demur and thanks. 'Not to worry, darling, it's an investment in both our futures. I'll take it out of you before I die, don't worry!'

John Chalmers, too, continued to keep an eye on her and although Molly was grateful for his kindness and his continuing interest she did not fully trust him. She went to dinner with him frequently and he was an escort at parties and functions but soon after she began work on *Blithe Spirit* she discerned that his attitude towards her had changed. To her annoyance she sensed he thought that since he had discovered her he had some sort of proprietary hold on her. She also recognized that his interest was becoming less avuncular – although, to be fair, he had never

205

made an overt pass. But she often felt uncomfortable under his scrutiny. And once, when he was drunk, eyes glittering, he had taken her by the arm. 'What gives with you, ice queen?'

She had managed to extricate herself and neither had referred again to the incident. Yet his words had upset her and had forced her to examine the fact that she was almost twenty-two years old and unlike most if not all of her colleagues in the theatre had never had a full sexual relationship with any man. The unconsummated episode with the priest in the dunes so long ago was dreamy in her mind, entirely unreal, but that was as far as she had ever gone with anyone. Her years in London had affected her, Molly knew, to the extent that she was no longer the wide-eyed convent girl who had arrived there but, because she had been catapulted into 'real' theatre life in such an unorthodox manner, she genuinely felt she had to concentrate on her work to the exclusion of everything else, including men.

Molly kicked off her shoes and began to undress.

Sometimes, observing the behaviour of her actress colleagues, she envied their blithe self-assurance and ease with men, their assumption that sex went with the territory of dates and dinner parties. She frequently wondered if she would be a different person if she, like most of them, had attended a drama school.

Stripped to her bra and pants, she studied herself critically in the large mirror. The lights burnished her pale skin, making it look almost golden. What was the matter with her? She liked men, enjoyed their company . . . but at a certain stage, usually when they became physically demanding, she always called a halt.

Molly had gone out on dates but had seen no man more than once, with two exceptions. The first had been a fellow actor whom at first she had liked very much but whose obsession with himself soon bored her; the second was an attractive young City broker whom she had met at one of Dolly's dinner parties. She might have liked to continue the relationship with him – it was easy and friendly. The broker, who was in his late twenties and originally from Liverpool, had a wry sense of humour which made her laugh. But their liaison came to an abrupt end and,

206

as usual, it had been her fault. They had been out to dinner together on their sixth or seventh date. It was a Saturday night after the show and Molly, knowing she had the Sunday free, was relaxed. After the dinner she readily agreed to go on with him to a nightclub.

But when they got there the cacophony of the disco music and overcrowding on the dance floor jarred and her mood of happy relaxation evaporated. She did not want to be impolite but on the dance floor when a girl who was gyrating wildly to a beat that had nothing to do with the music accidentally ground a stiletto heel into her instep, Molly used it as an excuse to ask the broker to take her home.

He was very apologetic as they left the club and Molly felt that she had been churlish. After all, he had spent a horrendous amount of money on her during the evening and Molly felt that it was she who had been at fault, she who had been paddling against the stream. She invited him back to the house for a nightcap. He came eagerly.

Molly realized too late that the invitation had been a mistake because the broker made the natural assumption that his being invited into her house meant an invitation into her bed. He started to kiss her the moment they got into her hallway.

She pulled away, laughing. 'Hey, hold on a minute!'

She turned on the lights and took him into her sitting room but when she was pouring him a drink he came up behind her and nuzzled his face into the nape of her neck, raising her hair. Molly liked the sensation and turned around to kiss him but his kisses were too hard, too insistent, and the usual alarm went off in her head.

'Simon, Simon, stop, please,' she managed to gasp.

'What's the matter?' He was genuinely puzzled.

'It's just that . . . that . . . '

'What?'

'Well, things are moving too fast . . . '

He reacted as though she had slapped his face. He moved away from her and sat on the couch. She covered her embarrassment by pretending to search in her drinks cabinet for a drink for herself, conscious of his eyes on her bent back.

After a few moments she straightened up and brought his whiskey across to the couch, concentrating on the glass. The cut surfaces of the crystal reflected several tiny rainbows in the soft light. 'Here you are,' she said, not meeting his eyes.

'Thanks.' He sipped at the drink and she went to an easy chair opposite the couch where he sat. 'Shall I put on some music?'

He shrugged. 'It's your house, Molly.'

She went over to the stereo. A record was already on the turntable, a new one, the soundtrack from the film *The Sting*. 'Do you like ragtime?' she asked.

He shrugged again so she turned on the stereo, keeping the volume low, and the Joplin pieces filled the room. Molly went back to her chair and sat down. She pretended to listen intently to the music. 'Simon,' she said after a bit, but he held up his hands.

'Don't worry about it, Molly, it's not the first time I've been rejected.'

'But I'm not rejecting you,' she cried. 'I'm really not. It's just that—'

'You don't want to make love with me,' he finished. 'But I want to make love to you. And when you invited me home with you, I naturally thought . . . ' He looked at her steadily. 'But I thought wrong, didn't I?'

'I can't explain it, Simon, I wish I could.' She could see how stung he was.

'I think I'd better leave,' he said. She wished the evening was not ending like this but she could not now very well ask him to stay, nor appease him. So she watched him drain his drink and stand up. He made a little gesture of finality, buttoning the jacket of his suit and she knew that whatever relationship they had had was over. She was sad about it but resigned.

He kissed her briefly on the cheek as she saw him to the door and said he would telephone in the next couple of days.

In bed later Molly stared at the ceiling and thought about the little scene. Objectively, she knew the broker was very attractive. He was athletic and intelligent, unattached – so was

208

she. There was no reason on earth why she would not go to bed with him.

Other than that he was the wrong man. They all were.

Because Molly, half horrified, admitted to herself when she was being really honest that she was not interested in anyone except her brother. The knowledge appalled but excited her. In one way she was glad he was absent, in another she wondered if it was his very physical absence which kept her passion for him alive, that if he were to be present in her life like a normal brother she would see him as such and get on with her own concerns.

Because, to her secret shame, it was the remembrance of Conor's spanking her on the afternoon their father died which most excited her sexual imagination. Many times, alone in her bed, she had re-created the scene, herself across his lap, his strong hands holding her, the wind against her bare legs. Molly kept that fantasy locked away in a secret, multicoloured box, bound in her imagination with ribbon like a Christmas parcel. But late at night, in the darkness, the ribbon slithered open – sometimes involuntarily, sometimes at her own tremulous tugging – a slow, pleasurable prelude to the release of the fantasy itself.

Molly wished she could talk things over with someone. She had plenty of acquaintances but no close women friends in London, with the possible exception of her agent – and Dolly was not exactly an agony aunt in whom she could confide her sexual doubts and longings.

She gazed at her half image in the dressing-room mirror. She was stuck in this trap of her own construction because how could she tell anyone the truth about herself? It was far too bizarre . . .

'Dammit, Conor!' she said aloud to the mirror. 'Where the hell are you?'

Far away, emphasizing the hush and peace in her dressing room, a telephone rang faintly. Molly stopped in the act of belting on her towelling robe and listened until it was answered. Then she kicked off her shoes and lay down on the scruffy little *chaise-longue* which ran along one wall of the room. She closed her eyes and let her mind empty but the image of her brother's face floated in front of her, superimposed on the stones of Inisheer.

In her letters home to her mother she was always positive and cheerful about Conor, reassuring Sorcha, whose health, battered by her life of hard work, was cause for worry. Molly did not want to add to her mother's troubles by revealing a single shred of doubt about Conor's welfare. The reassurance was easy. Molly was of the firm conviction that somehow, sooner or later, her brother would arrive back in her life again.

Her own telephone on the wall beside the door shrilled and she jumped up, heart thumping with its suddenness.

It was the doorman. Her agent was downstairs with a reporter. She had forgotten she was doing an interview. 'Send them up, will you,' she said and did a quick check of her hair in the mirror, at the same time making sure that the belt of her robe was tight.

Dolly jangled through the door, kissing her client on both cheeks. 'This is Una O'Connor from the *Irish Record* in Dublin,' she said introducing the reporter who came in with her. She was a freckled, red-headed girl of about Molly's own age.

The two shook hands. 'And congratulations on the run and your notices, Miss Bryan,' said the girl, seating herself on the *chaise-longue.* Molly sat beside her and Dolly plonked her bulk on the chair in front of the make-up table.

The reporter switched on a small tape recorder. 'Miss Bryan,' she began, 'I know a little about your background, your start in the Abbey Theatre and all that, but one of the things which intrigues me is why you felt you had to change your name?'

The implication was unmistakable: Margo Bryan had felt that her Irish name was not good enough for her. It was a bad start and Dolly jumped in. 'Oh, that was my idea!' she said, patting her hair so her bracelets rang. 'I felt, although Margo did not necessarily agree, that "Molly" was just too old-fashioned for the type of market I could see ahead of her.'

'I see,' said the reporter uncertainly and, to her relief, Molly realized that she was nervous. She hated giving interviews; when she read her words in print, they sounded trite and not at all what she had meant to say. This girl did not appear to be one of the smart know-alls to whom she had been sometimes subjected.

She smiled to put the girl at her ease. 'Well, it was really a joint operation,' she said. 'Dolly – Miss Mencken – wanted a new name but it was myself and John Chalmers who actually changed it. You've heard of John Chalmers?'

It seemed that the reporter had done her homework. She did know all about Chalmers's influence on her subject's career and from then on both women relaxed. For the next twenty minutes there were few problems with the interview.

Until they came to Molly's background. 'I've read a few interviews with you before, Miss Bryan, and although you have mentioned your mother as being a great influence on you I've never seen any mention of your father. Had he any influence on your career choice?'

Molly was off her customary guard. She hesitated and Dolly jumped in again, looking pointedly at her watch. 'Time's getting on, Miss O'Connor. Don't forget, Margo has a performance in two hours' time and she likes to have a period to herself before she goes on. I'm sure you have plenty there. Anything else you need, you can always give me a call. You have my number?'

The reporter switched off the tape recorder and stood up. 'Thank you, Miss Bryan,' she said politely. 'I really appreciate your letting me see you at such short notice.'

Molly stood up too. 'That's all right, Miss O'Connor.' Dammit, she mustn't show she was flustered. 'The home crowd is always the one to please,' she said, at her most charming. 'I'm sorry we have to stop it there but I do have a lot of mental preparation to go through. I'm sure you understand. I hope you have enough there?'

'Plenty,' said the reporter.

But as Molly saw her out she had the firm impression that the girl had made a mental note of the way the interview had ended. She might have been nervous, thought Molly, but she was sharp. 'I hope you enjoy the show tonight,' she said as they shook hands. 'And that the ticket is there for you.'

'Thank you again, I'm sure it will be – and I will!'

'And come back afterwards for a drink?' As soon as the words were said Molly wished them unsaid. She should be wary of reporters and she noticed Dolly stiffen. But somehow she was very anxious to have given a good impression. Respect in Ireland was important to her and she wanted this reporter to be on her side. She hoped that the cracks in her own performance during the interview could be papered over.

'I'd love to, Miss Bryan.' The girl seemed surprised.

The performance went well that night, Molly thought, smiling broadly during the waves of applause at her curtain calls.

In *Blithe Spirit* Elvira is a ghost, a troublesome one, who haunts her former husband and his new wife. For once Molly's unusual height worked to her advantage on stage. Both of the actors who played the 'live' married partners were a head shorter than she and the contrast between them and herself added to the comedy and other-worldliness of her presence. She had worked to develop a gliding gait for the part and tonight, she knew that – literally – she had not put a foot wrong.

She was very tough on herself and had frequently been told by directors and colleagues that her self-imposed standards were too high. But tonight, when the applause washed over her at the end, she felt that, for parts of her performance, at least, she had deserved it. As she usually did when the final curtain fell, she picked over the places where she could have done better. They were few tonight, she realized, and mostly to do with lapses in concentration caused by the knowledge that a reporter was in the audience. A reporter who was coming round for a drink, she remembered with an inward groan as, back in her dressing room, she plastered coconut oil all over her face. She was unusually tired. The skin on her face was pink and sore as she tissued off the last of the make-up.

She was still in the shower when her dresser let in the reporter. She heard the dresser's voice and the door opening and then closing as she turned off the water. 'Hello, Miss O'Connor,' she called. 'Won't be a minute. Make yourself comfortable . . . '

There was a mirror in the tiny bathroom and, looking at herself, she saw her face was blotchy and red from the removal of the make-up and the heat of the shower. To keep up appearances, she applied moisturiser and a light foundation of liquid make-up. No sound filtered in from outside except the soft clatter of hangers as the dresser hung up her costumes. From the corridor outside, she could hear the voices of the other actors, calling to one another through the open doors of their dressing rooms. The theatre was winding down into darkness.

She removed the white elasticated headband she used to protect her hair from grease and make-up and brushed her hair. Then she went out into the dressing room. 'Sorry—' she began and stopped dead.

The brightly lit room seemed to shrink. It was a man who stood there and not Una O'Connor.

Now thirty-three, he had changed subtly since the last time she had seen him six years ago. The face was deeply tanned and, by contrast, the eyes seemed brighter. The unruly dark hair was longer, curling over his collar, and even under the sports jacket and slacks he wore, she could see that his body had hardened.

'*Dia Dhuit* . . .' he said. Then he stood, waiting calmly.

She had not heard Irish for six years. '*Dia's Mhuire dhuit*,' she responded automatically.

He had carried into the room with him an air of purpose and energy and Molly became supremely conscious of the surroundings. The theatrical good luck cards, bright with black cats and green horseshoes, which were plastered all over her walls seemed tawdry; the 'Break a Leg' message that Jeremy, her co-star, had scrawled in carmine number two across the top of the mirror – with which at the time she had been delighted – now seemed cheap and ridiculous. She felt wrong-footed and then, for some reason, violently angry. She wanted to strike him.

He seemed to be waiting for an indication as to whether he should stand or sit. The dresser, not conscious of any of the undertones, bustled forward, removing Molly's street clothes which were draped across a small armchair, leaving it free so he could sit down. He thanked her, sat and crossed one leg over the other.

'This is Joan, my dresser.' Molly used English to introduce

213

him to the woman but did not complete the introduction. She turned towards the mirror and picked up a hairbrush. The dresser, a small, bespectacled Englishwoman, shook Conor's hand and went into the bathroom. There was another short silence while Molly brushed her hair. Finally she put down her brush and swivelled to face him.

'Listen, Conor, I don't know what to say – Where the—' Although she had not lost her fluency she stumbled on the Irish because she felt so confused. Her fury at the slip now added fuel to the confusion.

He was maddeningly serene. 'What's to say? I died, now I am risen!' He smiled.

'Where were you, where have you come from, what were you *doing* all this time?'

'Now, Molly – or is it *Margo* – all in good time . . .' He looked her so directly in the eye that she dropped her own. 'I might ask you the same questions, by the way,' he continued, unruffled. He might have been chatting to a fellow commuter he met daily on a train. 'I had you safe in a little frame in my mind, little sister, running all over the island. I had heard you'd gone to Dublin but that was all. I must say I had no idea that you had climbed to this exalted state until this very afternoon when I happened to be passing through a Tube station and something about the posters for this play seemed a little familiar.'

'Did you go to the play?' She was momentarily diverted.

'No, I'm afraid I was a little late – but I will! And I did buy a programme.' He held it up. 'I see by this that you're a star in a hit television show!'

But she was not to be flattered. 'Mam was very upset when you stopped writing!' she said, almost shouting.

'Yes, she must have been. I'm very sorry about that. I had my reasons . . .'

'Any chance you might *reveal* these reasons?'

'All in good time. Do you have . . . you know . . . a date or anything now?'

Dumb, Molly shook her head.

'Well, maybe we could go somewhere and talk?'

'I have all the time in the world,' she said. 'Let's talk *now*!'

'Look,' he said, his tone conciliatory, 'I stopped writing to Mam because I knew that sooner or later the Guards would be after her, asking her again had she heard from me – and I didn't want to put her in the position of lying for me all the time.'

'She's a grown-up woman!' Molly's own fury at him was absolute but she vested it on behalf of their mother. 'You might have given *her* the option of deciding whether she wanted to lie for you or not. And she's not well! You might have been interested in *that* – or then again, of course you might not—'

There was a soft knock at the door. She had forgotten all about Una O'Connor. Distracted, she shot to her feet. He had to pull in his legs so she could get to the door.

As she opened the door to admit the reporter, the steam went out of Molly's anger at her brother. She saw that the girl had changed out of her afternoon clothes of blouse and skirt and was wearing a softly cut dress which flattered her full figure. It always moved Molly when she realized the effort people put in to attend the theatre. 'Hello, Miss O'Connor,' she said warmly. 'Won't you come in?' She found it a relief to revert to speaking English; it seemed to place her relationship with Conor at a slight distance.

The reporter stepped through the door and then stopped. 'Oh, you have company!' she said.

'It's all right,' said Conor, standing up. 'I'm nobody really, just an old friend from the old country. Sean Molloy,' he said, holding out his hand.

'Una O'Connor,' said Una, accepting it.

Molly, trying to assimilate what was going on – *Sean Molloy?* – nevertheless saw the flash in the reporter's eyes as she looked up at him.

Conor offered Una his seat and moved to the *chaise-longue.* 'Are you in the theatre too?' he asked.

The reporter shook her head. 'No, I'm a journalist, actually, with the *Irish Record* in Dublin.'

'I see.'

Molly had the sense that in some way she was losing ground in a battle the spread of which she could not fully see. 'Miss O'Connor interviewed me earlier today,' she said.

215

'I see,' said Conor again.

There was an awkward pause broken by the reporter. 'Well, thank you for inviting me round,' she said and stood. 'I'd better let you get on with it . . . '

Molly, who had not sat down, turned to the fridge in the room. 'What am I thinking of! Please have a drink? What would you like?'

'No, really,' said Una, 'it's getting late and you must be very tired after such a performance. It was wonderful by the way,' she added.

'Thank you.'

'Don't go – do have a drink! I'd like one too, Molly!' Conor had crossed one leg over the other again. He beamed at the reporter and then at his sister.

'Well, if you're sure.' The reporter sat down again. She accepted a Perrier and Conor asked for a bottle of beer. Molly helped herself to a stiff whiskey. She felt she had earned it.

'And what do you do, Mr Molloy?' asked Una when they were settled.

'A little of this, a little of that. I travel.'

'How interesting. Are you a salesman?'

Conor laughed. 'In a way, I suppose. I sell myself. No, I'm nothing special. I'm just a worker, one of those who moves where the work is. I'm just back from Germany. I shot bolts into about nine million Volkswagens.'

Molly listened to the banter. This was a brother she did not know. Whereas the old Conor had been composed, the poise of this one was a revelation. And, what was more, as she saw the way Una O'Connor responded to her brother as a man she recognized, with a shock, that she was jealous – but as quickly as she recognized the feeling she squashed it. 'Would you like another drink, Miss O'Connor?' she asked, with Margo Bryan's sweetest smile.

At that moment her dresser came back into the room. 'I'm finished, Miss Bryan,' she said. 'See you tomorrow. Nice meeting you, sir,' she added to Conor, 'and you, Miss.' She nodded to them all and left the room.

Una stood up decisively. 'I'm going too, Miss Bryan, I've

overstayed my welcome as it is. Thank you very much for everything, I really appreciate it.'

She shook hands with Conor. 'It was nice meeting you, Mr Molloy.' Was Molly imagining it or did she stand a little close to him?

When the reporter had gone Molly, charm stripped, turned to him. 'Now what was *that* all about? Who's Sean Molloy?'

He was not put out. 'Could we go somewhere, for a drink or a meal or something? We've a lot to catch up on—'

His gall was breathtaking. 'I'm not sure you deserve any catching up, Conor Ó Briain—'

'Whether or not,' he said. 'Could we go somewhere?' He pulled at his collar. 'I find it very hot in here.'

'OK, just give me a moment.'

When Molly was ready they left the theatre and she directed the taxi to a restaurant she knew near Covent Garden. On the way, although they made tense small talk, they sat mostly in silence, a few inches apart in the dark vehicle. He seemed perfectly relaxed but Molly's confused mind raced. She was very conscious of his hands, one of which rested on his lap, one on the seat, palm up, between them. They were large and well shaped, with long, flexible fingers.

She had not relaxed by the time they got to the restaurant, which was Italian, small and intimate. The head waiter greeted her as they walked in and sat them in a small alcove. She ordered a beer for Conor and a Bellini for herself. It was a quiet night, only two other tables were occupied – one by three men, all moustached, who were drinking champagne while at the other sat a soft-eyed couple, gazing at one another, floating in a haze of love.

'All right,' said Molly when the waiter had taken their order. 'Why did you say your name was Sean Molloy?'

'That's the name on my driving licence . . . and on my passport and on my social security papers. Think, Molly! Why would you imagine I would not want to be known by my real name?'

'How did you get those papers?'

'Molly, I can't believe you are so naïve—'

"—and *I* can't believe *you* just showed up like this!' she hissed.

He looked surprised at her vehemence. With a renewed jolt she realized the row was not because of his false identity but because of that look she thought she had seen in Una O'Connor's eyes. She could not help herself. 'You must have known for months how to contact me!' she accused. 'I haven't heard *one word* from you since you left Inisheer.'

'Is that a fact? I did write to you, Molly, before I left Ireland for England. I asked Father Hartigan to send it to you—'

'Oh, *that*!'

'Did you find it wanting?'

'Well it was hardly enough for *six years*!'

'Yes, well, I'm sorry. Will you accept my apology? I won't do it again, I promise. I'll write to you every other day—'

'Be *serious*, Conor!'

'All right, all right!' He laughed. 'I am serious about one thing. I'm not going to lose touch with you again.'

'And what about Mam? Are you going to get in touch with her?'

The waiter arrived with their drinks and she stopped, keeping her eyes lowered so that the waiter would not see the expression in them. When he had gone again she looked at her brother reproachfully. 'This play has been running for six months. There has been publicity in the papers – you must have known.'

'Where I work we don't get the kind of newspapers your picture might appear in.'

'Where do you work?'

'Like I told that girl, the reporter, I move around—'

'Yes, but where?'

'The north of England, Holland, West Germany . . . '

'Doing what, Conor?'

'Working.'

'What kind of work?'

'Anything I can get.'

'Like what?'

'Hod-carrying, digging tunnels, harvesting shellfish, packing

218

frozen food in a warehouse – I told you about the work for Volkswagen.'

Her anger ran down again. 'But your qualifications!' she protested. 'What about botany and all the hard work you put into that?'

'Molly, botany is not exactly the profession of the masses. Those areas were obvious areas for the police to check and even with my changed name if I had tried to get work as a botanist – or even as a humble gardener – the police would have found me very quickly. You know as well as I do that the only way I could have escaped detection was to disappear into casual labour and keep moving.' He lapsed into silence and looked steadily at her.

'Conor, don't. Why are you looking at me like that?'

'I'm not looking at you like anything.'

'Conor, you are. You're embarrassing me . . .'

He took her hand. 'You have become very beautiful,' he said simply. 'I've missed you.'

In her hotel room, Una O'Connor ran the tape of her interview with Margo Bryan. It was all rather bland, she felt. There was some interesting stuff about the actress's exacting standards and her professionalism but, other than that, very little she did not know already.

She was intrigued by Margo Bryan's personal life. Something was definitely odd about the father and that relationship. She made a mental note to do a bit of digging. More to the point, she wondered about Sean Molloy. Was he a boyfriend? Una could not decide. Electricity had been pinging around that room when she had arrived but she had not been able to decipher the signals. At one stage she had thought that perhaps they were in the middle of a row which she had interrupted with her arrival but had changed her mind. Sean was too relaxed for that. She found she could not get him out of her mind.

Una was in search of a man of substance. She could not have described the quality, or multiplicity of qualities which went to make it up but Sean Molloy had it, whatever it was. His

219

physical presence was immensely powerful. By closing her eyes Una could recreate its impact on herself.

Una was sexually experienced, she had had several lovers, some she described as boyfriends, all of them nice and perfectly satisfactory in their own way but, to date, all of her relationships had sort of faded away like the Cheshire Cat's grin. Instinctively she felt that if she could organize this one it might be different. Una had learned always to trust her instinct.

But however was she going to meet him again? There was only one line of communication and that was Margo Bryan. She had better not do anything to cross Margo. First she had to find out whether she was trespassing on Margo's territory. Una was honourable about things like that.

The next day was Sunday and in a London pub Conor sipped slowly at a pint of bitter while he perused his copy of the *Observer* in front of a real-effect log fire fed by gas. It was lunch time and the pub, in a gentrified area along the Thames – which flowed grandly past the bay window at the back of the lounge – was decorated with chintzes and horse brasses to give it a 'homey' atmosphere. It was busy with the chatter of groups of friends, largely male.

Conor found it difficult to concentrate on his newspaper. The voices all around him were muted, very English – and, as usual in such circumstances, he longed to be standing at a dark bar counter in Dublin surrounded by the loud waves of talk, ribald, fatuous, even aggressive. The conversation all around him at the moment was, he noticed, mostly about house prices.

He tried to sort out his feelings. He had been shaken by his encounter with his sister. Ever-practical and pragmatic, in the six years since he had fled from Ireland he had come to terms with his status and sometimes quite enjoyed the independence of his new life as an itinerant jobber. He missed Ireland terribly and mourned the satisfaction and even tenor of his former life as a botanist. But, strong and very fit, he had always managed to find work which was well paid enough to ensure that he had plenty of leisure. He was abstemious in his habits – although he still ate like a horse – and was not interested in material wealth. Consequently, while working he had always managed to put money aside and then, when he had enough saved to buy himself some time, left his current job and moved on.

He used his leisure well. If he was in England he utilized the library system to keep abreast of botanical developments; if abroad, he learned the vernacular of his temporary residence. He spoke French, Dutch and German well enough to have a colloquial conversation and having acquired Latin in secondary school found it quite easy to understand Spanish and Italian although he did not speak those languages fluently. As a result he never had any problem getting a job. Once or twice employers had sensed that this calm, self-possessed person was perhaps over-qualified for the job he was seeking but he always managed to reassure them, genuinely, all he wanted to do was to make enough money to live.

There had been women in his life, never serious and never for long. He knew women found him attractive. Many with whom he had been involved had tried in various ways to prolong the relationship but Conor, knowing always that he was going to move on and being practised in self-protection, never allowed himself to become emotionally dependent or attached.

He looked around the pub, still pittering and tinkling with cool English voices. The colourlessness of the clientele and designer-created cosiness of the décor was getting on his nerves. He decided to telephone Molly and looked at his watch. It was one fifteen. He supposed actresses were late risers but this, surely, was a respectable hour.

She answered on the second ring, which meant that she was probably still in bed. His tone was bantering. 'Not at Mass, I see?'

She laughed. 'And what Mass did *you* go to, dear brother?'

'*Touché*! Did I wake you?'

'Well, no, actually. I've already had a telephone call from a Miss Una O'Connor. Remember her?'

'Sure. Last night in your dressing room.'

'Well, Miss O'Connor finds it necessary to turn her article

221

on me into a 'profile' and this apparently means that she has to talk not only to me but to others about me . . . '

'Yes?'

'And guess who she wants to talk to about me?'

'You tell me.'

'If you ask me Miss O'Connor has a little crush.'

'She couldn't have. We only met for ten minutes.'

'How long does it take in Holland or Germany or the north of England?'

Conor heard the needle. 'Well, it's out of the question. I can't talk to her about you.'

'But, dear brother, I'm afraid I've already told her I'll pass on the message. Co-operation with the press and all that.'

Conor sighed. Whatever was going on he had to divert it. 'All right, we'll talk about it later. It's a lovely day. I wondered if you were interested in taking a walk by the river?'

She hesitated. 'What time?'

'Any time you say. I'm at your disposal.'

'Fine. Well, how about half past three?'

'That's grand. I'll meet you at the entrance to Westminster Tube station. All right?'

'All right.'

'Goodbye, so.'

'Goodbye, see you later.'

He replaced the receiver and went back to the bar where he ordered a half-one. He brought the whiskey back to his table and attempted to concentrate once again on the magazine section of his newspaper but found he was reading the same sentence over and over again. He checked his watch. Two hours until he had to be at Westminster.

It was actually a few minutes earlier than that when he saw Molly walk towards him. He had been killing time looking at the T-shirts, miniature Houses of Parliament and Big Bens in the souvenir shop a little way along the footpath. She was simply dressed. It was a warm day and she wore faded jeans and a sleeveless button-through blouse of primrose cotton. She had tied her hair into a pony tail, her feet were bare in a pair of thonged leather sandals and, slung over her shoulder, she carried a light jacket in a shade of yellow deeper than the blouse. Except for her height and grace she might have been a teenager. She saw him and waved but before she reached him was intercepted by a middle-aged couple clearly seeking an autograph.

He walked up to her, waiting a few paces away while she dealt with the couple, signing the back of an old envelope the woman had produced from her handbag.

'Hello, Molly,' he said when the couple had left.

'Hello.' She smiled at him. She was her old sunny self, he saw.

They decided to take a trip on one of the pleasure craft which plied the Thames as far as Greenwich, descended the stone steps to the level of the river, paid their money at a little booth and, with all the other tourists, boarded one of the boats.

'Have you ever done this before?' She was gay.

He shook his head. 'There's always a first time.'

'Well, I've done it with Dolly – that's my agent, you'll have to meet her – she says that every visitor to London has to see the city from the Thames.'

She maintained her good humour as the boat, loaded with tourists of all nationalities, chugged ponderously out from the jetty and set off. There was little opportunity for talk because the barker kept up a running commentary through a loud hailer as they slid along the great waterway, under one bridge after another, past barges, fire tenders and pleasure craft. Several two- and three-masted sailing ships were moored behind one another, rocking in the swell created by a pair of light speedboats which raced one another, dangerously, Conor thought, up and down beside them.

'Far from currachs and the *Naomh Éanna*!' he shouted into Molly's ear as one of the speedboats, three-quarters out of the water, made a spectacular U-turn. But his words were drowned by a burst of tinny music, 'Tie Me Kangaroo Down, Sport!' from the loudspeaker on their own boat, prompting a party of Australians on board to raise a ragged cheer.

They got a potted history of London as the barker indicated the features along the banks on either side: Cleopatra's Needle, the dome of St Paul's, the grey bulk of HMS *Belfast*, London Bridge and the Tower. It was breezy out on the water and when they got to Greenwich Molly, who felt chilled, suggested that they disembark and have a cup of coffee.

This proved difficult. Sunday afternoon was a sleepy time, even along the tourist trail and they had to walk through several streets before they found a little newsagent-cum-café which was open.

There was no one in sight although through the doorway behind the counter, they could hear the sounds of a cricket commentary on television. Conor banged on the counter and after a minute a small dark-skinned man, Indian or Pakistani, appeared to take their order. They consulted the handwritten menu Sellotaped to the wall, ordered apple tart and coffee then sat at a little table inside the fly-blown window. When it came, the tart was tough and doughy, topped with synthetic cream, and the coffee had obviously been made hours ago and repeatedly reheated.

'Desperate!' said Conor as he tasted it. He pushed it away and took a pipe out from the inside pocket of his jacket.

'I didn't know you smoked a pipe,' said Molly.

'There's clearly quite a lot you don't know about me.'

'So tell me!'

'Well I filled you in on all the important stuff the other night.'

'Well, tell me about the unimportant stuff.'

'Like what?'

'Come on, Conor. Don't tease me.'

'All right, what do you want to know?'

'Can I ask you anything?'

'Anything.'

'Have you a girlfriend?'

'No.'

'Come on, there must have been someone! You're thirty-two years old—'

'Thirty-three actually.'

'Don't quibble! Just tell me about the woman, or women, in your life.'

'Nothing much to tell.'

'Conor Ó Briain! You're not going to have the nerve to tell me that you've got to this age and never been kissed?'

'Oh, I've been kissed all right!'

'By a lot of women?'

'A few . . . '

'A good few?'

'Yes, well, you could say that.'

'A good few or a lot?' The tone of her voice had changed subtly.

'A lot, I suppose.'

'Anyone special?'

'Umm . . . '

'So there was someone special?'

'Not any more.'

'Did you want to marry her?'

'No.'

She tried a different tack. 'Well, tell me who she was.'

He was enjoying himself. 'Why is this so important all of a sudden?'

'Did I say it was important?'

He did not answer but spent some time tamping down the tobacco in the bowl of the pipe with the corner of a matchbox. Then he swatted at a fly which was hovering near his untouched and congealing apple tart.

'Conor?'

'Yes?'

'Stop fiddling with that bloody pipe and tell me about this woman.'

'Why?' With the verbal joust his blood had started to tingle.

She was leaning forward, intent. 'You said I could ask you anything.'

Her blouse was gaping slightly. He became aware of the shadow which ran from her collarbone to a point between her breasts. He concentrated on his pipe.

'Why is this the only thing you're interested in?' he asked, keeping his eyes on the matchbox he held over the bowl of his pipe. 'I could ask you the same question, by the way. Anyone special in *your* life?'

'Don't change the subject.'

'All right.' He relented and sat back out of harm's way. 'I'll tell if you will.'

'All right,' she said. 'You go first.'

But when it came to it he could not maintain the level of lightheartedness. There had been no particular 'special woman' in his life, he told her quietly. There had been several who, should he have pursued matters, might have become 'special' but he had not chosen to pursue matters.

'Why not?'

'For the same reason I don't use my real name.' He pulled at his pipe. 'Your turn now.'

She considered for a moment. 'Well, I'm not thirty-three years old yet, so *I* still have an excuse!'

'Come on! You mean to tell me that all the time you were in the theatre in Dublin, ever since you came to London, there has been no one interested in you?'

'I didn't say that . . .'

'Well, what's wrong then?'

She bridled. 'What do you mean, what's *wrong*?'

'You know what I mean . . .'

'I don't. Are you implying that there's something *wrong* with me?'

'Is there?'

She sat bolt upright, gripping the table. '*I* wasn't interested in *them*!'

'Why not?'

'Don't know . . .' She began to blush. 'This is stupid! Let's change the subject.'

'Oh, so when *you* don't want to talk about it we change the subject?'

'Well, have *you* anything else to say?' She took a gulp of the awful coffee, now cold. 'Let's leave this. I'm sorry we got into it.'

226

'It was you wanted to get into it – remember?'

'Yes, well, I've changed my mind.' She sounded as if she were twelve years old.

'Anything you say, Miss Bryan. What do you want to talk about now?'

'I don't know.'

'Well, are you not interested in anything else about me besides women?'

'Of course I am.'

'OK,' he said, puffing on his pipe. 'Take your time, now. Don't want to rush you . . . ' He smiled, still teasing, but letting her off the hook.

There was a pause. Both looked sideways through the window beside which they were sitting.

'What about Una O'Connor? Do you fancy her?' Her voice sounded very young.

'Molly, don't be ridiculous. How could I fancy someone I met for such a short time in such circumstances?'

'It happens.'

'Well, it didn't. All right?'

'Well,' her face took on a determined cast and she rooted in her handbag. 'I promised I would give you her number so you could tell her all about me.' She handed over the piece of paper. He saw it was a Dublin number. 'She's in Dublin,' Molly said snapping her handbag shut. 'She said she'd come back over.'

'Do you not want me to talk to her?'

'That's up to you.'

'Well, I won't – all right?'

'Conor, of course you have to talk to her.'

He sighed and put the piece of paper in his pocket.

'Listen,' said Molly. 'I've got a great idea. I've a friend – she's an actress in the television show with me – she's having a birthday party tonight and I was dreading going alone. Why don't you come with me? I would really like you to meet her.'

'I hate parties. What television show, anyway?'

'*Where's Dad?*, the sitcom you read about in the theatre programme.'

'Oh, the reason you're *famous*!'

227

'Don't be so bitchy. It pays the rent. And, anyway, I doubt if I would have been cast in the West End in *Blithe Spirit* without being so-called famous.'

'When's it on?'

'Wednesday nights.'

'How can you do that and still be on stage in the West End every night?'

'It's all shot in studio, Monday to Friday – bankers' hours! And they shoot around me when I have matinées. They're used to that. I'm not the only one who's playing in the theatre at the same time. Dolly arranged it.'

'The famous agent?'

'The very one. Now,' Molly was tired of talking about herself, 'what about this party?'

'I told you I hate parties.'

'This won't be too bad. It'll be crowded and noisy so we won't have to stay long. We won't be missed if we leave early. Anyway, I'm dying for you to meet this girl. She's absolutely gorgeous.'

'So?'

'Well, maybe you'll like her.'

'So?'

'Well, maybe you'll *like* her, Conor!'

'I said – *so*?'

'For goodness' sake, don't be such an old fuddy-duddy!'

He could see she felt she was back in control of the situation.

Una paced the floor of her flat. She had arrived in from the airport only fifteen minutes before.

There was no way in the world he was going to telephone her.

He might already have rung.

He might not even have got the message yet.

She had left the door of the flat open just in case. Her flat was just across the hall from the communal public telephone which served the house. She went out into the hallway and lifted the receiver to make sure it was working. It was.

When she had telephoned Margo Bryan with the message that she was going to change the style of the interview, she had listened very carefully to the nuances in the actress's voice. But Margo had seemed only marginally interested. Granted, she had woken the woman up and she was sleepy. But when, holding her breath, Una mentioned Sean Molloy's name, Margo had responded quite calmly and taken down the telephone number. Was the calm natural or acted? Una could not decide. And, anyway, Una's request was so perfectly within the bounds of possibility that even if they were having a number together Margo need not necessarily smell any rat in a *bona fide* reporter wanting to talk to her boyfriend about her. Una was no nearer knowing what the relationship between the two of them was. She would have to wait until she spoke to him. If he rang.

The one thing Una could not stand was inaction. She was a bad waiter-around. She consoled herself with the knowledge that if she did not hear from him, she could ring Margo Bryan again on the pretext that since she was not always in attendance at her telephone she must have been out when he called.

She put on the electric kettle to make a cup of coffee and then switched it off again, fearful that the noise it made might drown the bell in the hall.

She was behaving like a lunatic. She walked to the door of the flat and closed it firmly.

Immediately the telephone rang. She scrabbled at the door and ran out into the hall but then stood in front of the instrument letting it ring while she caught her breath. It would not do to appear too eager.

'Hello,' she said.

But it was her news-editor. 'Listen,' he said briskly on the other end of the line, 'apparently there's been a mass streak at a soccer match at Dalymount. Seven of them have been arrested – they've been taken to Store Street.'

'I see,' said Una, her disappointment acute. Already she was calculating how long it would take her to get to Dalymount, the soccer stadium on the north side of the city and then to the Garda station at Store Street in the city centre. She decided instantly she did not want to go at all. Suppose he rang while she was out?

'But I'm just starting on this Margo Bryan interview,' she said.

'That'll keep,' said the editor.

'It's for features, they want it tomorrow – and you have me marked for the graveyard tonight.' Una was not normally scheduled to do the night-shift but the paper was temporarily short-staffed.

'Oh, yeah,' said the news-editor. 'Sorry. Forget it!' He hung up. Una sighed. She went back into the flat closing the door behind her and switched on the kettle again. Streaking, she thought as she made the coffee, that was this year's special offer. A bunch of adolescent male nudes with delusions of grandeur. In her own state of adolescent sexual tension she wondered wryly if she could have been truly objective . . .

Placing the coffee within reach of the rickety table which doubled as dining table and desk she pulled her typewriter towards her. She set up the tape recorder beside the typewriter and, using the pause button on the machine to start and stop Margo Bryan's soft voice, she sat down to begin the transcription of the tape. It was funny, she thought, how most actresses who could boom to the back of a theatre at will spoke so softly and intimately in normal conversation.

Having worked for about four minutes, Una got up and slunk towards the door and again propped it open.

Conor had not lied when he told Molly that he hated parties. He skulked in a corner of the little house, which he supposed the estate agents would have called a *pied-à-terre*, hating the noise and mindless chatter, the smoke, the awful bitter plonk which was put in his hand when he arrived. He hated most of all the prospecting, the sexual *frisson* that electrified the air. He had already had the same conversation with three women during which they assessed his exact degree of interest and availability. He was ill at ease for another reason: having to be watchful, careful to maintain the masquerade that he was a friend – and just a friend – of Molly's from the old days.

'Hello there! What's your name?' It was another one, blonde and skinny like most of them.

'Sean Molloy.'

- 'Is that an Irish accent I hear?'

She had raised an arch eyebrow.

'Yes! Excuse me!' Conor moved away from her and out into the hallway. Squeezing past a couple locked together at the foot of the stairs, he went up to what he presumed was the bathroom. He knew he had been rude and for Molly's sake, hoped that the woman was not important to her.

Mercifully the bathroom was vacant. He locked the door after him and sat on the edge of the bath, green with gold fittings. He stayed there a long time but after a while he became aware of a timid knocking at the door. He found he had been staring at two frilled bowls of *pot-pourri* on the windowsill.

The knocking continued. 'Yes?' he called.

'Oh, sorry!' said a female voice. 'Will you be much longer in there? There *is* only one bathroom – sorry!'

'I'll be out in a second!' He ran water and flushed the toilet and then, bracing himself, opened the door. He apologized to the woman as she swept in past him. He looked down at the open hall door and wondered if he dared walk down the stairs and straight out through it but thought better of it. Molly would be very hurt. He went in search of her.

From the vantage point of his height he spotted her easily, standing with a glass in her hand while a man, gesticulating, engaged her in earnest conversation. The man was about three inches shorter than she and she had inclined her head towards his mouth to hear him above the hubbub.

Conor pushed his way towards her. She saw him coming, smiled an excuse at the man and joined her brother. She led him towards the kitchen but they could not get in. The tiny room was more crowded, if that were possible, than the tiny living room. The hostess was under five feet tall, dressed like a bird-of-paradise. She looked around and saw Molly in the doorway.

'Well, hello!' she called. 'Bedlam, isn't it? Thought you weren't coming. You know everyone?' Then she saw Conor.

231

She wiped her hands on a tea-towel and threaded herself through the crowd towards the door.

'Who's this, Margo?' she breathed, seeming to get tinier, looking up and up and up at Conor.

'Jenny, this is a friend of mine from Inisheer – Sean Molloy. I hope you don't mind that I brought him . . .'

'Mind?' asked the bird-of-paradise. 'Is he yours?'

Conor had had enough. 'Nice to meet you,' he said as courteously as he could. 'Molly, I'm afraid I have to go. I'll give you a call at the theatre.' For a moment he was sorry – she looked as though he had hit her.

'Let me come with you as far as the door,' she said.

'All right,' he said, then, 'Nice meeting you, er . . .' he said forgetting the bird-of-paradise's name.

They pushed their way to the front door and stepped out into the evening.

'Are you sure you have to go? Was it terrible?'

'Pretty awful.'

'I'll come too—'

'No, you stay. They're your friends.'

She looked uncertain again but he kissed her firmly on the cheek. 'Bye!'

'When will you telephone?' she called after him.

'Tomorrow.'

'Promise?'

'Promise.'

He took deep lungfuls of air. They had come to the party by taxi and he was not quite sure where he was. Looking around he saw he was in a neighbourhood of mews houses and windowboxes. There was a pub on a corner, the Slap and Tickle. It was quiet and half empty. He ordered a half of bitter and sat in the corner. Searching in his pocket for change he pulled out the piece of paper Molly had given him with Una O'Connor's name and telephone number.

He crumpled it and put it in the ashtray in front of him.

*

'Are you warm enough, my dear?' In the back seat of the convertible, Malcolm Smith leaned over and tucked the rug more securely around Cordelia's knees. It was a balmy evening and they had decided to take the top down for the ride to the Chicago Opera House.

The chauffeur drove the Lincoln proudly, conscious of the stares of those on the sidewalk and the unfortunates in cars of lesser status. The car's maroon paintwork shone and the white leather upholstery gleamed with polishing. Malcolm's social engagements were few now and his daily commitments at the brewery had eased long ago so he and Cordelia had settled into a gentle, contented routine of domesticity. They went out rarely but when they did Malcolm, for Cordelia's sake, made a big occasion of it.

They had been a very good match, he thought as he looked at her. He knew she indulged him and his eccentricities, letting him be, respecting, for instance, his fondness for solitary breakfasts – a custom he maintained even though he no longer went daily into the office. He had a sweet tooth and over the years had developed a fondness for a certain variety of nougat, obtainable in just one Jewish delicatessen in Rogers Park. Cordelia ensured that each Saturday morning the chauffeur made a trip to the deli to top up his supply. Malcolm sighed contentedly. He liked the order of their days together and the gentleness of their nights.

Tonight, she was wearing the gift he had given her for her last birthday, a choker of beautifully matched pearls which lay on her skin, which was still good despite her age. She was dressed in a butter-coloured floor-length skirt and matching blouse in pure silk over which she wore a chocolate brown mohair wrap. Malcolm thought she looked as lovely as the day he first met her almost fifty years before.

As the chauffeur smoothly fed the car into the sweep of traffic from the Outer on to the Inner Drive, Cordelia noticed him watching her. She reached a hand over and touched him lightly on the arm. 'You look very distinguished tonight, Malcolm.'

'So you always say, m'dear.' To please her he had worn a tux, an outfit he detested although Cordelia was never done telling him that all men looked wonderful in tuxedos.

233

He loved this time of the evening in Chicago, particularly at this season of year before summer had wilted the streets. He felt energized as the city snapped from business to pleasure, with cabs ferrying people dressed in party clothes and streetlights coming on to compete with the hazy dusk rolling in from the lake. Ahead of them now, they could see the aggressive shape of the Hancock Center as it thrust itself protectively above the city like a latter-day Minotaur brandishing the twin horns of its antennae at the sky.

They joined the snarl of traffic along Michigan Avenue, crossing the sluggish Chicago river which was guarded on either side by the beautiful Wrigley Building and its almost-twin which housed the *Sun-Times*. The *Sentinel* building was a little further down the river. Malcolm's lightness of mood dimmed. The failure of the relationship with his grandson was a continuing sadness.

Christian's truculence towards Malcolm had abated somewhat with maturity but the two of them could not be in the same room for long before there was a row – or at least an argument. Malcolm never intended it to happen but somehow he always found himself criticizing Christian's clothes, his spending habits, his lifestyle, his neglect of his wife Jo-Ann. Malcolm had known from the start that Christian's marriage would be a disaster and it was no comfort to have been proven right. Christian's divorce had deeply saddened his grandfather and it was Malcolm who had ensured that Jo-Ann had been properly taken care of. If the business end of his divorce had been left to his grandson, Malcolm felt, the affair would have been protracted and very messy. Since he could see all too clearly that his grandson's treatment of his wife was largely to blame for the divorce, Malcolm's sense of fair play had revolted at Christian's *laisser-faire* approach to the financial end of the proceedings and he had stepped in, forcing Christian to make a decent settlement which he, Malcolm, had had to underwrite.

To Malcolm, meticulous in business, Christian's attitude of 'easy way out' was anathema. He was genuinely proud of his grandson's achievements in journalism, particularly since he had been given the foreign brief six years before. As frequently as he could, Christian wangled things so that Dick would be the photographer on his trips abroad and the two of them had become a sort of roving conscience, trying to make readers aware of atrocities in Central America, of apartheid in South Africa, of floods and poverty in Asia and South America and of appalling deprivation or injustice almost everywhere. Their pieces were frequently the subject for discussion at the country club, not always favourably because Christian often wrote about issues that many of Malcolm's friends and acquaintances wished could be kept under the carpet. But there was no mistaking the stature of his grandson as a journalist and Malcolm preened in it by proxy.

His admiration for Christian's professional prowess was tinged, however, with long-term dread. More and more, it seemed, when Christian returned from one of his trips abroad he hit the bottle immediately. And recently Malcolm had had to bail his grandson out of a charge of drunk driving.

'What are you thinking about, Malcolm? You look sad.' Cordelia touched his arm again.

He saw they were almost at the Opera House. 'Oh, nothing much, Delia. Just the usual . . .'

She nodded sympathetically. 'Not to worry. Just think what's in store tonight. Carreras!'

They alighted from the car at the kerb and joined the perfumed crowds milling around under the chandeliers which lit the plush lobby. Malcolm spotted a pair of country-club acquaintances who were half-way up the grand staircase.

'Hello, Sam! Hi, Dave!'

The two men turned and came back down the staircase to pump Malcolm's hand while their artificially tanned and glittering wives swept Cordelia with their fake lashes before mouthing a parallel 'hello'. She remained serene.

CHAPTER SEVEN

Christian's drinking bouts had begun to endanger his assignments.

Early in January 1974, he and Dick were in the lobby of the Addis Ababa Hilton, huge, tiled and air-conditioned, furnished with soft couches and easy chairs and decorated with flowers and native art of the more bland variety. They were sunk in a plush couch in the lounge area outside the bar and Dick's patience was wearing thin. For the third evening running Christian was drunk. He was just on the verge of becoming belligerent and Dick wanted to avoid that at all costs. If it had not been so tedious it would have been a constant source of wonder to him how his friend's personality changed so much with drink. 'Come on, Christian,' he said, 'let's go to bed.'

'But we have – we haven't discussed what we are going to do about the *story*.'

'We'll discuss it in the morning, Christian.'

'No! I want to discuss it now!'

Dick sighed and said as levelly as possible, 'Christian, we've been here for three days now and you have shown no interest at all in this story.'

It was all Christian needed. 'Whaddya mean, *asshole*?' he bridled. 'Whaddya mean? Thish – this is an im*port*ant story. We gotta be *thinking* right.'

'Yes, yes! For God's sake . . . ' Privately Dick was having serious doubts about whether they would get any story at all out of this trip. The telexes which arrived for them several times a day from their newsdesk in Chicago were becoming increasingly angry. Christian had refused to answer any of them. ('Tell them anything you like, Dick. Tell them I'll contact them when I have the story.')

Since they had arrived in Addis Christian had sunk into a state of such lassitude, fed by a river of alcohol, that he seemed incapable of making even the simplest decision. The front of the tracksuit he had bought at the hotel's gift shop on the evening they had arrived was now stained and his thick blond hair was tangled and unkempt.

Dick was afraid that Christian had lost his nerve. They had come to cover the famine which, rumour had it, was about to rage out of control in the north of the country but so far they had not left the city. While he continued to telex back that Christian was ill with tropical dysentery, Dick was seriously considering making his own arrangements, shedding Christian and going out by himself to send back a picture story with extended captions.

He knew from experience that there was no point at all in barracking his colleague. He would, as always, simply have to wait until Christian himself came out of the bender. They were lucky in one area – the newspaper had not yet succeeded in getting through by telephone although he knew this was merely a matter of time. He stood up. 'I'm going to bed whether you do or not, Christian.'

Christian had now fastened his attention on a huge fruit arrangement just outside the main restaurant, on the other side of the lobby. 'Look at that! The vul-vul-vulgarity of that . . .' He attempted to rise from his seat but stumbled and Dick had to put out a hand to save him from falling.

'Christian, will you go to bed?'

'Go to bed? Go to *bed*?' Christian could not have been more astonished had his friend suggested that they grow wings and fly. He flopped back into his seat. He clearly had difficulty focusing his eyes. 'How can I poss—' he hiccuped. Dick waited. 'How can I posh-*possibly* go to bed?'

'Why not, Christian?'

'Why not what?'

Dick gritted his teeth. 'Why won't you go to bed?'

'Because I don't *want* to!' Christian's handsome features set themselves stubbornly.

'All right, Christian, see you in the morning.'

237

'Wait a minute, Dick . . . '

'What now?'

Christian had fastened again on the arrangement of fruit. 'Do you not think it's vulgar, Dick?'

'Yes, I do— '

'Oh, so you *do* think itsh vulgar?'

'Yes, I do.'

'Well, then!'

'Well, what?'

'You *do* think it's vulgar?'

'How many times do I have to say it?'

'Well, then!'

Christian sat back, satisfied. Even when sharp and sober he had a peculiarly lateral way of thinking, which was disconcerting even to those who knew him. Dick had had enough. 'See you in the morning.' He walked across the lobby towards the lifts. Christian looked after him and shrugged. He closed his eyes and fell asleep. Alerted by a scornful barman, the receptionist on duty woke him half an hour later and escorted him to his room.

When Dick came down to breakfast next morning Christian was sitting in the restaurant eyeing a Bloody Mary. While the worn muzak tape wowed through a string version of the Beatles' 'Yesterday', he toyed with an American-style bacon, lettuce and tomato sandwich held together with a plastic cocktail spear which flew a little paper Stars and Stripes on its tiny masthead. His eyes were bloodshot and baggy and the lower part of his face was covered in thick blond stubble.

At least, thought Dick, he was not yet drunk. 'You look awful, Christian,' he said as he sat down.

'Don't rub it in.'

Dick saw that he had not even touched his Bloody Mary. 'You've got to eat,' he said. 'You'll feel better then.'

'I'm not hungry.'

'You need food.' He gave his own order, scrambled eggs and bacon. Then, 'Look, Christian,' he said, 'they won't be put off any more.' He took the latest telex from Chicago out of his pocket and placed it on the table between them. 'They want

238

to know when they can expect copy and some idea of what it covers and how long it will be.'

Christian would not meet his eyes.

'Christian?'

'I know, I've screwed up.'

'Don't give me any of that Uriah Heep humble shit. The question is, what are we going to do about it?'

Christian shrugged, his head drooping, and Dick sat back, disgusted but too fond of Christian to be angry. He had been looking after him all his life, it seemed. 'All right,' he said, 'we cut our losses and get out of here. We can't spend any more of the paper's money hanging around here. Anyway, your liver needs a break.'

'What'll we tell them?'

'We'll think of something,' said Dick. 'Stay here – don't move – and I'll go to the desk to see what the story is about flights.'

'Yes, Dick,' said Christian humbly. His contrition was absolute. Dick thumped him on the shoulder with affectionate exasperation and went out to the reception desk. They were in luck. An Alitalia flight would depart for Rome that night at nine o'clock and although they could not connect immediately with another to Chicago there was an Alitalia from Rome to London which would get them into London early in the morning. From there they could take any number of flights.

When he came back Christian had still not touched his food. 'Get your mouth around that sandwich!' ordered Dick. 'We have to get out to the airport by six thirty. There are no seats available but apparently there never are at this stage. We're on standby.'

Christian held on to the sides of the table. He told Dick he thought he might be sick.

'Come on.' Dick pushed the sandwich under his nose.

'I can't . . .'

'All right. I told them to prepare our bill but let's see if we can keep the rooms for a couple of hours more. You, my friend, are going to take a nap and a shower.'

'All right,' said Christian meekly. 'What time is it now?'

'Just after ten thirty.'

Christian closed his eyes. 'Christ, Dick, I feel absolutely awful!'

'You look worse,' said Dick. 'Now, why don't you go up to your room? I'll call you at four thirty. I'll go with you now and you can give me your room key. That way I can get into your room and won't have to break the door down to wake you up!'

Obediently Christian stood up, a good seven inches taller than his friend, swaying a little like a fragile, diseased tree. Dick looked at him ruefully. Getting mad with Christian was easy, he thought. Staying mad was impossible. He felt like a mother hen.

That evening they arrived at the airport early but so, it seemed, had everyone else in Ethiopia. When they got through the considerable security checks and into the airport itself it was Christian, by virtue of his height and weight, who took charge. Dick marvelled at his friend's powers of recuperation. Christian wore a new white track suit, had shaved and showered and except for a network of tiny red lines in the whites of his eyes, looked like an international tennis star. When he put his mind to it he could adopt an arrogant, commanding presence and Dick watched in admiration as he cut a swath through the heaving, gesticulating crowd, imperiously waving aside the protests of a woman in uniform with a walkie-talkie.

They were called first from the standby list but had to travel economy. It was uncomfortable, especially for Christian who had difficulty with his long legs, but shortly after they were airborne, Christian fell asleep. His head inclined towards Dick and after a bit fell on to Dick's shoulder. Not wanting to disturb him Dick turned his head gently to look at Christian's sleeping face. All that was visible was the curve of his cheek and that absurd cowlick on the crown of his head.

It was raining as they came into London. The drops of water ran horizontally across the windows as the Alitalia jumbo touched down at Heathrow and thundered along the runway on its braking run. Long before the aircraft slowed to taxiing speed the pre-disembarkation bustle began over the protests of the cabin crew as people snapped off their seat belts and stood to retrieve bags and parcels from the overhead lockers.

They had been so exhausted when they arrived in Rome that neither had wanted to continue directly on to Chicago from London and they had decided to overnight in London. They went through the weary process of customs and immigration and then queued in the arrivals hall to book a hotel. The only accommodation immediately available was in a small private hotel in Belgrave Square. They queued again for a taxi, in rain which, despite the sheltering roof over the taxi stand, squalled in on them and soaked them. They were both shivering in tracksuits, entirely unsuitable for the London weather on such an unseasonable day. 'Remember when we thought it was glamorous to go on foreign assignments?' said Christian, who suddenly saw the funny side of the situation. But Dick was too tired to respond.

They checked in just after noon and arranged to meet again in the lobby at four.

When they met, having slept and showered, they were both very hungry so took a cab to Piccadilly. Christian was anxious to make amends to Dick for all the care lavished on him over the past few days. He did not dare broach the subject of the *Sentinel* newsdesk – which was still blissfully unaware that not only had they left Ethiopia and were in London but that they had left with not an inch of copy.

The taxi let them off in the traffic flow which swirled around Piccadilly. Christian's eyes lit on a hamburger bar. Dick held up his hand. 'No, we're not going there, or,' he turned resolutely away and began to walk towards Shaftesbury Avenue, 'to any fast-food joint. Forget it, Christian!' Christian sighed. When he was hungry he did not care at all what he ate provided it was familiar and edible and available immediately.

They compromised on a medium-grade steak house and chomped their way through steak and chicken Kiev, with mounds of English chips and a limp, ancient salad.

'You still can't get a rare steak in this country,' moaned

Christian after the food arrived. He sawed savagely at his meat which, to be fair, did show a single streak of faint pink deep in its tough heart.

'How many times have I told you that you do *not* order steak anywhere east of Rio de Janeiro or New York City . . . '

'Well, remind me again next time.'

'I reminded you just before you ordered.'

'Yes, but it's been three years since we were here. How did I know things hadn't improved? How did you know for that matter?'

'This is just silly, Christian. Just shut up and eat.'

'The way you carry on you'd think we were married!'

'Well, we are in a way! We have to live together, don't we?'

Christian laughed and Dick joined in.

Still they had not discussed the newsdesk. The subject weighed on Christian's shoulders and tightened around his head like a band but, master-procrastinator that he was, he was again able to direct his mind elsewhere.

They strolled towards Leicester Square after their meal. It was just after five thirty and the streets were alive with office workers, who hurried along quite distinct from the tourists and visitors who looked vaguely lost.

They passed a Keith Prowse ticket agency and stopped casually to look in the window. 'Will we go to a show tonight?' asked Dick.

Christian hesitated. He looked at his watch. Five forty-five. Theatre was not his bag at all, but London was said to be its Mecca. Sir Laurence Olivier, all that . . . And he was on his best behaviour. 'What's on?'

'Let's have a look.'

They went inside and browsed through the leaflets and handouts at the desk.

South Pacific ('A Smash!' *Evening Standard*) was playing at Drury Lane. Christian was amenable to *South Pacific*, having played a soldier, one of Emilio's sidekicks, in a production of the show in his sophomore year at Evanston High School.

'At least I'll know the tunes.'

But *South Pacific* was booked out except for single seats at matinées.

'You could go along tonight, sir, and queue at the box office,' said the clerk. 'Sometimes there are returns.'

'Nah,' said Christian. 'That's OK, but thanks anyway.'

'What about this?' Dick was holding a flyer about a play at Wyndham's Theatre.

'What is it?'

'A revival of a Noël Coward play, *Blithe Spirit* . . .'

'What's that about?'

'I don't know, but I know about Noël Coward. And it's been running for months – must be good. As long as we're in England, we might as well see' he read off the flyer, '"A quintessentially English play".'

'Is it heavy?'

'No, not if it's by Noël Coward.'

'Are there seats available?' Christian asked the clerk.

'As it happens, sir, we've just had a release of a block of five seats.'

Christian shrugged. 'OK. Noël Coward it is.'

They took their seats five minutes before curtain. The old theatre, with velvet seats and gilt on the boxes, smelt dusty and faintly sweet and the audience, of all nationalities, spoke in hushed voices as if out of respect for a superior age. The muted lighting enclosed the space and cut it adrift from the outside world and Christian, whose experience of theatre had been limited to high school shows and The Icecapades, felt instinctively that he should walk on tiptoe.

Their seats were cramped and uncomfortable and as usual he found it difficult to fit his long legs in the space provided. 'Quintessentially English, huh?' he bitched. 'Promise that if it's a dog we leave at half-time – OK?' Then he spotted the little opera glasses fitted in their holder on the back of the seat in front of him. 'Hey, look at this!' There was a slot for a 10p coin to release the glasses. Dick had one and Christian pressed it into the slot. But the opera glasses proved to be a disappointment. No matter which way Christian twirled the little dial he could not focus them adequately. 'Leave them,

Christian,' said Dick. 'When the lights are on on the stage you'll find it better.'

The lights dimmed and the curtain went up.

A half-hour into the first act all thoughts of leaving the theatre at the intermission had left Christian's mind. He could not take his eyes off the actress playing Elvira. The image through his little opera glasses was fuzzy and distorted but he was fascinated by the way she held her head, the way the lights played on the planes of her face, the way she seemed to float about the stage. He barely heard her lines and cared not a fig about how she fitted into the plot. He lowered his glasses each time she made an exit and put them to his eyes again each time she came on. He thought her the most beautiful woman he had ever seen in his life.

He was in a state of high excitement at the interval. While Dick attempted to order drinks for them through the crush at the bar, Christian perused Margo Bryan's biographical note in the programme. 'She's *Irish*!' he said to Dick when the latter came back bearing two teaspoonfuls of liquor in two glasses.

'Who?'

'That actress, Margo Bryan, the one who's playing the ghost . . . '

'So what?'

'Don't you think she's really something?'

'I think she's very very good. I wouldn't have thought she was Irish, though.'

'No – I mean don't you think she's really a looker?'

'Christian, sometimes I can't believe you're the same age as me. You're incorrigible!'

'Yeah, ain't it the truth!' Christian grinned. 'She looks a bit familiar to me – does she remind you of anyone?' he asked eagerly.

'Now that you mention it, she reminds me a bit of Jo-Ann—'

'That *dog*!' Then, seeing Dick's expression, 'Sorry, Dick. I know I said I wouldn't call her that any more.'

Dick said nothing.

'But seriously, Dick, seriously, that girl has real class . . . ' He

244

searched again through the biographical note. 'It doesn't say here that she's married . . .'

'It rarely does,' said Dick drily.

'Well,' Christian made up his mind, 'I'm going backstage to see her after the show.'

'And how do you propose to get in?'

Juggling his drink Christian pulled out his wallet. He extricated his press pass and held it gleefully under Dick's nose. 'These things have their uses.'

'You think she lets media people in to see her automatically?'

'She might let the foreign correspondent of the prestigious *Chicago Sentinel* in to see her if I send word that she has just won the prestigious Foreign Actress of the Year Award from the prestigious Newspaper Critics Association of Midwestern America.'

'The *what*?'

'You heard me.'

'And what am I supposed to be doing while you're doing this?'

'Backing me up, of course. You're the photographer who will be taking pictures of the Foreign Actress of the Year while I interview her.'

'Will she not be a little suspicious since I don't have a camera?'

'Dick!' Christian stood back in mock horror. 'You know the way I work on these important pieces for the prestigious Association of Midwestern Critics.' He made a little gesture with his hand, flying an imaginary aeroplane. 'Recce first. Little reconnaissance mission to spy out the land.' He swallowed his drink. 'Tonight we introduce ourselves. Tomorrow we do the interview. At least *I* do the interview, you take the photographs. A *few* photographs.'

'Wouldn't it be simpler to ask to see her and ask for an interview? Most actresses like to see their names in the papers.' But Dick knew he was wasting his time. For Christian the elaborate side-plays were part of the challenge.

The ushers had begun to call the resumption of the play. Dick drained the last millimetre of Scotch in his glass. 'And after I take just a *few* photographs then I beat it?'

Christian, still smiling, put his arm round his friend's shoulder. 'That's the plan, pal . . . '

After the play the two of them found their way round to the stage door. The theatre was on a corner and to get to the stage door, they had to go round to the back, passing through a wide alleyway and picking their way through an overflow of drinkers from the pub on the other corner.

The lobby behind the stage door was an unwelcoming place although it was stuffy with heat from an electric fire. There was a public telephone and a noticeboard fluttering with cast calls and Save the Whale literature. There were no chairs or seats. 'Can I help you, sir?' At least the doorman was polite.

'Yes,' Christian answered with his most brilliant smile. 'I'm sure you *can* help us. I'm the Foreign Correspondent of the *Chicago Sentinel* – that's in Chicago, Illinois, of course – and this is my photographer, Dick Spielberg . . . ' He handed over his press pass. 'We're on temporary assignment here in London and we have just heard that Margo Bryan, your actress, has won a very big award in America. My newspaper has assigned me to interview her for her reaction.'

'This is the first I've heard of it,' said the doorman, but not in an unfriendly manner. 'Have you an appointment with Miss Bryan?'

'No,' said Christian apologetically. 'I got the call from the newsdesk about this award at about seven o'clock this evening. And of course I knew there was no point in trying to call Miss Bryan so close to her show.'

'Hang on a tick, I'll give her a call,' said the doorman and picked up the telephone.

'Is Miss Bryan available?' he said into the instrument. Then, after a minute or so, 'Miss Bryan, there are two gentlemen down here from an American newspaper. They say they want to interview you about your award . . . '

He listened and put his hand over the mouthpiece. 'What award?' he asked Christian.

'Foreign Actress of the Year,' said Christian, sincere yet casual. Dick was carefully studying the noticeboard, staring at the fuzzy type on a notice advertising a forthcoming anti-vivisection meeting.

'He says it's for Foreign Actress of the Year, Miss Bryan . . .' The doorman listened again then, replacing the receiver, told them they could go up to her dressing room. 'It's the first she's heard of it too,' he said, chuckling.

The dressing room was at the top of a short flight of stairs and along a brightly lit corridor, past other doors through which came the sounds of chatter and water running. A profusion of smells competed for prominence, of sweat, cats, Jeyes Fluid, concrete, dust – and a heavy smell which, from the days of his triumph as a soldier in *South Pacific*, Christian recognized as the smell of greasepaint.

Christian knocked at Margo Bryan's door. 'I don't know how you're going to pull this off,' hissed Dick. But before Christian could answer the door was opened by a rotund, bespectacled woman, who invited them into the room.

Another man was there, large and dark, but Christian barely noticed him because Margo Bryan emerged from the bathroom, her face scrubbed pink and clean and her hair loose but secured by a headband. She wore a man's white towelling robe. 'Hello!' she said.

Christian's heart turned over and fell into his stomach. He introduced himself and Dick.

'How do you do?' said Molly. She indicated the other man. 'This is a friend of mine from Ireland, Sean Molloy.'

The man shook hands with the two Americans. Professionally, Christian assessed him. Competition? But Conor's face was open.

They all sat down.

'It's very nice to meet you – and I appreciate your interest,' said Molly, 'but what's this about an award? Alfred said . . .' Her voice was entirely different from what it had been on the stage. It was soft and accented.

Dick spoke up. 'Miss Bryan—' he began.

But Christian cut in. 'We're very sorry to intrude like this,

247

Miss Bryan, but you see we've only just heard ourselves about this award. Perhaps you will hear later on tonight or tomorrow.'

'This is the first award I've ever won!' said Molly, her face alight with pleasure. She turned to Conor. 'Isn't it wonderful, Sean?'

Christian noticed a hesitation as she spoke to him. 'Are you in the theatre, Mr Molloy?' he asked.

'No.' The man did not elaborate but Christian was not fazed. Americans, he knew, blurted their pedigrees and salaries within five minutes of new acquaintanceships. Other nationalities had different rules of social niceties.

'Would you like a drink?' offered Molly.

'No, thanks,' said Dick.

'Yes, please,' said Christian simultaneously.

She looked uncertainly at them.

'We'd love a drink, Miss Bryan. My photographer here is a little slow . . . '

Dick clamped his lips shut.

She gave them a beer each from her little fridge. 'You, Sean?'

'I'll have a beer too.'

When they were seated, all the men piled up together on the small *chaise-longue*, drinks in hand, she asked Christian to explain to her what this award entailed.

'To tell you the truth, Miss Bryan,' said Christian, charmingly, 'we're almost as much in the dark as you are. I do know, of course, that it is prestigious and that it is voted on by the Association of Critics of Midwest America.'

'Who?' she looked puzzled.

'The Newspaper Critics Association of Midwestern America.'

'Is it only newspapers?'

'Oh no, it's television too – and radio,' he improvised.

'Well, why is it called the Newspaper Critics Association?' It was Conor. He did not turn his head but addressed his question to Christian straight ahead through the mirror.

'Did I say that? I meant, of course, the Association of Midwestern Critics,' said Christian, deprecating.

Molly looked doubtful. 'Please don't get me wrong, I'm very flattered – but how did they see me, these critics? I've never been in America.'

'Who knows?' Christian shrugged. 'I've never been much for the theatre myself and neither is my partner here – ' Dick scowled but Christian ignored him ' – and although I am, of course, aware of this award I've never had to interview anyone connected with it before. I will, of course, have all the details before I interview you.'

She paused and Conor cut in again. 'Who got Foreign Actor of the Year?'

Christian darted a glance at the Irishman through the mirror but he was studying his drink. Christian, the complicitous neophyte in all matters of theatre and awards, spread his hands and shrugged without answering.

The dresser, who had been moving around quietly tidying the dressing room, said a soft goodbye and left.

'What does the award entail?' asked Molly when the door had closed behind her. 'Would I have to go to America?' The vista of escorting the actress to the States, the two of them together for eight hours in the intimacy of the first-class cabin of an aircraft, spread itself before Christian's delighted mind. 'You may indeed, Miss Bryan,' he said earnestly while Dick spluttered and coughed on his drink.

'Are you all right, Dick?' asked Christian, banging his friend energetically on the back with his free hand. Dick, whose face was bright red, coughed some more but nodded as best he could.

Christian turned back to Molly. 'Sorry, Miss Bryan. You were saying?'

'I don't think I would be able to go to America,' she said. 'We only have Sunday nights off. When is this award?'

'All will be revealed when I meet you for interview, I promise. I'll call my newsdesk the minute I get back to my hotel and I will get all the details.' He decided to press his advantage. 'When can we meet tomorrow?'

'Let me see . . .' She took a little green diary from the make-up table in front of her and opened it at a ribboned page. 'Would sometime around lunch time be all right with you?'

'Perfect!' cried Christian. 'I'll pick you up. Where do you live?'

She hesitated. 'No, that's all right. I'll meet you somewhere convenient for you.'

'Let me buy you lunch?' He grinned. 'Don't worry, it'll be on expenses.'

'If you're sure . . .'

'Of course. Where would you like to go? The Ritz? The Dorchester?' He was getting carried away and he knew it.

She laughed, caught up in his enthusiasm. 'Oh, no! They're far too posh!'

'Well, where, then?'

'What about a place called Kettner's in Soho? Do you know it?'

'No, but I can certainly find it!'

'All right, see you there at one o'clock! I'll make the booking.'

They took their leave then. 'Goodbye, Mr Molloy! I hope we meet again,' said Christian to the Irishman and did not wait to hear if there was an answering 'goodbye'.

Nothing could have deflated him. He closed the door behind himself and Dick and bounded down the stairs two at a time. He felt like kissing the doorman, the actor who held the door open for them, Dick, the wino who stumbled aside when he burst out through the door . . .

Outside, he grabbed Dick's arm. 'I'm in *love*! I'm going to marry that woman!'

'Quite!' said Dick. 'Now, how are you going to tell her about the award?'

As it turned out there was no problem next day about the award. The beginning was a little shaky from Christian's point of view. He arrived at Kettner's, in his opinion five minutes early, to find Molly already ensconced at a window table. It was Friday and the restaurant was doing a brisk trade mainly from businessmen who sat huddled together over their soup.

'I'm really sorry, Miss Bryan. Have I got the time wrong?'

'No, that's all right. I'm always early for everything! I can't help it. It must be the boarding-school training.' She looked over his shoulder. 'I booked the table for three. Where's Mr Steinberg?'

'Spielberg. He was called out on another job.' What he did not tell her was that Dick had already departed for Chicago, furious that he had been left to carry the can for the débâcle in Ethiopia.

'Oh!' She looked uncertain again.

'Don't worry, there are plenty of freelancers in London. Everything'll be OK.'

They ordered. Since she was playing that night she asked only for a salad. He ordered steak.

'Have you any more news about the award?' she asked when the waiter brought their drinks – Perrier for both of them. Christian was absolutely determined to turn over a new leaf – never again would a drop of alcohol cross his lips.

He took a deep breath. 'About the award, Miss Bryan, funny you should ask.'

She looked puzzled and he plunged in the deep end. 'There's no award, Miss Bryan – Margo. It was a ruse. I wanted to get to meet you.' He put on his most dazzling, most boyish smile. It had served him well with women all over the world. On tenterhooks he watched as a succession of expressions chased across her face: bewilderment first, then annoyance and finally, to his relief, amusement.

'There's no award?' She said it flatly.

'Uh-uh!'

'Is there such an award in existence?'

'Uh-uh!'

'No Association of Midwestern Critics or whatever they are?'

'Uh-uh.'

'I see.' She took a mouthful of her Perrier.

'This is not to say, Miss Bryan, that you won't win every

award going. Oscars, Golden Globes, Nobel Prizes for Acting—'

'There's no such prize.'

'Well, at the very least, the prestigious award from the prestigious Association of New York Critics . . . '

'Is *that* a real award?'

'I have no idea.'

She looked at him and, for a brief moment, he thought it was touch and go.

'Why on earth did you simply not ask to meet me?' she asked.

He could not read the expression in her eyes. 'Because you might have said no.'

The waiter brought crudités. She took a sliver of celery. 'Suppose I stood up now and walked out?'

'Suppose you do? I'm willing to bet you won't.'

'Are you now?'

'Yep!'

'What's to stop me?'

'You are!'

'Why, may I ask?'

'Because you think I'm outrageous and as well as that you think I'm interesting, not to say good-looking. And you've never met anyone like me before.'

'That's for sure.'

She took a piece of cauliflower and chewed it in silence.

'Are you enjoying that, Margo?'

'It's delicious.'

'I can show you where there's a great pumpkin.'

She laughed then and he was giddy with joy and relief. It was going to be all right. 'I might marry you,' he said.

She laughed again.

Late the next night Father Pat Morahan, snug in his temporary bed on Inisheer, stirred in his sleep. The resident curate on the island was laid low with a bout of flu and not wanting to make more work for his elderly housekeeper Father Morahan, as locum, had accepted the offer of a spare room in one of the houses near the beach. He snuggled down into the warm cocoon of sheets and blankets, glad that he was cosy in here and not outside in the storm which battered its fury on the small window of the room and against the corrugated roof over his head. He was sleepily aware that the battering seemed somehow to be getting louder, more urgent. He half-opened his eyes, then sat up suddenly. There was a continuous knocking at his door accompanied by the voice of the woman of the house. '*A Athair, a Athair*!'

'*Nóiméad amháin*!' he called, but it was less than a minute when he got to the door, having put on the trousers which lay on the wooden chair beside the bed. The braces, still attached, dangled on each side almost to his knees.

The woman of the house stood outside in the main room of the cottage dressed in her nightdress but with a shawl across her shoulders. He saw immediately why he had been wakened because behind her stood a dishevelled Brendan Ó Briain. Rivulets of water dripped off his oilskin. He twisted his wet cap in his hands.

'Is it your mam?' asked the priest.

Brendan nodded without answering, his eyes large with fright.

'Give me a moment, I'll get dressed and come with you. Have you a lamp?'

Again, Brendan nodded.

The priest dressed quickly, putting a thick jersey under his black clerical waistcoat. As a matter of course he always carried the Holy Oils with him on pastoral visits and he retrieved them now from his valise, placing them carefully in the little travelling case. He knew that Sorcha had been ill and had actually planned to visit her after the Sunday Mass but he had had no idea that she was as bad as it now seemed she was. The islanders were hardy people and sent for the priest only at the end.

When he was ready, protected in oilskins, he left the room and accompanied the silent Brendan out into the storm. The wind, from the northwest, screamed as it assaulted them and they were drenched instantly by driving rain and sheets of salt spray from the sea they heard, rather than saw, crashing against the rocks about thirty yards to their left. The night was so black that they could see nothing at all, just the bolts of water driving through the inadequate cone of light cast by Brendan's torch. But Brendan, knowing every inch of the island, pitched his light on the ground a few inches in front of his boots and walked resolutely ahead. Father Morahan tucked himself in behind and, single file, they battled uphill against the wind, leaning into it at an angle of 30 degrees. Within minutes the priest, who was running a little to fat, was panting.

The storm was even worse up by the house. As Brendan pushed open the door it was torn out of his grasp by the wind which roared ahead of him into the kitchen. The door slammed against the inside wall and the wind rushed towards the chimney breast, plucking ash and smoke from the fireplace. For a few moments while Brendan, coughing, struggled to close the door, the kitchen was obscured in a swirling fine grey cloud. Eventually he managed to engage the lock and the ash settled slowly all over the kitchen as the two men removed their oilskins.

Brendan led the priest to the back of the house and into Sorcha's room.

The Ó Briains had only recently got electricity and the new plaster was still unpainted around the socket for the bedside lamp, which burned without a shade on the small table beside Sorcha's bed. In the bulb's bare light the lines of a hard life and a harsher climate showed on her spent face, adding many years to her real age which the priest estimated to be about sixty-five. Her thick grey hair, always so neat, was loose and tangled, matted around her head on the pillow and although the blankets on her bed were augmented by extra coverings of shawls and greatcoats she was shivering. Her eyes were closed and she made no sign that she knew anyone else was in the room. But when he placed a hand on her clammy forehead she opened her eyes.

When she saw who it was she tried to struggle into a sitting position but was too weak. 'Don't be fretting now, Sorcha,' said the priest gently, kneeling beside the bed and restraining her efforts with a hand on her shoulder. Her lips moved but her voice was so faint he could not hear what she was trying to say. He leaned forward, his ear right above her mouth. 'What is it, Sorcha?'

'You must be drowned, Father,' she whispered in English, each word costing her a great effort. 'Would you like a cup of tea?'

'No, Sorcha,' he answered. 'I'm absolutely fine. Don't be bothering about me. Brendan can get me a cup later.'

She tried to struggle up again. 'I'm sorry I don't have a chair for you – Brendan . . . '

He restrained her and put his finger on her lips. 'Please, Sorcha, I'm fine.'

She closed her eyes again and he moved the lamp to the floor to ease its harshness. Then, putting his lips close to her ear, he asked her if she wanted to go to confession. Without opening her eyes she nodded.

He took the purple stole out of his inside pocket, kissed it, put it around his neck and leaned towards her again, so close he could smell the fustiness of the greatcoats which covered her. The storm seemed to grow even louder outside the room as if trying to beat its way into the little circle of light and shadow.

She began her confession, making a tremendous, halting effort, but despite all his training in professional detachment the priest found it difficult to concentrate on this sad litany of wandering thoughts at Mass, of sins of omission against her long-dead husband and the son who lived with her. Of sins against an avenging, demanding God. As he often did in these circumstances he felt savagely ashamed at their relative positions with regard to sin. But in this case the irony that she should be confessing this childlike chronicle of pitiful transgression to him, of all people, was almost more than he could bear.

He forced himself to be the representative of God, as she so firmly believed he was, and tried to focus not on himself but on her words.

'And is that all, my child?' he asked softly when, exhausted, she seemed to finish. She did not respond and he put his hand on her shoulder. 'Is that all, Sorcha?'

With an effort she opened her eyes again.

The look in them was so fearful that involuntarily he tightened his grip on her. 'What is it, Sorcha? What is it?' The shivering, which had subsided, started again. Her head rolled on the pillow. 'Sorcha, whatever it is God forgives you. I forgive you in God's name . . . ' But she kept her head averted.

Her lips were moving and he leaned so close that he could feel on his cheek her tiny puffs of breath. Still he could not understand what she was trying to say. 'Say it in Irish, Sorcha, it'll be easier for you.'

He caught something. Something about Molly . . .

A cold fist in his stomach. He was afraid she sensed it. She had stopped trying to speak. He forced himself to be calm. 'Take your time, Sorcha . . . '

She closed her eyes again. His body, lit from behind, cast a huge shadow over the bed and the ceiling. Despite the storm their little circle in the room was quiet, now dangerously so. He could hear the big, double-belled alarm clock on the washstand. It ticked with a double tick every second time. There were small sounds from the kitchen as Brendan moved around.

She waited so long that he thought she had fallen asleep and did not know whether he was glad or not. He was just about to make the Sign of the Cross to give her absolution when again she opened her eyes. The shivering had stopped. She seemed to have gained a little strength.

'Molly is not my child, Father.'

Carefully, noting the interaction of every muscle and bone, he removed his left hand from her shoulder and placed it against the right one, folding both of them in an attitude of prayer. He called on all his professional reserves. 'I see, my child.' He swallowed hard. There was no way out. He was stepping way beyond the confessional but he had to know. 'Whose is she, Sorcha?'

He could see her face was already smoother with relief. She was speaking more clearly and strongly. 'I don't know, Father. Micheál found her from the sea.'

Father Morahan could not feel himself breathing. 'When was this, my child?'

'The first of May nineteen fifty-three.'

He forced himself to maintain the tones of a priest. 'But, Sorcha, how did you explain the child to everyone?'

'My own little Molly was poorly and died that night.'

'Did no one ask you?' He took a deep breath and slowed himself down. 'I mean, everyone on the island must have known that your child was ill. How did you explain it?'

'There was talk, Father, of changelings, but we keep ourselves to ourselves. The new child was about the same size and fair too. And I didn't care about the talk and I loved her like my own, God forgive me.'

'Where is she, Sorcha? The baby? I mean, your baby . . . '

'Micheál buried her under the potato drills.'

He had a vision of the potatoes he had eaten that evening for supper. How many other little corpses sweetened the potatoes on this blasted island? He forced himself to continue listening to the weak voice. 'I said prayers over her, Father, and she was buried with a rosary in her hands. I have prayed for her every single day of my life, Father.'

He lowered his head into one hand, assuming the confessional posture. 'Does Molly – I mean *this* Molly – does she know?'

'No, Father.' The little surge of strength was nearly gone. He could hear cups being rattled on the dresser. In the kitchen Brendan was making tea.

'Does anyone else know? Brendan? Conor?' he asked urgently. He realized he was behaving more like a detective than a priest. She shook her head. Then she closed her eyes again. Automatically, falling back on ritual, he made the Sign of the Cross, *Ego absolvo te . . .* Even as he murmured the words the revelation hammered at him: he was the only one who knew. Like an old, old man, he got to his feet. He saw she was quietly asleep, her hands still folded together. He tiptoed out of the room and into the kitchen.

Brendan looked up from his task of pouring boiling water into a blackened teapot which stood on the hob by the fire. The Ó Briains had a bottled gas cooker in the scullery but, like many of the others on the island, still used the hook over the fire to boil water. 'Would you have a cup, Father?'

He nodded and sat in one of the chairs by the fire.

They waited for the tea to draw. Brendan looked into the fire but the priest looked away towards the table. He focused his eyes on an empty sardine can, noticing that stuck to the oily surface of the metal lid, tightly rolled over its key, was a fine down of ash. The kitchen wore a forlorn, neglected look. There were two dirty plates on the dresser and a broom had fallen across the doorway into the scullery. He wondered what the house would look like after a few years in Brendan's sole care.

The storm outside was worse if anything. The wind howled in the wide chimney breast driving raindrops downwards into the fire which sputtered and hissed. They had to sit a little way back so as not to choke on the smoke which billowed out from time to time in clouds. But as the two of them sipped their tea Father Morahan was grateful for the din outside. It obviated the need for talk.

The longing to see her again was as strong as the storm outside. He felt that if he had been alone he would probably have wept. It was always dangerous for him to come to Inisheer but he had managed to push her into a secret, unthreatening place in his mind. Nevertheless he sometimes found it hard to breathe when he saw someone who reminded him of her, or absurdly, when he heard certain popular songs. The dead of night belonged solely to her.

Sorcha's revelation, in a way, was not so strange. Perhaps he had always known that Molly could not have been a child of this bare, tortured piece of battered rock. Staring at the ash-covered kitchen table, he saw again her pale shimmering body in the sand. He had to get away. He drank the last of his tea. Age seeped through his leg-bones when he got to his feet. Brendan stood too but Father Morahan pushed him gently back down into the chair. 'I'll be off, then, Brendan,' he said, 'but I'll be back early in the morning before Mass.' He shook Brendan's hand and turned away but the man jumped up again and caught his arm. 'I'll walk down with you, Father.'

'No, Brendan. You stay here with your mother. She needs

someone in the house.' He saw then that Brendan was afraid to be alone with the dying woman. 'I know it's hard, Brendan, but you won't be alone for long. I'll be back soon.'

'Father!'

'Yes?'

But Brendan hung his head. Father Morahan touched him on the arm. 'Lend me your lamp, will you?'

Brendan walked across to the dresser and picked up the torch. He handed it over. 'Will you telephone Molly, so?'

Father Morahan nodded and then had to wait while Brendan searched in a cracked milk jug on the dresser to find Molly's London number.

Outside, the storm sprang at him like a demon taking his breath away but he bent his head into its jaws and almost welcomed the black confusion of wind and water. He could lose himself. But the gale, now at his back, forced him headlong into a semi-run. Within yards he had tripped and fallen heavily. Pain shot through his shoulder.

With difficulty, panting, he pulled himself upright against a wall, grazing his hand on the rough stone. In an effort to catch his breath, he hung on to the wall, standing as still as he could, but the wind, gusting, impelled him again. Despite the oilskin the bitter, swirling rain had streamed under his hood and was running coldly down the hollow in the middle of his back. Holding on to the walls, trying desperately to keep the light from the torch trained on the ground in front of him, he moved on.

Twice more he fell. The second time the torch went out and rolled out of his hand. He stayed on all fours, crawling around in little circles trying to find it. The stones were slimy and freezing under his searching hands and then he cracked his head hard against the wall. The pain was intense and for the first time in his adult life Father Morahan lost control. He stopped searching for the torch and still on all fours, like a bull, raised his voice, prolonging it, screaming his rage, his pain and his frustration, challenging the storm.

He blasphemed. 'Fuck you, God! Fuck you!' He cried it twenty times.

He lowered his head in the blackness and let the storm take him, allowing his body to go slack until his back hit the wall beside him. He lay quiet then, curled into the lee of the jagged wall like one of the island collies or a ewe sheep in his native Mayo.

He stayed where he was for a long time with his head hunched down into his hood, not caring, glad of the lashing storm. He fantasized that he was a piece of rock, a small piece, a stone which could be driven down the boreen before the wind and buffeted out into the sea where it could sink without trace in all that quiet blackness. Such quietness. After a while he could no longer feel his hands and feet and his face had set into its grooves so that moving any muscle of it, even to lick the rain off his lips, was painful.

Gradually, a picture of himself – curled against the wall, a bathetic, middle-aged fool – forced him again to his feet but he found it even more difficult to move than before, doubly handicapped by the weather and by the numbness in his hands and feet. All he could feel in his boots were his heel bones on which, to move, he had to balance as if on two broom handles. Carefully, step by step, holding on to the wall, he made his way down towards the sea.

When he reached the woman's cottage he did not bother to be quiet as he knew she would be watching out for him. As he latched the door behind him she came into the kitchen wearing a man's raincoat over her Viyella nightdress and clucking over the state of him. She raked the ashes of the fire and placed a kettle to boil on the black range. 'Go and change those clothes, Father,' she said. 'I'll give you a cup of tea and a drop in it.'

He was too drained to protest or to be polite and handed over his oilskins so that she could organize some place to hang them.

In his bedroom, he splashed cold water on his face and bathed his grazed hand. Then he took off his soaked, filthy priest's trousers, changed into a clean pair of slacks and went back out to the kitchen where the woman bustled about. Bitterly he could see that she was more than half thrilled with her part in the drama. She made him sit in the seat of honour by the big fireplace and handed him his tea.

'Now, Father,' she said in her lilting English, 'get that down you. There's a drop in it too, you'll surely need it, because your work will be hard today.'

She settled herself in the lesser chair opposite him folding her hands in her lap. 'How's Sorcha, the creature?' she asked. 'Will she last the night?'

He was too tired to answer. He shrugged and sipped his tea made fiery by the poteen. It burned its way down his gullet and into his stomach.

She was not affronted. Together, in silence, they gazed into the fire which, like the fire in Molly's house, hissed under the raindrops which were driven down the wide chimneybreast. Like that they passed a quarter of an hour until he had finished his tea and his head fell forward on his chest. She rose and took the cup from where it drooped from his hand. Then she left him and went into her bedroom.

Molly woke just before the clock chimed downstairs. She was too comfortable to make the move necessary to check her bedside clock so she counted the chimes. It was eight o'clock. The street outside was still, no traffic, no delivery vans, and the storm which had rattled her windows in the early hours of the morning seemed to have passed. She snuggled deeper under her duvet, loving the warmth, the knowledge that it was Sunday. No interviews, no press agents, no work, hairdressers or make-up artists. She planned to spend the day pottering around the house, reading Sunday newspapers, watching television. In the meantime she could stay in bed as long as she liked.

Her mind drifted across the additions and improvements she was planning to make to her house now that she could afford them. Molly adored sunshine and light, pale colours, freshness. Her bedroom was typical of the rest of the house, creamy sheepskin rugs on the polished boards of the floor, sepia prints on the walls, a glowing patchwork quilt over the duvet on the bed, a pottery jug filled with the drooping heads of early daffodils on the desk in the bay of the window. This coming summer she was planning to add a conservatory, filled

261

with plants, to her south-facing kitchen – Conor would help her there. She might even include a small aviary.

Conor. Since he had come back it was inconceivable to Molly that Conor would not be in her life. Blessed with a vivid visual imagination, since childhood she had seen Conor in the form of different rooted objects – a giant oak, or a buttress on a bridge, or the tower of an ancient cathedral. She had often tried to imagine how he in his turn saw her and, on balance, thought he probably saw her prosaically still as a child, a small barefoot girl in a flowered frock, whose favourite pastime was searching for pink cowries on a beach.

She wriggled her toes in her smooth warm sheets. Once, when she was about seven, she had tried to explain to him her personal vision of heaven. She had been puzzled by the concept of heaven being infinitely expandable and had asked her teacher how God managed to fit all those trillions and trillions of souls, more trillions every day, into heaven. 'God is a great organizer,' her teacher had answered. For ever after Molly saw heaven as a sort of vast platform, floating along through eternal infinity, which was pale blue with cottonwool clouds. On this platform were rows and rows of wooden school benches on which were balanced trillions of identical white stainless souls. The souls were triangular, balancing on one of their points and angled sideways so that as many as possible could fit on each bench.

Molly tried to explain to Conor about this and about God's job in heaven, always busy welcoming hordes of new souls and fetching more and more benches for them to sit on. Heaven, in Molly's seven-year-old opinion, sounded dreadfully boring.

Conor had just shouted with laughter and tickled her and that was that.

He had telephoned full of plans late last night after she had got home from the theatre. He had landed a job as a general attendant at London Zoo and although his wages would not be high he would have enough money left, after paying the rent on his small studio flat in Battersea, to cover food and the fees for a night course in archaeology. He had sounded pleased and Molly had been delighted for him – and for herself. At least he would stick around for a while.

She debated now whether she should leave the delicious warmth – it was never the same when you got back in again – to make herself a cup of tea or coffee and was still engaged in lazy debate with herself when the telephone rang. She stretched out an arm and lifted the receiver. 'Hello?'

'Will you marry me?'

'Christian! Do you know what time it is?' But, warm and secure in her bed, she laughed.

'Of course I know what time it is. The question is, will you marry me?'

'For goodness' sake. We've had *one lunch* together!'

'Yes, but what a lunch.'

'Perfectly ordinary lunch, if you ask me. Salad, steak, nothing to set the world on fire.'

'It was the most extraordinary lunch in the history of the world. Marry me and you'll never have to eat salads again!'

'Suppose I want to eat salads?'

'I'll buy you a lettuce factory.'

'Christian, I'm going to hang up now. I've things to do.'

'So early in the morning?'

'Things you couldn't understand. You're *American!* She stretched lazily and yawned.

'English things?' he persisted.

'Irish things.'

'What things?'

'Mysterious things which have nothing to do with you.'

'Let's do mysterious things together.'

'Christian. Go back to Chicago! I'll see you next time you're in town.'

'I'm in town now. I can't go home without some indication that you'll marry me. It's cruelty. I'll have to get on to the association.'

'The same one which gave me the award?'

'No, this is a different association. This is the Association to Piece Together the Shattered Dreams of Smiths.'

'Oh, *that* association. Well, you'll just have to get on to your association then, won't you? I'm going to hang up.'

'All right, my darling Sleeping Beauty. I'll call you from the States.'

'That'll cost a fortune, Christian.'

'Oh, no, it won't. The *Sentinel* will pay – if I still have a job, of course!'

'Why would you not?'

'Don't worry your gorgeous head about it – just a technicality. Like I'm about three days overdue with no story . . .'

'Christian!'

'I told you not to worry, Beauty. It's my problem. You think about my offer. Best you'll get all day!'

'Goodbye, Christian!'

'Goodbye, Beauty . . .'

She had never been courted like this before and although she did not take him seriously the feeling was not unlike the one she got when she first drank champagne. This American's open, confident warmth and charm was like a bright breeze. She had never met anyone before who had laid his heart so readily on his sleeve. He was funny too, and entertaining and affectionate.

If Conor was an oak, what was Christian? She tried for an image for Christian. Christian was a silver fish, always moving, impossible to pin down. She pictured his body, lithe and athletic with wide shoulders, long legs and narrow hips. He was attractive, no doubt about that.

The telephone on her bedside table rang a second time disturbing her reverie. She picked up the receiver. 'I told you to go back to Chicago!'

But there was a crackling on the line and then the faint sound of a woman's voice, very far away. She could just make it out. 'Hello, hello, hello . . .' said the woman, obviously shouting.

'Hello?' Molly answered, alarmed now.

There was no reply from the woman, just more crackling.

'Hello?' said Molly again, louder. She had recognized the atmospherics. She had never before had a telephone call from Inisheer so early in the morning. And it was Sunday. Something was wrong. Swinging her legs over the side of the bed she sat upright on its edge. 'Hello?' she said again. 'Who is this? Is there anybody there?'

It was a man's voice now, also very faint, although she could hear by the tone that he too was probably shouting. 'Hello, is that you, Molly?'

'Yes,' she shouted back. 'Is that you, Brendan?' Brendan had long ago given up his job in Birmingham and was back on the island with their mam.

'This is Father Pat Morahan,' said the faraway voice. Molly's body went rigid.

'Hello! Hello! Are you still there?' the priest shouted.

She forced herself to answer. 'What's wrong, Father?'

'Molly, could you come as soon as possible. It's your mother . . .' His voice faded away altogether.

She gripped the receiver. 'Hello, Father, hello . . . hello . . .' she shouted. He said something she couldn't catch and almost crying with frustration, she put her mouth right down so that her lips were grazing the mouthpiece. 'Can . . . you . . . hear . . . me . . . Father?' But he said something which again she could not catch. 'I . . . can't . . . *hear* . . . you . . . Father!' More crackling.

Slowly and very clearly, calling on every ounce of her actress's training in voice projection. 'Just answer yes or no, Father. Is Mam alive?'

She heard the faint yes.

'How . . . bad . . . is . . . she?' She could make out the words 'gravely ill' – and something else she did not understand. 'I'm coming on the first plane I can get, Father!' she shouted.

'All right, Molly,' he shouted back. Then the line went dead. She sat holding the receiver, staring at it. Then she replaced it. Automatically, she looked at her clock. Eight forty-two. She got off the bed, walked into her bathroom and turned on the shower. She was just about to step into it when she stopped.

Conor!

She turned off the shower again, went back to the telephone and dialled Conor's number. It rang four times before he answered.

'I had a telephone call from Inisheer,' she said, trying to keep

265

the panic out of her voice. 'It's Mam. She's very ill. I'm going there straight away. Do you want to come?'

There was silence at his end of the line.

'Listen,' she continued, urgently. 'Why don't you meet me at Heathrow? I'll be there in less than an hour.'

'All right,' he said. 'See you, then.'

Since it was Sunday, with relatively traffic-free roads, the journey to the airport took only forty minutes but he beat her to it. She saw him immediately when she entered the cavernous check-in hall shared by all the domestic and inter-island airlines. He was standing by one of the Aer Lingus desks staring into space, unshaven and haggard, dressed in denim jeans and sweatshirt over which he had thrown a duffel coat. Her instinct was to run to him and throw her arms around his neck but she checked the impulse. When she reached him, she merely touched his elbow. 'Conor?'

His face was expressionless. She left him and walked the short distance across the hall to the ticket desk. She was lucky as there was a flight to Shannon at eleven o'clock. Using a credit card she bought an open-return ticket and walked back to the check-in area where Conor still stood. The clerk, smartly dressed in the familiar green uniform, was Irish. 'How many travelling?'

'Just myself,' said Molly.

The clerk completed the formalities. 'Any luggage?'

'No, just hand luggage . . . '

Conor still stood a little way behind Molly, staring into space. The clerk looked curiously at him. 'Is your friend OK?' she asked Molly. 'He doesn't look well.'

'He has just heard a friend of his at home has died. I'm going over to the funeral, actually, but he can't make it. Pressure of business . . . ' she added, improvising.

The clerk nodded sympathetically. With the huge Irish population in London she was quite familiar with people travelling home at short notice to bury friends and relatives.

'I'll tell you what,' she said, 'you have at least half an hour before you board. Why don't I see if I can get you into the VIP lounge? You'll have a bit of comfort and privacy there.'

She made a telephone call and within a few minutes another

266

clerk came to fetch them. He took them upstairs and along a mezzanine, through a door and into the small lounge furnished with a couple of sofas, an easy chair and a coffee table. He asked them if they would like coffee or tea or something stronger – all of which they refused – then he left quietly. As soon as they were alone, Conor put his head in his hands. 'What am I going to do, Molly?'

'Would you not chance coming with me?' she asked. 'It's Sunday morning, there certainly won't be many people about – and anyway, there is no immigration on the Irish side . . .'

He shook his head bitterly. 'For God's sake, Molly, have sense.' He was almost shouting. 'As soon as I step on to that island the Guards will know. You know that as well as I do!'

'I know, I know, I'm sorry. It's just that I wish I could think of something that might help.'

The tension crackled between them.

The windows of the room were double-glazed. Outside, the airport bustle proceeded as if it were being projected on to the grey sky in a silent movie.

'She mightn't die,' said Molly eventually, although she knew she did not sound convincing.

Again he just shook his head.

The minutes ticked away. Copies of that morning's Irish newspapers were arranged on a small table in a corner of the room. Conor picked up a copy of the *Sunday Independent*, opened it and bent his head into its pages. But after a while he flung the paper onto a table and rising, walked towards the window. 'I wish, I really wish . . . If I hadn't – if he hadn't . . . If that *thing* hadn't happened, with *him*—'

'Stop it, Conor!' she said, alarmed at their reversal of roles. He had always been the one in charge, the calm one.

'It was as much my fault as yours,' she said, appeasing. 'I provoked him.'

'Don't be ridiculous.' He was shouting. 'Of course you didn't provoke him. He was an awful, appalling human being.'

'But, Conor—'

'*You didn't fucking provoke him!*'

She was really frightened. Conor rarely swore. Her instinct

267

was to calm him down at all costs but she felt paralysed on the sofa.

He clenched his fists and pounded one into the other. 'You have no idea what I went through every time I saw him raise his hand to you.'

Molly watched him power up and down the small space between the two sofas. She had not felt this helpless since she was a child.

There was a discreet knock at the door. It was the young airline clerk to see if they needed anything. Conor kept his back turned to the door, facing out of the window. Molly, out of her depth, wanted to get rid of the clerk and asked for coffee.

The young man left, leaving the door slightly ajar. Conor remained where he was.

He turned round when the clerk left and looked at her in a way which sent slithering fingers through her blood. She had never been more conscious that he was a good four or five inches taller than she.

He came towards her and pulled her off the couch, gripping her shoulders. For an extraordinary moment she thought he was going to kiss her. But he dropped his hands and went back to the window. She saw his knuckles whiten as his fingers tightened on the windowsill.

Quietly, not wanting to make a sound, she bent her rubbery knees and sat again. An aircraft slid past the windows and the roar of its engines, muted by the double-glazing, filled the little room.

The clerk came back with the coffee, his eyes fixed on the little tray so he would not spill the liquid. 'Sorry,' he said, 'but I'm afraid you'll have to drink it pretty quickly. We'll be boarding you in three or four minutes.'

Luckily the coffee was cool enough to gulp. Conor picked up her coat from the arm of the couch on which they had sat. His face was a mask. 'Have you got everything?'

She took the coat and nodded, afraid to look at him. The clerk picked up her overnight bag and the three of them left the lounge. When they got within sight of the security barriers Conor stopped. 'This is as far as I go,' he said

268

quietly. He kissed her on the cheek. Then he turned and walked slowly away.

Molly was the last passenger to board the aircraft, which was only half full, and almost immediately the doors were closed. She declined to take one of the sweets offered by the air hostess and closed her eyes when the jet began to roll out to its take-off point. The memory of the extraordinary scene in the lounge was superseded by her terror of flying. As usual, when the engines roared for the take-off run her stomach began to churn. She clutched the armrests of her seat until her hands hurt and, although it had been many years since she had darkened the door of a church, began the silent childish litany: Sacred Heart of Jesus, in Thee I trust; Immaculate Heart of Mary, pray for us; our Holy Guardian Angels, protect us; St Joseph and St Jude, pray for us! She recited it mentally over and over again as the plane raced along the runway and opened her eyes only when she felt the change in angle and vibration which meant that they had left the ground.

During the flight she tried to blot out Conor's face by reading *Cara*, the Aer Lingus in-flight magazine, but his face floated over its glossy colourful pages. She forced herself to think not of him but of her mother.

It was a fine day in Shannon and she was grateful, as they travelled along the roads to the new airfield at Oranmore outside Galway, that the taxi-man was not inclined to talk. She leaned her head against the worn seat and watched as the countryside of County Clare sped by. Although the low January sun shone white, the storm of the previous night had left clear evidence of its passage. The poor land of the fields was waterlogged under the washed sky; many of the leafless roadside trees dangled half-broken branches and several times they had to negotiate around fallen trunks. The tyres of the taxi crunched constantly on the litter of twigs. If it had been this bad here, twenty miles inland, thought Molly, what must it have been like out on the islands?

They passed through the town of Ennis, slowing down behind the mini-rush-hour caused by cars and bicycles outside a church after a late Mass. She was already a million miles from London.

The familiar Irish names gave her comfort as the villages and signposts sped by. She mouthed the soft words to herself: Dromore and Crusheen, Carra Lake, Gort and Kiltartan, Laban, Ardrahan, Kilcolgan, Kilcarnan, Clarinbridge . . .

It was just after half past two when they pulled into the airfield at Oranmore. She paid the driver and walked across to the tiny one-storey building, not much more than a shed, which served as check-in, assembly point, passenger waiting area, parcel office and communications room for Aer Arann, the airline which served all three islands.

Word had obviously spread about Sorcha because the moment she stepped inside the hut the girl behind the counter, whom Molly recognized as one of the O'Flahertys from Inishmore, came forward to sympathize. 'We were expecting you, Molly. We were all very sorry to hear about poor Sorcha.' Faced with kindness and concern Molly's self-composure was threatened but she thanked the girl and accepted a cup of tea, which was produced for her from behind the check-in counter. 'It won't be long now,' said the O'Flaherty girl. 'Ye'll be going at three o'clock.'

The Islander aircraft, small and sturdy and specifically designed for island-hopping, was scheduled to call first at Inishmore before going on to Inisheer but in deference to Molly's life-and-death mission, the airline had rejigged the itinerary and she was to be landed first. There were only five other passengers, all going to the bigger island – returning, ironically, from a funeral on the mainland – but they did not raise any objection at the change in plan, looking at her with sympathy. At five minutes to three, one by one holding their baggage, the six of them were weighed on the big Berkel scale. The pilot himself did the weighing, chatting while he noted the weights on his manifest.

The flight was uneventful. They skimmed west, out over Galway Bay for fifteen minutes until Inisheer was in sight. It was Molly's first view of her home from the air and, despite the tragic reason for her visit, she was fascinated at the bare, treeless landscape, almost entirely light grey in colour, deeply scored with thousands of fissures and marked out in a crazy pattern by the drystone walls. The island looked like a limestone jigsaw on the surface of the dark green ocean.

It disappeared from her view as the pilot circled round again over the sea and lined up on the flat grassy promontory which served as an airstrip. She could see the tractor and trailer used to carry the freight and luggage and a couple of people standing on the grass holding their hands over their eyes and looking upwards. The arrival of the Aer Arann plane was always one of the highlights of island life and usually attracted a crowd but today, being Sunday, many people were still obviously at their dinners.

Although dry and bright, it was still very windy out here. The little plane seesawed as they lost height and Molly's stomach started to heave. She realized she had not eaten all day, having had only the lukewarm coffee at Heathrow and the cup of tea at Oranmore. But before she was actually sick, the plane skewed once more and thumped on to the grass. She looked out of her window and recognized one of the people there. Older, fatter but unmistakable, the priest's hair blew wild and he held the collar of his black clerical coat up around his ears.

Preoccupied with other events of the day this complication had not occurred to her. How could she have been so stupid? It was inevitable that he should meet her. Brendan was probably tending to her mam.

The plane bumped to a halt and the pilot unstrapped himself. He got out of his seat and opened the door and immediately the cold air gushed through the tiny cabin. There was no escape. Molly unstrapped her seat belt and, carrying her overnight bag, struggled out of her seat. One of the Inishmore passengers had to get out onto the grass to let her pass.

The pilot said goodbye to her. She delayed until he had climbed back into his plane and then turned to face the priest who was still hanging back. She walked across the short strip of grass which separated them and when she reached him, she extended her hand. 'How are you, Father?'

He took the hand but barely touched it before letting it drop. 'I'm fine, Molly,' he said. Then, 'I'm very sorry about Sorcha . . . '

271

She nodded. The silence beat between them. He broke it, leaning forward to take the bag from her hand. She noticed that his left one was bandaged. He turned and walked towards the little opening in the stone wall which ran along one side of the airfield.

'What happened to your hand, Father?' she asked, when they had squeezed into the battered car he had borrowed to drive her up to her house. One of the few on the island, it was rusted and very small and she had difficulty folding her legs under the dashboard, not least because there was a six-volt battery on the floor under her feet.

'Oh, nothing much,' he said. He jumped out of the car, muttering something about checking the water, and she had to sit uncomfortably for several minutes, her feet balanced on the battery, while he fiddled under the bonnet.

When he got back in he kept his eyes fiercely ahead of him. He seemed to scrunch his shoulders and hips so that not a millimetre of his body would touch hers – difficult in the tiny, constricted space – and reactively, she felt her calves begin to cramp as she strained to hold her own body away from him. She was very conscious of the freckled skin bulging slightly around the bandage on his left hand as it rested on the gearshift like a fat spider, just inches away from her thigh. She knew he was conscious of it too because he removed it after a minute or so and placed it in his pocket, not taking it out again for the remainder of the journey although the engine shuddered for a gear change as they went uphill.

When they came within sight of the house she saw a small group of men standing outside the front door, two of whom she recognized: one was an uncle, one his son, her cousin. All of the men wore caps and all had their hands in the pockets of their Sunday suits. Two hens and a cockerel pecked around in the dirt by their feet.

Molly told herself there was no reason to be embarrassed as the men stared at her from under their caps but their oblique gaze made her feel acutely uncomfortable. She hesitated as she and the priest approached the door but the group parted, some going to one side of it, two going to the other. As she passed through them, first one then another touched a cap. She kept her head high as she unlatched the door and walked inside. Father Morahan followed her in but placed her bag against the wall of the kitchen and went out again.

The kitchen was bright and clean, the fire was banked and a neighbour woman was in the little scullery washing dishes. Brendan was not in the room and she supposed he was with her mother. She greeted the neighbour but put off going in to Sorcha, steeling herself. While the woman organized a cup of tea Molly looked out of the window. The heads of the men outside had swivelled after the priest who had walked a little way along the boreen. He had stopped where two walls made a rough right angle and was leaning against them, pulling on a cigarette. The men, absorbed, did not realize she was watching them. She saw one of them snigger and was suddenly very glad she lived in a crowded, impersonal city.

Brendan came from her mother's room. He was very thin and a little stooped and she saw with a shock that he looked like an old man. '*Dia dhuit*,' he said awkwardly.

She returned the greeting. They had never been close, she and this brother, and she knew that he resented her career in England and the success it brought her. Nevertheless, seeing his plight now, she felt nothing for him but pity. She had an impulse to hug him but knew better. 'Is Mam inside?' she asked.

He nodded and indicating to the neighbour that she would have the tea later she went into her mother's room.

There was a low hiss from a bottled-gas heater under the window. The bed was neat, with fresh sheets and clean wool blankets under a spotless white candlewick counterpane. Someone had draped a white tea-towel on a makeshift frame over the top of the bedside light and the soft glow was kind to Sorcha's face where it lay on a white linen pillowcase. Sorcha's hands were folded on the counterpane, rising and falling irregularly as she breathed in shallow gasps. Her grey hair was loose to her shoulders but neatly combed and kept off her face with an incongruously childish Alice band of red plastic. It was this detail which almost broke Molly's heart.

She sank to her knees beside the bed. For several minutes

she gazed at the face of her mother and then gently took one of the old hands in her own. The skin was hard and calloused and the thin gold wedding band had all but disappeared into it but the hand itself was small and delicate. So little time now to tell her mother how much she was loved. Maybe no time at all. She stroked the fragile hand and then laid her cheek on it. It felt leathery and dry against her own soft wet skin. Sorcha's eyes opened.

'Is it you, Molly?' she whispered. She tried to struggle up but barely succeeded in moving her head.

'Rest, Mam, rest,' said Molly. '*Suan.*' She leaned over and kissed her mother's clammy forehead.

'But after the long journey, you'll be wanting—'

'Stop it, Mam. Rest yourself, rest yourself . . .'

Sorcha succumbed. She tried to smile. 'I'm glad you're come, Molly.'

'Darling Mam, darling Mam,' was all that Molly could say in response, still holding the small hard hand in both her own. Then, almost to herself, burying her head on the counterpane, 'What will I do without you?'

With a great effort Sorcha brought over her other hand and stroked her daughter's head. 'Hush, *a chroí*, you will be the one now to look out for the family.'

All Molly's great plans, all she had wanted to say to her mother, were no use now. There was no time, she could see that. 'I will look out for them, Mam. You rest now. I'll mind them.'

There was a movement behind her. Brendan had crept into the room and stood twisting his hands. His face was creased with misery.

When Molly turned back to her mother, Sorcha was looking straight at her. 'I just want to say,' she said softly, so softly that Molly had to lean close to hear: 'that a mother knows more than a daughter thinks she knows . . .'

Molly eased her arm under Sorcha's head so that she was cradling her and Sorcha's face was turned towards her. She brushed a strand of her own hair from where it had fallen across Sorcha's cheek and took one of her hands. She barely

274

heard the last faint words: '*Maith dom é! Maith dom é!*' Then Sorcha died.

'Whatever it is, Mam, of course I forgive you,' whispered Molly against her mother's slack fingers.

The funeral was lashed with January rain and Una O'Connor shivered as she waited to offer her condolences to Molly at the graveside. She was the last to do so and saw the struggle to remember on Molly's face. 'Una O'Connor,' she said, extending her hand.

'Oh, yes,' said Molly. She looked genuinely taken aback, 'I'm sorry I didn't recognize you, but I didn't expect . . . '

'I'm very sorry about your mother,' said Una. 'I didn't know her, of course, but I know how it is to lose a mother.'

'How did you know?' Molly still held Una's hand.

'My own mother died last year—'

'No,' said Molly. 'I mean, how did you know Mam had died?'

'The death notices in the *Independent*,' said Una.

'Thank you very much for coming all this way, I really appreciate it.'

Una was embarrassed. Her motives were, as usual, mixed. She had seized on the funeral as a way back into contact with Sean Molloy. She had even dared hope he might be present. But at the same time she liked Margo Bryan and genuinely wanted to show her sympathy. Molly dropped her hand. 'You'll come up to the house?'

'Oh, no! That's for family only.'

'Of course you'll come. You've come all this way. This is Brendan, my brother.'

Una had presumed that the tall, stooped man who looked old enough to be Molly's father was the brother. Throughout the exchange between the two women he had been standing quietly, hands clasped in front of him as though waiting for someone to tell him what to do. Una was familiar with the type, ineffectual and sad. She shook hands with him now. 'I'm very sorry, Mr Ó Briain.'

'Yes, yes,' he said, all in a rush, 'come up to the house, come up to the house.'

Una felt like an impostor. She wished with all her heart she had not come. She trudged after the rest of the mourners through the unrelieved grey of the streaming, rocky landscape as the waves and waves of rain beat at her city coat, useless against them. How could anyone live in a place like this?

The little house was as she expected. She felt like a ghoul. Nevertheless as the tide of Irish talk, so rapid that she could not understand it, washed around her, her professional eye noted and retained the features of the kitchen, the dresser and the blackened fireplace, the spotless starched linen on the table, the bottles of whiskey, piles of sandwiches and barrel of stout, the assorted, borrowed glassware and rows of wooden chairs.

She accepted a glass of whiskey from a woman. The woman smiled at her with such friendliness that Una was doubly ashamed of her mixed motives.

Molly came and sat beside her but they ran out of conversation fast. She moved across the kitchen and tried to talk to Brendan but he kept his eyes fixed on a far corner of the room and answered all her questions in shy monosyllables.

'Did Sean Molloy not come to the funeral?' she asked him at last, when she was sure Molly was at the other side of the room.

His long creased face puckered. 'Sean Molloy?' he repeated as though thunderstruck. 'Sean Molloy?' He threw his body backwards in the chair and raised his eyes to heaven as though thinking but it took Una only a moment to realize that the dumb-show meant that Brendan was being polite to a stranger. He had never heard of Sean Molloy.

Not a boyfriend then . . . But, on the other hand, would Margo Bryan have confided in this brother? She was no nearer. And the timing was hardly appropriate to ask Margo herself.

At least the actress would now look on her as a friend.

The moment Una allowed the thought she felt like a worm.

CHAPTER EIGHT

There was too much wind and rain in this bloody country.

Father Morahan shook his umbrella in the hallway of the presbytery in Tullyhalla and pulled off the plastic raincoat he wore over his ordinary coat. Despite the generous whiskey he had been given after completing the rituals of a sick call, he felt frozen through after the short walk from the sick man's house at the end of the village to his own bungalow, set back from the road in a little garden beside the church. And his shoes were letting in the wet. He was sick of it, sick of it, he thought irritably, pulling the laces open and kicking the shoes into a corner. He looked at his socks. There were twin half-moons of wet around the toes.

February was by far the worst month in Ireland, he thought, padding into the gloomy front room which smelt of polish. If it wasn't gales and sleet it was rain, bloody rain. And as for it being the official beginning of spring, he had yet to see snowdrops in his back garden that could survive intact the blasts of February.

He glanced out of the window at the village street. Not a soul about. The lights of the small grocery shop on the opposite side of the street glowed cheerily but through its steamy window he could see the owner sitting idly at the till, gazing out at the street. A young tree, planted by the Tidy Towns Committee outside his front gate, jerked at its stake under the onslaught. He shivered. This is an awful country, he repeated to himself like a mantra, opening the press beside the fireplace and taking out the whiskey bottle and a tumbler. Not only was this an awful country but this godforsaken village in the back end of nowhere was its apotheosis.

For one glorious year Father Morahan had lived differently.

In 1970, on sabbatical, he had filled in for a pastor in a wealthy suburb of San Diego, California. Sunshine, glorious sunshine, easy work, invitations to swim at the pools of rich parishioners; no endless rounds of raffles, bingo or mediating in disputes between teachers and parents about who was running the school, no memberships on delegations to the local public representatives seeking money to fund a community centre. No leaking church roofs. No pretending to like limp ham salads and seedy cake in the local convent parlour. No need to hide in the clerical undergrowth if you were having a drink outside your presbytery.

No scandal if you were seen walking down the street in conversation with a woman.

He took the first sip of his whiskey. A draught created by the open door swirled down the chimney and blew on to the floor a blurry snapshot of himself and a parishioner which had been propped against a toby jug on the mantelpiece. He looked at the snapshot with disgust. How he longed right now for the sun on his bare back and the feeling of indolence which spread through his body after a swim in a clear blue pool.

Even his obsession with Molly Ní Bhriain had lost some of its urgency during that year.

But then he had had to come home. An awful bloody country.

He retrieved the picture from the hearthrug and replaced it on the mantelpiece, then carrying his drink, he went into the kitchen. It was even colder in here – cold in temperature with the draughts curling under the badly fitting back door, colder in ambience. Not a cup was out of place and the tiled walls gleamed in the wintry light from the back garden. There was a note on the spotless draining board from Mrs Conway. She had gone to visit her mother in Galway and would be back in time to make him his tea.

He stood there for a moment indecisive, staring out through the window at the sodden grass, forgetting why he had come into the kitchen in the first place. Then he went into the little dining room which adjoined the kitchen and was his personal bolthole. At least it was warmer in here although the fire had burned low. He threw a log into the grate raising a shower of sparks and turned on the television. There was racing on the first channel and when he pressed the button for the second the air was filled with the sound of ricocheting bullets. He recognized Gene Autry and stood watching for a moment, tuning in to the action. Then he sat into his fireside chair and took the second sip of whiskey.

He realized after five minutes or so, when his tumbler was almost empty, that he had already seen this film – or if not this one, another very like it – and his concentration wavered. The decision he had been putting off for days tugged at his brain. It had been half made already the day after she had returned to London following her mother's funeral. It had been three-quarters made the day he travelled the twenty-odd miles to the public library in Galway to find the two addresses – of the Federal Aviation Authority in Washington and of Lloyds of London. He had not wanted to risk awkward questions from the local librarian. 'And what would you be wanting those for now, Father?'

All it needed now was the final push. A bit of action. He would have to stop messing and just do it; it was eating away at him, this knowledge about Molly without knowing exactly who she was. It had to be easy. There could have been only so many babies lost at sea in the Atlantic at the end of April or the beginning of May 1953. What he was going to do with the knowledge after he acquired it was another story. Cross that bridge when he came to it . . .

No point in waiting any longer: today was the day. Mrs Conway safely out of the house. Nothing on until confessions after tea.

A small, cluttered bureau stood beside his chair. Its leaded glass front was jammed shut against a chaotic pile of books and papers, but the desk part stood permanently open. It was territory forbidden to Peg Conway and her polish. So was the bottom part of the bureau, which was always locked and to which only he had a key. In there were his most personal possessions, photographs of his mother and from his childhood, books which had belonged to his father, a missal given to him by his Jesuit spiritual adviser when he had been ordained, a tin box containing the medals, now rusted, he had won for hurling in his youth and another one which contained his father's old IRA medal.

In there was also a shoe box in which he had placed over the years all the clippings and reviews of Molly Ní Bhriain's work that he could find. He had been careful, always clipping the material when he was alone, usually late at night, and when he had done so always burning the remainder of the page. In summer when there was no fire he had had to stand over the grate while it burned before raking the ashes through the bars.

He unlocked the bureau and reflexively checked to see that the box was still there. There was a surprising amount of material in it – hardly a month went by but there was something about her in the chauvinistic Irish newspapers, whether in the gossip columns, features or arts pages. The box was now more than half full.

On the writing surface of the desk was a pewter tankard, pitted with age and stuffed with old bills, rubber bands, pencils without points, pages torn out of the *Sacred Heart Messenger* in the margins of which were pencilled notes and telephone numbers. He put his drink down and picked up the tankard, shaking it around until he spotted the addresses he wanted, handwritten on a crumpled page torn out of a pocket diary. He smoothed out the page and placed it carefully to one side. Then, replacing the tankard, he took up his whiskey glass again tipping the dregs into his mouth. The whiskey stung his lips which, as always in winter, were chapped and sore. He knew he was drinking too much but did not care. More and more these days he was finding he did not care all that much about anything to do with himself.

He looked across at the television. Gene Autry was still shooting it out with the bad guys.

Father Morahan took a pen and a writing pad from another part of the desk and turned his chair round to face it. The chair was too low for the level of the writing surface and his back was uncomfortably strained. But this was how he always wrote letters and he was too old to change now.

Christian Smith stared at the scarred surface of his editor-in-chief's desk. The man was too thin. It was common knowledge that he suffered from a duodenal ulcer.

The editor was meticulously tidy, Christian saw. Although technology had caught up with the *Sentinel*, he kept a supply of yellow pencils, sharpened to razor points, in an old cigar box geometrically parallel to the edge of the desk. The box, his two telephones, his computer terminal and a single manila folder were all that was on the desk at present. The window of the editor's office was open, although it was snowing outside, and Christian could faintly hear the downtown traffic and the screeching of the El as it rounded a corner on the elevated tracks above the Loop.

Although he refused to meet the editor's eyes he was conscious of the man's unwavering stare and that he was picking his teeth with an open paper-clip. He saw, out of the corner of his eye, the movement as the editor threw the paper-clip into a metal waste-basket. Irrelevantly the thought struck Christian that since it had landed noiselessly the basket must be full.

Not wanting to open the conversation, Christian looked out of the window of the small office. The Chicago river, he saw, was partially frozen, the thin film of ice looping along its side walls in dirty opaque arcs. The snow was beginning to lie on it.

'This is the last one, Smith.' The editor dropped the words one by one into the heavy atmosphere of the room. He opened a drawer and flung a piece of card across the desk.

'Is that for me, sir?' Christian was careful to keep his voice neutral.

'Well it's hardly for me!'

Christian picked up the card. Letraseted on it were the words: 'If your mother tells you she loves you – check it!'

Christian knew all too well that for a while he had been living perilously close to his last chance at the *Sentinel*: his portfolio of work for the paper was impressive but his reputation for unreliability was growing. He had been put on notice after the Ethiopia episode of four weeks before but the present carpeting

281

was, in his view, for a relatively minor offence, a tiny error of fact – due to his taking a short-cut – which had led to the newspaper being sued by a State congressman and having to settle immediately to avoid going to court.

'Thank you, sir.' He placed the card face down in front of him.

'I think you get the message?'

'Yes, sir,' said Christian and then something, that treacherous sideways streak in him, broke through the tension and rushed out. He was fed up with being patronized and treated like a schoolchild. He heard his voice almost before he had thought of the words. 'Well, I have a message for you – *sir*!'

He picked up the card again and tore it savagely into little pieces. Some of the Letraset resisted tearing and fluttered off whole on to the editor's spotless desk. Christian stood back then and, pausing just long enough to note with satisfaction that the man's eyes were bulging, he stalked out of the office.

Flushed with exultation, brushing off enquiries from colleagues, he cleared out his desk and scribbled a note for Dick, pinning it on the bulletin board beside the newsdesk. Then he left the building. He went straight to the Shamrock Bar.

Dick joined him later and tried to talk him into apologizing. 'I'm sure he'll take you back, Chris.' But Christian's blood was up. Rationalization had always been easy for him. Anything bad that happened to him could be shown to be someone else's fault and in this case it was the troglodytes in management at the *Sentinel* as personified by the editor. He had never been properly appreciated. He was too talented for such a Neanderthal organ. His resignation stood.

They had a few drinks and Christian went back to Dick's apartment for a few more. He slept overnight on Dick's Murphy bed. He had been initiated into the mysteries of Murphy beds quite soon after he had left home to live downtown. Most of the older apartments had them and Christian's abiding fear was that some night, when he was fast asleep, the contraption would spring back up into its cupboard on the apartment wall of its own volition trapping him inside like a mummy.

Four days later, Cordelia travelled with him to O'Hare to see him off on the flight to London. He was far more comfortable with his grandmother than with Malcolm, not least because her gentle presence acted as a buffer and intermediary in the prickly relationship between himself and his grandfather.

There had been a time, before his parents' deaths, when Christian had been close to Malcolm although he had always been slightly in awe of his grandfather's imposing presence and never totally at ease. But in latter years their individual attitudes had become frozen and Christian had never been able – even if he had had the inclination – fully to bridge the chasm which had opened up between them during his teens.

Their goodbyes had been formal. Christian knew that Malcolm was furious that he had chucked his job and was off on what he considered a damn-fool expedition to try his hand as a freelance in London. But they had not fought openly and Malcolm had limited himself to behaving glacially in his grandson's presence. Christian was relieved to escape. Nonetheless it had occurred to him that this might be the last goodbye and he found he had been surprisingly emotional.

Malcolm was seventy-four now, as old as the century, and although to Christian he had always been indestructible and still was, it was a shock to see his hands so gnarled and liver-spotted as they shook hands on the front steps of Greentrees.

'Grandma, I'm sorry,' he said simply as the Lincoln crawled along through the sleety rush hour on the Kennedy Expressway towards O'Hare.

'I know, Christian,' said Cordelia. 'But it's all right, honey. We all have one life to live and you have got to live yours the way you see fit.'

The Lincoln came to a complete halt. 'There must be an accident up ahead, ma'am,' said the chauffeur over his shoulder. Sure enough, within minutes the emergency vehicles, red lights flashing, screamed by on the hard shoulder.

'Have you heard from Jo-Ann at all?' Cordelia asked, wiping away the condensation on one of the side windows of the automobile.

'No, Grandma. I hear from Dick she might get married again.'

'That's good. I always liked Jo-Ann. I was sorry when you divorced.'

It was on the tip of Christian's tongue to present, as usual, his side of the story but he held it and contented himself with a non-committal 'Ummm.'

They were crawling on again. 'Tell me again what your plans are, Christian,' said Cordelia.

Christian did not actually have anything concrete in mind; his portfolio reposed in the trunk of the automobile with the rest of his luggage. He had done his research – Britain was in the throes of recession and although he had faith in his own ability to get work he had no idea how much the general belt-tightening would have affected the newspaper world. He did hope, not without justification, that his experience of disaster reporting, for which there was never a lack of news appetite, and his being American at this time in history would be a help. The world was still fascinated by the soap opera surrounding the Watergate scandal – President Nixon was on the run – and he had good contacts among the Democrats.

'I have no immediate plans, Grandma,' he said truthfully. But then, for her sake, he embroidered, 'I have been offered several opportunities. I'm going to take my time. I need a break anyway. And . . . ' He hesitated, but plunged on. 'I've met a girl in London, Grandma.'

'Oh, yes?'

'I've only met her twice, would you believe, but we've talked a lot on the telephone. I'm crazy about her, Grandma.'

'What's her name?'

'Margo Bryan. Well, actually, her real name is Molly but she's an actress, a very good one, Grandma, and Margo is her stage name. She's Irish.'

'Have you a photograph?'

'No, I'm afraid not. But Grandma I know you'd *adore* her.'

'How does she feel about you, Christian?'

'I – I'm not quite sure. She certainly hasn't turned me down, or anything like that. She's very upset at the moment because her mother has just died. Grandma, I've already asked her to marry me.'

'On two meetings and a couple of telephone calls?'

'I knew as soon as I saw her that it would be the right thing. I've never been more sure of anything in my life.'

'I remember you said the same about Jo-Ann, Christian.'

'I know, Grandma, I know.' He deserved that. He knew his grandmother did not mean to rebuke him – it was not in her nature – but he was deflated.

Cordelia patted his hand. 'Christian, I wouldn't dream of interfering. I just want you to be a little cautious this time so you won't get hurt. But I do remember, believe me, I *do* remember what it is like when you fall in love instantly, like summer lightning. It was that way for me and your grandfather. So I am sympathetic. Just take your time, won't you?'

'Of course I will, Grandma.' He kissed her on the cheek. But he had no intention of following her advice.

'One more thing,' she opened her purse. 'This is for you, but it's just between you and me, Christian, not for anyone else's ears or eyes, OK?'

Christian unfolded the cheque. He gasped. 'Grandma!' The cheque was for ten thousand dollars.

'It's from my own funds,' said Cordelia calmly, 'and nothing to do with Malcolm or the family. Remember, the brewery was left to me.' It was something which had never seemed to matter; Malcolm had dedicated his life so completely to the brewery that no one in the family ever thought about it as Cordelia's.

'Grandma – I can't take this!'

'Why not?' She was serene as always.

'Well— ' He was overwhelmed. 'I just can't, that's all!'

'You'll be getting all of it anyway when Malcolm and I pass on so what's the difference getting a little of it now? I have a feeling you'll need it.'

He was still holding the cheque when finally they pulled up at the international terminal. She would not come inside with him. 'We'll say our goodbyes here, my dear. I hate goodbyes. Have a pleasant trip and, Christian, please call us when you arrive to give us your address. I know you don't think so but your grandfather worries terribly about you.'

'I know he does, Grandma.'

'And so do I, my dear. Take care now – and let us know what happens between you and your girl!'

'I will and, Grandma—' She was getting back into the Lincoln and Christian noticed that although she was still elegant she had grown very thin. He wanted to say to her that he loved her – and Malcolm too. But when she turned around expectantly he could not say it.

'Thanks,' he said instead.

He had treated himself to one last business-class flight. For once he did not sleep. Nor did he order a drink. All through the long flight he sipped Perrier and orange juice. Since the morning he had woken up on Dick's Murphy bed and decided to go to London he had a feeling that he was embarked on an adventure that was given to him on extra time, one last chance that he must not screw up.

He watched the flickering images of *A Touch of Class*. All around him people chuckled appreciatively into their headsets but Christian, lost in plans and dreams, did not pay attention to the film. After a while he took off his own headset. The engine note was steady and he was aware of the soft whoosh of the pressurized air system streaming cold air from the circular vent above his head. He closed his eyes but his brain, fed by adrenalin, would not let him sleep.

When there were only two hours to go before landing he did doze a little but snapped awake when the captain came on the PA to say good morning. The cabin staff were already coming through the cabin with trolleys laden with orange juice, coffee and breakfast rolls. The captain went on to say that because of strong tailwinds they were a good fifty minutes ahead of schedule, were therefore just over an hour out of London and were at present about sixty miles off the northwest coast of Ireland.

Christian had flown this route on countless occasions but he never crossed this part of it without acknowledging that somewhere in the sea thirty thousand feet below lay his mother, father and baby sister. He strained to catch the first sight of land. Should Molly agree to marry him – and he accepted it was a very, very big 'if' – the appropriateness of it struck him. It was as if fate, having devastated him in this part of the globe by removing those he loved, might now be willing to make amends by offering compensation.

There was no cloud of any consequence and the Irish coastline floated into view, a clear, jagged grey line, fringed with white all along its length as the ocean broke over it. They were flying so high that it was impossible to pick out individual landmarks but he thought he could see several islands, seven or eight, strung along the coast. One of them was undoubtedly Inisheer.

He sipped the orange juice, grimacing at its acidity. A memory of his mother, bright as a jewel, caught him unawares. He had run in from school into the morning room. His mom was leaning over the bassinet and picking up the baby who was about three months old. She had turned and smiled at him and then, sitting in his grandfather's wing chair, had taken him on her knee and given him the baby to hold. They had sat there, the three of them, he safe in her warm arms while the sunshine from the lake bathed them through the open door. The baby had sat still, examining his face with wide serious eyes full of surprise. He had been able to smell her, a clean, summery smell.

Carefully he put the juice beaker on the table in front of him. He turned his face fully to the window and stared hard at Ireland through the ragged wisps of white cloud until he had his face under control.

It was the middle of March when Molly agreed to marry Christian Smith.

She had been seesawing between depression and normality since her mother's death. *Blithe Spirit* had finished its run, heightening her sense of emptiness, and even the news that she had been nominated for a Keane Award for her performance in the show had lifted her spirits only temporarily.

She had accepted the formal expressions of sympathy from her friends about her mother's death but had no one in whom to confide. Shortly after she came back from Inisheer Conor, to whom she might naturally have turned for comfort, took leave of absence from his job at the Zoo and went

287

to Israel on a dig in connection with his night course in archaeology.

As soon as Christian had heard about her mother, he had stopped pressurizing her into romance but simply seemed always to be available with a willing, ready ear. In any event when he returned to London he was busy with his own career, hustling work, of which there was no shortage at present since the grand jury in Washington had announced that Nixon had been involved in Watergate. Christian, having made himself an expert on this, was much in demand not only for newspaper work but as an interviewee on radio current affairs programmes.

He had ceased making extravagant gestures too, contenting himself with bringing her flowers. Molly felt very comfortable with him and fell into agreement to marry as if he had been proposing a gentle walk along the Thames. It happened after a dinner at La Vecchia Rizzione in St Martin's Lane, a restaurant Molly loved.

The dinner was delightful. The restaurant was packed as it always was, the decibel level cheerfully high as the diners competed with the ambient noise. The waiters bustled up and down the long room, speaking to one another in loud Italian, singing along with the operatic and Neapolitan background music, dancing with the female customers and sometimes each other, dousing the lights for effect at a strategic point of the evening so that the fairylit giant mural which stretched the length of the restaurant on one wall could be seen to good effect.

Although she was in relatively good spirits Molly was feeling particularly vulnerable, being about to start work on her first film. Shooting was to start the next day but Molly was not required on location in Glasgow until the following Monday. Although it was low-budget, with a shooting schedule of only eight weeks, it was prestigious, cast with real stars; it had been an honour to have been asked to test for the part, a triumph when she got it. She was to play opposite Eugene Lothar, a handsome veteran, who had been voted Sexiest Man in Britain in a *News of the World* poll.

But as her film début drew nearer, the insecurities common to all actors became rife. She was excited about the film but terrified. She would not be equal to it. It was an illusion that people thought she could act. Everything else she had done and been praised for was a fluke. She was a one-role actress. She was too tall, too gawky. All the others on the film were more experienced than she was.

So when Christian showed up to take her out to dinner she had been delighted at the distraction.

She looked affectionately at him as he gave the order. The candlelight sculpted hollows in the fine bone structure of his face and, as usual she noted with amusement, the cowlick stood sentinel on the crown of his head. He looked so *American*. She wondered then if she loved him. She was certainly very fond of him. 'Christian?' she said as he pored over the menu.

'Yes, honey?' He looked up eagerly.

'Oh, nothing,' she said. She broke a piece off a bread stick and smiled at him.

They drank very little but very well – a fino each to start and, although it was an Italian restaurant, a really good Rioja Grand Cru with the meal. They compensated the waiter's injured national pride by having two sambucas afterwards. Christian was mellow, not talking much, allowing the conversation to take its own pace. By the time they were ready to go Molly was feeling better and looser than she had in weeks.

They went back to her house for a nightcap. She lit table lamps, drew the curtains and put Mozart to play on her stereo and the little house drew closely in around the two of them while they sipped drinks and chatted, their voices low in response to the tranquillity.

At about three in the morning she went out into the kitchen to open another bottle of wine. When she got back into the sitting room Christian did not raise his head. He was staring into the flames of the gas fire which flickered hypnotically in the converted fireplace.

'Come here, honey . . . ' he said and without turning round he held out his arms and she went towards him. He was sitting in a small easy chair so she sank to the ground in front of him between him and the fire, leaning her body against his knees. He opened his legs so she could prop herself comfortably against the seat of the chair, then, leaning forward, he wrapped his arms gently round her and cradled his cheek on her hair. 'Molly, we have to get married . . . ' he said softly. 'I can't live any more without you in my sight all the time.'

She gave in then. It was so easy, so peaceful. And she needed someone too, someone who would be on her side.

They stayed up all night, making plans. There was no sense of elation at first, just a quiet happiness between them in the spirit of the evening they had just spent. Christian held her hand tightly and told her that he was afraid that if he made a lot of noise now, she, the house, the evening, the future might all vanish in a puff of smoke. But as Molly's little clock chimed on into the early morning, he hugged her over and over again and kissed her, gently and fiercely, turn and turn about, until the kisses numbered in the thousands.

'Why don't we go to bed, Molly?' he whispered into her hair at about four in the morning.

She disentangled herself. 'Christian, there's no hurry—'

'But I want you so much. I love you – we're engaged. Why wait? What difference does it make now?'

Molly didn't know what difference it made but she couldn't do it. Not yet.

'Is it the Catholic thing?' he asked softly. He was stroking her hair, very gently, reassuring her.

'I can't explain it,' she said. 'If you love me you'll just have to trust me.'

He held her away from him a little. 'Is it that I'm not attractive enough?' he asked anxiously.

She smiled and shook her head feeling tender and protective, more like his mother or his big sister, she realized, than his brand new fiancée. She hugged his knees and leaned her head on his lap. 'Oh, no, Christian, you're probably the most attractive man I've ever seen.'

He hugged her back. 'If that's the case how can you resist me?'

'Difficult, I know – but then I've had lots of practice.'

'Well, all right,' he said with mock grumpiness. 'But just you wait! You'd better prepare yourself well for our wedding night. No quarter given then.'

Bingo! Una pounced on the wire copy. Margo Bryan, Irish actress, formerly of the Abbey Theatre, had been nominated for a Keane. Una knew enough to know that this award was the West End equivalent of a Broadway Tony and as far as she knew no Irish actor had been nominated before. This was news.

She brought the paragraph over to the news-editor. 'Have you seen this, Myles?'

He scanned it. 'This the one you interviewed before?'

'Yes. She's really good. She might even win. And I think there's probably a good background story there – if I can get it.' On tenterhooks she watched him consider.

'Could you do it on the telephone?'

Lying on top of his in tray Una saw the latest circular from management on cutting back on travel costs and expenses. 'I'll make you a deal,' she said swiftly, 'I want to go to London anyway for something personal. If you pay the fare, I'll pay everything else. Even taxis.' She saw him hesitate. 'I have a contact in a travel agency – I'll go Apex.'

'Apex will take fourteen days . . .'

'I told you I have a contact in a travel agency.'

The news-editor shook his head priggishly. 'The *Irish Record* does things legally.'

'No one'll know. It'll be our secret.'

'This something personal must be some guy!'

'He is.'

The news-editor pursed his lips. 'OK, you owe me one. It'd better be good!'

'It will,' promised Una.

She walked back to her own desk, took out her contacts book and dialled Margo Bryan's home number. There was no reply. She looked at her watch – she would get her in two hours' time at the theatre.

She was marked that afternoon to cover a news conference about a new industrial initiative in the fledgeling Irish electronics

291

industry. Una, who firmly believed that the only efficient mode of transport around Dublin was on two wheels, was parking her bike at the city centre hotel where the conference was being held five minutes before it was to start.

She signed in, accepted a glass of plonk and a press pack and scanned the room. They were all there, all the usual suspects, the obtrusive television presence of RTE, the Irish state broadcasting service, the suits from the 'quality' press and business magazines, newsdesk hacks like herself who could be marked on anything from a funeral to a bank raid, a few live wires who, she knew, would try to excite a bit of controversy.

'Hi, Una! What's new?' Mark Trimble bounced across to her. At one time she had thought Mark attractive and gone out with him a few times. But every man she met now paled into insignificance when set against the unattainable Sean Molloy. It was difficult for Una to believe that she had a crush on a man she had met for ten minutes. The last time it had happened to her was when she was eleven years of age.

Una prided herself on her practicality and this obsession made no sense. In one way she hoped that he would prove genuinely to be unattainable; then she could put herself out of her misery and work on something else. It was the not knowing that was killing her.

'Hi, Mark!' she said without enthusiasm and continued to scan the gobbledegook and bar-charts in the press pack. He was unabashed and opened his own documentation. Mark was rarely still. He bounced and jigged now while he was reading, as if he might fall over if he stayed still. The habit had driven Una bonkers while they had been going out together.

The conference started but Una could not muster interest. For once, she decided, she would stop being a perfectionist and simply take the press release at face value. But for the sake of quotes in her copy she went up to the podium after the formal conference had ended and asked for an interview with one of the Japanese who were opening the factory and with the Chamber of Commerce representative from the rural town in which the factory was to be located. She dispatched both of them in five minutes.

She all but ran to her bicycle to get back into the office and was already dialling the Wyndham's Theatre number with one hand while pulling out the chair at her desk with the other.

'Oh, no,' said the doorman when she asked for Margo Bryan. 'That run's finished, my dear. Got a musical in here now.' Una hung up and dialled Margo's home number again. She was lucky. This time Margo answered on the third ring.

'Hello,' she said, 'this is Una O'Connor.'

'Oh, hello, Miss O'Connor – Una. I'm sorry, I meant to write to you after Mam's funeral to thank you for coming so far. It was very good of you. I just didn't get around to it yet.'

'Please don't thank me, it was no trouble. I'm sure you're still very upset.'

'Well, life goes on, especially life in the theatre.'

She certainly did not sound depressed, thought Una. 'I believe congratulations are in order,' she said. 'You've been nominated for a Keane?'

Molly laughed. 'News travels fast! Yes, I believe I have.'

'That's wonderful and no one deserves it more.'

'Well, thank you.'

'Which brings me,' Una took a deep breath, 'to my reason for telephoning you. The newspaper, in the person of myself, would like to do a feature on you.'

'*Another* one?'

'Well, if you remember, the last one was cut way back to quite a small article because of pressure of space in the news pages that day. I – we – would like to give you one with more prominence in the features pages.'

There was a pause and Una held her breath.

'When would you want to do this?'

'Within the next couple of weeks, if it suits you.'

'Well, it would have to be sooner than that. This is Saturday and I'm leaving on Monday to start work on a film.'

'Better and better,' said Una.

'Could we do the interview on the telephone?'

Damn, thought Una. The woman was learning. 'Well, no,' she said persuasively, 'that would be really very difficult for me. I don't work well on the telephone. I think it would be far better for both of us face to face.'

'Well, all right,' said Molly slowly. 'I suppose we'd better leave it until I come back from the film, then.'

'How about tomorrow?'

'Tomorrow's Sunday. My fiancé is taking me to Oxford for the day.'

Fiancé? Shit!

'Who's the lucky man?' To her horror, Una heard her own voice actually squeak.

'He's an American. Actually, he's a journalist. From Chicago.'

All Una heard was the word American. She felt like throwing the telephone receiver up in the air and jumping up after it.

'Well, double congratulations! That's wonderful!' But she could not persuade the actress to give up her day off – or even to come home from Oxford early – but in the light of the great news was perfectly happy to leave the interview until Margo had fulfilled her film commitments.

'We'll have more to talk about anyway, then,' she said, 'and it will be nearer the time for the actual awards. It'll all work out for the best. Good luck on the film and again, double congratulations! I'll telephone you when you come back in three weeks' time and we'll set it up.' She slammed the receiver down on its cradle and the copy boy was treated to the sight of Una O'Connor throwing her arms around the news-editor.

'What's that for?' he said irritably, straightening out the copy she had crushed.

'I won't be doing that interview with Margo Bryan until three weeks' time.'

'That's good news?'

'That's very good news!'

'What about the personal business in London – the contact in the travel agent, the Apex? It all seemed bloody urgent an hour ago.'

'That was before!' said Una. 'It'll keep for three weeks!'

Three weeks wasn't long. She felt instinctively that if she could get to him on his own, she'd have a good chance. Una hammered out her copy on the industrial initiative as though she were Michelangelo who had hit a good streak while painting the Sistine Chapel.

She read over her copy but stopped abruptly before she got to the end. It had never occurred to her that Sean Molloy might have a girlfriend.

Four weeks later, Molly got out of bed at eleven o'clock on a Saturday morning. She knew that Conor had been home for three days yet she had not yet had the courage to telephone him. He had to be told about her engagement. She knew instinctively that Conor would be horrified and did not want to expose her fragile sense of equilibrium, so recently acquired, to the icy blasts of his disapproval. She did not want her soft new happiness put under a microscope.

While she had been away filming – a process she found she took to like a duck to water – she had had an excuse not to be in touch. But there was no putting it off any longer. The time was now.

Still in her nightdress she went downstairs and straight to the telephone in the hallway. But when she was half-way through dialling she replaced the receiver.

Furious with herself she went into the kitchen and slammed around, making coffee, squeezing oranges. Knowing it was irrational she transferred the fury to Conor. How dare he make her afraid of him? What business was it of his?

She marched back out into the hall and, before she could change her mind, dialled the number, the full number.

He answered on the second ring, sounding sleepy.

'Hello, Conor,' she barked. 'Still in bed?'

'Whoa,' he said. 'What's up with you? What happened to "Welcome home, Conor", "How did the work go, Conor?", "I've missed you, Conor!"?'

She kept her spine stiff. 'I'm ringing to invite you to lunch.'

'I've had nicer invitations!'

'Well, would you like lunch or not?'

'Yes, *sir*! How could a man refuse?'

'How about in one hour's time at Kettner's!'

'Kettner's is too expensive.'

'All right, a hamburger, then.'

'Come off it!'

'Well, where then? *I* like Kettner's. And in case you're still worried about the expense, I'm paying.'

'Whoa again!' His own voice, which had been good-humoured, changed. 'First of all, women don't pay for me for lunch in expensive restaurants. Second, I don't think I want to go to lunch with you at all in your present mood.'

She knew he was right. 'I'm a bit on edge, Conor—'

'*I'll* say!'

'Well, I'm sorry. But I really would like you to come to lunch.'

'There's nowhere to park near Kettner's...' Conor had recently purchased a battered Morris Traveller and was as proud and as careful of it as if it were a Rolls-Royce.

'It's Saturday, Conor. It'll be OK.'

'An hour is too soon. Make it an hour and a half.'

'OK. See you then!'

She replaced the receiver and realized she was shaking. What was she going to do?

She had a bath and dressed, a process which took three times longer than normal. All the while telling herself she was being ridiculous, she put on and discarded six different outfits. At the end of fifteen minutes her bed resembled a stall in a jumble sale. Eventually she settled on a dress of pale blue silk with Fortuny pleating on the sleeves.

She arrived at the restaurant early. Kettner's had a brown, comfortable glow and one of the reasons she liked it was that, compared to other fashionable places, the waiters did not harry or hurry the clients even when the restaurant was busy. As this was Saturday – an anniversary of her first lunch with Christian, she thought – there was plenty of space.

She was seated at a table in the bar area when Conor loomed through the door, dressed to match his Morris Traveller in old, sagging tweeds. He looked tanned and fit and his hair was shaggy. No one would have taken him for a humble zoo attendant, she thought fondly, temporarily forgetting her nerves

296

and waving to attract his attention. He spotted her immediately and came towards her.

He stood off a little in mock fear. 'Is it all right to kiss you, *mein Führer*?'

'Don't be silly, Conor! I'm sorry about earlier.'

'Well, let's start all over again,' he said, kissing her on the cheek and lowering himself into a chair beside her. 'Hello! How are you today?' He eyed her up and down. 'My! Don't we look smart!'

Even she had had to admit when she looked in the mirror before she left the house that she looked very well. 'Oh, this old thing!' she said and laughed. The laugh cracked. 'Would you like a drink?' she asked.

'Let's get this straight,' he said, taking off his coat. 'I hate this. Drinks cost a fortune in this place—'

'No more than anywhere else in central London,' she protested. 'But you're my guest and don't insult me.'

'I'm sorry, Molly,' he said, 'but this is way out of my league.'

'It's in my league now that I'm going to be a famous film star. So shut up, Conor, and just have a bloody drink.'

'I hate this,' he repeated.

'I know. But think, when you're a famous archaeologist, you can invite me to your digs in the desert and then you can be host and feed me ass's milk or whatever.'

'It's unlikely I'll even pass my exams at the rate I'm going now.'

She attracted the attention of one of the waiters and ordered a Bellini for herself. 'And what'll you have, Conor?'

He fixed the waiter with a steely eye. 'A glass of plain tap water, please!'

'Really, Conor,' she said after the waiter had gone. 'That was a bit unnecessary.'

He ignored the rebuke and settled into his chair. 'So, what have you been doing with yourself lately? Tell me about the film.'

'All in good time.'

She knew she should spit it out and get it over with. But she couldn't. She had not even had the guts to wear the ring. It was in a zippered pocket inside her handbag.

He sighed. 'Such suspense. Always the Sarah Bernhardt.'

When the drinks came they talked about his work, his real work, which was archaeology now as opposed to his work at the zoo which he regarded merely as employment. A lot of work was going on in Africa, he told her, where various expeditions in Tanzania, Kenya and Ethiopia were pushing back the frontiers of man's birth on this planet.

'You probably heard about the Leakeys, Molly, they're doing wonderful work but there's another expedition working in Ethiopia, led by a man called Johanson. Rumours are floating around that he has found a full skeleton of a woman which might prove that man, as we know the species now, could be two million years older than we thought it was . . .'

They were called to their table and ordered lunch. Conor continued to talk about his new vocation and tried to explain why it was so exciting. He peppered his conversation with technical jargon Molly did not understand. She realized she had not seen him so animated for years but all the time the flow of talk passed round the great dam of what she had to tell him.

She half listened, half rehearsed what she was going to say while nodding at suitable junctures and asking what she hoped were reasonably intelligent questions. The more work and study he had to do the better Conor liked it, it seemed. He told her that he had been up until four-thirty that morning completing a paper – hence the sleepy voice on the telephone.

After the food arrived Molly found it difficult to eat and pushed her salad around on her plate. She had to tell him – and soon. But now there seemed no natural opening in Conor's flow of enthusiasm. Maybe she had been making mountains out of molehills and her news would not be a problem after all.

Oh, by the way, I'm engaged . . .

She watched him digging into his steak thinking that it was one thing her brother had in common with her fiancé. Conor always ordered steaks in restaurants. If there was no steak he ordered chops. If there were no chops he grudgingly ordered fish. Plain fish. He had it all planned, he was telling her now. As soon as he could earn his living as a professional in the field he would give up his job and would offer his services as a researcher to one of the established digs.

'Of course, I'll have to do a post-graduate course before I'm accepted in the real world of archaeology. I've already decided what it's going to be on – I won't tell you, it'd take me ten minutes to explain it – but I will be able to go on real digs. Imagine, Molly! I might be the one to fill a gap in what we know about our ancestors. I might be the one to find a new type of axehead used by *Homo Habilis* or even *Australopithecus africanus*!'

'Imagine!' Molly said drily.

'Sorry.' He grinned.

He mopped up the gravy on his plate with his last piece of steak and put it in his mouth, placing his knife and fork carefully together on the plate and sitting back. 'Now it's your turn. How was the film?'

'It was really exciting.'

'That's all you've got to say about it?' He mimicked her. ' "It was really *exciting*!" '

'Well, it was.'

'Well, come on. Tell. What about this fellow Eugene Lothar? What was he like?'

No more procrastinating. Molly took a deep breath. 'I've something to show you . . . ' She reached under the table for her handbag and found the ring, slipping it on her finger before bringing her hand up to show him. He did not say anything. The chatter and clatter all around seemed to rise in volume.

'Who's the lucky man?' he asked flatly.

'It's Christian Smith, the American journalist you met in my dressing room the night he and his photographer came around. Do you remember?'

'That phoney!' She saw he was genuinely scandalized. She had told him, laughing, about Christian's ruse and the spuriousness of the award.

'Please, Conor, he's not a phoney.'

'I see,' he said again.

She must not panic. His face was like granite.

'When did this happen?'

'Four weeks ago. What does it matter when?'

'I don't suppose it does really. What's the attraction? Is he rich?'

'That, Conor, is none of your business.' She tried to hold on to her temper. 'I think, brother dear, that you might, for instance, say congratulations or wish me a happy life or whatever is customary on these occasions.'

They glared at one another. He was the one to give in. 'You're absolutely right,' he said quietly. 'I'm sorry. I do wish you a very happy life, Molly, I really do.'

To her annoyance, she found that she had her left hand covered with her right, hiding the ring. She uncovered it and laid the hand square in front of her beside her plate, still full of salad. 'I was hoping you'd come to Chicago and give me away at my wedding,' she said.

'I can't afford to go to Chicago.'

'Your fare would be a built-in part of the wedding expenses.'

'Oh! And I suppose *he*'d pay.' He was getting angry again.

'*His* name is Christian.'

There was another stand-off. She reached down under the table to pick up her handbag. She put it on the table and took out a handkerchief.

'Don't tell me you're going to *cry*!'

She scrubbed at a non-existent spot on the sleeve of her dress. 'No, I'm not going to cry. I'm not the crying type. I have no reason to cry. I'm not the one who is being irrational.'

'Have you told Brendan?'

'What has Brendan to do with it?' she asked, astonished.

'He's your brother. The head of the family.'

'Come off it, Conor!'

He picked up his knife and began to chase a piece of mange-tout around the plate. Molly knew Conor hated any vegetable that came only in French.

'*You*'re my brother,' she said softly.

He continued to push the mange-tout around. 'I think you're

making a mistake,' he said. 'But clearly anything I think or say will have no effect.'

'I'm afraid not. We're getting married in Evanston, in Christian's house, on the second of May. And I hope you'll be there.'

'That's only a couple of weeks away. I have my exams coming up less than a month later,' he said slowly. 'Even if I wanted to, I couldn't possibly take time off to go to America.' He placed his knife and fork carefully together again. 'And I don't want to. That's final. Now let's talk about other things.'

In a way she was relieved at his decisiveness. Not having him around the place during the wedding would mean one less thing to worry about.

They ordered coffee and Molly tried to keep the tone of the conversation light. She told him about the movie and when he seemed to be paying no attention, slipped in the news about the award. 'Oh, by the way, there are more congratulations in order! I've been nominated for a Keane Award.'

'Is that a big one?'

'One of the biggest in the West End.'

He was genuinely delighted. 'That's brilliant, Molly!' He seized her hand across the table and then dropped it. She realized he had felt the ring. 'I've only been nominated mind,' she said. 'There are a few other contenders. Heavyweights. But it's a real honour.'

'I'm so proud of you, Molly.'

She saw by his face that this was not what he meant.

'Bill, please, waiter!' she called and took her credit cards out of her handbag. She made great play of selecting the correct one.

'Would you give me a lift to the Cumberland, please?' she asked then. 'I've to do an interview.' She did not tell him that she was meeting Christian there, that Una O'Connor had persuaded her to bring Christian along to be interviewed too. 'You can just drop me outside. OK?'

'Sure.' He shrugged.

They left the restaurant. It was raining and neither had an umbrella so they sprinted to the Traveller, which was parked about fifty yards away. Breathless, they got into the car and

Conor started the engine. Molly was conscious again of his male smell, now overlain with the thick aroma of damp tweed.

He drove as fast as the traffic lights allowed.

When they pulled up outside the Cumberland at Marble Arch Molly spotted Una O'Connor, hurrying along towards the entrance.

'There's the reporter, Una O'Connor,' she exclaimed and jumped out of the car. 'Una! Hello, Una!' she called.

Una heard and turned round. Molly was standing by the door of a car, waving at her. She waved back and walked as far as the car.

'You remember – er – Sean Molloy?' said Molly, indicating the driver of the car.

Una's heart lurched. He was leaning across the steering wheel to say hello to her – at least his lips were moving and she thought that must be what he was saying. She had the confused impression that his hair was longer than she remembered.

'Hello, Mr Molloy,' she answered, mustering every ounce of *sang-froid* in her meagre store. 'What a surprise! How've you been?' she added.

'I've been fine,' he said.

'You've a great tan. Have you been away?' Her smile, she knew, was as cretinous as the remark.

But again he answered courteously. 'I was in Israel actually, on an archaeological dig.' If he was being sarcastic it didn't show.

She became uncomfortably conscious of Molly standing behind her back as she leaned into the car. Damn. She couldn't let this opportunity slip, it might be the only one. Desperate measures. Egalitarianism between sexes and classes was one of the few perks of her profession.

'Would you like to have lunch sometime?' she blurted. She saw him glance at Molly and registered the look for later analysis.

'I'd love to,' he said coolly. 'Here's my telephone number. Next time you're in London, Miss O'Connor?'

'Una, please!' she said faintly.

He fished a pen from his pocket and searched for paper.

Flabbergasted though she was, Una was more aware than ever of the actress standing behind her. 'Sorry,' she said, turning around. 'This'll only take a sec.' Her interviewee was staring off into the middle distance, away from the car.

Una turned back into the Morris just as Sean Molloy found an old playing card under the front seat. He scribbled a number on it and handed it over. 'Looking forward to it,' he said. 'Becoming quite a habit, being taken to lunch. Goodbye, Molly!' he called, leaning further across so he could peer out. 'Thanks for the lunch. Delicious!'

Una did not know what was going on and she did not care. She clutched the precious playing card in her hand and waved as he closed the door. She did not turn round to see if Molly waved or not. 'Well,' she said happily, watching the receding rear end of the Morris Traveller, 'shall we go in?'

The fiancé was in the lobby. There was no mistaking him – he lit up like a Christmas tree when they walked in. He was beautiful and charming and she could see other women in the lobby shooting glances at him. But, she decided as early as ten seconds into the introductions, he was definitely not a man of substance.

She smiled brilliantly at both of them and walked ahead into the coffee shop to do the interview.

303

CHAPTER NINE

A few days later, on 28 April, it was a pet day in Tullyhalla, the sort of day that called a truce in Father Morahan's long war of attrition with the Irish weather. The sun was as kind as summer and warmed the top of his balding head. There was only the gentlest of breezes and it was so quiet in the village that he could actually hear the leaves rustling in all the new trees planted along the street by the County Council and the Tidy Towns Committee. He came out of the church after morning Mass and stood for a few moments enjoying the air, listening dreamily to the whining of Silvie Cash's Honda 50 as, counterpointing the gentleness of the morning, it came up the street in fits and starts. Silvie was the postman, whose beat covered maybe nineteen square miles of isolated cottages in the bogs and scatterings of little villages.

'Hello, Father!' shouted Silvie, as he approached the church. The man's relentless cheeriness usually got on Father Morahan's nerves but today he waved back as the postman swerved into the churchyard, guided his red steed in a half-circle and skidded to a halt in front of him, spraying gravel into the flowerbeds. 'Not supposed to do this, Father,' he said, shouting above the nasal cough of his engine. 'Not supposed to dev-i-ate from the proper route!'

He pronounced deviate the local way, with the emphasis on the 'ate'. 'But sure since 'tis yourself,' he continued, sorting busily through his bag, 'we can make an exception. Isn't it a lovely day, Father, thank God and his Mother? Lovely entirely! Great out!'

He handed three letters to the priest, tipped his cap, revved hugely and shot out of the gate. Father Morahan looked at his letters and his heart jolted, making him feel nauseous. One of the letters bore an American postmark and the logo of the Federal Aviation Authority. He gripped it tightly, thinking that the letter must be blinking like a neon sign, that everyone in the village must have noticed the delivery. His impulse was to tear it open right away but he restrained himself. There was not a soul within thirty yards of him but across the road the grocer was raising the blinds on his shop and carting in the stack of newspapers thrown in his porch by the driver of the Galway bus. The grocer had eyes like a hawk.

The letter seemed to pulsate in his hands as he stood trying to decide whether to go to his house or back into the church. He remembered that it was a Fair Day in the nearby town of Toome and his heart sank. Mrs Conway always wanted to get breakfast over with quickly on a Fair Day so she could be ready when her nephew called to drive her into town. She would know that Mass had been over ten minutes ago.

The envelope burned his hand as he walked the fifty yards to his front door. It would now have to wait until after breakfast. Before he went into the kitchen, he stuffed the letters, all three of them, behind the glass of his bureau in the dining room.

Mrs Conway was sitting on a stool in the corner of the kitchen. He saw she already had her hat on. 'Sorry I'm a bit late, Mrs Conway,' he said with false heartiness. 'Silvie delayed me.'

She sniffed. 'That's all right, Father. It's none of my business, of course.' Peg Conway had been widowed at the age of twenty-seven and had kept house for priests ever since. She had a brother who was a bishop.

Father Morahan attacked the rashers, eggs, sausages and tomato she set before him, wolfing them, dying to get into the letter but afraid to arouse the slightest suspicion by behaving in any way differently from usual. So he ate the fry and two slices of toast spread with butter and home-made marmalade and drank two cups of tea as he did every morning. Then he thanked Mrs Conway and, leaving her to clear the table, went into the little dining room, which he always referred to as his study.

But it was not until he heard the buzz of the nephew's car

305

followed by the bang of the front door as she left that he dared to take the three letters out from behind the glass.

He took a deep breath and opened the letter.

It was signed illegibly, 'pp.' someone called Philip Froelich, and informed Father Morahan that some time between the night of 30 April and 1 May 1953 a DC3 had ditched in the sea somewhere off the coast of Ireland on a flight between Reykjavik and Shannon. The flight, which had originated at Midway Airport in Chicago, had been chartered by a family named Smith, from Evanston, Illinois, and including the crew of three, had been carrying seven persons, six adults and a one-year-old baby girl. No bodies had ever been found although several months after the accident some pieces of wreckage had been washed up along the coasts of the southwest of Ireland. An investigation had concluded that the aircraft had been caught in a bad storm, had gone off course and run out of fuel.

Now he knew.

Yet he knew nothing. Only that her name was Smith and she was from Evanston, Illinois, which he supposed, since the plane had taken off from there, was near Chicago. Her family had chartered an aircraft so they had probably been rich.

Not really knowing quite why he was doing it, Father Morahan took a piece of paper and wrote, 'Smith, Evanston' on it with a shaky hand. He folded the paper and put it in his pocket. He unlocked the bottom of the bureau, took out the shoe box, opened it and carefully folding the letter back into its envelope, inserted it under the pile of clippings, making sure it was completely hidden before he replaced the lid. Then he put the box back where it belonged and relocked the door of the bureau.

He stuffed the other two unopened letters, one which he recognized as a circular from his old school, the other a bill, into the pewter tankard on the desk part of his bureau. He looked at his watch – only nine thirty. He wondered if he dared have a drink so early in the day. He had a funeral Mass but since it was a Fair Day in Toome the Mass was at eleven instead of the usual ten o'clock and he had nothing formal to do until then.

He went into the sitting room, opened the press which contained the whiskey but closed the door again. He had better not. Even if he ate mints the mourners at the funeral were sure to notice the smell on his breath.

He stood looking out at Tullyhalla, at the wide street, the small single-storey and two-storey houses in varying degrees of order, some white, some colourwashed, some derelict, all leaning intimately against each other like the old, comfortable neighbours they were; at the chicken-mesh erected by the County Council around the boles of the sapling trees; at the two shiny new litter bins against the base of which drifted a sea of lollipop wrappers, crisp bags and half squashed soft drink cans. At the far end of the street, a County Council worker was alternately wheeling a pushcart and pushing a brush along the gutter. Directly opposite the house the grocer was using a small paintbrush and a bowl of whitewash to paint the details of special offers on his shop window. Mrs Moran, the woman in the house beside the shop, was cleaning the brasses on her door.

Father Morahan took out the piece of paper from his pocket. 'Smith, Evanston'.

He tried to picture Evanston. He saw it as sunny with good-looking American kids rollerskating on the sidewalks or carrying tennis racquets slung casually over their shoulders. If it was anything like the richer parts of San Diego it would be leafy with wide boulevards and all the houses would be in separate lots with no dividing walls. In the early mornings women would drive husbands in station wagons to the commuter train, manoeuvring past the large cars already parked neatly in the Park 'N Ride lot beside the tracks.

His Molly had been deprived of this sylvan, easy-going way of life and dumped into the wild barrenness of Inisheer. But now that he knew, the knowing was anti-climactic. He needed to know more . . . He looked at the drinks press again but turned decisively away. Like Scarlett O'Hara, he would think seriously about his problem tomorrow.

He went out of the front door of his house, leaving it open after him and crossed the road to the shop where he bought two Cadbury's Flakes for which he had long had a passion, never chewing them but letting the slivers of chocolate melt slowly and deliciously in his mouth. He picked up his daily copies of the *Irish Independent* and the *Irish Record* and, as usual, divided his change among the various charity boxes on the shop counter.

He went back to the house and into the cheerless kitchen where he put on the kettle for a cup of tea, savouring his first Flake as he waited for the water to boil. He made the tea, poured it out and carried it to the table. Then he opened the second Flake and spread out the *Independent*, turning first to the death notices followed by the sports pages.

He was only half-way through the paper when he was interrupted by the telephone. He hurried back into the kitchen, washed up his cup, rinsed out the teapot and refolded the *Independent*, taking it with the *Record* into his study for later perusal.

His pastoral work kept him out all day and it was actually after six o'clock that evening before he got back to reading his newspapers.

It was well past his tea time when he let himself back into his house. Mrs Conway was nowhere to be seen but, as a reproach, a plate of congealed lamb chop and chips sat on the table in the kitchen, symmetrically placed between his knife and fork. Father Morahan had already had a huge funeral meal with the mourners. Feeling guilty, he took the unappetising mess and scraped it into the bin by the back door, put the plate in the sink and then went into his study via the cupboard in the front room from which he poured himself a substantial whiskey.

In the study, whiskey by his side, he opened the *Independent* and tried to concentrate on the news pages. The paper was full of the Beit art robbery. According to the newspaper the paintings were said to be worth £8 million. Eight million pounds, thought Father Morahan enviously. What he could do with that kind of money . . .

After a few minutes he threw the *Independent* aside and picked up the *Irish Record* which was also leading with the art raid. He checked the death notices on the back page, then

308

paged from back to front through the rest of the paper, almost too tired to turn its broadsheet pages.

She was there on page five.

Galvanized out of his torpor, Father Morahan read Una O'Connor's page-long feature with growing horror. The story was unmistakable. Margo Bryan, local girl, successful actress and film star, was due to marry Christian Smith, heir to a brewery fortune in the United States.

Mr Smith has at last found happiness after a lifetime of tragedy. Born with a silver spoon in his mouth, his sheltered life was shattered when his mother, father and baby sister were killed in an air disaster.

Ironically [the piece went on] although she was too young to have been aware of it, the DC3 in which her future husband's family was travelling ditched into the sea within a hundred miles of where Margo Bryan, whose real name as is well known in Ireland, is Molly Ní Bhriain, was born and reared . . .

The rest of the page blurred in front of Father Morahan's eyes.

Molly, his Molly, was about to marry her brother.

The paper rattled as his hands started to shake. He always knew she would get married some day and had tried psychologically to prepare himself for the notion of her in some other man's bed. But even that awful prospect was superseded by the knowledge of this billion to one chance.

He railed at the unfairness of his dilemma. He felt he had to do something to stop this incestuous marriage yet how could he reveal that he knew the truth? He was solemnly bound by the secrecy of the confessional. He had already betrayed that warrant by writing as he had to the FAA and Lloyd's. And to whom should he confess? To Molly? How could he approach *her*? He felt weak and nauseous.

He made it up the stairs to the bathroom just in time to void the half-digested funeral meal. Again and again he vomited violently until he was retching dry and the tears ran freely down his face. Exhausted, he flushed the lavatory and sank to the floor, resting his wet cheek against the smooth coolness of the bowl.

He struggled to his feet after a minute or so, washed his face and went into his bedroom where he sat on his bed and faced the truth. He had been weak all his life; now was the time, whether he liked it or not, when he had to behave with honour and courage, no matter what the personal consequences.

He went back into the bathroom and brushed his teeth to get the sour taste out of his mouth, then went downstairs and picked up the *Record* from where he had dropped it on the floor. He read the piece again. There was no time to lose: the wedding, which was to be at the bridegroom's house, was scheduled apparently for 2 May. That was only three days away. Molly and this fellow – he could not bring himself to think of him as her fiancé or even as her brother – were probably already in America so that removed one option. It was not the type of news he could announce over the telephone and he could hardly arrive at their doorstep. He was relieved. At least he would not have to face her directly.

Since no bodies had been found, would the FAA's accident investigation files on the air crash have remained open? Could he telephone the FAA anonymously, telling them he had certain information about the accident?

But would they act quickly enough? Would they contact Molly before they went through their files? And what possible reason could he give them for wishing to remain anonymous? They would think him a crackpot and dismiss him.

He looked at the article in the *Record* once again. This Una O'Connor – she would surely be interested in the story. And reporters were known to respect anonymous tip-offs and never to reveal their sources.

He quailed at the notion of talking to her but before his imagination could run too far with him he went into the hall and dialled Directory Enquiries, asking for the telephone number of the *Irish Record* in Dublin.

'*Irish Record*.' The call was picked up by a woman.

'Could I speak to Una O'Connor, please?'

'One moment please . . . '

He heard another tone and then, after the telephone had been lifted, a background hubbub – voices, typewriters, machinery. Immediately the sound was muted. Whoever had picked up the extension had covered the mouthpiece. It was a man. He could hear the muffled voice. Father Morahan was now in an agony of impatience. He wanted to get it over with, whatever 'it' was.

At last, the man came on. 'Sorry for holding you, can I help you?'

'May I – may I speak to Una O'Connor, please?'

'Una's on a few days off. Can I take a message?'

'When will she be back?'

Again the background noise was muted as the man obviously made enquiries. He came back on again. 'Not till Wednesday, I believe.'

'It's very important that I get in contact with her. Could you tell me where she is, please?'

'Is this to do with a story?'

'No, it's personal.'

'I'm sorry, we don't give out telephone numbers or details about our staff.'

'But it's a matter of life and death!'

'If you care to leave your name and number,' said the man patiently, 'I'll make sure she gets it if she calls in. *If* she calls in . . . '

'No, that's all right,' said Father Morahan and hung up abruptly. His heart was thumping. He looked stupidly at the silent black instrument which seemed to leer back at him.

He would write anonymously to Una O'Connor and would hand deliver the letter to her office in Dublin. It would be perilously close to the wire; her colleague had said she would not be back at work until Wednesday and Wednesday was the 1st, the day before the wedding. But once she read the letter she would surely see the importance of urgent action. Miss O'Connor would also be morally obliged to do something about the information once it was in her hands. Indeed she would be happy to do so since, no doubt, it would provide her with material.

311

He hurried to his desk and before he could change his mind, pulled his writing pad towards him and took a Biro out of the breast pocket of his black jacket.

He put no return address on the top right-hand corner of the page.

Dear Miss O'Connor [he wrote],

Please forgive my intruding like this, and the haste in which I write, but I feel I must inform you of a matter, arising out of your article in today's newspaper concerning the actress Margo Bryan – Molly Ní Bhriain – and her forthcoming marriage to the American journalist, a Mr Christian Smith.

Before I tell you of my concerns, please do not believe I am a busybody or a gossip and please be assured that I write from the highest moral standpoint.

He reread the second paragraph and realized that it made him sound as if he were indeed a moral snoop. So he tore up the letter and began again.

Dear Miss O'Connor,

I am sorry for bothering you, but I read your article in today's newspaper and I think I have some very urgent information concerning it in which you may be interested.

I have followed Miss Bryan's career with great interest and was at first happy to see from your article that she was going to be married. Unfortunately, I have received knowledge, I cannot reveal how, but believe me, the source for this knowledge is absolutely unimpeachable, that by a million to one chance, Molly Ní Bhriain and the American journalist, Christian Smith, are in fact brother and sister.

I know it sounds absolutely extraordinary, but if you write or telephone the Washington-based Federal Aviation Authority, they will confirm that on the night of 30 April 1953 – the very night you mention in your article – a baby was lost at sea in an aircrash off the coast of Ireland.

Miss O'Connor, that baby was not killed in the crash

312

but survived. She was washed up on Inisheer and was brought up by a poor family there named Ó Briain. I enclose a letter I received from the FAA, confirming the crash, as I had reason to make this investigation myself.

I know that this is very difficult to believe, Miss O'Connor, but for professional, ethical and moral reasons, I cannot reveal how I came by this information in the first place. It was revealed to me on an absolutely confidential basis and I have tortured myself since I received the letter from the FAA as to whether I should break this confidentiality. Were it not for this million to one chance, I would have carried the secret of Molly Ní Bhriain's true identity with me to the grave. But, as I think you will see clearly, I am now taking this serious step only to prevent a greater moral problem and possible disaster for the two young people involved. As God is my judge, Miss O'Connor, I have nothing but their best interests at heart. For the same ethical and moral reasons for which I cannot reveal my source, I cannot myself approach the couple.

I am sure you will appreciate the significance of this information and I hope I can rely on your good sense to see, like I do, that this marriage cannot go ahead.

I took the liberty of telephoning your office and your colleague there informed me that you were not due back from holiday until Wednesday 1 May. But as you can see from your own article, which I also enclose, this marriage is to take place in Evanston, Illinois, on 2 May. As you can see, the matter is one of extreme urgency.

I hope I can also rely on your discretion. And as an intelligent woman, you will possibly understand from the foregoing why I cannot sign my name.

Before he could change his mind, he unlocked the bureau, removed the FAA letter from the shoe box and carefully tearing off the 'Dear Father Morahan' at the top, he folded it inside the letter he had written to Una. He put the two letters in an envelope and addressed it to Una O'Connor, marking it

'By Hand'. Then he stuffed into his jacket pocket the fragments of the first letter and the 'Dear Father Morahan' piece he had torn off the one from the FAA.

There. It was done. He stared at the envelope on the desk. It mocked him. This was too dangerous. If and when she rang the FAA, they would have a copy of the letter to him on the Smith file and he had no guarantee that his cover would not be blown.

He was being despicably cowardly and selfish. How would Molly react to a reporter giving her such news, which wrecked her marriage prospects and exposed her to the possibility of public exposure?

There was only one other option open to him: the advice of the church – venerable as she was, there would surely be a precedent for this situation. He would have to confide in someone in ecclesiastical authority. Not his bishop, who was old and very conservative. That would be too difficult and too galling. He decided to go to see Ned O'Neill.

Father Edward O'Neill, a Jesuit, had been Father Morahan's spiritual adviser in the seminary in Maynooth. Ned, who was now nearly ninety, was tolerant, wise with a bubbling sense of humour. Nothing, or hardly anything, could surprise Ned. He had been confidant and friend to hundreds of young seminarians, many of whom, including Father Morahan, had stayed in touch. Ned would know what to do.

Father Morahan had taken a few steps towards the door into the hallway when he heard the key in the lock of the front door. Mrs Conway! He had temporarily forgotten Mrs Conway.

He dashed back to the bureau and picked up the envelope addressed to Una O'Connor. Panicked, he looked round. There was no fire in the grate. He scooped the clippings out of the box and shoved the envelope under them, replaced them, put the lid back on and threw the box into the bureau. He was locking it when she came into the room.

'Good evening, Father,' she said.

To his horror, he saw as he turned around towards her that one of the clippings had fallen out. 'Hello, Mrs Conway,' he said with phoney cheeriness, straightening up. He took

314

a step towards her so he stood on the clipping. Had she seen it?

She gave no indication that she had. 'I was down the village, Father, visiting Sarah Sheehan. She isn't long for this world.'

'Well, Mrs Conway, she's a great age, God bless her . . . ' A corner of the clipping was sticking out from under his foot.

'Well, I just came in to get my prayer book, Father. I'm going over to the church to do the Stations.'

'Right, right, Mrs Conway.' Still he didn't move. If it had not been so fraught the scene, he thought, might have been from a Marx Brothers comedy. He was even tempted to giggle.

'Will I put down a fire for you, Father?' she said, looking at the empty fireplace. 'It's turning chilly.'

'No, that's all right, Mrs Conway. But would you mind turning on the half six news on the radio?' The radio was in the kitchen.

'It must be nearly over, Father.'

'Well, it's the weather forecast I'm interested in.'

'All right, so!'

Mercifully, she left the room. He bent and picked up the clipping and it too was mushed in with the rest of the paper in his jacket pocket, which, he thought, was beginning to feel like a waste-paper basket. When Mrs Conway came out into the hallway again, clutching her tattered prayer book, he saw her to the door and closed it after her, then went immediately to the telephone. He was in luck. Ned O'Neill was there.

'Pat!' The old priest's voice, still strong, was filled with pleasure.

'Sorry for the short notice, Ned, but can I come to see you this evening?'

'That urgent?' Ned's voice was cheerfully noncommittal. 'Not thinking of leaving at this stage, I hope?'

Father Morahan laughed uneasily. 'No, nothing like that, Ned, but it is very important.'

'Well, whatever it is can it wait for a couple of days?' asked the other man. 'I'm invited to Maynooth tonight – in fact you just caught me, my lift's just arrived – and one of my grand-nephews is bringing me to Cavan tomorrow to do a bit of fishing.'

315

Father Morahan clenched his fist on the telephone table. 'I'm afraid it's a little bit more urgent than that, Ned.' He checked his watch. 'It's only a quarter to seven and there's still an hour or two of daylight. How long will you be in Maynooth? I could be there in less than two and a half hours if you could see me tonight. That's if I wouldn't be intruding on your dinner . . . '

Ned O'Neill's tone had changed subtly yet again. 'I see. Well, Pat, certainly. And you certainly wouldn't be intruding. It'll be just a lot of old fogeys like myself and I'm sure we'll run out of steam long before you arrive. I'm staying overnight in Maynooth tonight anyway and at my age old bones don't need all that much sleep. I'll expect you so . . . I'll leave a message at the front where I can be found. Don't worry, I'll stay up for you so don't kill anyone on the roads in your hurry.'

'I won't, Father,' promised Father Morahan as he hung up. After he replaced the receiver he again felt weak and clutched the edge of the half-moon telephone table to steady himself. He ought to eat something, he thought, since his stomach was now completely empty. Instead, forgetting he already had a whiskey in the study, he went to the drinks press in the sitting room and poured himself another one which he drained in one long draught. The liquor warmed him all through making him feel instantly better.

He poured himself a second, smaller one and took it with him into his study where the television still laughed at itself in the exercise of a quiz show. He turned off the set and, moving decisively now, scribbled a note to Mrs Conway telling her he had been called away urgently overnight but that he would see her around dinner time tomorrow. It was the luck of God, he thought draining his second whiskey, that she was out in the church and he didn't have to face any questions. If he got a move on, he would be well away before she got back . . .

He left the note on the draining board in the kitchen, put in a call to Wynn's Hotel in Dublin where he always stayed when in the capital and took a clean pair of pyjamas and underpants from the hot press beside the Aga. Then he collected his toothbrush, toothpaste and electric razor from the bathroom, his breviary from the bedroom and, rolling the whole lot together, put them in a briefcase he pulled out from under the bed. Before he left he went back into the sitting room and, watching out of the window for Mrs Conway's return, he poured one more whiskey, a small one, just to give him courage.

Luck stayed with him. He had started his car, a three-year-old Ford Escort, when he saw her leaving the church. Pretending not to see her he gunned the engine and shot out of the gate, roaring off up the street in the direction of Loughrea and the main road to Dublin. The roads were relatively clear and he drove fast, concentrating, aware that he had had a couple of drinks. There was a symphony concert on the radio, Beethoven's Pastoral, a piece he had loved all his life.

It started to rain just outside Aughrim and he turned on the Escort's wipers but their rhythmic swishing combined with the lush strings of the symphony so that by Athlone, despite having opened the side window of the car, the drinks he had taken earlier were affecting him and he was really having to fight hard to stay awake. He pulled into the parking lot of the Monarch Hotel to take a break.

The lobby was hopping and two separate sing-songs were in progress, one in the bar, the other in a function room. As far as he could make out Father Morahan realized that there had been two separate wedding receptions in the hotel and the guests were now intermingling into one huge party.

'Have a drink, Father?' Father Morahan looked around. The man, enormously fat with long strings of hair crossing his bald pate like a five-barred gate, was seated in an armchair in the lobby holding up his own pint, which wobbled dangerously in his hand and threatened to spill over his gaping shirt front. 'No, thank you,' said Father Morahan politely and went into the bar.

The staff, two young girls and a man, were running up and down along the spirit measures, barely able to keep up with the demand. Half-pulled pints stood in neat rows along the counter. Father Morahan found a vacant spot at a corner of the bar and managed to attract the attention of one of the girls. 'Could I have a sandwich, please?'

317

'What kind of sandwich, Father?'

'Anything you have,' he said, in deference to the chaos.

'I'll have to go into the kitchen. Would ham be all right?'

'Ham'd be fine.'

'Do you want a drink, Father?'

'Yes,' he said, 'I'll have a whiskey. Make it a double,' he said then. It would be all right. The sandwich would counter the effect. He had finished the whiskey before the sandwich arrived and ordered a glass of beer to drink with it. He felt very uncomfortable, perched on a high stool with the corner of the bar cutting into his stomach as he leaned over it to eat the sandwich. He became aware, from all over the room, of eyes on him although out of respect for his clerical garb the wedding guests, augmented by regular drinkers, gave him a wide berth. He bolted the sandwich and gulped down the beer and left as quickly as he could.

It was a quarter to eleven when he reached Maynooth but seeing the enormous gates his courage failed him and instead of turning right, which would have brought him into the seminary, he kept to the main road and drove through the town and out again on to the main road towards Dublin.

He thought briefly of getting out to have a walk to clear his head but decided instead to have another sandwich in the next town of Leixlip. He saw a pub in the main street but each side of the road was choc-a-bloc with cars and there was nowhere to park. He drove on, turned right over the bridge and spotted another pub at the end of the bridge. This one had a car park.

He pulled into it. He felt quite good now. It would not be long before Ned O'Neill would help him sort the whole thing out.

The pub was doing a brisk trade but again he found a vacant stool at the bar. All that was available in the food line was yet another ham sandwich. 'Anything to drink, Father?' asked the young barman.

'I'll have a beer,' said Father Morahan. 'No, better change that,' he amended. 'Make it a mineral.'

'Britvic?' asked the barman.

Father Morahan changed his mind a third time. 'I'll have

318

a coffee and a small Irish.' The barman sighed and looked pointedly at his watch but set the whiskey in front of him and then went off to fetch the sandwich and put on the kettle for the coffee.

As he sipped the whiskey Father Morahan saw that he was the only person there who was alone. People, men and women, sat in groups laughing, chatting, enjoying each other's company. A blue cloud of cigarette and cigar smoke hung in strands in the air above their heads. On one side of him at the bar sat a group of three men, obviously well heeled and old friends, guffawing loudly; the couple on Father Morahan's other side were oblivious to everything except one another. Their drinks were untouched on the bar counter as they sat, his knees clutched around hers, gazing ardently into one another's eyes.

The priest stared into the golden depths of his own whiskey. He had come to this, he thought, sitting on a bar stool alone, half-pissed. No matter how kind Ned O'Neill was going to be tonight he would never be able to obliterate the memory of what it was he had done. Everyone had someone but no one cared for him.

Through his fog of self-pity he saw that the barman had returned with the sandwich and the coffee and had asked him something. 'What?' he managed.

'That'll be two pounds sixty altogether,' repeated the young man. Then, 'Are you all right, Father? You don't look well.'

Father Morahan held up his hand, 'I'm fine, son, I'm fine.'

He removed the Cellophane wrapper and took a bite out of the sandwich but it tasted like wallpaper and he could not face any more of it. Leaving the coffee untouched, he drained the whiskey and stood off his stool. There could be no more running away.

In the car park he switched on the engine and the wipers, too, sprang into action, forward and back, forward and back. They made a little thunking sound on the 'back' part, before pushing aside the river of rain on the glass. He put the car in gear and drove out of the car park and on to the bridge, facing back into Leixlip.

His eyes were dazzled by the high beams of a truck which was just coming to the end of the bridge and had pulled out a little to negotiate the tight left turn. Father Morahan put his right hand over his eyes to shield them against the glare and instinctively jerked the steering wheel to the left with his other hand. The lorry driver sounded his klaxon, a horrendous blast when heard close-up – and Father Morahan jumped in fright. His right foot gunned the accelerator. The Ford Escort shot towards the ironwork of the old bridge and crashed through it.

He was strangely relaxed as the car sailed through the air for a second or two. He was more surprised than frightened. When the car hit, thirty feet below, the steering wheel cannoned into his chest and winded him although there was no immediate explosion of pain. He supposed that would come later. Everything seemed to be in slow motion. The car was at a strange angle, leaning forward, half sideways. There was a great roaring sound and simultaneously his feet, which were bent under him at an odd angle, were getting very, very cold. Water. Water was gushing in. He fumbled for the door handle but such was the position of the car that he was leaning heavily on the driver's door and the handle was behind him. He could not bend his arm to the angle required. The car started to spin and to make a grinding noise as the water rushed farther up his body. He supposed he and the car were impaled on a rock or something. He was very cold and started to shiver. He noticed that the water was up to the level of his car radio and wondered if a radio could survive immersion in water. Still he was not frightened. He just wished that the roaring sound would subside.

Father Morahan never swore. He swore now.

'Ah, shite!' he said.

His last conscious thought, as the freezing, earth-tasting water rushed down his throat and up his nose and made his eyes opaque, was absurdly not of his immortal soul, nor of Molly, nor of Ned O'Neill who was by now getting concerned. He regretted that he had not eaten his ham sandwich.

At the subsequent inquest, the coroner was unable to determine whether Father Morahan had made any effort to get out of the car after it hit the water, which was in flood. And since the priest's nearest living relatives were all abroad it was Mrs Peg Conway who travelled to Dublin to claim Father Morahan's personal effects. Everything found in the car had been packed into the sodden briefcase.

'Here's his wallet,' said the official, 'and here are his watch and the contents of his pockets.' He gave Mrs Conway the wallet and a plastic bag containing the watch, some coins, a pocket appointments diary and some sodden pieces of paper.

At home that night, she opened the plastic bag. One piece of paper had obviously been torn off a letter, the heading of which showed it was from Washington DC. The second had Father Morahan's writing on it: it was smeared but seemed to say 'Smith, Evensong'. The third was a piece of newspaper, soft as tissue but still legible. It was about Margo Bryan. Mrs Conway took all three pieces and burned them, setting a match to them in the empty grate in the priest's study. They burned slowly but she stood and watched until they had curled and turned to black ash. She went into the kitchen then and sat at the table, lost in thought for a while. Then she seemed to make a decision.

Although Father Morahan's keys were in the briefcase, she took her own set out of her handbag and went into the little dining room. She fitted one of the keys into the bureau lock and opened the bureau, extracting the shoe box.

Mrs Conway had not been shocked when she had discovered its contents several years before. He was not the first and would not be the last priest to harbour such a passion. If anything, Mrs Conway empathized secretly somewhere deep in a Celtic soul which no amount of Roman or puritan churchifying could entirely subdue.

She had decided out in the kitchen what she was going to do with the box and its contents. She could have burned the clippings but she was superstitious about dead men's property. She was damned, however, if she was going to leave them for others to find, to paw over, to snigger and speculate and to sully his memory with innuendo about something they could not possibly understand.

She pulled a piece of Father Morahan's unheaded notepaper to her and scribbled on it in capital letters:

FOUND AMOUNG THE AFFECTS OF FR PATRICK MORAHAN

She opened the lid of the shoe box and put the note inside on top of the clippings. Then, carrying the box and the lid, she went back into the kitchen, sat at the table and, taking them out one by one, read through three of the clippings until she found what she was looking for, a feature article that mentioned the name of a theatre in which Margo Bryan had played. She copied down the name of the theatre on another piece of paper and replaced the three clippings.

She pulled open the drawer of the dresser in which she saved wrapping paper, string, rubber bands, anything that might come in handy. She searched for a few minutes, then found a piece of strong brown paper large enough. Smoothing out the creases as she brought it back to the table along with a ball of twine she wrapped and tied the box into a neat parcel and wrote, MISS MARGO BRYAN, WYNDHAM'S THEATRE, LONDON, ENGLAND on it in big lettering.

Then she made a cup of tea and went to bed.

Her nephew collected her next morning in time for the funeral which was in Father Morahan's home parish of Kilmacslea in County Mayo. She put the parcel on the back seat of the car before settling herself in the front. 'I want to stop off in Tuam to post this,' she said.

'But, Auntie Peg, the post office here is open,' he protested. 'We'll maybe have difficulty getting parking in Tuam.'

'Just do as you're told!' she snapped. At present, Peg Conway trusted no one in Tullyhalla. Particularly postmistresses.

The Church in her wisdom had given Father Morahan the benefit of the doubt with regard to suicide and allowed him the full panoply of its funeral rites. The two shops and three pubs in Kilmacslea closed for the morning and the tiny stone church, which dated originally from the twelfth century, was packed. There were thirty-one priests and three bishops on the altar for the concelebrated funeral Mass. Mrs Peg Conway was the only one of the congregation who wept at the graveside.

Molly had expected to be dazzled by the splendour of the house in Evanston but the moment she stepped into the wide entrance hallway she had felt immediately at home.

She stood for a few moments, looking upwards along the beautiful sweep of the grand staircase, while Christian fussed about with their bags and coats. Malcolm, who had met them at the airport with the car, rushed off to tell the housekeeper they had arrived and Cordelia, hearing them come in, came out of one of the rooms off the hall, extending both hands. 'You are very welcome here, Margo,' she said in her soft voice. 'I hope you will be very happy.'

Molly liked her instantly. 'Thank you, Mrs Smith,' she said. 'I already feel I will be.'

'I wish you would call me Cordelia? I hate Mrs Smith. If you call me Mrs Smith I'll call you the same!'

Molly laughed. 'All right, Cordelia. And please, would you call me Molly? Margo is only my stage name.'

'I much prefer Molly anyway.' Cordelia smiled.

Christian took her arm. 'Come on! I want to take you down to the lake.'

'Christian,' protested Cordelia, 'I'm sure Molly's very tired and would like to wash up.'

'Are you, Molly?' Christian was contrite.

'I'm not that tired but I would like to change my clothes.'

'Well, we'll go down to the lake first thing in the morning – OK?'

'OK.' She laughed.

Malcolm, who had returned to the hallway, intervened. 'Anyway, it's bitterly cold out there and I've already ordered supper.'

She turned towards him. He had not yet removed his coat and she had the strong impression he was watching her closely. The impression did not diminish as, throughout supper, she continued to feel that he was scrutinizing her. He was the perfect host, chatting lightly, making her feel at ease, yet she could not shake off the feeling that behind it all he was puzzling something out.

'Your show in London,' he said. 'I believe it's a hit and that you have been nominated for an award?'

'That's right,' said Molly. 'The run of the show is over but I've been nominated for a Keane Award. The ceremony is in ten days' time and the producers say I have to be there for it. That's why no honeymoon, I'm afraid.'

Cordelia, who had had less than a month to plan the wedding in the house – 'You didn't give me much time, Christian!' – explained to Molly what remained to be done. 'Did you bring your dress?'

'To be perfectly honest, Cordelia, it was the last thing on my mind.'

'Oh, good!' said Cordelia. 'We'll go to I. Magnin's tomorrow.'

'Say goodbye to your fiancée, Christian!' Malcolm laughed but Molly noticed that Christian didn't. All through the meal she had sensed an undercurrent of antagonism from Christian towards his grandfather which, now that she had met Malcolm, she could not understand. Malcolm, she thought, was bending over backwards to be accommodating and pleasant to Christian but Christian seemed to be resisting all overtures.

The arrangements for the wedding were relatively simple. Neither Christian nor herself had wanted any fuss but Cordelia was apparently anxious about Molly's Catholic background. 'Are you quite sure, Molly,' she asked, 'that you don't want a Catholic ceremony? I'm sure we could arrange it. Malcolm is on nodding acquaintance with the Cardinal, aren't you, dear?'

'I'm quite sure, Cordelia,' said Molly, before Malcolm could answer, 'that even the Cardinal couldn't fix things this quickly. There is really no problem, honestly. Whatever ceremony you have organized here will be absolutely fine.'

'And you're absolutely sure you're happy with getting married here in America? I'm sure Malcolm and I could have made the trip to Ireland.'

Molly knew there was no way in the world that she could have been married to a divorced man on Inisheer. She had not bothered to go into the ins and outs of Catholic marriage law with Christian, telling him simply that on the island it would have been thought outrageous that she was getting married less than four months after her mother's death. 'Please, Cordelia, don't worry,' she said. 'It's no problem to me where I get married.'

'Well, if you're sure,' said Cordelia, who went on to talk to Christian about where he was to pick up his morning suit.

Dick Spielberg, whom Molly had briefly met in her dressing room three months previously, was to be Christian's best man but there was still the problem of who would be Molly's bridesmaid and who would give her away. 'It's such a pity,' Cordelia said, 'that none of your family is coming over.'

Molly knew it would have been a waste of time inviting Brendan – he would not have travelled even to London. And Conor had ruled himself out. 'I've a very small immediate family, actually,' she said. 'I'm sure Christian has told you that all I have are two brothers and unfortunately one of those is out of touch altogether, working abroad. But please, Cordelia, I'm just as happy that things are working out this way. I couldn't bear all the fussing that usually goes with weddings.'

'Well, we'll have to find you a bridesmaid,' said Cordelia briskly. 'And Malcolm will give you away – if that's OK with you?'

'Of course it is! I'd be delighted.'

By the coffee stage Molly was dropping with tiredness and asked to be excused. Christian got up from the table too, kissed his grandmother and said that he, too, was going to bed.

They went up the stairs together and outside the door of the room she had been given he kissed her lightly. 'You're very welcome, Molly,' he whispered. 'I've dreamed of bringing you here. I love you very, very much.'

'I love you too . . .' she whispered back. As she closed the door she realized it was the first time she had said it.

She thought back over the conversation at supper, reflecting on how easily she had shed the practices and strictures of her church – as easily as a snake sheds its skin – when she had gone to London. At the same time, she would always feel like a Catholic. What would Sorcha have thought? And would she be marrying Christian at all if Sorcha was alive?

She was too tired to puzzle it all out, too tired even to unpack.

She washed her face in her little bathroom and climbed naked into the cool, linen-dressed bed. Her room was at the back of the house overlooking the lake. She had not drawn the curtains and when she turned out her bedside lamp the room went black but then everything in it came gradually back into view, in shades of grey and silver in the moonlight reflected off the water of the lake. Molly felt secure and comfortable. In that floating state half-way between consciousness and sleep she became aware of a sort of whispering sound around her. It was low and gentle, like a sigh which arose from the lapping of the lake and the breeze outside her window.

She woke next morning at 4.00 a.m., her body clock, despite her tiredness, still on London time. She could not go back to sleep and was reading one of the books from the shelves in her room when a maid brought her a cup of tea. Shortly afterwards Cordelia knocked at her door. 'We're early risers in this house,' she said apologetically as she came in. 'I hope you don't mind me calling you so early but if we're to get all our shopping done we should get an early start. It will take a good hour to get downtown through the rush hour.'

Molly, who was not in the least interested in shopping as a general rule, found she loved shopping with Cordelia. She saw that Cordelia was known and popular in all the ritzy boutiques and shops on Michigan Avenue and the two of them had a wonderful time. To her surprise Molly loved this unaccustomed feeling of fizzy recklessness.

Cordelia had contacted the stores in advance and selections of dresses were available for inspection. Molly whirled and twirled for Cordelia's approval in clouds of silk and satin and fichu lace. Eventually, in Saks, she settled for a simple elegant dress of cream silk jersey which draped itself in sensuous folds against her skin. She pirouetted in front of the shop-floor mirrors. 'I look like Isadora Duncan! What do you think, Cordelia, do you like it?' She looked past the saleswoman to Cordelia and immediately stopped her prancing. There were tears in Cordelia's eyes. 'What's wrong, Cordelia?'

326

'It's nothing, Molly. It's just in that dress you remind me of someone else, long ago.'

'Oh, I'm sorry. I wouldn't want to upset you. I'll take it off immediately. There are plenty more dresses.'

'No,' said Cordelia firmly, blowing her nose. 'It was just a passing fancy. Of course we'll take that dress. You look spectacular, Molly.'

That afternoon Molly was temporarily alone in the morning room, which the family seemed to use daily instead of the more formal and cavernous drawing room off the hall. Curiously, she roamed around the walls examining the books in the bookshelves, the pictures on the wall. In one corner stood a piano on top of which was a collection of photographs. There were several of Christian in all stages of childhood – and of another baby, which she assumed was his dead sister. But it was a full-length photograph of a bride and groom that caught her attention. She saw why Cordelia had reacted the way she did in Saks. The bride was dressed in a straight white dress, not dissimilar in style to the one she had chosen. This woman was tall and angular with broad shoulders like her own. The face was squarer and the hairstyle completely different. Nevertheless the resemblance to herself was remarkable. No wonder Cordelia had been taken aback. This must be Christian's mother. She heard footsteps approaching and put down the photograph guiltily as if she had been caught spying through a keyhole.

It was Christian, come to take her sightseeing in a little Fiat Ghia which belonged to Cordelia. 'And if you're not too tired I've got tickets for the hockey game tonight. Dick'll come too. Would you like that?'

For Christian's sake Molly tried very hard to enjoy herself at the Chicago Stadium that night. But the noise and violence of the game appalled her as players skated deliberately into each other or tripped each other when they thought the referee was not looking. She spent a great deal of the time with her hands over her ears, her eyes closed, and was exhausted when the game was over.

The next night Malcolm and Cordelia took the two of them and Dick to dinner in the restaurant on the ninety-fifth floor of the Hancock Center and the contrast to the previous raucous evening could not have been greater. When she emerged from the lift Molly gasped with pleasure at the panorama spread below and all around her, the floodlit skyscrapers set against the black lake, the strings of lights along Lake Shore Drive, the streams of car lights along the expressways, the coruscation of stars, lighthouses, airport control towers, aircraft warning lights on cranes, the twinkling planes themselves moving slowly through the sky, landing and lifting off at Chicago's three airports.

Cordelia delighted in Molly's reaction. 'I hope you'll be very happy in our city, Molly,' she said.

'I know I will,' said Molly. She glanced at Christian who was beaming like a full moon.

All through the week before the wedding Christian continued to be an exemplary companion, gentle and loving. The only niggle in Molly's mind was his aloofness from his grandfather. She saw a side of him, cold as ice, which worried her. But she had little time to worry, with wedding rehearsals and meeting Malcolm's and Cordelia's wide circle of friends and relations. A little girl, daughter of Christian's second cousin, had been chosen by Cordelia as combination flower-girl and bridesmaid. Molly found her enchanting.

The whole week passed in a whirl of activity until it was her last night as a single woman. The house was a bower with white flowers everywhere, threaded through the banisters of the staircase, framing the doorways, banked in huge drifts in the corners of the entrance hall and the drawing room where they were to have their reception.

The wedding itself was to take place in the morning room and the decorators had erected a floral arch of lilies and white roses in front of the french windows. Molly would marry Christian looking out at the lake.

Cordelia had insisted that, as a matter of tradition, Christian should leave the house to sleep elsewhere. Grumbling, he had gone to stay with Dick. Molly went to bed early but she could not sleep. As she lay looking at the patterns made by the moon on her bedroom wall, she began to worry about sex with her new husband. He had not put any pressure on her in that direction, although he referred to it a lot semi-humorously, telling her frequently that her beauty was more than a saint could bear . . .

Her virginity was not a problem, she was not afraid. And she did love Christian, she was sure she did, but he did not excite her physically and she would happily have settled for their current level of affection. This, she knew, was neither possible nor fair. She had to be fair to Christian. She concentrated on the positive: she did love his body, it was good to feel it against her own when they kissed. She knew she would have a good life with him. Surely it was just a matter of building on that feeling . . .

There was a soft knock at her door. She sprang out of bed to open it, certain it was Cordelia with some last-minute arrangement.

It was not Cordelia who stood there but Malcolm. He was still fully dressed in his navy blue pinstripe suit and breathing heavily, obviously from the exertion of coming up the stairs. Cordelia had confided to Molly that she wanted to have a chair-lift installed for him but he steadfastly refused to ruin the aesthetics of the staircase. 'I'm sorry to come up so late like this,' he said, 'but we haven't had much opportunity to talk and I would so like to have a chat, just the two of us, before the wedding. May I come in?'

'Of course,' she said, opening the door wider and standing aside.

He sat in a small bucket chair by the window while she pulled the covers back over the bed and put on her dressing-gown. She felt she should feel embarrassed but did not. Malcolm was the one who seemed to be nervous as she finished tidying the bed and sat on it, looking at him expectantly. In Molly's experience, all the old people she had known tended to fidget a lot but Malcolm was an exception. He was always calm and carried an aura of stillness around with him. He sat still now. 'I suppose you're wondering what's so important that I should come barging in here like this?'

'No, that's OK – I'm glad to have the opportunity to talk.' She decided to help him out. 'Is it something to do with tomorrow?'

329

'In a way,' he said. 'In another way not. But I have been debating with myself whether to show you this . . . ' From the inside of his suit he pulled out his wallet and extracted a small, passport-sized photograph and passed it across.

Molly studied it. It was a colour snapshot of a blonde girl with high cheekbones and a wide mouth. Apart from the eyes, which were round, Molly could have been looking at her own sister. 'Who's this?' she asked.

'It's Jo-Ann, Christian's first wife,' he answered. 'When I saw you first at the airport, I was immediately struck by the resemblance. Jo-Ann was small, much smaller than you are, Molly, but outside of that you bear a remarkable resemblance to one another. But that's not really why I brought this up. The point is,' he went on hesitantly, 'when he first brought Jo-Ann home, I was worried about her too. You see both of you are . . . are very, very like Christian's mother Maggie . . . ' He put the photograph back in the wallet and took out another one, older and in black and white, a miniature of a studio portrait, preserved in a plastic wallet.

'I've already noticed that particular resemblance,' she said simply, taking the photograph and glancing at it. 'I saw the wedding photograph downstairs on the piano.'

Malcolm was studying her reaction. 'I just thought you should know,' he said.

Molly was not as dismayed as perhaps he thought she should be. She had been present at many dinner parties where it was discussed, this male search for mother-substitutes and where the discussion ended when it was decided at one end of the table or the other that it was a perfectly adequate psychological basis for a relationship.

'You're not upset?' asked Malcolm.

'No.' She shook her head. 'It's not surprising really. If what you're suggesting is true – *if* it's true – he's not the first and won't be the last to do that.'

'You're a very mature young lady,' he said. 'Christian hasn't told us much about your own family background. Your parents are dead? You have two brothers?'

She nodded. 'Yes, they're both older than I am. One of them,

Brendan, is at home still, he's the eldest of the family. Conor, he's the younger one, he was a botanist.'

'Was?'

'Well, I don't know what he is now . . .'

His eyes were in shadow but she thought she saw his expression sharpen as though he detected something odd in her tone. She realized that she had spoken as though she felt guilty.

'The other thing I'm worried about,' he said, 'and please stop me if I'm getting out of line, my dear, is the difference in your cultures. I don't know very much about Ireland, shamrocks and shillelaghs and dyeing the Chicago river green on St Patrick's Day – that sort of thing!' He grinned. 'Typical American view of the old sod.'

She grinned back.

'Well, that's not strictly accurate,' he went on. 'I know a bit more than that. You know I'm a fellow Celt? You know I'm Welsh?' She nodded. 'But I'm sure our world of coalfields and slag was light years away from what I've always imagined Ireland to be,' he continued. 'Green, soft, everybody reciting poetry, singing at parties . . .'

She laughed. 'Well, there wasn't all that much difference between you and me, maybe. There wasn't much green on Inisheer. And I can tell you that the only poetry I ever heard was in the classroom of the national school!'

'You're a Catholic, for instance, and he's not,' said Malcolm. 'Is this not a problem for you?'

She shook her head. 'Not at all. I'm afraid I march to my own drum these days.'

'Well, that's all I have to say. Please forgive me, my dear. I'm an old man.' He looked down at his hands. 'Seem to be saying that a lot these days . . .'

'Malcolm, you're not to worry,' she said. 'I'll take care of Christian, I promise.'

'Were you happy as a child?' The question came out of the blue, forcing her to think carefully.

'Yes, I was happy, I think,' she said slowly. 'I don't remember all that much, really.'

331

Then she had the sense that she was about to hear what he really came to say.

'Forgive me, my dear,' he said quietly, 'but I am an old man – There! I've said it again! – and since they have nothing left to lose old men can be daring. I hope you won't be insulted if I ask you if you really love Christian. He and I do not always see eye to eye – you may have noticed this yourself – but I don't think I could bear it if I thought he was going to be hurt again. I've watched him go through so much and I've felt so helpless.'

Her heart went out to him. 'Malcolm,' she said firmly, 'I wouldn't hurt Christian for the world.'

'Again forgive me, my dear, but that's not what I asked.'

She felt cornered. There was no way she could dissemble. 'All I can say truthfully,' she said, searching, 'is that I *think* I do. I have certainly never loved anyone the way I love Christian.' She was telling the truth but it was not satisfactory. She knew it even as she said it.

He got up from his chair. She stood up with him. He took one of her hands and in a strange, courtly gesture kissed the back of it. 'I think you're a lovely girl,' he said, 'and I am really looking forward to the wedding and to having a new granddaughter. Please forgive an old man's ramblings.'

He left the room then, turning towards her again at the door. 'Goodnight, my dear, and I'll see you tomorrow. And I'd like you to know you will always be welcome in this house. No matter what happens . . .'

'I already know that,' she said.

As he pulled the door closed she experienced, as she had several times since she had come here, that curious sense of *déjà vu*.

Next day, the ceremony went ahead without a hitch. Conor, to whom she had given the Evanston address in case of emergencies, sent a telegram: GOOD LUCK TO BOTH OF YOU. LONG LIFE AND HAPPINESS. He signed it SEAN MOLLOY.

As Molly and Christian woke in the bridal suite of the Palmer House Hotel on their first morning as man and wife, in London

332

Una O'Connor was waiting nervously for her lunch guest in the restaurant of the Cumberland. She had been waiting for fifteen minutes. It was not that he was late – she had been twenty minutes early and there were still five minutes to go until their one o'clock appointment.

From her table she could see the door but she was determined that he should not catch her looking out for him. So she kept her head down over the novel she had brought. Una, whose life was governed by the timekeeping habits of others, never left home without a book.

He arrived punctually and once again she was struck by his sheer physical size and presence. He was absolutely unaware of it, she decided as they shook hands and he slid into his chair. She played the introductions very coolly. Una was always cool when she was not taken by surprise. She already knew the menu and, playing her advantage as hostess, pointed out various options.

'Do they have any steak?' he asked, looking at the long list in front of him.

'I'm sure they can cook you one,' said Una. She raised her hand to a waiter who padded over. 'Is it possible that you can do steak?'

'There's steak on the menu, Madame,' said the waiter.

'*Plain* steak,' said Conor.

Una was grateful. She led the conversation, 'interviewing' him. 'Tell me about life at the zoo?' she asked.

'Nothing much to tell,' he said, shrugging his shoulders. 'I'm a general attendant there, I can help out anywhere.'

'Do you actually like animals or is it just a job?'

'No, I like animals – but it is just a job. My real interest is now in archaeology.'

She caught the 'now'. 'What was your real interest before?'

'Botany,' he said.

There was something in his tone, a warning. She went back to archaeology. 'I know absolutely nothing about archaeology,' she said. It was like pressing a button. All she had to do was to sit sipping her wine and toying with her monkfish while he attacked his steak and poured out his enthusiasm for his subject. 'I'm doing exams in a few weeks' time,' he said. 'I started my

333

course late, only last January, and I'm up to my eyes trying to keep abreast of the class.'

'When will you be qualified?'

'Probably never. I'll never learn enough, there isn't time in a lifetime and as soon as you get caught up with what's going on in one area another area leaps ahead. But I'll be accepted as a *bona fide* archaeologist, all going well, in two or three years' time.'

Una was having difficulty in concentrating on his answers. As he continued to talk she felt as alert as if a high-tension wire were passing through her body. This was all very well and he was totally at ease but what on earth was the next step? She had no plan further than this lunch and she began to panic. He was finishing his steak and mopping up the meat juice with a piece of bread roll.

She became aware that he had stopped speaking and was looking at her expectantly. *Jesus. Had he asked her something?*

'Sorry,' he said. 'Was I boring you? I do that a lot, I'm afraid.'

'No, you weren't boring me.'

He looked at her without comment and then smiled. 'It's your turn.'

'No, I'd like to continue talking about archaeology.'

Conor placed his knife and fork precisely where they bisected his clean plate. 'Una,' he asked, 'why did you ask me to lunch?'

'Because you were there – like Mount Everest?'

'That's as good a reason as any, I suppose.' Then he continued, his voice casual. 'What do we do now?'

'What – do you mean?'

'Well, I gather you didn't ask me to lunch because you thought I was fading away from hunger . . .'

She gathered together the remnants of her self-possession. 'Well, if it comes to that why did you accept?'

'Oh, a variety of reasons! Including the fact that I quite like red hair,' he said.

She saw he was still smiling although for the life of her she could not interpret the smile. 'Are you – are you on a day off from work today?' she managed.

'Yes – I should study, of course!'

'Oh, of course! Right!'

She made a gesture to call the waiter for the bill when he spoke again. 'Why did you ask?'

'Well, I was hoping you might be able to take me to the zoo!'

It was a brazen effort and he laughed outright. 'All right, Una. The zoo it is!'

Molly inserted the key into the lock of the Vernon Street house while Christian paid off the taxi and struggled up the short pathway with their luggage, including a trunk they had acquired to accommodate some of their wedding presents.

Molly's cleaning lady, Mrs Sharma, had placed fresh flowers on the hallstand and had stacked the heap of mail neatly alongside it.

'I'm going into the kitchen, Christian,' Molly called and she went through the hall, taking the mail with her. She put on the kettle – always a reflex action when she walked into her kitchen having been away – and sat at the table sorting through the envelopes. She did not open any of the brown envelopes, junk mail or circulars but set aside a heap of invitations, a letter from Brendan and one in Dolly's flowing script. She opened this first. It contained the shooting schedule for her film and a little scribbled note in which Dolly had written that she had received for her client, a 'very intriguing parcel', readdressed to her from Wyndham's Theatre.

The kettle whistled. She could hear Christian humping suitcases up the stairs. 'I'm making tea, darling,' she called through the door. 'Do you want a cup?'

'Coffee, please!'

'Instant all right?'

'Oh, OK,' he said grumpily, heaving at the trunk. 'I can't manage this up the stairs on my own. I'll need help.'

'Why don't we unpack some of it down here?' she called. 'It'll be easier to get it up then.'

'Oh, very clever! Just when I've nearly broken my back!'

'Christian! Don't be so crabby! You'd think we had been married for thirty years instead of three days.'

'Four days,' he corrected, coming into the kitchen. 'Don't forget the time changes.' He came up behind where she stood pouring water out of the kettle into two mugs and squeezed her to him.

'Christian! I'll spill the water!'

He removed his arms from around her waist and raised both hands in the air. 'Sorry!' He went and sat at the table.

She brought the two mugs across, determinedly bright. 'Would you do me a favour?'

'What?'

'I've just had a note from Dolly that she has a parcel for me. She says it's intriguing, whatever that means. But I'm dying to see what's in it. Would you be a darling and take a taxi to her office to collect it?'

She saw he was not inclined to be helpful. 'I'll do *all* the unpacking while you're gone, Christian,' she said. 'Then we can go to bed.'

'For a sleep?' The sarcasm was unmistakable.

'Aren't you tired?'

'I suppose you are?'

'Well, isn't it normal to be tired after a transatlantic flight like we've just had?'

'Yes, it's normal. Sorry, Molly, I'll go get your package.'

She was in the bedroom, hanging up her clothes in her wardrobe, when he returned with it. She sat on the bed to unwrap it.

'It doesn't look like a script,' he said curiously, sitting down beside her. He was right. When she had ripped the paper off Molly found she was holding a battered old shoe box, the condition of which had not improved with the handling it had got from the post office. She prised off the lid and found a note.

FOUND AMOUNG THE AFFECTS OF FR PATRICK MORAHAN

The name, unexpected, came as a jolt.

Christian was looking over her shoulder. 'Who's Father Patrick Morahan?'

'Ah, it's just a priest I used to know,' she said. 'He must be dead . . . '

'They're all cuttings about you,' he said, reaching over and riffling through the top layer. 'Was this guy sweet on you, Molly? A priest?'

'It's all a long time ago,' said Molly, trying to put the lid back on the box.

'A woman with a past, eh? A *priest* yet!' He made a playful grab for the box, his customary good humour restored. 'Let's see those cuttings.'

'Christian, don't!' she said, laughing, snatching the box to herself. She felt bashful about letting him read all that old stuff about her. But he grabbed for it again and they wrestled on the bed for possession. She eluded him and keeping the box tight to her chest, ran out of the room with it, flitting down the stairs two at a time.

'Give it here!' ordered Christian, thundering after her. 'Wife! Listen to your master!'

'Master, me eye!' she said and dodged out of his reach down the hall and into the kitchen. He caught her from behind but she managed to hold on to the prize. 'It's only a pile of old rubbish,' she said firmly, 'but it's mine! Nothing to do with you.' Dragging him with her she took a few steps across the kitchen and, while he continued to cling to her back like an oversized monkey, she reached up and put the box on top of the kitchen dresser.

'All right,' he said playfully, nuzzling her back. 'Come on, confess. Who was this guy Morahan?'

'Nobody that need ever concern either of us, Christian,' she said diverting him, kissing him on the mouth.

He broke the kiss, gasping. 'Molly, I warn you, kisses like that can have consequences . . . '

'So what? We're married!'

He struck his head with his open palm. 'Now she tells me!' Then he stood back from her and took her hand. 'You mean it, Molly? You really mean it?'

She nodded. She began to shake a little.

'Come on,' he said, his voice tender. 'Upstairs, wife!'

PART THREE

PART THREE

CHAPTER TEN

'It's a little girl!' cried the midwife triumphantly.

The tears poured down Molly's face as the baby finally slithered out of her.

She felt flattened and empty, exhausted yet exhilarated, all at the same time. Making a tremendous effort she raised her head to see her daughter but the baby had been taken to the other side of the room, to a table where they were huddled over her.

She lay back and held Christian's hand. She searched his face but only his eyes were visible over the surgical mask he wore and his eyes were not looking at her but across at the baby.

She was glad Christian was with her. She had really needed him to be with her.

There was another contraction. She closed her eyes and pushed out the afterbirth.

'Good girl,' said the midwife.

Molly felt ludicrously pleased at the praise. The strong lights of the delivery room were hurting her eyes but she looked up again at Christian. Although he was still holding her hand his head was now swivelled round and he was looking away from her altogether, towards the door. There was some kind of hubbub at the door. A nurse was running.

A young doctor came and sat on the stool at the end of the delivery table. She saw he was West Indian.

'Just going to give you a little stitch,' he said. 'You won't feel anything.'

'Where's the baby?' she asked him. All she could see was the top of his dark head as he bent to his task of stitching her episiotomy wound.

'Easy, now,' said the doctor softly.

'Where's my baby?' Molly felt panicky. Her body felt as

delicate and stretched as the thinnest glass. She looked from the doctor to Christian. Christian's eyes were full of tears. Something was wrong.

'They've taken your baby to the nursery to put her in an incubator, just as a precaution,' said the doctor, still without looking at her.

'What kind of precaution?' asked Molly. Her voice rose in pitch but then a nurse came and gave her an injection.

'For the pain, my dear,' said the nurse. 'And so you won't get sick.'

Molly was unaware of any pain. And she did not feel sick. 'What's wrong, Christian?' she asked Christian, begging.

He did not answer but he had stripped off his mask and she was terribly afraid when she saw the expression on his face.

'Is the baby dead?' Molly struggled to get off the table but she was still strapped in to the stirrups and the nurse and the doctor rushed to restrain her. She thought she heard herself screaming but her voice sounded very strange.

'There, there, my dear,' said the nurse. 'Everything's going to be all right. Just lie still and have a little rest.'

The doctor said something which Molly could not understand because everything was suddenly so distant and she felt so, so tired, much tireder even than she had been before. The tiredness descended on her like a soft black blanket, so soft that it muffled all the words she was trying to say. She tried to fight, to throw it off, but it overpowered her, cutting out all the light and all the sound. She dropped into sleep as if she were falling down a deep well.

When she woke again it was dark and for a few moments, she drifted, full of delicious laziness having no idea where she was. She had been dreaming, a very vivid, lovely dream in which she had been getting married all over again and the house in Evanston was floating on the lake like a flower-filled barge. Everyone was there in the dream, even Sorcha, her mother, looking beautiful, standing proudly as Molly walked up the short aisle. Jo-Ann was there, blonde in a pink dress, standing beside another lovely lady in grey, who smiled gravely at Molly as she walked by and Molly knew that this was Christian's mother. She smiled back at the lady as she passed and the lady seemed very pleased. Malcolm was at the top of the room, playing some sort of bouzouki-type musical instrument; he had multi-coloured ribbons and streamers pinned all over his navy pinstripe suit. John Pius, his pink face wreathed in giggles, was the preacher. Even Beauty, the little collie Molly had loved as a child, was an honoured guest. She sat at John Pius's feet and wagged her tail, her ears pricked, as Molly approached. Beauty wore a tiny peaked clown's hat on her black and white head and a garland of flowers round her neck.

And after the ceremony when Christian lifted the veil off her face it had not been Christian but Conor. And it had felt warm and right, there had been no surprise.

She stretched in the warm smooth bed but when she moved there was an uncomfortable tug between her legs. She remembered. The baby. She was in hospital. She had had a daughter.

The filaments of the dream evaporated as with difficulty, her head swimming, she raised herself off her pillows and switched on the light over her bed. The room was clinically clean but bright with flowers. Someone had been in and arranged them. They spilled all over the windowsills, lockers and tables, even the television set, dozens of them, orchids, roses, dahlias, chrysanthemums, in baskets and vases and little posies. She had a sense of unreality, as if she had died and been transported in death to somewhere else. She had not seen anyone bring flowers.

She eased herself out of bed, feeling dizzy when she attempted to stand upright. Keeping her head low she groped her way along the wall towards the window and pulled back the heavy curtains. Although the streetlamps were on outside it was not really dark yet but still dusky. Off on the horizon to the west she could see the remnants of a red-gold sky.

She made her way back to the bed and collapsed on to it. A flex ran from a wall socket under her pillow. She followed its length and uncovered a rubber bulb at the end with a red button in its middle. It was a call bell. She pressed the button and a light went on over her door.

Within seconds, a nurse came in. 'Good heavens, my dear! You shouldn't have got out of bed.'

The nurse assisted her back under the covers and settled her down. 'We didn't expect you to be awake for a little while yet. How do you feel?' plumping the pillows behind her, professionally smoothing down the counterpane.

Molly felt more disoriented than ever. 'Where's my baby?' she asked. Her voice sounded far away and very faint.

'We'll bring her in to you in a little while,' said the nurse. 'She's in the nursery now, the doctors are with her, we're running a few little tests on her.'

Tests. Through the fog the word struck fear into Molly's heart.

'What kind of tests?' she managed to ask.

'Don't worry now, dear, the doctor will be in shortly and he'll explain everything. Would you like a little drink?'

The nurse poured some water from a turquoise-coloured plastic jug into a turquoise-coloured plastic beaker and held it to Molly's lips. The water tasted very sweet.

'Is there anyone here? Where's my husband?'

'You were asleep for such a long time, my dear, you were absolutely exhausted. He went home for a while but he said we were to telephone him just as soon as you woke up.'

'Will you telephone him? I'd like to speak to him, please.'

'Certainly, my dear. We have the number out at the desk. You rest now.'

'When can I see my baby?'

'Won't be long now. You rest, dear.' The nurse left the room, the crêpe soles of her shoes making a sucking sound on the parquet flooring. It was very quiet in the room after she had closed the sound-proofed door behind her.

Molly tried to hold thoughts in her mind but they kept slipping away. She knew something was wrong with the baby. It was not just the behaviour of the staff. She felt it in her bones. Where was Christian? Where were Malcolm and Cordelia? She tried very hard to focus. Malcolm and Cordelia had definitely been at the clinic at some stage. She was sure she remembered their faces floating vaguely somewhere above her own.

344

Or was that before? Had she only dreamt they were here? They were definitely in London – they had been staying at the Dorchester for the past week. Malcolm had insisted on coming for the birth of his first great-grandchild. He had been tremendously excited over the past few days.

She concentrated. Where were they all now? Christian should be with her. Cold fear assaulted her: he wasn't with her because he was drinking. He had promised he wouldn't. He was supposed to be on the dry. He had promised.

She thought she heard someone at the door. They were bringing in her baby! But whoever it was passed on down the corridor.

Christian should be here with her. She would make it all right for Christian and herself. They would make a go of it now they had a baby.

Her thoughts struggled out of the fog, showed themselves, but slipped away before they crystallized.

Christian would cut down on the drinking. It was a girl, they had said. He would be able to cut down on the drinking because now he had a daughter . . .

She would make more effort to respond sexually. That side of things was all her fault. It should be better from now on. Some books hinted that women did not mature sexually until after they had given birth. She would really try harder. The soreness between her legs would heal and she would be much better.

They would all be better, all three of them – Christian and herself and their daughter. A family now . . .

After all, she loved Christian.

She held on to that thought. She *loved* Christian, she would love him better than she had. A lot of their problems were to do with her not loving him enough . . .

Where was her baby?

She tried to remember the moment of birth, the cry of her baby. Try as she might, she could not remember any cry. 'It's a little girl!' someone had said. Then the hubbub at the door of the delivery room. She had not seen her baby, they had not given her her baby to hold . . .

She rang the call bell a second time and when the nurse

345

came in again, the same one as before, she demanded to see the baby.

The nurse saw her agitation. 'Yes, dear,' she said in a soothing voice. 'I'll go now and get the doctor for you.'

Immediately after the birth of his daughter Christian accompanied his sleeping wife when she was wheeled into the recovery room and from there to her room, where it appeared that she would continue to sleep soundly for hours. He sat in a chair in the room feeling useless and superfluous as the efficient staff came and went, monitoring her condition. The gynaecologist who had presided at the delivery, an elderly, silver-haired man called Sinden who was beautifully and expensively dressed, came in at one stage and spoke to him in a low voice. He was kind but not very informative, telling Christian that he would return later as soon as there was any definite news.

Christian already knew that the news would be bad; it was now just a matter of degree. He had seen his daughter, bluish and stiff in a nurse's hands as she was rushed to the nursery incubator, and had recognized that she did not look at all like the newborn babies he and Molly had seen in the training films at the antenatal classes they had attended.

As he sat in the quiet room he tried to make sense of his tremendous feeling of detachment. After the initial trauma of the birth his brain had seemed to slip out of gear into neutral. He had the faraway impression that he should be panicking, feeling sad or tragic or even fearful of the future – yet all he felt was this great grey flatness. He stared at his wife where she lay on her back, propped up on pillows, her head fitted into a small hollow. Her hair was tangled and unkempt and spread out in dark strings on the white bed linen, made faintly luminous under a blue nightlight above the bed. Her mouth was open and she snored slightly as she breathed.

He had made a mess of this marriage too. Just like it had with Jo-Ann, the successful conquest of Molly had been the end of his desire. It had taken a while, of course. His physical desire for her had been frenzied in the beginning and the first time he had seen her naked in his bed he had felt like falling on his knees to worship such perfection. He had been patient with her, knowing she would need time to flower.

But as the weeks went by he had become irritated and then frustrated. If he was to be fair, there was nothing on which he could actually fault her. He had failed to make some connection.

With hindsight he felt it had been a mistake that she had given up her career – even though they had agreed it would be just for a year. It had been his idea that she should relax for a while, get to know her new family in America. She had seemed happy enough about it at the time and the first month or so in Evanston had been blissful – at least he thought it had been. His grandmother and grandfather adored her and the atmosphere in the house was happy, even gay.

But then she had got pregnant and the situation had changed. The delight in the Evanston house had been enormous – the years seemed to drop off Malcolm at the prospect of a great-grandchild – and at first Christian had been able to rejoice in tandem. But his joy had faded quickly. Molly, sick for the first two months, was wrapped up in the pregnancy with Cordelia as a confidante. She shut him out. And as the months passed their sexual life had dwindled away to nothing. He had tried to talk to her about it and she had always participated politely but each time he had had the futile sense that he was talking to someone buried deep in a secret place, completely out of his reach. She had asked him to be patient, promising him that this aspect of their lives would improve as soon as the baby was born . . . But he had felt with certainty that it was a promise she would not – could not – keep. Nor, he now admitted, did he want her to.

He looked at her now, sleeping the sleep of the dead in her hospital bed. She was beautiful in repose, despite the untidiness of her hair and the dark shadows around her eyes, beautiful like an alabaster statue. The truth was, he thought, Molly did not seem to need sex.

So because he had loved her, or thought he had, he tried to convince himself that sex wasn't everything and buried himself in his work. He was now working freelance for a number of

347

publications all over the world and had been happy to come to London for the last two months of the pregnancy as, for some reason, she had taken a strong dislike to the efficient but impersonal American way of birth. He had even imagined that, away from the cushioned, supportive atmosphere created by Cordelia in Evanston, they might have a chance of recreating the intimacy of their first month together. But the move had made little difference. She remained unreachable. They spent their days politely and their nights apart, although they were separated by only a few inches in a large double bed.

Deep down, Christian admitted to himself that his drinking might be a contributory factor. She closed up on him when he had had a few drinks and although he tried, he really tried, not to drink so much, he couldn't seem to help himself. There were times when drink was his only friend ... And although he blamed his circumstances, her lack of appreciation, his bereavements, when he was low and sober like this he knew that the blame lay firmly with himself.

All in all, his sense of failure was enormous.

She sighed in her sleep and he leaned forward, ready for her to wake up. But she was merely changing position and he sat back again.

He had no idea what he felt about the baby. It was too soon and the scale of the difficulties ahead was unknown. But Christian's sense of self-loathing and failure was tempered by a feeling of deep resentment at the trick fate had played on him – on them both. *That* surely wasn't his fault.

They were now in a trap, the two of them, in a net which was tightening round them, binding them together. It was grotesque.

Christian looked at his wife and all he saw was an eternity of dust. She would be better off without him ...

He stood up and went to the window, parting the curtains and peering out at the street below. People, ordinary people, men with briefcases, were hurrying home from work. Cars nosed slowly into and out of parking spaces. A taxi picked up a fare. Why him?

He glanced back over his shoulder at his unconscious wife.

348

He had been sitting with her for nearly an hour and she had not stirred. There was no point in staying here. In any event, no one had seemed to care very much whether he was around or not and it mattered least of all to Molly. He knew he should call Malcolm and Cordelia who were probably getting anxious for news by now. He had promised that he would call immediately after the delivery. But it was hardly the kind of news a person could deliver on the telephone. 'Hey, Grandpa, guess what's happened to your first great-granddaughter!' He would have to go in person to the Dorchester.

He went back to stand again for a moment beside Molly's bed. The blue light from above reflected off her teeth and made translucent the satiny tissue of her eyelids. With a shiver he realized she looked like a cadaver. Strangely he felt an impulse to kiss her. He bent over her face and touched his lips to her forehead, which was cold and faintly damp.

He left the room and told the nurse at the station in front of the lifts that he was leaving the building for a while to go home, that he had a couple of errands to do but could be contacted at his home number after an hour and a half or so. He scribbled the number on a pad, then crossed the carpet to wait for the lift.

Outside, the heat was bleeding away from the May day, which had been unseasonably warm. He got a cab immediately and asked to be driven to the Dorchester. But when the cabby was taking a short cut through Berkeley Square, on an impulse he asked the man to pull up at the flower stall on the pavement. To the stallholder's astonishment, he bought fifty pounds' worth of flowers – orchids, roses, chrysanthemums, dahlias, all the showiest of blooms the woman had on display. She tied them up as best she could in two huge bouquets and, carrying them, Christian got back into the cab.

As the taxi got nearer to the Dorchester, and the moment when he would have to break the bad news to Malcolm and Cordelia, Christian began to funk it. He tapped the glass partition between himself and the driver and when the man slid it back, Christian told him he had changed his plans, that he wanted to be driven to Soho. The man threw his eyes to heaven and slammed back the partition.

When they got as far as Brunswick Street, he slid it back again. 'We're in Soho now, sir, where do you want to be let off?'

'L'Epicure restaurant,' replied Christian. It was the only name he knew in the district. He could not immediately remember the name of the restaurant where he had lunched with Molly that first time. Perhaps it was an omen, he thought bitterly.

It took another five minutes for the cabby to get to the corner over which blazed the restaurant's distinctive flaming torch. Christian got out, leaving the flowers behind him on the seat. He asked the driver to take the bouquet back to St Catherine's, scribbling the address and Molly's name on a piece of paper. Then he paid him twice what was on the meter, which was only £5.30, plus another five pounds. The taximan took the money. 'Whatever you say, guv! Have a nice day!'

Christian watched the taxi move off into the distance. The desire for a drink was now irresistible. He looked around; a pub was kitty-corner to the restaurant and he crossed the road to it and went inside. It was noisy and cheerful, a babbling place full of young people, obviously workers in the nearby garment district. There were a few advertising agency types too, young men with pony tails and thin girls in very tight dresses with long painted nails and straight expensively bleached hair.

Christian found a corner of the bar and ordered a double bourbon on the rocks. When it came he drained it in one swallow, then, catching the barman's eye, immediately ordered another. He took this one to a corner of the room where there was a free stretch of windowsill and perched himself on it, sipping it, thinking back over the past few hours.

He had difficulty in contemplating that limp bloodied scrap he had seen being rushed out of the delivery room of St Catherine's less than three hours ago as his daughter or as a child at all. He took a large swig of his drink. With the press of bodies and the remnants of the day's heat outside it was getting oppressively warm in the pub. He took off his jacket, drained his glass again and went to the bar to order again.

Another American stood at the counter, about the same age as himself but there the resemblance ended. The other man was small and tubby with sandy hair and pale eyes. 'Hi!' he said. 'A fellow American, eh?'

Christian was in no mood for pleasantries but he acknowledged the greeting. 'Hi,' he said shortly and fixed his eyes on the barman.

But the man was determined. 'On vacation?'

'No,' said Christian, hoping by his tone to deter him. 'I live here actually.'

It was a mistake to have admitted any detail at all. The man fastened on it. 'Well, how about that! Maybe you could give me a few pointers.' He held out his hand, 'Ferdy Cameron. It's a Scottish name. Professor of English at Modena in Oshkosh, Wisconsin. I'm on sabbatical here in England.'

Christian took the hand. 'Hi! Christian Smith. I'm a journalist.'

'My God! Not the Christian Smith who wrote that great stuff about the Convention in Chicago?'

It had been so long since this had happened to him that Christian was temporarily disarmed. 'Yes,' he said, surprised.

'Well, put it there, Christian!' said the other man. 'I've used that article in my classes. That was some piece!' He seized Christian's hand again and pumped it enthusiastically. 'This is great! Christian Smith! I gotta buy you a drink, Christian!' There was no escape.

Three drinks later Christian, in that state which presages outright drunkenness, began to feel that old Ferdy was not a bad sort and suggested they have a meal together. Ferdy was delighted. He had been lonely in London so far, he confided. Londoners were cold fish. Christian, loosened by the drink, was tempted to confide his current problems in his new friend but something, a sense of incompleteness, held him back.

He and Ferdy crossed the road and entered L'Epicure and, after a short wait, managed to get a table. They talked of America and their college days and Christian managed to keep at bay the awful empty feeling in the pit of his stomach. He and Ferdy had a couple of brandies after the meal and ignored the flapping of the waiters around their table.

351

Just as the doctor was coming through the door of Molly's hospital room to tell her the truth about her baby, in another part of London Conor was in bed beginning a row with Una O'Connor.

It had been a hot day for early May. The windows of Conor's tiny third-floor flat were open but he was sweating as he lay on his back in the narrow bed, Una's soft round body, also damp, snuggled into him. He wished he could get up straight away but tried to be patient as she cuddled into him, making him feel even sweatier.

He stifled a yawn. Not for the first time he wondered how he had got himself so deeply immured in this situation. He liked Una, she was an intelligent companion and sex between them was fun, or had been fun – but she took far more out of their relationship than he was prepared to donate and increasingly he felt she was a drain on him. She was able to manipulate her roster to spend a great deal of her time off in London; he wished she wouldn't but on the other hand he felt ungrateful because he knew she spent all of her spare cash on air fares.

'Did you see the piece in the *Standard* about Margo Bryan?' she asked idly.

He used the opportunity to remove himself gently from her arms and to get out of the bed. 'No. What piece was that?'

She turned on her back and stretched her body into a wide, sensuous X. 'Apparently *Streams of Hope*, that movie she made with Eugene Lothar, has been nominated at Cannes and Margo herself is an outside chance for an award. Of course, they called her a *British* actress!' Una, Conor knew, felt proprietorial about her journalistic protégée.

'Well, I suppose in a way they're right.' He crossed to the sink and began to sluice some of the sweat off his face under the running tap. 'After all, most – all – of her success has been here in England.'

Una raised herself on one elbow. 'Sean Molloy!' she said indignantly. 'How dare you? You of all people!'

'What difference does it make, Una?'

352

'Well, it makes a great deal of difference to me – and I'm sure if Margo were here it would make a great deal of difference to her! How would you like it if you discovered some new fossil which was going to revolutionize the world's thinking on the origin of the species or something and the papers all called you an Englishman?'

Conor continued to splash water on himself. Una, who tended to become vehement at the drop of a hat, was getting on his nerves. He knew it was unfair. 'Uh–uh!' he said, muttering into the water.

She would not be put off. 'Well?' she demanded and he heard the bedsprings creak as she sat up in the bed. He did not turn round but he knew that her eyes would be wide with indignation. He was tired and fed up with the argument. He wanted to remove himself completely from the room, from her, from this stifling day.

Immediately he was ashamed. Una was a decent person, probably as decent a person as a man could find, and he knew that she was genuinely in love with him. She deserved better than this from him. He had never even told her his real name or revealed his true relationship with Molly. Poor Una was still under the impression that he was Sean Molloy from Inisheer, old friend of Molly from the year dot. He dried his face and padded back to the bed, sitting down on the side of it.

She moved over to make room for him and came close to him, wrapping her arms around him. 'Well? You didn't answer me. Englishman!' She began to move against him, arching her back, moving her thigh so it lay across both of his, nuzzling her breasts against his side. He was repelled. 'Stop it, Una!' He had spoken more harshly than he had intended and could see that she was hurt. He tried to make it up to her. 'Sorry, I didn't mean it . . .'

But she made a little 'hands-off' gesture, removing herself from him and standing up. He made no move towards her. 'Sorry Una, I really didn't mean it. I'm hot and tired and I've had a really hectic week.'

'So have I, Sean!'

'I know. Let's go out and have a meal or something?'

353

'No, that's OK. I'm tired too. I'll just have a shower.' She took the loose cotton dress which lay on the floor, slipped it over her head and walked the few paces away from him towards the bathroom. He heard the water running in the shower. He sighed. This weekend was going to be tough.

He admitted to an acute longing to see Molly. Una was lovely but she was no substitute. He had to see Molly. He knew her baby was due around this time. They had not met since her marriage to Christian – in fact, since she had told him about the marriage at that lunch. It would have been difficult for them to meet, even if they had wanted to, because they were frequently on different continents. As well as Molly being in America, he, with the co-operation of the zoo which continued to grant leaves of absence, had immersed himself in archaeology and was frequently away participating in excavations.

On the other hand, he had mixed feelings about not seeing her during the past year. He missed her dreadfully and jealously and often woke up in the middle of the night thinking of her. But, given her new status as Mrs Christian Smith, he knew that if he did see her he could not behave naturally towards her in a manner befitting a brother – or even, if there were others around, as the supposed old friend Sean Molloy. It was far easier on them both if they did not meet at all.

They had spoken. She had telephoned him to thank him for his telegram and his present – a damask tablecloth of Irish linen – and on a few occasions since. But mostly they communicated by letter, stilted, formal epistles which might have been between penpals who had tired of the correspondence but who were still committed to it. She wrote about the doings of her new family, particularly of the old man, Malcolm, of whom she seemed very fond. Her visit to Inisheer with Christian to meet Brendan was good for two months' letters. But she was already five months gone when she told him about her pregnancy.

In his turn, when he was abroad he wrote her long involved descriptions of whatever desert or gorge he happened to be in at the time – and since there was every possibility his letters would be read by Molly's husband, he always signed his letters 'Sean'.

The sound of running water continued from the bathroom. He looked around at the tiny room, cluttered and claustrophobic, made more so by Una's scattered belongings and her half-unpacked overnight bag in the middle of the floor. Conor, who had lived alone for so many years, was meticulous and personally very neat and Una's untidiness was an additional source of irritation to him. He had to get out and get some space . . .

He went over to the bathroom door and knocked. She didn't hear him at first and he knocked a second time. The sound of the shower stopped. 'Yes?' she called.

'Una, I'm going out for a few minutes. Won't be long.' He waited.

'OK,' she said then and he heard her resume her shower.

He threw on his clothes, which by habit he had folded neatly on a chair beside the bed, and left the flat taking the three flights of stairs two at a time.

He would have to confront the issue of Una once and for all, he thought as he hurried towards the Traveller, parked a short distance away. Keeping the situation going like this was not fair to either of them.

He got into the car and sat for a few moments, his chest pressed against the steering wheel of the little car, staring at the old-fashioned dashboard without seeing it. The feeling that he should go to Molly was growing more urgent. But how? How could he walk calmly into her life after an absence of more than a year? On what pretext?

This was ridiculous. He did not need any pretext to go to see his own sister. The imminent birth of her baby was the perfect opportunity to contact her – he was family, after all. He would be the baby's uncle. And if Christian answered the door he would deal with that as it happened – say he was just passing or something like that.

He started the car and sped off in the direction of her house in Vernon Street.

When he got there the street was as quiet as usual. He checked his watch – it was just after ten thirty and the streetlamps were lit. Many of the houses showed lights in the windows but there were no lights on in Molly's house. He rang the bell anyway, just in case she – or they – were somewhere in the back, perhaps in the kitchen. He was regretting his impulse – what was he going to say? – and was almost relieved when there was no reply after his third ring. He was just about to leave when he heard the sash on the upstairs window of the adjoining house being lifted.

A head emerged, lit by the streetlamp below. 'Looking for someone?' asked the owner of the head, a middle-aged woman with blonded hair escaping from a headful of curlers.

'Yes, I was looking for Mrs Smith. Sorry to have bothered you,' he called back. 'I hope I didn't wake you up.'

'That's OK, luv,' said the blonde head, 'but you won't find Mrs Smith there tonight. In the hospital, she is. Had the baby by now, I expect. She was taken off at about eight this morning.'

'Thank you very much!' called Conor, feeling silly. 'You don't happen to know which hospital?'

'St Catherine's, I believe,' said the head.

'Thanks again!' called Conor.

'You a relative?' called the woman.

'Friend,' shouted Conor.

'Give her my love, then, when you see her, dear. OK?'

'I will,' he promised.

The window above him closed and he got back into his car. He drove out of Vernon Street and towards Earl's Court. The traffic was light and he risked parking near the Tube station while he ran into the entrance where he knew there would be public telephones. He dialled 142, got the number of St Catherine's private clinic from the operator and then dialled the clinic. It was answered on the second ring.

He said he was making enquiries about a Mrs Molly Smith.

'Just a moment, sir,' said the girl on the switchboard and the line went dead. When it came back a different voice was on the line:

'You're enquiring about Mrs Molly Smith?'

'Yes,' said Conor.

'Is that Mr Smith?' asked the voice.

'Yes,' said Conor immediately, on instinct.

'I'm very glad you telephoned, Mr Smith. We've been trying

356

to contact you at the number you left but there was no reply. Mrs Smith has been asking for you, she is very anxious to talk to you. Can you come in as soon as possible?'

Conor's heart started to thump. 'Yes, certainly I will,' he said. Then, 'Is everything OK with her?'

'The doctor is with her now,' said the voice crisply. 'I've just come on duty myself but I know that things are under control. I'm sure the doctor will fill you in when you arrive.'

'Thank you,' said Conor. He rang off. He stared stupidly at the telephone, at the graffiti, at the little stickers which advertised the services of various strict head-teachers and mistresses. Something was wrong.

He had forgotten to ask for the address of the clinic. And as 'Mr Smith', who should know, he could not call back.

He ran out of the station and, not caring about the hazardously parked Traveller, flagged down a taxi. The cabby knew where the clinic was; it was less than a mile away and getting there would be a matter of only a few minutes.

The hospital was tucked into a Regency terrace of houses in a quiet cul-de-sac. Conor paid off the cab and ran up the short flight of steps. The lobby, furnished with armchairs and coffee tables, was peaceful with Mozart piped discreetly through the greenery which hung from a three-sided mezzanine around the stairwell. The only hint that this was a hospital and not a private hotel was the starched white uniform of the girl behind the reception desk.

'Mr Smith,' he announced, 'to see Mrs Molly Smith.'

He felt like a criminal and in his nervousness and guilt at the impersonation – suppose Christian had arrived since he had made the telephone call? Suppose this girl had seen Christian earlier and remembered him? – his voice was hoarse.

But the girl did not react, merely checked a circular card index file in front of her and directed him to the mezzanine and the lift which would take him to the third floor.

A nurse and a doctor were waiting for him when the lift door opened. The doctor introduced himself as 'Anderson' and asked him to step into the office for a moment. Conor seized the doctor's sleeve. 'Is Molly all right? Is she all right?'

357

'She's fine, Mr Smith. A little agitated and we have given her a light sedative but she is really fine . . . Dr Sinden apologizes that he is not here himself to talk to you – we were trying to contact you for quite a while and eventually he had to leave, I'm afraid. But before he left he familiarized me with the details of the case and asked me to fill you in when we did manage to get in touch.' His voice was serious, urbane, soothing. As he spoke he propelled Conor towards an office. The nurse came with them and closed the door after the two men, seating herself discreetly in a chair half hidden by a filing cabinet.

The doctor indicated that Conor should sit on a chair in front of the desk and himself sat on its edge.

'Is it Molly or the baby?' Conor asked, impatient with the man's scene-setting.

'Your wife is fine, please don't worry about her. She's had a shock and she is naturally depleted and exhausted after giving birth but in time she will come to terms with what has happened.'

'So what's happened? What's wrong with the baby?' It occurred belatedly to Conor that he did not know whether Molly had given birth to a boy or a girl.

The doctor hesitated, then, 'Your daughter may, I stress *may*, be suffering from a condition we call cerebral palsy.' He put his hand on Conor's shoulder, a professional gesture which Conor immediately resented. He forced himself not to shrug it off.

'There is no easy way to say this,' the man went on, 'but your daughter is brain-damaged. It is too early to say how badly or how it happened, whether it is genetic or caused by something during pregnancy or labour. We will do our very best for her, of course, you can rely on that, but I'm afraid the prognosis is not good.'

'You mean she's going to die?'

'Some people with this condition live to be quite elderly.'

'But what do you think about *this* person?'

'It's too soon to tell.'

'You think it's bad, don't you?'

The doctor nodded. 'We always say there is hope in these situations but yes, it's bad.'

'What are the symptoms?'

'Each patient is different, of course, depending on the severity of the brain damage and where in the brain it has occurred. In the case of your daughter it is far too early to tell. We will have to watch her development.' He paused, giving Conor time to assimilate the information.

'In the case of your daughter, Mr Smith,' he continued, 'it appears she might be quadriplegic. In other words – she is largely paralysed. There may be other problems as well. It is quite likely, Mr Smith, that if your daughter survives she will have to be institutionalized.'

Conor had quite forgotten that he was not Molly's husband. He wanted to shake off this man, well intentioned though he was. He stood up. 'Can I see Molly – I mean my wife – now, please?'

'She is probably sleeping,' warned Dr Anderson, 'but of course you can see her.' He got off his perch and held out his hand. 'I'm very sorry. You've had a shock, I know. And I'm sure you think it's easy for me to stand here telling you not to worry too much. But I can assure you that your daughter is in good hands at the moment. Everything which can be done will be done for her, please be sure of that. And we will arrange for a psychologist to see your wife, of course.' He hesitated. 'I'm really sorry . . .' he said again.

Conor took the man's hand and shook it briefly. He no longer felt like an impostor. All thoughts of Christian Smith had left his head.

He followed the doctor out of the door and down a corridor lit with shaded wall lamps. Their footsteps made no sound on the thick carpet. Anderson pushed open a plain heavy door, then stood aside to let Conor go in alone.

The only light in the room was from a dim blue bulb directly over the bedhead. She was asleep on her side breathing softly, her knees pulled up like a child. Her skin was like fine china under the ethereal glow of the nightlight and he thought her more beautiful than he had ever seen her.

Moving very quietly and keeping his eyes on her all the time, he carried a chair from a corner of the room to a spot beside the bed and sat in it as close to her as he possibly could without actually touching her. She did not stir and slept peacefully on. A strand of her hair which had fallen across her cheek wafted on her breath and he longed to touch it, to brush it off. He noticed that the room was full of flowers.

It was very quiet: the sounds from the street outside were muffled by double-glazing and heavy curtains on the windows. On the other side of the door he heard a single clink, bottle against bottle or spoon against glass. He became aware of the blend of scents in the room, a fusion of the hygienic hospital smell and the heady mixture given off by all the different flowers and something else he recognized with surprise as the heavy, bloody scent of parturition. During his island childhood Conor had occasionally been present at the birth of a calf or a litter of puppies. This smell was not dissimilar.

After ten minutes or so she opened her eyes. She looked at him for a moment without recognition and then smiled as guilelessly as a child. 'You came,' she whispered.

He nodded. He thought his heart would split open.

She took her hand out from underneath the coverlet and held it towards him. He gripped it. It was warm and soft from its lair. 'You know about my baby?' she whispered. She was very calm. He nodded again. Her lovely face creased between her eyebrows as she tried to remember something specific. 'There's something wrong with my baby, Conor . . . '

He tightened his grip on her hand and then relaxed it. He was afraid he might crush it. 'Molly, we'll face it together. We'll all help.'

'Where's Christian?'

'I don't know, Molly, but after I leave I'll find him for you.'

'I don't know if he knows yet . . . '

'I don't know either, but this is not something you will have to face on your own, I promise.'

He sat very still. Even under the faint illumination he could see that her eyes, which she held steady on his face, were opaque.

'Did you see her?' she asked, still whispering. He shook his head. 'I did,' she said. 'I saw her. They brought me down to

360

see her. She's in a little glass case. She's very beautiful, like a little delicate shell.' She had difficulty getting her tongue around the words.

'Have you decided on a name for her?' He felt instantly stupid. What difference did it make what this baby was going to be called?

But she answered. 'Margaret Susanna,' she whispered.

'That's a lovely name,' he said. 'Margaret Susanna Smith,' he repeated, barely able to get the words out. 'It's a lovely name.'

'Yes,' she said, 'I know. It's a lovely name.' She closed her eyes.

'I don't suppose you saw the *Evening Standard* this evening?' he asked gently.

'No . . .'

'They say you're an outside chance to win an award at Cannes.'

'Am I? That's nice . . .' She did not open her eyes and Conor thought she had fallen asleep. He hoped that her dreams could be pleasant for a little while.

But her lips moved again. 'Don't leave yet, Conor.'

'I won't.' Very soon after that her hand slackened in his.

When he was sure she was soundly asleep he disengaged himself, finger by finger, and stood up not making a sound. Then, as though he were venerating a shrine, he bent over her and kissed her on her slightly open mouth. Her lips were dry but very soft.

He stood for a few moments looking down at her and left her then, closing the door behind him. From some other part of the building, a great distance away it seemed, he heard the high, frantic mewling of a very young infant. Within seconds another had joined in. He wondered with fleeting bitterness if either of them was Molly's or if, indeed, Margaret Susanna could cry at all.

The dark-skinned nurse at the station in front of the lift looked up as he pressed the call button but he did not acknowledge her smile.

The night air outside was cool and fresh after the overheated

361

hospital. He remembered that in his haste he had forgotten to lock the Traveller. He hoped that it would still be there and went in search of a taxi.

Luck was with him: the car was still where he had parked it. He looked at his watch as he paid off the cab and to his surprise it was not yet midnight. So much had happened to him emotionally in the past two hours that, had he been asked to guess, he would have put the time at nearer two in the morning. He discovered he was very hungry.

The next task was to find Christian but before that he simply had to have something to eat. He saw there was a Wimpy Bar still open near the station. He drove the Traveller along Earl's Court Road and parked it in a small side street, then walked back to the Wimpy. He was the only customer in the glaring, garish shop where he ordered two hamburgers and a bag of chips, wolfing them while standing at the counter, thinking furiously as he ate. He had no idea where Christian might hang out, knew none of his friends or even his acquaintances. They had not a single mutual friend. He regretted bitterly now that he had not kept in touch with his sister. Had Molly given any clues? Had the hospital?

That was it: 'We've been trying to contact you at the number you left but there was no reply . . . '

He finished the last of his chips and walked back towards the Traveller. There was a telephone booth on the corner of the street where he had parked. He had forgotten the number of the hospital and once more had to dial Directory Enquiries to get it.

The hospital again answered on the second ring. Conor took a deep breath and feeling ridiculous, like an actor in a bad B movie, did his best to assume an American accent. 'This is Gerald Smith,' he said. 'I'm the brother-in-law of Mrs Molly Smith who has just had a baby there. I'm trying to get in contact with her husband, who is my brother Christian. I understand he left a number with you?'

'Oh, yes, Mr Smith,' said the receptionist helpfully. 'Just a moment . . . '

There was a click and for a moment the line went dead.

Then she came back and read out the telephone number of Molly's house in Vernon Street. That was no use whatsoever. He thanked the girl and rang off. But at least he knew now that Christian intended to be at home at some stage. He dialled the number but there was no reply. The best thing to do was to go home and keep trying to telephone at intervals throughout the night. Christian was bound to turn up sooner or later – he might even go to the hospital. He might be at the hospital now.

To his surprise Conor felt no dart of jealousy at the thought of Christian at Molly's bedside. He found there had been some sort of catharsis he could not explain but he felt, at least he *hoped*, he would never be jealous of Molly's husband again. It was certainly true for tonight. From now on whatever made her happy would make him happy even if that happiness was in someone else's bed. He started up the car and sped off. He was crystal clear now as to what he would say to Una.

The Friday night crowds in Soho swirled around Christian and Ferdy as they stood outside L'Epicure. Christian, who despite all the alcohol he had consumed had failed to anaesthetize the horror, urged his new friend to come on somewhere with him. 'Come on, Ferdy – it's far too early yet to go home!' If he could have a few more drinks he could postpone going back to the empty house where, alone, he would have to face his demons. Worse, if he did not have somewhere else to go he should, in all fairness, go back to the hospital.

'I – I don't know, Christian.' Ferdy's little face was doubtful. 'Where would we go?'

'Plenty of places,' said Christian. 'London is full of night-clubs.'

'No, I don' think so, Chrissian.' Ferdy was slurring.

'Oh, all right.' Christian was tired of the man anyway. They parted from one another with exchanges of addresses and prom-ises to keep in touch, promises which, in Christian's case, were empty. Then each went on an individual search for a taxi.

The street was so busy that it was twenty minutes before Christian secured one.

'Where to, sir?' asked the cabby. Christian dithered. He should go back to the hospital. He checked his watch – half past midnight. She would undoubtedly be sleeping and his presence would be superfluous again. The cabby waited patiently.

Christian made up his mind. He would salve his conscience by telephoning. And he would then go to the Dorchester to see Malcolm and his grandmother. No one could fault him then. 'Would you take me to the Dorchester, please?' he said. 'But would you stop at a telephone booth on the way?'

The hospital answered on the second ring but he had to raise his voice to be heard above the traffic noise.

'Oh, yes, Mr Smith,' said the receptionist. 'I'll put you through to the floor now.'

'Hello?' said another voice, after a few clicks.

'Hello,' said Christian, speaking slowly and clearly because of the traffic but also so as not to betray that he had had a few drinks. 'This is Christian Smith, Molly Smith's husband.'

'Yes, Mr Smith?'

'I'm just checking on my wife, Molly Smith.'

'Well, there's been no change . . . '

Even through the noise he thought she sounded puzzled. 'I see,' he said, 'is she sleeping?'

'Yes, she is – and I'm sure she'll sleep now till morning.'

'I see. Well, will you take a message, please? Will you tell her when she wakes that her husband telephoned and sends his love and that I'll be in early in the morning.' The voice at the other end made no reply. 'I'm sorry, there's a lot of noise here,' said Christian. 'Did you hear me?'

'Yes, Mr Smith,' said the voice slowly. 'I'll see your wife gets your message.'

'Thanks a lot,' said Christian. He hung up and got into the cab again. 'The Dorchester, please,' he said.

The inaction was driving Malcolm up the wall. He could wait no longer. For the twenty-fifth time that hour he raised the sleeve of his jacket and consulted his watch. After half past midnight. Suppose something was wrong?

He looked across at his wife wishing he had her temperament. She was comfortably ensconced in a couch in the bay window of the small sitting room of their suite, reading a tattered volume she had picked up that day at a second-hand bookshop, *The Making of a Queen – Victoria at Kensington Palace* by an author named Eleanor Graham. This was Cordelia's first time in England and to Malcolm's amused surprise she had revealed a fascination with the British Royal Family.

He sighed noisily. Even the suite was beginning to irritate him. It was decorated in the Regency style with a profusion of pastels and stripes, tassels and furbelows, and now that he had nothing much else to occupy him its repro opulence was beginning to look tasteless to his educated eye. He knew that Cordelia, God bless her, was doing her best. They had eaten in the suite and all evening since they had finished the meal she had been trying to distract him by imparting little titbits of information garnered by Miss Graham for her hagiography of the Princess Alexandrina Victoria.

It was four hours since he had telephoned the hospital. 'There must be some news by now.'

Cordelia lowered her book. 'Malcolm,' she protested in her soft voice, 'it's not all that unusual for a first labour to go on this long. I've known some women who were in labour for up to thirty-six hours. Molly has been at that hospital for only sixteen. Why don't you go to bed and I'll stay up? I promise I'll call you the very minute that telephone rings. Christian won't forget to ring us – he knows how anxious you'll be.'

'There's no point in going to bed,' he said fretfully. 'I couldn't possibly sleep.' He was seated in an armchair with the telephone by his side on a little side table. He gave the side of the instrument an angry thump. 'I want to go over there, Cordelia!'

She put her book face down beside her on the couch, came towards him and went behind his chair, massaging his neck. 'Listen, you old coot, why don't you listen to your wife and go to bed? You know very well that there's nothing you can do over there and sitting here like this you're just going to work yourself up for no reason at all! And then, when the news comes through, you'll be in no condition to appreciate it.'

He put his hand behind his neck and stroked the back of one of hers. 'I'm sorry, my dear, you're right as usual. How come you're always right? I don't know how you put up with me . . . '

'Because I love you, that's why.'

He pulled her round and kissed her. 'Malcolm Smith!' she protested. 'You need a shave!'

'So what? Sign of a real man, m'dear!' They smiled at one another and Cordelia went back to the couch and again picked up her book.

Malcolm sighed and picked up a copy of *Tatler*, one of the magazines the hotel management had supplied as decoration for the coffee table in front of his chair. He turned the pages irritably but could not concentrate on the parade of debs' balls and country weddings.

He jumped when the telephone rang. 'This is reception,' said the voice in his ear. 'Your grandson is here. Shall I send him up?' At last! 'Yes, please, send him up!' he said excitedly into the telephone mouthpiece and replaced it. 'Cordelia, it's Christian! There must be some news!'

He went over to open the door but it was a minute or so before the lift doors opened and Christian emerged. The happy expectation died in Malcolm's soul when he saw his grandson's face. And even before Christian got up to him he could tell he had been drinking. But he bit back the retort which shot to his lips. Remonstrations would be counter-productive if there was, indeed, something wrong. 'Come in, Christian,' he said, standing back to let his grandson through the door ahead of him. 'We were getting worried, we really were.'

Christian walked into the room and across to Cordelia, who still sat on the couch. He leaned forward and kissed her.

'There's something wrong, isn't there, Christian?' she said quietly.

Malcolm came and stood in the centre of the room. He had

not closed the door to the suite. Nervously, he jingled coins in the pocket of his trousers. 'What is it, Christian?'

Christian did not turn round to answer Malcolm but continued to address his grandmother. 'Yes,' he said, 'there is a problem.' Malcolm heard the shake in his voice and saw that he seemed to wobble a little on his feet. 'Sit down, Christian,' he said. He walked to the door of the room and closed it quietly. Then he crossed to the chair he had recently vacated and sat again in it. Christian seated himself beside Cordelia.

'The baby is handicapped, Grandma,' he said. 'She's – it's a girl – she's badly handicapped. Brain-damaged.' He turned his head away and looked into the middle distance. Malcolm stared at him. This could not be happening. Not to this family. Not again.

'Have you seen her, Christian?' Cordelia touched her grandson beside her.

'She's sleeping,' he said. 'They sedated her . . . '

'The baby?' She was puzzled.

'I thought you meant Molly.' Christian's voice was toneless.

'No, I meant – have you seen your daughter?'

'I saw her when she was born. She was blue. It was dreadful.' He put his head in his hands and Malcolm realized that it was, in fact, happening.

'Could I have a drink, please?' Christian asked, muffled.

'Is bourbon all right?' Malcolm went into the bedroom. Cordelia always packed a bottle when they were travelling – to help them sleep in strange beds, she said.

He came out with the bottle in his hand and a glass and handed both to his grandson. Christian poured out a measure and gulped it. He held on to the bottle and was still clutching it when he left the suite five minutes later. For once Malcolm did not have the heart to try to take it away from him.

Before he got to the flat, Conor stopped at a telephone booth and dialled the Vernon Street number again just in case. Still no answer. Then he rang the hospital yet again and said he was making enquiries about Mrs Molly Smith.

There was the usual click before the line went dead and then the woman's voice came back on. 'Are you a relative?'

This time, he said, 'I'm her brother.'

'Yes, well, Mrs Smith is asleep and she is doing fine.'

'Is there anyone with her?' he asked. 'Should I come to sit with her?'

'Just a moment, sir . . . ' said the voice and the line went dead again. After a minute or so, the woman came back on. 'I've been on to the floor, sir, and the staff nurse believes that Mrs Smith should be allowed to sleep.'

'Yes, but is there anyone with her? She shouldn't be alone at a time like this.'

'There are no visitors in the hospital at this hour, sir, only husbands in exceptional circumstances and during labour and birth.'

'Is her husband not with her?' asked Conor.

'Sir.' He could hear she was getting impatient. 'Mrs Smith is *sleeping*.'

'Thank you, I'll call again in the morning.' So at least Christian wasn't there. Now he had to face Una.

Five minutes later he let himself into the house and climbed the stairs making no effort to be quiet. Friday night was party night in the building. There was a fanlight over the door into his own bedsitter and he could see that the light was on. Una was still awake. He realized that, like a coward, he had been secretly hoping that she would be asleep.

'Hello,' she said as he opened the door. She was sitting propped up in the bed, a book in her hands. Scrubbed and in her nightdress, her red hair curling around her face, she looked small and vulnerable as a child – and he felt that what he was about to do was despicable.

'You were a good while!' she said.

'Yes, sorry! Would you like a drink or a cup of tea or coffee or something?'

'I have some duty-free in the bag. I brought it for you but when you were so long I was going to open it myself.'

'All right,' he said. 'I'll get the glasses.'

While he rinsed out a pair of tumblers under the tap at the sink and filled a jug with water she hopped out of bed and rummaged around in the bag, scattering underwear, books and cassette tapes all over the floor. 'Here it is! I always pack it in the bag. I hate carrying those yellow Duty-Free bags through customs at Heathrow. I feel they look at you with contempt, those officers. Ta-raa!' She held up the bottle of Paddy. Then she climbed back into the bed, smoothed the covers around her and looked at him expectantly, the bottle still in her hand. 'Well, come on, slowcoach!'

He brought the glasses over and sat beside her on the bed. She poured two generous measures into the tumblers and replaced the cap. He topped up each glass with water from the jug and then put the jug on the night table.

'Here's looking at you, kid,' said Una, raising her glass in a toast and then taking a sip.

'Are you not going to ask me where I was, Una?' he said quietly, without touching his own drink.

'That's your business. None of mine. We're not umbilically linked, you know!'

She wasn't making this easy for him. He put his untouched drink on the night table beside the jug. 'Una,' he said gently, taking her hand, 'we have to talk.'

'Uh-oh!' she said. 'I don't like the sound of *that*!' Despite the flippant tone he could hear the seriousness.

'There's something I have to tell you.'

'Don't tell me! I knew it all along. You've a wife in Clacton!' She withdrew her hand and took another sip of her drink.

'Una, I'm not married. But I have been deceiving you.' She wrapped both hands around her tumbler and stared into it. 'Are you listening, Una?'

'Oh no, I'm not listening. I'm singing. What do you think I'm doing?' She looked at him then, a straight, direct look. 'You're trying to tell me you're in love with someone else.'

He almost admitted it. The temptation was strong to tell someone, anyone. But not Una. 'It's not that, Una. I'm not who you think I am.'

'What?'

369

'My name is not Sean Molloy.' He watched her while she digested this information.

'I see. Well, am I to know who you are?'

'Do you want to?'

'I'm not sure I'm going to like this but we've come this far . . . ' She made another little gesture which tried to be devil-may-care and failed miserably.

'My real name is Conor Ó Briain and I'm Molly's brother.' She looked genuinely bewildered. As well she might, he thought. 'I'm Molly's brother,' he repeated. 'I've just come from the hospital where Molly has had a baby girl. The baby is handicapped, Una. There are things I have to do now for Molly – for my sister . . . '

He watched her face. To his horror he realized he had made a mess of it. She thought it was going to be all right for them – and of course, from her point of view, why not?

'Oh, Sean!' She put down her drink and hugged him. 'I'm so sorry – I mean I'm so sorry about the baby, but I'll help! I'll do anything I can to help.'

'No, Una.' He removed her arms gently from around his neck. 'That's what I want to tell you. I don't want any help, not from anyone. I want to be on my own.'

She lowered her arms and folded them but he could see it took a while for his meaning fully to register. 'I see,' she said quietly. She picked up her drink again. 'But why, Sean? What difference does it make to us? And by the way,' she added conversationally, 'why the deception? *Why* are you Sean Molloy?'

'If you really want to know I'll tell you but it's a long and very complicated story. I have to find Molly's husband now. He has temporarily vanished.'

'Why, Sean – Conor? I hate that name by the way!' she said with some savagery.

'Why what?'

'You know. The real why. I know you well enough to know you must have your own good reasons for changing your name – and for your sister to collude with you. Are you IRA by any chance?'

He smiled in admiration. 'No, you can take it that I'm not IRA.'

'Well, thank heaven for that!' She attempted to laugh and again failed. 'But the real why is why should your name change affect us?'

'Again, that's a very, very long story. Let's just say that a lot of things have happened together to me – and very suddenly – and that I do, really, need to be on my own for a while.'

She tried one last time. 'For a *while*?'

'Una . . .'

'All right, all right!' She adopted a stage-Irish accent. 'I know when I'm beat!' She tossed her drink back in one gulp and placed the glass with exaggerated care on the side table. Then, business-like, she looked at her watch. 'Do you want me to leave straight away? It's a bit late . . .'

He thought again she looked like a child pretending to be grown-up. He took her in his arms. 'Oh, Una!'

But she disentangled herself. 'Now now! Mustn't be sentimental about these things!' Her mouth set itself in a parody of a smile and Conor felt abjectly guilty. He stood up. 'Of *course* you don't have to leave now, Una. And I hope you'll stay the weekend?'

'*Please*, Sean!' She shouted it at him and picked up the book which lay discarded beside her on the bedcover. Turning away from him she threw it with all her strength, not at him but away from him against the wall on the far side of the bed. The book was a paperback and it crashed harmlessly against the wall making no mark, falling with a soft thud on the carpeted floor.

Conor held up his hands in surrender. Although he was feeling so guilty about causing her such obvious pain the last thing he wanted was a scene. 'All right,' he said, 'but please stay as long as you like. I have to go out now to see if I can locate Molly's husband.'

Una swallowed. 'Yes, Molly. Well. Mustn't keep you from Molly.' Her voice was bitter. She swallowed again, hard, and Conor saw that she was having difficulty fighting back the tears.

371

'Una,' he said again, taking a step towards the bed.

But it was her turn to hold up her hands to stop his advance. She kept her eyes fixed on one of the buttons of his shirt. 'I really am very sorry about the baby. You know that. Please give Molly my love.' Her voice wobbled.

'I will.'

'And,' she said, bringing her voice under control again, 'I'm putting you on notice that I *will* want to know about all the mystery. It's just that I can only handle one thing at a time . . . at the moment . . . '

He felt as though he was whipping her. He now wanted badly to get away. 'You will know. I promise.' He looked back at her from the door as he let himself out. She was out of the bed, her back to him, picking up her book from the floor. He saw her shoulders were shaking and wavered for a moment. Then, resolutely, he closed the door.

He got to the house in Vernon Street just after one thirty, parked a little way down the street and turned the engine and the lights off to wait. He wished he had brought a coat because the night, after the earlier heat, had turned quite chilly. He managed to doze a little, however, and it was after two when he became aware that a taxi was turning into the street. Thank God!

The taxi stopped in front of the house, diesel engine ticking quietly, and after what seemed like a very long time the back door opened and Christian got out into the pool of yellow light cast by the streetlamp. Even from a distance of twenty yards Conor could see that he was in a state. His hair was dishevelled and his shirt collar open. His knees buckled under him as he got out of the cab and he had to lean against it with both hands or he might have fallen.

Conor felt the bile rise in his throat but took a firm hold on his emotions. He must stay calm and in control.

After the taxi drove away Christian stayed where he was on the pavement looking after it, his hands slack and hanging, knees still bent, head wobbling slightly on his neck. When it was turning out of the street he made a peculiar gesture in its direction, raising both arms in the air as though he were a victorious general saluting his victorious troops. Then he let his arms drop, shrugged at the now-empty street and turned, aiming the crown of his head at his front door.

Conor got out of his car, closing the door very quietly so he would not startle him. He walked towards him. 'Christian,' he said when he had got within earshot.

Christian reacted without surprise, turning his head. 'Oh! Who're – who're you?' he said, mystified.

'Good evening, Christian,' said Conor. 'I've been looking for you. Molly would like to see you.'

'Molly?'

'Yes! Your wife, Molly!' Conor clenched his fists by his side.

'Moll – Molly wants to – wants to see me *now*?' Christian staggered a little into the gutter. 'But who're *you*?'

'You may not remember but we met once,' said Conor. There was no point in fudging now. On the other hand, the man was so drunk he probably would not remember. 'I'm your wife's brother, Conor,' he said crisply.

Christian gave the impression he was dredging through his memory. 'I've never met you . . . Wait a minute . . . you – you – you're the guy in the dressing-room, Mallarkey . . .'

'Molloy,' said Conor crisply. 'But believe me, I'm Ó Briain, Conor Ó Briain, Molly's brother. Could we go inside now?'

But Christian was still stuck two sentences back. 'Molly wants to see me *now*?'

'Come on, Christian.' Conor took his arm. 'Let's go inside and we'll have a cup of coffee. No point in talking out here.'

Christian tried to shrug off his arm but he was no match for Conor's iron grasp. 'OK, OK!' He extracted his keys from his jacket pocket and Conor, whose impatience was getting the better of him, took them from him and opened the front door.

He switched on the lights. The hallway bore the marks of a hurried departure. There was an empty paper bag lying on the floor and a single shoe abandoned under the coatstand. The mail had not been picked up.

373

He shepherded the shambling Christian down the three steps towards the kitchen at the back of the house. When he switched the light on in here he saw further evidence that Molly had left in a hurry. Dirty dishes were piled in the sink and the lid was off the coffee-pot as if she had been about to empty the stale grounds but had changed her mind – or been interrupted.

Conor, totally in charge now, found the packet of coffee and filters in a cupboard, rinsed out the old grounds into the sink and measured out enough coffee to hype up an elephant. He filled the percolator and plugged it in. While he waited for it to bubble he glanced at Christian. To his dismay he saw that his eyes were closed. He was nodding off over the table.

'Hey!' he called loudly. 'Hey, Christian! Wake up! The coffee's just ready.'

Christian opened one bleary eye. 'What are you doing here, Mallarkey?' he asked in astonishment.

'I'm making you a cup of coffee, Christian. We have to go to see Molly.'

'Molly?' asked Christian blankly.

It was clearly no use. Christian would do more harm than good tonight, anyway. 'All right, man,' said Conor. 'Come on, I'll help you up the stairs.' Christian shrugged and allowed himself to be helped up from his seat and co-operated willingly as Conor half carried, half frog-marched him up the stairs.

When they got to the bedroom Conor aimed his burden at the bed and heaved. Christian landed face down, his feet dangling over the side. He fell asleep instantly.

Conor drew back, panting a little. Christian was almost as tall as he was and, being dead-weight, had been very heavy. He looked around the room. He had never been in it before. It had Molly's stamp all over it – fresh flowers in a jug on a little desk in the window, soft sheepskin rugs on the bare floor.

There was a Moses basket, draped with *broderie anglaise* and sprigged cotton, in one corner of the room and piled underneath and around it were unopened boxes, which, he could see by the illustrations on them, held baby equipment. Beside the basket, an archway had been broken through the wall into the next room, which had been converted into a sort of dressing room. It contained two huge Victorian wardrobes, two tallboys, several chests of drawers and a dressing-table in front of the window, the wooden frame of its mirror bristling with electric bulbs. There was also a wooden clothes-horse, now bare. The wardrobes both hung open. One, obviously Christian's, was disorderly with suits, jackets and shirts. Ties were strewn untidily on the floor in front of it and shoes stuffed any old how underneath its graceful arched front. The other wardrobe was Molly's, hung neatly with dresses, blouses and skirts in the soft fabrics and plain colours she favoured.

He looked back at Christian, who was snoring, and then went over to Molly's wardrobe. He ran his hands over some of the dresses she had worn and the rough skin snagged on some of the filmier fabrics. He recognized the dress of pale blue silk with the pleated sleeves, which she had worn on the day she told him she was going to be married. It was as soft as a cobweb when he touched it and still smelled of her. The hanger rattled slightly, causing him to check over his shoulder again. But Christian had not stirred.

Conor went back into the main bedroom and took off the other man's shoes, which still dangled over the side of the bed. They were slip-on and came off easily. Then he crossed the floor to open the window to cool the room as he thought it might help in the sobering-up process. He was leaning across the desk to pull up the sash when his eye was caught by a silver-framed photograph lying flat on the surface of the desk. It was Molly's portrait of their mother, Sorcha. And in a corner of it, tucked into the frame, was a blurred black and white snapshot of the whole family. They were all standing, Micheál and Brendan in front of the cottage, stiff and unsmiling, staring straight at the camera, Sorcha between them, her hand up to her eyes to shade them from the sun and Conor himself, in short pants, looking away from the photographer towards the edge of the picture. He had one hand outstretched towards his baby sister. Molly, about two years old, was standing, back to the camera and feet planted firmly apart. She held both hands clasped behind her back and her head to one side, obviously defying her brother's blandishments to stand into the picture.

375

There was another beside it, also framed in silver, a formal wedding photograph of Molly and Christian. He was looking at her, an expression of happy adoration on his face. She was solemn and very beautiful. Conor forgot his mission to open the window and, feeling he was trespassing, left the room, closed the door after him and went down the stairs.

The aroma of coffee was thick in the kitchen. He poured himself a cup and added three teaspoonfuls of sugar to it to assuage its bitterness. He opened the door of the small refrigerator and his nostrils were assaulted by the aroma from something liquid and red in a small bowl – but there was no milk. There was hardly any food in the fridge at all, apart from the contents of the bowl, a small piece of cheese, a head of lettuce and the heel of a loaf of bread. As ever Conor was hungry. It was Friday, he thought – no Saturday now. Molly probably did her shopping at the weekend.

He looked at the piece of cheese and, sighing, picked it up and put it on the bread. Then he carried the makeshift sandwich over to the table, pulled out a chair, angling it so he could prop up his feet. It was going to be a long night.

He stayed at the table for what remained of the darkness, getting up now and then to walk around the kitchen stretching his legs. Once, just before dawn, he went through the conservatory which led off the kitchen and out into the miniature garden Molly had created on her flagged patio. It was south-facing and she had trained all sorts of creepers and flowering plants to grow on trellises fastened onto the whitewashed walls: clematis, lobelia, various ivies, old-fashioned climbing roses. There were geraniums and pelargoniums in pots and huge tubs filled with red and orange nasturtiums. The pearly light which precedes the dawn was not yet strong enough to make much of a differentiation in the colours of the flowers – and many were still curled tightly closed – but their combined scent was already riotous. He remembered Molly, lying so still in her blue, flower-filled grotto at St Catherine's . . .

He stayed on the patio, breathing in the inert moist air, watching the flowers come slowly to life as the sky flushed first salmon-coloured, then gold, then the palest shade of blue

376

patterned with clouds of pink and white. It was going to be another warm sunny day.

He went into the kitchen and brewed more coffee. If St Catherine's was a typical hospital it would not be long before Molly was wakened. It was time to wake her husband.

He remembered something.

He let himself out of the house, propping the front door ajar with a newspaper, got into his car and began to tour the streets. He was searching for somewhere to buy milk but there were no all-night shops in the neighbourhood.

He gave up and drove back to Vernon Street but as he turned off the engine of the Traveller he spotted that many of the houses had had a delivery from the early-morning roundsman. Moving and feeling like the thief he was, Conor selected a house a few doors up from Molly's and picked up a bottle of milk from in front of its door.

CHAPTER ELEVEN

Christian did not know what hit him. He was woken violently by a crashing sound and then, a second later, the pain descended on the poll of his head like a pile-driver. He risked opening his eyes to find that the crashing sound was of both windows in the room being raised. To his surprise, then outrage, he saw that they were being raised by a man he did not recognize. If the man was a burglar why was he opening windows? But when he tried to remonstrate, to ask what the devil was this man doing in his private bedroom, the pain strangled the words in his throat. He closed his eyes again, he was too sick to care if there was a whole army of burglars in his room.

He was so sick he felt like crying. Something cut uncomfortably into his stomach and he realized it was his belt buckle. He must have gone to sleep fully dressed. He could remember nothing of how he got home, nothing after he had gone to see his grandfather in the Dorchester.

Sick as he was he was outraged when the burglar came over and shook him. He groaned into the bedspread under his face and tried to lift his head to tell the man to get lost but the pain shot all the way down to his toes and no words came out of his mouth. The shaking was rattling his teeth as though they were electrosensitized steel bearings in his painful jaws. Even his ears hurt. 'Go away!' he managed thickly but the burglar would not let up.

'Come on, Christian, come on!' The man's voice was like sandpaper on Christian's painful scalp. 'You have to get up. I'm not leaving you until you do. If you don't get up I'll pour cold water all over you.'

Christian was too sick to fight. It seemed far easier to do what the man wanted. He inched his knees upwards and, still without lifting his pounding head, sought the floor with his feet. Then he crept backwards off the bed, leaving his head as the last part of his body to be lifted. He kept his head low, at right angles to his body, while he stumbled towards the bathroom.

His torturer was there ahead of him and the shower was running. 'Who the hell are you?' he managed, but the effort caused him to retch.

'We met last night,' said the man. 'My name is Conor Ó Briain. I'm your wife's brother.'

'You're in Aus-Australia or something!'

'No, I'm not. I'm right here and you're going to take a long shower.'

Christian was too sick to resist. Keeping his head low and sideways in an effort to minimize the pain, he stripped off his clothes and, leaving them where they lay in an untidy heap, stepped into the shower.

He screamed. The water was as cold as ice and the shock made his heart beat so savagely that to add to the pain in his head he now had a sharp pain in his chest. He crashed out of the shower again but the man was there, a stone wall, blocking his way. 'Get back in there!' he said.

Christian had had enough. 'Fuck off!' He pushed his head upwards under the man's chin like a butting ram. '*Fuck off!*' The pain swelled and nearly split his skull.

The man did not move, neither did he seem in the least perturbed by the outburst. 'We have to get to the hospital as soon as possible,' he said. 'Please get back into the shower. You are in no condition to go anywhere at the moment.'

Christian made a canopy of his hands over his eyes as if by doing so he could tie the pain inside and stop it bursting out through his forehead. He glared at his enemy from under them. '*We* have to go to the hospital?'

'Christian, we're wasting time. Your wife has been trying to contact you. I happened to go in to see her last night. I promised her I would bring you in.'

Chilled by his encounter with the cold water, naked and dripping, Christian started to shiver. He stared at the man from under the little tent of his hands. He was standing in his own bathroom, after all. The man was an intruder. 'Have we met before?' he said, with as much hostility in his voice as he could muster.

'Yes, we have. The first night you arrived in London with that phoney story about interviewing my sister.'

'Mallarkey!'

'Molloy. Now are you going to get back in that shower or do I have to push you?'

For a few seconds more they continued to glare at one another. Christian was shaking all over now but he saw that no quarter would be given and in his present condition he knew he would be no match for his implacable adversary if push came to shove. So he caved in and stepped back into the shower, taking care not to let the water hit him before he had turned the mixer tap to a respectable temperature.

He stayed in for a good twenty minutes, letting the water beat on his sore head, massaging its warmth into his face and the back of his neck. He felt marginally better when he turned it off and went back into his bedroom to dress. He could smell coffee from downstairs and the aroma of something cooking. It turned his stomach.

When he got to the kitchen the other man was standing at the sink with his back to him and clouds of steam arose round his head as he drained something out of a pot. Potatoes. The man was cooking potatoes at this hour of the morning!

'Are you crazy?' Christian managed to ask before he found himself being forced by a strong hand to sit at the kitchen table while a quantity of soft boiled potatoes were poured out of the pot on to a shallow dish already set between a knife and fork.

Christian looked with horror at the steaming, soggy potatoes which had been boiled so soft they were almost mashed. The mound was bleeding a substance like lumpy wallpaper paste at the edges. Worse was to come. From a small pan, Conor poured hot milk all over the mess in the dish. He passed over the salt and pepper shakers. 'Eat!' he ordered.

'I don't want them. I couldn't eat them. I'll get sick!' Christian tried to muster some degree of self-righteous outrage. 'Fuck off!'

380

he said, pushing back his chair, which scraped horribly on the tiled floor.

'*Eat!*' thundered the other man, restraining him from standing up. Christian looked from the plate to Molloy and saw the menace in the man's eyes. For the third time in half an hour, he gave in. He picked up his fork and took a tentative mouthful. To his surprise, he did not gag.

He shook a liberal helping of salt and pepper all over the food and in a few minutes had finished what was in the dish. Then Molloy poured out a cup of strong tea and put it in front of him while he poured coffee for himself. Christian wanted to say that he would prefer coffee but accepted the black tea and drank it meekly without comment.

'If you're Molly's brother how come your name's Molloy?' he asked.

'It's a long story,' said the other man and Christian did not have the energy to pursue it. Although he was still feeling very sorry for himself he had to admit that in whatever Irish bog this man had learned his hangover cures, they were effective. He was feeling more human than he had forty-five minutes ago.

'Right,' said Molloy when he had finished his coffee. 'I have my car outside. It's nearly a quarter to seven. I'll have you at the hospital before a quarter past.' The horror of his situation was re-borne on Christian.

They drove through the Saturday streets in silence and Christian opened the window and held his face out to the cool morning air. They got there all too soon.

If their mission had not been so fraught, thought Conor as he turned off the engine, he would have enjoyed this quiet part of London. The sunlight was filtered on to the pavements through the branches of the plane trees and, in the absence of weekday traffic, the chirping of sparrows was loud in their branches. He turned to Christian. 'Here we are!'

The other man's face was haggard and Conor felt almost sorry for him as he opened the door, swung his legs onto the pavement and said with some dignity, 'Thank you for the ride.'

381

Then, with something approaching an appeal, 'Are you coming in too?'

Conor shook his head. 'I'll come in later. You'll need some time alone with Molly.'

Christian got out and closed the door. The Traveller was parked about twenty yards beyond the clinic and Conor watched him in the driving mirror as he walked slowly back towards it and climbed the flight of steps to the front door. He decided to get out of the car too to get some fresh air. The end of the cul-de-sac was formed by one side of some railings which enclosed a small park and, not bothering to lock the car doors, Conor strolled towards them, letting himself into the park through a wicket gate.

It was a pleasant place, cool and green boasting flowering shrubs and trees, flowerbeds, an expanse of daisied lawn and a pond not much bigger than a large puddle. He had it all to himself and walked a slow circuit of the railings. Then he flopped on to his back on the grass beside the pond. As his ears adjusted to the quietness he could hear, alongside the birdsong, the minute paddling and scudding of water insects going about their business above and below the surface of the stagnant water, its smell warm and fusty in his nostrils. There were other insects at work too. Under his palm on the grass he felt tiny movements, of ants probably and spiders. A cabbage butterfly fluttered across his line of vision, making him blink and he realized how tired he was. It was a relief to close his eyes and, thankful it was his Saturday off, he did not resist as he felt himself drift off into a gentle doze.

As soon as Christian entered the hospital lobby his queasy stomach began to heave again. He asked the receptionist where the lavatory was and she pointed to a doorway, half-hidden behind a flowering tree. He got into the cubicle just in time to vomit.

He stood for a long time, knees quivering, before coming out to wash his hands and face. A discreetly lit mirror hung behind the wash-basins and as he ran water over his hands Christian

382

studied his reflection. He was very pale, he saw, but other than that quite presentable. He thought of his wife waiting for him in the bed – and of his brain-damaged daughter, probably in an incubator. One of Christian's lifelong habits was to add the sums of his life in plus and minus columns to see how they balanced out. Looking in the mirror now, he examined his present situation as objectively as he could.

On the positive side:
He was healthy.
He was young.
He was a good journalist.
He was a good provider for his family.

On the negative side:
He was the father of a handicapped baby.
He did not love his wife.
He drank too much.
He made his wife unhappy.
His wife had no respect for him.
His wife was right.

The conclusion was inescapable. He was professionally competent and personally a loser. He would be no good for this baby and this wife – or any wife.

Even if Molly never worked again, which, with her talent, was doubtful, she and the baby would have no material problems – his grandfather would see to that. Only one course lay open to him. Molly would see in time that he had done her a favour.

Christian dried his hands very carefully and combed his hair. Then he left the lavatory and went back out through the lobby of the hospital. The receptionist, busy on the telephone, did not give him a second glance as he passed out into the London day.

Conor woke with the snuffling of a dog at his ear. It was an over-fed Jack Russell and its owner, a small elderly lady dressed more for a winter drawing room than a stroll in a summer park, was calling it in a quavering voice from the perimeter of the park. 'Toddy, Toddy! Come back here! Come here this instant!' Conor sat up feeling lightheaded. He patted the dog, which wagged its tail, barked and then trotted busily back to its mistress who leaned down and gave it a slap on the nose for its trouble.

Conor bent his head to his knees until the dizziness cleared and then looked at his watch. He had been asleep for nearly half an hour, he reckoned, and he thought he might decently venture now to join Christian and Molly in the clinic.

He felt scruffy, however, and longed for a shower and a change of clothes. Luckily, since his beard needed shaving twice a day, he kept a battery-operated razor in the glove compartment of the car. He walked back to the Traveller and sat in it, angling the driving mirror towards him, scraping the buzzing razor over the dark stubble. Although Conor used mirrors for his daily ablutions, he rarely saw himself. His own face was of no interest to him. But through the car window this morning the sun caught his face obliquely and he saw with some surprise that his beard was now well speckled with grey. He was getting old he thought.

He finished his task and ran his fingers through his unruly hair, smoothing it down as best he could. Then he got out of the car, locking it this time, and walked towards the clinic.

There was a different atmosphere in the foyer this morning. The doors had been propped open to admit the air and sunshine and a woman was passing a whining vacuum cleaner over the carpet. Another was moving along the mezzanine, using a can with a long spout to water the plants. Conor saw that someone different from last night sat at the reception desk but this time did not announce himself. He smiled in her direction and passed up the stairs as though he belonged in the place.

He was not so confident, however, when he emerged from the lift onto Molly's corridor. He had not thought out how he was going to explain his impersonation of last night should he encounter any of the people he had met. Now that Christian was around there could be no doubt in anyone's mind but that something fishy was going on. Christian and he bore not the slightest resemblance to one another.

He recognized the dark-skinned nurse he had seen the night before and braced himself for an awkward question. But she just smiled at him. 'Hello, Mr Smith,' she said. He smiled back, relieved. Christian must have walked past her or she might have been absent from her post for a few minutes.

He was almost at Molly's door when he heard a man's voice call. 'Mr Smith! Mr Smith!' What was he to do? It was the doctor, Anderson, who had spoken to him the previous night. Obviously the man had not yet met Christian. He waited while the doctor caught up with him.

'Good morning, Mr Smith,' said the doctor, slightly out of breath. 'I've just had a call from Dr Sinden and he would like to see you when he gets here. He should be in at about nine o'clock.'

'Thank you,' said Conor. 'How is the baby?'

'There is little change at the moment although we should know more when we get the results of the tests we did yesterday. Normally we would have to wait until Monday but, thanks to Dr Sinden's status here, we managed to jump the queue in the lab.'

'Thank you,' said Conor. The doctor turned and went back the way he had come and Conor proceeded to Molly's room.

The room was bright with sunshine and colourful with the masses of flowers, very different from the dim blue grotto he remembered. She was sitting up in bed, propped high against a heap of pillows and was facing away from the door gazing out of the window so that at first she did not hear him come in. Her hair had been combed, he saw, but dark circles shadowed her eyes and the eyes themselves were puffy. He thought she must recently have been crying.

No one else was in the room, which he thought odd. Perhaps Christian had come in and left again immediately? 'Hello, Molly,' he said softly from the doorway, not wanting to startle her.

She turned to face him and her face suffused with pleasure. 'Hello, Conor,' she said. 'You came again. I'm really glad.'

'Has Christian left?' he asked.

She looked puzzled. 'He hasn't been yet,' she said. 'I'm expecting him, though. He rang some time during the night and left a message that he would be in first thing this morning. He's probably still asleep,' she added loyally.

Perhaps Christian was in the lavatory. It had been a long time since Conor had had a hangover of the type he was sure was afflicting Christian but he did have some idea of what the other man was suffering. 'Has the doctor been to see you this morning?' he asked, pulling a chair to the side of the bed.

She shook her head. 'Not yet, but the nurse said he'd be in quite early.'

Conor was still wondering about Christian. He had seen him come in, after all. Perhaps he was down at the nursery. 'Are you *sure* you haven't seen Christian?' he asked.

'No. Why do you ask?'

'It's just that ... oh, never mind. How are you feeling this morning?'

'I'm fine, grand ... ' Then, hesitantly, 'Would you like to see the baby?'

He nodded and she got out of bed and reached for her dressing-gown. He noticed that the nightdress she was wearing had a peculiar buttoned flap at the breast and realized that it was to facilitate breast-feeding.

As she led him towards the nursery he braced himself for what he was about to see. He was not in the least squeamish but he had never encountered a brain-damaged newborn baby before and did not know what to expect. He hoped that for Molly's sake he could make the right responses.

Margaret Susanna was the only baby in the nursery. The others, explained Molly, were all with their mothers being fed. Her voice was matter-of-fact, too matter-of-fact, thought Conor as he looked at his only niece through two glass walls, the outer wall of the nursery and the wall of the incubator in which she lay.

She was naked, lying on her stomach, her tiny, fleshless buttocks almost non-existent. She had a thatch of reddish-blonde hair and her eyes were closed. Rubber suction pads were fixed to her back and arm; her face was turned towards him and he could see tubes in her nose and coming out of her mouth. The wires and tubes led to a variety of machines and monitors around the incubator and yet another tube trailed from a bag which hung on a stand, the end of it fixed to one of her matchstick arms with a miniature splint. She was so puny and still – it was difficult to believe that she was alive at all but he assumed that the blinking lights on the monitors attested that she was. Even at this distance and allowing for the tube he could see that her mouth was misshapen.

Desperately he searched for the right words but Molly saved him. 'Isn't she beautiful?' she whispered. She looked up at him with an appeal in her eyes.

'She is absolutely beautiful, Molly,' he said. He felt once again that he would go to the ends of the earth, fight any foe, to protect this sister from further harm. He looked again at Margaret Susanna. Even this situation was not insuperable. He would help her.

But where the hell was Christian? 'Are you sure Christian was not in earlier?' he asked softly. 'He couldn't have come in without your knowing? Were you out of the room for any length of time?'

She looked at him, puzzled again. 'No, Conor. Anyway, even if he had come in and I was out he would have waited, surely, or left a message. Why do you ask?'

'No why,' he said and she did not pursue it. It was very odd.

They stood there for a while longer but the baby did not stir at all although the monitors continued their steady green vigil.

Eventually they walked slowly back towards Molly's room. When they pushed open the door the room was not empty. Malcolm and Cordelia were sitting stiffly side by side in two chairs beside the bed. Molly exclaimed and crossed the floor, giving each of them a hug. Malcolm tried to stand but she pushed him back down. 'Oh, Malcolm!' she said. 'Have you heard?'

The old man was older than Conor had expected from reports in Molly's letters. Even through that stilted, formal prose Malcolm had appeared to be lively and full of energy. But this Malcolm Smith, although distinguished and aristo-cratic-looking, sagged in his chair, his knobbed hand clutched, clawlike, around the handle of a cane. In the bright morning sunlight he was as pale as a tallow candle. His wife Cordelia was a handsome woman who looked interrogatively towards the door where Conor lingered, uncomfortably unsure whether he should come in or not.

Molly hesitated, not knowing how to introduce him, but he let her off the hook and took charge, walking towards the couple and holding out his hand. 'Good morning, Mr and Mrs Smith,' he said. 'Your daughter-in-law has told me a lot about you. I'm her brother, Conor.' Molly gasped. He turned to her. 'It's all right, Molly,' he said. 'All that's over and done with as from today.'

Conor was somewhat surprised to hear the confident tone of his own words. 'I've made up my mind that I'm going to sort things out,' he continued and then turned back towards Malcolm. 'I'm sorry we have to meet in such circumstances.'

The old man extended his hand with grave courtesy and Conor wished he did not look so scruffy. He fancied he saw what Molly liked in Malcolm. Even in his present sad state, there was a sort of nobility about him.

'I'm very glad to meet you,' said Malcolm. 'And I'm glad Molly here has you around at a time like this.' He turned again to Molly who was sitting on the edge of her bed, facing him. 'This is the brother you told me about, the one who's the botanist?' She nodded.

Conor thought it pointless and inappropriate to go into lengthy explanations as to his present lowly occupation at London Zoo, so to forestall any more talk about himself he moved a little across the room to support his tired back against the wall.

'I'm so sorry. I feel really helpless,' the old man said then. 'And if I feel bad I can imagine what you must feel, you and Christian. Where is Christian, by the way?'

Molly shrugged. 'He'll be in soon, I'm sure. He sent me a message. It's still very early.'

The old man's expression seemed, to Conor, to sharpen but he did not press the issue of Christian's whereabouts. 'Molly,' he said, with something which sounded to Conor like an appeal in his voice, 'please be sure that we, Cordelia and I, we'll do anything, I promise . . .'

A picture of Margaret Susanna's immobile, skewered little body rose in Conor's brain and he knew in his heart that, with the best will in the world, there was very little that anyone could do. He studied the carpet, which was expensive and of a misty blue like immature heather.

'I already love her, I really do . . .' Molly whispered, close to crying.

'I'm sure you do, my dear,' said Malcolm, 'and we'll all take care of her together. This is one area where money can help and, thank the Lord, we have no problems on that score. I'll organize the best help, the best medical advice and the most advanced treatment that money can buy.' He paused and looked across at his wife, then back at Molly. 'Do you think we could see her, my dear?'

'Maybe Molly's not up to it, Malcolm.' It was the first time Conor had heard Cordelia speak. She had an attractive, low-pitched voice.

'No, that's all right, Cordelia,' said Molly. She walked round the bed, took a tissue from a box on the night locker and blew her nose. 'Sorry for blubbing like this,' she said. 'I'll bring you to the nursery now.'

Conor felt that his presence was not needed for the moment. And he realized he was fired with new energy. Having made the first great leap, the admission as to his identity, his urge now was to continue, to tie up all loose ends, to get rid of anything extraneous to this new certainty in his life. 'Molly, I'll head off,' he said, 'but I'll come back again this afternoon.'

She was in control of herself again. 'I'll walk with you to the lift,' she said.

The lift was stuck on some floor below. They could hear a clanking noise as something big, probably a bed with a patient on it, was loaded. While they waited she blew her nose again. 'Sorry about that outburst back there, Conor,' she said, 'I'm afraid I don't know whether I'm coming or going.'

'Don't apologize,' he said and lapsed into silence. He was again very conscious of her physical nearness and, even if she were not his sister, in her present state his desire – even the thought of desire – was so inapt that he felt he must be some sort of monster. She was holding her arms crossed under her breasts which, swollen with milk, strained the buttons of her dressing-gown. He could just make out the dark circles of the aureoles through the gown, which was of fine lawn, and he had the insane urge to put his mouth over them to suckle them.

The lift came at last and, shaken, he got into it.

Una took a last look round the small bedsitter and picked up her bag. She stood for a second or two, deep in thought, then sat at the counter-top which separated Conor's kitchenette from his living space and served as dining table and desk. She extracted from her shoulder bag a shorthand pad and pen and scribbled Conor a note.

> Dear Conor,
> There is nothing so trite, I know, as goodbye notes so I will make this as brief as possible. If you think this is a bit undignified (to write at all, I mean) I'm sorry. My motto in life has been 'nothing venture . . . etc'. Strange as it may seem, I'm not used to being dumped! I'm tempted to tell you simply to fuck off. There are lots of really terrific bitchy things I could think of which would make your hair curl even more than it does already! But even if I did tell you to fuck off I wouldn't really mean it. It would be pride speaking and I have found that pride is a very lonely virtue.
> So, my dear, this is it, it seems. I want to think of something noble and Jane Austenish to say, but can't for the life of me. Some wordsmith I am!
> I suppose I'm hoping that if I'm patient, we might

sometime get together again. Anyway, I've enjoyed it.
Can't say any more without getting all smarmy.
Una
P.S. I think, actually, I'm brilliant to be taking this so
calmly. What do you think?

Una did not reread the note in case she changed her mind. She folded it, left it under Conor's tea caddy on the counter-top and replaced the pad and pen in her shoulder bag. She picked up her other bag from the middle of the floor and, without again looking back, let herself out of the flat.

At the clinic Dr Sinden left Molly's room, leaving Molly, Malcolm and Cordelia in a state of despair. None of them spoke after he went. He had been very kind but had put no gloss on the facts. Margaret Susanna was quadriplegic. She had a hole in her heart, a cleft palate and would be, as far as they could judge at the moment, profoundly deaf. It was too early to tell about her sight. The results of the tests were not all available so he had no definite explanations to offer as yet. The birth had been normal with no significant deprivation of oxygen. It would be weeks possibly before it was known for sure what factor or combination of factors had caused the baby's multiple handicaps. 'It could even be genetic,' he had concluded, 'and to eliminate that possibility we will probably have to do tests on yourself, Mrs Smith, and on your husband.'

After he left Molly stood gazing out of the window with her back to the other two. Malcolm and Cordelia sat side by side facing Molly's empty bed. It was Cordelia who broke the silence. 'Do you think we should pray?'

'No!' Molly and Malcolm had spoken simultaneously. Molly turned round. 'Sorry, Cordelia, I didn't mean to speak to you like that.' She crossed the room and got into the bed, arranging the covers over her. Then she lay on her back, eyes wide open staring at the ceiling. She had been on such a see-saw of emotions over the past twenty-four hours that she felt now she should be hysterical. But all she experienced was a great anger. And, well

391

intentioned and loving though Malcolm and Cordelia were, she wanted to be alone. The silence dragged on. She could hear the breath of the old man wheezing slightly in his chest.

'Where's Christian?' he asked out of the blue. 'Christian should be here . . . '

'What time is it?' Molly, who up to now had felt the need to be loyal to her husband in front of his grandfather and others, did not care any more.

'It's just after ten o'clock,' said Cordelia.

'Well, then, I don't know where he is,' said Molly. 'He's probably in some public house.'

'Is he drinking much?' asked Malcolm quietly.

'I don't know,' she said. 'Stands to reason, doesn't it?'

'Would you like us to leave, Molly?' Malcolm had sensed her mood.

'I am a bit tired, to tell you the truth.'

He stood up. Molly looked at his dear face, lined with suffering about the baby and concern for herself. She regretted her rudeness and sat up, holding her arms out for a hug. 'Malcolm, I feel so alone. Everyone is being so kind but I feel so alone. I've never even held her, you know.'

Leaning heavily on his cane with one hand, he bent over to give her a one-armed hug. 'It is just terrible and . . . ' He struggled to find words as he straightened up. 'Would you like a priest to come to see you?'

She shook her head. 'I do talk to God but in my own way. I'm very angry with God and the last thing I want to hear is about some Divine Plan.'

Malcolm looked helplessly at Cordelia, then back at Molly who kept her eyes fixed on the ceiling. 'You know where we'll be if you want us, honey,' he said. 'Please don't hesitate to call if there is anything at all you want – even if it's just to talk. I'll be in touch anyway. I'll call this afternoon and, if you feel up to it, we'll come back again this evening after supper. And tell that grandson of mine when he does turn up that he has me to answer to if he doesn't pull himself together!'

She nodded, keeping her eyes glued to the ceiling, not trusting herself to speak.

They left then, Malcolm leaning heavily on his cane.

But Molly was not to be allowed her solitude because as soon as the door closed behind them it opened again to admit two nurses, who announced that they had come to take her for her bath. She protested that she could happily bath herself but the older of the two nurses, who seemed to be in charge, would not hear of it. 'Part of our job, dear, first baths always to be attended – and you'll be surprised how tired you'll be after it. We don't want you conking out on us and drowning! It'd look bad on our record now, wouldn't it?' Molly heard an Irish accent, overlain with many years of London, and was grateful.

She went with them into the bathroom attached to her room and while the younger nurse drew the bath and shook Dettol and a handful of salt into it, the Irish one wrung out the face flannel in the sink and proceeded to wash her face with gentle but firm strokes. Molly, who was much taller than the nurse, had to lean over so her face could be reached properly. Nevertheless, she felt like a child and, to her surprise, found it a comfort.

She surrendered herself to them as, deftly, they removed her nightgown and helped her into the steaming, milky water. It stung a little between her legs at first but not for long. They sponged and flannelled and soaped her and one of them combed her hair. Soon the water was like balm.

Both her breasts felt very heavy and seemed to be getting sorer all the time and she asked them if this was normal. 'Have you had your injection?' asked the nurse with the Irish accent.

'I've had so many injections,' answered Molly. 'I don't know which one you mean.'

'Well, you would have been told about this one. It's to dry up your milk.'

'I don't know. I can't remember. Such a lot has happened.'

'You poor darling,' said the Irish nurse who, Molly saw by a badge pinned to her ample chest, was named Mrs Bridget Slevin, SRN. 'I'll go and check when we've finished here and we have you all dry and comfy in your bed,' she continued. 'We'll sort you out, never fear.' She soaped Molly's back. 'Yes, we'll sort you out.'

For the first time since the birth Molly consciously relaxed as she surrendered to the competent and kind ministrations. The nurse had been right about the bath promoting tiredness: a languor was drifting over her and she longed for her bed and a long sleep. 'Sit back there now and relax,' said Bridget Slevin, 'while we organize your bed. We'll leave the door open, though, so we can see you.'

Molly lay back in the antiseptic water and watched as the whiter strands left by the soap pooled and separated and joined, then separated, then pooled again, like rivers in a delta. She heard the nurses moving around the bed and the shirring and plumping as sheets and pillows were removed and replaced. They talked quietly as they worked but she could not hear what they were saying. Lulled by the warmth and comfort of the bath, she was drifting, ever so peacefully, towards a misty sleep.

'Are you all right in there?' It was the Irish nurse, popping her head around the door.

'Yes, I'm fine.' Molly came to and straightened up a little.

'Don't want to lose you. Important lady like yourself.'

'Not that important!'

'Oh, come on now! Such modesty! Aren't you on the television and don't you have your name in the papers and everything? Margo Bryan, the famous actress!' The accent was pure Galway, absolutely familiar to Molly. 'Come on now, darling, time to get you back to bed.' Bridget helped Molly out of the bath and threw a towel around her, scrubbing her with it energetically until Molly's skin tingled. Then she handed her some clean underwear and pads. 'Have you got a clean nightdress?'

Molly indicated the locker beside her bed and Mrs Slevin opened it, pulling out one of the beautiful new maternity nightdresses made of lawn which Christian had bought for her in Harrods. 'Isn't this absolutely *gorgeous*?' She held it up to her nose, smelling the newness. 'What a lovely thing!' She gathered it up like a ring and popped it over Molly's head. 'There we are, darling, all nice and clean. In you get!' Molly noticed that the other nurse had left.

Bridget held the crackling sheets apart so that Molly could slide in between them then, when she was settled, tucked them in around her. 'Annie's gone to check about that injection,' she said. 'I'll be back in a little while. You rest now and have a little sleep if you can.'

Molly responded to the mothering like a blind starved thing. She felt warm and snug and cared for and somehow safe. 'You know about my baby?' she asked.

'Musha, I do!' said Bridget, plumping pillows already as fat as Christmas geese. 'You poor old darling, you're having a time of it, aren't you? But try not to fret too much – God is good.' In her mouth the aphorism, familiar from Molly's childhood, sounded fresh and new and Molly did not resent it. She closed her eyes and the nurse left.

She must have slept then because the next she knew there was a sort of muted commotion around her bed. Molly opened her eyes. It was Bridget Slevin again but her kind face was creased with concern. 'Mrs Smith!' she was calling softly. 'Mrs Smith!'

Another nurse stood behind her and in the doorway Molly thought she saw a male figure in a white coat. She groped for consciousness. 'What is it?'

'You're wanted in the nursery, Mrs Smith,' said Bridget, coming to the head of the bed. 'Come on, darling, I'll help you.'

She reached under the bed and taking Molly's slippers turned them towards herself so Molly could slip her feet into them. Molly's dressing-gown was hanging up on the bathroom door and Bridget took it off its hook and held it out.

'What's the matter?' Molly asked as, helped by the nurse, she put her arms into the sleeves and tied the ribbons which fastened the robe down the front. Bridget's face gave the answer away and Molly stood as still as a stone. 'How bad?' she asked.

'I don't know, darling,' answered the nurse.

The short walk to the room with Bridget beside her and the other nurse walking behind them passed as though in a dream. Molly felt her heart had stopped beating and she was somehow floating. Her head felt light and she could not feel her own breath.

As she entered the nursery she heard one of the infants in the corner of the room grizzling, making tentative little yelps, but there was silence around her own baby's incubator. A little crowd waited around it and seemed to be doing something, but the monitors told the story. Instead of blinking and bleeping they were quiet. Margaret Susanna, less than twenty-four hours old, had given up her fight.

Molly moved towards the incubator and stood beside it. It was open. A doctor was removing the suction pads from the baby's back. They made little plopping noises as they came unstuck. The tubes were already gone from her mouth and nose and her tiny arm was free of the feeding drip.

The doctor, a young West Indian (the same one who had stitched her up? Molly could not tell), completed his task and stood aside respectfully. 'We are very sorry, Mrs Smith,' he said. 'We did all we could.'

'Can I pick her up?' asked Molly.

He nodded. The others around the incubator left and, after a small hesitation, so did the doctor. Molly reached into the transparent box and carefully picked up the little body. She was still warm to the touch since the temperature within the incubator had not yet cooled. Her head flopped on her neck and, instinctively, Molly caught it.

She felt someone at her side. It was Bridget who was holding out a soft nursery blanket. 'Here,' she said, 'let me wrap her for you.' She took the corpse and with expert hands swaddled it in the blanket, then handed the little bundle back to Molly.

Molly cradled her daughter for the first and last time. With her forefinger, she traced the line of her eyelashes and the curve of her tiny cheek and leaned her own cheek against the damp thatch of hair. One of the baby's hands protruded a little from the fold of the blanket and Molly touched the fingers, as delicate as the stalks of the wild flowers which grew in the crevices of the limestone on Inisheer.

'Would you like to baptize her?' It was Bridget, whispering. Molly nodded.

Bridget left on soft feet and returned a few moments later with a pitcher of water. She poured a few drops over the baby's head and said in a low voice, 'I baptize thee in the name of the Father and Son and Holy Ghost.' The water ran off the baby's head and down along Molly's side, wetting her.

Bridget moved away again and picked up the baby in the corner of the nursery who had now discovered his voice and started a full-throated, despairing roar. She came back towards Molly. 'I'll bring this fella down to his mother and then I'll be back,' she said quietly. 'Sit down, darling.' With her free hand she led Molly to a little stool which was set against a changing table in the room.

Another nurse was busy writing at a little desk but, tactfully, she did not look up and kept her head bent over her task.

Molly felt very calm. She sat and gazed at the peaceful face of her baby, committing every line of it to memory. Margaret Susanna weighed as little as a bird and the little head felt snug in the crook of her arm and pillowed on her breast. She wished she could open the eyelids to see what colour her eyes were but contented herself with smoothing her hair which, having been wetted in baptism, was now springing back over the soft fontanelle.

'The poor little creature,' said Bridget softly at her elbow. 'Isn't she beautiful?' Being Irish Bridget had none of the reticence about death which sometimes characterized her English colleagues. 'You can be sure of one thing anyhow,' she continued, herself stroking the little head, 'you have a little angel up there now to look after you.'

The tears began then, but they began in Molly's heart, big tears of mourning and grief, cleansing her of bitterness. She made no attempt to stem them or conceal them as they poured up from her heart and down her face.

'You poor darling,' murmured Bridget, putting her arm around her shoulders. 'There, there. Poor old thing . . .'

The other nurse got up quietly and left the room while Molly pillowed her head on this kind woman's breast and wept for herself and her baby.

Up to the last minute Molly thought Christian might show up for his daughter's burial, which took place on the afternoon of the following day, but he did not. They had searched for him, of course. Conor had gone out again in his Traveller, had staked out the house and toured the pubs nearby and in Soho, which they knew Christian liked. But London was a city of ten million people and, as Conor well knew, a man who wishes to go missing can do so with ease.

Then they had tried to trace him through the police but the only information they could get, even with Malcolm's contacts, was that Christian had left the country on a PanAm jumbo bound for Chicago and had arrived in that city. He had not gone home, contacted Dick or Jo-Ann – who was married again – or any of his former colleagues on the *Sentinel*.

The funeral took place in the grounds of a convent of elderly nuns near Willesden in a plot which had been organized by Bridget Slevin. Her aunt was one of the community. There was no pomp. The Mass of the Angels was celebrated by the convent chaplain who, like his charges, was too old to be on more active service in the wider community. It was sung by one of the nuns, a lady whose wavery voice had once obviously been quite good. She was accompanied by another nun who stretched her arthritic fingers over a cracked harmonium and did not always make the octaves.

Throughout the Mass Molly was very calm. She was tired and her body, which had given birth only forty-eight hours before, ached but not enough to be a distraction. The oratory reminded her of her schooldays, its cleanliness, simplicity and ambience of women at peace together, its windows of plain glass letting in the sunshine to splay over the plain furniture and the floor, tiled in black and white. The Stations of the Cross were not pictures or illustrations but discreet black crosses at intervals on the white walls, designated in Roman numerals from one to fourteen. The Paschal candle and altar candles were lit for the Mass, their flames almost invisible in the sunshine, but other than these, the oratory was decorated only with two sprays of white lilies on both sides of the white infant coffin, just two feet long, which reposed on a low step at the entrance to the sanctuary. Although she had not been in a church since her mother's funeral, Molly found herself soothed by the gentleness of the service in such surroundings.

Malcolm sat behind Molly, lost in his own thoughts as the Mass progressed. His mind ranged over a gallery of the people who had passed through his long life – his business partners and social acquaintances, most long dead. All those business deals which had seemed so important at the time and which mattered not at all . . . Such huffing and puffing . . . The people he had loved: his mother, dimly remembered, his father and brothers, Alan and his dear Mamie, Maggie and Cal and Susanna. All lost. Even Christian, now, it seemed . . .

He had come to London with such excitement, such high hopes. He had come for a birth and found only another funeral. His eyes were drawn continually to the coffin, free of all ornamentation except a six-inch plaque of sterling silver on which were engraved the names, Margaret Susanna Smith. There were no dates. He had held her, too, after the autopsy and just before they put her in the coffin. His great-granddaughter. Lost too.

Malcolm was tired deep in his soul in a way he had never been before. It was time to give up. When the Mass was over he allowed Cordelia to help him out of the oratory and if she felt his weight heavier on her than usual she said nothing. Molly herself carried the white coffin in her arms out of the oratory and into the convent grounds. It was another hot sunny day. The sun blinded Malcolm and caused him to squint. He had the beginnings of a headache.

They started out for the cemetery. It was a short walk and the unceremonial nature of it made it all the more poignant. The stooped chaplain, stole and surplice drifting in the breeze, walked ahead of the coffin. Conor walked at Molly's side and Malcolm, still leaning on Cordelia, walked behind her. The only other people in the baby's funeral procession were the Reverend Mother and her community of seven nuns, who walked or hobbled, two by two, along the gravelled pathway towards her grave.

Malcolm thought he could not bear it. He closed his eyes and allowed Cordelia to guide him, becoming acutely aware of the sound of the feet scuffing all around him in the gravel. All the other funerals ... No more funerals. The next one would be his own and he would not have to bear it.

But Cordelia would have to bear it. He opened his eyes and looked at his wife, so patient and supportive, walking solidly in step along beside him. He didn't deserve her. He was a self-pitying old fool, wanting to bow out when people still needed him. He straightened his spine and took some of the pressure off her supporting arm. She noticed the change and smiled slightly up at him. Malcolm decided there and then to pull himself together and to live as long as Cordelia loved him and as God willed.

The graveyard, neatly tended with rows of plain white crosses, was in a corner of the nuns' small apple orchard which buzzed with bees and butterflies and which, in hands other than theirs in this part of London, would have been a priceless piece of real estate. The little procession halted in a place a little apart from the lines of crosses where a high hedge of fuschia screened the nuns' property from the surrounding houses. The hedge had been trimmed recently and in the process a profusion of the deep pink and purple bells had littered the ground like gay confetti around Margaret Susanna's grave.

Malcolm kept his head bowed as a mark of respect while a decade of the rosary was recited by the chaplain and the nuns. Molly's face was set and inscrutable. Conor's was watchful. He had his arm linked underneath his sister's.

When the time came for Molly to place her daughter in the little space prepared for her she did it carefully, bending her knees until she was squatting by the grave. She laid the coffin inside it, taking care not to jolt it or bump it against the sides. Then she straightened up.

The chaplain sprinkled a few drops of water on the coffin and said some more prayers, which Malcolm did not understand, and then Conor stepped forward. Malcolm wept at last as, with his bare hands, Molly's brother pushed the soft earth back into the hole until the coffin was covered and the hole was filled. He continued until he had packed all the displaced earth into a little pyramid.

CHAPTER TWELVE

In October, four and a half months after her daughter's death, Molly started pre-production work on her second film.

The first, *Streams of Hope*, had been successful at the box office. Despite British newspaper speculation it won nothing at Cannes but took two Oscars – Best Supporting Actress for a newcomer, Tracy Sullivan, and Best Score for the composers, the rock band Morgan La Fay. Molly's own work in *Streams* had won almost unanimously good reviews from the critics both in Britain and the States and, with the Oscars under its belt, the movie attracted great attention – so much so that Dolly Mencken was up to her fat ankles in offers for her.

Taking Dolly's counsel, Molly took her time about accepting any of the offers and chose, as her second foray into the cinema, *Emerald Night*, a semi-fantasy based loosely on a children's fairy tale. It was another small-budget movie and she knew that she was probably cast in her own role because of her West End success in *Blithe Spirit*. This worried her because although it was a wonderful part, a mysterious other-worldly creature who casts a spell on a middle-class, conventional professor of mathematics at Liverpool University, she was wary of type-casting.

Dolly had no such qualms. 'Listen,' said Dolly, who could barely be seen behind the mounds of paper on her desk, 'when you've nothing else on your table except an offer to play your fourth ghost, or fairy or mermaid, then we'll worry.'

Her bracelets jangled as she opened a drawer, took out a compact and, squinting, applied rouge to her wrinkled cheeks. 'Margo, this is tailor-made for you. And listen, darling, they didn't ask you to *test* this time. That's something. That means we're really on our way. After this one we'll get you one where you'll stomp around in handknits and tweeds followed by a pack of dogs. All right, darling?' She snapped the compact shut. 'All right?'

'All right,' agreed Molly.

'And you'll be playing opposite *David Croft*, darling.' David Croft, who was to play the professor, was an international star.

Molly had gone off happy.

As the first day of shooting approached, however, she became sick with nerves and the night before she had to travel to the location in Liverpool she came down with aches and pains and had to go to bed.

At about eight o'clock in the evening Conor, who was now living at the house in Vernon Street, knocked at her door. 'I've made you a cup of Bovril, Molly.'

'Thanks, Conor, but no thanks. I couldn't face it.'

He opened the door. 'You have to have something. Anyway, hot liquids are good for aches and pains.'

'Who says?' She felt really miserable.

'I say. Now listen, Molly, I think you should try to pull yourself together.'

'What?' She was outraged.

'You know what I believe?' he went on. 'I believe you're just scared of tomorrow and your body got sick on purpose to give you an excuse not to go. I think your pains are psychosomatic, Molly.'

She struggled to a sitting position, tears of rage in her eyes. 'How dare you? I'd like to see *you* cope with what I have to cope with.'

'And just what do you have to cope with, Molly?' He ignored her wrath and remained infuriatingly calm. 'I know you've had a rough time emotionally but you have a good career, people clamouring to hire you, a nice house, plenty of money, even a live in house-boy who puts up with your nerves and brings you hot drinks when you, as you put it, "can't cope"!' She glared at him but it had no effect. He held out the steaming mug. 'Are you going to take this drink or not – or shall I just leave you to your misery?' He smiled as he spoke so that if she refused she would look utterly churlish.

402

She took the drink. 'Well, as long as I don't have to have lectures with it.'

'Lectures over.' He bowed like a mandarin and left the room.

Molly, propped on her pillows, sipped the Bovril. He was probably right, she thought grudgingly. He was nearly always right about everything to do with herself and her life. After Margaret Susanna's funeral, she had accepted his suggestion, tentatively made, that he should move in to Vernon Street temporarily to keep her company. He had not disposed of his own flat and continued to pay the rent there but had moved a few clothes and personal belongings into the spare room of her house. Four months later he was still here and the arrangement looked like continuing.

Life ran on an even keel in the house as both of them came and went and became re-immersed in their own lives. Each had a separate circle of friends – the more discreet of whom now knew who Conor really was – but when they were home together they spent the time quietly, reading or, in Conor's case, studying. They watched quite a bit of television.

'Like two old frumps,' Molly joked whenever her friends asked how she and her brother got along. 'Typical Irish bachelor brother and sister set-up!' This was not strictly accurate, she knew. For brother and sister they were unnaturally respectful of one another's privacy and if, by chance, one touched the other while passing in a room or in the narrow hallway, there were elaborate apologies. But by and large they were both calm and even happy and the frisson between them became a part of normal life in the house, simmering but under control. She felt cherished and cared for and, from time to time, Molly had the strongest impression that she was a child again and that she and her brother were playing house. She found she could talk freely to him about her grief and sense of loss over the death of the baby.

They also discussed Christian but not a lot. It was a relief to confess, late one night as they shared a nightcap, that she would be relieved if her husband did not come back at all. Malcolm, she knew, was considering engaging a private detective agency to look for Christian but was hesitating about it. Reading between the lines Molly saw and understood that he was afraid of what the agency might find. She felt the same herself.

She had squarely faced the fact that she did not want Christian as a husband any more and discussed with Conor how she should handle the situation if and when he was found. Conor's advice had been that she should do nothing immediately but should, in the interim, take legal advice.

She finished the Bovril. Was she imagining it or had the aches in her joints lessened? She tested her legs: they were stiff and painful as before but she decided to try to ignore them and think positively. She got out of bed, put on a dressing-gown and, carrying her empty mug, went downstairs. 'Thanks, Conor,' she said when she went into the kitchen. 'Sorry I was crabby.'

'You're welcome – feeling a bit better?'

'A little,' she admitted.

'Dr Ó Briain's magic potion again.'

He was writing a letter at the kitchen table.

'Who's the letter to?'

'The usual.'

'I see. How's it going?'

'Pretty well, I think, but we can be under no illusions. It will be a long haul, Molly . . . ' She clucked sympathetically and rinsed out her mug at the sink.

Conor had begun negotiations with representatives of the Irish police. Caution had become a byword with him, however, and he approached the problem by a circuitous route. He had telephoned a friend in Amsterdam who had hired a Dutch solicitor. This solicitor was briefed by the friend and approached the Irish Embassy for advice. The embassy had made enquiries of the Department of Justice in Dublin and had come back to the solicitor with the information that the file on the case was still open and that technically Conor was still being sought.

He was now engaged in tripartite negotiations with the Dutch solicitor, an English solicitor and the Department of Justice via the embassies in both countries. In the meantime, as a precaution, he had ceased to travel outside England and continued to work and maintain his documentation under the name Sean Molloy.

'That reminds me,' said Molly, finished at the sink. 'I must write to Malcolm and Brendan. Anyway, it'll take my mind off tomorrow.' She opened a drawer of a small chest against one wall of the kitchen, took out her writing materials and carried them across to the table. She sat opposite Conor. 'I'm still sore, you know, still full of aches and pains.'

'Of course you are,' he said without looking up from his own writing. 'Why wouldn't you be? You'll see, though, once you get on that set tomorrow you'll be fresh as a daisy!'

Conor had been right as usual, Molly thought next afternoon as she sat with the director and David Croft in the latter's trailer to discuss the first scene they were to shoot together. Both she and David were made up and in costume – since the budget was so tight, rehearsal time was limited – and Molly felt not a trace of an ache or pain in a single bone.

David Croft paced around the trailer, talking like a machine gun. He was large, lithe and thin as a whip, a chain-smoker. He smoked incessantly now as he suggested script changes which would accommodate what he saw as his character's motivation in certain scenes. Molly had been nervous about meeting him since he had been cast by the media, particularly the tabloid press, as an impatient, volatile hellraiser, as likely to throw something and walk off the set as he was to turn in a good performance.

He also had a reputation as a ladykiller. Molly had vacillated between worrying that she would not be able to handle him and shame that she should have the arrogance to think that he might be interested in her in the first place. And even if he was, would she be interested in him?

The truth was that Molly was perfectly happy to be celibate and unattached. Her brother was the only person, male or female, who could penetrate her emotional defences and since he was out of bounds sexually she had accepted their companionship in lieu.

405

On the other hand, watching David Croft's clever, animated features as he paced and expounded in the trailer she could see clearly why he was considered to be so attractive. His very agitation relaxed her. She empathized with him, seeing how vulnerable he was beneath all the noise and aggression. Molly recognized that, experienced star though he was, David Croft was as terrified about this first leap into the film as she was. And as he continued to bombard the film's director with questions and theories, answering the questions before the director had a chance to do so, Molly's instinct was to wrap him up in a blanket and say 'There there . . . '

Finally, when his star ran out of steam the director, who was Welsh, stood up. 'Some of those suggestions are really excellent, David, and I'll talk to the script-writers. But I've to see to the set-up now. Maybe you would run the scene as scripted, just for the first time, so we see what we can improve on?' Croft was left with no option but to agree. 'I'll see you on the set for rehearsal, then?' The director left the trailer and Molly was left alone with her co-star.

'Want one of these?' He offered Molly a cigarette.

She shook her head. 'Would you like me to leave too, David?'

'No, stay, darling, stay, please. You're a good influence on me!' He lit a cigarette for himself and threw himself on his day-bed. He looked consideringly at her. 'Have you met Tammy yet?'

'No.' Tammy Simms, who had won a BAFTA and an Oscar nomination for previous work, had been cast as Croft's bewildered wife.

'Well, watch out for her,' said Croft. 'She's actually quite sweet but she's insecure. She doesn't like competition.'

'But why?' Molly was genuinely astonished. 'We're different types and we have completely different roles.'

'Yes, darling, but like you Tammy's blonde, or was, is fifteen years older than you and is at her peak now. You're only starting. And just *look* at you!'

Instinctively Molly looked in the mirror a few feet away from her and became instantly embarrassed. 'I think Tammy is beautiful,' she said.

'And what do you think you are?' His eyes were green, she saw, flecked with brown. Her embarrassment increased. 'You're a strange one,' he said curiously. 'I saw *Streams of Hope*. Did you enjoy making it?'

'Yes, very much.'

'The camera likes you.'

She saw he was raking her with his eyes. It was a try-on look with which she had become familiar since becoming an actress and she had learned to counter it. That he was no different from any of the others gave her confidence. She was not going to be another notch on his bedpost and diversion was the name of the game. 'If we're to be friends, David,' she said boldly, 'you should call me by my real name, which is Molly!'

'Molly,' he said, repeating it, drawing out the ls. 'Mol-lllll-ly . . . That's nice. Soft. Like you—'

'I'm not soft,' she retorted. 'Don't ever think I'm soft.'

'Great!' he said. 'A toughie! I hate soft women!' Again he gave her that long, raking look but before she could think of a suitable riposte he jumped up from the day-bed and resumed his pacing. 'What do you think of this script? Do you like *your* character? Do you think he's overwritten, my professor?'

'I think it's a very good script,' said Molly, calmly.

'Do you, indeed?' He rounded on her. 'And how many scripts have *you* read in your lifetime?'

'What do you expect me to answer to that?'

'Just answer me. How long have you been in the business?'

'Oh, my! A touch of tetch?'

'I'm sorry, darling!' He was instantly contrite. 'Don't pay any attention to me. I'm always like this on the first day of shooting. You'll get to know and love me.'

'Maybe I will, maybe I won't!'

'Yeah, no softie!' he said and threw himself back on the day-bed. 'You didn't have any love scenes in that one. How do you feel about the love scene we're about to do in fifteen minutes?' It is a fact of life that since films are not shot in sequence people who do not know one another sometimes find themselves making love within an hour of meeting.

'I'm nervous about it.' Molly decided she had nothing to lose by being honest although she knew this particular love scene was relatively innocuous. According to her script, she visited the professor in his sleep, hung above his bed and in close-up kissed him languorously but chastely, leading him to wake in fright.

'It'll be all right,' he said. 'You really are a beauty, Molly. Can't wait to kiss you.' But he was looking past her at his reflection in a mirror.

Molly was used to this type of vanity in actors. 'Hope you're not disappointed,' she said – and was saved from further answer by the second assistant's knock. They were wanted for rehearsal.

Croft put out his cigarette and took up a phial of breath spray from his make-up table. 'I've been shredded by hundreds of leading ladies for kissing them with cigarette breath! Never travel without my Gold Spot!' He sprayed two puffs into his mouth. 'Ready for anything now, ducks!' He grinned and Molly decided that she liked him.

For the next six weeks she threw herself into the work and from the beginning she had fun. Her first meeting with Tammy Simms was a delicate affair but forewarned as she was Molly behaved demurely, the neophyte at the feet of the Great Actress. Tammy Simms was reassured and then charmed.

It was a very happy set and cast and crew melded around the director to become a unit. Shooting went smoothly and they were all working so hard that there were few opportunities for off-screen dramas. David Croft, who was going through his third divorce, laid a half-hearted romantic siege to Molly throughout the schedule although his sense of humour saved the situation from being embarrassing and allowed it to become a running gag on the set.

He grabbed her and kissed her frequently – to the great frustration of the make-up crew – and when she wriggled, eel-like, from his grasp he would clasp his chest theatrically with both hands, 'Look, look!' to the assembled gallery of technicians, continuity girl, assistant directors and runners. 'See what I have to put up with!' He sent her drifts of flowers. Every morning when the car came to collect her from her hotel, there was a fresh bouquet of white roses on the back seat. She found white carnations on her pillow when, dog-tired, she got back into her room at night.

Molly enjoyed all the attention. She was laughing more than she had in months. But towards the end of the shooting schedule she began to worry a little. It was too much fun. Christian, too, had courted her like this.

When they met on set for the first day of the last week's shooting, Molly carried the latest bouquet, of baby's breath and white freesia, in her hand. 'Listen, David,' she said, 'I think really that this has gone far enough. I have enough flowers to fill a florist's and while I love flowers and I'm really grateful to you for everything, you've got to stop it now.'

He looked down at her and she was conscious that he was probably the first actor she had ever worked with who was a good head taller than she. In some respects his imposing physical presence reminded her of Conor.

'Why?' he asked.

'No why. You know why,' she said, her resolve teetering. 'Just *because* . . . ' she said then, lamely.

'Because why?'

'I told you! No why – just because.'

'Is that some sort of Irish reason? Do you not like flowers, Molly?'

'I love flowers. I told you that a million times. But I also told you a million times that I had enough flowers to do me a lifetime. And, and . . . '

'And what?'

'And I don't need any more flowers.'

'But I love sending flowers.'

'Look, David . . . ' Molly was stuck then. He had never said explicitly that he was serious about her.

'Yes, Molly?'

She became aware that one of the unit drivers and a boom operator were standing together close by and were obviously listening to the exchange. She took him by the arm and led him behind a cyclorama. '*Why* are you sending me all these flowers?' she asked. 'Why me?'

'You know why – or have I lost my touch?'

The green eyes were, for once, very still. She wavered for a split second. It would probably be great fun to have a full-blown fling with this attractive, amusing and talented man. But as she wavered the expression in his eyes changed to one of tenderness. Molly retreated immediately into her stockade.

'David,' she said, 'I like you very much. But that's all.'

'The lady's wish is my command . . .' He bent low over her hand and kissed it.

'I – I hope you don't mind . . .' she said hesitantly.

'My dear Molly,' he said, 'never has a man been rejected with such finesse!'

'I'm not rejecting you.'

'Please, my darling, no remonstrations of innocence. Wish I could be the man, that's all.'

'There's no man, don't think that.'

'Oh no?' He raised his eyebrows. 'Must dash. Pity!' he added, turning away. 'It might have been good fun!' Molly was almost tempted to call him back. What the hell was the matter with her?

There were no more flowers and he behaved impeccably during the last week of shooting. Luckily all the love scenes were in the can and in the scenes they did have, mainly shot in filthy weather on the Mersey ferry, they were so preoccupied with rain and make-up and wet costumes and keeping on their marks on the rocking vessel that the week passed quickly.

The unit had a party on the final night and they all had a great deal to drink as work tensions unwound and spirits heightened. David, who had been sitting opposite Molly at the dinner-table paying a great deal of attention to the continuity girl, leaned across when the girl went to the lavatory. He was a little drunk, she saw. He took her hand. 'Are you really, really not going to sleep with me?'

She had been drinking champagne and was herself feeling loose and warm and, for a wild moment, was tempted. But the moment passed and she shook her head. 'David, I'm really, really not. Anyway, you seem to be getting on very well without me.'

He dropped her hand and patted it. 'Well, if you ever change your mind –' he said.

' – I know where to find you!' finished Molly.

She left the party shortly afterwards, kissing him on the top of the head, and next day, when she woke, there was a final card from him, slipped under the door of her room some time during the small hours of the morning while she slept. It was a plain white card, with two words written inside in his large uneven handwriting: *Forse ancora* . . .

Molly smiled. She knew that *ancora* meant 'again' – and could guess, having studied Latin at school, what the first word was. 'Perhaps again . . . ' he had written. He had signed it simply D.

The film company had reserved a first-class corner seat for her on a mid-morning train to London and, to her relief, her carriage was half-empty. Two middle-aged housewives, who recognized her from the television show, approached her shyly for an autograph before the train left Lime Street Station, but she was left in peace for the remainder of the journey.

As the train clacked smoothly along, Molly took David Croft's card out of her handbag, contemplating his message and another lost opportunity. It was time, she knew, seriously to examine her present life, her constant rejection of emotional ties. She had read as many pop-psychological articles as the next person and from what she understood from them many problems of this nature were experienced by people who had been abused, traumatized or neglected in their childhood. She had no such excuse. Up to the time her father was killed she had had a relatively normal life.

Only on stage or in creating a character not her own did she feel in any way whole. Because, whatever the cause or character defect, she seemed somehow to be a spectator in her own offstage life. No matter what effort of will she made, she continued to feel displaced, a partial person, a mother without a child, a wife without a husband, a child without a mother or father, a woman without a man. Yet every time a life-saving line was thrown to her she threw it back.

She continued to wonder about that episode with the priest in the sand dunes. Had she suppressed some aspect of it in some way? Was this a contributory factor to her sense of detachment?

411

In her mind that experience had been insignificant and ethereal, a minor thing which might even have happened to someone else. If it was a cause of her adult problem with men, surely she should feel Father Morahan had done something awful to her? But she did not. The memories of that eventful period of her life, which had spanned only a few days, were dominated not by Father Morahan and his clumsy seduction or even her father's death – but by that mental picture of Conor pulling away from her in the black currach.

She watched the tidy undulating landscape rolling past her window as she travelled home. London was not her home, she thought, but, then, neither any more was Inisheer. She tried to conjure up her childhood, the storms and sunrises and harshness of that place of stones, her taciturn father and gentle mother. But they had all shrunk, like framed pictures on the walls of a soulless gallery. Except for Conor. Guiltily, she admitted to furtive excitement that she was going home to Conor. She wondered then, not with any real intent, if she should consult a psychiatrist.

Decisively, she abandoned all this self-analysis – which, any-way, she had been taught in school was pure self-indulgence – and opening a magazine tried to concentrate on an article about the Queen Mother. But the excitement and anticipation of seeing Conor again grew in the pit of her stomach as the train neared London.

To her disappointment he was not at home when she got to the house in Vernon Street. The Traveller was not outside and when she let herself in the house had the forlorn, musty smell of emptiness. Some mail lay where it had fallen on the mat inside the door and she picked it up adding it to the neat pile on the hall table.

She went through to the kitchen to put on the kettle and found a note from him on the dresser. He had gone away for the week-end to York and was not due back until the following Tuesday.

Molly, feeling as empty as her house, collected her mail and opened it at the kitchen table. In her absence, she saw, Dolly had been busy and had organized several meetings about future work and press interviews.

She telephoned Dolly who, recognizing post-work anti-climax when she heard it, immediately invited her out to dinner.

By the time it was coming up to Margaret Susanna's first anniversary Molly had completed a limited run of *Hamlet*, playing Ophelia in an art-house on the outskirts of London. Dolly had thought it would be good for her reputation. The critics, luckily, had agreed.

One Friday morning in May, she was invited to see a rough-cut of *Emerald Night* in a small cinema hired for the occasion. The director had begun the process of hyping his movie and had invited – as well as cast, crew, moneymen and friends – a carefully selected group of press, five critics whom he respected and knew personally. When the house lights came up at the end of the screening, cast, crew, moneymen and friends stood up in their seats and applauded and cheered.

The critics, Molly saw, were applauding too, but discreetly. They had chosen single seats apart from everyone else and apart from each other. While they clapped slowly and reflectively, islands of gravitas in a sea of enthusiasm, each watched the other four out of the corner of his eye – they were all men – none wanting to lose face by revealing immoderate enthusiasm. Of course, they had all agreed in advance to be bound to secrecy until the actual release of the film, a promise which the director well knew was about as reliable as a twopenny watch. He had complete confidence that not one of them would be able to resist leaking little hints and innuendoes and each would rush to score against the other, to be the first with the news, to be seen by the public – and most of all by rival critics – as an insider.

After the screening there was a lunch in the upstairs room of a pleasant restaurant in Covent Garden to which the critics, as befitted their independence, did not go. But Molly did and enjoyed herself thoroughly. She had been pleased with her work and found to her surprise that she was able to suspend disbelief and watch her performance as a character rather than as herself. Because they were both abroad on other projects, neither David nor Tammy, the lead stars, could be present at the screening so

Molly was the most important cast member at the lunch and was treated accordingly.

She drank some champagne and after the second glass felt light and insubstantial, like a feather. Her habit was to alternate alcohol with Perrier but today she allowed herself to be wafted along in the flow of the general good cheer and high hopes and drank glass after glassful of the champagne.

'The hell with it,' she said to herself after her fourth glass, 'it's not often a woman gets to see herself in her own movie. Thank *you*!' she said graciously as her glass was filled up again by the attentive waiter.

The more she drank, the more tender grew Molly's affection for cast and crew, the more brilliant and entertaining she found their conversation. She loved *everyone*, she decided. Film-making was a funny old world.

She filled her glass again without waiting for someone to offer her the bottle, spilling a little of the wine on the tablecloth, and smiled apologetically and widely up and down the table. Everyone told her it was OK, not to worry.

Such lovely people . . . She refilled her glass. Molly loved acting, movies, the continuity girl, who was seated to her right. 'And how's David?' she asked, aiming her chin on to her hand and missing slightly.

'David who?' asked the continuity girl in return, a little frown of puzzlement between her china-blue eyes.

'David!' said Molly. 'David, you know, David Croft, our star! *Your* David . . . '

'Oh, *that* David!' said the girl with a laugh, brow clearing. 'He's not my David. Why would you think he's *my* David?'

'Ohh!' said Molly, her elbow slipping off the table. 'Oops!' She giggled and turned to the lighting cameraman, an Australian. 'Of course. He's not her David at all. He's nobody's David. *Forse anc-ancora*!' She waved her hand across the table like a benediction and bowed her head. 'How are you, Bluey?' she asked the cameraman.

'Who's Cora?' asked the continuity girl.

It was Molly's turn to be puzzled. 'Cora? Cora who?'

'Never mind, dear,' said the continuity girl, patting Molly's shoulder.

'I'm fine, Margo!' said the cameraman to Molly's left and she swivelled to look at him. He was supporting, Molly knew, at least two wives and about seven children.

'And how 're, how 're all the chi-children?' She was hit with a bout of hiccups.

'They're fine, Margo, ace!' said the man, chuckling. 'Have a drink of water. Maybe you should go home?' Molly decided that might be prudent. She looked at her watch and was amazed to find it was almost four thirty.

She bid a sentimental goodbye to the director, who called a taxi for her and stood with her in the entrance to the restaurant until it arrived. Before getting into the taxi Molly embraced the director and told him she loved him *dearly* . . .

All the way home Molly, who had never been so drunk before, revelled in the frivolous, mellow feeling. She thought sentimentally about all her dear friends on the cast and crew. David, dear David. She would have to send David a card. As the taxi wheeled round corners and darted in and out of the traffic Molly, utterly relaxed, rolled from side to side in her seat and giggled. 'You all right, luv?' asked the driver indulgently, shouting over his shoulder after a particularly daredevil turn.

'Never better – I'm – I'm in a movie!' She felt loving and loved and airy as swansdown. When the taxi pulled into Vernon Street she was cheered to find the Traveller parked outside her house. Conor was in. She paid off the cab tendering a ten-pound note and telling him to keep the change.

'I'm home!' she carolled as she turned her key in the lock. 'They loved it, they loved it – and I was *terrific*!' she continued, dancing into the kitchen. 'Meet *Mar*-go *Mar*-go *Mar*-go Bryan!' she sang. 'I'm going to be a *film* star!' She pirouetted around the room, picked up a vase of flowers off the kitchen dresser and, using it as a particularly large microphone, began to mimic Louis Armstrong's version of 'What A Wonderful World'. Her singing voice had never been Molly's strongest attribute and she cracked on a high note. 'Sorry!' she said, stopping abruptly and putting her hands over her mouth like a child. She giggled again.

Conor, who was sitting at the kitchen table, smiled at her happiness. 'Carry on. And, anyway, film stars can sing in their own kitchens any time they like.'

'Any time?'

'Any time,' he assured her.

'Whee!' she said and scattered the flowers all over the kitchen in handfuls.

'You're drunk, Molly!' He was amused rather than scandalized.

'Yep! And issa lovely feeling. "All I want is a room somewhere . . . " ' and she was off again with *My Fair Lady*.

Conor waited until she had finished the last chorus of 'wood-int it be *Luv*-er-ly . . . luv-er-ly . . . Luv . . . er . . . lee!' and had bowed to his laconic applause before telling her his own news. He had had a telephone call from his solicitor. He was going to Dublin the following day and a formal interview, in the presence of his solicitor, was set up for him at the Department of Justice on Monday.

'Oh that's wonderful. *Wonderful!*' Molly replaced her vase and, crossing the kitchen, threw her arms around Conor's neck. He did not respond and she withdrew hastily. She hiccupped. 'Sorry!'

'That's all right,' he said wryly. 'It was nice. Don't apologize.'

The director had chosen his critics well. Within two days columns with titles like 'Under The Arcs' or 'Cyclops' began to bristle with sentences and paragraphs mentioning – in passing – that the eagerly awaited *Emerald Night* was now in the can.

One critic, Clive Treethorne, wrote in an 'I hear'-style paragraph that newcomer Margo Bryan, who had 'so impressed' in *Streams of Hope*, had fulfilled all that promise and was 'one to watch' in the Oscar stakes.

Another, Trilby Owens, wrote that he had heard from reliable sources that the on-screen chemistry between David Croft and newcomer Margo Bryan ('one to watch for an Oscar?') was 'truly electrifying'.

A third, Derwent Reed, did not bother to disguise the fact that he had had a preview of the film and thus infuriated the other four. He wrote that while Tammy Simms turned in 'her usual sterling comedy work',

> 'it is fey, willowy newcomer Margo Bryan, who appeared from nowhere like a shooting star in the firmament to impress greatly in *Streams of Hope* (as this reviewer pointed out at the time) and who now fulfils that promise by carrying off the acting honours in *Emerald Star*. This is no mean feat when one considers that she is up against old hands like David Croft and Tammy Simms. Watch out for Bryan for an Oscar early next year . . . '

All this hype did not pass unnoticed through the sieves employed by the British wire services and a small paragraph on Margo Bryan, rewritten with an Irish emphasis by a showbiz stringer, was transmitted and received in the wire-room of the *Irish Record* in Dublin, ripped off the machine and placed with the other copy in the news-editor's basket.

The news-editor, having read the telex, took it across to the desk of one of the reporters. 'Isn't this one your baby?' he asked.

Una O'Connor read the paragraph. 'Do you want anything on it?' she asked.

'You don't sound all that enthusiastic.'

'If you want something on it, I'll do it.'

The news-editor considered. They were coming up to the slow summer season and the features area of the paper was always on the look-out for personality pieces. Even if that did not work out, if this woman, Bryan, did get an Oscar nomination, it would be as well to have established a prior relationship with her.

'Yes,' he said. 'See what you can do with it.'

Una took a deep breath. She got Molly at home on her first telephone call. 'Hi!' she said brightly. 'Remember me? Una O'Connor, *Irish Record*?'

'Oh, yes, Una, of course I remember.' Molly hesitated and Una knew what she was thinking. Sean.

'Look,' she said, 'this is probably as embarrassing for you as it is for me and I'm sorry, but this is a professional call. My newsdesk wants yet *another* piece on you because of all this speculation about you and an Oscar and your film.'

'But the film hasn't even been released yet!'

'I understand it's imminent, though. The piece on you would run to coincide with the release here.' Again Una heard the hesitation. She would just as soon not get entangled in anything to do with Sean Molloy again but this was work. She appealed to the actress's sense of duty. 'I'm sure that the piece will help the film attendance here. We'll give it a good spread.'

'What kind of piece would you do?'

'Well, it would be another personal piece catching up on what you've been doing over the past year – which I understand has been considerable.'

'Would you leave my personal life out of it?'

'You mean your marriage?'

'No,' said Molly quietly. 'I mean the death of my baby.'

It was Una's turn to hesitate. 'I think you know by now that you can trust me not to let you down.'

'All right, so.'

She told the news-editor that she had secured the interview.

'All right,' he said, 'but do it immediately. Abbey Street and Burgh Quay get the wires too.' The offices of the *Irish Record*'s rival newspaper groups were located there. 'What about photographs?'

'I don't want a photographer with me on this one,' answered Una immediately. 'We can pick up the photographs later.'

Una went back to telephone Molly a second time and they arranged to meet, this time in Molly's house, at ten o'clock the following morning.

When she was in London Una always stayed at the Regent Palace, not for its luxury – it was far from luxurious – but for its location. It was right beside Piccadilly Tube station, across the road from a Boots and with several fast-food restaurants nearby. All a journalist needed.

She was up at seven and by nine, breakfasted and alert with new batteries in her tape recorder, spares in her pocket and new cassettes broken out of their Cellophane wrappers in her handbag, she was out in the rush-hour flagging down a taxi. She had received directions from Molly as to how to get to Vernon Street by Tube but on an assignment where she did not personally know the interview venue always took the most reliable form of transport, which in London was a taxi.

On the way she resolutely refused to think of Sean Molloy – she had never been able to think of him under his real name of Conor. In the long nights alone in her bedsitter Una knew that he had ruined her for other men but she was resilient and fatalistic. It was her own fault that she had got herself into that situation. She had pushed, she had used Margo Bryan but she had failed in her primary objective. Her secondary objective, the continuing professional relationship with the actress herself, was independent and must be preserved.

The cab deposited her at Molly's front door with twenty minutes to spare so she walked out of Vernon Street. It was worse to arrive too early for an interview than too late since the interviewee, particularly one who was uneasy and who had to be seduced, would probably be found at a disadvantage. If they were to open up he or she had, above all, to be made to feel secure.

Vernon Street – which, she saw, was a street of well-maintained terraced Victorian houses – was in a very quiet part of London but she spotted a corner shop on an adjoining street. More to kill time than because she wanted it Una went in and bought a Mars Bar. It was nearly ten minutes to ten. She walked back to Vernon Street slowly, employing her observer's antennae to the full, in case she needed to pad out the piece, noting the types of houses, gardens, cars.

She stopped dead when she turned the corner. The Traveller was parked outside the door. It had not been there when the cab dropped her, she was positive about that, she certainly would have noticed. Her heart raced with all the old feelings and nerves. What was she going to do? She tightened her lips. She was going to do an interview. That was what she was going to do. It was one minute past ten when she rang the doorbell.

To her relief Molly herself answered. Automatically Una

419

noted what she was wearing – jeans and a man's shirt – and how she looked – older but more relaxed. Still spectacularly beautiful. During the hellos, she took a mental photograph of the hallway – red and white tiles, one small watercolour – an abstract – antique hall table, small bowl of white roses – and registered the smells and ambience of the house – coffee, brightness, warmth, cosiness.

Molly took her into a small drawing room off the hall, beautifully and simply furnished with smallish chairs and tables appropriate to the scale of the room and a lovely old Victorian fireplace, which now housed a gas fire. Again, there were bowls of white flowers everywhere.

'You're welcome, Una. This is becoming quite a habit, isn't it?'

'Well,' said Una, 'some journalists specialize in the Iron Curtain, some do flower shows, I do you!'

Molly laughed. 'Would you like coffee?'

Una nodded that she would and Molly left the room. Where was he? In the kitchen? Would she see him at all? Her fear of seeing him and her longing to see him flip-flopped, distracting her. She stood up to take a look at the titles of the books in the glass-fronted bookcase which took up an alcove beside the fireplace. She shouldn't have. The bookcase contained a mixture of plays, paperback novels and tomes on botany and archaeology. *Was he living here?*

'I've been looking at your books,' she said when Molly came back with the fragrant coffee and a plate of biscuits.

'Nothing brilliant there.'

There was nothing for it, she had to ask. 'Is your brother here?'

Molly flashed her a quick look. 'He is, actually. He lives here now – but he'll be leaving in a few minutes,' she added quickly. 'He's going to Dublin.'

'Right, shall we begin?' asked Una, busying herself by taking out her tape recorder.

She began briskly, bringing herself up to date with the actress's career development since they last spoke, mainly the filming of *Emerald Night*. She concentrated fiercely and although now and then she thought she heard a noise from another part of the house managed successfully to conduct the interview on two levels. Trusting her tape recorder to take the narrative of the questions and answers, which were relatively standard, she was also listening intuitively to the subtext, watching her subject's changing expressions and hearing the tone of her voice, the little pauses, hesitations and rushes. All the time she was waiting for the right moment when it would be opportune to lead Margo into the area of her personal life.

It came quite easily and naturally. Molly had been talking about scenes she had particularly enjoyed filming in the two films she had done and Una was following along gently, eliciting information about acting techniques and why one particular scene was more enjoyable than another when the first side of the first cassette tape clicked off in the tape recorder. Una, who had worked hard but unobtrusively to weave around the two of them a warm cloche of intimacy and understanding, reached to turn it over. While she did so, keeping her eyes on the tape recorder and making her movements more elaborate than necessary, she asked casually, 'Was it difficult to get back to work after the death of the baby?'

Molly did not answer but Una kept fiddling with the tape recorder as if there were a problem fitting the cassette back into its compartment. Eventually she seemed to get it working again and put it back on the little table between them which held the remains of the coffee and biscuits. She leaned forward and looked expectantly and empathetically at her subject.

Very few people can withstand a long pause in a conversation and Molly was no exception. 'It was a bit,' she admitted eventually.

'Did you find everyone else sympathetic?' asked Una, dropping her voice to match Molly's tone exactly. Again she waited. Molly hesitated but Una did not lose her nerve.

'Yes, they were,' said Molly, 'but I don't think anyone who has not gone through it could understand how bad it is.'

Una knew she had struck gold.

For the next half-hour, Molly spoke about the birth and death of the baby, in fits and starts at first, but then headlong. She had the actor's sense-memory and eye for detail and Una felt that prickling sensation at the back of her neck which told her she had good material. In any terms she had a great story. When the second side of the first tape ran out she did not immediately change it but kept her eyes on the actress, who was telling her at that point about the kindness of Bridget Slevin. She was crying. Una threw a switch in her brain which acted as a substitute recorder, memorizing the quotes while slowly reaching into the handbag at her feet, extracting a second tape by sense of touch. She succeeded in substituting it for the first one in the recorder without jolting her subject out of her narrative. She switched the machine on and relaxed again, letting it do its job while she concentrated on keeping the story going.

It came to an abrupt end when Conor opened the drawing room door. 'Sorry to interrupt but I have to leave now or I'll miss my plane.' He walked over to Una. 'I couldn't leave without saying hello,' he said.

She stood up. Molly had obviously told him she was coming. 'Hello,' she said. To her fury she felt her heart start to thump.

Conor looked across at Molly who was tearstained and drained. Una now felt absurdly guilty. 'Is everything all right, Molly?' he asked.

'Yes, yes, everything's fine,' she said. 'Honestly! I was just reliving a few old memories . . .'

Conor turned back to Una. 'How've you been, Una?'

'I've been fine.'

'Thanks for your letter, by the way.' Many was the night Una had clenched her toes in bed at the memory of what she had written in that letter, not regretting or repudiating it but because she had no idea how it was received.

'I've saved it,' he said now, 'and I'm sorry I didn't reply. I will some day – I promise.'

Una nodded, speechless.

'Well, I have to be off. Cheerio! Wish me luck, Molly.'

'Of course I do, Conor!'

He kissed each of them on the cheek and went out of the door.

Una realized her recorder was still running. She switched it off. In the silence they heard the door slam and the engine of the Traveller start up. Una was unusually at a loss. She had to keep the intimacy she had built up between herself and the actress. She wanted Molly to be secure, to feel easy that the personal stuff would be in context, but at the same time she was still trembling inwardly from the contact with Conor. She had to force herself not to touch her cheek where he had kissed it.

'Have you any cuttings about your career to date which I could refer to for the piece?' It was safe, neutral ground.

The actress looked almost startled to be brought back to the subject of acting. She wrinkled her forehead. 'I don't think so,' she said. She thought. 'Dolly has files of them, though – you know my agent, Dolly Mencken?'

Una nodded. 'I'll contact her when I get back to my hotel.' Privately she eschewed any notion of going anywhere near that old battleaxe. She stood up. 'Thank you very much. I'll leave you in peace.' The priority now was to get out before Margo Bryan realized she had said too much and started imposing conditions.

'Would you like more coffee?' Molly had recovered her composure.

'No, thank you – but you mentioned you like gardening. I'd love to see your garden,' Una answered quickly, not wanting to betray her anxiety to leave.

Molly seemed genuinely pleased at the request. 'Certainly. It's lovely at this time of year.' They went down the little hallway and out towards the conservatory and the little patio.

'What a lovely kitchen!' said Una, admiring the big sunny room which was one of the best features in the house.

'It is nice, isn't it? I brought some of the furniture from Ireland to remind me of home – that little chest there, that dresser – Oh!' said Molly, spotting something on top of the dresser. 'I forgot about these. You asked about clippings?'

She reached up and took down from the top of the dresser a battered old shoe box. She blew dust off the top of it. 'Sorry! I guess my cleaning lady doesn't reach that high. I haven't actually read through these,' she went on. 'Dolly has a clippings service and she keeps everything anyway but there

423

is probably some early stuff in it. Would they be any use to you?'

'Thank you very much. That'd be great.' Una took the box.

'Just get it back to me some time at your convenience,' said Molly and then she seemed to remember something. She took the box back from Una, opened it and extracted a piece of paper from the top of the pile inside and, crumpling it, put it in the pocket of her jeans. There had been writing on it but Una had not been quick enough to decipher what it was. Molly replaced the lid, handed the box to her and then led her outside through the conservatory.

The patio was indeed lovely, with all sorts of flowers Una could not name in planters and tubs and pots although she did recognize the beautiful blooms of a rhododendron. It was only May but out here the sun was hot and bees were making a racket, clustered around a bush with bluish-purplish flowers.

They stood together in the sun and made small-talk about the possibility of its being a fine summer this year. She admired the patio and the flowers and then said she really had taken up enough of Molly's time and that she must be going. Juggling the shoe box, her tape recorder and her shoulder bag, she shook the actress's hand at the front door.

'I'm sorry I got emotional,' said Molly. She hesitated, then took the plunge. 'I'm not going to say you can't use that stuff about the baby but I'm trusting you not to make it sensational?' There was an appeal in her voice and Una's heart went out to her. Now that the stuff was safely on tape she could afford the luxury of humanity.

'Don't worry,' she said and she really meant it. 'I promise it will be OK. Anyway, I'm sure that what you said will be a great help to other women in the same situation.'

'Yes, there is that,' said Molly but Una could see she was unsure.

'Please believe me,' she said, 'you *can* trust me!' Again she meant it. There would be no future for herself or the paper in betraying the woman by cheapening the piece. They might need her again. As she walked away from the house she was already composing the opening paragraphs in her head. At the same time she wanted to be alone to think about Conor. She longed to be safely back in Dublin.

Where was he going to be in Dublin? That was a treacherous thought with no future. She squashed it.

By the time she got back to the hotel from which she had already checked out she had calmed down. She retrieved her overnight bag from the porter and stowed the tape recorder carefully inside. She tried to stuff the shoe box in, too, but it would not fit. Blasted nuisance! she thought, sorry now that she had asked about the clippings. She'd have to nurse it all the way back to Dublin and then she would have the bother of parcelling it up again and sending it back. She considered briefly posting it on right now, from London, but then thought it would look ungrateful.

In any event, there might be something in it she could use – although she already knew she had more than enough on tape to write one of the best human-interest stories of her life.

To keep herself from moping about Conor, Una began writing her story within ten minutes of letting herself into her decrepit, untidy bedsitter. She had not planned to live in such circumstances for as long as she had – and could certainly have afforded better – but there had always been something more interesting than flat- or house-hunting to occupy her mind and her time.

She hung her jacket on the back of the door and threw her overnight bag and the shoe box on the bed. She did not even make herself a cup of coffee but extracted the tape recorder from the bag and set it up on the table in the centre of the room, which served as dining, kitchen and work table, one leg of which was shorter than the other three and was supported on a small block of wood.

Una debated for a few moments whether she should telephone the news-editor but decided not to. It was always possible that the editor's input might be negative. She would deal with that, if and when it happened, after she had written the story. The worst thing that can happen to a journalist's

425

conviction about a story is an argument about it before it is written.

She first typed the quotes she remembered from the time she was changing tapes. Then she switched on the tape recorder. Omitting only her own questions she transcribed the interview, a task which took almost four and a half hours. It was after eleven when the sound of Molly's drawing room door opening, followed by Conor's voice, filled Una's flat.

Abruptly Una switched off the tape recorder and stood up. She realized she was very hungry. She went to the refrigerator in her 'kitchen', divided from her 'living room' by a curtain strung on sagging wires. There was nothing in the fridge except a carton of milk and two mouldy tomatoes.

She left the flat and walked the few hundred yards on to Rathmines Road and the local Kentucky Fried Chicken, which always did a roaring trade at this time of night after the pubs closed. She had to queue for her fried chicken and Coke and, since all the tables were full, decided to take it home with her. She let herself into the flat again and, still carrying her food, crossed to her bed to turn on the radio which stood on the bedside table. Her overnight bag lay half-open on the bed where she had left it and beside it lay the shoe box. She turned on the radio, tuned it to the national pop station, RTE Radio Two, and eyed the shoe box with distaste. She had more than enough material but a sense of duty and her own perfectionism prodded her. There might be something here she did not know. Anyway, she had hawked it all the way from London, she might as well get some value out of it.

She sat on the bed, cracked open the Coke, opened the snack box and put a chip in her mouth. Then she took off the lid of the shoe box and shook it upside down so that the clippings would fall on the bed beside her. They were soft and greying, some were even yellow, but they had been carefully folded exactly to fit the dimensions of the box and were slow in coming out. Wiping her greasy fingers on her dress so she would not dirty the clippings, Una prised out the ones which were stuck. There was more than clippings in the box. There was an envelope. The envelope had her

426

name on it. Was this some kind of joke played on her by Molly?

Her heart stopped. Conor! He had said he would reply to her letter 'sometime' . . .

Before she opened the envelope, as though to slow herself down she took one more chip.

Una did not know whether she was disappointed or not when she saw the heading. Dear Miss O'Connor . . . It wasn't from him, then. But from whom? She began to read.

Dear Miss O'Connor,
I am sorry for bothering you but I read your article in today's newspaper and I think I have some very urgent information concerning it in which you may be interested . . .

She had to read the letter twice before she had fully comprehended it and its enclosure.

However this letter had got mixed up with Margo Bryan's clippings, the implication was unmistakable: the woman had married her brother. Did she know? The questions hammered in Una's brain. Answers too. This probably explained the handicap problems with the baby.

Her brain clicked into automatic. One thing to check.

She went to her own 'filing system' – a series of canvas sports bags under the bed, but kept loosely in order – and searched through it until she found her own story on Molly and Christian. She checked the dates with the dates mentioned in the FAA letter.

They tallied. There could be no mistake.

If she thought she had a good story before, this was a story to beat all stories. And if Molly got an Oscar . . . !

Steady, steady. She should not fly off the handle but had to take this one detail at a time. Who could have written the letter to her and why to *her*?

She read it again. The latter part of the question was easy: 'I read your article in today's newspaper . . . '

But who?

427

'I have followed Miss Bryan's career with great interest . . . '

That explained the clippings.

'I had reason to make this investigation myself . . . ' Why?

The only reason for making such an investigation could have been personal interest. This man, or woman, was personally interested in Molly. It was too much of a cliché to imagine that it was a man in love. The more logical thing must be that it was a woman. Molly's real mother?

She checked her own article again. The Smith baby had been from a wealthy family, lost at sea in a chartered aircraft. The mother's body had never been found – even if she had survived somehow, unknown to her family, would it have been likely that she would have known where her daughter was, followed her progress and not come forward?

That was all too far-fetched. She was thinking rubbish, Una decided. To steady her thoughts she crossed the floor of the flat, threw open the single, rickety window and put her head out into the night air. It was drizzling but she closed her eyes and allowed the mist to cool her hot cheeks. There was only one explanation. The letter had been written by a man who loved Molly but who could do nothing about it.

Married?

She remembered something from the end of the letter. She withdrew her head, closed the window and went across to the bed from which she picked up the letter again.

' . . . revealed to me on a confidential basis . . . revealed . . . '

Revealed . . .

Confessed! The man was a priest.

Una's knees went weak and she sat down on the bed. She rooted around in her bag and took out the Mars Bar she had bought the day before, unwrapped it with shaky fingers and bit off a huge mouthful.

What to do?

The first thing was to contact Margo Bryan. She looked at her watch. It was a quarter to one in the morning. It would have to wait – she could not wake the woman with this kind of information. In fact, she should not tell her on the telephone at all. She should go to see her again as soon as possible.

She stuffed most of the rest of the Mars Bar into her mouth, turned up the radio and chewed furiously. (For ever after when Una thought of Margo Bryan she associated the actress with a mouthful of glutinous chocolate and toffee and the sound of the Average White Band.)

She threw off her clothes, turned out the light and tried to go to sleep. The situation begged other questions. Conor? He was not Molly's brother after all, it appeared. Did he discover this somehow? Was this the reason for his very sudden disengagement from herself?

Una tried not to think of that aspect of the problem. It would serve only to complicate the already complex journalistic task she now had. But she could not get to sleep. At one point she turned on her bedside light and reread the letter. She turned the light off again and lay down. Dare she ask Molly about Conor?

At about four o'clock Una gave up on sleep. She took her coffee jar full of 10p pieces and crept down the hall to the communal bathroom. It was cold and damp but in her feverish state she welcomed the chill. She fed the meter, turned on the gas geyser and took a long hot bath.

She was at the airport just after seven o'clock. She used her American Express card to buy a ticket to London and although the first flight, just before eight o'clock, was fully booked, she managed to get a seat through the standby desk. She had only a short time to spare before boarding but she went to the public telephone and dialled Molly's number.

The telephone rang six times before Molly answered. Her 'Hello?' sounded sleepy and Una's stomach danced with nervousness while the coins fell into the slot. She was afraid the actress would have hung up.

'Hello?' she said immediately the last coin had clinked in.

'Yes? Who is this?'

'Molly, it's Una. I'm awfully sorry to wake you up, I really am, but something very, very urgent has come up in connection with the piece I am writing about you—'

'Do you know what time it is?'

'Yes, I do, and please believe me, I would not disturb you if

429

it wasn't extremely urgent. I'm at the airport – I'm actually on my way to London to see you.'

'*What?*'

Una could hear the annoyance in the voice at the other end of the line and rushed on. 'I have some information for you.'

'What kind of information?'

'It's about your husband,' said Una, inspired.

There was a short pause. Another coin fell into the slot.

'What about my husband?' Molly's voice was wary.

'I can't tell you over the telephone, I really can't. But I do really, really think you should let me come to see you.' Una heard the last call for her flight booming over the public-address system of the departures terminal.

'Well, it does seem you're on your way already!'

'I'll come straight to your house from the airport.'

'All right.'

'Again, I'm sorry for waking you, Molly.'

'That's all right.'

Una hung up and raced for her plane. She was the last to board and flopped into her seat, panting. As soon as the aircraft took off her stomach began to churn with nausea and nerves. 'What am *I* worried about?' she repeated to herself – but it was no use. Although professionally she was still excited, she dreaded the coming scene and projected it a hundred ways: Margo incredulous, angry, indignant, threatening, weeping, violent, hysterical? All of those? How would she herself feel or react if someone, if a *reporter*, arrived out of the blue with proof that her husband was her brother?

Behind it all was the insistent, thumping question of her own personal interest. Where did Conor now fit in? First he was the friend, then the brother, now what? Una refused to think about Conor. She would think about him *after* she had done what she had to do with Molly.

She wondered if she should take flowers – there was a flower-stand in the arrival-hall at Heathrow – but rejected the idea as being too schmaltzy and insincere.

She had the shoe box with her in, of all things, a string bag and as she travelled on the Tube into London she was conscious of how incongruous it looked, shabby and ancient. The anonymous letter was stowed in her handbag which she clutched under her arm, and the overnight bag, which she had not unpacked from the previous day, again contained the tape recorder fitted with a brand new tape and another set of new batteries. She had no fixed idea about how she would handle the situation as a story. She could not, in all decency, whip out the tape recorder immediately.

The central problem remained. How would she break the news? Should she go bald-headed for it or pussyfoot? She had still not decided when the taxi dropped her on the corner of Vernon Street. She paid the driver and walked, heart thumping, towards Margo Bryan's bright yellow door.

Molly's heart was thumping too as she waited for the reporter's arrival. Enemies do not wear horns or carry tails but speak in soft, beguiling voices and she had developed a foreboding about this Una O'Connor, with her open, freckled face and mop of bright red hair.

She felt wound up and jittery. In an effort to calm her apprehension after Una's telephone call she had taken a scented bath and dressed in one of her favourite, most comfortable outfits, a jumpsuit of white cotton. But she could not rest easy as the minutes dragged into hours. It was still early, only ten minutes past ten. Who knew what time the woman would come?

She tried to read a script that Dolly had sent her with a recommendation that she should consider it favourably. This one was to be filmed in Argentina and was a big-budget, star-cast project from one of the major studios. Dolly's covering note had advised that the part envisaged for her was ideal but had warned that since the budget – and therefore the risk – was so high she might have to test for it. She tried to concentrate on the print but found she was reading the same page over and over again. She threw the script on the kitchen table but then picked it up again, brought it back into the living room and filed it neatly away on the bookshelf. She turned on the radio but could find nothing that had no religious overtones except on Radio Three, which was playing music she did not like. She turned off the set again and continued her pacing of the house, straightening

431

cushions that did not need straightening and wiping down the already immaculate work-surfaces in the kitchen.

She went out on to the patio. After a succession of glorious warm days the weather had changed overnight and the morning was overcast with a wind from the northeast which had torn petals from the early-flowering roses and some of the more delicate of the pot plants, discarding them to drift like pastel snowflakes around the flagstones. She shivered and went back into the house, moving again from room to room in search of something productive to do. Everything was gleaming, Mrs Sharma had been in the afternoon before so not even a speck of dust was visible to be banished. She got a cardigan, pulled it around her shoulders and went back out to the patio. She swept up the petal debris and when that was done began to dead-head the potted geraniums and pelargoniums. The wind stung her face but the steady work settled her a little.

What could this woman know about Christian other than what Molly herself had told her in the interviews? Her terror was that the reporter had managed somehow to find her husband. If she had, what condition was he in? And was the fragile tranquillity of her life to be snatched away from her again? Yet surely it would have been impossible for Una O'Connor to find Christian in the time between her leaving the house yesterday morning and seven o'clock this morning? There would not have been time. Unless, by some extraordinary coincidence, she had bumped into him in Dublin and recognized him from the time of the first interview. Or maybe he had contacted her . . .

Molly vacillated wildly between wanting to know what this information was and not wanting to know. She had a premonition that whatever it was it was going to affect her radically. Or was she panicking unduly, mistaking fear for foresight?

For the last few months she had been living in a fool's paradise, playing house with Conor, burying Christian's existence, wherever he was, at the back of her mind. But she saw now that she had been a coward. Christian was her husband, her responsibility. She should not have let things slide, left efforts to find him to Malcolm. She should have instigated a proper search.

When she hung up after Una's telephone call, her instinct had been immediately to telephone Conor. She knew the name of his hotel in Dublin. But she resisted the urge. He had enough on his plate without hysterical calls from her about information, as yet unspecified, which was threatened by a reporter and which may or may not prove to be important or even true.

She heard the doorbell ring and her stomach gave a great lurch. At least the waiting was over. Forcing herself to move at a normal pace she went into the kitchen and removed her cardigan, hanging it over the back of the chair. As she went to open the front door the doorbell rang again, this time prolonged and strident. She felt a flash of irritation at the reporter's impertinence and stopped deliberately in front of the mirror over the hall table to check her appearance. When she opened the door, no one would have known she was feeling anything but her usual self. 'Good morning,' she said. 'Won't you come in?'

As Una stepped into the hallway Molly noticed that the girl's skin was blotchy and that there were dark rings under her eyes. She also seemed nervous. A wild suspicion flashed through her mind that this woman might be having an affair with Christian and had come to confess – but it was so ludicrous, she almost laughed out loud. Her own confidence increased.

'Would you like a cup of coffee?' she asked.

'No thank you. I'm up to here with coffee,' Una gave a half laugh and made a gesture to indicate a line somewhere between her collarbone and her chin, 'my own and the airline's. I've been up all night.'

Molly hesitated, then, 'Come on into the kitchen, Una – it's a bit more homey at this hour of the morning.'

Una followed her into the kitchen and stood awkwardly, not knowing where or if to sit. Molly indicated one of the chairs at the table. 'Are you sure you won't change your mind about the coffee?'

'Yes, I'm quite sure, thank you – oh! Before I forget!' and she took the shoe box out of the string bag and handed it over.

Molly took the box and put it back on top of the kitchen dresser. She sat at the kitchen table, facing Una. 'Let's get this over with. What is it you want to tell me about my husband?'

Una stared hard at the table and Molly waited – for an age it seemed to her. Finally Una looked her straight in the eye. 'I've rehearsed how to say this over and over again, all last night and coming over in the plane, but I still find it very difficult.'

Molly would not help her. She continued to wait.

'I have something to tell you about your husband and yourself.'

'Yes?'

'Molly, it will be a terrible shock to you!'

'For God's sake, get on with it!' Molly's nerves were strung tight.

'Yes, well, but before I tell you there is something else I have to say.' Una took a deep breath. 'You must remember I am a reporter and my job is to cover stories.'

Molly's nerves could stand no more of the preamble. '*Please* will you tell me what's on your mind?'

Instead of replying Una opened her handbag and took out a white envelope which she passed to Molly in silence. Molly looked at it. 'But this letter is addressed to you . . .'

Una nodded. 'Read it.' Molly took out a handwritten letter and another one, typed, with the top torn off. She read the handwritten one first and, as she read, time stopped. The fridge, which had been humming quietly, clicked off and the silence which took its place seemed as loud as rushing water. The second letter confirmed what the first one said.

'Who's the second one from?' she asked, whispering. 'The top is torn off.'

'Yes,' said Una. 'But as you can see the name under the signature shows that whoever wrote the letter belongs to the FAA – that's the Federal Aviation Authority in America.'

Molly continued to stare at her. Her face felt cold as ice. 'He's my *brother*?' she whispered. 'But that couldn't be . . .' She pleaded wordlessly with Una that this be a mistake, some practical joke.

Una started to put out a hand but retracted it. 'I'm really sorry to be the one to do this to you, I really am . . .' She

434

was whispering too. 'Could I get you a drink – a brandy or something?'

Molly looked again, stupidly, at the two letters which she still held in her hands, one in each. 'Where did these letters come from?'

'From the shoe box you gave me with your clippings. I don't know why the person who wrote me that letter didn't send it.'

The shoe box. Father Morahan. FOUND AMOUNG THE AFFECTS . . .

Molly stared at Una. 'How could this be? It's impossible. That means that if he's my brother then Malcolm is my father, no, my grandfather . . . ' She looked again at the letters which seemed to waver in her hands. 'Conor,' she whispered, 'he's . . . he's . . . '

Molly had never before fainted but the room began to spin around her and she felt as though she were going to. The letters in her hand began to rattle loudly as she started to shake. 'Are you OK, Molly?' asked Una anxiously. 'Would you like a drink?'

Molly pillowed her head on her arms on the table in front of her. 'Could I have a glass of water, please?' she asked.

Una took a glass off the dresser and ran the cold tap, testing its flow until the water was icy cold. She filled the glass and brought it back to the table. Molly picked it up but could not hold it and some of the water slopped out. Una helped her raise it to her lips.

'I'm sorry, Una.'

'Put your head down to your knees . . . ' Molly did so. After a while, she felt a little less dizzy and sat upright.

The letters had slipped from her grasp and lay on the floor underneath the table. 'Would you get them for me please?' she asked.

Una reached under the table, picked up the letters and gave them to her. Molly hesitated. 'They're yours, of course, they were addressed to you.'

'I think,' said Una wryly, 'that you can lay some claim to them . . . '

Molly read Father Morahan's letter again.

435

I have received knowledge, I cannot reveal how . . .
for professional, ethical and moral reasons, I cannot
reveal . . .
revealed to me on an absolutely confidential basis . . .

There was only one conclusion. Confession. He had to have
learned it in confession. And it had to be from someone who
was involved. Her father? Sorcha? She would never know now.
And she would have to get used to the idea that Micheál had
not been her father, nor Sorcha her mother.

She raised her eyes to Una. 'Could I keep these letters
for a few days?' she asked, trying to keep a tight rein on
herself. 'Obviously I'll have to . . . there are some things that
I have to . . .'

Una nodded. 'Keep them as long as you like,' she said.
Then she pulled her chair forward until she was close to
Molly. Instinctively Molly knew she would not like what was
coming next.

Her instinct proved correct because after clearing her throat
Una launched into a speech she had, Molly realized, clearly
prepared. 'I've said already that I'm a reporter doing my job,'
she started. 'Now I've no wish at all to make life difficult for
you – more difficult than it is going to be. But if you put yourself
in my shoes you must see what a big story this is. In a sense,
because the information was sent to me, it is my story now as
much as yours . . .'

Despite her own shock Molly saw that Una was finding this
difficult, that she was embarrassed. But she was damned if
she was going to help her out. She pulled around her what
shreds of self-possession she could grasp. 'And maybe you'll
appreciate, if *you* put yourself in *my* shoes—' she started but
Una cut her off.

'I know how you feel,' she said, 'I really do – and of course
I'll wait a few days.'

She paused now and Molly noticed that her freckles joined
over her nose. 'Really?' she said, trying to force irony into
her voice.

'I can't just do *nothing* about this story, Molly.'

'I'm sorry but I think you can.' Molly tried to be strong, but the voice which came out was high-pitched and weak.

There was a brief stand-off.

'Listen,' said Una softly, after the pause, 'I'm sorry for being the messenger but I didn't ferret out this information, you must know that. I didn't look for it – it was written to me unsolicited by someone who, if I may say so, really seemed to have your best interests at heart. Whoever wrote me that letter trusted me to do the right thing. Well, I think I've done the right thing in coming to you but, as I said, I'm a *reporter*.'

Molly felt trapped.

'What I'm suggesting,' Una continued, 'if this is OK with you, is that I do nothing at all with this story for a month to give you time to sort out what you need to sort out . . . And I'll help you – honest! If there is anything I can do to help find your husband – I mean your brother – ' Molly winced ' – I'll do it. My paper has considerable resources and contacts in the most surprising areas all over the world. We're not detectives but it is surprising how much journalists can find out when they put their minds to it.'

'But the publicity—'

'Believe me, I'll make it all right. You will not be ashamed of anything I write. I never ever do this – and my editor would probably kill me if he finds out I'm even breathing this – but if you like I'll let you see the stuff before it's printed. There will be no guarantee that I'll change anything, mind you, but it should put your mind at rest. And if there is something that I've got wrong or something that really causes you or your family pain or embarrassment I'll have a rethink about it. If you co-operate with me, I'll co-operate with you and I *promise* you that things will work out all right!'

Molly looked at her with her carrotty hair. The urgency of her argument had wiped the veneer of sophistication from her speech patterns and the accent had reverted to its Galway origins. Molly was reminded a bit of Bridget Slevin, another Galway woman who had helped her in an hour of need. She had got over her anger and was inclined to trust this one again.

She decided that, in any event, she had no choice. 'Would you really help us look for my – for Christian?'

'Yes. Mind you,' added Una, who suddenly became conscious that for someone who was only a base-grade news reporter she was promising quite a lot on behalf of the *Irish Record*, 'I'll have to check all this out with my editor,' she said, 'but I think I can persuade him.'

'I think you probably can!'

They half smiled at one another.

'After all,' said Una, pressing home her advantage, 'none of this is your fault, any more than it's mine. You can hardly be blamed for an air crash that set you adrift in the Atlantic and for the deception which was perpetrated on you when you were one year old!'

'Has this ever happened before?'

'I've heard of it happening before,' Una lied on instinct.

'In Ireland?'

'No, I think there was a case in America that I read about recently. I'll find out for you.' She made a mental note to comb newspaper and library archives.

'If you could,' Molly said anxiously. 'Maybe I could get in touch with those people, find out how they coped . . . '

'I'll do that,' Una promised. The conversation petered out. There seemed nothing left to say, thought Una, but she was worried about leaving Molly alone. 'Have you anyone you could go to for the rest of the day?' she asked gently. 'I don't think you should be alone.'

Molly thought. There was no one at all she could go to, flopping on to their shoulders with this thunderbolt, at least not in London. She could go to Conor in Dublin but deliberately excluded Conor. That subject was something to be considered in isolation and the implications of it had not fully sunk in. She thought of John Pius, also only a plane ride away, but then remembered that John Pius was on holiday in Mauritius. That left Malcolm and Cordelia, so far away in Chicago. But they would have to be told anyway and the telephone was not the proper medium for such momentous tidings. She had no work to hold her here for the moment and Conor was planning to go to Inisheer to visit Brendan if the interview in Dublin turned out as he hoped.

She made up her mind. She had quite a healthy bank balance, thanks to Dolly's shrewdness, and she could afford to fly to the States at will. 'I'll go to Chicago to see Malcolm, my – my grandfather.' The words were very strange. She had never had a grandparent since both Sorcha's and Micheál's parents had been dead when she was born – or had they? Things were very confused.

They would not have been her grandparents, anyway. She had not been born on Inisheer. Sorcha and Micheál were not her parents. All along she had had no parents, just like Christian, but she had had a grandfather. She did have parents too, they were Christian's parents but they had died in an air crash like Christian's parents had . . .

'So my real name is, is . . .' She thought of the array of photographs on the piano in the Evanston house. The photograph of the baby, of herself. She could hardly bring herself to say the name 'Susanna'.

'Susanna,' prompted Una.

'Susanna,' repeated Molly, barely audible. And then she thought of her own baby Susanna, the still, warm little body she had held in her arms in the nursery of St Catherine's, the head downy against her cheek.

Una let her cry. It was probably very good for her, she thought. She felt unusually helpless. She stood up from the table and did what all Irishwomen do in a crisis. She made a pot of tea.

CHAPTER THIRTEEN

When Molly took a mouthful of the tea she almost gagged but
Una ordered her to drink it. 'I put four spoonfuls of sugar in
it. You need it.'

Molly sipped at the sweet liquid. She felt surreal as though
she were in a movie and at the same time watching it.

Una suggested they travel together out to Heathrow so Molly
went with her up the stairs to her bedroom and sat on her bed
while Una went into her dressing room. But Una opened the
wrong wardrobe. 'They're Christian's,' said Molly quietly. 'I
never had the courage to get rid of them . . .'

She watched as Una selected a few clothes from the correct
wardrobe and packed them in a small suitcase and then went
into the bathroom and came out with armfuls of cosmetics and
toiletries. The whole operation took less than ten minutes.

Una called a taxi and then turned to Molly just as they were
about to leave the house. 'Have you got your credit cards?'

Molly picked up her handbag from the hallstand and nodded,
obedient as a child. She was still dazed. It was nice to have
someone taking care of you.

'Passport?'

'No, sorry . . .'

'Where is it?'

'It's in the little chest in the kitchen.'

'I'll get it. Don't move.'

'Thank you, Una.'

Una came back with the passport, looking through it. 'Are
you sure your visa's OK?'

'It's fine, it's a five-year one.'

Una took Molly's handbag, opened it, put the passport in and
closed it again. She hesitated. 'Are you sure you're all right?'

'Yes, really,' said Molly.

Una asked her twice more in the taxi if she was all right and twice Molly said she was. But when she got to Heathrow she had not shaken off the surreal feeling and left all the arrangements to Una. Although it was Sunday the noise was frightful.

Since there were no seats on a direct flight to Chicago she agreed to go via New York. Una organized her credit card to pay for the tickets and all Molly had to do was sign the counterfoil.

She did notice that the tickets were red. 'First class,' said Una, shortly. 'You can afford it – and you deserve it. You'll need looking after and a bit of sleep.'

Molly was grateful for all Una's care and attention but suddenly afraid of travelling alone. 'Would you not come with me?' she asked. But Una shook her head. 'I can't. I wish I could but I really can't. I have a job, you know. As a matter of fact I'm supposed to be in the office in two hours' time.'

'Of course. I'm so sorry.'

'Molly, please don't apologize like that. I hate myself for what I've done to you.' They were still standing at the ticket desk.

'Well, could you stay for a little while?'

'Yes.'

Molly again watched as Una, showing her press card and smiling a lot, wangled it so that she could go into the first-class lounge with Molly. And when they got there she held Molly's hand.

'It's a bit difficult to take it all in, you know,' said Molly.

'It will take a bit of time,' said Una. 'I think you should go and see a doctor when you get to Chicago. Give me the telephone number of the house and I'll call ahead and get them to meet you.'

'Would you do that? You're very kind.'

'Stop saying I'm very kind. I'm not very kind. I feel like a shit at this very moment. Now give me the number.' She copied it into her own contacts book. 'Now remember, I won't have told them anything. I'll just alert them to the fact that you're coming and they're to meet you.'

'Maybe they won't be able to meet me . . .'

'So what? Have you money? You can get a taxi.'

'I'll change money in New York.'

'Attagirl!' said Una, and went to fetch coffee for them.

'Do you think I should telephone Conor?' asked Molly.

Una looked at the floor. 'That's one area I can't help you with.'

'Sorry . . .'

They sat there, Molly still holding Una's hand. Then Molly said, looking away from Una towards a painting on the wall of the room, 'I think I love Conor.' She said it not to Una but to herself.

Una said something, so low that Molly could not catch it. She had her head down so Molly couldn't see her face.

'I beg your pardon?' she asked politely.

'I said, "Of course you do, Molly,"' said Una, quite loudly. But she didn't lift her face.

When she had seen Molly safely off, Una walked slowly back towards the main hall. Since Molly's need had been greater than her own she had reacted instinctively by playing nursemaid. Now Molly was gone she had time to think about herself. First things first: she realized her stomach was rumbling – she had not eaten since the night before. Although she knew she should check to see what time the next flight to Dublin was due to take off, or even if there were seats on it, she decided that for once she would be good to herself. She climbed the stairs to the restaurant and seating herself at one of the tables ordered a large steak and chips.

But when the food came, although there was nothing wrong with it, she found she could not eat it. She took a few mouthfuls but her earlier hunger had disappeared.

She had lost him irrevocably now.

She stared at the food. And then she realized clearly that whatever she had told herself when he had broken it off with her she had not told herself the full truth. She had been secretly hoping against hope that somehow she would find a way to get him back again. Una despised herself for that self-delusion.

442

She had to face the fact that she had truly lost him.

'Is everything all right, madam?' The waiter was indicating the almost untouched food. Una raised her eyes. Through her tears his oriental features were blurred. She attempted to smile. 'Yes, it's just that I was not as hungry as I thought.'

The waiter picked up the food and took it away.

She grasped her bag and unconsciously shook her head angrily to remove the tears. It was all such a big cliché, the great empty space inside her, the pain . . . She had always prided herself on her toughness and invulnerability and here she was crying like a wet. He was only a man after all. She would concentrate on her story.

She paid for the uneaten meal and went down the stairs to the Aer Lingus ticket desk but every step drummed in her head. She had lost him, lost him . . .

Half-way across the Atlantic Molly became irrationally convinced that Malcolm would die before she could tell him the news. The first-class cabin of the jumbo was only half full and she had a window seat but no seat companion and, as her panic mounted, for that at least she was grateful. Her earlier mood of calm acceptance, when she had let Una run her as though she were a clockwork toy, had evaporated during the horror of the take-off and since then the implications of Una's discovery had run around in her head as though on a train track, flashing by each time before she could fully see them.

Christian was her brother.

Conor wasn't her brother.

Sorcha wasn't her mother.

Micheál wasn't her father.

Malcolm was her grandfather.

Cordelia was her grandmother.

Her mother was Maggie, her father was Cal.

Her mother was Maggie – that grave woman in the wedding photograph.

She had grandparents and cousins in America.

She knew that she would be making discoveries about herself

443

now for the rest of her life. All that time lost – but was it?

The chances were she would never have met Conor.

She understood Una's reticence now about Conor.

Poor Una.

But once, when the thought of Conor came round again, it broke her through into the sunshine. She smiled so widely at the stewardess who was serving her with canapés at the time that the woman smiled back but looked puzzled.

Now Molly willed the plane to go faster. She pushed it on with all her might. She wished she had taken Concorde. She had to get to Chicago to see Malcolm but, more urgently than that, she had to get to a telephone in New York so she could talk to Conor.

She called the stewardess and ordered champagne. Her excitement was mounting to such a fever pitch that she thought her head would fly off. She changed her mind when the champagne came and ordered beer instead. Champagne would fizz inside her, beer might slow her down. She needed to be slowed down.

'Certainly, ma'am,' said the stewardess, taking away the champagne. The stewardess must think she was on drugs. That was the way she felt. As though she was drugged.

She picked at the rich first-class food but drank her beer and the combination of the beer and the soporific sun on her face through her window calmed her. Molly managed to sleep when they still had more than two hours to go before landing.

The stewardess woke her gently with a hot towel.

Kennedy airport was bedlam and Molly, disoriented, muzzy from the sleep and the travelling, found that her urgency about telephoning Conor had lessened. What would she say to him, anyway, on the telephone? It was something she had to tell him while she watched his eyes.

She let the airline shepherd her gently through the first-class transit procedures and into another aircraft to Chicago. This flight took another two hours but it seemed no time at all when the familiar streetscapes along the lake appeared beneath her window.

Cordelia was waiting for her at the exit gate.

Darling Cordelia.

Molly burst into tears and flung her arms around Cordelia's neck.

'Molly! What is it? What is it? My poor Molly. What is it?'

The other people in the arrivals area gave them space. Molly continued to sob, laughing and crying alternately.

'Come on, Molly,' said Cordelia at last. 'Come on – you can tell me all about it in the car.'

It was dark in the morning room. Malcolm was sitting in his wing chair, which was now showing its considerable age. The brocade was rubbed shiny at the corners and threadbare along the padding where his head had rested for so many years. The only illumination was cast by a tall standard lamp almost as venerable as Malcolm's chair but the french windows stood open as it was a warm night and the lake, like a thin sheet of pewter, gleamed beyond them through the screens under a three-quarters moon.

Cordelia came into the room with Molly.

'Malcolm, look who's come to see us!'

He might have been sleeping because he started, making a low guttural sound, before attempting to push himself upright leaning heavily on the armrests of the chair.

'Molly! My dear! How lovely to see you!'

'No, please don't get up, Malcolm,' she said, rushing forward and restraining him. 'I'll sit here.' She fetched a tapestry stool from its place in front of another chair and positioned it in front of him.

Cordelia made for the panel of light switches just inside the door. 'Let's turn on a few lights in here—'

'No, it's OK, I like it like this,' said Molly.

'All right. I'll leave you two alone. I'll get coffee . . . '

'I'm sorry I didn't go to the airport with Delia to meet you, my dear. I was a bit tired today.' Half of his face was in shadow but Molly saw that whereas in repose Malcolm's face showed his years, when he was talking he looked like a much younger man.

'Oh, Malcolm,' she said, 'of course you didn't have to come to the airport. I – I have something really extraordinary to tell you . . . ' Then she did not know how to continue. It had been easy with Cordelia. The words had undammed on the flood of tears. 'Is it getting a little cold in here for you?' she asked. 'Should I close the doors?'

'No . . . it's not cold and I'm not cold. What is it you have to tell me that's so extraordinary?'

'You're going to find this very, very hard to believe,' she said hesitantly, 'and I hope it won't be too much of a shock.' She leaned forward and gripped his hands. 'A reporter came to see me today – yesterday – no, today, with a story about myself. She had absolute proof – I know where she got it and who supplied it and I think I know how *he* got it – with proof that I'm not who I've thought I was. I'm not Molly Ní Bhriain from Inisheer.' She stopped. 'This is very hard.'

'Go on, please go on.' Malcolm had stiffened, tense as a cat.

'Malcolm, I'm your granddaughter. I'm Christian's sister.'

He didn't move.

'I know it's very, very hard to believe. But that air crash, that plane that went down. Apparently, I survived and I was washed ashore in a life raft . . . on Inisheer. I don't know the full details about what happened but I was found by my mam and dadda – at least, I mean by the people I thought of as my parents. But I wasn't. I'm yours . . . ' She dropped his hands in despair. 'Oh, I'm making a mess of this . . . '

Very slowly, he folded his hands in his lap. 'I think somewhere deep down, I've known this all along,' he said, very calmly but the effort to control himself was showing. 'It will take me a while to adjust but I don't need convincing that you're who this reporter says you are.'

'I really am your granddaughter!'

The old man continued to sit very still but the expression on his face was one she was to remember for the rest of her life. He began to talk as though to himself. 'When you came out of that customs hall, that first day with Christian, I could have sworn you were Maggie in the flesh. I think I must always

446

have known something like this. But it was just so improbable. It was not only how you looked, it was something about the way you walked and held yourself . . . '

He banged his fist on his knee. 'When we were told about that empty raft we should have searched those islands. I should have gone there myself, house to house, I would have recognized you immediately . . . All those years . . . '

Cordelia came back in the room and saw his agitation. 'What about Christian?' she asked quietly.

Malcolm looked across at her over Molly's head and then stood up. 'This makes it imperative we find him. I'll reactivate that agency tomorrow.' He looked back down to where his granddaughter still sat. 'You're my Susanna?'

'I'm your Susanna, Grandfather – but it's going to take me a while to think of myself with that name!'

'Names, names,' said Malcolm. 'You're back!'

Molly did a childish thing that night. She took a lipstick and wrote 'MY NAME IS SUSANNA!' in scarlet block capitals all over the mirror of the dressing-table in the guest room. Although she had turned the lights off she had not pulled the curtains and the mirror glittered in the moonlight so that she could dimly make out the letters from where she lay in the bed. It was the first opportunity she had had all day for reflection.

She placed her left hand in the path of the pale light which slanted from the window across the room on to the counterpane where the diamond of her engagement ring caught it and shone. She could hardly continue to wear it now.

For the first time in her life she wished she was a writer or, more likely, a composer or a painter. She tried to imagine what her painting would look like. Swirling circles. On the periphery it would be full of yellows and oranges and bright reds for the highs: for the good work she had done, for her lovely, bowered wedding day, for the moment of happiness when her baby had been born. But these brightnesses would whirl around a central vortex, menacing with mustard and vile greens and dirty browns: the instant snatching away of her baby, Christian's drinking and desertion. And right in the middle would be a white circle which represented the unknown. Her future.

Conor. It must be six o'clock in the morning in Ireland, she thought. His image had hovered all day just out of the span of her attention but she had refused to grasp for it. The implications were too new, too exciting and in a way too terrifying to examine.

She laughed aloud in her bed. It was ironic, she thought, that just as he had come out of the closet to declare he was her brother, she was about to reveal that he was no such thing.

She sat up suddenly. That was something which had not occurred to her until now. How did Sorcha and Micheál explain the sudden arrival of a one-year-old baby in their midst? Had Conor and Brendan known all along that she was a foundling?

It became imperative that she ring him. She jumped out of bed, hurried down the stairs as quietly as her urgency would allow and went into the drawing room, which was little used, but was the farthest room from any of the bedrooms. She did not turn on the lights, her eyes were accustomed to the darkness and the moonlight was bright enough to see the telephone, which was conveniently on a little side table by one of the floor to ceiling windows. She pushed the buttons for the operator and giving the Dublin hotel name asked for the telephone number.

'Is that north or south Ireland, miss?'

'The Republic!' she said. Normally that kind of question irritated her but not tonight. Illinois Bell, despite its ignorance of the capital cities of the world, operated with its usual efficiency and she had the number within thirty seconds. 'Thank you!' she said politely to the operator and punched out the digits immediately before she could forget them.

The number rang and rang, for so long that she was in despair and was about to hang up when it was answered and a male voice, not exactly the product of a charm school, came on the line.

'Yes?'

'May I speak to Mr Conor Ó Briain please? He is staying there.'

'Hold on . . .'

To her relief she heard Conor's voice a few moments later. 'Hello?' He did not sound sleepy.

'Hello, Conor.'

'Is that you, Molly?'

She felt giddy. 'Well, yes, in a manner of speaking.'

'What?'

'Yes it is me, Conor.'

'Molly, are you drunk? Where are you calling from? You sound as if you're on the far side of the moon.'

'Well, I sort of am. I'm in Chicago, well, not Chicago, Evanston, actually.'

'I see. What are you doing there?'

'Oh, I'm here on a sort of mission.'

'I see.' Now he sounded impatient. 'Look, Molly, why are you ringing me at this hour of the morning? This is a very important day for me and I've been up since five o'clock, going over and over what I have to say in less than four hours' time.'

'I'm not playing games, Conor.'

'What?'

'I'm not playing games! I have a very important question to ask you. Now you might think it is very, very odd but it is part of the reason I'm here. It's a matter of life and death, Conor, and I'm half afraid to ask you.'

'What is it, Molly, for God's sake?'

'Do you know anything about my birth?'

There was a pause and when he answered she could hear the astonishment in his voice.

'Your birth?'

'Yes, my birth.'

'Well, I wasn't at it, if that's what you mean. I was away in school at the time.'

'What age was I when you first saw me?'

'Oh, Molly, for crying out loud, what's this all about?'

'I'll tell you when I see you, Conor. Now will you just answer me? What age was I when you first saw me?'

'You must have been about two months old or something like

449

that. I came home from school at Easter with Brendan and there you were.'

'Are you sure you saw me that Easter?'

'Of course I'm sure. You wouldn't remember but I was the one who brought you down to the beach for the first time. And it was definitely Easter Sunday because we had chicken for dinner.'

She laughed. Dear Conor. Always food.

'Are you sure you couldn't be mistaken?' she asked. 'Could I have been one year and two months old, d'you think?'

She could hear him sighing.

'You were a very small baby when I brought you to the beach, Molly. You couldn't walk or talk or sit or even babble. Now does that answer your question?'

'Yes!' said Molly, irrationally happy.

'And now can I get back to preparing for my interview with the massed ranks of the hierarchy of the Irish police force?'

'I want you to listen to me very carefully, Conor. I've to stay here for a couple of days, there are a few things I have to do, but I'll be coming back to Ireland later in the week. I'm going to come over to Inisheer and see you and Brendan.'

He paused again, then said carefully. 'Are you over there looking for Christian? Will you be bringing Christian with you?'

'I have no notion of where he is. But I am going to try to find him. But even if I do, I will not, repeat, will not, be bringing him with me.'

'I see.'

'Conor, something really extraordinary has happened but I want to tell you in person and I want to tell you on Inisheer.'

'Just tell me one thing – is it good or bad?'

'You'll just have to wait and see – but I think you'll be impressed.'

'You've been nominated for an Oscar!'

'For goodness sake! That doesn't happen for months and months. Anyway, it's better than an Oscar.'

'So it's good, then.'

'Just wait and see. And good luck today. I've a hunch nothing at all can go wrong today.'

'Goodbye, Molly.' She could hear he was smiling.

'Goodbye, Conor!' She sang it.

She raced back up the stairs to her bed. He had seen her when she was two months old. That was a mystery they would have to unravel together. It must have been a different baby. Poor baby. But her brain couldn't deal with that now. Nothing could dampen her exhilaration now . . .

Malcolm was already fully dressed when Molly came downstairs early the next day. The desk in the morning room was open and he was sitting at it, notepad in front of him. He slammed down the telephone receiver in frustration when she came in to the room. 'Damned agency! I keep getting an answering machine.'

'Malcolm,' she protested, 'it's only seven fifteen in the morning.'

'Yes, well!' he said. 'Anyway, good morning, Susanna.'

'Susanna, Molly, Margo – I think I'll just call myself Fred and be done with it!' She walked across and kissed him on the cheek. 'Good morning, Grandfather.'

Malcolm managed to contain himself until eight o'clock when the agency telephoned back. He fired rapid instructions at them and then informed them that he was hiring a second agency to augment their efforts. To find his grandson had now become absolutely essential.

Christian was already on the streets but he was a hundred miles from Chicago and light years from Evanston. The sun shone red from the sky but it was not because of a pretty dawn. The town of Gary, Indiana, reeked of the furnaces and smelters that belched fumes into the air twenty-four hours a day.

The flophouse on one of the back streets which served as Christian's current residence turned its guests out at seven o'clock, hail, rain or shine. Christian shuffled along the sidewalk. His feet, neglected to the extent that he had the beginnings

451

of two ingrown toenails, hurt him dreadfully and the torn sneakers he wore were a size too small. At least he had something to do today, an appointment. He was to see someone from Social Security. But the appointment was not until nine o'clock. He stopped a man hurrying in the opposite direction. 'Excuse me, sir?'

The man hurried on, ignoring him.

'All I wanted was to know the time!' Christian shouted after him but the man did not stop.

A woman did tell him the time – it was twenty-five minutes to. Only twenty-five minutes to go. Christian was looking forward to going in somewhere and sitting down. The appointment was to review his situation. He might even get a job out of it – but sober as he was at the moment he knew the prospects were dim. His efforts at jobs in the last six months had failed miserably. He had had piecework on the railway yards and in the mills but he never lasted long. Christian knew his whole life was now a cliché – from the kind of stories he used to cover in a life which now seemed centuries away. The world was a bitch to him and his only friend was the bottle. He had to laugh sometimes at the irony of it.

He was going to see the Social Security people because two nights ago he had had a terrible shock when the man beside him in his current flophouse had choked on his own vomit and Christian had been the one to find his corpse.

Christian had seen his own future.

When he had arrived in Chicago after leaving London, he had checked into a hotel with a bottle of bourbon for company. When he was sober enough next morning he went to his Michigan Avenue bank and closed all his personal accounts drawing out all the money, which was a considerable sum. Then, instinctively wanting to lose himself, he took a bus to Milwaukee where again he checked into a downtown hotel.

He had looked around the room, clean, large, air-conditioned and as impersonal as an airport waiting room. It was the end of family life or any attempt at it. He could not bear to think of what he had done. He knew then that the only way he could keep living was to keep drunk.

Not wanting to attract undue attention, he moved hotels after three days and kept moving by bus through the cities of the Midwest, skirting Chicago, checking into good hotels in each place. He lived like that for nearly five months until all the money was gone. He had lost forty pounds in weight.

He got a job in the stockroom of a hardware store in Detroit but could not concentrate on the inventory and was fired.

That became the pattern of his life. He would clean himself up, work for a few days and then be fired with enough cash to keep himself in sleazy motels and drink until he ran out of money again.

Eventually he could not get a job at all and went on welfare. For the last few months he had been indistinguishable from the derelicts, winos and drop-outs who frequented the flophouses of all the major cities. They all had stories to tell but none, including Christian, told them. They all got by, they got some money from welfare, they sold their blood, they picked up food from the back doors of restaurants and although there was a degree of camaraderie among them from time to time they all lived their lone lives like pieces of flotsam that never touched.

Occasionally Christian thought of his former life, of his grandfather, of Molly, of journalism. But he was always able to bury the thoughts in drink – someone always had a bottle. The loneliness dimmed and after the first few months it was never acute, just a part of everyday life.

The Social Security office opened on time and Christian shuffled in with the rest of the clients. But the woman with whom he had an appointment was late. He sat on a bench in the large, green-painted room to wait his turn while clients were called to one of the little booths which lined the counter at the top of the room. The sporadic flurry served only to counterpoint the dead, hopeless atmosphere which enveloped the place. Christian's need for a drink was becoming urgent. He was just about to leave when his woman arrived and called him from the door. She brought him out of the main office and into her own, a partitioned square open at the top, little bigger than four telephone booths.

'Mr Smith,' she said, settling herself behind her desk and pulling a legal pad towards her. 'Is that your real name?'

'Yes,' answered Christian, then, 'John Smith.'

The woman sighed. 'Look, Mr Smith, we have a lot of John Smiths. Could you not at least be a bit more original?'

'Smith is my real name,' said Christian truthfully.

She sighed again. 'All right, Mr Smith. You married?'

'No. Yes – *no!*'

The woman sighed again. 'Any living relatives?'

'No, ma'am.' This time Christian's voice was emphatic.

'You sure, Mr Smith?'

'I'm sure.'

'Last permanent address?'

'Some place in Detroit, Michigan.'

'I mean a *permanent* address, Mr Smith.'

'That was as permanent as it got.'

The telephone on the woman's desk rang and she dealt with the call, scribbling on her pad. She replaced the receiver. 'Now, Mr Smith, our records show that you have been without a job or visible means of support for a relatively short period. Do you want rehabilitation?'

The abruptness of the question fazed him. His motives for coming had been to seek help but now that help was so imminent he quailed. The need for a drink became overpowering. 'What – what do you mean?'

'You heard me. I said, do you want rehabilitation?'

Christian moved uneasily in his seat. His feet were throbbing. 'What kind of rehabilitation?'

'You know very well, Mr Smith. Detox.'

Christian had never been through detox but he had heard enough lurid stories about it. 'I – I don't know.'

'Mr Smith,' said the woman, kindly enough, 'you either want rehabilitation or you don't. It's not my job to persuade you, just to facilitate you. Why are you here? Detoxification is your only chance. You're still a young man, Mr Smith. I don't know what your background is and that's not relevant. But just think of it. You'd be taken care of . . . Make yourself a new life. Give yourself a chance.'

She pulled a manila file across the desk and flipped through it. 'I see from this that you have no major medical problems to speak of. You would come through easily enough and then you'd have a chance to put your life together again. How about it?'

Christian looked at the homely black face which gazed back at him from across the desk. Apart from anything else she was the first person who had spoken gently to him in weeks. 'Would I get my feet fixed?' he said.

'What's wrong with your feet, Mr Smith?'

'They hurt a lot. I think it's my toenails.'

She made a note on the file. 'We'd take care of that.'

'OK,' he said hesitantly. 'What do I have to do?'

'You don't have to do anything, Mr Smith. Uncle Sam will take care of you now. Do you have your social security card?'

He shook his head. He had sold it.

'No matter.' She picked up her telephone.

Conor's interviewer was tall and slim, he wore his inspector's uniform well. He was flanked on one side by a junior Garda officer and on the other by a civil servant from the Department of Justice. Conor and his solicitor sat on the other side of a vast boardroom table, french-polished to satiny perfection.

The interview, Conor felt, was not going well. There were long pauses between the Inspector's polite questions while he and the two men on the other side of the table took notes. The five of them were going through one such pause now.

There was a degree of unreality about the whole thing, he thought, waiting for the next question: the thick quietness, the too-shiny table, the Inspector's gloves neatly placed beside his cap in front of him and, a little to one side, his own lack of something to do with his hands. The room was high and wide with long windows through which, faintly, he could hear the roar of traffic. All those people outside, just going about ordinary lives. He had made a mistake in initiating this process. He had been having a perfectly satisfactory life in London.

The Inspector, whose name was Silke, stopped writing. 'Tell

me again, Mr Ó Briain, why you felt it necessary to change your name.'

Conor's solicitor jumped in. 'With respect, we've already been over that.'

'Well, with respect, if you don't mind, we'll go over it again.' The Inspector's voice remained impeccably polite but Conor, not for the first time during the interview, was uncomfortably aware of his solicitor's smooth English accent.

'Well, as I told you,' he said, 'I felt that I had to submerge my identity so that if the police were looking for me—'

'*If* the police were looking for you – but, Mr Ó Briain, if, as you have told us, your father's death was an accident, why should it be necessary to run from the police in the first instance?'

'With respect—' the solicitor interjected again but it was Conor's turn to cut him off. 'I think, Inspector,' he said, 'if you were in my shoes, you would have done the same thing. My father and I were fighting viciously, I have made no secret of that. There could be an interpretation that when he tripped and fell, as he did, that some action of mine had killed him.'

'Surely that would have been for the courts to decide?'

'Inspector Silke, I did not stop to think of the courts. I just saw my father lying on the ground, dead. I was his son, Mr Silke. I had killed him.'

'Ahh,' said the Inspector.

'I really must insist, here,' said the solicitor. 'My client in no way admits to the killing of his father—'

'But he has just done so, Mr Carthew.'

'In my view what he has said was not an admission of liability but—'

'I would prefer to hear Mr Ó Briain's version of the incident in his own words, if you don't mind, Mr Carthew!'

The solicitor opened his mouth to say something else but changed his mind. He shot Conor a warning look but Conor ignored it. It was out now and what was said was said. 'All right, Inspector,' he said looking directly across the table at the other man. 'I know it looks bad. I know perhaps I should not have run like I did. But . . . ' He hesitated, then plunged on. 'My

456

father and I had a history of arguments and fights. He beat me a great deal when I was growing up, even into my late teens. That day, the day he died, he was spoiling for a fight with me. I don't know why, I just know it was not unusual with him. I can't go so far as to say my father hated me because I don't know what was in his mind but certainly, on that day and on many others like it, he wanted violence. I was then in my late twenties, Mr Silke. My late twenties. He insulted me, my mother, my sister. I couldn't take any more of it and when he lunged at me I was not going to take it lying down as I had *quite literally*—'

Conor's voice had begun to shake with passion and he stopped. No one in the room moved. The two men, who had been taking notes on either side of the Inspector, kept their heads bent, pens poised.

After a few seconds, Conor continued, his voice under control. 'I was not going to take it as I had on so many occasions. He and I had fought before but this day there was something different about it. I think this was the first time I was fighting for someone other than myself. He had insulted my *sister*.'

Again he stopped.

'Would you like a glass of water, Mr Ó Briain?' The Inspector pushed the carafe and a glass towards him.

'No, thank you.' Conor stared at a point above the Inspector's head. 'My father and I went outside the house – I can't remember what was said or who said what. I just know that this fight was something to do with settling things once and for all.'

The solicitor made a move but Conor turned to him. 'It's all right, John. I don't care now.' He turned back to the Inspector. 'We took off our jackets, my father and I, and suddenly he was not my father any more, just an opponent. We started to fight. He hit me hard – he was a fisherman and very strong – and I hit back. People, neighbours, children started to gather. I remember a warm sticky feeling over my eyes and even while we were fighting I remember the shock of realizing it was my own blood. I couldn't see very well, I just kept hitting and he kept hitting me and suddenly he wasn't there any more he was on the ground. That's all.'

An electric clock hung on the wall of the room and in

the silence its hands could be heard moving on, a second at a time.

'I see,' said the Inspector at last. 'One question, Mr Ó Briain, can you remember which of you hit the other first?'

'No,' said Conor.

'I see,' said the Inspector again and made some notes.

The silence ticked on.

The Inspector stood up. 'We'll be in touch, Mr Ó Briain.'

Conor, drained, was shocked. 'Are you—' he began to ask and then could not remember the rest of the question.

The solicitor stood up too. 'My client has been through a great deal of mental anguish in the last few years, Inspector. We would greatly appreciate if you could give us some indication as to how you think our appeal might progress.'

The Inspector held up his hand. 'I'm sorry, that is for my superiors to decide.' He stood back, placed his chair neatly under the table and walked around it. Automatically Conor stood.

The Inspector came right up to Conor and he was almost as tall as him. 'Thank you for coming in, Mr Ó Briain. Please don't leave the jurisdiction until you hear from us. Have you got your passport with you?'

'I have it.' It was the solicitor. He opened his briefcase and rummaged in it. While he was thus engaged Inspector Silke held out his hand to Conor. 'Goodbye for now, Mr Ó Briain.'

As Conor took his hand the Inspector interposed his body between himself and the two other officials, who were getting their papers together at the other side of the table. And then Inspector Silke gave Conor a huge wink.

Christian sweated and shivered in his bed. The initial sedation had worn off and he felt wave after wave of panic sweep over his body, wringing him out and leaving him alternately rigid and limp. He wanted to cry out but some remnants of sanity warned him that to cry out would be useless. What he really needed, what every pore cried out for, was a drink. Anything. On the street he had always prided himself that at least he had not descended to the level of the meths heads but now he would not have cared. Meths, spirits, beer – anything.

He had to get out of here. He had really wanted to go straight but it was impossible. No man could go through this. He looked around for his clothes. They were nowhere to be seen and he was dressed in hospital-issue pyjamas, frayed and worn so that there was a hole in one of the knees.

He got out of bed and was too panicky to stand upright so he crawled across the floor on his hands and knees to the door of the room. It was locked. Again and again he tried the handle, pulling on it, twisting it with all his strength until the sweat poured off him in increasing claustrophobic panic.

He began to scream. 'Help! Help! Help!' His voice sounded weird, faraway and amplified as if it were coming back at him from the top of a high mountain.

'Help!' he screamed again.

To his horror the room was moving. The walls were pulsating in and out, bulging and writhing, crawling with maggots. He crawled over to a corner and huddled in it avoiding the maggots, clutching his hands around his knees for safety, while the walls continued their grotesque square dance. All the time he continued to scream for help.

The door burst open and two men came in, one carrying a syringe. They lunged at Christian but he saw them not as men but distorted like fairytale beasts. He fought the beasts off as though he were a wildcat. The three of them struggled but Christian's panic made him strong and he managed to get away from the beasts and make for the door. They were coming after him down a corridor. He didn't recognize the corridor, he didn't recognize anywhere at all. He went through a door and found himself in some sort of laundry place. Huge machines, turning on giant rollers, pulled in long white sheets like shrouds and spewed them out again. There was steam everywhere and a bitter smell.

The people in the laundry stood at their machines, their mouths in big round Os as Christian tore through them. He nearly fell over a big hamper but steadied himself.

He saw another door at the far side and looked behind him.

The beasts were coming. He sprinted towards the door. His feet were light and he didn't feel them touch the ground. The door gave when he crashed into it and he was in a boiler room, blasts of heat and rumbling and miles of pipes. EXIT, said a sign on a big green door. He made for the door, pushed the silver bar and was free in the open air in a parking lot. He dodged behind a car and then another one and then another one again. He did not stop to see if the beasts were coming. He collapsed on the ground behind a panel truck at the far end of the parking lot. His heart was hammering and he felt sick, sicker then he had ever felt in his life. He looked at his feet. One of them was bleeding.

But he had to get out of here.

He knew he wouldn't get far in the pyjamas. He looked around. A few feet away from him was a high embankment. The parking lot ran along one side of the railway tracks. Even in his fright and panic he knew that this was a stroke of luck.

Now and then on the streets he had met men, hobos, who had stories to tell of marathon journeys made on boxcars. This was surely his way out. If he could get into a boxcar, he could rest a while and then, surely, he would find some help, another hobo, a fellow traveller who would lend him clothes and maybe share a jug.

Christian stood up and checked the parking lot. One car was moving out but away from him. He had a chance. He scrabbled up the overgrown embankment clawing at the stones and grass until he reached the top. The tracks were just his own height below him and he lowered himself onto them.

His body was shaking like a leaf but his mind was clear. This was where salvation lay. Boxcars. Hobos.

Almost buoyant, he hugged himself to try to stop the chattering of his teeth as he heard the train approach. It was coming too fast, he thought. It wasn't a goods train. No boxcars. He would have to get out of the way and wait for a train with boxcars.

He turned and began to climb the wall to the top of the embankment again to get out of the way of the train. But the worn pyjamas slipped from around his waist and down over his bleeding foot so he couldn't get a toehold. Spreadeagled against

460

the wall he yanked at the pyjamas to free his foot but the train was upon him. There would have been plenty of space between himself and the train if he had not moved but the gush of wind the train brought with it frightened him and he tried to flatten himself against the wall. The pyjama-covered foot slipped and he skidded down the wall. He held on desperately, clawing, but in a split second one of his legs shot out behind him and onto the track where a wheel of the train caught it. Christian spun and jack-knifed with the impact and his other leg and arms went under. The train caught him under its speeding wheels and carried him for a hundred yards before he died.

It took quite a while for the police to identify Christian and it was almost midnight of the next day when his family came to collect his body. Molly sat beside her grandmother in the back of the Lincoln while Malcolm sat up front with the chauffeur. They travelled south on Interstate 90, past the Robert Taylor Projects, taking the cloverleaf onto the Skyway. They passed open fields and farmhouses and the turn-off to The Dunes and it seemed no time before they saw in front of them the red glow of the Gary sky.

CHAPTER FOURTEEN

After the funeral, Molly waited a few more days and then, promising her grandparents she would come back within a month, she went home to Galway. She had a few hours to kill before she could get a plane to the island so she took the taxi past Oranmore and into Galway. The emotions of the past week had heightened her senses. She had not been sleeping well and fatigue combined with adrenalin to produce an excitement so intense that sometimes she had to stop to catch her breath. She walked through the bustling Galway streets, gay with shopping mothers, the first sprinklings of tourists and posses of schoolchildren just let out for the day but she barely saw them. Conor jigged around in her blood.

She found she had walked as far as St Nicholas's. With a pang, she remembered Sorcha telling her gravely that Christopher Columbus had stopped to pray in this very church on his way to discover America but then adding sympathetically that poor old Christopher had been too late: St Brendan the Navigator had already found it centuries before.

She went into the church and lit a candle to Our Lady in memory of her mother, who was not, after all, her mother. It was peaceful and cool in the church after the brightness outside. A sacristan moved silently around the sanctuary, performing quiet rituals with books and markers and patens and genuflecting every time he passed the tabernacle. Molly stood gazing at the steady yellow flame of the candle and finally understood what Sorcha had meant when she had asked on her deathbed for her forgiveness.

She could not pray but sat in a pew and watched the flame, which burned quietly alongside its fellows until a draught issued from the door and it guttered. Sorcha felt very near.

'Oh, Mam,' she whispered. 'I loved you.'

Christian's funeral had been small and quiet and very sad but in a strange way it had taken the newness off Molly's new relationship with her grandparents. Try as she might, she could not grieve for Christian in the way she felt she should. Her sadness was more for the waste of Christian's life than for its loss. Seeing her grandparents' sorrow, however, she was able to grieve for them and it brought them close.

In the days after the funeral she, Malcolm and Cordelia had talked and talked and talked. She had asked innumerable questions about her real parents and they had told her every little detail they could remember about Cal and Maggie Taylor, even about Maggie's odd, silent parents who had been her other grandparents. Her real father, she discovered, had been very like Christian. He had even had a cowlick.

She had tried to assimilate it all, to picture Maggie and Cal and their lives in the Evanston house. She had tried to feel like Maggie's daughter.

She had stared at Maggie's picture and tried to regress, emptying her mind of everything else but the picture, trying to remember anything at all of her own brief span with Cal and Maggie in the house. And once or twice she had an illusion that she did remember something, a look, a feeling, a sunbeam in the morning room. But realistically she recognized it was probably her overactive imagination. Sorcha would always be her mother.

She sat on until the candle she had lit for Sorcha had puddled at the base. It flamed briefly and then went out.

She went back out into the day to walk up to Moon's to buy Conor a present and one for Brendan too. She supposed she should probably have brought both of them something from America. It was funny. When she thought of both of them together, they were still her brothers.

She raked through the racks of sweaters and men's clothes in the store, picked up pieces of Waterford and Galway crystal and eventually decided on a sports jacket of Donegal tweed for Brendan. She had not seen him for so long that she hesitated about the size but the assistant assured her it could be changed if it did not suit or fit.

She could not find anything suitable for Conor and left the shop. There was a jeweller's just across the street from Moon's and she walked across to it. It offered nothing of any interest in the window, which was full of Claddagh rings, Claddagh necklets and even lumps of Connemara marble embedded with Claddagh plaques. She went inside and found she was the only customer. She told the assistant she wanted something very special for a man, for a very special occasion.

The assistant thought for a moment and brought out a tray of gold identity bracelets. 'You could have it engraved?' she suggested.

But they were vulgar things and Molly could never see Conor jangling with a bracelet. She looked along the glass cases. In a corner of one of them, half-hidden by a silver-plated bear with a slit at the back of its head, she spotted a tray of unusual gemstone rings.

'Could I see these?' she asked. The assistant unlocked the case and extracted the tray.

One ring was exactly right. The craftsman had set an oval moonstone signet-style in a square setting of heavy silver. Molly held it in her hand. It felt substantial and smooth and warmed immediately in her palm. The moonstone was pale, a paleness that was no colour, but as she moved it around under the jeweller's spotlight it glowed with faint pink and grey and blue. It was a beautiful thing.

'Do you know anything about who made this?' she asked the assistant.

The girl shook her head. 'I think it's second-hand, madam,' she warned. 'Sometimes we have the odd second-hand piece. Do you know the gentleman's size?'

'No,' said Molly, 'but it's not important. Could you engrave the inside of it for me right now?'

The girl hesitated. 'I'll check.'

She went behind a curtain and emerged again within seconds. 'All right, so.'

'Do you have a piece of paper?'

The assistant tore a piece off a pad and handed it to her with

464

a pen. Molly thought for a few seconds and then scribbled, 'For ever'.

She hesitated, holding the pen above the paper. Then she added a dash and the initial M. She gave the piece of paper to the girl, then asked for it back. 'Sorry,' she said to the girl and scribbled out the M.

She paid for the ring with a credit card and left the shop, walking the short distance to Eyre Square and the taxi rank. The trip out to Oranmore was uneventful and the plane was ready for her when she got there. She had been unable to get on the scheduled flight and had had to charter this one.

As she was the only passenger, the embarkation procedures were swift and Molly strapped herself in beside the pilot. He chatted cheerfully to her as he took off and trundled his plane into the sky. In less than fifteen minutes they were circling over Inisheer.

Below her on the airstrip she could see several figures looking up at the plane. She had pictured herself slipping in unannounced and walking into the kitchen of the cottage, surprising him. Too late, she realized that the pilot would have radioed that a special unscheduled flight was coming in and word would have spread like wildfire amongst the islanders, to whom anything out of their ordinary routine was a welcome break. Children were running along the boreen towards the strip but she did not recognize Conor among the people waiting. All to the good. Was it the French who said that anticipation is the best part of a love affair?

The plane landed and bumped to a halt and, bidding goodbye to the pilot, she got out, blinking in the evening sun. She had been wrong about Conor. He was coming across the grass towards her from the west. If he noticed anything unusual about her manner he made nothing of it. 'Hello, little sister,' he said and took her bag.

They walked off the airstrip and out into the boreen. Conor greeted several of the men, who tipped their caps to Molly, and the children clustered around the entrance to the field stared at her but fell back a little as the two of them approached, leaving a passage.

465

She had not been in touch with Conor since her wild, middle-of-the night call when he was still at the hotel in Dublin and his account of the interview with the Gardai took up most of the walk to the house. He had not heard back, he told her, but was going to the mainland the following day to make enquiries.

She was barely listening. She was now openly admiring the set of his shoulders and the length of his thighs and the way his hair curled over his collar and frosted a little at the temples.

Once, he looked directly at her to make some point and she was almost shocked at the extraordinary clarity of his eyes. Immediately she felt like giggling. Molly knew she was acting like a schoolgirl but happily gave herself a temporary licence.

'Are you listening?' he asked, stopping dead.

'Yes, Conor,' she said demurely.

'What are you at, Molly?'

'Nothing, Conor.'

'Are you going to tell me what the big secret is?'

She made her eyes wide. 'Of course, Conor!'

'Well, tell me!'

'Not *now*, Conor, not *here*!'

He sighed in exasperation but they were nearly at the house and they walked the rest of the way in silence. Molly was delighted at the effect she was having on him. She could hear tunes in her ears. But her heart sank as she came close to the house. Even from the outside she saw that Brendan had neglected it. It badly needed whitewashing; each year Sorcha had painted the door and the two small windows at the front but the colour was now faded, the paint flaking in patches around the hinges.

'Oh, Conor!' she said, jolted for a few moments out of her mood. 'If Sorcha could only see what's happened to her lovely house.'

'I know,' said Conor. 'It was as bad inside but I've forced him to help me over the past couple of days and it's a bit more presentable than when I came. Be warned, Molly. Even in this short time, he's changed a lot.'

Brendan certainly had changed since Molly last saw him. He

466

had always been thin but now he was cadaverous, stooped and ill-looking. He had been sitting at the empty fireplace smoking a cigarette when they came in and when he jumped up to greet them he was caught with an appalling attack of phlegmy coughing which bent him double. He looked old enough to be Conor's father and not his brother.

They waited until the spasm had passed.

'Have you seen a doctor for that cough, Brendan?' asked Molly. She was genuinely fearful of the awful wheezing and rattling sounds he was making.

'Arrah, not at all,' he said, still wheezing. 'Them doctors is all shite-hawks. Take your money and gives you a bottle and bye-bye and that's the end of you. How are you, Molly?' he said with a ghastly attempt at joviality, smiling and showing two blackened eye-teeth in his top gums. The four between them were missing. 'Grand to see you,' he went on. 'You're looking great, anyways. London must agree with you. And I'm very sorry about the babby. That was a dreadful thing altogether. Very, very sorry.'

It was a speech he had obviously rehearsed. Molly could have cried.

'I'm absolutely fine, Brendan,' she said. 'Now let me show you the great present I brought you. I want you to try it on straight away.' She took the jacket from her holdall. She had taken it out of the Moon's bag and had packed it rolled only in its tissue paper. 'I hope it fits you now, Brendan,' she said. She heard herself talking more loudly than was necessary in a hearty tone she did not recognize. Appalled, she realized she sounded as though she were a matron in a mental hospital.

'Ah, you're too good,' he said, 'and I with nothing to give you in return.' He shook it out of its tissue paper. 'Oh, isn't it lovely entirely. A lovely thing. Too good for the likes of me.'

'Of course it isn't, Brendan.' Again she felt like crying. Was this the mean sniveller of her childhood – this shambling, pathetic creature? She would almost have preferred the original.

'Put it on you, Brendan.' It was Conor, who had not taken part in the little scene up to this.

'Did you bring it all the way from America?' Brendan took

467

off the suit jacket he was wearing which might once have been brown but was now so worn that it was an oily grey. 'Conor told me all right you were in America.'

'I did, Brendan,' she lied. 'All the way from Chicago.'

'I hear Chicago's a great city. The Windy City! And they dye the river green there on St Patrick's Day!' He put the jacket on. It was far too loose and made him look even worse than before but he did a little shuffle of appreciation with his feet. 'Molly, it's lovely. It's the bestest jacket I ever did see. And all the way from the Windy City!'

He was making such an effort, trying so hard to be pleasant that the overall effect was like something out of a freak show and Molly realized sadly that since Sorcha died the man probably never spoke a full sentence to anyone from one end of a long year to the other.

'I think it's a bit big for you, Brendan, I'll change it for you—'

'Wirra's trua, you will not! What change! Divil a change! This jacket fits me so well I'll be buried in it! It's a beautiful coat. Now!' He clapped his hands together. 'Ye'll have a cup of tea or something stronger?'

He turned, stepping on his old jacket and the tissue paper and walked towards the dresser to fetch the mugs. Conor intervened. 'Molly and I are going for a walk, Brendan. She told me on the way up that she wants to see all over the island again before it gets dark. Why don't you go to the pub and we'll join you there later?'

'Right, right, right. Right you are!' said Brendan. 'I'll see ye there, so. There's a lot to talk about, eh? We'll have a fine night tonight!' He raised his hand in salute, jerking it upwards like a sort of marionette and went out of the door. Too late, Molly saw that the sales tag was hanging out of the back of the collar on the new jacket but she did not have the heart to run after him.

Conor shrugged. 'Don't worry, Molly. He'll settle down. It took me a day or two to get used to it but remember the kind of life we live now. If we still lived here we'd be used to this kind of thing.'

'But Conor . . . '

468

'Now I said don't worry about it. Brendan is not your problem. As a matter of fact, he's probably quite happy . . . ' He picked up the tissue paper off the floor, balled it and threw it onto the ashes in the cold grate. He hung Brendan's old jacket on the back of a chair. 'Now, would you like to go for that walk I invented? You're probably tired, though, are you?'

She pulled off the scarf she had tied around her head and shook her hair loose. 'To tell you the truth, Conor, I would love a walk.'

They started in silence. It took a while for Molly to get over her distress at seeing the state to which Brendan had brought himself and Conor respected her mood, sometimes leading the way, sometimes falling into step beside her, adjusting his own long stride.

They climbed up beyond the post office. It was a glorious evening and few were about. The children were at their homework or already in bed and the men who were not in the pub or clustered around the television in the Óstán were down at the pier. The calm evening and the soothing sound of the quiet sea seeped into Molly's bones. Bit by bit she recovered her earlier mood of mischief and gaiety and with it excitement at Conor's presence again began to swell.

Without her realizing it they had come to the place they knew so well together, the little grassy hollow at the top of the cliff. She almost laughed out loud at the appropriateness of it.

'Let's sit down awhile, Conor, it's so lovely,' she said. He obviously caught something in her tone because he looked at her oddly but flopped down obediently on his stomach, his chin on his hands facing the western sky. It was getting late, after half past nine, and the sun was beginning to set. Molly sat too but cross-legged and upright and chastely apart from him. Now that the moment had come to tell him the truth she was suddenly very nervous.

They let the evening settle around them. He moved a little away from her, wriggling like a caterpillar. It might have been, she thought, to get more comfortable on the uneven ground. She was not sure. He was tense.

They watched the sun as it descended slowly into the flat

469

gun-metal plate of the sea, pulling gold and crimson fingerlings with it. The lower it dropped, the tighter the silence between them stretched until it was as painfully taut as a violin string. A little breeze got up and riffled the grasses around them but the ground was warm from the day and they were not cold – or at least Molly was not.

She risked a look at Conor. He seemed lost in contemplation of the scene before them but, highly tuned as she was, she could feel the rigidity of his body in her own. He kept his head raised a little on one fist and with the other hand picked, as if to a hidden rhythm, pieces of grass, lichens and mosses from an area about six inches square. He placed the blades and velvety pieces in front of him in some sort of order and after a while she could see he was building a small green pyramid. Briefly, she was reminded of the little mound he had made over the baby's grave. But even that could not deflect her excitement.

She was sitting about two feet from him and on a level with his waist. He was wearing a pair of dark green corduroy trousers with a toning sweater of light wool, an outfit she had bought him as a Christmas present five months before. The trousers ruched slightly at the knees and in the crease where his buttocks met his thighs. The jumper had ridden up a little, exposing an inch of skin above his waist. She longed to touch it.

She continued to watch him play with the grasses and could not stop her imagination prompting her as to how his hands would feel on her breasts . . .

Suddenly, he threw himself on his back. The movement startled her and she jumped a little. He stared at her, placing both his hands behind his head as a pillow. All the sounds around came sharply to her ears, the heaving of the sea below, the calling of a sea bird she could not identify.

'Are you going to tell me what this game is about?' he asked softly. His gaze was so direct and so tender that her body answered with a surge of lust. But she turned away from him and lay on her own back.

'I thought this would be easy to say,' she began, staring up at the sky which was draining slowly of colour, 'but now that it's here I don't know how to begin.'

'Try at the beginning.'

'That's just it. That's the hard part. Let me try with this. I have a present for you, Conor.'

She felt around in the pocket of her jeans while he continued to lie on his back, looking at her with that uncompromising stare. She handed over the tiny box containing the ring. He took it and ripped off the red paper, decorated with pictures of bows and engagement rings, in which the jeweller's assistant had wrapped it. 'It's a ring,' he said, when he opened the box.

'Yes. I hope it fits you.' Then she realized that this was exactly what she had said to Brendan. She took a deep breath. 'Conor, before you look at the ring or what I have had engraved inside, I want you to listen to me now. And please listen until the end. In fact I want to start at the end, if you don't mind.'

But his eyes were on the ring. She saw him look at the engraving. For ever.

He made a movement towards her. 'Molly—'

She put her hand out. 'Shush . . . let me speak, please.'

She turned away from him and faced the sea. 'The end is that I love you, Conor. I love you with all my heart. I have loved you with all my heart, I think, since I was two years old. And I have felt guilty about loving you all these years because I thought it was unnatural. And, of course, it was unnatural for a sister to love a brother in that way. That is the way I loved you, Conor, physically, emotionally, sexually, without realizing it sometimes but it was always there. I wanted you in my bed, in my body, in my mind and my heart. I still want you. I want you now more than I've ever wanted anything in my whole life . . . '

She noticed the haze of dusk on the sea. She wished now that he would do something, say something, anything at all . . .

She risked a glance towards him. He was still staring at her. His eyes seemed to have darkened and she could not fathom the expression in them. There was nothing for it and she went on. 'That's the end of the story, Conor. The beginning of the story is more complicated and this you will find probably more difficult to believe than the end of the story because after all I'm not the only sister to love her brother throughout the course of the world. The beginning of the story, Conor, is that I am not your sister.'

She heard a movement behind her and she sat up like a whiplash to be quicker than he. Quick as a leopard she leaped on him and pushed him back down again with her full weight, leaning with both hands on his upper arms pinning him to the grass. 'Don't say anything yet. Listen to me, Conor, listen!'

Under her hands, his biceps felt like knotted iron through the fine wool of the jumper and he could easily, she knew, have thrown her off had he wished to do so. She slid her hands down his arms until her palms met his. The warmth of them shocked her. She could actually see his heart hammering in his chest.

'I am not your sister. I am Christian's sister.'

He made a little movement but she tightened her grip on him, using every atom of strength and willpower to force him not to move, to continue listening. 'But that is not what I want you to know. I want you to know I am not *your* sister.'

He was absolutely still under her.

'That plane crash which killed Christian's family, I was in that plane and by some miracle I was washed ashore here in a life raft and Micheál and Sorcha found me and brought me up as their own, as your own. But I was not their own or your own and someone brought me proof a week ago. The only real proof is blood tests, I suppose, but I have a photograph of my real mother with me, Christian's mother, and you will see the resemblance. I will tell you how I found out later but that is not important. What is important to realize is that there is no blame attached to any of the people in this story, not Mam or Dadda or Christian or me or you.'

She loosened her grip a little. 'I'm sorry I'm rushing like this with you. I didn't mean to. I meant to lead you on, tease you a little. Oh, I had great fantasies about how I would shock you, Conor, take all my clothes off in front of you and seduce you into real sin and then when we were both well and truly damned, then and only then, I was going to tell you the truth.'

He looked past her, out beyond the cliff and she thought he was revolted and was going to stand up and walk away. Suddenly she felt horribly embarrassed.

She had miscalculated . . . She had made a fool of herself. She removed herself from him and sat back on her heels looking out over the sea. One of the local fishing boats had moved out of the harbour, the sea had turned blue-black and the boat was already showing a light.

Behind her, she heard Conor sit up but she did not react. Then he put both hands strongly around her waist and pulled her to him. In one swift movement, he turned her around and fastened his mouth over hers. She answered him with her own mouth, opening it, feeling the warmth of his tongue, pulling his soul into her own.

They were on their knees and he urged her backwards until she gave way, sliding her legs around until she lay underneath him and his full weight was on her. She pressed up against him with the hunger of years in a kiss which went on and on. He had wrapped his body completely around hers and because he had both his hands underneath her it seemed that he was lifting her into him, fitting their bones together until they were one melded skeleton.

Molly could not believe the strength of her desire. Because of her previous experiences she had thought of herself as repressed or even frigid and this tumbling rush caught her unawares. She moved again, catching his thick hair in both her hands and wrapping her legs tightly around him. But he caught hold of them and looked directly into her eyes. 'Not here,' he said.

She was in such a state that the stopping was like a douche. 'Where?' she whispered.

He stood up and pulled her up with him. They stood a little apart, not touching now.

'I want to make love to you in our bed, Molly,' he said.

'It's not our bed.'

'Not yet . . . '

They walked back down the hill towards the house, excitement continuing to build between them but as far apart as the boreen would allow. They fell rigidly into step with each other as though they were marching.

It was dark inside the house but Conor did not turn on the new electric light. He took the battered paraffin lamp, which

473

was still kept for power failures and emergencies, and found the matches where they had always been kept to one side of the high, oil-clothed mantelpiece. He raised the wicks and lit them, held the glass chimney over the flame for a moment to warm it and fitted it into its crenellated brass holder. Molly, standing just inside the door and leaning against it, trembling, watched the way the gentle yellow light made his eyes shine and created an intimacy in the cottage she remembered from the better days of her childhood. He carried the lamp through to the bedroom, the same bedroom where so long ago she had cut him free with a kitchen knife. That, she remembered now, was the only time she had ever seen him naked.

Through the open door of the bedroom she watched him place the lamp carefully on a table by the window.

Then he came to the door. 'Come here, Molly,' he said.

She did not move, not yet. 'Suppose Brendan comes back?' she asked.

'Brendan won't come back.' He said it with certainty.

When she walked towards him he stopped her, put his arms around her for a moment, then stooped to pick her up and carry her to the bed. He laid her on it and the old springs creaked loudly.

He stood over her then and she looked fearlessly back up at him. Everything in the room was golden. He leaned over and undid the zip fastenings of her boots, first one, then the other. He made a ceremony of undressing her, taking his time, undoing the buttons of her sweater and blouse and slipping them over her shoulders. She co-operated by lifting herself off the bed. He rolled her over on her stomach and undid the clasp of her brassière and then rolled her back again, taking the straps down her arms. Each time a piece of her was uncovered, he stroked it with long firm strokes as though she were a young horse who had to be gentled. He cupped her breasts in his hands and kissed them, one after the other, tiny reverent kisses so soft that they were like a warm breeze.

When she was completely naked he started a long, slow, stroking pass over her entire body, starting at her neck and moving over her shoulders, keeping his palms on her sides and allowing his thumbs just to brush her breasts, stroking along the curve of her hips and tracing a line with his thumbs, downwards from her navel. She arched upwards towards his hand but he did not stop, moving on to her thighs and knees and calves, ending smoothly with her toes. She was trembling like a leaf and every hair on the surface of her skin was raised.

'Please, Conor,' she said.

For reply he leaned forward, raising his arms so that she could ease off his jumper. His skin was tanned and firm. He never took his eyes off her as he kicked off his shoes and peeled off his socks and then took off his trousers and pants in one swift movement. She saw that his body was just as she had imagined it, beautiful, hard and strong, with fine dark hair on his chest, legs and forearms.

Perversely, she now wanted to delay and as he climbed back on to the bed, she attempted to hold him off.

But he was too strong for her. He made an inarticulate guttural sound and pulled her towards him. She pressed her length against him so, at last, they held each other, skin to skin.

He turned a little on his side and taking her buttocks in his hands, fitted himself into her. He made another sound deep in his throat. They were both trembling hard and when they began to move it was with such increasing intensity that Molly felt he was penetrating not her body but her mind and every corner of her soul. She had never had an orgasm and when it came she cried out and clung to him for safety and in ecstasy and soon afterwards he came too, burying his head in her neck and riving her with everything he had saved for her for all his adult life.

The golden light from the oil lamp spilled over their bodies like a benediction.

Conor got off the bed without a word and returned with a quilt he took from a trunk in the corner of the room. He lay down again beside her and pulled the quilt over the two of them and then took her in his arms again, covering her face with gentle kisses, first her forehead then each of her closed eyes, her cheeks, her nose, her chin and finally her lips, the softest of kisses. She had so often dreamed of what his lips would feel like, thinking

475

they would be hard and firm but now they were anything but that: they were soft and warm and tasted on her own like sweet milk. She put her head under the quilt, redolent with old smells from their childhood in the house, leather and stone, turf and paraffin. She smelled the smell of them together and pulled the quilt over both their heads, kissing the point at his throat where she found the little hollow under his Adam's apple.

They lay together then, without moving, safe. 'What's next?' Molly asked, her voice muffled under the quilt and against his chest. She could feel him smiling although she could not see his face.

'Remember Messalina,' he said.

'Where's that?' she asked, bewildered.

'It's not a where it's a who. Look it up in your Robert Graves. She was a sort of a sister too.'

Like the last time they had lain together on this bed, she made herself small and curled into him like a little kitten.

SKY

For Pat Brennan
with gratitude.

Acknowledgements

As always, there have been many who helped over the long haul. My thanks are due to Mairéad Coyle of the Conrad Hotel in Dublin, Evanna McGilligan and Clare Tuohy of the Canadian and British Embassies, Tim Kelly of the European Commission office in Dublin, Tom Davitt of the Department of Justice, Gerry Martin of the Tae Kwon Do Centre, Phena O'Boyle of Bord Iascaigh Mhara, veterinary surgeon Michael Hatton, Dr Jim O'Connor, director of the Natural History Museum of Ireland, my mother and father, Bill and Maureen Purcell, who helped gather details. Thanks to Ciarán Gavin of Computing Workshop who helped me out more than once when I demanded too much of my machines. And thanks to Michael Cuddihy, Tom McCaughran, Martin McGowan and to my friend and ornithologist, Killian Mullarney.

In Montana, I must thank Karen Huff for her generosity in loaning her cabin on Flathead Lake to a complete stranger – and John and Mary O'Conor for arranging it. Valerie Hemingway also extended wonderful hospitality, as did Father Sarsfield O'Sullivan of Butte (and Béara); I must also thank Ellen Crain of the Butte/Silver Bow Archive.

Deepest thanks to all my loving friends who stuck with me throughout. I hope they won't take it amiss if I single out Pat Brennan, Treasa Davison, Gill Bowler, Frank and Patricia Byrne – and Patricia Scanlan, fount of boundless, hard-hitting encouragement.

Thanks to Macmillan in Australia, New Zealand and

London, particularly Susan Robbins, Jill Rawnesly, Hazel Orme, and my tactful editor, Suzanne Baboneau. As ever, thanks to Treasa Coady, Charles Pick and Martin Pick, who always steer me through.

To Kevin, Adrian and Simon: there would be no point to it without you.

And finally, delighted gratitude to Northwest Airlines who so kindly upgraded me to business class on my research trip to Montana so that I, like Sky, could experience those wide plushy seats.

Prologue

Trinity burns. The old cobblestones of Front Square are alight with passion as students and ordinary Dublin citizens gather to listen to a powerful denunciation of Bloody Sunday.

Thirteen civilians shot dead by British soldiers in Derry – Londonderry to the Brits.

Speaker after speaker, breath spuming in the foggy, frosty air, parades on to the platform: boys newly become men in the aftermath of the shock, girls with women's faces. The smallest and the last is a girl who had been there that day. Who had seen the purple dye, then the bullets.

In the centre of the crowd, Rupert de Burgh, a young man with curiously light-coloured eyes, face waxen in the makeshift lighting, is transported with the fire of this young woman's rhetoric. His friend jammed beside him is so spellbound he cannot even cheer – Rupert can feel him trembling.

Someone at the front lights a rolled newspaper, tossing it in the air. Many hands, black stars against the flame and sparks, reach for it until it splits and sputters out. 'They're killing our brothers up there.' Rupert's companion turns to him. 'Rupert, they're murdering our brothers.'

'Come on, Rupert! Come on.' He turns and pushes through the press of bodies behind.

'Where? Where are we going?' Rupert pushes on behind him. 'She's not finished – where are we going, for God's sake?' His accent is not Irish. Rather, it is upper-crust English. Home Counties' Blue.

'To burn the bastards, burn them out—'

'Burn who?' But Rupert finds he is trembling too. He is panicked – and yet threaded through the fear are strands of joy.

The young woman's rhetoric reaches new heights; all around, students raise clenched fists, wave their scarves, punch each other's biceps. Rupert's friend is joining in the chant now, louder, louder. 'Burn the bastards . . .'

It is taken up by stragglers at the back. '*Burn the bastards.*' They turn and run towards the covered archway, which leads towards the street outside. '*Burn the bastards.*' It spreads towards the front. '*Burn the bastards . . . Burn the bastards,*' splitting and rippling in a widening V until row after ragged row wheels and runs.

The stewards appointed to marshal the event jump on to the stage in horror. One grabs the microphone: 'Come back, come back,' he shouts. 'Order, please, *order* . . .' Too late. 'BURN THE BASTARDS, BURN THE BASTARDS.' The crowd has become a mob.

Fergus Lynskey, tall and rangy with floppy hair and a profile like a falcon's, is passing as the crowd pours through the archway through the gate and into College Green. He presses against the railings as the run begins towards Nassau Street, sweeping all in its path. 'What's happening? What's happening?' he calls to one after another.

In response, one boy, his face transfigured with joy, waves both fists in the air: 'BURN THE BASTARDS!' before running on.

'What's happening?' Lynskey asks a breathless girl with stringy, waist-length hair, who squeezes in beside him to remove her platform shoes.

'I can't run in these,' she explains, wrenching at the buckles which hold them round her ankles.

x

'No,' he shakes her arm, 'what's happening – why is everyone running?'

'We're going to burn the bastards!' The girl kicks off the first shoe and begins to struggle with the second. Across the road, someone throws a brick or a stone through the front of Cook's travel agency. The shattering of plate glass is lost in the uproar.

'Burn who?' Lynskey, whose Kerry accent is as thick as cream, has to shout to be heard above the roars and screams, the noise of pounding feet.

Another crash as someone throws another brick, this one through the window of Barnardo's, the furrier's. 'Tell me,' he wants to shake this girl, shake someone, 'where are ye all going? Burn *who*?'

'The Brits, of course.' Breathlessly, the girl kicks off the second shoe and is away, rejoining the stream.

Lynskey, who wants to join the Gárdaí and, confident of getting through the recruitment process, is waiting for the advertisements to appear, hesitates then dodges through the stragglers at the back of the crowd. He heads for the telephone box on the other side of the street, dials 999, passes on the information, then dials again – Store Street Gárda station this time. He asks for a sergeant, a friend to his family. 'To the British embassy? They're too late, son.' The sergeant is laconic. 'The place is already on fire.'

Rupert de Burgh, who has lost his friend somewhere along the way, arrives at the embassy, but instead of pushing through to the front hangs back. Watching. Exulting.

Some time later, it could be ten minutes, it could be fifteen, the authorities are gradually taking control when Rupert becomes aware that a tall young man has materialized beside him. This youth, whose most prominent feature is a long, hooked nose, seems appalled at what is going on. 'What do they think they're going to achieve?' He shakes his head and Rupert is glad to be standing in the shadow of a tree beyond the reach of the street-light so the newcomer cannot see his expression.

A pair of youngsters start to rock a nearby car. 'Stop it.' The newcomer rushes over and grabs the nearest boy by the scruff of the neck. 'Get away out of this—'

The youths, of an age when larger people can still frighten them, run away down the street. 'I can't stand this,' the hawk-like man comes back towards Rupert. 'I wish I was already in Templemore.'

'I beg your pardon?' Outside his parents' home, Rupert is always polite.

'Templemore,' says the other man. 'The training centre. I'm going to be a Gárda.'

As sometimes happens in the most unlikely situations, Rupert de Burgh instantly sees his own future.

Mayville, Montana, June 1992

Sheriff Brian O'Connor, heavy-set, black quiff oiled straight back from a low forehead, replaces the telephone receiver and stares at it. Now and then, not more than once a year, maybe, the little hairs stand on the back of his neck. This is one such occasion.

His call had been from Joe Mason of Santa Barbara, California. A plumber by trade and no more than an acquaintance, what Mason had had to say made perfect sense. The time for pussyfooting with so-called 'peaceful' – or even protest – solutions to Ireland's problems with England was past. And now Joe tells him that even the IRA, that last line of defence, might be going soft. Secret political talks, for God's sake, with the covert blessing of the yellow-livered, pandering Irish government. If this was true – and it seemed it was – it made a mockery of the reasons for which Pádraic Pearse and his fellow patriot martyrs had died in 1916. It made a mockery of the patience of people like himself, and other patriotic Irish-Americans and Irish-Canadians, who had waited all these years for justice.

The sheriff gets up from his desk and walks across to the window of his office. It is a perfectly ordinary Montana summer day and out there are ordinary automobiles parked in an ordinary lot but his life is about to change. He knows it like he knows his own name. Joe Mason is a member of a select new Irish-American-Canadian group, membership of which is restricted to ten people and is by invitation and personal recommendation only. And, as of one minute ago, Brian O'Connor is a member.

An odd common denominator among the ten is that not one has ever set foot in Ireland. So far.

Chapter One

At the time, the mutiny seemed such a little thing. If she had not flared up that day Sky would never have been switched to the shamrock assignment, might never have made the connections.

The early-June day was hot. Hot for Butte, where 80 degrees is a heatwave. So hot that the weatherman on KLFM was forecasting storms. And maybe it was the wet patch on the back of her blouse that was the final straw, that made her jump up from her desk and march after Jim – or Jimbo – Larsen into his office, just seconds after he delivered the flyer.

Holding the piece of paper as though it were radioactive, she pushed open his door before he had time to resume his seat. 'I'm sorry but I told you last year was the end of it. That I wouldn't do it again.' She smiled then, daring her boss to do something. Like fire her. Eight years was too long in the one job, particularly in a two-bus town like Butte.

While she waited for him to say something, Sky, as tidy as a hurricane, sniffed with distaste at the disorganization of Jimbo's office, which offered barely space enough for one human, let alone two. The editor of the *Butte Courier* had never been seen to throw out a scrap of newsprint, his own or anyone else's, and he peered out at her from a grotto carved into bluffs of yellowing paper. 'We've got to cover it.' He seemed caught in disbelief at this unexpected revolt and settled into his chair to argue. 'What do you suggest?'

'Send the kid.'

This was mean: Lindy, the junior in question, was a beautiful, vague creature whose employment by the newspaper owed more to Jimbo Larsen's long-standing friendship with her father than to her skills, or even ambitions. Sky nurtured a suspicion that, far from paying her, Jimbo was actually accepting money from the girl's father to keep her off the streets. The kid showed flair for dress, however, and for the first time in its sixty-year history, the *Courier* sported an occasional fashion page. 'Be good for her.' Sky hardened her heart. 'She could do with a solo ride.'

'Come on!' Jim changed tack, pressed Save on his keyboard in case this proved a long haul. 'This isn't like you,' he wheedled. 'Just once more? I'll do it myself next year – or maybe by that time the kid'll be OK on her own. Where is she, by the way?'

'I'm not her mother—' Sky stopped, noticed the way a spray of sunlight from the window glinted on the bald patch in Jimbo's sandy-coloured hair and remembered how long they had soldiered together. She softened a little and studied the press release again as if reconsidering. She knew how important the upcoming rodeo was to the paper: the owner of the *Courier* was also the proprietor of the rodeo ground, and some of the cowboys from his ranch were expected to do well. It was the same every year: the purses were small, but a win, in a state as underpopulated as Montana, translated into prestige because everyone got to hear about it.

Sky had hated rodeos since, as a child, she had attended her first one in Augusta and had egged on the four-legged participants rather than the humans, no matter how skilled. 'If I do it, let me ask you for the last time – *if* I do it – will you change your mind and send me to the nationals?' The Montana primaries were imminent and Sky, convinced that nationally this was the Democrats' year and that November would see the end of George Bush, had been campaigning for months to be allowed to join the big boys at the national conventions.

'Get real, Sky, you know there's a squeeze on.' Circulation of the weekly had been trickling away. Competition was steep, with titles from other towns and states muscling in, and with the decline in newspaper reading. In some ways, the *Courier* was a victim of its own high editorial standards; Montanans, like the rest of the United States citizenry, tended now to prefer their news and information pre-digested and in seven-second soundbites.

'No conventions, no rodeo.' She widened her smile. The task of the rodeo reporter was to record everyone and everything which moved that day within a five-mile radius of the ground, every breeder, dancer, wrangler, roper, their sons and daughters, mother and fathers, if possible their high-school teachers. Each name printed translated into at least one newspaper sale, many more if the named one had relatives and friends out of state.

'That's blackmail!' But Sky could see Jimbo's heart wasn't in it. He hated carrying the dreary lists of names as much as she hated collecting them. 'Call it greymail.' She dangled the press release between her index finger and thumb. 'You know as well as I do that you could do with some good national politics. This state has a stake in this election, you know, and Perot has more support than some around here'd like to think.'

The editor glared for a second, then seemed to think better of what he had been about to say. 'I'm not hopeful,' his long Finnish face, always lugubrious, settled deeper into itself, 'but I'll see what I can do.'

'Good.' Without giving him any further opportunity to slide under her defences, Sky turned and left the office, making sure the half-glassed door clicked behind her. She knew the chances of her going to the conventions, either in Houston or in New York, were about as good as Dan

3

Quayle's prospects of winning the presidency but she had gone too far now to backtrack. She balled the release and aimed it at the empty trash-can across the room. The metal rang satisfactorily. 'Good one.' She patted herself metaphorically on the back as she slid behind her desk and peered to locate the cursor she had left to flicker in mid-sentence on her screen.

She was writing up her notes on a routine piece about the city's annual water shortage but, after a minute or so, she got up again and crossed to the coffee machine. The row with Jimbo was symptomatic of a deeper discontent. Somewhere, over the course of this spring, impatience with her doe-like existence, which had rumbled under the surface for so long, had erupted to demand action. 'R. Sky MacPherson, you're bored, bored, bored. I'm *bored*.'

'Hi!' Behind her, she heard the door open. The kid was back.

'How'd it go?' Sky looked round: she had to admit that, given the heat, the girl looked pretty good in cropped T-shirt and tiny skirt, which exposed her long brown legs to sensational advantage.

'All right, I guess.' The kid had been sent to interview Butte's newly appointed public librarian. 'Look what the cat dragged in.' She held up a piece of brown paper, tightly folded to the shape of a small rectangle on which were scrawled in vivid purple the words *Edditor. Urjent.* 'Some guy gave it to me on the way into the building. Will I trash it?' She held it over the garbage can.

'No.' Sky resumed typing. 'Bring it in to him. It's addressed to him, isn't it?' *Nice one, kiddo*, she thought with satisfaction, thinking of the editor's reaction. Served him right.

The junior, carrying the paper as though it was on a silver salver, crossed to Larsen's door and knocked, while Sky, sighing, gazed at her keyboard. Ten seconds later, while she

4

was paging through her notebook, she heard the kid come back into the room. 'What was it?' She looked up.

'Haven't a clue, he said just to leave it on his desk.' The kid sashayed to the coffee machine. 'Hot today, isn't it, Sky?'

'Sure is.' Sky cut off the follow-up complaint with a burst of furious typing. 'Must be at least eighty.' She knew the sarcasm was wasted; never having been outside the borders of her home state, this dipstick had no idea what heat was.

Immediately after graduation, in an effort to get away from Montana but most particularly from her mother, Sky herself had spent three years, including three squelching, sweaty summers, in Chicago as a junior on the *Sun Times*. By contrast to the humidity and discomfort there, Montana heatwaves were short-lived, flares of light and balm that were supremely welcome after the long, blue-nosed winters.

The telephone bleated but before she could say 'hello', she heard the familiar sound of daytime TV in the earpiece then, 'Is that you, Sky?' Her mother's voice plummeted like lead to the pit of her stomach.

'Yes, Mom?' She grabbed a strand of her hair and tugged until it hurt.

'If you're not too busy this evening, would you take me to Franklin's?' Shopping for gew-gaws was one of Johanna's vices. The Ben Franklin chain, with its enormous range of goods ranging across hair ornaments, dried flower baskets, hideous sweats, dinky stationery and sports equipment, called to her like a siren. 'Aren't you meeting the girls tonight, Mom?' Sky was falsely gay. The 'girls', in their fifties, were the relicts of her mother's past, two divorced matrons who, like Johanna herself, persisted with incense, dirndls and long hair.

'Buffy can't make it, her son's coming in from Wisconsin.' Johanna's voice was charming, low-pitched and retained its Irish lilt, and it drove Sky through the roof.

She pulled the hair tighter, stretching the skin on her

forehead until it felt as though it was going to tear. 'What about Hermana?'

'She's menopausal today. So will you drive me?'

'I wish you'd learn to drive, Mom.'

'You know I can't master machines, Sky. Some people are just not meant to know about machines.'

Sky gritted her teeth. 'What do you need from Franklin's?' In her present mood she dreaded the thought of gliding down those wide, somnolent aisles in the wake of her mother, who always fell into a sort of trance the moment she pushed through the store's offer-clad doors. 'You know there's a perfectly good store within walking distance of the house. Anyway, Mom,' she improvised, 'as it turns out, I may have to work.'

'Well, golly, why didn't you say? If you have to work, that's all right. I'll keep a nice salad.'

'See you later.' Sky replaced the receiver and took out her frustration on her keyboard.

All her friends thought her mother delightful. What drove Johanna's daughter to distraction, however, was the assumption that everyone was on the same airy wavelength as she was. The pronoun most frequently used by Sky's mother was 'we'. Yin, yang, Jung's collective unconscious, mysterious herbs and teas, ginseng, strange powders and remedies recommended by Johanna's friends on the Blackfoot reservation – 'we' all subscribed. It was just that 'we' had all covered our real selves with phony selves piled on by the false brain-god of Thought. Johanna always turned off the news and *Sixty Minutes* on TV, watched only movies and her daytime soaps.

Knowing she was being perverse, Sky's response was to insist on engaging her mother in conversation about every disaster and treachery consuming the world, on eating packet cereals and processed meats packed with E numbers. Yet even these ostentatious and childish ploys did not succeed in raising so much as a pained expression to her mother's unlined face. Johanna listened patiently without interrupting, constructed nourishing and tasty health-food concoctions and removed them without complaint if her daughter left them untouched. 'We' – including Sky – all knew Sky was in denial. It was just a matter of time before she came to her senses.

Sky read back what she had poured on to her screen and found it was garbage. 'A-aaagh!' She swept both hands across the surface of the desk sending paper clips, cuttings and Xeroxed press releases cascading on to the floor.

The junior, surprised at the ferocity of the yell, turned round from her contemplation of the alley outside. 'Do you have nothing to do?' Sky picked up the telephone and shot her a venomous glance while punching at the numbers. 'Turn down the damned TV, will you?' she hissed into the sound of television glop before her mother could get a word in, then, 'It turns out I'm not working, after all.'

A storm hit Butte just as Sky and her mother pulled up at the kerb near Franklin's, and rocked the little car with a barrage of pebble-sized raindrops. 'We can't get out in this, Mom.' She switched off the useless wipers. 'It's forty yards to the door and it would be like swimming up a waterfall. This is no shower either – we'll have to go home.'

'Wait just a little.' Johanna inclined her head like a child determined on winning over an adult.

'Don't *do* that, Mom. You'll drive me crazy.' Sky, who could think of a million better places to be than here, had to restrain herself from knocking her own head on the glass of her window. Her mother fixed her with a cornflower gaze as penetrating as a paring knife. This look was by far Johanna's most effective weapon, simply because it was not a weapon. 'And don't do that either.' This time Sky did crack the side

7

of her head on the window. 'What is it with you? I'm thirty-four years old and a divorcée and you make me feel as though I'm ten and caught with my hand in the cookie jar.'

'I'm listening.' The older woman's eyes did not blink or waver. 'Only you know how you feel, Sky, or why you react like this. We'll go home if you want to.'

Sky groaned and lowered her head to the rim of the steering wheel. The storm vibrated through her forehead, wormed a tunnel into her brain. 'Mom, I'm going to have to leave again. This place – living at home – it's killing me.' She looked over. 'It's not you, personally, don't be hurt.'

Then, finding herself still held in Johanna's gaze, 'All right, it's partly you. It's a personality thing between us but you mustn't take it as an insult or that I don't love you,' she heard herself getting worked up, 'but you know what I mean – thirty-four-year-olds shouldn't be living with their mothers. No other species on the planet does it. It's the whole thing, Mom, you, Butte, that deadbeat paper. I've got to go somewhere else, be on my own.'

Still her mother said nothing. In the livid light within the car, Johanna's dark halo of hair was imprinted against the window, which streamed red and blue from the blurred Special Offer posters on the store frontage outside. She was too close, too blameless and, in the end, her silence proved unbearable. Before she knew it Sky had the door open and was outside in the fierce warm rain, blinded, her boyish haircut melding to her scalp. 'All right, all right, forget it,' she was having to yell above the bucketing, 'we'll go inside. Who cares that this is a hundred-dollar sweater?' She struggled with the folding umbrella she had picked up on the last Franklin excursion but by the time she managed to raise it it was no longer of any use and she threw it into the Nissan's back seat.

Johanna did not emerge from the car until her polka-dotted foldaway plastic raincoat was fully buttoned and the matching headsquare tied under her chin. 'All righty,' she closed the car door with careful attention to the handle, 'I'm ready,' and smiled with neither recrimination nor triumph.

'Great.' Sky took her arm and bundled her ahead towards the store.

They had the cavernous spaces inside almost to themselves. The staff moved through the aisles at a leisurely pace, reticketing and repositioning sale items and taking advantage of their unexpected leisure by calling to one another, their voices taking on a peculiar disembodied quality in the soft whoosh of the air-conditioning.

Sky left her mother and headed back into the rain and then into a nearby coffee shop where she stacked paper napkins into the seat of her moulded plastic chair to absorb the damp from her clothes. Unlike Franklin's, the air here was still and humid and before long she was steaming gently. Determined to suffer, she gulped decaffeinated coffee as flavoursome as boiled tractor oil and chewed her synthetic jelly doughnut. She was the only customer and, ignoring the glances from the waitress behind the counter who tried to stare her into hurrying, she forced herself to quieten down and think.

How had she allowed herself to become trapped like this? But, of course, she knew the answer to that. Sky thought of her ex-husband, so loving, attentive, naturally witty – and so crocked.

He had been dry when she met him, and stayed dry for the first three months after their marriage, but it did not take long after that for her to learn that the normality was a veneer and that he was severely messed up, not only with drink but with drugs. At the time he had loved her so much, promised her so much, including the carrot – crucial to a girl who had trailed around the western states for so long in the wake of her mother – of living with her in the same place for the rest of their lives.

9

In many ways, she knew that her ex had done her a great favour. If he had not plunged so low and so quickly, she might still be trying to make the best of things with him, clinging to the hope that things might improve. Unlike the way in which she conducted her professional life, Sky had always shirked confrontation in matters of a personal or emotional nature; no matter how firm her resolve, at the first sight of someone else's hurt or confusion she caved in.

Her misjudgement of her husband's character and behaviour had been a severe lesson and it meant that, while she continued to date and was never short of boyfriends, no one since Randy had succeeded in gaining her confidence. Sky considered that she had had a lucky escape and was determined she would never get caught like that again. For almost a year now she had sometimes enjoyed, sometimes endured the on-again-off-again relationship with her present boyfriend. Greg Landos was handsome, big into fishing, hunting, flying his dad's plane any time he could borrow it, riding in his pickup – on the surface a typical Montanan who thought that only poncy Easterners removed their hats while eating. If conversation was not about one or other of his hobbies he floundered. She was on one of her downslides with Greg, and in her heart, knowing she was being unfair to him, was casting around for some gentle way to move on. It was certainly time. How to do it without devastating him was the crux.

She surveyed the dispiriting gunge in the bottom of her Styrofoam cup, as flat and uninteresting as her life: stuck in Butte, in a job with no possibility of promotion, with a boyfriend who did not interest her. And in a mother–daughter scenario she knew was classic: she could live neither with Johanna nor without her. The only-child chains were too strong. If only Johanna had an ugly, brutal, or even parsimonious temperament; if she drank, or was vulgar or had cheap affairs, like other women's mothers, it might have made things easier. But, deep down, Sky knew she took perverse pride in her mother's quirky individuality. She was doomed.

That evening, 350 miles upstate from Butte in the town of Mayville, Sheriff Brian O'Connor was stretched comfortably in his recliner in front of the TV in his untidy living room. The Cubs were slaughtering the Dodgers: Cubs at the plate in the ninth, bases loaded, pitcher winding up.

The telephone shrilled beside him. 'Hot *damn*!' The sheriff put down his beer and, keeping his eye on the screen, lifted the receiver. 'Yes?'

The Cubs man on the plate struck one and the home crowd went wild, but something his caller said made the sheriff search wildly for the TV's remote control to kill the cheering. He sat upright to concentrate on what the other was saying. 'I see.' He frowned after about two minutes, then said, 'May I ask who gave you my name?' He listened again, then: 'I see. You know I've never done nothing on this scale before—'

The caller obviously interrupted because the colour drained slowly from the sheriff's florid face. '*How* much? Could you repeat that?. . . Give me a day or two to consider,' he said hoarsely after the other had complied. 'I'll see what I can do.'

He hung up slowly. This was unbelievable, the opportunity of a lifetime.

He had been worrying about how he was going to raise the five thousand dollars he would need as his contribution to the scheme being cooked up by his new *ad hoc* group of patriotic friends. The budget for what they were planning was modest and was being met largely by one of the Canadian members, a millionaire sexagenarian by the name of Jerry Flynn. However, in the interests of democracy, and

11

on the basis that each member of the group would have more at stake if he contributed financially to the endeavour, everyone was expected to chip in. So far, any time Sheriff O'Connor needed to raise extra cash, all he had ever had to do was to identify and target individuals in his own catchment area for simple blackmail. Nothing moved in his jurisdiction without his knowing so he always had a readily available list of possible victims and an armoury with which to ensnare them. He had, however, used his ammunition only when it was necessary to subsidize his meagre salary – when he had to buy a new automobile, for instance. It had always proved successful because he had kept the scam small and was not greedy. Five grand was way out of the league in which he had played.

But, out of the blue, here was an invitation to take part in a deal that would not only allow him to pay his dues in one fell swoop but would net him a lot more besides. His telephone caller had been from the state capital, Helena, and although not connected with the group – the deal he was offering was a commercial one – he had given as his introduction someone from that city whom the sheriff recognized as a fellow traveller. It seemed so fitting, somehow, and although he felt a little daunted by the scale of what he was being asked to do, the sheriff liked the clean, quick sound of the operation.

If he accepted the commission, he was to speak only to his contact in Helena who would telephone him from time to time. Otherwise, provided he adhered to a time-scale, he had a free hand in how he set things in motion. The job itself, which was to be once-off and lucrative, was to find a method of shipping to Ireland a certain body-sized and weighted consignment in a genuine casket, with paperwork. That done, he would be paid immediately.

The sheriff knew that procuring the casket shouldn't be too difficult, given that he was a lackadaisical member of the

St Patrick's Brigade in Butte, an outfit that saw itself as one of those keeping the flame, but which fired up only on St Patrick's Day. The present incumbent of the presidency was a funeral director, Bill Collins.

He reached for the telephone; he had been given two weeks to get going.

As he waited to be answered, he reflected that the stiff would be more problematic: what he had to find was a corpse with no relatives. Come on, he thought, surprised that a funeral home would not answer more quickly. It was a pity they couldn't just send off one of those famine coffins – reusable boxes with hinged bases through which the corpse was dropped into the grave. If they were discovered they could always pretend the stiff had fallen out.

The telephone was at last picked up. 'Hello, Bill.' The sheriff forced warmth into his voice. 'When's the next meeting of the old Brigade?' He listened, then: 'I know, I know, but I'm busy and Butte's a long ways away. Why don't you all meet up here sometimes?'

A little later on that night, in Ottawa, Canada, investigators with a search warrant were letting themselves into the luxury home of a former government member. The ex-minister, who was in his sixties and now very rich, was vacationing in Europe with his wife.

In a matter of seconds, they had disabled the alarm system with a sophisticated scanner and easily gained access through the front door by inserting what appeared to be a thin, credit-card-sized piece of flexible plastic into the door jamb.

Once in, as if they knew exactly where they were going, the four men walked quickly through the sunken living room, their feet making no sound on the thick pile carpet.

Efficiently, they searched a room fitted out as a study, opening every drawer, rifling the neat desk. It took them some time to unlock a large filing cabinet, but one of the dozens of needle-like devices on a key-ring yielded results and the cabinet gave up its secrets.

One of these secrets was to have far-reaching effects on both Sky MacPherson and the sheriff of Mayville.

Chapter Two

Almost a week later, on the other side of the world, in Co. Kerry at the southwest corner of Ireland, two walkers were crouched low over the fluttering, struggling body of a small bird. They had come upon it while taking a walk across a remote headland near a beach. The pair, who were on holiday from Dublin city, had no idea what type of bird it was. Long-legged, it was about a foot long from the tip of its thin, curved beak to the end of its tail; its plumage, through which the wind browsed, was dark brown and buff. 'Is it some kind of a seagull?' the woman offered.

'I don't think so.' The man touched the bird with an index finger. It responded with a pathetic effort to get away, managing to put less than two feet between it and its human knights errant before flopping down again into the boggy grass. 'Seagulls are much bigger and stronger-looking. And sure don't they have webbed feet?'

'I dunno. Let's leave it.' The woman stood up and tugged at his arm.

'Ah, no, we couldn't do that.' The man reached out to stroke the bird, which reacted with a frenzy of wing-flapping, producing no forward progress. 'I think we should bring it to a vet. The poor thing, it looks all in.'

'Suppose it dies in the car?' The woman stepped back as though the very mention of death might contaminate her.

'We'll wrap it up warm and put it in the boot.' Gently, the man scooped up the creature, which offered little resistance. 'Take the sandwiches out of my pocket. We'll wrap him in the tinfoil. I've seen the ambulancemen on the telly do that with people who've been in accidents. It'll keep him warm at least and we'll leave a little space so he can breathe.'

Gingerly, avoiding the long beak, the woman did as she was bid. As they swaddled the bird, it was so exhausted that it seemed to give up and lay still. 'Is it dead?' The woman stepped back again.

'No, I can feel its little heart. Come on, we have to get to Tralee as quick as we can.' They walked fast back to the car, trying not to joggle their patient, the man holding it as though it were made of eggshell porcelain.

When they got to the surgery, however, they were too late: the vet opened the little parcel to find the bird dead.

'What is it, Doctor?' The man, who seemed unwilling to leave, stroked the mottled feathers. The woman had waited outside in the car.

'Don't know.' The vet, more used to dealing with mange, hoose and foot-rot, looked doubtfully at the pathetic little heap on his table. 'Could be a whimbrel or something, but I doubt it. There's a fella up the town, a Dutchman, wouldn't you know, who knows a lot about birds. I'll ask him if you like – after all, you've gone to a lot of trouble.'

'You done good. No, don't stay, but thanks for the call, I'll take care of the ambulance and all of that. You go home now to your wife and kiddies. But stay in touch, won't you?' *Yes!* The sheriff of Mayville, who had been mooching around his empty house while waiting for his TV dinner to heat up, slammed down the receiver and scrambled to belt on his gun. One week into the two weeks he'd been given and he had still been shy of his corpse. This one looked like a prospect.

The call had come from the cab of a truck that belonged

16

to a bonehead logger of his acquaintance named O'Shaughnessy on whom he kept a file of unprosecuted violations, reasoning that either he or his truck might, some day, come in useful: the man himself as a target for a few extra dollars, his truck for the haulage of something the sheriff might want moved.

While travelling north along 506 O'Shaughnessy had apparently come on a dead hobo half on, half off the road. And a woman, who smelled strongly of booze, maybe dead or maybe nearly dead at the steering wheel of a nearby Volvo.

Right away, Sheriff O'Connor had known who that woman was. She had to be Midge Treacy, lush, wife of Daniel Treacy, one of Butte's most respected and successful citizens. The sheriff had particular reason to know her because, only three weeks ago, the same woman, driving a different Volvo, had almost totalled him and his own newish Buick on the same stretch of highway. Her blood-alcohol count that first night had been over 500. She was – or had been, depending on whether or not she was dead – on bail for that little package of charges and the case was due to be heard within a few days.

As he raced out to his car, getting soaked in the process, the sheriff could almost feel those little cogs and wheels whizzing round in his brain. And, as he gunned the automobile out of the driveway, he saw an even better prospect than the gods' gift of a hobo's funeral uncomplicated by mourners.

He had not heretofore included Treacy as a possible target for blackmail. Sure, after the Buick incident, he had toyed with the idea of stinging the guy for a few bucks over and above the replacement value but, it being the wife's first offence and no one having been injured in the crash, he knew she would probably get off with a slap on the wrist. As a blackmail possibility Treacy had seemed pretty weak, not least because, in his business dealings, as far as the sheriff had ever heard, the man was clean.

This was the good thing about staying in a small burg like Mayville, one of the reasons he never sought higher office in Helena or Missoula or Butte. Here, he was king. Here, everyone could owe him favours, even a judge and a medical examiner. And those who owed him nothing right now knew that to do a good deed for the sheriff was a sort of investment in the future.

The location O'Shaughnessy had given was less than two miles outside the city boundary. Not wanting to draw attention to himself, O'Connor put on neither screamer nor roof lights and, although the temptation to drive fast was strong, tried to keep within the speed limit. Because of the storm there were fewer people about, which was lucky. The sheriff going anywhere was always a matter of speculation in Mayville. If there was trouble, he thought, if there was a big gaper block, for instance – although at the best of times 506 was not a busy place – he could forget Treacy as a hot prospect for a few bucks and revert to Plan B, by which he would just use the hobo as a convenience to get the use of a casket.

His luck held. He got there so promptly that the gaper block in attendance consisted of one auto and a pickup, both from out of state. Wipers still swishing uselessly, the Volvo's nose was buried in the metal crash barrier, which had served its purpose by preventing the car from going over into a ravine.

A little way in front of it, the hobo was as dead as last Christmas, his ragged clothes so wet now that they blended seamlessly with the runnels made by the rain on the surface of the highway. 'There's nothing we could do for the poor man but the woman's still alive.' The long-haired driver of the pickup, who could not have been more than seventeen, was overcome with the drama of the situation as, pushing his

18

streaming hair out of his eyes, he crowded in behind the sheriff as he crouched over the body.

'We didn't like to move the woman, Officer.' The woman from the automobile was also pretty shook. 'She's in bad shape, she needs to get to hospital quickly.'

'Thanks, lady, I've already called for an ambulance.' The sheriff straightened and walked across to the Volvo, stuck his head through the open door.

Midge Treacy was breathing slowly and heavily. Her head lolled sideways on her neck. Blood trickled from her nose and from a cut along her hairline, but otherwise she was as clean as a baby. The stink of booze, however, would knock a person down. 'Show's over, folks, clear the highway now.' The sheriff withdrew his head. 'This is a dangerous spot here and in this storm we don't want to be causing any more accidents.'

'Shouldn't you take our names and addresses, officer? Won't you need us as witnesses?' The woman, who was sheltering under a golf umbrella, looked from the corpse to the sheriff and back again.

'Looks like both you guys are from out of state. You really want to have to come all the way back up here, give evidence, all that expense and trouble? Ain't nothing no one can do for that poor old tramp now. I know the guy, no relatives, no home. He's better off.'

'Well, if you're sure . . .' The woman still did not look convinced.

'Of course I'm sure.' The sheriff was geniality itself. 'Poor old guy,' he shook his head sympathetically, 'he had no life. And don't worry about the lady, we'll get her squared away.' Relieved, the woman went back to her vehicle to be followed by the kid to his. After a last lingering look, both of them drove off.

After their tail-lights vanished around the bend, the sheriff listened hard, waiting until the sound of both vehicles died

19

away. The accident had happened less than half a mile from where Midge Treacy had almost driven himself and his Buick off the road. Although the blacktop was good, 506, which was narrow and had only two lanes, swooped and twisted treacherously right through the Purcell Range from Libby to Yaak; clusters of little white crosses, Montana's quirky highway markers to denote scenes of fatal accidents, grew along it like spinneys of little ghost trees.

Rain pattered on the sheriff's hat and on the hood of the Volvo. He turned up his collar and, confident no one was around, opened the trunk of the police car, packing the tools and office supplies in it towards the back. Then he walked swiftly to the dead hobo and picked him up, skin and bone and weighing as little as a fawn. Water streamed off the dangling arms and legs as the sheriff carried the body to the vehicle and stuffed him in, tidying the hands and feet until he was all nice and neat. He closed the trunk then walked around to the front. It was only then that he radioed for the ambulance.

It arrived within minutes and he acted real friendly. 'Terrible thing, terrible . . .' After Treacy's wife had been lifted out and placed in the ambulance, he brought the driver round to the front of the Volvo. 'Look at that,' pointing to the streaming traces of the hobo's blood on the fender, 'that's what musta happened. She musta hit a deer. Easy to do, this weather.'

Then it was a simple matter to 'discover' old Leon's body in the early hours of the morning while on a routine patrol further up the highway. By that time the sheriff had cleaned him up a little.

The following morning, Sheriff O'Connor put a call through to the offices of Treacy Resources Inc. in Butte. Her boss, said the man's snooty secretary, was naturally at his wife's bedside at the hospital.

'Naturally,' the sheriff agreed. Very connubial. He pursed

his lips as he called the hospital number. Hobo, shmobo. He had thought about it overnight and the prospect of a little cream from Treacy was just too rich to resist. After all, she'd had two accidents within three weeks: the woman was clearly a menace to herself and society.

Called to the hospital phone, the guy was chilly at first, as might have been expected, but when he heard what the sheriff was proposing, he agreed to meet.

National Headquarters of the Gárdaí in Dublin stands inside a set of gates to one of the biggest and most unspoiled city parks in Europe. A long, straggling building in grey stone, it looks like the barracks it is.

Inside, in one of the meeting rooms, a balding, ruddy-faced chief superintendent was wrapping up his conference. He looked around at the force assembled from various specialist units within the ranks. 'That's as much as we can do for tonight, kiddies. I've got to get home.' He yawned. Although he was inclined to speak in clichés more suited to the Hollywood movies for which he had a passion than to the sober circles of the force, everyone knew that the verbal style masked a mind as incisive as a scalpel. 'I'm in the doghouse already,' he continued. 'I'd promised the missus I'd take her to the pictures tonight.'

As the others started to gather their notes together and pack them away, no one dared offer the truth that the same missus would, no doubt, welcome a night off from the pictures. 'We're all agreed now, are we?' the chief superintendent asked one more time. 'Lynskey should go to the States.'

Everyone in the group, twenty-seven men and two women, returned his gaze and indicated assent. Whatever they thought personally about Fergus Lynskey, none disputed that he was a good policeman. They were an oddly

21

assorted bunch: with the possible exception of the chief super himself and Lynskey, not one would have chosen to socialize with any of the others. Drawn from Special Branch, the Emergency Response Unit, the Anti-terrorist Squad and the Drugs Squad, each member had been hand-picked. The group's size reflected the scale of the impending investigation. The chief, whose surname was Daly and who therefore attracted the nickname Joxer, screwed the cover back on to his fountain pen. 'How about you, Rupert?' He eyeballed the man directly facing him at the opposite end of the table. 'Do you think he should go? As usual you're not saying much.'

'No problem.' Rupert de Burgh had eyes that seemed to absorb the colours of his surroundings, like camouflage. 'We definitely need our own man there.' The chief super nodded. He had never liked Rupert de Burgh but no one would have known it. Although the detective was technically an Irishman, having been born here because his mother had been on holiday in one of the crumbling great houses where her relatives still eked out an existence, in the chief super's book he was essentially English. He had lived in England until his late teens. He betrayed little vestiges of his origins now, however: his accent was indistinguishable from that of the educated Dubliner.

Bill Daly was familiar with the contents of his man's personnel file and knew he had come over from London to attend Trinity College in 1971 but had dropped out of academia after only a few months, applying to join the Gárdaí during a recruiting drive early in 1972. He had been promoted rapidly and had proved a good detective, conscientious, punctual, with a better than average record of detections and arrests, which was why he was on this special task force. He was also a bit of a whizz at computers and other electronics, skills that were in high demand. Unlike many members of the Gárdaí, his marriage seemed stable too, which would indicate a fairly well-balanced individual.

So what was it about him? Daly could not identify exactly what made him uneasy about the man: perhaps it was the watchfulness in his peculiar eyes. As the last of the stragglers made for the door, the chief super told himself, not for the first time, that there was no law which said policemen had to be nice guys. There were a few others on the force who could give Rupert de Burgh a run for his money in the lack-of-personality department. 'Stay a minute, Fergus, will you?' he asked, as Lynskey followed the group to the door.

Despite Lynskey's easy manner, he was not much more popular with his colleagues than de Burgh. Many of them felt, rightly, that he bucked the rules and got away with it; that he had it both ways, respect and a long rein from the brass while continuing to get all the most active assignments. Whereas the others were frequently buried in drudge work, Lynskey sailed past the paperwork and was always attached to any group put together to crack something big. He spoke French and German fluently and so had travelled widely. His expenses claims were legendary.

Now he sat down again in the chair he had just vacated. Daly and he had met during training in the Gárda depot at Templemore but while one had opted to climb the promotions ladder, the other, who hated more than anything else on earth to be confined to a desk, no matter how prestigious, had resisted all urgings – of his superiors, of his former wife, even of his mother – to go the pen-pushing route, preferring to continue work in the field. Bill Daly was perhaps the only man on the force who knew that lurking under Lynskey's cynicism lay an unquenchable idealism, an unusual trait in an experienced detective. Apart from their friendship, it was why the chief superintendent played favourites with him.

23

When the door had closed behind the last of the group, Daly looked across his desk at his old friend. 'What do you think? What are we dealing with here? I can't see a clear line through this. Is the intelligence accurate?'

'It's a bit murky, all right, but if you ask me,' Lynskey stretched and yawned, 'with the two situations we're looking at I think one could well be feeding off the other.'

The chief superintendent sighed. 'Nothing's ever simple, is it?'

'What I don't understand is how, if this guy the Canadians raided is so high up, they could have kept it quiet. I haven't seen anything in the papers about it.'

'They chose their time. Apparently he's on holidays. And, as for the second part of what we're interested in, the FBI is pretty good about identifying subversives. If they say there's a new group in town, I'd believe them. And, as you know, they've been watching a few of their own guys for a while now.' The chief superintendent paused. 'I wish we had the latitude they have when it comes to tapping telephones . . .'

'What worries me, though,' Lynskey studied the ceiling, 'is who's feeding information from here. It's their timing that bothers me. Seems a bit neat that Ireland is flavour of the month for everyone all of a sudden, especially with – ahem – Operation Omega pending!' He delighted in teasing Daly about the fanciful names he dreamed up for problematic operations.

Daly did not rise to the bait but mulled over what Lynskey had said. 'There's no proof there's anyone feeding from here.'

'Doesn't it seem a little convenient that this group – if we're on the right track and if it *is* a group, of course – suddenly springs into action just when our friend across the water takes a vagary to come here?' Lynskey watched his boss. 'And that they seem to be piggybacking on traffickers – which *is* known here?'

24

'I hate royalty, do you know that?' The chief superintendent spoke with genuine passion.

'Oh, come now.' Lynskey raised his eyebrows over his long hooked nose so that he looked a little like a surprised eagle. 'You can't blame poor old Big Ears for considering an honest invitation. And go on, admit it. Your so-called Operation Omega will be a lovely test of your security skills.'

'I hope that's all it'll be, a test.' Daly tugged at his ear, a habit when he was thinking dark thoughts.

'Come on, Joxer, cheer up. You know very well why our political masters are so anxious to facilitate our friend. Photo-opportunities, a few nice snaps of firm handshakes and history being made and all the rest of it. Do wonders for our Taoiseach's ailing image. Not to speak of our own dear Minister.'

'Why are you so sure there's a leak from here? I've kept it absolutely tight.'

'I have what your screen detectives call a hunch.' Lynskey grinned.

'All right, you and Kojak!' At last Daly smiled and reached for his jacket, thrown carelessly across the back of a chair. 'You'll start with this fella Treacy in the States. He's been getting a few interesting calls lately. There isn't much time, you know, and I'd feel a lot better if I knew exactly what they were planning. Given what we've been told about their backgrounds, it has to be something to do with bombs and bullets.'

'Maybe . . .' Lynskey was thoughtful. 'But that's why you're upping the national debt by sending me to America, surely? So I can find out?' He stood up.

'Do you need a lift?' Daly shrugged himself into the jacket.

Lynskey walked beside his friend towards the door. 'I'll walk.'

'Of all the weekends for that royal so-and-so to decide he

wants to come over here.' The chief superintendent stopped with his hand on the door handle. 'As if we didn't have enough complications with the Association picking that weekend to implement its bleddy overtime ban. You know Bodenstown's on as well?'

'Forgot that. I must say Bodenstown doesn't impinge all that much on my consciousness.' The cemetery around Bodenstown church in Co. Kildare, not far from Dublin, is the burial place of the Irish patriot Wolfe Tone. It is the site of an annual June commemoration march at which national-ist convictions and sentiments are reiterated, not only by committed thirty-two-county republicans, such as Sinn Féin, but in latter years by some government members. To nation-alists, the march to Bodenstown is an important aspirational symbol and, in the more fervid past, from time to time had been banned. 'But sure it's not much of a headache these days.' Lynskey was fidgeting – he wanted to be off.

'Maybe it's no headache to you,' Daly pulled at his ear, 'but it is to me. The force still has to be there. So that's even more of us missing from the streets on a weekend when there are three business conventions and the World Irish Dancing championships in the city. Did you know that? The place'll be swarming with pickpockets, our own and uninvited guests. We might as well throw our hats at it.'

'I heard,' Lynskey's tone was blithe, 'but you'll come up with something. That's why you get paid your enormous salary, Joxer, and I'm just a humble foot-slogger!'

At just about that time, a Dutchman in the town of Tralee in Co. Kerry identified the little bird found by the two Dublin holidaymakers on the grassy headland.

In high excitement the Dutchman, who had access to a worldwide library of bird lore, broadcast the news that they had on their hands a *Numenius borealis*, an Eskimo curlew.

26

A migrant that bred in Arctic tundra, probably in Alaska – although a nest had not been found for more than a hundred years – the species had been hunted mercilessly in the middle of the last century, to extinction, most experts thought, until one or two showed up at the beginning of this century. Since ornithological records began, only six had appeared in the geographical British Isles. And this, the seventh, was the first to be seen for a hundred and fifteen years.

Chapter Three

Obituaries! Sky glanced back at her computer screen with contempt as she poured her coffee. As if she had not written enough of them to last several lifetimes. And this one was turning out to be as interesting as watching paint dry.

It was now just over two weeks since her little mutiny about the rodeo began. As the date for it came closer her defiance rumbled on, under the surface, but as yet she was no nearer getting the go-ahead to travel to the conventions.

The door opened and the kid came in, carrying a high-school yearbook. She dropped it on their communal desk. 'The stuff you want is about in the middle. Maybe page thirty, forty, something like that – but I wouldn't hold my breath, Sky. There's not much there. If you ask me she was pretty mousy.'

Of course there was nothing there, Sky thought. Why would anything go right?

She took the coffee to her desk and stared once again at the dispiriting words in front of her. She was trying to write about Midge Treacy, wife of one of Butte's finest, the powerful Daniel Treacy, who was benefactor to every good cause in the city.

Mrs Treacy's life, by contrast to that lived by her husband, had been so private as to be almost invisible. According to the paltry few paragraphs Sky had managed to dredge from the newspaper's cuttings library, Mrs Treacy had been sweet and gentle. But that was about it. For the past fifteen years or so, it appeared she had retired to the couple's hunting lodge in the northwest of the state, and was seen in public only rarely. To fill the space allocated for her piece, Sky had been forced to telephone around for anything she could find.

She found little – certainly nothing that might have been helpful as background for an obituary writer. The only drama in the woman's life had arisen a few weeks back when she had been charged with drunk driving. But the charge had never been heard because of her unfortunate death. Other than that, it seemed that she had led an invisible, perfectly blameless little life.

As drinking habits were hardly an appropriate slant to take in a woman's obituary, and as it seemed to be universally accepted by everyone she contacted that Mrs Treacy had preferred the silent company of the Rockies to that of so-called Butte society, as a last resort Sky had had to plunder the office thesaurus, regurgitating 'charming', 'lovely' and 'generous' in as many ways as possible. Sighing, she reached again for the despised but well-thumbed volume. Definitely time to move on, she thought again as, on her screen, she deleted 'hideaway'and replaced it with 'retreat'.

In the early years of her marriage to one of Butte's
most prominent citizens, Daniel Treacy and, before
she retired to seclusion in her beloved Rocky
Mountain retreat, his wife, Midge's hospitality was, if
low key, always generous. As one of Butte's most
charming [Sky backtracked and overwrote this with
'stylish'] stylish if elusive society hostesses, in those
early years she made her husband's guests to their
remote but lovely [Never having been in the house
and therefore ignorant of what it was like, she
highlighted 'lovely' and substituted 'turn-of-the-
century'] turn-of-the-century home feel not only
welcome but as if

29

'Even if you're not available for the rodeo, I can assume you're available for this?' Jimbo was beside her, holding out a piece of paper on which was scribbled the time and location of the monthly meeting of the St Patrick's Brigade. Although the meeting itself was always private and this marking required only the briefest attendance to collect the secretary's notes and handouts, it was one he always assigned to himself. The Brigade took itself seriously, would not take kindly to anyone but the editor. Especially a woman whipper-snapper. 'Look, Sky,' he dropped the press release on her desk, 'I know – we *both* know – you're too good for this rag but there's only the two of us' – he took no notice of the junior's gasp – 'and while you're here you'll have to do the best you can. Just like me.'

He went back to his office, leaving her to ponder the unfairness of her fate.

Before she went home later that afternoon, Sky took a detour to call into the funeral home where Mrs Treacy's remains reposed. The piece did not have to be filed until next morning and, if she could not get details about the woman's life to fill the required page, she might as well pad it with descriptions of how serene she looked in death. And maybe she could glean a few apposite sentences from the relatives.

The shingled building stood in a wide alleyway between Porphyry and Silver and not far from Interstate 90, easily found by out-of-towners by virtue of the neon cross permanently lit over its front door. Owned by the Collins brothers, third-generation Irish whose grandfather had coughed his life away underground in the Orphan Girl mine, it was not the biggest parlour in town but quite impressive. Its stained-glass windows and brass door furniture gleamed and Sky, her reporter's eye desperate for detail, noticed that today even the veins of mica and quartz scattered through the freshly raked gravel in the parking bays sparkled as though it had been passed through a polisher.

On the streets outside, the rush hour – or what passed for rush hour in Butte – was betrayed only by the muffled toot of an automobile horn and the alley was quiet, just a handful of vehicles in the bays. She had obviously chosen a valley period in the respect-paying business and, before going in, took advantage of the lull, leaning against the Nissan to catch a few moments of quietness.

The smell in the alleyway remained impregnated with heat, a soft stew of buttery tar and warm stone, engine oil and the indefinable spice that means city, no matter how big or small the population. For to be strictly accurate, although its residents always referred to it as a city, Butte was barely town-sized. From where she stood Sky could see a narrow vista of its loose folds falling from the end of the alley to the Flats below the plateau.

Today there was no breeze, an unusual phenomenon at this altitude, and she pulled at the front of her white cotton blouse to peel the fabric from the damp skin under her breasts. She pushed up her sleeves and, taking off her sunglasses, raised her face to what was left of the sun, hazy and whitish now, as though already capitulating to the yellow thunderheads piling up to the west.

'Sky! How ya doin'?' She opened her eyes to find Teddy Morzsansky, a school contemporary with whom she shared a desultory interest in photography and who, with his wife, worked in the parlour. 'Fine, just fine, Teddy, gathering forces for the next onslaught, you know.'

'Sure,' he sympathized. 'You look sensational, as usual, the tan suits you. So does the length of that skirt. Always loved those legs – sure you won't change your mind and marry me?'

'Tried it, didn't like it!' Sky, unselfconscious, smiled. It

31

was an old joke between them, its familiarity pleasant. It had been a long time since the nine days' wonder of her spectacularly disastrous marriage had cast any shadows. 'Anyway,' Teddy was a head shorter than she and she rumpled his hair, 'I believe Melinda might have something to say.' The Morzsansky marriage was reputed to be happy.

'I've always said that guy was out of his tree – what was his name again?'

'You know what his name was. Randy.'

'Yeah, Randy.' Teddy loosened his tie. 'You're here for Treacy, I suppose?' Without waiting for her affirmation, he turned back towards the door. 'I'm going off, but I'll come in back with you. Not that there's much to see.'

'What do you mean?' Sky unrolled the sleeves of her blouse and rebuttoned the cuffs.

'Casket's already closed . . .' He scanned the sky. 'Looks like another storm's about due.'

'It couldn't be closed. Isn't there some sort of wake?' Sky was annoyed. Not much she could write about a lidded casket.

'Sealed all right.' He ran his fingers through his mussed hair. 'It's being shipped back to Ireland, you know.'

Sky removed her keys from the ignition. 'Was she badly cut up? Is that it?' According to the local reporters' accounts in Libby, Daniel Treacy's wife had been killed when her car tangled with a logging truck on the plunging road between the Treacys' hunting lodge and Libby itself.

'Don't rightly know how bad she looked.' Teddy walked ahead of her and pushed at the parlour's front door, then stood aside to let her through. 'Did you hear the local news this morning? Truck driver's not to be charged – apparently he didn't have a chance, she was on the wrong side or something. You heard he had a phone in the cab and it was him called for help.'

Teddy would never change, Sky thought, as she waited

32

for him to lead her towards the chapel. He had always been a chatterbox – perhaps his cheerful nature helped him through the more dismal parts of his profession.

The inside of the parlour was as well kept as the outside and their feet made no sound on the thick red carpeting of the lobby. 'Melinda must've gone to the powder room.' Teddy surveyed the vacant reception desk. 'She won't be long. Anyway, as I said, I didn't see her, the boss insisted on working on her himself. Stands to reason, I suppose, she being who she is an' all. Looks like your visit's wasted, Sky.'

'I'll go on in anyway, now that I'm here.' Such was the hush that both had instinctively lowered their voices while he led her into the short corridor that opened to the left of the reception desk. They stopped outside the furthest of four doors and he tapped briefly on it before looking inside, 'No one at home except the sti—' Recollecting that, friend or not, he was talking to a reporter, Teddy amended himself. 'You're safe. She was driving a Volvo too, you know.' He nodded sagely. 'So much for those commercials. But you've seen how big those loggers are. Must have been a doozy.'

'The casket's very big.' Sky searched her memory. Nowhere had she seen anything about Mrs Treacy's unusual height for a woman.

'It's because it's being shipped. There's an inner and an outer one. There are a lot of regulations about it.' They spent a further minute or so chatting about a forthcoming camera circle meeting and then Teddy moved away. 'I'll leave you to it – anything you need, you just ask Melinda.'

'Thanks.' Sky pushed open the door and was immediately struck by the bare look of the place. Given the prominence of Midge Treacy's husband, she had been expecting a vulgarity of floral tributes, but instead, the heavy casket, made of dull metal in battleship grey, was adorned only with one pink rose, placed on the crucifix fixed to the lid. The vases, urns and wreath stands that usually swarmed in these

33

chapels had been removed, as though someone was being either tactful or unwelcoming.

She pulled a miniature tape recorder from a pocket of her purse. When working on features, as opposed to interviews, she rarely took notes, reasoning that anything worth remembering would stick. She was in such trouble on this one, though, and had such an amount of space to fill that she felt she needed every tiny detail, however unimportant. She listened for a second or two at the door and then, sure she would be alone for a while, took up a position at the foot of the casket, flicked on the recorder and, using verbal shorthand, described to it everything she saw and sensed: 'Feeling of being isolated but not alone . . . subdued, pinkish lighting . . . profound hush . . . as if the room – no – it's not the room . . . as if *all* physical matter is sort of on tiptoe . . . waiting . . . For what?. . . Tall twin flicker of candles pooling yellow on smooth grey curve of metal . . . clean lines of the brass – gold? – handles – casket so still, solid . . . density . . .

'Moving closer now . . . One of the pink rose petals on the lid is wider, looser than its sisters, wilting in the stagnant air . . . Inscription on silver plate . . . "Mary Dorothy Treacy, née Shelton, born 6 April 1943 died 18 June 1992 . . ."' She pressed the pause button to calculate how old the woman had been and was shocked to discover that Midge Treacy had been only forty-nine at the time of her death.

For some reason, the yearbook vintage had not registered and in the single adult photograph she had been able to find Mrs Treacy had worn an ageless, classic suit and her blonde hair had been pulled back from her pretty face in a severe French pleat. Sky was in the habit, when in difficulty with a piece, of not writing the opening paragraph until the rest of the article showed some shape and this was probably how she had managed to overlook her subject's age.

At least now she had a slant – 'Killed at a tragically young age . . .'

Now, for the first time, she felt a twinge of interest in the subject of her obituary. This woman had been far, far younger than her husband and that single fact seemed to give her independent life. It suggested wooing and courting and flying in the face of convention – no hint of which Sky had unearthed so far in her research. Could it suggest love out of the ordinary?

Too late now to be speculating. She shrugged and reactivated the recorder. 'Moving on again, thick oak – mahogany? teak? – panelling of the room . . . tall wooden crucifix carved in angular, modern manner on its own brass stand in its own corner . . . The absence of flowers is a puzzle . . .' Her back to the chapel entrance as she continued to murmur into the microphone, her concentration was such that over the machine's tiny whir she did not hear the door open.

'May I ask what you are doing, Miss MacPherson?'

Her tape still revolving, Sky turned and was staring up into the eyes of Daniel Treacy. She extended her right hand. 'Please accept my sympathy on your loss, Mr Treacy.'

'Thank you.' He shook her hand briefly. 'Would you mind?' He indicated the tape recorder. In the restricted acoustic of the chapel, his voice was surprisingly strong and resonant for a man thought to be only two years off seventy. She had seen him before but had never until now noticed, despite the authority he wore like a crown, quite how gaunt he was.

'I'm sorry.' Startled but not intimidated, Sky turned off the machine. 'I'm writing your wife's obituary and I came to pay my respects.'

'I see.' He stared hard at her. 'Do you usually use a tape recorder to pay your respects?' Sky had noticed before that brown eyes fade less with age than blue, and it was those deep, impregnable circlets of dark brown that were undoubtedly Daniel Treacy's most arresting feature.

'How do you know my name?' she countered, holding his gaze, aware nonetheless of the incongruity of the occasion. 'I mean, we've met only a few times, always in company and for very brief periods.' She heard her official, reporter's voice.

'I know your work,' curt now, 'but I also know your family. Your father has a cabin not too far from our hunting lodge in the northwest. And many years ago in Ireland I knew your grandmother Elizabeth.

It was a shock – not only that he knew her father, whom Sky herself saw so seldom that she felt she hardly knew him, but that he had spoken of her mother's mother, whom Sky herself remembered, from her one visit to Ireland when she was a very young child, as a tall, gracious lady of about a hundred years old. That she had clearly not been a hundred years old was demonstrated subsequently in photographs and letters, but it was still strange to have her referred to by her first name. Yet Sky knew that most of the Irish in Butte were descended from family in the same small area somewhere in the south of Ireland so it stood to reason that the older generation would know one another. This man, however, unlike many others of Irish extraction in Butte, did not wear his nationality like a badge, a trait which she of all people should understand. Through the years, her own family connection with Ireland had become tenuous: her mother had chosen her friends in Montana from different ethnic minorities.

Unlike many of her classmates of Irish ancestry, Sky had strenuously resisted imprisonment in the tight grasp of what she regarded as the Irish ghetto mentality. Although she went to a Catholic school, she declined to learn Irish dancing and always refused to participate in the parade on St Patrick's Day. And on the grounds that she supported only what she understood, she did not contribute time or money to the many collections for the 'fight-for-freedom' cause, still espoused by some of the more radical Irish in Butte.

Her memories of that one, far-off visit had faded until they were simply little flashes, like a slowly turning magic lantern: a big feather bed in her grandmother's house in Cork city, a fluffy white hen in a farmyard to which she had been taken on a long, long drive, the smell of a peculiar soda they called red lemonade. Dreadful rainstorms. She had been taken to Ireland to visit her grandmother by her aunt Goretti, now also just a distant voice on the telephone, albeit only from New York. 'We're not a close family.' She had spoken without thinking.

'I beg your pardon?' Treacy was startled in his turn.

'Sorry, it appears that I've acquired the habit of voicing my thoughts.' Her smile, intended to be rueful, died as she stared into those inscrutable brown eyes.

He was not afraid of silence, waiting for her to form the bridge. 'Perhaps we could meet for coffee or something so we could talk?' She had to make an effort not to gabble. 'I mean when – after – ' gesturing towards the casket, 'perhaps it's inappropriate at the moment.'

'Perhaps.' She could hear no trace of irony or sarcasm. 'I'll get in touch. Now, if you'll excuse me?'

Wishing fervently that he had not caught her in the crass activity with the tape recorder, Sky reiterated her sympathies and eased herself out of the chapel.

Outside, the gun-metal sky had overcome the sun, and when she got back into the Nissan she rolled up the windows in expectation of rain. She sat for a few moments, in the hot, unmoving air staring at the dash and unable to shake off the impression that she had been in some sort of fight. In the habit of placing every thought and feeling in neat boxes, she tried to analyse this disquiet but could find no label for it.

One thing she did know: she was aggrieved that her

mother had not mentioned family acquaintanceship with Treacy. Sure, Sky had given her no opening: her own encounters with the businessman had been so transient as to merit no discussion at home. Yet she felt now that Johanna, who talked a blue streak about all her other friends and acquaintances, might have at least mentioned him. To annoy her mother, Sky picked up a giant-sized pizza on her way home that evening. Larded with pepperoni, anchovies and E numbers, she planned to eat every single piece of it.

She never got to, however, because when she opened the door, Johanna was standing just inside, the telephone to her ear. 'Oh, here she is, sorry, hold on a minute, will you?' Johanna was never at ease with the telephone. She liked to see the expression in people's eyes when she spoke to them. 'Here she is now,' she repeated, holding out the receiver.

'Who is it?' Sky mouthed, as, juggling the pizza, the keys, her laptop and her purse, she struggled to take it. 'I don't know,' Johanna mouthed back.

'Hello?'

In her surprise, Sky almost dropped everything. The caller was Daniel Treacy and he wanted to meet her for dinner that night.

Chapter Four

'This is strange.' Sky's mother watched her daughter's preparations to go out again. 'His wife is not cold in her grave.'

Since she and her mother had moved into the duplex, Sky had been meaning to do something about the décor in her bedroom: the landlord's taste ran to wallpaper covered in pink rosebuds, matching pink drapes and a green carpet, but every time she came to the point of action, something more important intervened. 'His wife is not *in* her grave, Mom,' it was typical of Johanna to have no sense of time, 'she's still at the parlour. I told you.' Sky was less impatient now than defensive but if she had learned anything in her career as a journalist, it was to remain open-minded. So Daniel Treacy's behaviour was not normal for a widower so recently bereaved? Not necessarily: the words 'normal behaviour' applied differently to different human beings. And she could hardly complain since she was the one who had suggested a meeting.

'M-mmm.' Johanna picked up a hairbrush and began smoothing her daughter's cap of fine blonde hair – an inheritance from her father – and, despite everything, Sky, who had been going to tackle her about Treacy, felt immediately stilled. She suspended operations with a mascara wand and luxuriated in the sensuous feel, the way her hair rose a little off her scalp in response to the strokes of the brush.

The squalls outside continued to buffet the double-glazing, but within the room she could hear not only the rhythmic shushing of the bristles against her hair but the purring of her mother's two cats, which habitually followed their mistress from room to room, and which had now nestled among the tumbled bedclothes.

Sky still fitted an early description of one of her high-school friends: she was a 'clean slob'. Everything about her person and her surroundings sparkled with cleanliness, but no matter how many good intentions she had, she could never seem to keep her bedroom tidy. Right now, however, because of the premature darkness the lights had been switched on and, bathed as it was in yellowish light, even the clutter all around seemed to have assumed its own surreal beauty.

'Maybe he wants to offer you a job?' Her mother's voice was low as if she, too, was responding to her ministrations with the brush. 'I'd be careful, if I were you.'

'Why? I'm a big girl now.' Sky closed her eyes the better to enjoy the sensations.

'Well—' Her mother stopped brushing for a few seconds as though thinking out what she was going to say next. When she resumed, her voice was a little higher. 'We know him a little, dear. Hermana and Buffy and I met him at a St Mary's fund-raiser and we were a little worried about his aura. So if he's thinking of offering you a job—'

'What job, Mom?' The spell was broken. Sky jerked her head away and worked again at putting on her mascara. 'With all due respect, he couldn't be offering me a job, he doesn't own a newspaper. And how come you never said before now that you knew him?' Then she was sorry for snapping. 'Thanks for doing my hair.'

'Well,' Johanna examined the bristles, 'I still think it's a bit strange. A few hairs here, Sky, maybe a little selenium . . .' It wasn't worth another argument, Sky thought, she would take up the matter of Daniel Treacy and her mother some other time.

She bit her lip as her mother picked her way over heaps of

40

discarded clothes, books and piles of newspapers, and went towards the kitchen; she would also shut up and swallow the supplement. The stuff might even do some good – who knew?

She stood up from her dressing-table and kicked a path through the mess to stand in front of the cheval mirror. Not normally vain or self-regarding, she took the opportunity for a critical, full-length look at herself. She had to admit that her skin was still excellent and, even at the age she was, her eyes sported only marginal circles. Maybe her mother's pills and potions did counter all the black coffee and other pollutants she put into her system. She was wearing the best outfit in her closet, a straight-skirted silk suit of dove grey, a colour that highlighted her wheaten hair. Her father had also donated his rangy physique, long arms and legs, wide shoulders, narrow waist and flat belly, while her mother's contribution had been the cornflower eyes, wide mouth and prominent cheekbones. But there was that ski-jump of a nose. The lamp on the dressing-table cast an oblique light against it, throwing the bump into relief. That nose belonged to neither of her parents and, in Sky's opinion, was the physical cross she had to bear. All through high school and college, she fought with anyone who could not see the nose through her eyes, got into the habit of using it to bat compliments away.

'*You're so beautiful, Sky.*'

'*For Chrissakes how could anyone with a nose this crooked be beautiful? Don't make fun of me!*' At the same time she could not have borne to have it fixed. Something about her Catholic education had stuck. *Don't tamper with God's handiwork* . . .

'Here,' her mother was back with a glass of water and two pills, 'in case we forget in the morning. You look lovely, Sky, you really do. But be careful when you meet him. Dark thoughts are catching.'

41

Sky covered a retort by swallowing the tablets as her mother excavated her purse from the mess on the floor. 'Thanks, Mom,' she checked that her little tape recorder was ready, 'for everything.' She gave Johanna a perfunctory hug and hurried out.

It would be too much to expect that Daniel Treacy was responding to her invitation to talk about her own relatives, she thought, as she gunned the Nissan into the evening traffic. It was far more likely he wanted to influence her obituary piece.

Her hunch proved accurate.

He had asked to meet her in the restaurant of the Copper King Mansion on Granite. She arrived a little early and, while she waited for him, perused the menu and chatted with the hostess – younger sister of another schoolmate – revealing casually whose guest she was. In response to the girl's barely concealed astonishment, she let it be known exactly why she was here. The last thing she needed was gossip about herself.

The mansion, a three-storey, brick building, which had been the home of William Clark, the billionaire mining boss, had been restored to its former glory in the sixties, and its heavy furniture, old silver, crystal and china pieces gleamed with care. The Copper King Mansion represented the height of fine dining in Butte but it was a Monday night and during a brief scan of the dining room, Sky saw to her relief that her fellow diners were all strangers, tourists mainly, most looking uncomfortable in what was, no doubt, the one dressy outfit they had brought with them on vacation.

Through a window, she saw Treacy pull up and park his imported Saab convertible across the street and had to stifle her instinctive reporter's reaction that this was hardly a suitable vehicle for someone that old. She was already building a scaffold of impressions around this man which had nothing to do with the matter under review.

'Good evening.' She was waiting for him inside the door. 'I was surprised to get your call.'

'Shall we go through?' He seemed unwilling to participate in social niceties and, aware once again of the chilling depths of those eyes, she nodded meek assent.

Their corner table was discreet, with the buffer of an empty one between them and the nearest couple. As they were given their menus, a busboy hurried over to clear the vacant table of cutlery and glassware.

'I booked both tables.' Daniel Treacy had noticed Sky's look of surprise at the boy's action.

'I see.' She busied herself shaking out her napkin. Whatever he had to talk about was well planned. 'Is this how you always eat? At two tables?'

'Do you eat meat?' He looked up from the menu. 'May I order for you?'

'Sometimes.' Sky felt she was being bullied but, given the circumstances, decided to allow him run the agenda. 'Yes and yes.' She folded her copy of the menu and placed it on the table in front of her. 'Please do.'

He beckoned for service and ordered lamb for both of them with a bottle of French Châteauneuf du Pape. 'I'm assuming this is acceptable?'

'Fine, Mr Treacy.' Where was the spousal grief? 'I must say at the outset that this is a very unorthodox occasion. I think you must know how unorthodox.' Then Sky, who frequently saw the funny side of the most inopportune scenario, felt the treacherous clutch at her chest in response to the question that had shot to the tip of her tongue. She had nearly asked at what time tomorrow was Midge Treacy's flight.

She stifled both the question and the laugh by pretending to cough. 'Sorry,' she gasped, pouring iced water into one of the glasses in front of her, 'I got very wet today, think I must be getting a summer cold.'

43

He watched her in silence while she drank the entire glassful and poured herself a refill. Then, 'Yes, it is unorthodox. But I thought I could help you with some of your research. I don't want half-assed speculation about Midge masquerading as fact in the newspapers. Since you seem bent on writing the stuff, I would prefer to talk to you and get it over with and for you to get it right.' It was the longest speech she had ever heard from him – he tended to leave public speechmaking to underlings – and she heard echoes of her mother's lilt. He spoke much faster than Johanna, however, with a sense of urgency.

As she had felt earlier at the funeral home, Sky sensed peculiar disquiet in this man. She tried not to think of her mother's warning about auras and about dark thoughts being catching. 'Please forgive me, Mr Treacy,' she was not afraid of him and had to show it early, 'but I can't help thinking that you are very composed for a man so recently bereaved.'

She braced herself for an explosion but none came. Instead, he stared at her for several seconds and, knowing it was important not to flinch, she held his gaze.

The tension broke when the wine waiter held out a bottle for his inspection. 'Thank you.' Treacy reached into the breast pocket of his jacket and took out a pair of half-moon spectacles to look at the label. 'That's fine. Please pour.' Then, putting the glasses back in his pocket, 'I'm not sure what business my composure or otherwise is of yours, Miss MacPherson, but since you ask, I do not wear my heart on my sleeve. My feelings don't concern your piece about my wife, surely.' He was addressing her as though the waiter was not there.

Sky should have felt rebuked but, for some reason, did not. Instead, she continued to wonder why he had asked her here. This whole occasion was so out of kilter as to be bizarre. Of course it was: the man's wife was lying dead less than a mile away covered in lead or steel or whatever it was that had been used to seal the poor woman into eternity.

Yet she felt something deeper going on. If she was to recognize it when it arose, she must suspend ordinary disbelief. Johanna, she thought wryly, would be delighted with her.

As it stood, she knew hardly anything of any value about her host, other than what everyone in Butte knew: that Daniel Treacy had arrived from Ireland nearly fifty years ago and had never gone back, even for a visit, that he became rich out of his original mining company, Treacy Resources Inc., had diversified into lumber and other commodities, had worked hard, married late – in his mid-forties – had led a private personal life, had supported nearly every charity in Butte and lent his name to the letterheads of a few of the health and arts organizations. Up to now, Sky had never been all that interested in businessmen, preferring to profile or interview people in other professions or the arts. In her experience, people who were successful at making money became so because they were single-minded and tended to cut out everything else, even in some cases, personal relationships. It made for short and boring copy.

The wine waiter was yet another of her acquaintances, this time from grade school. As he retreated, he raised an eyebrow behind Treacy's back at the company she was keeping. She shot him a quick smile. That Butte seemed more like a large village than a fully grown city frequently caused her to grind her teeth, but there were times, such as now, when it was pleasant to have complicitous company. She redirected her attention across the table. 'Was your wife from the same part of Ireland as yourself?'

'From the other end of the country,' he shook his head, 'from north Mayo. Being of Irish extraction yourself, I'm sure you're as aware as I am that most of the Butte Irish are

45

from West Cork. Midge felt quite isolated. Mayo people are as different from Cork people as' – he hesitated, searching the depths of his wine for an analogy she would understand – 'as New Englanders are from Texans or Californians – or even Montanans.'

'I see.' But Sky did not. As she well knew, Ireland was only three hundred miles end to end. How anyone could postulate that such a tiny geographical distance could make any notable difference was odd. 'You never went back? Do you miss the old country?'

'No.' He shook his head in a way that precluded development of that line of enquiry. 'How is your mother?'

'You did mention my grandmother and my father, but you know my mother too?'

'Only in so far as I know who she is.' Treacy let Johanna off the hook.

Their meal arrived and, as she watched it being served, she thought she had better continue with the enquiries about his wife although, if the truth be told, Daniel Treacy himself was turning out to be a far more interesting subject. 'While we talk about your wife, would you mind if I recorded our conversation?' She hesitated before taking up her knife and fork. 'My deadline is tomorrow morning and I won't have time to recheck anything.' For the first time he looked unsure. 'It's standard practice, I promise you,' she reached into her purse for the machine before he could object, 'but if it worries you that the tape is lying around afterwards, although I usually reuse them over and over, I'll send it to you or destroy it.'

'That won't be necessary. I trust you.' He was a man who made quick decisions.

In spite of Sky's best efforts over the fifteen minutes that followed, however, the picture of Mary Dorothy Treacy painted by her widower proved so sketchy that it served merely to arouse curiosity. For instance, how could a man

46

be married to a woman for twenty-four years and not be able to give any plausible reason for her lack of interest in going back to visit her home place and people? Sky's own family might have been cited in evidence but hers was most peculiar. She had always believed that the reason for Johanna's lack of interest in going back home was a symptom of her general come-day go-day attitude to life. Even taking Treacy's word for it that Midge had felt isolated from her fellow Mayo people, as he had maintained, would that not have meant she would have desired even more to go home at least once a year? After all, it was almost a cultural imperative among the Butte Irish, most of whom had far less money and opportunity. In Sky's experience, most of these expatriates managed to scrape together the wherewithal for annual or bi-annual trips to the 'old country', and even those of the second and third generation frequently nurtured pipe-dreams of settling back there some day. But now, if Daniel Treacy was to be believed, here was equal apathy from himself and his late wife. It seemed that at different times both had shaken the soil of Ireland off their heels for good.

And yet Midge Treacy had felt 'isolated'.

The story did not gel somehow. Sky concentrated on the staccato answers she was getting to her questions. According to Midge's husband, her life at the hunting lodge seemed to consist mostly of working on watercolours of the surrounding mountains or reading. She got up late every morning, never went shopping and, if she drove at all, it was never further than the forty miles or so to Libby. The owner of an art-supply store there supplied her with materials, and also obliged her by keeping some of the supplements from his own Sunday editions of the *New York Times* so that she could select books and order them from New York and Toronto.

'I'm sorry, there's not much more . . .' The conversation

47

petered out and Treacy speared a small potato. Sky noted that just as her own food reposed virtually intact on her plate, a standard hazard of interviewing someone over a meal, he had not eaten much more than she. Perhaps, given the circumstances, it was understandable. As though conscious of her incipient sympathy, he glanced at her, and she saw an expression in his eyes that might, just might, have indicated a thaw.

Feeling he was giving her a cue, she searched for what she should say or ask. 'I heard rumours that you were thinking of running for public office?' Although she had heard no such thing, asking a question from left field was a technique that sometimes freed up a conversation.

Not on this occasion. 'Never in a million years. You were misinformed,' Treacy closed up again. 'And, to get back to the matter in hand, as I'm sure must now be evident to you, Miss MacPherson, Midge lived – *liked* to live – a very, very quiet life and to keep herself to herself.'

If the woman was that fond of the quiet life, what was she doing driving alone along a dangerous highway that evening? Something was definitely not kosher here. It was not the time and the place to behave like a public prosecutor, however. 'What did she like to read?' Sky put in her mouth a sliver of her meat, virtually cold now, and chewed.

'Popular fiction, mostly, women's novels, that kind of thing.' He waved a dismissive hand.

She flushed with indignation but again controlled her tongue. So what if feminism was not his strong suit: the guy was nearly seventy. She swallowed her mouthful, then said, 'Where was your wife bound for that night, Mr Treacy?'

'God alone knows.' He sighed. 'She was heading south but it was unlikely she meant to get to Butte that night. The accident happened near Mayville, just north of Libby, as you know – maybe she was going there although, as far as I know, she had no friends or acquaintances there. If only I'd been at home at the time. Never mind,' he took the first sip of his wine, 'life is full of "if onlys", isn't it?'

There was no answer to that. 'What about your wife's schoolfriends or their relatives?' she asked. 'Has – sorry, had Mrs Treacy kept in touch with anyone anywhere else in the States?'

Again he shook his head. 'She went to boarding school in Ireland until she came out here for senior year in high school and, as far as I could see, lost touch with all her classmates soon after graduation. This is why we're bringing her back there. She will be buried in a small village called Crossmolina. All her people are there, and her friends, those who remember her, of course, will have the opportunity to attend. We put the death notice in the Irish newspapers.'

'So how do you feel about going back after all this time?' Sky thought she had little to lose by moving the goalposts a fraction. 'Of course, it will be a sad occasion—'

'Very.' He found something interesting on his plate. 'I'll not be staying for very long. I'll be coming back immediately after the funeral – there's some urgent business I need to attend to.'

'You won't take advantage of the opportunity to go to your own home, visit with your own folks?'

'I'm afraid there will not be time.' He looked up at her at last, his eyes in shadow. 'But to forestall your next question, Miss MacPherson, some of my own relatives will no doubt come north for the funeral and I shall visit with them then. Please, could we stop talking about me?'

Sky accepted the reprimand and toyed for a while with her food. She waited for a decent interval while the tape beside her bread plate wound on, recording nothing but the useless clatter in the dining room. 'You never had children?' she asked abruptly, as if it had just occurred to her.

'No.'

She saw she had touched a nerve but was not to be put off. 'Was this a source of sadness to your wife? To Midge?'

'It was her decision. I'm sure you must have enough by now, Miss MacPherson.' He looked pointedly at the little tape recorder.

'Nearly finished.' Sky was not going to be instructed as to how to conduct her business, no matter how sensitive this situation. 'If you don't mind my saying so, sir, I couldn't help noticing that there were no flowers at the funeral parlour—'

'By my request,' he interrupted her. 'They would have to be left behind. I can't see any purpose being served by transporting wreaths across the Atlantic, can you? And before you ask, that was indeed my rose on the coffin.'

She responded to the challenge and went fishing. 'How was your wife's health, Mr Treacy?' She kept her voice level. 'We didn't see much of her in town and, as you've outlined, she did prefer her own company in latter years, could it have been because she was, well . . . delicate?'

'Who told you that?' His outrage was genuine and Sky recognized she had crossed the border of what was seemly. 'I'm sorry, Mr Treacy, I meant nothing by it. I realize how painful this must be for you – but there was that drunk-driving charge—'

'I really must insist now that the interview part of this meeting is over.' He spoke across her apologies, then recollected himself. 'Since you ask, my wife's health was good for a woman in her forties. Yes, there was that one charge. But search if you like, you won't find any other. She did not like crowds or the pollution of the city and chose her own lifestyle, with my full co-operation and enthusiastic support. Now, please turn off that machine.'

Sky complied. The woman was at rest now and what had gone on within her marriage was none of a reporter's

50

business . . . yet if the truth be told, her initial astonishment at the extent of this man's co-operation had yielded to the suspicion that he might be clouding the issues surrounding his wife's death. But consideration of that would hold. 'I'm truly sorry if I upset you.' She put the machine into her purse. 'I guess I'm just naturally a nosy-parker. Like all reporters, I never have enough.'

He stared hard at her, but then placed his cutlery on his plate over the half-eaten meal and sat back in his seat. 'I'm sorry I was gruff,' he said, 'but these past few days, I've been under a lot of personal strain. I'm sure you understand.'

'Of course.' She smiled into those cold brown eyes. 'Sometime in the future, when you feel comfortable about it, I should like very much to do a profile on you, Mr Treacy.'

'Out of the question.'

Sky did not argue. There was a story to be told here and some day she would be the one to tell it. 'Then would it be possible that I could talk to you some more on a personal basis?' She was undeterred by his grim expression. 'I'd find your memories of my grandmother fascinating. My mother has told me a lot, and we do get letters – my grandmother lives in Cork city now, did you know?'

'I did not.' He shook his head, took out his spectacles and polished them.

'So would you?' Sky took advantage. 'Sometimes it's nice to get another perspective.'

'No tape recorder?' He held up the spectacles to the light.

'Definitely no notes, Mr Treacy. This would be a personal favour you would be doing for me.'

'Then perhaps some time in the future – must keep in with the press.' He gave her a wintry smile but before she could respond he looked at her half-cleared plate, and went on, 'I don't wish to be rude, but I have some friends waiting for me at home, and tomorrow, as you might imagine, is going to be a difficult day. I wonder if you would mind if we skipped dessert?'

'I hate to waste this delicious food but like you, as it happens,' Sky indicated his own unfinished meal, 'I'm not very hungry. Must be this summer cold.' She folded her napkin and was content she had scored an opening.

Chapter Five

The air in the small kitchen was cloudy with incense when Sky got home: the Bliss Sisters were in session. This was the name she had given to her mother's trinity of like-minded friends. And, to judge by the number of mugs, used tea bags and scented candle-stubs in evidence, the group had been in residence for a couple of hours.

'Greg called while you were out.' Sky's mother was sitting behind Buffy, massaging her friend's neck. 'He says to tell you everything's all set for Friday.' He and Sky were going to his parents' cabin on Flathead Lake for the weekend and, while she loved the place, she wished she could go there alone. Buffy, who was holding the two cats on her lap, sniffled and blew her nose but Sky did not feel up to listening to a recital of her woes or of the Bliss Sisters' interpretation of them. 'I thought you weren't meeting tonight, Mom?' It was after nine thirty, and since her own room was so untidy, she had been hoping for vacant possession of the dinette table to transcribe her notes and finish her piece.

'We weren't, but it's a crisis. Buffy's son was supposed to come in from Wisconsin,' Johanna continued kneading, 'but he telephoned an hour before she was leaving for the airport to pick him up. Buffy hasn't seen that kid for fourteen months, Sky. How was your dinner?'

'Young people! Anyone like more camomile?' Hermana got up from her chair and lumbered to the stove, saving Sky the necessity of reply. In every sense of the word Hermana was the heavyweight of the Sisters: a two-hundred-pound six-footer with chopped hair and a face like a scrubbed dinner plate, her bluff manner hid a huge, marshmallow heart. She was not the brightest of the group: she had looked blank when Sky once asked her if she had adopted her name, the Spanish for 'sister', as a homage to feminism. 'Chuh-heez . . . ! Is that what it means?' Her face had pinkened with pleasure and astonishment. 'That's not it, though, Sky. You see Mom and Dad wanted a boy – Herman, you know?' In the moments when she was not being driven crazy by all three members of the Bliss Sisters, Sky adored her. She declined the offer of camomile tea and turned to leave, 'I have to write an article, I'll do it in my room. Take care now.'

'You bet.' Hermana tore the outside wrapper off a store-bought box of sunflower-seed cookies and flung it on the table.

The single-storey duplex Sky shared with her mother stood in its own circular lot; the other apartment had been vacant for more than six months, an arrangement which suited them fine because the party walls were paper thin and allowed neighbour-to-neighbour access to the most private activities. For many years, when she wasn't longing to escape altogether, Sky had wanted to move the two of them out but it was all a matter of money. Johanna was without means – her only income came from twelve hours of weekend work in the coffee-shop of a nearby hospital. Her unworldliness, so attractive to everyone else, was another source of irritation: she would wash used paper plates or use the same tea-bag ten times over, but then would hand out whatever money was in her wallet to the first bum or shiny-shoes with an appeal bucket who knocked on her door.

The other members of the Bliss Sisters helped look after her: Buffy, who was a good cook, frequently brought over some food, and Hermana, whose guilt-ridden ex-husband paid alimony way over the odds, now and then 'lost' a few dollars somewhere in the duplex, to be found gladly by Johanna as money she herself must have put away some time and forgotten.

Sky's salary kept them in reasonable comfort, but a rent increase would have meant serious curtailment of trips to Ben Franklin, and that Sky would not have been able to take her weekends away, with or without Greg. These breaks from her mother and her job were essential for the maintenance of her sanity.

She closed the door of her room, cleared a space on the folding card table she used as a desk and went to work, trying to blot out the murmur of the women's voices from the kitchen. She was ruthless with the piece, writing directly on to her laptop as she transcribed from the tape recorder. Somewhere within the hour it took her to finish, she became aware that the therapy exercise in the kitchen had wound up, heard the goodbyes and the slamming of an automobile door. Both Johanna's soulmates lived on the Flats, a mile or so on the other side of town.

When the obituary was at last finished, Sky felt sluggish because of the wine she had drunk earlier so she stood and performed a few stretching exercises, somewhat proscribed because of the lack of space on the floor, and then went down to the kitchen to brew a last cup of decaff.

Johanna was sitting staring dreamily at her own reflection in the dark glass of the window over the sink. Declining the offer of something to drink, she began to wind a strand of her curly hair around an index finger, a mannerism she usually affected when upset. 'Tonight's weird, Sky. There's something really strange going on. I haven't thought about your father for yonks and now, out of the blue, in he comes.'

'In where? Sorry, Mom.' Sky's retort had been automatic. 'What were you thinking about Dad?'

55

'Oh, just . . .' her mother wound faster, 'he's definitely around. I feel him very strong.'

'Come on, Mom, don't be so aggravating.' Then Sky noticed that, unusually for her, Johanna looked uncertain. 'Want to talk about it?' She poured hot water over the brown powder in her mug and carried the drink over to the table.

'Not really.' Her mother's voice was sad. She came and sat beside Sky: 'I suppose what brought it on was Buffy and all she's going through. I suppose it's a young man's disease, being casual.'

'Is this what you're feeling about my dad?' On her last visit to her father nearly eight years ago, and shortly after she had returned to Montana from Chicago, Sky had found Larry MacPherson alone and supremely happy, making a living from guiding rich men through the hunting and fishing territory he adored.

Johanna and he, who were members of a commune when they met, had not married, preferring, as Sky's mother always maintained, to preserve untainted memories of their glorious time together. The split had been friendly: Larry, who had been only about eighteen, had hung around until after Sky was born and then had drifted northwards, first to Alaska, from where, having worked his way through northern and western Canada, he had come finally to settle near Yaak, Montana, in a corner made by the northern and western borders of Canada and Idaho. Over the years he had sent money – sporadically, but as much as he could afford – right up to Sky's twenty-first birthday. 'Do you miss him tonight, is that it?' Sky grimaced at the bitter taste of the decaff and spooned sugar into it from the bowl on the table.

'I don't know how you keep that figure of yours, Sky.' Her mother sighed. 'No, it's nothing like that, if I had to do it over, nothing would change.' Then she smiled. 'Guess it's hormones, darling. I'm as menopausal as Hermana.'

'Don't talk such nonsense, Mom, this isn't like you.'

'I know.' Johanna got up from the table and began clearing off the debris. 'Must be that storm this evening. Something's about to break – I can feel it – ahh!' She gave herself a little shake. 'Sure the apple will fall on the head that's under it, as the old people used to say.'

'Less of your Irish blarney.' Sky enjoyed these times of ceasefire when, for short periods, her mother did not annoy her as much as she usually did. 'Here, this is too hot anyway. Let me help with that.' Leaving the coffee, she took the dishrag and used it to sweep cookie crumbs off the table into the palm of her cupped hand. 'Listen, Mom . . .' Reluctant to break up the truce, she hesitated as to the best way to broach what was on her mind, then went for it anyway. 'Daniel Treacy seems to know a lot about our family. Even Dad. How come you never told me?'

'I never knew he knew your dad.' Something about her mother's voice caused Sky to cease operations with the dishrag. She peered at Johanna, who was turned away from her, again staring into the blackness of the lot. She was being unusually evasive. 'Mother! What gives here?'

'You know as well as I do, Sky, that the Butte Irish all come from my part of the country. Of course we all know – knew – each other.'

Sky sent dates and years flying through her head: if her mother had come here aged sixteen in 1954 and Treacy had arrived forty-eight years ago, in 1944, that would have made Johanna only five and him twenty or so when he had left their home parish. 'Why the mystery? Why didn't you tell me this before? You led me to believe earlier this evening that you didn't know the guy—'

'I didn't!' Johanna's indignation was too strong. 'You never asked me directly before. It never arose.'

'Mom,' Sky threw down the dishrag, 'I'm sick of hearing stories about Lahersheen and all the rest of it, about Grandma and my precious uncle Francey!' Johanna's

57

brother, Francis Sullivan, was the only one of the clan who could have been said to have made good. He was a rich man, and his visit to his American relations had been long promised. 'Look at me, Mom.' Sky sank on to one of the chrome and plastic dinette chairs. 'I know the names of your ex-neighbours, your horses, cows and dogs, even your goddamn farmyard chickens. How come the name of Butte's most prominent citizen never fell from your lips before?'

'Language, Sky! I told you before, you never asked.' When Johanna turned round, Sky saw that her lips were set.

'Don't think it rests there, Mom.' She accepted a good-night kiss.

'I'm tired, I'm going to bed.' Her mother placed a finger over her own lips. 'It's late now, we'll talk tomorrow. Stardust! Moondancer! Come on, you guys!' Followed by the two tail-high felines, she left the kitchen.

Having filed her piece early next morning, Sky informed Jimbo that she was going to the funeral parlour for the removal prayers.

He was surprised. 'All we need are the names of the guy who says the prayers and the chief mourners and we know them already. You don't need to go.'

'I'll go anyway, I want to.' Sky was annoyed she had mentioned it in the first place.

'Suit yourself.' The editor shrugged and picked up his desk telephone.

As she had expected, the funeral parlour was crowded. Although she was in plenty of time for the ten o'clock ceremony, there was no space left in the chapel and she had to stand outside in the corridor, pressed against the wall in the crush. She exchanged pleasantries with other reporters and faces she recognized among the dark suits and chains of office, and wondered where poor Mary Dorothy Treacy was now and what would she think if she could see this parade of respect she had neither sought nor received in life.

Daniel Treacy arrived on the dot of ten, ushered through the throng in the corridor by the officious funeral director. From her vantage point against the wall, Sky watched his bearing as though she was writing a colour piece about him. Immediately she felt like an emotional voyeur. Whatever Treacy's state of mind or heart this morning, he did not want others to see it. His stare was fixed on a point somewhere ahead of him and above the crowd as Bill Collins cleared the way for him into the chapel. One or two of the suits tried to sympathize with him as he passed, but he moved on as though he had not noticed.

As the murmur of prayers began inside the chapel Sky wondered again why her mother had not come. Johanna, although not an official churchgoer, was a great one for the satellite societies and support groups which surrounded all of the Butte religious organizations. She and the Bliss Sisters were always ready to help out with collections and cake-bakes, and were frequent attenders at the funerals of those whose relatives they knew only peripherally. 'But you knew this man from your home place, Mom.' Sky had assumed that her mother would come with her to the ceremony.

'Ah, no, I don't think I'll come today. No.' Her mother had concentrated on her bowl of nuts and seeds. 'I'll think about the poor creature. That'll be all that'll be necessary.'

If proof were ever needed that she should pursue whatever story her mother had about Daniel Treacy and his wife, this was it, but Sky knew that, in her own sweet way, Johanna could be the most stubborn of people and she did not interrogate her any further.

As she heard the prayers in the chapel drone into the final decade of the rosary, she wondered if she should follow the cortège out to the airport. She would quite like to see for herself what procedure was followed – for instance, was the casket just loaded on to the plane as though it was a crate of fruit? Or was there some prescribed ceremonial such as there was with military bodies being returned? On balance, however, she decided not to go: she was now determined to keep Daniel Treacy to his promise of an interview after a suitable interval, and she might spook him if she appeared to be taking too personal an interest in him now.

The prayers ended and Collins, helped by Teddy Morzsansky, cleared the corridor outside the chapel so that the casket could be taken to the waiting hearse. Outside, the alleyway sparkled: chrome, wing mirrors and metallic automobile paint winked and flashed with prisms from watches and jewellery, gold glinted on wrists and in ears, the gravel glittered underfoot. A quick morning storm had lifted the weight from the air and the day now promised perfect Montana summer.

What awaited Midge Treacy in her native County Mayo? From everything Sky knew about Ireland, the cold, wet clay of that country would close over her like a suffocating blanket. Poor woman – Sky turned to watch as the casket was loaded into the back of the hearse – is this what she would have wanted?

She sensed that Daniel Treacy was impatient now to get going, although his features remained frozen as he shook hands briefly, or nodded in acknowledgement of the condolences of his peers, colleagues, employees and their well-groomed wives. As soon as the hatch door of the hearse was closed, he walked briskly to the following limousine and got in. To the super-alert Sky, this haste, too, seemed inappropriate. It was not as though the flight was a scheduled one and they had to catch it: she knew the casket was being carried on Treacy Resources' private plane. It was as though Daniel Treacy had already washed his hands of his wife and wanted to get on with next business.

Like a dark, ragged guard of honour, the crowd parted to

line both sides of the alleyway as the hearse and limousine moved slowly away from the front of the funeral parlour. It would be a small, sad procession to the airport and Sky wondered, not for the first time, about the lack of correlation between money and happiness.

She found herself standing beside Teddy and Melinda Morzsansky, the three of them making a subgroup a little apart from those on their side. As the limousine passed, Sky, who somehow continued to harbour the absurd notion that her profession afforded her some sort of invisibility, stared hard into the vehicle to gain a last glimpse of Daniel Treacy. The window glass was slightly tinted but she could make out his face. Just as his eyes met hers.

The small hairs on her forearms rose a little and she knew, without doubt, that her presence disturbed him. So much so that she failed to notice that two of the mourners, appropriately dressed and with neat haircuts, had detached from the crowd and were walking purposefully down the alleyway towards a plain, beige-coloured sedan.

BUY DAD A SIX-PAK!! ONLY $23.95!! The sign shrieked at them from the canopy of a gas station as Sky and Greg drove into Polson, the town which stood at the southern tip of Flathead Lake. The six-pack in question comprised six car washes, some bright spark's idea of a novel gift for Father's Day. 'You getting your dad anything for the twenty-third?' She looked across at her boyfriend, whose driving style was casual to say the least. One booted foot on the dash beside the steering wheel, which he held with just one pinky.

'What?' He removed his hat and, with his arm, mopped his forehead along the line of the sweatband, then replaced it. 'You gotta be kidding! Support Hallmark?'

'Relax, relax, I only asked.' Sky was not in the mood for discussion or argument. As it happened, she had been

61

thinking of her father even before she saw the sign; the open road – more open, perhaps, in Montana than in any other state – always reminded her of his free spirit. Although not in the habit of contacting Larry on Father's Day, she had been thinking it was time she wrote him a letter. Their last exchange of correspondence had been at Christmas.

'You grumpy or sump'n?' Greg swung the pickup into the parking lot of a grocery store. 'This place OK?'

'It's where we always stop, isn't it?' Sky surveyed the store frontage, the piles of watermelon inside the glass, without enthusiasm. 'And no, I'm not grumpy.'

'Coulda fooled me!' He turned off the engine. 'Now move that cute little butt and get me ma vittles, woman!'

'I wish—' Sky stopped. 'Never mind.' She hopped down from the cab of the vehicle and slammed the door. 'Come on, pick yourself a cart and follow me.' It would have been too easy to puncture him: Greg's posturing always swelled in direct proportion to his insecurity. Women's silence made him uneasy and she knew she had been unusually quiet on the trip.

Although he had not worked up the courage to ask her, Sky knew only too well that Greg wanted badly to be married. He had had dozens of ultimately unsuccessful relationships with women. She also knew that his apparent inability over the long haul to sustain a woman's interest – despite his physical attractions – bewildered him. The main reason that she always returned to him after trying to walk away was that she could not stand to remember the hurt look in his eyes. He would never be Iron John, but he was straight and kind-hearted and to leave him seemed tanta-mount to branding a puppy with a hot iron. 'Maybe you're right, I am a bit crabby. Forgive me?' She took his arm and felt a renewed stab of guilt as she saw the look of relief that crossed his handsome face. Then he had to wreck it. 'Course I forgive you, babe!'

62

'Just do me a favour, please, Greg?' She pulled him around to face her.

'Name it!'

'This weekend, just for once, would you cut out the western shit? And before you ask, you know what I mean, the babe, woman, macho crap. I'm feeling a bit sensitive and it would make things so much easier.'

He looked sheepish. Then, after a small hesitation, 'Sure. Sorry, Sky, didn't realize it was that bad.'

'It's not.' Sky did not want to get into it. 'Not yet. Just heading it off at the pass, so to speak, OK?' She turned away and walked into the store ahead of him so as not to give him any further opportunity to show how vulnerable he was and make her feel guiltier still.

They stocked up: beer, deli meats and salads, chips, barbecue sauces and charcoal, steaks, sausage, bread, cookies and packs of their secret vice, Snickers bars. As they emerged into the sunlight they carried enough food to provision a small weekend army.

The cabin was eight miles from the town, at the end of a wooded private road. Sometimes, when contemplating the length of time it took to get here from Butte, Sky thought she and Greg must be out of their minds. And yet, no matter how endless the journey to get here or how early the start, on arriving at the house again Sky always marvelled at her good fortune in being given access to this magical spot. And there was some comfort in knowing that they were not the only ones who behaved in such an irrational manner, spending almost as much of the precious weekend on the road as at the cabin. A great number of their fellow cottagers were in exactly the same situation. It was the American way.

Greg backed the pickup into a little clearing and they carried the groceries into the house, which was right at the water's edge. The first thing Sky always did on arrival was to open all the waterside windows and doors and walk out on

63

to the sundeck, built on stilts so that to stand at its rail felt like riding the prow of a little ship at anchor. Although Flathead's shore was full, all lots taken, there was no sense of crowding: zoning was tight here and the house sites were large and heavily wooded. They had been late starting from Butte this morning and already it was getting on for dusk. Barbecue smoke curled through the trees from several fires along the shore. 'OK, ba—? Sorry – OK, Sky?' From behind, Greg put his arms around her waist. 'Want a Snickers?'

'Sure.' She accepted the candy and leaned back into his embrace, hoping he wouldn't ruin the peace by making sexual overtures to her right away. 'It's a beautiful evening, isn't it?'

'Hungry?' He squeezed her waist.

'M-mmm.' She did not respond physically. 'Not yet, this'll tide me over.' She unwrapped the chocolate bar. 'Let's just stand awhile and enjoy this, it's so lovely.'

'Sure.' Accepting the reflectiveness of her mood, he stood back a little.

Slowly, savouring its nutty sweetness, Sky munched the Snickers and let the peace of the place infiltrate her soul. As the sun sank below the rim of the hill behind the house, the snowcaps on the Mission range to the southeast glowed pink and a little breeze sprang up to riffle the weeds that came through the boards of the deck on which they stood.

Far out on the rapidly darkening water, engine note no louder than a mosquito's whine, a lone speedboat pulled a skier. Abruptly, the skier somersaulted, a flash of bright blue swimsuit against the dark of the treeline and then was gone. Instantly, the boat slowed and came round in a wide, slow arc, gentle as a moorhen rounding up her chick, then motored quietly to her berth about a quarter of a mile away along their own side. As she came near, a dog gambolled into the shallows to greet her, and Sky heard laughter, thinned by distance, as the craft's occupants tied her up and then, raced by the dog, ran up the foreshore. In front of where Greg and she stood, the leaves on a young birch whose roots were in the water shivered silver in the belated wash that had been sent towards it.

Then, one by one, the lights on the docks and in the houses on the shore opposite came on so that the dark collar of trees which fringed their bay was pierced with points of gold.

'Happy?' Greg's breath was warm on her neck. As she turned to kiss him she managed to subdue the niggle. She was definitely happy. For now.

That weekend, like all weekends at Flathead, passed more quickly than any single day in the city. They arrived Friday evening, it was lunchtime Sunday and they were going back. 'I wish your hours were more flexible.' Greg, who worked for his father's liquor store, had leverage.

'Tell that to the *Courier*.' In spite of her ambivalence about Greg, Sky was as reluctant to leave as he was. 'Maybe they could change publication from Wednesday to Thursday to suit us.'

'Aw, shucks!' He grabbed for her and she kissed him but then pulled away.

'We'd better get rolling, huh? Won't be home until after midnight even if we leave now, this minute.'

'Sure.' He turned away to buckle the straps on his backpack and she could have cried on seeing the set of his shoulders. All weekend long he had been on his best behaviour, considerate in bed, more gentle than she had come to expect, and she could have nothing to complain about. But pacing around every conversation, like a hungry wolf, was the knowledge that sooner or later the question of their future together would have to be addressed seriously. The animal was there now, yellow eyes glinting with greed,

65

waiting for one of them to let down the fence. They both knew it and each recognized the knowledge in the other. It was breaking Sky's heart – not for herself, but for him.

She was exhausted when she let herself into the duplex at about one o'clock on Monday morning. Johanna had left a light burning over the kitchen stove, signal that there was an urgent message.

Thinking that it had to be from Jimbo, she almost did not bother to go pick it up but then, in case it was an unexpected early marking, walked wearily over to the bulletin board.

Mr Daniel Treacy called about the interview. You're to call him at his office Monday a.m. See you breakfast, Johanna, XXX.

Her mother had never, ever signed herself 'Mom', even when Sky was in grade school and begging that she try to be as like other mothers as possible.

Before she went to sleep, Sky summarized what she knew to date about Daniel Treacy into her tape-recorder, a habit she had developed which always ensured that, no matter how fast her brain was racing on the night before a challenging day, she got some sleep. If what she needed to remember was written down or in the recorder, her brain could let go.

'Here goes.' She switched on the little machine and dictated to it what she already knew, where to find the other references, who to contact for background.

But then, willy-nilly, she found herself enumerating facts that had been nagging at her about the death of Treacy's wife. 'Like, for instance, the newspaper stories say she was driving south, probably to Butte. And that she'd told no one she was coming. But the accident happened in the middle of the night and she couldn't have made Butte without stopping. Where was she going to spend the night?'

She pressed the pause button and decided to summarize

66

what she knew about Midge Treacy. She set the machine in motion again. 'One, the woman was very young, much younger than her husband. How did she get here to Montana – to the States, even? What did she work at before she met him?' While the little tape rotated, Sky tried to remember if the late Mrs Treacy's profession had been mentioned in any of the material she had been able to find. If it had, it had escaped her notice – but, then, she had not been looking for it. She had assumed, like everyone else, that the life of Mary Dorothy Treacy, née Shelton, had been of interest to the general community as 'just' a professional man's wife.

'Two,' she murmured, 'when did she get here? He says she did senior year in high school here. So she had to have come as a child. And yet Treacy had said all his wife's relatives were in Ireland and that she went to boarding school over there. Why did she switch schools? Could she have been an orphan? Sent out here? Sponsored?' Again she strained for answers, any hints she might have missed in the obituary research material, but came up with nothing. 'Three, only a small detail, why a *pink* rose? It's worth asking. Four—' Sky pressed the pause button. After a few seconds, she clicked the machine off altogether and lay staring at the ceiling. This was supposed to be a personal interview she was doing with Treacy, not an interrogation about his wife. And yet her brain was prompting that his relationship with his wife in life and in death was proving to be what was most interesting about him. The fourth question she had been about to dictate to her machine related to the possible existence of a third party in all this. Could the shy Mrs Treacy have had a lover? Perhaps she wasn't heading for Butte that night, as it had been put about, but going to meet him? Or her?

And was this the reason that the rose was pink and not red? Treacy knew of his wife's affair? Anyone among those at the funeral chapel who had hung back or seemed particularly grief-stricken? None that she could recall. Sky put her tape-recorder on her night-table, turned over and stared through the window at the trees ouside. She was letting her imagination run away with her. And now that the woman was dead, was it any of R. Sky MacPherson's business if Mrs Treacy did walk a little on the wild side?

But as she drifted off to sleep, her brain continued to worry at the question that underpinned all others. Why was Daniel Treacy, the reluctant subject, suddenly so eager to talk?

Chapter Six

'May I take that for you, sir?' The palace official, in full dinner regalia, held out his hand to take the newspaper cutting from the Prince of Wales, who had just finished perusing it. The two men were being driven home from a public dinner engagement at the Guildhall.

The cutting had been given to the Prince after a discussion on ornithology with one of his table companions. Well-known as a watercolourist and for his love of the countryside, it was not as widely known that the heir to the British throne was also a closet twitcher, one of that band who will go anywhere in the world at a minute's notice to see a rare species of bird.

Before folding the cutting and putting it away, the official glanced at it: apparently the Irish Natural History Museum in Merrion Street was mounting an exhibition centred around a new acquisition. An Eskimo curlew.

FANCIERS EXPECTED TO FLOCK TO MUSEUM

. . . harassed museum staff are already under siege as fanciers from around the world seek details of when the bird can be seen. 'We are very short-staffed at the moment,' said a museum spokesperson last night, citing cutbacks in the general public service, 'and the fact that right now is a holiday period does not help.'

Like everyone else, the palace official knew that the Prince was attracted to the holistic, more mystical side of existence and reckoned he would think it not a coincidence that he had been given this information just as he was considering an invitation to go to Dublin for the first time.

The Dublin branch of Amnesty International was hosting a huge international conference. The centrepiece was to be the first European appearance of Naboom Kebele, the Nelson Mandela of the central African state of Kaman, a country which, after gaining independence from Britain, had just emerged from a period of devastating tribal and civil war. Kebele had been imprisoned for even longer than Mandela and, like the South African, the longer he had been incarcerated the more his cult status had grown. Against immense odds, he had orchestrated a peace movement which culminated, after forty years of unrest, in the signing of an agreement to hold nationwide elections.

The palace official, who was dead set against the visit for security reasons, knew that the Prince held the African leader in such high esteem, despite Kebele's well reported anti-British rhetoric, that he was longing to meet him. He had also expressed the desire many times to visit the Irish republic. But no heir to the British throne had visited Éire – even in a private capacity – since the setting up of the state in 1922, and the official guessed that the Amnesty invitation had been sent as a stunt, that its issuers had not entertained much real hope of it being accepted. The main caveat, as the seemingly endless campaign of violence continued to rage on in Northern Ireland, was whether or not the Irish felt they could guarantee the Prince's safety.

The official sighed as he folded the newspaper cutting and put it away. This would strengthen the Prince's desire to get to Dublin.

*

The answer to why Daniel Treacy had called Sky was not long in coming.

Next morning, while she waited to be put through to his office, she tried, as she always did, to visualize the scene at the other end of the line. She had been to the corporate headquarters of Treacy Resources before – a modest glass and steel structure at Prospect and Park near the Montana College of Mineral Science and Technology – but always as part of a hack pack, when the company's PR machine wanted the press there for some reason of its own. She had never seen beyond the public spaces. Somehow, she imagined Daniel Treacy's office would be Spartan yet affluent, no-nonsense furniture and technology combined with corporate good taste.

'Thank you for calling, Miss MacPherson.' He was on the line.

In the normal course of such a conversation, Sky would have injected enough warmth into her response to melt the permasnow on the Rockies, but instinct warned her that Treacy could probably detect bullshit at a hundred paces. 'You're welcome,' she said, in a neutral tone. 'I'm delighted you called so soon. I hope everything went well in Ireland.'

'Everything went according to plan. It was a sad occasion but life must go on.'

'Of course.' They were already fencing, she could feel it. 'I'm so sorry – did you get back this weekend?'

'Last night.' She heard the shutters come down. 'Now, about this damned interview.'

She wrestled for control. 'When would be convenient for you?'

'We could have lunch today. Here, if it would suit you. I could have our people rustle up something.'

Sky thought fast. She liked to meet people in their own environment yet, in Treacy's case, she thought the invitation too pat. He was attempting to haze her through the arena,

71

like a cowboy running one of Jimbo's damned rodeo steers. In her hesitation the skirmish was lost and she heard herself agreeing to be at his building at a quarter of twelve the following day. Since she had not much to do this morning, she could easily have acceded to his first suggestion, that she come over right away, but she was not going to yield everything. 'The paper goes to bed at noon Wednesday and,' she decided to stretch the truth, 'I already have some stuff lined up to do for it today so tomorrow would be better.'

'Fine. I'll have you collected from reception. Looking forward to it, Miss MacPherson.'

She was left with a humming receiver in her hand. 'Missing you already . . .' she murmured, in a nasty sing-song tone, and then had to explain herself to the kid.

By the time she was shown into Daniel Treacy's office, Sky was as prepared as she could ever be about her subject. The depressing result of research conducted through the entire Monday was a slim folder containing PR handouts about Treacy's companies, a few puff pieces from the local press over the years and a sprinkling of three-paragraph cuttings from those few nationals and business organs that had been enticed into Butte by the efforts of the Butte–Silver Bow chamber of commerce. For instance, in 1989 *U.S. News and World Report* had included a thumbnail sketch of Treacy in its half-page on the 'resurgence' of business in the city. The writer had profiled him as 'taciturn but effective' and had tagged him and his companies among those to be watched.

Johanna might have been able to help, but all that had greeted Sky when she came into the kitchen before going to work on the Monday morning was another note: her mother had apparently taken it into her head to go visit one of her Blackfoot friends, who had moved in from the reservation and now lived near Helena. She had taken an early bus and asked Sky to make sure to feed the cats in case she was delayed. Which almost certainly meant she was not coming home that night. Sky caught herself being as indignant as though she was the mom.

She had even sought help from the Butte–Silver Bow Public Archives, a well-organized source that had proved invaluable to her in the past. By the end of the day, however, she had had to conclude that there was precious little of personal interest available on Daniel J. Treacy who, for the forty-eight years he had lived in Montana, seemed to have been able to exercise remarkable control over everything written about him. Apart from mentions of his birthplace as County Cork, there was nothing of his childhood, education and early life. In other states, this might have appeared more peculiar than it was, but in Montana everyone, or almost everyone over a certain age, had come to the state from somewhere else. The native Montanan of over thirty-five sometimes seemed to Sky as rare as a genuine gold nugget in Hellroarin' Gulch, the mecca for Butte's tourists at the World Mining Camp and Museum.

As she was ushered into his office, she was pleased to see that her guess at his taste in office décor had not been wide of the mark. Except for a framed photograph of his wife – the same one used by the *Courier* over its obituary – Daniel Treacy's office might have been furnished from an upmarket office-supply catalogue: pale wood and steel, parquet floor-ing, a large abstract oil in a metal frame. His desk was immaculate. The floor-to-ceiling windows, which ran all along one wall, showed a fairly standard view of Butte – defunct pithead machinery towering like skeletal dinosaurs over the rows of shingled roofs, the mile-wide slash of the Berkeley Pit beyond, and beyond that again the white-tipped snaggle teeth of the Rockies. 'Are you Catholic, Miss Mac-Pherson?' The question startled her as he came from behind his desk with hand outstretched.

'I'm sure you must know from my pedigree that I am, or at least that I was born that way.' She took his hand and he shook hers formally before shepherding her towards the window where a small, white-clothed luncheon table had been set up.

'It's just that from this office, as you can see, I have a fine view of our statue.' He smiled widely at her – his smile took years off his face, – which unbalanced her to the extent that she could not decide whether or not he was making fun of her. The 90-foot-high statue of Our Lady of the Rockies that dominated the peak shadowing the city from the northeast, although supposed to be a non-denominational tribute to motherhood, was Catholic Butte's pride and joy, its Rushmore, its Christ of the Andes, visible for miles around and illuminated at night. But hardly what she would have expected as an object of veneration for Daniel Treacy.

'So you have,' she murmured, pretending to gaze up at the white figure while waiting for him to make the next move.

'Yes.' He held out a chair for her. 'Treacy Resources helped out a little with the funding and labour.'

The first course, smoked salmon and crayfish, was already laid out, wine cooled in a bucket to one side of the table and, as Sky took her seat, a waiter materialized through a doorway into an annexe room without any visible signal from her host. The weather had held and, despite the central air-conditioning, the heat radiating on to her right shoulder and neck from the sunlight that shafted obliquely through the window felt familiar and comforting. She declined wine when it was offered. Her glass was immediately taken away and a tumbler filled with Perrier. This was a class act, she thought, watching Treacy through her lashes. 'Shall we begin?' he looked expectantly at her.

'Thank you.' Sky chose deliberately to misunderstand

him, shaking out her napkin and taking a dainty piece of the smoked salmon. Not wishing to irritate him, however, she made small-talk, asking him general questions about the way his companies operated and meshed, the answers to which she already knew from the research in her briefcase.

'Let's cut to the chase, shall we?' After a few minutes of this, he signalled to the waiter to clear away their plates. 'All of this is in the public domain, Miss MacPherson, as I'm sure you know. I was under the impression that you had a different sort of profile in mind.'

'I have indeed.' Sky took her recorder out of her purse. He frowned but said nothing. 'I know I promised no taping,' she kept her tone casual while activating the machine, 'but I'm sure you can appreciate that writing notes while eating is virtually impossible and holds up the proceedings. And since you're such a busy man . . .'

'Go ahead.' He stared into his consommé.

Although she was burning to know why he was coming out of the woodwork now, of all times, she hoped this would become clear in the course of the conversation and began with his childhood. After a few minutes this seemed to have been the usual stuff of the Irish immigrant, shoeless, four-in-a-bed large family, small farm, tiny fishing village, education truncated by lack of funds and opportunity. It was textbook *Quiet Man* or that other bible of the Butte Irish, *Man of Aran*, and she became impatient. She moved him as quickly as she could through the reminiscences about his hard-working mother and father, his boyhood excursions to catch salmon or shoot rabbits, wishing he would get to the part where he decided to emigrate.

'You seem bored. How much of this do you know already, Miss MacPherson?' he asked suddenly, startling her out of her own train of thought.

'None of it, I assure you.' If he saw through her that easily she was losing her touch.

75

'Not from your mother?' Those merciless eyes missed nothing.

'She never spoke about you.'

'I find that hard to believe. Her family and mine lived in adjoining townlands. Treacy Resources has not been hiding its light under a bushel – there have been photographs of me in the newspapers from time to time.'

Always the same ones and carefully controlled, Sky thought. 'My mother and I moved to Butte only eight years ago,' she said aloud, 'and, forgive me for saying it, the difference in your ages meant that she was only five or six when you moved to the US. Anyway, she is a very unworldly woman. The names of businessmen, however prominent, do not feature much in her conversation.'

He continued to stare at her and Sky knew that he did not believe her. What she had said was entirely true – she and her mother had lived in various small towns in the western half of the state before Sky had gone east, and part of the deal between them, if Sky was to come back to Montana after the break-up of her marriage, had been that they live in a city. Butte had been the result. 'You don't know my mother,' she repeated, 'and she never mentioned you until we spoke about you in connection with your wife's death.'

'And what did she say about Midge's death?' He was very still, as tense as a length of steel cable, and Sky knew that she must pick her words carefully.

'She said she would be thinking about your wife.'

'Thinking about her?'

'It's how she is. She believes in the Oneness of thought, that sort of thing. That we can all connect somehow. That, in many ways, concentrated thinking about someone is as beneficial to communication as actually being in that person's presence.'

'I see.' He raised an eyebrow and Sky felt absurdly that she should defend her mother. It was one thing for her to criticize and be sceptical, quite another for an outsider to disparage Johanna's beliefs. 'I'm sorry, I'm not expressing it very well. It's not *Star Trek*, but with my own eyes I have seen evidence that extra-sensory perception does exist. The telephone ringing a second after you think of someone you haven't seen for ages, that sort of thing . . .'

His expression remained quizzical. 'And do you believe something similar, Miss MacPherson?'

This was it. He was on a fishing expedition too. He was afraid she – or her mother – might be psychic. He definitely had something to hide about his wife's death. 'I believe anything is possible, Mr Treacy,' she said coolly, 'but no, I do not subscribe to my mother's wilder notions.'

She had passed the test. He relaxed visibly. 'I'm sorry if I appear somewhat on edge.' He resumed spooning his consommé. 'I'm quite tired, as I'm sure you will understand.'

'Of course I do.' Sky studied him covertly while she let him rest and the main course was served. His appetite had not improved, she noticed: he had eaten only half of the starter and a third of the consommé. He was good-looking, in an ascetic, Gary Cooper way, with one of those lean faces, peculiar mostly to males, which improve with age. Judging that he would not be the type to indulge in vanity, she did not bother to search for traces of transplants or expensive hairpieces in his springy, iron-grey hair, which would probably have been curly had he not worn it severely cropped.

'Will I do?' He did not raise his eyes from his plate and she had the grace to be embarrassed.

'I'm sorry.' She shrugged. 'Guess I'm not as good as I think.'

'On the contrary, I've long been an admirer of your style. Wasted in this town, if I may say so.' Then, before she could respond, 'May I ask *you* a question, Miss MacPherson?' He sat back to let the waiter serve small boiled potatoes and broccoli.

'Sky, please. "Miss MacPherson" makes me sound like a Scottish schoolteacher in *Little House on the Prairie*.' She was rewarded with a grin, the first sign of genuine spontaneity since she had become interested in him as a subject. 'Very well, Sky, my question is about your name – your byline. You sign your pieces "R. Sky MacPherson." I've wondered, now and then, what the R signifies.'

Sky, who hated the flower-child name with which she had been afflicted by her hippie parents, always told strangers the R stood for Roberta. She felt she had little to lose by revealing it to this man. 'I'll tell you if you won't laugh.' She raised her chin.

'I promise I won't laugh – shall we eat?' He picked up his knife and fork.

'It's Rainbow.' She braced herself for ridicule but none came.

'If you hate it, why not change it? This is America, after all, land of the free and so forth.'

'It would hurt my mother too much.' She did not accept the bait. 'She raised me mostly on her own and I thought I owed her. I used R.S. back east but then I discovered that R.J.s and D.J.s and S.J.s are ten a penny in Montana. At least "R. Sky" is distincitve. And people here don't seem to worry about it too much.'

'Rainbow Sky,' he said, without a trace of irony. 'That's even more distinctive.'

'I think we'd better get back to the interview.' She was uncomfortable at the turn this was taking. 'I did some research on you.'

He inclined his head to indicate he would have expected as much and Sky, noticing that the tape had run out, reached to turn it over. 'Excuse me.'

'Look, I asked you here for a reason.'

She looked up. His voice had changed completely and his eyes were no longer like agates. 'I thought you had.' She held his gaze, while flipping over the tape.

'Without that, if you don't mind.' He put a hand over hers on the machine.

'On the record, however?' They were coming to the nub of it. His hand was warm and strong but the skin had the papery feel of age.

He hesitated, then: 'Is there any median way between on and off the record?' He let go her hand and pointed at the machine. 'Such as mutual trust?'

Sky decided to go with it. 'You can trust me.'

'Very well.' He became still again. 'Look – this may seem odd to you—'

'I'm thirty-four years old, Mr Treacy. I'm a Catholic-educated divorcée, who had more than twenty communes and squats throughout Oregon and Montana on my housing list before I was ten. I have a mother who talks to trees and a drop-out father who says he loves animals but who shows people where and how to kill moose and bear. I've an alcoholic ex, who lives in his parents' basement. My boyfriend thinks only fairies drink wine and, for good measure, my name is Rainbow Sky. Nothing seems odd to me.'

The corners of Treacy's mouth twitched. 'When you put it that way . . .'

Sky knew she could not help him further, and waited while he made up his mind. He regarded her gravely for a few moments. 'You have your grandmother's hair. Your byline photograph does not do it justice.'

Sky, astounded at this turn of events, involuntarily touched her bangs. 'I was always under the impression I got this colour from my father.'

'Your father has ordinary blond hair, American hair. Yours – your grandmother's – is very distinctive. It's called strawberry blond where I come from. As far as I remember, your uncle Francey has it too. How is Francey, by the way?'

'He's fine, as far as I know. We hear from him now and again.' Knowing she had to bide her time until he felt able to say what he really wanted to say, Sky had recovered some of her poise. 'He struck it lucky, inherited money and married well. He is happy and quite rich.' As she spoke, she saw that Daniel Treacy, so sure of himself, so powerful and successful, was now swallowing so hard that his Adam's apple jumped in his throat.

Finally he came out with it. 'Actually this is about your – your grandmother. I'm very anxious for news of her. She will be seventy-five years old on the eighteenth of August next, as I'm sure you're aware.'

He swallowed again and she had to struggle not to show how astonished she was at his precision. The man had been – perhaps still was – in love with her grandmother. Where did that leave poor Midge? 'H-have you continued corresponding with her?' Her stammer annoyed her.

'We have never been in correspondence. And before that stinging intelligence of yours inspires you with your next question,' his stare intensified, 'I do, did, love my wife.' He stopped to let it sink in. Then: 'Your grandmother and I were friends of old. I continue to have the Cork newspapers flown to me. I don't want to see Elizabeth's name in the death columns of the *Examiner* without meeting her again.' He looked down at his unfinished meal. 'However, for reasons I hope presently to make clear, I don't want to go back to Cork. Miss MacPherson – Sky—' He leaned forward, and for a moment she thought he was going to catch her arm so she kept absolutely quiet, afraid to encourage him by moving a single muscle.

'I wonder if you could influence your mother, or perhaps your aunt in Chicago, to invite your grandmother to come to Montana as a treat for her seventy-fifth birthday?' His expression had changed so suddenly that she was taken aback: far from being forbidding and powerful, he looked like a child. 'I'll pay all expenses. She need not know this. If you think it would not upset her, I'll send a plane. You could say the whole family saved up.'

He saw then he had gone too far too fast. The light in his eyes died and he folded his napkin. 'Very well.' Now he might have been offering a business deal. 'I can see you believe that the private plane is out. It's just that to get to Butte from Cork by scheduled transport is such hard work and she is not in the first flush of youth. Of course, she would have to have someone travel with her. I'd take care of that, too.'

'I've no aunt in Chicago.' Sky at last found her voice. 'Perhaps you mean Goretti. She moved to New York a number of years ago.'

He held up his hand to stop her. 'No matter. I can understand quite well what a shock this is to you. And, having disturbed you to the extent I have, I hope you don't mind if I make things even worse. You see, Sky,' he picked at a crumb on the white tablecloth, 'I can save you a lot of digging around in dusty old files nearly fifty years old. Maybe even a trip to Ireland. All I ask is that you keep an open mind and remember that, although it is a cliché, there really are two sides to every story.' His face carved itself into fierce lines. 'Are we still in a state of mutual trust?'

Not a muscle, she said to herself, don't move a muscle . . .

'The reason I came to America and have never been back is that, as you have no doubt guessed, I was in love with your grandmother but it couldn't work out.'

'I see.' Sky recognized his choice of syntax. There was more to come.

'I'm going to tell you something which has not ever been made public in this country, something I have dreaded being made public ever since I came here, although I am quite sure

81

your mother and many of the other Irish with antecedents on the Béara Peninsula – particularly the older ones – well know. You are not the only one with name problems. I changed my name when I got here. My real name is McCarthy.'

She frowned in bewilderment. 'Is that all?'

'No, that's not all. It didn't work out between your grandmother and me,' the tan on Treacy's face was turning yellow as the blood drained from underneath it, 'because I killed your grandfather.'

She half rose from her seat but this time he put a hand across the narrow table to restrain her. 'Ask your mother or any of your aunts, Sky. It was an accident, I swear to you. An accident.'

Chapter Seven

Hoping that her mother would have returned, Sky drove straight home, only to find the house still empty. She resisted the urge to call Greyhound and Intermountain for the bus times and instead, reasoning that she had every right to find out what had been kept from her all these years, gave herself permission to go into her mother's room to look through the letters she knew Johanna kept in the bottom drawer of her low-boy.

The drawer, which was deep, was so full it was difficult to open fully and as she tugged impatiently it jerked on its runners, spilling its top layer all over the floor. As well as the personal letters there were old bills and receipts, snapshots, empty envelopes, flyers, junk mail, shopping lists and sheaves of yellowing newspaper clippings. A few of these had been taken from Irish newspapers but most had been carefully culled from Sky's own work and were right up to date. The last piece was her obituary on Midge Treacy.

Never having pegged her mother as a sentimentalist, the unexpected sight of this chronicle of love and pride was unsettling and moving; it was a reminder that no matter how old or confident or successful the child becomes, the mother continues to hold out her arms to assist the first steps of the little baby.

Worse was to come: as she picked a few of the pieces off the floor she revealed underneath a series of snapshots of herself on her First Communion day, all serious smiles and blonde ringlets tied up under her white veil. Naturally Johanna had never got around to putting them into an album: 'I must sort out my paperwork one of these days,' was a constant refrain and yet she always found something far more interesting to do. 'Oh, Mom,' Sky's throat closed over, 'I'll help you with your paperwork – and I'm sorry for all I said to you . . .' although she knew this soft resolve was unlikely to last. She cleared her throat and began the systematic search for clues.

It was not long before her softness dissipated. Although tidiness was foreign to her nature, Sky's work practices were methodical, and half an hour after she started she had several orderly piles all around her on the patchwork quilt which covered the big bed, all the Irish relatives' letters put to one side for sub-sorting. 'Grandma, Uncle Francey, Aunt Goretti, Aunt Margaret, Grandma again, Aunt Abbie, Aunt Constance, Uncle Francey, Uncle Francey again . . .' Her lips moved in litany as she went about her task. It emerged that her mother's most prolific correspondent by far was Sky's grandmother. None of these letters covered more than two pages, however, and could hardly be called profound, consisting as they did of straightforward news of the doings of the aunts and of Francey. Not one mention of anything to do with her husband's violent end, and no mention anywhere of Daniel Treacy/McCarthy.

Although it was difficult to have any genuine attachment to someone she had seen only once, of all her Irish relatives Sky imagined herself closest to her grandmother, despite the pedestrian nature of the correspondence and occasional telephone calls between them. Like her mother's scattiness, her grandmother's straight, strong script had always been a given in her life, giving her as real a presence in grade- and high-school conversations as other kids' grandmas. Sky had always thought she had plenty of time in which to make the long-promised adult trip to Ireland. Now, confronted with the fact that the old lady was nearly seventy-five, she saw that maybe she had not.

Her uncle Francey's letters gave her a shock of a different nature. Quite a few of the envelopes contained personal cheques, some for hundreds of English pounds. All, except the two most recent – for two hundred pounds apiece – were hopelessly out of date.

Sky stared at them in disbelief. There had been weeks when she had had to borrow money from Greg to pay utilities and here was this small fortune – she totted up the amount, which came to £3,450, maybe as much as six thousand dollars – lying here all the time. Her recent upsurge of tenderness forgotten, she folded the two good cheques and put them in the pocket of her skirt. Her mother would try the patience of a saint.

Francey's letters proved no more helpful than her grand-mother's and contained no reminiscences of past lives in Ireland, although they did report on the writer's sporadic trips back to Cork to see his mother. If Francey had noticed that his cheques to Johanna had not been cashed, he did not mention it. Too rich, Sky supposed sourly.

Constance's letters, from her sheep station in Australia, were the longest, describing the strangeness of life out there, begging for photographs of the Rocky Mountains to coun-teract the flatness of where she lived. The other aunts' letters, gossipy but rushed, and which appeared to owe more to duty than the pleasure of corresponding, were no more helpful. It must be difficult, Sky thought, looking at her mother's family relationships spread all around her on the bed, to maintain contact purely through the good offices of the US postal service. Johanna always fell on these letters with pleasure yet never seemed to feel the need to meet in person any of the senders.

It struck Sky then that her mother was not alone in this. That not one of these people seemed to have any need to see the others. She picked up one of her aunt Goretti's letters again: here was Johanna's sister, just down the road, relatively speaking, in New York, not married, no family ties and yet even she had never yet managed to make the long-promised trip west. She had preferred, as she admitted guiltily in her letters, to spend her annual two weeks' vacation soaking up the sun in Florida.

Sky looked again at the outdated cheques she had arranged in a fan shape to one side of her uncle Francey's stack; if she had known about all this money she would certainly have insisted that her mother go east. It was not as though Johanna was tied to the house and, working only at weekends, she was free all week. She was not slow in going walkabout on the reservations.

Here was something else that had not occurred to Sky since grade school, when everyone in the class compared family circumstances with everyone else: of her grandmother's six living children – there had originally been eight but one girl had died in an accident and another was missing, presumed dead – Sky was the only grandchild. Margaret, Goretti and Abigail were spinsters, and neither Francey nor Constance, the only two who had married, had had children. Unusual for an Irish Catholic family.

This was a weird bunch she had inherited, although, she thought grimly, her mother would fight her on that one. One of Johanna's more treasured ideas was that birth was not a random accident of genetics; if she was to be believed, we choose to come into existence from some other, ethereal plane we have inhabited since our last earthly outing and, what was more, we choose not only where we will be born but to whom. She had no answer to the question as to where that left the abused and the starving.

So what did that say about Sky herself? Supposing, just supposing, there was an inkling of truth in Johanna's theory, what baby in her right mind, having decided to be born in

America, would 'choose' to be born to Johanna and Larry and as a result to be lumbered with a name like Rainbow Sky? As she gathered the sub-files of letters into one neat stack, Sky thought it was no wonder she had rushed to stand in front of a justice of the peace with the first man who had appeared half-way normal.

Greg. She looked at her watch. It was still only mid-afternoon, and it was unlikely her mother would be home before nightfall – it was conceivable that Johanna might even stay away a second night. Sky felt she would go out of her mind if she had to stay in the house and wait.

She bundled all the letters and papers back into the drawer of the low-boy and then called Greg at the liquor store. He was surprised and delighted to hear from her, and yes, he could get off for a few hours. She changed out of her working clothes into jeans and a T-shirt and then, before picking him up, decided to check in at the office, although she knew she had no markings.

Tuesday afternoon, after the paper went to press, was always the slowest of the working week. 'Oh, hi, Sky!' The kid was pecking at a keyboard with two fingers; in trawling to find something useful for her to do, Jimbo had hit on making her Letters Editor. Her job was to select some of the most controversial pieces of mail for publication and to type them. Not a very taxing occupation. 'Mr Larsen was looking for you – oh, phooey!' The junior sighed as she examined a broken nail.

Sky checked the board, saw she had no messages and crossed to Jimbo's door. She put her head around it: 'You wanted me?'

'Don't forget the shamrock lot. It's tonight.'

As it happened, Sky had completely forgotten that she was to cover the St Patrick's Brigade meeting and was too keyed up about her personal affairs to engage the editor in another argument. Anyhow, the job would take less than ten minutes if she timed it right. 'If that's all, I'll see you tomorrow,' she said as sweetly as she could.

'How was the interview with Treacy?' he called after her as she left his office.

Daniel Treacy's momentous revelation had put the profile of him on the back burner as far as Sky was concerned but at this point she was not anxious to engage the editor. 'Fine, fine,' she called over her shoulder, 'I'll talk to you about it tomorrow.'

'Please do.'

'You bet!' Sky, detecting Jimbo's unusual interest in this one, registered it, filed it at the back of her mind but did not stop.

A few miles away, at Mooney airport, the little Horizon Air plane disgorged its passengers, who had travelled from Billings. Most were Butte residents, but one or two, like Lynskey, were coming to the city for the first time.

Most airports at which he had landed exuded a sort of anxious calm: in Butte, he saw, people strolled around the tarmac, even coming right to the steps of the plane to greet those arriving. The chief would have loved it: although it lacked the urgency of wartime, the layout of the airport, the low scale of the buildings, the little planes, would have reminded him of the closing scenes of *Casablanca*.

He took a cab to his hotel, which rejoiced in the name of the War Bonnet Inn, and along the way asked the driver to stop at a drugstore, where he bought a bottle of mineral water and all the current newspapers they had in stock.

The War Bonnet proved as unexotic as all the other tourist hotels in which he had stayed in the course of his career, but it was comfortable and clean and, having unpacked – a matter of a minute or so since he believed in travelling light – he lay on the bed and scanned his papers.

One of them, the *Butte Courier*, had what he was looking for: a long piece on Daniel Treacy's wife. It was written by someone called R. Sky MacPherson, whose thumbnail picture byline showed her to be as wan and big-eyed as all the others who posed for these publicity shots. The piece told him very little he did not know already.

Lynskey was tired but refused to sleep just yet. New places always excited him – it was one of the perks of the job. He decided to take a walk.

After Greg dropped her back to the Nissan, which she had parked in the yard behind the liquor store, Sky drove immediately to a call-box. At the other end of the line only her own voice answered her from the duplex.

She debated whether to go home – perhaps her mother would come back in the meantime – before she went to dance attendance on the St Patrick's Brigade. She felt sticky and dishevelled, and could have done with a long shower and clean clothes but decided that, since the job required little more than being a messenger, she would not bother. Who cared what the Luddites of the St Patrick's Brigade thought of her appearance? The only reason Jimbo continued to carry their stuff was because they were advertisers, sponsoring three premium-priced colour supplements for Christmas, at Easter and for St Patrick's Day. He subtly disassociated the *Courier* from the wilder anti-British sentiments behind most of the articles he had to carry in those supplements but the newspaper needed the Brigade's money.

Could she confide her indefinable unease about Treacy to Jimbo? The thought occurred to Sky as she drove slowly across town. The *Courier*'s editor had a finer mind and wider experience than his present job might indicate to an outsider. It had taken Sky the best part of a year after joining the *Courier* to recognize that this man, with permanently furrowed forehead and tired eyes, had once been a whizzkid. Originally from Missoula, with a good degree from the University of Montana and a postgraduate qualification from the Columbia School of Journalism in New York, he had worked for both the *News* and the *Post* in Washington – which had led to a healthy contacts book – and had been marked out as a rising star in the profession. But at the age of thirty or so, he had chucked in the rat race, for no good reason that Sky could see except that he had a beautiful wife who was a native of Butte and who could never settle anywhere else. His sons were both at Harvard Medical School.

Jimbo could be irascible and vengeful, as in his marking her to cover the St Patrick's Brigade, but she had deep respect for his journalistic instincts. She also liked him – except for the rare occasions, usually about once a year, when he went on a monumental bender lasting two or three days, during which everyone knew to steer clear of him. On those occasions he would stay in the office and not go home, rambling on about projects he would do if it wasn't for the f---ing rest of the world, becoming by turns aggressive and self-pitying until shortage of sleep and lack of physical capacity to take in any more booze rendered him unconscious. He would sleep among his paper towers for about twelve hours and wake up remorseful and ashamed. The rest of the year he worried over his computer and his calculator and performed to less than a third of his journalistic talent. In Sky's view, he had just given up.

Having examined the pros and cons of telling him what was on her mind, she rejected the idea. Her imagination was probably running away with her – after all, Treacy had insisted that the killing in Ireland was an accident – and it had been almost half a century ago. It was stretching it a little to connect it with what everyone else accepted was a tragic auto wreck in understandable circumstances; after

Mayville, the road to the northwest was a narrow, tortuous nightmare and those logging trucks were monsters. No, she decided, she would not speak to Jimbo, at least until after she'd heard her mother's version of the story and maybe had done a little more digging into the car wreck that had killed Midge Treacy.

The meeting of the shamrock lot, as the editor so inelegantly termed the group, was being held as usual in a private room in the War Bonnet Inn on Cornell. Much of what went on socially in Butte happened in either the Plaza or the War Bonnet, both run by Best Western.

Sky pulled in in front of the hotel and, because it was not eight o'clock, sat listening to a country station on the dash radio until it was time to go in. She had covered this event a few times before, when Jimbo had been unavailable, and the trick was to be sitting outside the room a few minutes before the end of the meeting to let them think you had been there all the time.

She had parked in a spot fairly close to the inn's front entrance and, having killed fifteen minutes or so, was just about to go in when she spotted the funeral director, Bill Collins, who was king of the shamrocks for this year, coming through the entrance door. She shrank down in her seat so he would not see her.

She need not have worried, Collins looked neither right nor left as he hurried to his automobile. Assuming he had been called away from the meeting to the parlour, Sky, watching through her wing mirror, waited for him to drive away before she got out but was surprised to see that he continued to sit in the driver's seat as though expecting someone to join him.

The minutes ticked by. Then Sky, whose hearing was acute, heard the faint buzz of a mobile phone. She saw Collins pick up the receiver, hold it to his ear for a few moments and replace it. His windows were closed and he had his back to her so she was unable to tell whether he had spoken or not.

She leaned over the passenger seat as though searching for something under it as he hurried past her again and – still without looking around – towards the doorway of the hotel. Just before he went inside, another man, whom Sky did not know, heavyset and with powerful shoulders, came out on the steps and then performed an about-turn to accompany Collins through the doors, as though he had been sent to fetch him back to the meeting.

The call had been by arrangement. Sky laughed aloud: could Bill Collins, good ole daily-communicant Bill with his pious face, conservative suits and lace-up Oxfords, be involved with someone other than his wife? Although it was none of her business, she was charmed: maybe she should run it up the flagpole with Teddy – he'd know.

One way and another, she thought, as she got out of the car, this was certainly turning out to be an interesting day. She was still smiling as she walked towards the front door and did not see the man coming obliquely at her from the side. 'Having fun?'

'Oh.' She was startled. He was tall and thin with a curved nose that would not have disgraced one of Johanna's friends on the reservation, and fell into step beside her. 'You looked as though you were having a great time.'

'Are you Irish?' It was a rhetorical question: his voice ran and rilled and could only have been from that country.

'Bingo.' He did not offer his name. By that time they were at the door and he opened it for her.

'Thank you.' She smiled at him as she passed through. 'This your first time in Butte?'

'First time anywhere near the Rockies, actually.'

'Well, have a great vacation.'

'It's getting better by the minute.' His frank stare would have made her blush, had she been the blushing type.

'Thanks again. Goodbye.' She walked off towards the room where the meeting was being held but, as she went, was conscious that the man watched her every step of the way.

She got there only seconds before the secretary, an old bat with the thin, pursed lips of the self-righteous, came out with her Xeroxed notes. As she handed them to Sky, who was the only reporter there that evening, she looked around as though disappointed. 'Anything you'd like me to highlight here?'

Sky scanned the two pages but could see nothing she had not expected: badly phrased calls on President Bush to use his influence with the United Nations and/or on the EC to mount an enquiry into the torture perpetrated by a biased police force on unfairly arrested Catholics, a reiteration of the standard motion condemning the British army of occupation in Northern Ireland, announcements of forthcoming benefits for the families of prisoners-of-war. 'Would you like to interview anyone?' The woman sniffed. 'Our President, Mr Collins? Mr Larsen usually does.'

'Yes, that'd be good.' For no reason other than she was fed up with this old biddy, Sky decided to ruin King Shamrock's day. If, indeed, he did have an assignation, the assignation would have to cool her heels.

The interview lasted all of five minutes. Bill Collins, although tense enough – Sky was not well enough acquainted with him to know whether or not this was his natural state – seemed delighted to see her. He complimented her on her work and behaved as though he was perfectly happy to settle in all night with her to lead her through the labyrinthine history of the conflict in Northern Ireland.

'I've told Jim Larsen all of this already,' he cracked his knuckles, making Sky wince, 'but nothing ever appears. I guess I'm just not persuasive enough, but then he's not Irish, not like us.'

'This is really wonderful background, Mr Collins,' Sky saw the danger of being cast as a co-conspirator and rushed to cut him short, 'but, as you know, the space for the community notes is quite tight. We are a commercial operation, after all—'

'But this is *news*. Why can I never get that across to anyone?'

'I agree it's news, of course it's news, Mr Collins, but, given everything else I have on my plate, I would not be able to do this story justice.'

'Another time, perhaps? I don't think the general run of the American population fully understands what's happening over there in occupied Ireland, Miss MacPherson. They're killing our people, yours and mine. Day after day,' he grabbed her arm but such was his intensity that Sky knew he had not noticed he had done so, 'it's just terrible. The British propaganda machine is given such a free rein over here. It's all this stuff about "special relationships", especially since Reagan and Maggie Thatcher hit it off so good!' Gently, Sky extricated her arm and he looked down at his hand with surprise. 'I'm sorry, Miss MacPherson, I do get carried away. I know that.' He tried to smile. 'But as a person of Irish extraction yourself, I'm sure you'll appreciate how frustrating it is for us. We find it very hard to get our message across and we're blocked at every hand's turn. We're not lunatics or fanatics, you know' – he cracked his knuckles again – 'but if we got an opportunity from a fine writer like yourself, we could start getting our message into the mainstream of Montana politics. In our own way we're as important out here, you know, as they are in New York or Boston. Every cog turns the wheel.'

'It certainly is fascinating and you're right, I don't know half enough about it.' Then, fatally, 'Maybe we'll get together sometime.'

'When?' He caught her arm again.

'I'll call you.' Annoyed at herself for giving the opening, she added, 'How's Mrs Collins?' watching for him to blink.

To her sneaky admiration, his eyes gave no more than a surprised flicker. 'She's fine, fine – do call me, won't you? Larsen is always promising coverage and never delivers.'

'I'll call you,' she promised.

And pigs will fly, she thought as she walked back to the Nissan.

Back in the duplex, she took a long, long shower and then, snuggled up in a towelling robe, emptied her mind of everything to do with work and settled down to read. Greg had given her a gift of E. Annie Proulx's *The Shipping News*.

Chapter Eight

The north Mayo rain was colder and wetter in the pre-dawn blackness than at any other time of day. This far from Greenwich, the mid-June skies began to lighten before four o'clock in the morning. It was now half past three.

The first part of the job now accomplished and the phone call having been made, bang on time, from the public box in Crossmolina, the Hiace van, was nearing the town of Ballina. White because this was the most common colour in Ireland, it wore 1990 registration plates, neither new nor old enough to excite comment, and was being driven at a steady pace just below the speed limit in case there was a nosy Gárda not tucked up in his bed. The van's three donkey-jacketed occupants were jammed close into one another along the front bench seat. They were burly men. Three workers, maybe in construction, going out on an extra early start because of the long daylight. Or fishermen travelling north to Killybegs to catch the tide.

The van's engine was well tuned and the regular swishing of the wipers was the predominant sound in the cab. No one spoke. Perhaps, being Irish, they were not all that keen on grave-robbing, after all.

'At last!' Sky threw aside her novel and ran towards the door at the sound of her mother's key.

'Hi, sweetie.' Johanna struggled through the door, her arms filled with an enormous package wrapped in brown paper. 'How was your day? Come on in, Hermana.'

The questions died on Sky's tongue as she saw her mother's friend.

'You sure it's not too late?' Hermana seemed uncharacteristically reluctant as she eased herself through the narrow frame.

'Not at all.' Johanna was already in the kitchen and lowering her burden on to a chair. 'Come on in, take the weight off your feet – ooh, sorry, Hermana! You know I didn't mean anything odious by that, darling.' Sky's mother giggled then turned to her daughter. 'Hermana picked me up from the bus, Sky. I didn't like to call you, thought you might be busy or with Greg or something.'

'I was worried, Mom, it's after ten o'clock, you could have called.' Sky closed the door and followed them.

'Now, Sky, I'm an old middle-aged lady. Who's going to mug me, for heaven's sake?' Johanna's laugh, as false as a two-dollar bill, echoed from the cubbyhole under the sink where she was foraging for cans of catfood. 'The very idea. Here we are, my little ones,' cooing at the cats which slalomed around her moccasins, 'poor mites, did you miss me? Like some tea, Hermana? Put some water on, Sky.'

Sky bided her time, making the tea and bringing it over to the table while her mother's verbal torrent continued to spew all over the can-opener and the catfood she was dispensing. Hermana's presence was not serendipitous: Johanna was ducking an interrogation about Daniel Treacy. It was why she had gone away so early, stayed overnight.

Eventually, she wound down and sat at the table with them, still avoiding Sky's eye.

'There's something I want to ask you, Mom.' Sky spoke quietly.

'Yes, dear?' Johanna darted a look at Hermana.

'What's in the package?' Annoyed at the confirmation of her suspicion, she decided to keep her mother in suspense.

'It's a rush basket Freda Little Calf gave me.' Johanna's relief was almost comical. 'Her sister's making thousands of 'em for the tourists. I thought I'd let the cats sleep in it – put in that little blanket Buffy made for me for last Christmas? She wouldn't mind, I'm sure—'

'Mom,' Sky was through being subtle, 'that's not what I want to know and we all know it. What gives with Daniel Treacy and Grandma? And how come you never told me that was not his real name?'

'Is it not?' Her mother tried her best to sound ingenuous as she busied herself squeezing the last drop of liquid out of her tea-bag with the back of her spoon. 'My, my! How about that!'

'No, it's not. His name's McCarthy. And you know it as well as I do. Don't bother to deny it, Mom! So tell me what happened.'

'Gracious!'

The fluttering about was getting under Sky's skin but she let her mother be for the time being. 'Yes?' She bit her lip.

'It was all a long time ago, dear, and I was so young at the time – let me see, what age would I have been . . .'

'Let me help you, Mom, he's already told me his name is McCarthy. He's already told me he killed my grandfather. But he said it was an accident and he said you'd be able to tell me what happened. Does that jog your memory?'

'It's not *my* fault, Sky, don't talk to me like that!' Johanna found refuge in maternal indignation.

'This is very upsetting for your poor mom, honey.' Hermana, whose bulk dwarfed the cheap chair on which she was sitting, almost overbalanced in her eagerness to rescue her friend. 'It's something she doesn't like talking about.' She steadied herself by catching on to the sides of the table. 'Dark things are better left buried, don't you think?'

Sky kept her eyes on her mother's face. From behind came the sounds of the cats' fastidious chomping at their food. 'There was a court case,' Johanna said at last, 'but he was set free, Sky. It was all a storm in a tea-cup. Here, kitty, kitty, kitty,' she bent to pick up both cats, 'good girls, you finished, then?'

Sky counted mentally to three. 'Mom?'

'Yes, dear?'

'Please tell me the truth. He says it was an accident. Was it?'

'I think so.' Johanna raised the cats' bodies until she was holding them like a furry shield across her chest. 'Why don't you write to your aunt Margaret? Or even Goretti? They're much older than I am, they'd remember better. The whole truth is that all I can recall is a great drama in the house one night and then a funeral. My father's funeral. I didn't *know* Daniel Treacy, Sky, I've told you—'

'But you did know, you *do* know, that he was in love with Grandma. And that he killed my grandfather. And then he ran off to the States.'

'It wasn't like that – I told you, the judge wouldn't have let him go. Oh—' Johanna looked to Hermana for support. 'It was an *accident*, I'm sure of it. Yes,' she nodded vigorously, 'it was definitely an accident.'

'I think you should write to your aunts, Sky.' Hermana patted her friend's hand. 'Or, better yet, why don't you call them?'

'I'll have to call them anyway.' Sky got up from the table and went to the sink to rinse her cup.

She might have known. Her mother could not face even the tiniest measure of unpleasantness. She let the silence behind her develop, then turned around and said, casually, 'By the way, he wants to invite Grandma over here for her seventy-fifth birthday.'

'Wow!' Johanna's gasp of excitement was audible. 'I was

afraid I'd never see her again – it's so expensive to go over to Ireland.'

That's your own stupid fault, Mom. Sky thought of all the out-of-date cheques in the drawer. She had had enough: she needed to think things through before she delved into the minutiae of the story or made concrete plans for her grandmother's visit, which was so clearly on the cards now. 'I'm very tired, Mom. We'll talk again in the morning.'

'Of course, Sky.' Her mother looked like a teenager. Sky kissed her cheek, Hermana's too, and left them to it.

It might have been an accident and it might not, she thought, as she closed her bedroom door. Either way, she was going to make a few discreet enquiries about the death of Mary Dorothy Treacy, conveniently out of the way just before her grandmother's birthday. It was a little too tidy to be coincidental.

Long after she turned out her light, she heard the buzz of talk from the kitchen, Johanna's light, excited lilt, Hermana's baritone rumble.

She extracted the story bit by bit from her mother over breakfast the next morning. Johanna was reluctant to resurrect her own mother's colourful past but the bones of the story proved quite simple. Sky's grandparents had had a row late one night, something to do with her grandmother flirting with Daniel McCarthy at a local dance. Things had gotten heavy and out of control, her grandfather had gone out for a walk to cool down, had met McCarthy, who was out shooting rabbits, they'd had words, there'd been a struggle and McCarthy's shotgun had gone off. McCarthy was charged but had been let go.

'That's not too bad.' Sky looked at her mother with compassion. 'Why the secrecy? You could have told me all this long before now. As a matter of fact, I think it's quite romantic.'

Johanna stared at her then. 'Well, it was your grandfather,

100

but I suppose since you didn't know any of the people involved ... For us at the time, though, it wasn't at all romantic, we were marked people in the parish. Not everyone believed Daniel McCarthy was as innocent as he seemed.' Johanna looked at her lap. 'Or my mother.' This last was so faint Sky barely caught it.

'What about Grandma?'

'Well, I was a child, I keep telling you. No one in the family ever, ever talked about that time, Sky, maybe now ...' She looked bravely at her daughter. 'Why don't you write to your aunts, like we suggested last night?'

'I will, Mom, but I want to hear it from you.'

Her mother looked away. 'I do think she loved him, yes.' Her voice was small as a child's. 'But she got married to my stepfather not too long after.'

'He died too.'

This brought Johanna's head whipping around. 'Much, much later. Mossie Sheehan just fell off a roof. It was an *ordinary* fall – wash out your mouth with *soap*, Rainbow Sky MacPherson!' Her indignation would have been amusing if the subject was not so serious. 'Lord save us from journalists, you're all such Dramatic Annies.' Johanna took too large a mouthful from her cup and hiccuped. 'Sorry—' she hiccuped again, then: 'You all see complicated stories in the simplest things! I can assure you, Daniel McCarthy had nothing whatsoever to do with our stepfather's death. He had already been over here for years. I was long gone myself by that time – I didn't even make it home for the funeral.'

'Aha!' Sky pounced. 'So you've known all along that Treacy and McCarthy were one and the same.'

'So what?' Johanna had recovered and the cornflower gaze was much in evidence.

'So, I want to know when did you suss Treacy and McCarthy were the same. And how come it was never mentioned at this breakfast table?'

'He was at a funeral I attended,' Johanna was on her dignity now, 'and I recognized him from a photograph my mother kept in a drawer in her bureau at home on the farm. As far as I know, you never asked me anything about him, Sky, so how was I to know you might be interested?'

Helplessly, Sky looked at her. For a woman who seemed so gentle, her mother always managed to do her own sweet thing.

'He hasn't changed all that much, you know.' Johanna settled herself more comfortably – as far as she was concerned, the difficult part of the conversation was over. 'And he's quite handsome, isn't he? My, my! After all these years, to think that he still loves her . . .' Her nose crinkled over a sentimental grin.

'Don't change the subject.'

'Oh, isn't it sweet!' Like the guileless smile of a child, Johanna's lit her face and was always irresistible. Now she clutched both hands to her kaftaned bosom. 'Wouldn't it be wonderful if she still loved him too and they could live happily ever after?'

'It's obvious we're going to have to agree to Mr Treacy's – Mr McCarthy's generous offer and have her over here in August.' Sky found herself willy-nilly caught up in this geriatric love story. She got up from the table to pour herself another cup of coffee. 'Why don't you be the one to make the first move and call her? Don't get too wound up in advance, though, Mom. She's an old lady. She might not want to come, you know.'

'A call to Ireland? Oh, Sky, you know we can't afford it.'

Slowly, drawing attention to the action as though she were a stage magician, Sky reached for her purse on the kitchen counter and pulled out the small wad of cheques. She separated the two that could still be negotiated. 'Sign those, Mom,' she said softly, 'and write on them the following words: "Pay to R. Sky MacPherson".'

Open-mouthed, her mother took the cheques and the pen offered with them and did as she was bid.

'I'm not going to say anything about this at the moment,' Sky took the two cheques back, 'but if you don't write this very day to your brother and ask him to replace that lot,' she indicated the pile of useless paper on the table, 'I will.' Then Sky, to whom the telephone was as essential to life as strong coffee, finished the thick brew in her mug. 'And make the goddamn call to your mother, Mom. We have four hundred dollars here,' she waved the two good cheques under her mother's nose, 'and, anyhow, it's Treacy's invite. We'll bill him for expenses.'

Throughout that day, she was so busy with routine work that she had no opportunity to pursue her private agenda with Daniel Treacy. She typed up the shamrock report and a couple of quotes from Bill Collins, and set up the stories which would pass for news in the next edition, including the hated rodeo. Not that she would cover it, a principle was a principle, but efficient work-habits were ingrained. At least the kid or the freelancer or whatever sucker eventually got to report on it would not want for the preliminary research.

She was due to interview one of the planners at City Hall about zoning violations and was immersed in the stack of bumf on the relevant regulations, when she realized Jimbo was standing at the desk. 'Got a minute?'

'Sure.' She rose and followed him into his office.

'Tell me about the interview with Treacy.' The editor leaned back in his chair and put his feet on the only clear space on his desk.

'It went fine, he's an interesting guy – well, I'm sure you know that.' Sky was cautious. Although the story was a scoop of sorts, Jimbo's persistent interest in it alerted her that something out of the ordinary was going on. He usually let

103

her get on with her stuff and made his comments when he saw the copy. Could he know about her personal angle? Or even about Treacy's past?

She dug a little: 'I haven't transcribed it yet, Jim, and you know I can't ever judge these things until I've done that. Any particular hurry on this one? I may have to see him again, so if there's anything special you'd want me to ask him . . .'

'Hm-mm,' he looked through his window, 'nothing at this stage. You're talking to him again? That's good. Just stay alert.'

'What about?' Then Sky wished she had not asked. Given her family involvement, she would have preferred to have done her own investigations outside the ambit of the newspaper.

'It may be nothing.' He looked speculatively at her and, removing his feet from the desk, seemed to come to a decision. 'Anyhow,' he continued, as though the conversation was already over, 'I don't want to say anything which might influence you in the wrong direction. Best to approach these things open-minded. But after you've talked to him again and transcribed your notes, come in and we'll discuss it. Before you write up your piece.'

Sky was almost through the doorway when his voice stopped her again. 'Did he talk much about his wife?'

'Not a great deal, no.' She searched his face for clues. 'Look, Jim, have you heard anything I should know?'

His expression was bland. 'Just thought I'd ask. We'll talk again.'

Sky did not know as she closed the door behind her whether she was glad or sorry they had had the conversation. On the one hand Jimbo had confirmed her own unease. On the other she had her mother and grandmother to consider.

'Shit,' she muttered under her breath, picking up the

telephone on her desk and punching out her home number. 'Did you call Ireland yet?' she asked her mother, without bothering with preliminaries.

'No, darling.' Johanna sounded surprised. 'It's still far too early over there. At least I think it is . . .' Her voice trailed away.

Sky had no time to go into the ins and outs of time zones. 'Good,' she said, 'hold off for a little while, until tomorrow, will you? Something's come up.'

'Oh, Sky! Have we got our hopes up for nothing?'

'Of course not. All I'm asking, Mom, is to give it just twenty-four hours. I have to talk to Treacy again and I don't want to present him with a *fait accompli*. I just want to make sure he really meant what he said, OK?'

'Oh, I'm sure he did, Sky. Don't worry.' Johanna's voice cleared happily. 'There's plenty of time. Do you think we should maybe paint the living room before she comes? It's a bit dingy, you know.'

Assuring her mother that they could discuss it that evening, Sky got rid of her and then for a long time sat staring at the silent telephone.

'Everything all right at home, Sky?' The kid looked over from the cabinet where she was replenishing the files from a small stack of new reports and publicity material.

'Everything's fine.' Sky snapped to attention and checked her watch. She was due at City Hall within five minutes.

The dreary interviews at the planning office took much longer than she had expected and it was after five when she got back to the office. The kid had left a Post-it note stuck to the telephone: *Mr Daniel Treacy called. Wants you to call him urgently.* Loath to let him set her agenda, Sky stared at the little yellow sticker. Then curiosity won the battle and she flipped open her contacts book.

She was put straight through, but all Treacy wanted, it

seemed, was to ask her if she had mentioned his invitation to her mother. Although his language was formal, even brusque, his tone was breathless and apprehensive.

She filled him in, fibbed that they had not yet been able to get in touch with the house in County Cork, and said she would pass on any developments. Then she asked for a further interview for her profile, assuring him that it would not take long and that all she needed was to flesh out a few details. After a brief pause he agreed, and they made an appointment. At her suggestion it was for the following Monday. That would give her a little time.

She hung up and, on impulse, crossed to Jimbo's office. Before she went careering off on what might well turn out to be a non-story and one that might embarrass the *Courier*, she decided to come clean. 'Busy?'

'Accountants!' Jimbo pushed the concertina of computer printouts away from him. 'You're working late for a Wednesday. What can I do for you?'

'It's Treacy, and this is confidential. I have a personal interest in it, too, so can I trust you?'

'Jesus! You've fallen for the guy!'

She looked at him in amazement: the thought was so incongruous and so far from the truth that it threw her completely. 'Of course not!'

'Sorry!' Jimbo waved her to a seat. 'It's all these numbers. Putrefy the brain.'

Sky took a deep breath. She told him about the long-ago love story and Treacy's invitation to her grandmother, the name-change after the death of her grandfather, letting the editor believe that Daniel Treacy had fled to the United States not only because of her grandfather's death but also because of a broken heart.

Then, as she moved on to the next phase and recounted the reasons for her unease about Midge Treacy's death, she saw the sceptical expression in Jimbo's eyes switch to one

106

she could not interpret and began to realize how ridiculous her theory sounded: other than linking the two deaths through Treacy, she had no basis for thinking that the automobile wreck was anything other than a tragic accident. 'Sorry,' she said limply at the end. 'Butte's finally got to me, I guess ... I know, I know, keep taking the pills, it's laughable. Sorry I've wasted your time.'

'Do you see me laughing?' Jimbo's face was impassive.

'You mean to say you think I might be right?' Sky was astounded.

'Not necessarily, but it's worth thinking about. I wasn't going to show you this until I saw your piece – you know how it's good to keep puzzle pieces separate until we've enough of 'em to put together in some sort of order – but take a looksee at this. Now, it's not exactly along the same lines as what you were just telling me, but what do you think?' From a drawer in his desk he took out a garish piece of paper and passed it over.

Across a set of four discount coupons for Folger's coffee, which had been torn from a magazine or weekend supplement, someone had scrawled, in lurid purple marker:

Ask Daniel Treacy about his prescious darlinge wifey
and the hobo she muredured. What kind of a
fuenereal did HE get? One Law four the Poor and
one four the Hog Muck Rich.
Signed,
Someone Onley Interesteded in Justise.
(One Of The Few.)

'How long have you had this?' Sky turned over the coupons to see if there was anything further on the back. There was not. 'A few days.' He was watching her closely. 'It came the day after the Treacy funeral.'

'How was it delivered?'

107

'By hand, in this.' Jimbo drew out a brown paper bottle bag addressed, in the same purple marker, with: *Edditor. Urjent.* Ironically, it bore the name of the liquor store owned by Greg's father. Sky recognized it not for this, however, but because it was the same bag that the junior had held over the trash can and that she had diverted into Jimbo's office.

Over the years, the *Courier*, like every newspaper in the world, had received its share of anonymous so-called tip-offs, which invariably proved to be the products of insane or revenge-filled minds. Sky figured this was one of those; even way out in the boonies, where Treacy's wife spent her time, a murder was unlikely to go unreported. 'Anyone remember who delivered it?' She passed the coupons back across the desk.

'Apparently the guy was black.' Jimbo put them and the makeshift envelope back into the drawer. 'Or, to be more accurate, that air-head out there thinks he *might* have been black but, knowing her, he might just have been dirty.' He shrugged in resignation.

'Oh, come on,' Sky felt she had to defend the kid out of female solidarity, 'she's not that bad. If he is black, he shouldn't be too difficult to track down.' African Americans were generally thin on the ground in Montana. She peered at her boss. 'You're taking this one seriously, aren't you? What have you heard?'

'I'm not sure.' He closed his drawer as gently as if it were made of Sèvres china. 'And I haven't heard anything, honest. Normally I wouldn't read something like this twice, as you know, but—'

'But what?'

'You sure you hadn't heard anything about the wife before now?' Jimbo was wearing his faraway look, which always meant his brain was trawling at high speed.

'Look,' she was getting impatient, 'the woman never registered with me until she died. Why should she? All right, she was a recluse – to each her own – but the only thing that could possibly go against Midge Treacy's unblemished character was that she apparently took a few drinks now and then.'

'I see.'

'Jim, I'm due home, I'm going into overtime now.'

'It was more than a few drinks.'

Instantly, Sky remembered Daniel Treacy's reaction when she had asked about his dead wife's health. 'So what?' she countered. 'I gathered from people I spoke to when I was writing the piece that that was all in the past.'

'I'm not so sure.' Jimbo stared at her. 'I heard the woman was a lush. Big time. By all accounts we're not talking amateur here but world-class. And not in the far distant past either but right up to her death.'

'But that message on the coupons talks about murder,' Sky argued. 'Drunks rarely commit murder. They're too interested in getting tanked, Jim. And, more especially still, drunks with as much money as Mrs Daniel Treacy don't need to kill to get their hands on a hobo's bottle of wine.'

The editor's expression did not change. 'Keep your eyes and ears open – and a call to the Mayville cops mightn't be a bad idea. Why don't you fly up there tomorrow? Maybe call in on Libby too. Check it out. I've to finish this for the accountants by six o'clock tomorrow evening,' he waved a disparaging hand at the printouts, 'or I'd go up there myself. I have my own theory as to what happened but I'd like to see what you come up with.'

Sky sighed. 'For God's sake, Jim, the woman's dead—' Then she stopped, her reporter's instincts sparking up. If Daniel Treacy's wife had killed someone during her lifetime, the bagatelle of her death was no bar to a great story. 'What's your theory?'

'Not yet.'

She tried for five minutes but Jim refused to yield another

iota of information or even guesswork. 'Better you get it for yourself. As I said before, I don't want to influence you.' She had to settle for this.

Back at her desk, she tried to see the potential story from as many angles as she could. If Midge Treacy had been involved in something illegal, that was big news for a newspaper like the *Courier*. But if Treacy himself knew and had used his money to hush it up, that would be sensational. Sky was punching the number for Libby Information when she remembered that her mother and her grandmother were personally involved in this. But she did not hang up.

Chapter Nine

Surrounded by thick forest, Libby is a pleasant little city, its low-slung buildings and wide parkways typical of most conurbations in Montana where space is a commodity always in plentiful supply. It is also a Godfearing place, with gaggles of sparkling clapboard churches and chapels setting out their wares on discreet noticeboards. As she came in from the little airfield in the rental car, Sky noted the billboards and banners advertising the city's centenary year and took a note that it might be worth a feature some time.

As she had passed through a few times before on her way to visit her father, she knew the layout of the city and found the county sheriff's office with little difficulty. The young deputy at the front desk was casual but friendly. He did a cursory check on the computer files, and told Sky that as far as he knew, no hobo had been found dead in Libby in the past few months. 'You say it could even be a murder? You'd need to check with the troopers and the feds.' He let his gaze fall to the white linen V over her cleavage.

'That's our information.' Sky willed her hands not to fly to her blouse buttons. 'And I thought I could short-circuit a little. You know how the feds are . . .' but as she went on to tell him that the tip-off had been anonymous, she could see he was far more interested in her body than in her story. She took a breath. 'I'd appreciate it, officer, if you'd listen rather than look.'

His neck suffused with colour as he turned again to the

keyboard in front of him. When next he spoke his voice was prim: 'I can assure you, ma'am, that as far as Libby is concerned you're wasting your time. We have investigated no murders of homeless persons this year.'

She asked him then about the accident at Mayville that had killed Midge Treacy.

'I'm not sure we handled that. Are the two events connected, ma'am?' He forgot his embarrassment and was instantly alert.

'No, not as far as I know at present,' she became conciliatory, 'but they might be. Our informant seemed to hint that they were. I'd sure appreciate some help on this one – my editor will not be amused if I arrive back with zilch.' She saw that he was still smarting and smiled brilliantly at him. '*Quid pro quo* – could I buy you lunch? Where's the best place in town?'

After some cajoling, he thawed and, although he refused lunch, agreed to drive her out to the scene of the accident when he knocked off duty an hour later.

She filled in the time by having a cup of coffee in a motel and then taking a stroll through the park-cum-graveyard behind it. After the break in the weather, the heat was building up again and, conserving her energy, she sat on a bench to watch the comings and goings at a block of apartments nearby – obviously custom-built for senior citizens since zimmer frames were much in evidence and no one she saw seemed a day under seventy.

Sky hoped death would take her quickly and not let her linger on until parts of her fell irreparably into dysfunction like pieces of old mosaic peeling off the façade of a building. She thought about Midge Treacy. Had alcohol made her unsteady and feeble? Had she been drunk that night? After the post-mortem nothing had been said in the papers about the alcohol content of her blood.

Autopsy. Try as she might, Sky could recall nothing about

it; she reached for her tape-recorder and made a note to check into the medical examiner's report.

Mayville was about twelve miles from Libby. The deputy found a safe place to pull off and park when they were still quarter of a mile away from the place where the Volvo had plunged off the highway. Montana Power was stringing wires along the route and while the road crew slung the cable across the road ahead, traffic was temporarily halted in both directions.

Sky and her escort got out of the car and climbed the steep gradient along the line of stalled vehicles, many of whose drivers were shooting the breeze while they waited for the delay to clear. The two-lane road had been cut into the side of a wooded mountain; the trees towered from the bluff to the left but on the sheer drop to the right, the ferny tips were well below them.

A knot of people stood at the accident site, which was the apogee of a sharp bend, just ahead of where the utility workers had pitched their cherry pickers.

Volvo or no, Treacy's wife had not stood a chance.

Sky and the deputy joined the group, exchanged good-natured banter about the inefficiency of utility companies, and then Sky moved a little away. The quick growth of summer had not yet healed the scars of Midge Treacy's death. Hundreds of feet below where Sky now stood, a wide, irregular brown stain marred the dense symmetry of green. No wonder the casket had been closed, she thought. The Volvo had evidently burst into flames when it hit. She examined the highway: no tyre tracks or skid marks, no twisted metal or even a single glint from the smallest shard of glass.

'Seen enough?' The deputy came over to her.

'Something strange here. If she hit the logging truck, surely it's odd that, even after a clean-up, there isn't even the tiniest piece of debris around—'

'Who said she hit the truck?'

'I assumed—'

'As far as I know, she just cut in front of him and off.' He made aeroplane gestures with his hands. 'He pulled up and called for help. He got a fright but there was no contact between them.'

Sky searched her memory for the precise wording of the newspaper reports. The deputy was right: none had mentioned collision. Now the conclusion seemed obvious: Midge Treacy had driven straight across the bend and off. It was so dangerous she need not even have been drunk.

She felt sympathy for the unfortunate logger. 'How about the truck driver?' she asked. 'You say he got a fright – I'd say it was more like cardiac arrest. He was on the side of the drop, after all – a split second more and he would have gone over too.'

'Yeah.' The deputy was looking at his watch. 'These guys are good though. They might seem to be reckless but they're always on the watch for renegades. Now if there's nothing more?'

Sky thought rapidly. It looked as though her journey was wasted. She was not ready to relinquish the story just yet, however. 'But what about debris? There aren't even any skid or tyre marks.' She peered again at the road. 'Don't you think that's a bit strange?'

'Lady, this is a bad bend – a *bad* bend.'

'But it looks as though she didn't even try to stop.' Sky paused. Could the Volvo's brakes have been tampered with?

'She'd had two previous accidents, miss.'

'Who came up to this one?' Sky saw he was becoming impatient.

'State troopers, I guess.'

'Who in the state troopers? Could you give me a name?'

'Don't rightly know. I was on vacation. It was probably

some of the brass. The Treacy name is big in Montana and brass attracts brass.'

'Don't I know it. Did they bring the ambulance crew? Did she go to the local hospital or straight to Butte?'

'I can check when we get back. Look, Miss MacPherson, I really better get goin'. My wife don't like it if I'm not home afternoons. She sees little enough of me as it is.'

'Sure. Sorry. Just one more thing, where's the wreck?'

'They're usually brought in to Deke 'n' Skippy's Auto. If you like, I'll show you where it is when we go back through Mayville.'

'OK.' Sky let it rest for the moment, then, 'Thanks. But maybe you should let me off in Mayville? I'll call into the auto shop but I'd also like to make a few enquries of the police there.'

The Mayville cop shop was similar to many Sky had seen before, not dingy, not smart. Utilitarian – that was the word, she thought, as she waited for a subordinate to fetch Sheriff Brian O'Connor who, she was told, had come to the scene of Mrs Treacy's accident. On one of the desks by the window, the base of an electric fan was in contact with a metal filing tray and was making a tremendous racket; she moved it slightly, then stood in front of the cooling draught.

'May I help you?'

Wheeling round, Sky instantly hated the man she saw standing a few feet away in front of the door into an inner office. It was chemical hatred, the type that flares for no reason. She judged him to be in his mid to late fifties and, despite his name, he seemed almost Latin in appearance, with over-full lips, eyes of a nondescript hazel, and black, oiled hair groomed without a parting. His belly strained the flimsy material of his shirt but, for all that, his forearms and

115

shoulders were well muscled and he moved as though he worked out. Slung prominently low on the pants of his uniform, his gun rode his fleshy hip like a monstrous excrescence and, overall, the sheriff gave the impression that he would be a person with whom it would be unwise to tangle.

'I sure hope you can help me, sheriff.' She introduced herself and smiled with what she hoped was disarming sweetness.

But he interrupted: 'Is there a problem?'

'I'm not sure.' Sky was not going to let him take over: it was time for a little dissembling. 'You see, my newspaper is running a series of articles on road fatalities—'

Again he interrupted, 'To what purpose?'

She attempted to stare him down, with no success. Then: 'It's a newspaper, sheriff. We run stories we believe will interest our readers.'

He did not react to her sarcasm. 'You the one that wrote the obituary on Mrs Treacy?' Despite his name his accent bore no trace of Ireland, rather the flattened vowels of the Midwest; he had to be second or third generation. He sat behind his desk, shuffled up a handful of pistachio nuts from a dish beside his telephone and started to crack them open with a thumbnail.

'Yes, that was me.' She decided, after all, that it would be in her interest to let him run the show.

But if she was expecting a comment on her literary style, or even on the factual content of the obit, she was disappointed. He said nothing, just loosened his belt a notch and opened a drawer in his desk, searching through the papers inside. 'What's your interest in the dead lady?' He looked up as though the question had only now occurred to him.

'I told you—'

'Yeah, yeah! You told me – road fatalities. But how come it's *this* wreck you find so fascinating?'

116

Sky had been expecting either co-operation or stonewalling, not an interrogation. 'I've been working on a profile of Mrs Treacy's husband, as it happens. It's to be a major piece—'

'What happened to the road fatalities?'

'If you would let me finish a sentence, sheriff, I was going to say that the two pieces are connected only by coincidence. Reporters work on more than one story at a time, as I'm sure you're aware.'

'Treacy's co-operating with your story?' His eyes were now as immobile as a basking lizard's, and he seemed to have forgotten whatever it was he had sought in the drawer. Sky could not figure out what he was at. She nodded assent to his question, then, in an attempt to win him over, smiled again. 'It's quite a scoop for my paper, but I wouldn't say, sheriff, that he's co-operating exactly. It's more like he's putting up with me. He has spoken to me. Do you know him?'

His features relaxed slowly. 'Who doesn't?' he muttered, resuming his search.

Sky waited, unwilling to antagonize him further. As she watched him leaf through the papers, the suspicion niggled at her that she had seen this man somewhere else. Before she could work it out, he snapped the drawer shut and locked it. 'It's not here.'

'Were you looking for something in connection with the accident?'

'My report from that night.'

'It's not in the computer?' Sky flicked a glance towards the purring monitor on the man's desk.

'Not yet.'

She did not bother to ask why not. She was tired of this guy. 'Here's my telephone number.' She fished in her purse and gave him the standard-issue business card with its blue-and-white *Courier* logo. I would appreciate it if you would give me a call as soon as you find your report.'

117

He took the card without comment and she knew that dinosaurs would lay eggs again in Montana before he would call her. But she wanted to cut her losses now, to get out of this man's office. Perhaps the truck driver would be more help.

It was only when she was outside that Sky remembered that she had not asked him about the hobo.

She had even less luck with the logging company, drawing a blank when she called the human resources manager in the firm's Helena headquarters. After what seemed like an interminable delay she was told that the driver in question was off duty and it was not company policy to give out home addresses or telephone numbers. 'When will he be back at work?' She was finding it difficult to continue to sound sweet: this whole exercise was turning out to be a bummer.

'One moment, please.' The line went dead and she had to insert four more quarters into the coin slot. Jimbo was going to hear about this: budget constraints or not this was the last time she went out of town without a mobile telephone – she had been campaigning for one for months.

The manager came back on the line with news that did not improve her temper. The truck driver had taken some vacation and was not expected to return for a week.

After another fruitless hour spent in the mortuary of the local newspaper, where she found only mirror-images of the *Courier*'s own coverage of the story and obits, Sky found she had a headache and decided she needed a coffee top-up. A bell jangled as she pulled open the glass door of the nearest coffee-shop, a wood-and-chequered emporium with café curtains and smiley faces painted on the windows. Immediately, she saw she had company. A high-school couple held hands across a table in a booth on one side of the room, but in a corner, Sheriff Brian O'Connor and another officer in a deputy's uniform were hunched over glasses of iced tea. At the sound of the doorbell, both turned round. O'Connor returned Sky's glance with a look that could have felled a moose. Then he twisted towards the lunch counter where the waitress – big hair, violet eyeshadow and a bosom that defied the attempts of her pink gingham uniform to subdue it – was filling sugar dispensers. 'Hey, Velma,' he called loudly, 'you layin' those eggs?'

'Keep your britches on, they're comin'.' The waitress continued serenely about her task.

Sky slid into a seat on the unoccupied side of the shop and outside the sheriff's line of vision.

'What's your pleasure, honey?' The waitress came out from behind the counter and plonked a glass of iced water in front of her on the 'rustic' wooden table.

'Just coffee, please, black.'

While she waited for her order, Sky reviewed her single page of notes. Until the police report from that night showed up, the only thing new she had learned from this sorry expedition was that Midge Treacy's Volvo had gone over the cliff all by itself.

'Here y'are, honey, black as the heart of Satan!' The waitress was back with the coffee jug. Her spectacular cleavage trembling, only a few inches from Sky's nose, she flipped over a cup and filled it. 'You on vacation?'

'No, just passing through.'

'Shame,' the waitress cleared off the rest of the place setting, 'it's pretty around here.'

'Velma!' O'Connor glared across at her.

'You're on my patch now, sheriff. She smiled complicitously at Sky and threw her eyes to heaven. 'Men and their stomachs!' White nurse's shoes squelching on the floor, she walked off towards the serving hatch between the lunch counter and the kitchen, calling, 'You want another soda there, kids?' as she passed the lovestruck teenagers.

As Sky watched her hold sway in her small domain, it

struck her that if anyone knew of a murdered hobo anywhere around Mayville or Libby it would be Velma. She waited it out until the sheriff and his sidekick, ignoring her, got up and left the shop. She noticed they left without paying.

Chapter Ten

Sky called the waitress, who had sat in the booth with the teenagers.

'Sure thing, ma'am, more coffee?' Velma collected the coffee jug and brought it over.

'Thank you.' Sky introduced herself.

'A reporter, huh? I thought so.' Velma indicated the spiral-bound notebook, which did not appear to impress her. 'What can I do for you, honey?'

Sky came straight to the point. 'I was wondering, Velma – you don't mind if I call you Velma?'

'Don't answer to nothin' else!'

'I was wondering if you'd heard anything about any unusual death around here recently. Probably a hobo. Has any stranger died lately in suspicious circumstances up this part of the state?'

The waitress used her free hand to puff out her hair to even bigger proportions as she thought. 'Suspicious circumstances? You mean murder, suicide, that kind of thing?'

'That's right.'

'Not that I can think of,' Velma said at last, 'unless you mean old Leon.'

'Old Leon?'

'Yeah, we're not even sure that's his real name. He was found dead up on the side of the highway, poor old guy, but that certainly weren't no murder or suicide. That was, let me see—' Velma raised her voice and called to the teenagers,

'You kids hear anything about old Leon being murdered? Anything like that?'

'Not me,' the girl piped up. 'My dad said he musta froze to death.'

'Drank himself to death, more like.' The boy sniggered.

Sky knew that once she had a name it would help in getting the other information. 'This man, Leon, he was homeless, was he?' She flipped over a page in her notebook and included the teenagers in the question. 'How did you know him?'

'But I told you,' Velma objected, 'that weren't no murder or suicide – sure the guy drunk a bit—'

'That doesn't matter for now.' Sky sat with pen poised over the virgin page. 'Did he used to come in here?'

'Yeah, we never knew when to expect him. He'd no teeth, and Vern back there,' she indicated the invisible chef behind the hatch, 'used to make him special meals he didn't have to chew, eggs sunny side with mashed potato, corned beef hash, stuff like that, y'know?'

'Tell me about his death.'

'Well, I don't know too much.' The waitress sat in the seat opposite Sky. 'All I heard is he was found by the highway. By the sheriff, as a matter of fact, it was him brought the poor old guy in. I think the kids are right. He probably froze. You know, a few drinks, lie down for a little sleep . . .'

'But if it's spring . . .'

Velma considered this. 'Yeah, but spring nights up this far north can be cold sometimes. You never heard of eupathermia?'

Sky forbore to correct her. 'If he was found beside the highway, could he have been hit by an automobile?'

'Weren't a mark on him. So the sheriff said anyhow. That right, kids?' Velma hollered at the pair. 'You two hear anything different?'

122

'Uh-huh.' The teenagers left their own seats and came to sit at the table opposite Sky's booth. 'My dad knows the sheriff, says the sheriff told him several of old Leon's toes were almost fallen off.' The girl was pretty, in a cheerleader way, until she opened her mouth and showed severe overbite. 'Is this going to be on TV?'

'I'm only a newspaper reporter, I'm afraid.' Sky fished out three business cards and handed them round. 'You sure the sheriff was the one found him?'

'Sure thing! Not much pie around here Brian O'Connor don't have a finger in.' Velma put the card in the pocket of her uniform and hitched up her cleavage until it rested more comfortably on the table-top.

Since Sheriff O'Connor had also found himself at the scene of Midge Treacy's death, Sky's conviction was beginning to grow that she was glimpsing some of Jimbo Larsen's so-far-disconnected puzzle pieces. 'Tell me a bit more about this Leon.' She sipped her coffee. 'I know he was a hobo and he had no teeth, but how old was he? How did you all know him? And can any of you remember where he was found?'

They all knew to within a few hundred yards where on the highway the body had been found but, for the rest of it, old Leon's personal details proved sketchy. None of the three knew how old he was – he was just known around town as old Leon and could have been anything from forty-five to seventy-five. He was a long-haired tramp of inoffensive temperament and relatively discreet drinking habits, who had been coming through Libby at no particular time of year and at no regular interval for years. 'Spring, summer, fall, any time,' the boy volunteered. 'My mom used to give him my old sneakers.' From what they could remember, old Leon, who never stayed around more than a couple of days, could have stood anything from five feet six to six feet. 'He was sorta hunched over,' this from the girl.

He walked with a shuffle and had blue eyes or maybe grey

or maybe light brown. 'Couldn't tell, but then no one looked overmuch.' Velma eased herself out of the booth and went to fetch more coffee.

'Where is he buried?' Sky thought she might find another puzzle piece if she could establish the tramp's last name.

'Don't even know if the poor guy had a funeral. Maybe Vern could help – HEY, VERN!' Sky fancied she saw cups rattle with the ferocity of the yell. Too late, she realized the hobo was unlikely to have a headstone.

Vern, thin as a rod and a perfect foil to Velma's opulence, knew little more than the others and, figuring she had gleaned all pickings in the coffee-shop, Sky declined a further refill and got up to leave.

'This going to be on TV?' It was Vern's turn to ask.

'I've told you all I know.' Sheriff O'Connor's thick brows now all but concealed his eyes.

Sky would have put her last dollar on a bet that he was concealing something important. 'And thank you for that, sheriff, but could I ask you something else, please, that I meant to ask you when I was in before. It was you found Old Leon, wasn't it?'

If she had not been watching so closely, she would have missed the brief flicker through the dark eyes. 'If you're back to your road fatalities, Mizz MacPherson,' he brushed something from the surface of the desk into the palm of his hand, 'you're on the wrong track.' With care, he deposited the contents of his palm into the trash can beside his desk and looked back at her. 'That vagrant died of drink and exposure.'

Sky saw that somehow she had rattled him. She pressed her advantage: 'It's just that . . .' Then intuition kicked in again. With this man she had to be cautious. 'Oh, never mind, it's not important.'

'Oh, but it is, Mizz MacPherson. You have a theory, perhaps? Were you about to tell me that you thought old Leon's demise was in some way connected with Mrs Treacy's accident?'

'Just something else flashed through my mind. Nothing at all to do with this story. I've been very busy lately.'

He scribbled a telephone number on a message pad, tore it off and handed it across the desk. 'I'd like to be kept informed, Mizz MacPherson. It's in all our interests that the number of – ah – road fatalities be brought down.'

'Of course, sheriff.' As she took the piece of paper, she saw that flicker again. 'My newspaper is always anxious to help the law. Catch you later.'

He nodded and picked up the handset on his desk.

Outside, Sky paused outside the sheriff's office and shook her head as though to dislodge something unpleasant from her hair. She saw the pair of teenagers from the coffee-shop walking slowly along the opposite side of the street – the boy slouching self-consciously, the girl animated and graceful – and was jealous: those kids could write whatever they liked on the blank page of their lives. They had it all ahead of them.

'You wired, Mizz MacPherson?'

Sky jumped. She had not realized she had spoken aloud – or she had been followed outside – until she heard the sheriff's voice at her shoulder. 'No, I'm not, and I'd thank you not to sneak up on me like that. You startled me.'

'You sure you're not wearing a wire?'

'You want to search me?' She faced down his stare until he turned on his heel and went back inside.

Deke 'n' Skippy's Auto (*You Bend'm We Mend'm*) spread itself over a littered half-acre behind a chain-link fence on the outskirts of Mayville.

Deke was absent but Skippy proved tall and rangy – and about as talkative as basenji. On seeing Sky's press ID, he scratched his freckled scalp as he considered her request to view the Volvo wreck. 'I dunno,' he said at last.

'Why not?'

Another eternity of indecision as he looked at the ground, then at the clouds. 'Sheriff say it's OK?' he asked eventually.

'I didn't ask him. What's the harm in just looking? Would you like me to go to his office and ask him if it'd be OK? I'm sure he wouldn't mind – but I'm on a tight schedule . . .' Sky, who saw no reason to reveal that she had already encountered the man who seemed to run everything in Mayville, smiled and touched his arm. The gentlest, most 'trust-me' of touches.

'I dunno.' This time, however, Skippy dared to meet her eyes. 'Maybe.'

'Thanks a bunch.' Sky did not wait for him to make up his mind. 'I won't be a moment. If you'd just point it out?'

Silently, he pointed a bony finger in the direction of the far corner of the compound. Then: 'She's silver. Or was. Pity. She weren't more'n two weeks old.' Skippy pursed his lips, as though he had said too much. Sky might have suspected he was hiding something if she had not already categorized him as one of Mayville's least voluble citizens. She turned her attention to the car.

The snub-nosed frame that sat on its four wheel-pods, although bent, was still recognizably a Volvo but the fire-blackened frame was no longer silver and it was missing any shred of glass, cloth or rubber; Sky touched it and flakes of black snow fell on to the ground. She peered inside: all that was left were twists of iron, a few bolts and a stalk that had once been a steering column.

Realizing she had been expecting some revelation or clue from looking at the wreck, she was disappointed. Nothing

126

could be deduced from this sad black hulk, drowsing in the sunny ordinariness of the Montana summer afternoon.

A plane droned overhead as she walked round the wreck, trying to determine if she was overlooking anything. She glanced up at the plane and, out of the corner of her eye, caught a flash. She looked towards it and saw Skippy: he was facing in her direction while talking into a mobile telephone. She had no idea what had caused the flash, perhaps his watch. And although she had no proof that he was talking about her, the goosebumps rose on her forearms.

Skippy knew more than he pretended.

'Hi, Skippy!' She went over to him, waving and smiling brightly. Seeing her come, he terminated the call and put the telephone in his pocket. Too quickly. He looked uncomfortable when she reached him. 'Thanks a lot.' Sky maintained her breezy façade. 'You were right, Skip, not much to see, I'm afraid.'

'Sure.'

'Well, any time you're in Butte,' she pulled out one of her cards, 'you just give me a call. As it happens, I'm in the market for a good second-hand compact.'

'Is that so?' The mechanic's relief was comical.

'Nothing too fancy, a VW or a Hyundai or another little Japanese, maybe? They don't pay me too good down there in Butte. You got anything right now?'

'I don't do the sellin'. That there's Deke's department.'

'Deke your boss?'

'We're partners.' Skippy's face gleamed with pride.

'Well, now you and I are acquainted, Skip,' Sky felt that in all compassion she could not put him through much more, 'you be sure and tell Deke I'm interested, OK?'

'You bet.'

As he took the card, putting it into the breast pocket of his coverall without reading it, Sky scribbled Deke's name

127

into her notebook. 'Just a couple more things, Skip.' She beamed brighter than a lighthouse. 'Is there any way of knowing what the condition of the brakes of this thing were like before she took off on her sailing trip?'

Skippy looked desperately from the wreck to Sky and back again. 'Nope,' he said uncertainly. 'Leastways, I don't rightly think so. I gotta go.'

'Yeah. Sorry to take up so much of your time. I suppose that was the law you were on to there on the telephone? To say there was a pesky woman reporter looking at the wreck. Were you told to report in if someone showed an interest?'

Skippy's expression was now of pure terror. 'I gotta go,' he repeated, almost breaking into a run as he hurried away from her.

Back in Butte, Fergus Lynskey was sauntering towards the registered office of the *Courier*. Mizz R. Sky MacPherson had been a revelation to him: he had recognized her on the instant he had seen her emerging from her car outside the hotel. Despite the fey picture in the paper he had expected a termagant – these women reporters always were. Yet R. Sky MacPherson was so beautiful she stopped his heart. As dishevelled as though she had been pulled backwards through a bush, she nevertheless exuded sexuality: even her carelessly combed tomboyish hair had glowed with it. He refused to think about it.

To say that Fergus's love life was no great shakes was an understatement. He took full blame for the shambles of his marriage. He had loved his wife, an air hostess with Aer Lingus, to distraction. But the pull of their jobs, both involving long periods away from home, had stretched their love so thinly it had snapped. Their separation had not been angry – rather, it had been puzzled, as though neither quite knew what was happening or why. But for him the result had been catastrophic.

For a short period after they parted he had played games with himself, kidding himself that it was wonderful to be free again. He became a regular patron of Dublin's subterranean late-night dance-clubs and wine-bars along Leeson Street, dancing, inhaling cigarette smoke, drinking indigestible and overpriced wine, even having the odd joint or two. Getting off occasionally with long-legged, blonde-haired girls with angels' faces.

Once, however, just before the four o'clock dawn of high summer, he had tottered out as usual to chase after a taxi, of which there were never enough. An hour later, he was still waiting, his back sore from leaning against a set of railings. The street glowed with gentle light, dimming the blue of the quietly revolving roof lights of the Gárda car on watch. It was not the first time he had been here at dawn but he saw, as though it was the first time, the empty chip bags that eddied around his feet, the pools of vomit that stained the footpaths; and although frantic inebriation was part of the scene, he was now repelled by the sight of a drunken girl, barefoot, kohl streaming down her cheeks like a pair of sooty rivers, being helped along the street by two equally drunken youths.

He sobered up. For the first time, he saw the seediness of the cave-like existence he had led, where he had been feeding chat-up lines not only to women of his own age – some still defiantly wearing their wedding rings – but to girls young enough still to be at school. Now he saw not fun but an entire street glittering with suppressed unhappiness. Relieved, he gave up going there.

This was not to say he was entirely celibate. Dublin was overflowing with available women, lonely civil servants and bank clerks from the country, girls attending night-time carpentry and mechanics' courses in the techs in hope of meeting men – only to find a preponderance of women like themselves. In pubs and rugby clubs and hotel bars, women everywhere were on the prowl and, now and then, Lynskey, hating himself, went home with one, usually to some bedsitter or flat as dingy as his own. He always tried to sew silk purses from these encounters, arranging to meet the girl again, hoping against hope that this one might be different. It never was.

Then he heard his wife was pregnant and the thought of her having a baby without him sliced him open. Less than six months after he had split up with her she had taken up with an accountant, with whom she now lived happily in a Dublin suburb. Her new life of tennis clubs and coffee mornings was far removed from her modest existence with Lynskey. Although he wished her well, he could not bear to think about her having a child that should have been his.

While growing up, he had always imagined himself settling down in a ramshackle house like his own in Kerry, a house rattling with hordes of children. He was the youngest of ten siblings, six boys, four girls, whose father had died when the eldest in the family was just fourteen. His mother, now retired, had been a national schoolteacher, and she had had to struggle hard to bring them up on her own.

It had been a struggle with a successful outcome. Now they were spread all over the world: London, Canada, Germany, Saudi Arabia, Tanzania, the Philippines. Six were married – seven if Lynskey was to be counted – three, a priest and two nuns, were celibate by choice. His mother had eighteen grandchildren and four great-grandchildren.

Lynskey had married in high hopes of adding to this number but his ex-wife's pregnancy seemed to seal off for ever his own chances for the life he had always assumed he would have and he shut down his heart. He became a good policeman, always the first to volunteer for night work or the

130

messiest assignments. And although he did not give up women, he gave up hopes of love and family. Ever since, he had projected the cynical self-confidence that the world admires yet does not like. Except in the minds of the only two intimates in his life – his mother and his friend, Bill Daly – who both knew the truth about him, to his co-workers and acquaintances he was a clever, smart-assed git.

The office of the *Butte Courier* was located in a nondescript, flat-topped building of only one storey, indistinguishable from its neighbours except for the lettering on its glass front door.

'Can I help you?'

Lynskey's eyes widened as a gorgeous creature, with legs so spectacular she could have modelled tights, looked up from the open drawer of a filing cabinet and spoke to him. Did this place breed these women? 'I'm looking for R. Sky MacPherson.' He kept his eyes firmly on the girl's face.

'I'm sorry,' her voice was breathy, 'but Sky is not available right now. Could I take a message?' This was delivered singsong, as though learned by rote.

'No message, I'll catch up with her.' He leaned confidentially on the front desk. 'I'm an old friend from Ireland. Do you know where she'd be?'

'Ireland, huh?' The girl looked doubtful. 'Well, I'm not sure I should be telling you this, but she did say she had to go to a barbecue tonight. This one.' She picked a leaflet from an in-tray on the top of the filing cabinet and gave it to him. Crudely printed, it advertised a fund-raising event for a sick little girl in a local high school.

Chapter Eleven

On her return from Libby, Sky, who had promised to accompany her mother to a benefit to raise money for a child who needed liver treatment in the Mayo Clinic, was so whacked after the events of the day that she asked to be excused. But she perished as usual on the twin spears of Johanna's cornflower eyes.

'OK, OK.' She threw up her hands in capitulation. 'But I'm not staying long. Hermana or Buffy can give you a ride home.'

The event was being held in the parking lot of the local Catholic school and, while it was relatively well attended, the lot was so vast that by huddling within range of the heat emanating from the row of home barbecues commandeered for the occasion, the crowd made itself look smaller than it was and the atmosphere felt flat.

Sky hated small-town small-talk and hung back, happy enough to stand alone in the shadows by the wall of the school building. She was peering without enthusiasm at the blackened hamburger and wilted shreds of coleslaw on her paper plate, and wondering how soon she could decently leave, when she was joined by a very tall, very skinny man.

'It's the soot I like.'

'Beg pardon?' Sky was taken aback. If this was a joke, the man's expression showed no sign of humour as he bit into his own burger. Then she recognized the eagle's-beak nose.

This was the Irishman who had held open the door for her at the War Bonnet.

'Soot. I like it.' He held the hamburger up to the nearest light – a security fitment on to which some optimist had taped a coloured gel. 'What about yourself?'

'You're not following me, I hope?' She could not remember what he had been wearing on their first encounter, but tonight, as though his accent were not enough, he was advertising his nationality on a washed-out sweatshirt that declared his love of Guinness. 'Yep. You got it in one. I'm not following you. This is a public event, isn't it?' He juggled plate and plastic fork and stuck out his right hand. 'Fergus Lynskey.'

Sky shook it. 'Sky MacPherson.'

'That's quite a moniker.' He whistled as they shook hands. 'And I know who you are now. You're that famous reporter. I'm pleased to meet you.' He popped the last of the hamburger into his mouth. 'Nice state you have here, Miss MacPherson. I've always loved the Rocky Mountains. You're from around here yourself?'

'Sort of.' Sky was unused to a man with such breezy self-confidence. The effect she usually had on men was to render them shy. 'Do you know them well? The Rockies?'

'From books.' He pronounced it 'bewks' and, despite herself, Sky had to suppress a delighted smile. 'This your first time in Montana?'

'Or anywhere west of Manhattan.'

'I'm Irish—' Then Sky, annoyed with herself, moved quickly to correct any erroneous impression he might have that she wore shamrocks in her hair on St Patrick's Day. 'At least, my mother and her family are Irish. I was born over here. But I'm not at all famous, I'm afraid.'

'It's not a crime to be Irish, you know,' he grinned, 'and you are famous. I've been reading your stuff in the local rag. And you've got your picture over your byline. In my book that's famous. Tell us about the name, why don't you? What does the R stand for?'

Once again, Sky found herself confessing her real name. And, once again, the revelation prompted not ridicule, merely another whistle. 'No wonder.' Lynskey dumped his paper plate into a nearby container. 'I can see why you wouldn't want to go through life with *that* hanging around your neck.'

This was such a refreshing change from the customary reaction – people usually tried to come up with something jocose or, even, words of comfort – that Sky found herself taking to him. 'Glad you think so.' She trashed her own plate and its untouched load. 'What do you do?'

'Secondary teacher – you'd call it high school. I do it solely because of the holidays. In Ireland we get three and a half whole months off in the summer. If that's not a solecism.' His long face lightened up as he grinned, showing good, if uneven, teeth. 'Now if only we had the weather.'

'Solecism, eh? You're a teacher, all right. Yeah, I hear the weather can be a bit capricious over there.' Sky grinned back.

'"Capricious"? *Touché*, R. Sky MacPherson. Must write that down.'

'That's enough, Mr Lynskey. What do you teach?'

'A shower of reprobates and chancers! Actually, I teach Irish and religion. Irish teachers usually get landed with religion. They seem to go together at home. Like Mutt and Jeff.'

Sky was charmed. 'Lynskey. *That's* not an Irish name if I'm not mistaken.'

'You are indeed. It is very much an Irish name. And I'm from a very Irish county. Kerry.'

'You and my mother are – were – neighbours, then. She's from the western part of Cork.' She pointed to where the Bliss Sisters were presiding over the coffee urns. 'That's near Kerry, isn't it?'

134

'In a manner of speaking. In many ways, there are no two counties which are further apart.' He held up his hand. 'Don't ask. It would take centuries to explain that. Suffice it to say that the inter-county rivalry in that part of the world can sometimes make the Trojan wars seem like a bunfight. Which one's your mother?'

'The one with all the colours.'

'What a marvellous woman!' He sounded sincere and for once Sky did not feel the need to explain Johanna's odd attire. Tonight, she was wearing one of Freda Little Calf's deerskin outfits, complete with head-band, neck thongs and cross-gartering. It was decorated with beading and fringes and little silver bells and over it she had thrown a cotton shawl in vivid reds and blues, which she had kept from her days of psychedelia.

'Marvellous might be a bit strong . . .' But Sky found herself looking at her mother and the other Bliss Sisters through this stranger's eyes. She was so used to apologizing for them – to herself and to others – that she was surprised to find that this man could be right. She outlined a brief history of the Sisters and her mother's relationship with them.

Lynskey listened easily, making no effort to sound those approving 'm-mm's and 'really?'s, which bedevil getting-to-know-you conversations, and Sky was suddenly enjoying herself. Apart from Jimbo, this was the first man she had met for years whose conversation might offer more than sport, the price of wheat, automobiles, cattle or real estate.

'Would you care for some coffee?' She heard the first tentative tunings of the Catholic school band, always a signal that the meal was over and that the entertainment was about to begin. She wanted very much to continue talking to this man.

'Never drink the stuff. Rots the stomach lining. Any tea, by any chance?' Fergus Lynskey settled himself comfortably

135

against the wall as if he had lived in this parking lot all his life and was accustomed to being waited on by women he had known for ten minutes.

Sky was so used to men reacting sexually to her – or at least to her minor celebrity – that his self-possession and confidence were exhilarating. She hurried off and practically tore a paper cup of hot water and a tea-bag out of her mother's hands. 'What's the rush?' Under the coloured lights strung around the barbecue area, Johanna's eyes were sparkling. She was always at her best at these charity functions.

'No rush.' Sky's own good humour was bubbling to the surface and made her reckless. 'It's not for me. See that man over there?'

Johanna turned round and looked to where Lynskey lounged against the wall. 'Which one?'

'Don't stare, Mom. The tall one – the one with the long legs and the tatty sweatshirt.'

'He's new.' Her mother put a finger to her lips, considering. 'I wonder, now, who would have brought him? What's his name, dear?'

'Fergus Lynskey. He's a teacher from Ireland. And guess what, Mom? He already thinks you're marvellous, just by looking at you. How about that for a first, huh?' Before the astonished Johanna could react, Sky had bussed her cheek, taken the tea and was walking away with it.

'Thanks. Is there sugar in it?' Fergus Lynskey prised himself off the wall and looked askance at the watery liquid with its appurtenances of string and label. 'Sorry, I forgot—'

Sky was about to go and get it when he stopped her. 'No matter. When in Rome . . .' He dunked his finger in the cup, pressing the tea-bag against the side.

The band was forming up and the child for whom the benefit was being held, a swollen-faced little girl of about four, was being carried on in the arms of her father. 'Listen,'

136

Sky turned impulsively to Lynskey, 'I know where you can get better tea. Or even a real drink. Do you like pasta?'

He raised an eyebrow. 'I've heard about you American women. And do you kiss on the first date?'

'Come on, don't be snide.'

'I'm being no such thing. It was a perfectly serious question.'

The proprietor of Pirelli's restaurant and bar, a Finn who was distantly related to Jimbo Larsen, had gone all the way with his Italianate theme. He had commissioned a mural of an erupting Vesuvius for the wall behind the bar, the candles on the red chequered tablecloths were held by wax-encrusted Chianti bottles and the Muzak looped itself endlessly through selections of Neapolitan songs. 'At least the decibel level is tolerable,' Sky apologized, after they had ordered their meal.

'It's nice. I like it.' Lynskey looked around. 'People don't eat late in Montana, I see.' The threesome at the only other occupied table were already arguing over who was going to pay for what.

'Not during the week.' Sky discovered she was hungry and broke off a piece of breadstick. 'Tell me about yourself. I forgot to ask you if you're married.'

'Something you probably should have asked me before you brought me here.'

'All right. But are you?'

His face clouded and, for a split second, Sky was shocked at the depth of her disappointment. 'Don't worry about it,' she said quietly. 'I had no designs on you anyway. Let's just enjoy the meal.'

'Have you ever heard of the Irish solution to the Irish problem?' His expression remained serious.

'You mean the IRA?'

Lynskey's shout of laughter was so unexpected and startling that even the busboy looked up from his apathetic laying of tables for the following day. 'No, you goose.' Lynskey chuckled. 'God, you Americans!'

Sky stared at him, not because of her gaffe, whatever it had been, but because, despite the beaky nose, he was so attractive when he laughed. *Stop it!* she warned herself. *Stop it* ... One of the principles by which she had always conducted her love life was that other women's men were out of bounds. 'I always thought the IRA was the main Irish problem.'

'It is, it is, of course it is!' He chuckled again. 'But that's not "the Irish solution to the Irish problem".' Again he became serious. 'I'm separated from my wife. There's no divorce in holy Ireland, as I'm sure you're aware, so what we do is separate officially through the courts. Hugely expensive and that way everyone gets to be equally miserable and stay miserable. Except the lawyers and bishops, of course.'

'I'm sorry.' But Sky was not. She sipped some wine. Then: 'Don't talk about it if you don't want to, but was it recent? Have you any children?'

'No, to both questions – do you mind if I dig into this garlic bread?' She took this as a signal not to probe any further and changed the subject, asking him why he chose Montana as a vacation spot. Apparently, it had been a spur-of-the-moment decision. 'Normally I spend my summers washing trains.'

'What?'

'Part-time job. My wife's maintenance payments are rather a drain.' This was a lie as Lynskey's wife had eschewed maintenance payments from the day she had moved in with her new partner. Yet the penniless-teacher cover story was the one he habitually used.

'So why aren't you doing that this summer?' The mental

138

picture of him sloshing buckets of soapy water over locomotives was irresistible.

'Because I'm forty next birthday,' he took a deep slug from his glass, 'and I've seen nothing of the world.'

Over the next hour or so, they chatted easily about Kerry and Cork, about Montana, about films they had each seen and liked, and discovered their tastes were similar. Sky wondered how best to slip in the facts about her own marital situation but the natural time would have been after his own semi-confession and the moment had passed. To bring it up now might look too forward.

The conversation flowed easily over the coming presidential elections, about which Lynskey was well informed, and then moved to the situation in Northern Ireland, about which he was reluctant to talk: 'It's just that there is no way to explain it in one conversation, or even two or three or a dozen. It would take years, especially – saving your presence – to explain it to an outsider. Almost as long as it's been going on.'

Sky did not push him but was intrigued to learn that he had already encountered Irish patriotism, Butte-style. In the War Bonnet's bar, he had encountered some of the shamrock lot after their meeting there.

'That's why I was there. I was covering that meeting.'

'Well, if I'd known *that* . . .' He grinned.

'*I'd* have run a mile in the other direction!' She took up the joust.

'You and what army?' It was an expression new to her but the gist was clear and, faced with such a speedy onset of intimacy, Sky felt shy. Lynskey seemed to suffer no such qualms, however, and took her hand. 'I'm glad I came to that barbecue tonight. Will we have one more for the road?'

She hesitated, aware that the proprietor of Pirelli's was sitting stony-faced behind the cash register at the door. They had already had two post-prandial Sambucas, their waiter and the busboy were long gone. She looked at her watch. 'It's after eleven fifteen, I had no idea it was so late. We'd better not – but can I drive you to your hotel?'

He cocked his head to one side. 'Only if you let me kiss you goodnight, R. Sky MacPherson.'

Sky knew she should have been offended. In the past she would have been offended. Now, looking into this man's eyes, she experienced something she thought she had long ago outgrown: an adolescent thrill somewhere deep in the pit of her stomach. 'You'll be lucky, Lynskey.'

They drove the short distance to the War Bonnet in silence and she was glad to find that this Irishman apparently saw as little need for small-talk as she did.

She saw no activity in the parking lot and, feeling somewhat silly, she pulled up the Nissan a little way from the front door of the hotel, outside the circle of light cast from within the lobby. Lynskey squeezed her hand. 'I'm definitely glad we met.' Then he leaned over and kissed her briefly on the lips. 'I'll ring you tomorrow.' He was gone before Sky could register the anti-climactic nature of the kiss.

As she drove home she thought of a thousand questions she should have asked him, a million things she should have said. Like, how dare he assume so much? Like, how did he know she'd be at work? Like, how come he never bothered to ask her if *she* was married – if she had a boyfriend . . . ? Like, how long was he staying? Like, when would she see him again?

Johanna was already in bed when Sky let herself into the duplex. As she tiptoed down the hall to her bedroom, she thought of an add-on. How come Fergus Lynskey was at the benefit in the first place? It was an unlikely attraction for a lone tourist.

*

For his part, getting ready for bed in his anonymous hotel room, Lynskey was giving himself a severe talking-to. He had been out with beautiful women, had been to bed with them, for God's sake. Why should one chaste kiss, a few hand squeezes, reverberate like thunder through his body? He had been afraid to kiss her properly, although she had seemed ready for it.

Lynskey's world was threatened by this woman. She had shaken his usual composure to the extent that he feared he would not be able to keep intact the breezy, bright façade, which camouflaged his loneliness. Up to now he had managed quite well, thank you, and his colleagues, and many of the women he had met and superficially loved, believed him to be quite a ladies' man.

He went to his briefcase, undid the combination locks and took out a cumbersome satellite telephone.

The chief superintendent, who was shaving before going to work, was peremptory. 'Any developments?'

'Nothing significant. I've made contact with a local reporter here, R. Sky MacPherson. She wrote a pretty good obituary on Treacy's wife but, as far as I can see, knows nothing.' He was testing himself: testing his ability to use her name without betraying interest. It seemed to have worked because his boss did not react. 'Anything else?'

'The St Patrick's Brigade seems innocuous, I had a good look at some of them last night. Didn't get to talk to the president, the one who runs the funeral home where the coffin came from. I'm going to do that first thing tomorrow.'

'Do that.' Daly was impatient to get off. 'Next time, have something to tell me. The meter is ticking.'

Lynskey pressed the 'end' button and returned the phone to the briefcase. He got into bed and lay with his hands behind his head. He wished he still smoked.

Chapter Twelve

'You're not trying to convince me that your turning up like that out of the blue last night was a coincidence?' Sky fiddled with the digital tuning on the Nissan's radio. She had been delighted when Lynskey had telephoned that morning. She usually worked Saturdays, but she had raced through a few catch-up calls in the morning and decided to take the afternoon off. Now, with Lynskey in the passenger seat, she was driving them on a picnic. She had turned off the interstate at Three Forks, and they were heading towards Madison Buffalo Jump.

'Do you want it to be a coincidence?' He was staring straight ahead. 'It can be anything you want.'

'I want a straight answer.' She gave up on the radio.

'I was out for a walk and I smelled the burning.' Lynskey paused. 'Will that do? Remember, I told you I liked soot.' When she glanced over at him his expression was deadpan and she could not help but laugh.

He was wearing the faded sweatshirt again today but instead of last night's jeans had donned a pair of cotton shorts, which looked as though he had borrowed them from a much smaller man. On his bare feet he wore old-fashioned buckled sandals and Sky thought that his prehensile toes and long, muscular legs had to be as white as the day he had been born. What she had heard about the Irish climate had clearly not been exaggerated. 'You still haven't given me a satisfactory answer,' she prompted. 'Did you not worry about integrating with a pack of total strangers? Or that you might not be welcome?'

'Listen, love,' he pulled playfully at a strand of hair sticking through the back of her baseball cap, 'what are you bothered about? It was a good cause, wasn't it? Where there's a good cause going, I'm your man. And when you think of it, MacPee, wouldn't you say I'm still getting quite good value for my few dollars' donation?' He made an expansive gesture that embraced her, the car, and half of Montana.

'Anyway,' he looked away from her through his window, 'you'll discover that teachers have no finer feelings. They get thumped out of us in training school. Blushing violets don't survive for long in front of classfuls of sixteen-year-old brats stuffed to bursting with hormones. Now, let's stop talking about me. I'm bored with me. What are you working on at the moment?'

Sky looked across at him. 'Oh, this and that. The usual.'

'Sounds riveting.'

'It's a job, you know.'

'Seriously,' he smiled, 'anything interesting?'

'I don't think you'd find it interesting. Well, maybe. Can I trust you with something I've just started? It's pretty confidential – at least at this early stage. And I'm a bit out of my league. I've no training as an investigative reporter – oh, I know we're *all* supposed to be interested in turning up rocks and seeing what's underneath, but somehow those kinds of stories don't come my way.' She hesitated. 'Until now, I think.'

'Now you've really got me curious. Of course you can trust me, my lips are sealed.' He made the gesture, both index fingers crossed over his clamped mouth. Then, when he saw she was still dubious about telling him, 'Sure what's it to me, R. Sky MacPherson? I'm only an Irish teacher and all that bothers me is the *tuiseal ginideach*. Anyhow, I'll be gone in a few days, won't I?'

Before she had thought about it, she had stretched out her hand and touched his hair, 'What's that – those words?' Its softness under her fingers surprised her. It was curly, longish, already flecked with grey, and although there was a lot of it, it felt fine and silky. Warm, fine and silky. She was already fantasizing as to how it would feel in her hands when – *if* – he were to kiss her breasts . . .

'Are you sure you want to know? It's grammar, the Irish genitive.' He responded to the invitation, leant over and kissed the skin under her jaw. 'You're gorgeous,' he whispered, 'do you know that? You're temptation incarnate.' Then he pulled away. 'I'm sure this is against some very, *very* severe code of the American highway.'

'I'm sure it is.' Sky was glad for the rush of the wind through the open windows of the automobile.

Luckily he did not seem to notice her confusion. 'Hey, MacPee, spill the beans to your uncle Fergus. What is it about this work that's so secret? Is it an undercover job?'

'Don't think that I'm fooled for a second by your clever impersonation of a dweeb. Undercover job, indeed!'

'All right.' His grin was broad and unabashed. 'So, anyway, what are you working on?'

'You're really interested?'

'Really, *really.*'

Tentatively at first, she began to tell him about the previous day's trip to Libby and points north. As she had suspected, he proved an attentive listener and, within minutes, she found she was using him as a sounding board. She was still talking when she turned off the engine and let the Nissan freewheel to a stop on the flat ribbon of highway near their destination. 'You see, the thing is,' she leaned into the back seat for the picnic basket Johanna had packed that

144

morning, 'I've nothing at all to go on. But every instinct in my body says something's wrong. And that this Sheriff Brian O'Connor's in it up to his neck. But what "it" is I don't know. It's very frustrating.'

She trailed off and looked towards the buffalo jump, an extraordinary cliff that erupted like a carbuncle from the floor of the prairie and was the only height for miles around. Through the open window, the shush of the breeze through the grasses was like a cool waterfall. 'I'm missing something, I know it.'

'This Skippy fella,' Lynskey's voice was slow and considering, 'you're sure he was talking about you into that cellphone?'

'As sure as I can be. But he's not bright enough to have much to do with anything. No, it's that sheriff. And I just know Skippy was on to him about me.'

'Now who's being melodramatic?' Lynskey pushed open the passenger door and unfolded his long legs on to the grass. 'Come on, maybe the fresh air'll clear our brains. Over here, is it?' He took the basket from her and, without waiting for her acquiescence, set out for the buffalo jump.

Sky registered his use of the word 'our' and as she got out to follow him realized that he was making partners of them. She let him get way ahead of her while watching with pleasure the easy way his long legs covered the ground. Over the past summers, Montana had suffered from drought; the recent storms were not enough to prevent the yellowing of the knee-high vegetation and she tried to find an analogy for the image Lynskey presented as he strode through it. All that came to mind was a picture from one of the nature books she had loved as a child, and it was hardly flattering: what she saw was a giraffe at full stretch through the African veldt. With his beaky nose, long, thin frame and pale skin, Fergus Lynskey should not have been attractive. Yet somehow he

145

was not only attractive but devastatingly so to R. Sky MacPherson. 'Take it easy,' she cautioned, 'the guy's just passing through.'

He was waiting for her at the peak of the buffalo jump, seated in the scrub, a gleam of triumph in his eyes. 'You're not all that fit, are you, MacPee?'

'I'm not about to win a medal at the Olympic Games, if that's what you mean.' She smiled down at him, noticing for the first time that although she had originally thought his eyes to be grey, in the brightness of this light they were, in fact, dark green.

'Too much skulking around in smoky bar-rooms in search of scoops, I'll betcha!' He reached up and pulled her down to sit beside him. 'Can we eat straight away?' Eager as a child, 'I'm starved.'

When Sky's mother packed a picnic, she went all out. They unwrapped chicken breasts, a Thermos of chilled cucumber soup, individual packets of Saltines and two types of cheese, a salad of peppers, carrot sticks, raw cauliflower, broccoli and mushrooms. For dessert, Johanna had put in two small pots of Jell-O and to drink, a second Thermos of iced tea. 'Terrific!' Lynskey surveyed the feast. 'But I'll have to teach you Americans the art of trotting mice on tea. *This*,' he sniffed disparagingly at the insipid yellow liquid Sky was pouring into two paper cups, 'doesn't even smell like tea. I hope you're not insulted?'

'On behalf of the American nation, I apologize.'

Catching her off guard, he leaned forward and smacked a quick kiss on her lips.

'What was that for?' Instinctively, Sky's hand went to her mouth.

'Do I need a reason?' He was staring at her in a way that made the hair on her forearms rise. Then he grinned and was the cheeky self she was coming to know. 'Because it's a gorgeous day? Because this little breeze blowing through

146

your hair is the freshest and warmest little breeze I've ever felt? Because I'm now feeling sorry for all them poor buffalo that were driven off the edge of this cliff just so we could have such a perfect picnic here?'

'It was the most efficient way to slaughter them.' Sky found refuge from the effect of his proximity – and the kiss – in adopting tour-guide mode. 'The Native Americans were very ecologically minded.'

'Were they, indeed?' He sank his teeth into a chicken breast.

'Stop it, Fergus!'

'Stop what?' He was innocence personified.

'Stop looking at me like that.'

'Right. Done.' He dropped his eyes. 'But hold on there, a second, willya?' He chewed swallowed and carefully placed the chicken breast on the paper napkin beside him. 'Now, is this look better?' He crossed his eyes.

'*Fergus!*' Sky was laughing now.

She stopped abruptly as he reached out and took her in his arms. 'This is the second date, MacPee,' his voice was husky, 'so I think a proper kiss could be in order, don't you?' This time, there was no playfulness. With his free hand, he brushed her hair away from her face and looked into it for what seemed like an hour. Sky met his gaze and then dropped her own eyes to watch his wide mouth, the depth of the channel above the upper lip, the fullness in the centre of the lower one. The sounds around became louder. She could hear the grass bend to the wind, the peeping of a bird she could not identify. On and on it went, that eternal moment as she waited for him to kiss her. She knew that when he did, everything would be different between them.

'Everything will be different if you kiss me.' As usual, the words popped out as quickly as she thought them.

'I know.' He did not change his position. 'I think maybe we shouldn't. Maybe it's better keep to things as they are for the time being. What do you think?' She felt as though she were made of fragile plaster. That if she were to be the one to make a move, she would shatter. 'I think so too.' She tried to say it without moving her lips.

'We'll kiss again. We'll do more than kiss. That's a promise, R. Sky MacPherson.' He stroked her forehead and then, gently, he raised her face. 'Here's a little taste to be going on with,' brushing her cheek lightly with his fingertips.

It took a little time to get back to the way things had been. At first, they ate in silence, not the companionable silence Sky had so quickly got used to, but one filled with darts.

'Come here, Sky.' When they were almost done eating, he took her and settled her with her back to him and both arms around her, facing both of them across the lip of the jump. 'Settle down. Just look at that.'

Sky looked. The jump was four, maybe five hundred feet high, in the sweep of prairie that spread like a great golden plate as far as the horizon on three sides, rising on the fourth to meld with the blue and purple Rockies. In all this honey-coloured space, Butte was just an irregular, brownish stain. The few visible farms were little clusters of red-roofed insignificance climbing out of folds in the grasslands; the highway they had left was visible only because of three puffs of brown dust, miles and miles apart, which appeared in line with one another.

The soft west wind was warm on Sky's face and she closed her eyes, revelling in it, in the feeling of Lynskey's arms around her. 'How could anyone go back to Ireland after seeing this?' The whisper in her ear was low.

'*Don't go, then* . . .' This time, to her relief, the words remained unsaid.

'Now, let's demolish everything that's left.' Quietly, he kissed the nape of her neck and loosed his hold on her. 'I'm still starving.'

They polished off the remnants but then, as she was repacking Johanna's picnic basket, Sky remembered Greg. 'Oh, my God!'

'What's wrong?' Lynskey turned from where he was framing a picture through the viewfinder of his pocket camera.

'Greg. I forgot.'

'Who's Greg, when he's at home?'

'He's my boyfriend.' Squarely, Sky faced him. 'I was supposed to meet him today and it went clear out of my head.'

'I see. We'd better get you to a telephone, then.' Sky had to admire this man. She found it difficult to believe they had known one another for less than twenty-four hours. It occurred to her then that not only had she forgotten the appointment with Greg but that he had not entered her head since she had met Lynskey. She had to end it with him: it would be grossly unfair not to. 'What are your plans for tonight?'

'Nothing much. I thought I'd see if there was a film I haven't seen yet. But what about this Greg?'

'Leave Greg to me. Would you like to have dinner? Look, Lynskey—' Sky stopped walking. She took a deep breath. 'You'll probably think I'm being too forward – too American – but if what is going on between us is what I *think* it is, well, actually – even if it's *not* – then Greg and I are no longer – well – Greg and I . . .'

She hated pussyfooting and here she was, behaving like the queen of the pussyfooters. 'What I mean is,' she amended, 'that even if I hadn't met you last night, Greg and I were finished. I was planning it anyway. I just haven't had the guts to do it.'

He let out that whistle she was beginning to know. 'Poor guy. Come on, Sky, get a move on. You've got to ring him.' He strode on ahead of her and unexpectedly Sky felt let down. He had not responded to what had been almost a declaration of undying love. Was she being as foolish as always?

All right, she thought, hurrying to catch him up – he was now fifty yards ahead – maybe she was reading too much into it. From now on, she would play it cool. Whichever way Lynskey's wind blew, she'd blow with it. 'You always walk so fast?' She was out of breath when she finally reached him and they were getting into the Nissan.

'I always walk when I'm thinking,' he held open the driver's door for her, 'and I was thinking about your dilemma. Tell us a bit more about this Daniel Treacy.' He closed her door, walked round to his own side and got in. 'You seem to think he's a bit of a mystery man.'

Sky engaged the gear shift and moved out on to the highway. 'I've told you all I know.'

'Oh, sure.' He changed the subject and in the hour and a half it took to get back to within sight of Butte, told her about his home town of Tralee, its history, the annual festival that brought girls from all over the world in search of a title commemorating some local heroine called Mary who was known for her beauty and virtue.

'A beauty pageant?' Her good humour restored, Sky was lulled by the rise and fall of his rapid-fire English.

'You could call it that,' Lynskey chuckled, 'but it's hard to explain. It's not swimsuits, and the girls don't have to have the body beautiful. Not even the face beautiful. It's more goodness, personality, that sort of stuff. They do party pieces—'

'Forget it. You're right, it is hard to explain. It's too Irish for me.'

'It's a pity your mother wasn't born two miles north of where she was or you'd be eligible.'

'Give us a break! I'm a bit elderly for beauty pageants – hey!' she looked across at him. 'How come you know the exact spot where my mother was born?'

150

'You told me yourself last night.'

'I said the name of the place, but no one, not even anyone from Ireland, has ever heard of it.'

'I have,' he said quickly. 'I used to play football. There's a couple of lads on the Cork team from around there.'

'You've done everything, haven't you? And you certainly seem to know a lot about me.'

'You talk a lot, MacPee. You told me a lot last night.'

'And just why *were* you at the benefit?'

'I wanted to meet you,' he said slowly, after the briefest of pauses. 'I saw your photograph in your newspaper. I went into your office,' he had the grace to sound embarrassed, 'and a young lady said you were probably going to be there. I'm sorry, Sky. Do you forgive me for the deception?'

The city was now ahead of them, far below. 'All right, I forgive you, I suppose I should be flattered. Now, Mr Schoolteacher, have a look at that. There's my city.' She had always loved the surreal look of Butte from up here, the way the derelict pithead machinery towered like giant insects over and among the house roofs. As they descended, she offered to take him on a tour of the city, 'That's if you're staying, of course – if you don't see a photograph of someone you like better in the *Great Falls Tribune* or the *Bozeman Daily Chronicle*.'

'I said I'm sorry. And you did say you forgave me. Of course I'm staying. I told you I have three and a half months' holidays.'

'Teaching must pay better in Ireland than it does in Montana.'

'I'll be a shadow of my former self by the end.' He smiled mischievously. 'The War Bonnet is my little treat for the beginning. To stoke me up, like . . .'

*

151

The white Hiace was again being brought into use. Just before dawn it had been driven into the garage of a semi-detached house on the outskirts of Sligo, where it had remained during the hours of daylight. The house belonged to a national schoolteacher, married with five children, who lent his garage from time to time. Not too often. Maybe once every two years.

Now, just after midnight, the van, with its complement of three men, was being driven out as quietly as it had come in. 'I wish it was over.' The driver was younger than the other two.

'Shut up. Just drive – you're being paid well enough.' The man beside him spoke with the authority of long leadership.

Meanwhile, in the Dublin suburb of Churchtown, the dawn chorus, more disturbing than melodious, had reached full pitch, blackbirds, song thrushes and sparrows, starlings and robins swamped by the chuckering of magpies, as raucous as adolescent boys.

Rupert de Burgh was oblivious of them as he walked quickly to the telephone kiosk at the corner of his road, which was lined with solid, semi-detached houses. He had to make the call and get back into his house and bed before his wife woke and noticed he had left.

He inserted two fifty-pence coins and waited. 'Toby?' He never bothered with the preliminaries. 'You got the cutting?' He listened, then: 'I do trust you. Just be sure to choose the right moment and watch his eyes. Good luck.' He replaced the receiver and hurried home.

When he had first arrived at Trinity College in the early seventies, Rupert, who was the son of a well-to-do Tory MP, had been like any other expatriate middle-class English student. But, on his first day, while sitting quietly in the buttery, a pint of beer in his hand, he had been befriended by the boy sitting on the next stool. Perhaps it was the attraction of opposites, perhaps his charismatic new friend recognized fertile, virgin ground when he saw it, but Rupert's true education began that day.

He had been aghast to find, over the weeks and months which followed, that what little he had thought and been taught about the Irish had been filtered through the self-satisfied sieve of English Tory revisionism. Within a short time, he had performed a *volte-face* from his upbringing and had become estranged from all his former friends in England, even from his parents.

Christmas that year had not been a success: Rupert's quiet public persona had never been mirrored at home, but this time his behaviour was exceptional. He found fault with everything, not only with his parents' views but with their wealth, their house, their staid way of life. Even their singing of English carols at the traditional Christmas service in the local Anglican church.

During that Christmas break he had gone to work on his brother. Toby, who hoped to go up to Oxford, had always been in awe of his more energetic elder sibling and would have done anything Rupert asked of him. Rupert tutored him about Cromwell, about the Penal Laws where the English treated Catholics as less than vermin, about the devastating famine in Ireland that halved the population while England continued to extract its corn taxes, about gerrymandering in the North, about systematic discrimination against nationalists. About Pádraic Pearse and the other heroes of the Easter Rising. And when the IRA was blamed for the killing of fifteen people in the bombing of McGurk's bar that Christmas, Rupert was able to show Toby how it wasn't the IRA that did it: it was British intelligence agents who wanted to up the ante.

His poor bewildered parents, who had sent off a super-ficially compliant, well-mannered boy to read English at a long-established university, albeit a provincial one, found themselves playing host to a raging, angry radical. The conflict had come to a head on Boxing Day, when Rupert refused to accompany them for the traditional visit to an elderly bachelor uncle, a retired Guards' colonel who babbled away harmlessly about Winston Churchill and the war. As his mother wept, Rupert ranted on about colonialism and the oppression of Irish civil rights. Finally his normally placid father had had enough. He issued an ultimatum: either Rupert came with them to visit their relative or he was out. Rupert was delighted. His Trinity fees were paid for the year so he went back to Dublin. When term resumed, however, he went to no more lectures or tutorials but hung around the bars or used the library for his own purposes.

And then, after Bloody Sunday, he had run with the rest to set fire to the British embassy where he had stood in the shadows and had been inspired to join the police by the young and unwitting Fergus Lynskey. Who had been too caught up in his own passion to have noted anything distinctive about Rupert de Burgh.

Chapter Thirteen

To take advantage of the spectacular vista of the Continental Divide, for which the site of Daniel Treacy's house had been chosen, the south side was virtually all glass, with floor-to-ceiling windows curving along it like petrified waves. Expensively but simply furnished, the large living room had a parquet floor, which shone in the dazzling light, three white sofas placed in a U shape in front of a marble fireplace on the fourth wall, a couple of easy chairs, also in white, and occasional tables in glass and dull grey steel. Even the lamps were shaded in white and there was only one picture: hanging over the fireplace was a large, steel-framed abstract in pale greys and white. The sparse simplicity was deliberate. Nothing was to detract from the scene outside.

The house was twelve miles northeast of the city, tucked away at the end of a private road near Elk Park Pass at almost six thousand feet. In front of the windows at which Treacy stood, the yard surrounding the house fell away in a series of terraced lawns, lush as Oriental paddy-fields, towards the edge of a bluff. Beyond this was a wide green ocean of fir and pine and beyond that again were the mountains, jagging the intense blue hem of the sky.

Treacy knew that in the bars and restaurants of the invisible summer-Saturday-evening city only a few miles from his house, everyone was gearing up to have a good time. Down there, people were having conversations and spats; they were laughing and being silly and eating cheap food, drinking convivial glasses of beer and wine, making plans to meet for Sunday brunch, to go to local fishing holes or to have barbecues or picnics.

It was a scene on which he did not care to dwell. King of the Castle, he thought sadly, remembering the game he had played as a child in Ireland. Sometimes vicious, always rambunctious, it involved pushing and shoving and clawing your way to the top of whatever elevation – a rock, a clump of furze – was designated for the day. As a child Daniel had never achieved the status of king, always having been overcome by bigger, heavier and more determined boys. 'Well, you've made it now,' he said, to his empty, elegant room and stupendous view.

Damn that girl. It had been at least six hours since he had first called and he was not accustomed to having to leave three messages for anyone.

At least her mother had had good news for him.

Almost furtively, although no one could be observing him, he took a slim silver case out of the inner pocket of his jacket. Opening it, he looked at the photograph it contained, an old black-and-white snapshot of Elizabeth Sullivan. It was one of those old-fashioned group shots, taken by amateur box Brownie owners the world over in the thirties and forties. She was Sky's mother, who was tiny, perhaps five years old, and was standing at the front, surrounded by her large family.

It had taken all of Daniel Treacy's ingenuity and a lot of his money to secure that photograph, which was more than forty years old. He had had it enlarged and enhanced, but even American technology was unable to obliterate the fact that the unseen photographer's hand had shaken a little as the shutter snapped.

Nevertheless, to Treacy, Elizabeth Sullivan's luminous beauty shone from it as clearly as though her image had been painted by Titian. She was holding the youngest of her eight

156

children, whom he knew to be Constance, now on a sheep farm in Australia.

There was little he did not know about Elizabeth's family.

What marred the photograph for him was that she was standing beside Mossie Sheehan, her second husband, long since dead, but the memory of whom could nevertheless inspire him with hatred. Elizabeth's first husband had been a mean fool, but Mossie had been the one who had deprived Daniel of the woman he had loved for more than forty-eight years. He had rejoiced savagely on learning of Mossie's death but by then, cruelly, he himself was married. But now that Midge was out of the way . . . His heart jumped as the image of his wife's waxen face rose before his eyes.

He closed the case and replaced the snapshot in his inside pocket, then crossed the perfect room, the clicking of his shoes on the parquet emphasizing how alone he was. He sat on one of the sofas, picked up a book and attempted to concentrate. Having read a paragraph, however, he had to begin it a second time. When it still made no impression on his brain, he threw the book from him. Nothing, he thought, could be worse than this emptiness.

Instantly, he rejected this idea: he must not feel sorry for himself; self-pity was the most ignoble of human failings. He picked up the TV remote control and pressed a button. Smoothly, doors in a console slid open and the television came on. He spent a minute or so flicking around the channels but could find nothing he wanted to watch. He switched it off again.

He looked at his watch: Elizabeth's granddaughter was turning out to be good at her job; he could see she was not to be put off. Where was she? Why was she not returning his calls? He wanted to impress his own version of his story on her before she discovered too much. Monday, when they were due to meet, might be too late. And he doubted if he could wait that long to find out if Elizabeth was coming. He wondered if he could risk calling Sky's home yet again. Time was getting shorter and shorter. He reached for the telephone but decided against it. Even reporters probably took Saturday nights off.

Daniel Treacy left his beautiful room and walked towards the cantilevered staircase that curved to the second floor and the bedroom suites. His shoes felt like concrete blocks.

On the roadway outside the house, a man in a plain beige sedan noted the lights going on in the upper storey.

As Sky pulled in, the parking lot of the War Bonnet Inn was teeming with conspicuously ID'd conventioneers who, in high spirits, were being disgorged from the coaches that had taken them in from the airport. 'Oh, great!' Lynskey groaned, as they stopped behind one of the vehicles. 'This is all I need. I've read about these conventions. I probably won't get a wink of sleep.'

'You'll survive.' Sky left the engine running and looked across at him. Now that she had decided to finish with Greg, Lynskey's presence made it imperative that she did so tonight. She said, 'Look, after I've talked to Greg, would you like to eat dinner? What kind of food do you like?'

'Home cooking. I want to eat at your house.'

'But my mother's there.' Sky was thunderstruck.

'That's just it. I want to meet that wonderful woman. Thank her in person for that picnic. Would she mind?'

'I'll have to call her.' This was definitely a first. No man with whom she had ever been involved had looked to meet her mother. 'Why don't you give her a shout from the telephone in my room while I have a quick shower and put on some real trousers? You can call your Greg too, see if he's in. If he is, you go off and meet him, I don't mind waiting, however long it takes. But if you can't reach him we could go straight to your house. And if that look in your eyes

158

means you're worried about the proprieties, I promise I won't jump you – honest!'

'What look?' But as Sky turned off the ignition, she felt a little like Pinocchio, or any puppet she had known in her childhood. It was still less than twenty-four hours since they had met and Lynskey was running her life. 'Anything else you'd like to organize for me?' she asked, as he opened the door and unrolled himself from the passenger seat.

'Not for the moment. Come on.' Then he bent down and grinned at her. 'Unless, of course, you'd like me to help you buy a bigger car. Me legs are crucified!'

His room was as Sky had expected, inoffensive, beigey décor, two beds, a TV, a mirrored dressing-table, which doubled as a desk, a coffee-table flanked with two chairs and windows framed with thick, swagged drapes. She sat on the side of one of the beds, staring at the telephone. What was she to say to Greg? From behind the closed bathroom door, over the rushing of the shower, she could hear Lynskey's baritone warble. Quickly, before she lost her nerve, she picked up the receiver and punched out the number of the liquor store.

Greg had already left. She called his home. Busy.

Guiltily relieved, she called her mother. Johanna was bubbling with delight. She had finally got through to Ireland and Sky's grandmother was seriously considering the invitation. And of course she would be thrilled to have Sky's young man to dinner. 'There were a few calls for you.' Sky heard the rustling of paper and the scrape against the receiver as her mother put on her glasses. 'One from Bill Collins – and – Greg and oh! Yes – guess what? Daniel Treacy called *twice* for you. We had a nice chat the second time. I told him about my mother. He's lovely, really, when you get to know him, isn't he, Sky?'

'Sure, Mom, lovely. I've got to run. See you soon.' She tried Greg's home number again and, when it was still busy, checked in at the office. Her voice-mail repeated the messages she had taken already from her mother. Bill Collins. Treacy. And Greg. Collins could wait until Monday but Treacy? Twice?

She copied the number he had left into her contacts book and was punching it out when she heard the shower being shut off. She hung up. But the singing started again and the sound of running water. Lynskey must be shaving, she thought, and decided that Treacy could wait. She was on time off and she deserved it.

Before her nerve failed, she tried Greg for the third time. This time the phone rang but the receiver was picked up by his father. Greg was out, and no, he had not said when he would be back. Sky asked him to say she had called and, hating herself for feeling so pleased at a further postponement of what she had to do, looked around the room to try to discern what type of person Lynskey was.

He certainly seemed tidy. His suitcase was nowhere in sight and, through the slightly open door of the closet, she could see a jacket and pants hanging. Apart from these, the edition of the *Butte Courier* on the dressing-table – the one that held the Treacy obituary – and a little travel alarm clock by the bed, the only other sign that the room was occupied was a briefcase on the coffee table.

What type of man travelled on an extended vacation through the Western states of the US of A lumbered with a briefcase? Sky smiled affectionately. This guy was fascinating but a definite oddball. Did she dare? She glanced at the bathroom door: the water was still running. Quickly, she crossed to the coffee table. The briefcase was locked.

The singing stopped and the water was shut off again. Sky had barely time to get back to her original seat on the bed before the bathroom door was opened a crack: 'You finished? Is it safe to come out?'

She nodded, trying to keep her conscience from shrieking aloud about her snooping. The sight of him wearing nothing but a towel around his waist compounded her agitation; his torso was hard and muscular, if a little on the skinny side. He noticed her scrutiny. 'I know,' he said cheerfully. 'I'm no Chippendale. But you should see the rest of my family. I'm the fat one. What's the matter? You look like a guilty child. Was it very bad?' he asked gently, coming to sit beside her. 'Was Greg upset?' He bent and kissed her softly on the lips.

Sky, who was losing count of these chaste kisses, managed not to grab him. 'He wasn't in. I feel dreadful about this. I was never very good at tough love or whatever it's called.'

'You've done it before, surely?' He pulled back, his expression sceptical.

'Only once, when I left my husband.' Sky knew she sounded like a weakling. 'I suppose I do things obliquely, show by my behaviour that it's time for a break. They usually get the message.' She looked down at his hands, square on his lap, and noticed that he bit his nails. 'That sounds appalling, as though I'm whatever the female equivalent of a womanizer is . . . I'm not, you know, I don't think I could flirt to save my life.'

'You don't have to.'

When she glanced up, his eyes seemed to be emitting light. She was uncomfortable in its blaze and also with the tenor of the conversation but felt that she should carry through to the end. 'Greg's different, somehow, I've tried to tell him, I mean to show him . . .' Miserably she trailed away.

'There's only one way to tell him, you know, and that's to tell him.' He made it sound easy.

'I know.' She looked directly at him. 'It's my problem, not yours. Now, about dinner, my mom says it's OK for you to come over.'

161

He reacted with the shout of laughter that had so startled her the night before in Pirelli's. 'Thanks a million.' He got up and padded to the closet, 'I can't wait. I'm starved.'

'You always seem to be starved.'

'I'm a big fella, MacPee. Now turn your back like a good girl so I can get dressed.' She complied and then asked why he had a briefcase on holiday. 'Oh, that!' His voice was airy. 'You wouldn't want to know what's in that.'

'Why not? Is it a secret? I've told you all my secrets—'

'All right, all right, you win. But you're not to laugh.'

'I won't.'

'I'm writing a book.' No matter how she begged, he refused to tell her any more. 'It's just a book, Sky,' he said at last. 'Every teacher – no more than every journalist, I dare say – thinks he has at least one book in him.'

'I want us to kiss properly.' Sky could have torn out her unruly tongue. Nevertheless she turned round to face him. He was still bare-chested but he had donned his pants and she had surprised him in the act of putting on his second sock.

He dropped it. 'Only if it's skin to skin.'

Watching his eyes, she unbuttoned her cotton blouse, then felt behind her and unhooked her bra. She shed the garments and sat, head high, to wait for him. He continued to hesitate, however, face working as though he did not want to touch her – and for a few awful seconds she thought she had made a fool of herself. Then, in two strides, he was beside her and had pushed her back on the bed.

His hands felt cool and surprisingly delicate on her breasts, like the wing feathers of a bird. She arched her back and he held both nipples gently between finger and thumb, rolling them so they swelled and hardened to bursting point. He kissed them, fluttering his tongue over first one, then the other, and the skin over her entire body seemed to contract until it felt as tight as a drum.

162

He moved to her mouth and this time his kiss was anything but chaste. Sky tightened her arms around his neck and pulled, tumbling them over until they were entangled. His lips were all that she had fantasized, full, warm and demanding.

Then he stopped, as suddenly as a guillotine. Holding himself still above her, he looked into her eyes. 'You wait, MacPee. You just wait.'

Sky could not read his face. 'Why not now?' She was breathing hard.

'Now is not right.' For a brief instant, she detected fear in him.

One thing was certain, though: this was not the cocksure Paddy she had taken with her to Madison Buffalo Jump. Although her body pulsed, she managed a smile. 'Whatever you say, Lynskey. I can wait.'

The silence between them as they both got dressed and drove to the duplex was of such complexity she did not dare begin to analyse it. She began to worry how Johanna would react to him. As she took him in, however, she heard laughter from the kitchen and realized the Bliss Sisters were in session. 'Sorry about this,' she whispered, 'I didn't know.'

Before her eyes, Lynskey reinvented himself, wading in with all verbal guns firing, even moving his accent up a notch so that all three women were instantly snowed.

During his enthusiastic demolition of Johanna's meatless meatloaf, he blarneyed and flattered the three outrageously, telling yarns, even flirting. Within half an hour of his arrival, they were behaving like teenagers, Sky's mother most of all: Johanna's eyes sparkled the brightest and her voice took on the lightest timbre.

'Woodstock?' The meal over, Lynskey pushed aside his tea and gaped theatrically. 'You don't mean to say I'm actually in the presence of three people who were at *Woodstock*? Ladies, I'm lost with awe, not to speak of envy.'

This sent Johanna rushing into her bedroom to find the photograph album, which contained the proof. As she returned with it and all three crowded around to show themselves off to Lynskey as girls, he winked at Sky, who was sitting, chin in her hands, wishing she could begin to understand this man.

It might be a help if she could be alone with him. The memory of their half-complete encounter was still raw and she wanted him so badly she felt it must be written on her forehead. Far from seeming to wish the same thing, she thought wryly, as far as Lynskey was concerned she might as well be one of the cats who were snoozing in their basket at her mother's feet.

Chapter Fourteen

At Hermana's prompting, Sky's mother finally agreed to sing for their guest, but only if someone would help her. 'How about you, Sky?'

Then Johanna turned to Lynskey. 'She has a beautiful voice, Fergus, beautiful, but she won't use it.'

Embarrassed, Sky batted away the chance to make a show of herself in front of the Irishman. She knew she had an unusually rich speaking voice – she had always been chosen in grade school to read the finale in the Christmas pageant – but she felt her singing voice left a lot to be desired.

After much discussion, during which dusk stealthily withdrew light from the kitchen to gild the sky outside, Buffy agreed to sing and the two women launched into 'Blowin' In The Wind', Buffy's breathy mezzo making a perfect blend with Johanna's sweet soprano. Throughout the song, Sky's mother plucked shyly at her hair so that by the time they were embarked on the song's penultimate verse, the braid was undone and, like dark candy-floss, her hair was drifting around her face and shoulders.

In normal circumstances, Sky would have been so mortified she could not have borne to watch the display but she saw it through Lynskey's eyes and was glad he had afforded her an opportunity to see her mother as the unique individual she undoubtedly was. An endangered species. She resolved to be less impatient with Johanna but knew immediately that her resolution was a waste of brain cells.

The telephone shrilled in the hallway just as the last notes of the song died away and, as she went to answer it, Sky looked back to see a tableau she reckoned she would remember for a long time: her mother and Buffy locked in sentimental embrace, Hermana surreptitiously blowing her nose and Lynskey's beaky face wreathed in benevolent smiles.

'Hello?' Sky's voice sang as she answered the phone.

'I've been trying you all evening. Did you forget we had a date?'

'Oh, God.' The sound of poor Greg's aggrieved voice was like a blow. 'To tell you the truth, Greg, I did.'

'Where the hell were you? They said at the office—'

'Don't take that tone with me. You don't own me, you know.' Sky took refuge in moral outrage from her guilt. During the pause that followed, she could almost see his huff: thick, grey and dense as iron, it crushed the air between them so she felt claustrophobic and flat. 'I'm sorry,' she offered, 'I didn't mean to yell.'

'I never pretended to own you.' He was stiff. 'I just thought—'

'Look, Greg—' She got stuck. Use of a blind telephone was the cowardly way to break up a relationship.

'What?' His belligerence made it easier for her.

'We have to meet.' She forced herself to be crisp, 'I'm real sorry about this evening but we have to talk.'

'Please, Sky, please!' His pain shocked her.

'We have to talk,' she forced herself to repeat.

'You want to break up with me.'

Visualizing his ravaged eyes, she wavered but then went through with it. 'I want to *talk* to you about it.'

The panicked silence crackled. Behind her, she heard the scrape of chairs from the kitchen, heard Hermana and Buffy talk over one another in their eagerness to impress their fond goodbyes on their new friend, Lynskey. 'Greg, are you

166

there?' She could still hear him breathing at the other end of the line. 'Greg?'

'I'm here. If you've decided on this, Sky, there's nothing to talk about, is there? But standing me up is a helluva way to let me know.'

'I told you that was a genuine mistake. Honest.'

'Yeah, well—'

To her horror his voice broke and she rushed in again, 'Greg, I want to be your friend—'

'*Don't!*' he cried. 'Don't patronize me, whatever else.'

'I won't patronize you.' She was feeling his grief for him now, 'I'm sorry – I really am.'

'Yeah, sure. Goodbye, Sky. See ya around. Have a nice life.' He clicked off.

She stood for a few moments with the receiver still jammed against her ear. This was not as she would have planned to do it but now that it was done, through the surge of shame and regret, trickled the threads of something lighter, brighter: a sense of infinite relief, akin to the feel-good sensation of childhood after she'd unloaded all those misdemeanours in the confession box. As she replaced the receiver, Sky was infused with a need to fill her room, the house – the world – with daffodils. 'Going already?' She turned to Buffy, who, with Hermana at her shoulder, was coming through the doorway from the kitchen into the hall.

Buffy leaned over and mouthed into Sky's ear, 'He's peachy. I'd hang on to that one if I were you!' In a normal tone, she continued, 'Look after your mom, now, Sky, you hear?'

'Thanks, Buffy. And thanks for the song. It was lovely.'

'What a guy!' Hermana enfolded Sky in a bear-hug and then held her off. 'What a guy!' she repeated. 'I might even take him myself if you don't want him.' Then, furtively: 'Take my advice, honey, and you think about that Greg. He's not up to your intellectual level.'

167

Around Hermana's bulk, Sky saw Lynskey twinkling up at Johanna, who was refilling his tea-cup. 'I think I have competition, Hermana.' She nodded in the direction of the kitchen.

'Oh, *you*!' Hermana chuckled and took Buffy's arm. 'We'll see ourselves out, dear. Now remember what I said.'

'Who was that, darling?' Johanna picked up one of the cats as Sky came back into the kitchen.

'It was just Greg.' Sky did not trust herself to look in Lynskey's direction.

'Your mother was telling me all about Daniel Treacy and her own mother, Sky. What a wonderful story.'

'You don't mind?' Johanna planted a kiss between the ears of the cat she held. 'Fergus knew a lot of it anyway, dear. He says you told him earlier.'

'I did.' Sky wondered briefly at Lynskey's persistent interest in Daniel Treacy but dismissed it.

'In all the time I lived in Ireland, you're the first Fergus I ever met!' Johanna beamed from Lynskey to Sky and back again.

'Don't encourage him, Mom.' Sky plonked herself at the table. 'He's insufferable enough.'

'Do you miss the old country?' Lynskey drained the herbal tea and held out his mug for a refill. He seemed to be settling in for the duration.

'I can't say I do.' Johanna's voice was now as full of rills and runs as his own. 'My family, of course, I miss them. Although I can't say in all honesty that we have been close. Odd that . . .' She trailed away, a faraway look in her eyes. 'My mother and my brother, Francey, in England . . . I was very close to him growing up. But we've all scattered now.'

'I hear your mother's maybe coming over for a visit?'

Johanna looked at Sky, unsure of how much she should divulge. 'I've told him, Mom.' Sky sighed. 'And he knows it was Daniel Treacy's idea.' She yawned. 'Speaking of Treacy, he's left several messages for me and I suspect he'll try to see me tomorrow, rather than Monday. I'm really tired. I think, if you guys don't mind, I'll drive Lynskey home now.'

Lynskey took the cue and got to his feet. 'Sorry. I've overstayed my welcome as it is – and I want to walk. I really do. It's early morning on my time clock.'

'Don't go yet, we were just getting started.' Johanna's disappointment was genuine.

'I'll be back, Johanna, don't worry. One of the advantages of having such superannuated holidays is that you can travel with few plans. And having met you and your daughter,' he straightened and looked directly at Sky, 'I've already changed mine. You'll be seeing a lot of me,' his eyes gleamed with wicked *double entendre*, 'I guarantee it.

'The dirty deed done?' he murmured, as Sky accompanied him along the little corridor to the front door of the duplex.

'M-mmm.' Sky was wondering if he would kiss her.

'Thank God for that.' He was enigmatic.

'That's a bit much, isn't it?' Although she found his honesty exhilarating Sky's guilt prompted a spurt of loyalty to her former boyfriend. 'You might at least *pretend* you're sorry for poor Greg.'

'Oh, I am, I am,' his smile belied it, 'but I'm happy for me. C'mere to me.' He enfolded her in his arms and kissed her strongly, but again broke off before she could respond. 'There. That'll hold us for a while.'

'Christ, you're something else, you know that? Are you sure you want to walk?'

'Sure. Tomorrow's Sunday. But if you don't want to see me, I'm a resourceful fella. I'll find something to do.' Before Sky could remonstrate he held a finger to her lips. 'There's always the king-sized bed in the War Bonnet Inn. Grand place, the War Bonnet.'

As she closed the door behind him she wondered if this on-again off-again stuff, which was driving her crazy, was a deliberate technique. But that fleeting look of fear on his face back in his hotel room had been real.

Before she turned in for the night, Sky called Daniel Treacy. Her suspicions had been correct. Something had come up for him on Monday and he wondered if they could meet in the morning instead.

In Killybegs in Co. Donegal, the omens were favourable. The weather was perfect: although it was not yet raining, the livid clouds, so low that the hilly landscape beyond the town was obliterated, were about to burst. Out to sea, a gale whipped long sheets of white foam from the crests of huge Atlantic rollers. Cold as winter and blowing sharply from the northwest, it might have been December rather than June.

The big inner harbour was sheltered from the worst of it, and although the timbers of the trawler fleet, lashed tightly together, creaked and screeched as they ground against each other, they were safe.

Even had the weather been fine it would have been unusual to see commercial activity in Killybegs so early on a Sunday morning, yet it was not unknown and the few people out and about paid little attention as fish boxes were loaded from the small lock-up garage at the end of the main street into the white Hiace van backed up against it. An elderly man, walking his fat, arthritic spaniel past it, did not even glance at what was going on.

The men worked efficiently and in silence. Loading completed, one climbed into the driver's seat, one secured the vehicle's back doors, the third scanned the lock-up's interior, making sure that nothing untoward would show to the prying eye. He went back inside and twitched at a pile of old nets and canvas sheeting in one of the back corners. Satisfied, he came out into the overcast day and secured the door with a rusty chain and padlock. Then he joined his colleagues in the van and they moved off.

As the Hiace travelled out of the town and towards the coast road, behind it, at the pier, one of the smaller trawlers, the *Agnes Monica*, slipped her moorings and nosed carefully out from between the companions tied on either side of her. As the captain took her forward, the hands on deck made sure that the vessels they were leaving exposed were tied up again. Then, as the trawler came clear and chugged slowly across the harbour towards the open sea, the men busied themselves with ropes and boxes and a general tidy-up. All the activities preparatory to a day's or a week's fishing.

The captain knew they would attract little attention, even putting to sea in such filthy weather. Those who fished from Killybegs were not faint-hearted but, in any event, unlike the super-trawlers which tracked the shoals across the open Atlantic, the *Agnes Monica* was a coaster, plying the inshore waters along the heavily indented shoreline and augmenting its usual catch of mixed fish with the contents of a few lobster pots. Everyone in the town would know that although she might be in for a bit of bumping, it would be nothing she had not encountered before.

They had spread the word that they might head around and over towards Rathlin and that they would be gone for a few days. That should cover them with their colleagues; as for the law – the captain grinned to himself as he chugged towards the harbour entrance – the Gárdaí were as transparent as children. They entrusted most of their so-called undercover activities to the night hours and were all snugly tucked up by now. The day shift was still turning over under its duvets and resisting its wives' exhortations to get up and get ready for early Mass.

The transfer of the fish boxes on to the *Agnes Monica* was effected in a tiny cove, invisible from the road above, about eleven miles west-northwest of Killybegs. Swirling sheets of rain obscured all but the nearest of the stony fields, which sloped steeply towards the cliff. The three men in the Hiace could not have asked for better conditions.

The trawler was hove to just outside an inlet, and if there had been anyone around to see, he would have assumed that the yellow-jacketed deck hands were priming the lobster pots stacked neatly along the rails, prior to throwing them over. What he would not have seen, unless he was right on the shore, was the Hiace. Having bumped down a tortuous little track, no wider than the span of its axles, the van was now tucked into a rocky indentation eroded into the cliff face. The three men jammed into the seat spoke little but it was clear that one was in charge. As the rain and wind pounded against the vehicle, and the other two swore at the discomfort, this man, gloved hands folded in his lap, sat as patiently as a sphinx, while the dinghy from the *Agnes Monica* was driven before the wind through the entrance to the cove. Although the distance to the beach was less than eighty yards, the craft was travelling so fast it was virtually surfing on the breakers. As it beached heavily, the two men in it jumped clear and dragged it up on to the packed wet sand.

This cove was shaped like a horseshoe; on either side, a pair of rocky promontories extended like protective arms into the sea, almost touching each other at the entrance, which was less than ten feet wide. The narrow mouth acted like a funnel for the wind, concentrating its ferocity so that the whirling spray and spume rebounded off the streaming cliffs, black and shiny as onyx.

The trip back to the top of the cliff was even more difficult than the descent. At one point the Hiace got stuck on the track, tyres spinning and spitting pebbles in all directions. Cursing, the men got out and wedged small boulders under the back wheels and pushed – no small task against the hill – until it lurched free.

But they still had to rejoin the road, which ran along the clifftop, where the risk of exposure was greatest, and they halted in a little hollow about thirty yards away. As one of the men got out and climbed the slope to check that their exit was clear, the young driver was on edge and sweating. He pulled at the collar of his oilskin after less than a minute. 'Where the fuck is he gone?'

'Shaddap. You and your nerves – you've been gettin' on *my* nerves all morning.' The accent of the sphinx-like man, although obviously cultivated in Donegal, was overlaid with transatlantic vowels.

The driver shot him a venomous glance. 'It's all right for you. When this is over you're safely back in America. And I know where *your* money's going and it's not to feed kids like mine is.'

'I said, shut up.' The man in charge reached into the pocket of his oilskin and took out a gun: small, black and snub-nosed. Almost casually, he levelled it at the head of the driver, who was struck voiceless with horror.

Seconds passed. Steam rose from their wet clothes and obscured the windscreen. Still holding the gun, the commander leaned forward and cleared a patch, the sleeve of his jacket squeaking against the glass. 'Are you going to be quiet?'

Still speechless, the driver nodded.

'Good.' His companion lowered the gun and put it away.

Just then the third man reappeared and jumped in. 'All clear. Come on, get the fuck on with it!' He, too, was showing strain.

Still badly shaken, the driver swallowed with relief as he felt the bite of potholed tarmacadam under his tyres. 'I'm not doing this again, d'ye hear me?' He felt safer now that the third man had rejoined them. 'This is the last time. I promised Marie. There's too many fuckin' eyes in this fuckin' country.' When neither of the others responded, he threw the Hiace into top gear and put the boot down.

The road they were on was not the main route back to Killybegs: narrow and twisting, it wound along the top of the cliff and joined the main road a few miles outside the town. 'You're going too fuckin' fast,' the third man yelled, as the tyres squealed on a bad bend, 'you'll attract every fuckin' policeman from here to Letterkenny.'

The driver did not reply, concentrating on the few yards of roadway ahead of the speeding vehicle. The rain was now so heavy that the wipers were useless, and as for the light – it was less like half past eight in the morning than nightfall. The driver flicked on his headlights but they were of little help, illuminating spears of rain and drifts of mist. 'Slow – fuckin' – *down*!' the third man yelled again.

'Jesus!' The driver swore. A white Gárda car, blue roof lights revolving slowly, was parked against the verge about fifty yards ahead. Standing beside it, in yellow slicker and Sam Browne, which glowed in the headlights of the oncoming Hiace, the officer was flagging them down with a torch.

'Don't stop. Run it!' snapped the commander.

Instinctively, the driver obeyed, flooring the accelerator so that the Hiace leaped. The Gárda jumped backwards, crashing heavily against the bonnet of his vehicle as the van sped past.

'Jesus, now they're on to us, Jesus, Jesus—' Having screeched around the first part of a corkscrew at the end of the short straight, the driver barely made the second, spinning the tyres in the soft mud of the verge. 'Why did I agree to this?' His voice was high and thin. 'We were doin' rightly as we were, Marie'll kill me—'

'Shaddap and slow down. You'll kill us all.' By this time they were almost at the T-junction on to the main road and the commander's voice cut through the driver's panic so he again obeyed, moving his boot from the accelerator to the

174

brake. But the rubber sole was wet and his foot slipped. The van shot through the junction and on to the main road, squealed into a skid, its rear swinging wide and ricocheting off a telegraph pole sending it across the crown of the road and on to the wrong side.

The elderly driver of a Toyota Starlet coming towards them had no chance to get out of the way before the Hiace hit him head-on.

Back on the secondary road above the sea, the Gárda, still badly shaken after his own near miss, was calling into Headquarters. He did not hear the crash above the crackling of his radio and the continuing roar of the storm.

The only survivor was the Starlet driver's greyhound.

The news reached the chief superintendent in Dublin later that morning. 'Who's the fucking independent operator who decided to do a Dan Dare?' He glared around the table at his task force. Some members, still at Mass maybe, had not yet come in but he had not wanted to wait.

'He's new in Killybegs.' The only woman present spoke quietly. 'He was just starting to drive in to work, along the main road,' she leaned forward and pointed to an Ordnance Survey map spread over the table, 'this one here—'

'I know where the fucking road is.'

'Sorry.' The woman was not put out. 'He was coming out of his gateway on to this road and he had stopped for a second. He thought he caught a glimpse of a vehicle driving too fast on the coast road that runs below the main one—'

'I see.' Daly's tone was larded with heavy sarcasm. 'Well, him and his fucking great ocular appendages can get themselves to hell on some offshore island. It took a lot of resources to set up this operation.' Again he scowled around the table. 'Where's de Burgh?'

'He's on his way in, sir,' the woman officer ventured.

Then, knowing better than to say anything more, they all sat waiting.

The chief got up and went across to a little side table. He poured coffee from a Thermos flask into a cup, added three spoonfuls of sugar and brought it back to the table. 'No one can find that bloody trawler,' he said quietly. 'It seems to have evaporated into thin air.'

'Does Lynskey know what's happened?'

'I've left a message for him to ring in – *shit*!' The chief threw his plastic spoon across the room.

Chapter Fifteen

Toby de Burgh was of average height and build, and although his face was passably handsome, he was one of those men who could, with ease, fade into the background of any gathering. His only memorable feature was the light colour of his eyes. Unlike Rupert, who was still estranged from their parents, he had taken full advantage of his family's money to set himself up, and was now wealthy in his own right from his activities in the City. He was a bachelor but not one who featured in the society columns, and his flat, furnished with massive Queen Anne and heavy Victorian furniture, showed no sign of a designer's hand. He was bidding farewell to his guests, the Prince of Wales and his detective.

He closed the door and sat at the table to review the course of the conversation. It had not gone too badly. Toby had no illusions that his illustrious guest had come because of his charming personality: he knew that the Prince was hoping he would donate a substantial sum to one of the organizations which received his royal patronage. Pleading another engagement, His Royal Highness had stayed less than forty minutes and had refused even a glass of wine.

It was not as though Toby himself was enamoured of a prince who held the honorary post of Colonel-in-Chief of the Paratroop Regiment, the very regiment responsible for Derry's Bloody Sunday.

He poured himself a glass of Calvados and gathered his

thoughts for the telephone call to his brother. The tabloid cutting Rupert had sent him, FANCIERS EXPECTED TO FLOCK TO MUSEUM, still lay on the table. Sipping his drink, Toby reread it then carried it to his desk, where he picked up the telephone.

When the call was answered, he did not identify himself. 'Nothing much,' he said softly, 'but I could tell by his reaction. I'd bet strongly, more than strongly, that the venue is go. He pretended not to be interested. So much so that I could see he knew too much about it.' Without waiting for an answer, he hung up.

Alone in the sitting room of his house in Churchtown, Rupert put down his own telephone and went to the door to listen: the bass thump-thump of the stereo unit in his sons' room continued unabated while, from the kitchen, he could hear his wife in heated argument with his daughter. Family as normal.

Quickly, he made a call to Sheriff O'Connor in Mayville, Montana: 'It's go. The venue is as we discussed. And there's one other thing, there's a man called Fergus Lynskey,' quickly, he spelled it, 'L-Y-N-S-K-E-Y, out there to Butte. Be careful, he's posing as a teacher. I don't know where he's staying, some hotel in the town, but try the biggest. He's one of ours, on the lookout.' Like Toby, he did not wait for a reply and, after he had hung up, turned to look at himself in the mirror over the fireplace in the sitting room. He had never liked it, a wedding present from his wife's sister: it had too many curlicues and cherubs in its thick gilt frame. But he liked the look of himself. In that mirror he was a man of substance.

From these two telephone calls grew a daisy-chain of further calls. Within ten minutes, plans for the operation had moved into high gear.

*

'Hire a car if you have to. Just get a move on your end, Lynskey – hold on—' The chief superintendent broke off in response to a knock on the door. 'Yes?'

It was ten minutes after the meeting at Gárda headquarters had broken up and, seeing his boss was on the phone, Rupert de Burgh reversed out of his office. 'I'll come back.'

'What is it, de Burgh? Tell me now, or I'll be gone. I'm on my way to Killybegs.'

'It was that I wanted to talk to you about.' De Burgh was apologetic. 'I'm sorry I missed the meeting – I couldn't get here on time. But I've done a bit of work up in Donegal before, I know the lie of the land and I'm sure I could spot a few faces for you. Could I be useful to you if I came along?'

'Hang on a mo',' Daly said into the phone, then, to de Burgh again, 'Come back when I'm finished this and we'll discuss it.' He waited ostentatiously until the detective had left the room, then: 'You still there, Fergus? Right, I've got a new name for you. Again, the feds got it from the Mounties in Ottawa – they seem to be really on the ball up there. This is a fella called Jerry Flynn.' He listened, then, 'I know, it's the first we've ever heard of him but until a few days ago we'd never heard of this Sheriff Brian O'Connor either. Apparently this Flynn character is flying down to a rodeo somewhere in Montana today – he has horses as well as everything else. And guess who his guest is going to be?' He listened, then: 'Bingo. But no, I don't know where the effin' thing is. That's what you're out there for. Just do it yesterday. Our friend across the water is getting itchy for an answer about the famous visit. So's the Taoiseach – another two points down in the polls today.'

Out in the corridor, de Burgh, who had been chewing gum, popped a new piece into his mouth as he leaned against the wall. 'Waiting to see the headmaster, are we?' another detective slagged as he walked past.

'Yeah.' De Burgh did not smile. The walls and doors were thick and largely soundproof, and although he strained his ears, he could hear nothing but a faint murmur, and then the dim percussion of the telephone being slammed down.

He eased himself off the wall and had his hand on the door handle when it was wrenched away from him. 'Oh,' the chief stood inside, 'I was just coming out to get you. We'll be leaving in about ten minutes.'

'There's another couple of things. Could I have a moment, chief?' De Burgh's face was serious.

The chief sighed, walked back into the room and behind his desk. 'Grab a pew.' He indicated the chair in front of it.

'Thank you.' De Burgh put his notes on the table in front of him. 'Oh, sorry,' he seemed only then to remember the gum in his mouth, 'where's your bin?'

'Here.' The chief gestured towards the side of the desk. 'What's on your mind?'

'It's nothing much, chief.' De Burgh went around and pulled the bin towards him so the desk was between himself and the chief. He sat down. 'I just wanted to tell you that, some time soon, I'll need a few days off. My sister-in-law's having a baby and my wife is going over to England to help.' As he was speaking he had leaned forward to deposit the wad of gum. 'I'll have to hold the fort with the kids.'

What the chief superintendent did not see was that de Burgh had transferred the gum from his right to his left hand. And while he made a movement towards the bin as though discarding it, he was sticking the gum under the lip of the desk, as far back as he could manage. 'Filthy habit,' he apologized again, 'but it keeps me off the fags.'

The chief superintendent made no difficulties about the time off but instead of standing up to go de Burgh sat on. 'The other thing I thought I might mention, but it may be a hoax . . .'

'I'm all ears.'

The chief tilted his chair so far back it was in danger of falling.

'I got an anonymous telephone call at home just before I left. The guy was trying to disguise his voice but he might have had a Cork accent.' De Burgh hesitated. 'He seemed to be saying that what we're looking for is buried in the grounds of a hotel in Glengarriff.'

'That's at the opposite end of the country from Killybegs. You're sure he said Glengarriff?' And when de Burgh nodded assent, 'Did he say which hotel?' The chief superintendent had gone very quiet.

'No.'

'Do you realize how many hotels there are in Glengarriff?'

'I did say that maybe it was another hoax.' De Burgh shrugged. He knew that Glengarriff, one of the most beautiful places in the southwest of Ireland, was a tourist Mecca. Just now it was coming up to the height of its season.

'Leave it with me.' The chief pursed his lips.

A few minutes later, de Burgh was speaking to his brother from a call-box outside the gates of the Phoenix Park, less than half a mile from Gárda headquarters. 'Done.' He listened, then: 'That won't happen, Toby, you don't know our cleaners. Anyway, there're cutbacks in overtime among them too, it's unlikely they're going to be that thorough. In any case, it won't be there for long. Talk to you tonight from Killybegs.'

He hung up and walked fast back through the park towards his office. It suited him that the Gárdaí were at sixes and sevens.

The previous year, at his wife's insistence, he had increased his mortgage so that he and his family could take a once-in-a-lifetime holiday. They had chosen California. On the last night, in a hotel bar in San Francisco, the Irish detective had, unusually for him, struck up a desultory conversation with a plumber from Santa Barbara whose name

181

was Joe Mason. The two had stayed up talking long into the night. They had exchanged telephone numbers and addresses, as one does on holidays, and de Burgh had largely forgotten about his new friend.

But then Mason's call had come, with a careful, obliquely worded request. It did not take de Burgh long, however, to realize that he was being asked to collaborate in a plot to infiltrate the annual republican commemoration of the patriot Wolfe Tone at Bodenstown in Co. Dublin. The plan was to take the Taoiseach hostage just before he read his speech and then to read their own proclamation of national-istic defiance.

Initially Rupert had thought the plan daft but even as Joe Mason continued to speak he had seen the glimmer of possibility that these people could be useful.

He had flown to London to confer with his brother, and the more they discussed it, the more they saw how they could use these misguided and outdated idealists for their own purposes – or, rather, de Burgh had seen it and had managed to persuade Toby.

Up to now, the de Burghs had remained independent of any of the recognized subversive groups. Yet they constituted a two-man organization which had bided its time and watched for an opportunity to make its contribution. Rupert was content to wait, for decades if need be, as he wormed his way closer and closer to the heart of the Irish security service. This quisling service which now doffed its cap to the English.

The beauty of Joe Mason's call was that it had dovetailed nicely with the chance for which the brothers had waited so long.

It arose because of Toby's lifestyle. He was gay and one of his lovers, who had not come out, was a senior official in the Foreign Office in London. It was for this reason alone that his urbane and wealthy City friend had cultivated him.

The arrangement, in which Toby and his friend met only at parties and at the houses of people with equal need for anonymity, suited the de Burghs' purposes very well, although until recently, the gossip and inside Foreign Office information had been of such little significance that Toby had begun to think he was wasting his time. Until he had hit the jackpot.

He and his friend had been enjoying a cognac in their palatial bedroom during a weekend houseparty in Surrey when the civil servant had gossiped about a possible trip to Éire for the Prince of Wales.

Within hours of receiving this nugget, Rupert was in touch with Joe Mason: he would help with Joe's group effort and would let them know the timing. But, of course, he did not tell him what he and Toby really intended. He was not sure if the Americans would have the guts for it.

Unknown to Bill Daly or Fergus Lynskey or anyone else, another thread had been added to the skein of mayhem.

After a restless night, haunted by erotic fantasies wherein she was being pleasurably engulfed by the huge soft lips and sinuous limbs of a fabulous creature resembling a benign praying mantis, Sky woke just after dawn. Reluctant to let the dream dissolve, she kept her eyes closed and tried to maintain it while her body revelled in the warm hollow of her mattress. Then, with a sensation like walking under a cold waterfall, she remembered Greg.

Her eyes flew open on the salmon pink day. Dammit. Why did every silver lining come with a cloud? She would not be able to live with herself unless she spoke with him face to face.

She tumbled out of bed and not bothering to cover her nakedness – Johanna would not be up for hours yet – padded towards the shower. Inside, she kept both hands on the controls, letting the water pour over her, alternately hot and cold. Johanna insisted that showers were essential for cleansing the aura and, for once, her daughter did not disagree. She concentrated on directing her mind towards the first task of the day. Daniel Treacy.

She rehearsed the headlines of the story: the mysteries surrounding Midge's life, the opportune crash that had killed her, the closed coffin, the sheriff's attitude, the scrawled note on the coffee coupons, the feeling that Skippy was part of an upstate conspiracy, Treacy's odd rush away from the funeral home, his long-time obsession with her own grandmother. His questionable past. By the time she stepped out of the shower and was towelling herself dry, Treacy occupied every corner of her mind.

She arrived at the offices of Treacy Resources exactly on time. 'I'm sorry to call you in on a Sunday,' Treacy was sitting across from her behind his desk – no hospitality today – 'but, as I told you last night, I'm afraid I have meetings all day tomorrow and the coming week is busy. I will be out of town for most of it. What are these one or two details you wish to know?' He began to drum the fingers of one hand on the desk-top. This from a man who had called her three times and who was, in a sense, bent on infiltrating her family.

Sky decided once again she would not be intimidated. 'Do you never take time off, Mr Treacy?'

He stared at her, then, slowly: 'As you are aware, my wife is not cold in her grave. However, as it happens, Miss MacPherson, I have acceded to well-meaning pressure from a business acquaintance and I am going on an – ah – outing this afternoon. Not that it is any of your concern.'

'It transpires that some of the details I need to ask you about concern the death of your wife.'

'Indeed?' His tone was icy. 'I would think that as my wife is so recently dead and buried, the *Courier* would have the decency to desist from prying into such a painful and personal area of my life.'

'May I ask what you were calling me about, Mr Treacy? I got one message at the office and two at home.'

The fingers stilled. 'I am a tidy man, Miss MacPherson, with a tidy mind. I do not like loose ends. And, since you ask, I do know that you have been digging around about my wife's death in the north of the state.'

'Sheriff O'Connor?'

'Never mind how I know. Why are you poking around?' His composure slipped a fraction.

'Because it's my job.' She kept her voice cool. 'You could save us both a great deal of trouble, even grief, if you would talk to me and tell me the truth about what happened to your wife.'

'The truth, Miss MacPherson,' he locked his eyes with hers, 'is that I genuinely do not know. I was not there that night. I do not know in what state poor Midge was when she drove to her death.'

'Wasn't there a post mortem?'

'There was very little for the medical examiner to work on.'

Suddenly, Sky felt dirty, with little entitlement to the high moral ground she had claimed earlier for herself and the *Courier*. 'I'm sorry,' she said.

'Are you? Sorry enough to desist from pursuing this non-story?'

'There is just one thing.' Nettled again, Sky took a deep breath. 'Had your wife anything to do with the death of a hobo on the highway somewhere north of Libby?'

Treacy got up and turned to gaze through the window towards the statue of Our Lady of the Rockies. He clasped his hands behind his back. Seeing traces of white on the knuckles, she let him be. If he was ever going to tell her, now was the time.

As she waited, Sky committed this room and everything

185

in it to memory. On her last visit she had noted its austerity, but now she went further: unusually for an executive in his position, there was no clock, no memento, no award, framed certificate or executive toy. Except for the single photograph of his dead wife, it was as though Daniel Treacy had had the place scoured so that no clue to his own personality or interests could possibly be divined.

Around them, in the unnaturally quiet building, the internal workings of the structure – the humming of the air-conditioning, the odd creak – which highlighted his silence might have been unnerving, had she not been so concentrated on the man at the window. 'I knew it would come out eventually.' He spoke so quietly she almost missed it.

He turned to face her and, with the blaze of light at his back, his features were in shadow. 'Midge did kill that hobo,' he said, 'but it was a genuine accident. She was drunk at the time. Too drunk to do the right thing.'

Sky held her nerve. If she said anything now, she might ruin what was next to come.

Treacy walked slowly back to his desk and sat down again. 'It's been a terrible burden on me. Now you know. What are you going to do about it?'

'That depends on what your wife did not do. Do you mean it was a hit-and-run?' Treacy nodded and, such was the pallor of his face, she felt almost sorry for him. But she hardened her heart. This man was rich – rich enough for others, including the police, to do dirty work for him. 'And there was a cover-up.' It was not a question.

'Yes.' He folded his hands in his lap and looked down at them, an uncharacteristically humble posture that puzzled Sky. He was also avoiding her eye.

'Was the sheriff involved in the cover-up?'

'He's an old friend of Bill Collins. Bill Collins is an old friend of others. That's the way it works, apparently. And that man she hit was drunk.'

186

Sky, ignoring the implicit appeal, remembered she had had calls from Collins, had assumed that the funeral director wanted to talk to her about the shamrock lot and had been in no hurry to return them. 'Look,' she had no wish to torture the man in front of her, 'I'll be honest with you, Mr Treacy, I don't know yet to what use I'm going to put this story. I have to think about it. But we have a bit of time, there's no rush. Your wife is dead, after all. In a way,' she softened her voice, aware that the man's bereavement was so recent, 'she already paid a terrible price. I'll talk to my editor. We're not in the business of persecuting people.'

'Thank you.' Still Treacy did not look up.

'We'll talk again. Anyway,' she tried to sound cheerful, 'we have to talk about my grandmother's visit . . .'

He looked up at last. 'Do you think she'll come? She certainly won't come if she thinks I've—'

'Try not to worry.' Behind the awful weariness of his eyes, she could see hope and heard herself tell him that her mother was going to call Ireland again that night. 'They're eight hours ahead and she imagines it will be less expensive and they can talk longer if it's late night here and early morning there.'

'But it's Sunday, and, anyway, there's no need—' he began, but Sky held up her hand.

'You can't control everything, Mr Treacy.'

187

Chapter Sixteen

An hour after Sky left Treacy's house, although it was only ten thirty in the morning, heat already shimmered inches above the tarmacadam and baked the paintwork of the vehicles in the McDonald's parking lot. Inside, however, the patrons, clad mainly in T-shirts and cutoffs, felt the chill of the super-efficient air-conditioning and rubbed at their goose-bumped flesh.

'It was an amazing change.' She and Lynskey were eating Sunday brunch, although for Sky the meal began and finished with strong coffee. 'In retrospect, I have the impression that he was sort of *waiting* for the bad news, you know?' She looked around, irritated at the level of chatter in the echoing room. 'It's terribly noisy in here.'

'Reminds me of Dublin Zoo.' Lynskey bit into the second of his Egg MacMuffins. 'But to get back to your man, I wouldn't blame the poor chap. You certainly ruined his day. You're pretty sure that note's the real thing?'

'It appears so now.' Sky watched in fascination as he poured two packets of salt over his second carton of french fries, then said, hearing echoes of her mother, 'That stuff'll kill you, you know.'

'What?' Lynskey paused a fraction. 'All these chips?'

'All that salt.'

'Listen, my mother's eighty-two and she likes a bit of mashed potato with her salt. We like salt in our family. So your man was poleaxed, what happened then?' With his left hand, he scooped up a fistful of the fries and put them in his mouth.

'Are you left-handed?' Sky tended sneakily to subscribe to the unproven notion that left-handed people are more intelligent than their more numerous right-handed brethren. She had always been attracted to intrinsic intelligence the way some women are attracted to power.

'Ambidextrous,' he chewed with evident enjoyment, 'comes in handy, no pun intended.' He grinned, then: 'So go on, did you get the feeling there was more to tell?'

Considering her answer, Sky looked away. They were seated beside the wall of plate glass facing the parking lot and, as she watched, a big Lincoln, springs bouncing under the exuberance of what seemed to be dozens of children, was turning slowly through the entrance. Multicoloured balloons streamed from every open window and even through the thickness of the double-glazing she could hear the high-pitched excitement from within the vehicle. 'I wish I was that age again,' she said.

'A birthday, obviously.' Lynskey paused long enough to look affectionately at the festive Lincoln then went back to his meal. 'Can't say it makes me homesick, though. Thank God I won't have to deal with kids for another three months at least. So did you? Feel that McCarthy had more to tell?'

Startled, Sky looked back at him. 'How do you know his real name's McCarthy?'

'You told me, silly. That first day, on the way to the Buffalo Jump.'

Had she? Sky could not pinpoint any conversation in which she had mentioned it. 'You keep bringing us back to this subject,' she said suddenly.

'Do I?' Lynskey tore open another packet of salt. 'It's a fascinating story, you've got to agree. It has everything, money, sex – albeit over a long distance – death in mysterious circumstances. Yeah. Even the possibility of a happy ending.'

As usual, Sky could not contain her suspicions. 'You're not thinking of using this for your novel, are you?'

Lynskey's shout of laughter caused several of the restaurant patrons to look round. 'Give us a break, love,' he said, when he had managed to control himself. 'I'm a schoolteacher. My novel, when it comes, will be small and perfect and full of serious *angst*. Stuff like money and love and possible murder is too trivial for me.'

Sky smiled and, as the birthday party erupted into the restaurant, began to go through what Treacy had said, how he had behaved. The more she talked, the more convinced she became that she was seeing only the tip of the story. Lynskey seemed to agree, nodding over his rapidly diminishing pile of fries, encouraging her with astute prompts.

'What do you want to do?' They were walking to the Nissan.

'I dunno.' He shrugged. 'What do people do in Montana on a Sunday in late June? What's on that I can boast about back home? Anything really special? I have my camera.' He patted a bulge in the back pocket of his awful shorts. 'I thought of asking you to take me out to the Little Big Horn battlefield but then I remembered it's Sunday and I'd prefer to do it when there weren't so many people about.'

'I don't mind taking you out there, but it's quite a distance, you know – it's beyond Billings—'

'I know.' His long face lit up. 'I saw a newspaper ad for a rodeo somewhere around here this weekend. That has to be the most quintessentially American Western thing I could see. Would it still be on, do you think? Could we go?'

'It's on, all right.' Sky hesitated. Briefly, she told Lynskey about the spat she had had with Jimbo the previous week.

'Well, of course, we don't have to go, I'm sure I can catch one somewhere else along the way.' But he looked so crestfallen that Sky changed her mind. The wretched rodeo would be a way of entertaining him and would earn her a few Brownie points.

'Are you sure you don't mind?' His pleasure was infectious when she told him they would go.

'Everyone has to go to a rodeo at least once in his life – I think.' She laughed as he kissed her cheek.

Jimbo was delighted too, once he had gotten over his astonishment. 'I'll contact the photographer – he can meet you there. And I'll pull off the kid, give her something else to do next weekend.' Even from home, Jimbo's telephone voice was different from the one he used for face-to-face encounters. Flat and snappy, it gave the correct impression that the instrument was not his favourite medium of communication. 'Bye.' He hung up abruptly.

'All set.' Sky joined Lynskey in the Nissan. 'I'll just wheel by the office to collect the bumf I need and we'll go straight away. It's not all that far, just over ninety miles.'

'I'll never get used to the distances here. You say ninety miles like we say three. That Little Big Horn must really be far away.'

'Welcome to Montana, buddy.' As they pulled out of the lot, heading towards the newspaper office, Sky looked doubtfully at the pale freckled skin of his upper arms; Lynskey had at last dumped the sweatshirt and, in honour of the heat, now wore a T-shirt in bright green emblazoned with legends supporting the Irish national soccer team, which had evidently taken part in some festival or competition called Italia 90. 'You'll need a hat in this sun,' she pulled her sunglasses from the glove compartment, 'but we can buy one at the grounds. You're already looking a bit pink.'

'I'm grand. Sure I can't go home without a suntan, can I?'

'You never heard of melanoma?' But Sky grinned. His

191

enthusiasm was impossible to resist. She might even enjoy the rodeo for once.

The man from Helena, the state capital, who had engaged Sheriff O'Connor in the matter of the casket, was speaking on a secure cellphone to a woman in Vancouver.

This woman, slight of form and with Oriental features, lived frugally in an expensive apartment, which had a view across the water towards Vancouver Island. Her furniture was of carved or lacquered wood and brass, her wall-coverings and soft furnishings in shades of gold and red. She had bought her home ten years previously, paying cash and finding little difficulty in passing scrutiny by the building's interviewing committee. She had no family ties, no pets and, being new to their city, no local friends. The committee members expressed a doubt among themselves that her aura of self-sufficiency might border on eccentricity but they approved her anyway.

They were not disappointed. She proved an exemplary tenant with perfect manners, paying her service and mainten-ance charges promptly. Although she had never agreed to serve on any of the subsequent committees, or to attend any meetings called to discuss affairs of mutual interest, she was exceptionally polite to her neighbours when she met them in the elevators or in the lobby. And, indeed, her lifestyle was so quiet and unobtrusive that if it had not been for these fleeting encounters, she might not have been in the building at all.

What the interviewing committee had not known was that, before moving to their exclusive block in Vancouver, this woman had been the mistress of many politicians and scions of industry in Toronto, Ottawa and, being bilingual, in French-speaking Montreal. Neither did they know that she was not planning to stay among them for much longer but was *en route* to her retirement destination, the house she had had built on a tiny, so far uninhabited island she owned off the coast of Brazil, which did not enjoy reciprocal extradition treaties with Canada. They could not have known that although her tax returns showed her to be a woman of substantial means, whose income was derived from shrewd investments in stock, they bore little relation to the true extent of her holdings.

Through diligent and imaginative use of her assets, this woman's wealth, hardly any of which was held in Canada but was spread over the Cayman Islands, Switzerland and the Isle of Man, was more than enough to fuel the economy of a European statelet for at least three months. Her turnover was as big as that of a modest multinational corporation which, in a sense, she had become. She was answerable to no board, however. And none of the operations she master-minded took place within the borders of her domicile. Instead, she controlled them through a network of five trusted deputies in Anchorage, Los Angeles, Orlando, Mexico City and Helena, chosen because it was so relatively obscure and crime-free that it would attract little unwanted attention. These deputies, her only full-time employees, were each paid a salary higher than that of the President of the United States, and provided the woman received the profits she expected in a given endeavour, any excess they garnered, through favourable fluctuations in exchange rates, for instance, was their own business.

The lieutenants also had a free hand in the recruitment of underlings, provided that these minions adhered to the pyramid structure the woman laid down in the blueprint for her organization: temporary workers received and relayed orders only from and to the layers directly above and below. This precaution ensured that no one except the woman and her five lieutenants had a full picture of any operation. And not one of the five knew about the work of any of the other four. The woman did not believe in consultation, democracy or round-table meetings. She did almost all of her business by electronically secured telephone and her only face-to-face engagements were in Ottawa with the pricy accountant who had once been her lover.

She listened carefully as her man in Helena, who knew that his boss always wanted the facts, no matter how unpalatable, explained what had gone wrong with the operation in Ireland.

The crash of the Hiace – which could not have been foreseen – had served to galvanize the attentions of the Irish police and government. The goods in the northwest of Ireland were safe, her man assured her, but it would be unwise to access them.

He then outlined the problems within the state of Montana, which could be contained: the newspaper was only a two-bit outfit with a cash-flow problem and would have to back off sooner rather than later. The FBI angle was well covered – he knew that the woman had a well-paid mole – and although the Irish cop's presence in Butte was a wild card, it was wound in with the work of the newspaper reporter and a method could be devised to deal with them both at once.

It was the first full briefing the woman had had. Normally, having set up an operation and provided the seed money, she let the others run it. Her genius lay in identifying niche markets: in knowing what product was most profitable in what part of the world. Her apartment was cabled and also sported a satellite dish and, as she spent a good proportion of her time watching television, she was well versed in foreign affairs. She made it her business to know which organizations might need funds for their own purposes. And exactly where.

Although she knew she was not the first to identify Ireland as an entrypoint into the lucrative European market, the present Irish operation was her first foray into that country.

Cautious as always, she had instructed that this test operation be kept small. The follow-up, however – ready to be put in motion the moment she gave the go-ahead – was the biggest she had ever prepared.

Now, as she listened to the bad news pouring down the line from Helena, she was weighing up her options: whether she should cut her losses and shut the whole thing down, or whether she should order damage limitation and proceed with the test. She had a great deal at stake: the main business, which was to follow this exercise, was not only the biggest of her career, it was to be her last, before the curtain fell on her retirement.

Sky and Lynskey held hands like high school sweethearts. Even for Montana, it was a gorgeous day and, as the miles unrolled under the Nissan's tyres, she felt young and irresponsible, even happy. The steady wind through the open windows was warm on her cheek and neck; to the west, under the crystal sky, the amethyst of the mountains seemed further away than usual, while eastwards, the recent storms, not enough to count as full-blown rains, had refreshed and softened the prairie, hazing its straw with pale and supple green.

After a bit, almost shyly at first, Lynskey began to tell her about his geographically far-flung but close-knit family.

After he had finished, Sky could not help but compare his mother's view of child-rearing to Johanna's laid-back and *laissez-faire* approach. 'That's quite a group of achievers, she must be some woman. All those vocations and professions scattered all over the globe.'

'And then there's yours truly.'

'Teaching is an honourable profession.'

He was silent and, for once, she did not leap to bridge the gap. She had to give herself a stern talking-to. Although she felt as though she and Lynskey had known one another for aeons, they had met less than forty-eight hours before. She had to slow herself, and it was obvious he wanted to take things easy. She shifted down a gear to negotiate a non-existent bump in the highway. 'So, you're all away from Ireland except you?'

'Yeah. Us Lynskeys could field a modest international think-tank. Between countries of residence and spouses, at last count we covered eleven nations.'

'It's nice for your mother that she has one of her children left in Ireland. At her age she must rely on you a lot.'

But this assumption, too, was misconceived. Apparently, Lynskey's mother was as spry as a forty-year-old and had filled her retirement years with twice as much activity as when she had been in harness. 'Remember she's a Kerry-woman.' Lynskey smiled affectionately as though this explained his mother's stamina. 'She loves cards – she's a member of three different poker schools. She's in a creative-writing circle and last year she took up Italian because she intends to travel to Verona in August and wants to under-stand first-hand what the operas are about.' He reached for Sky's hand and squeezed it. 'She reminds me a bit of your mother. Same spirit.'

Sky thought of Johanna's willow-like attitude to whatever life threw at her and raised her eyebrows at the notion of there being the remotest similarity between her and Lyn-skey's redoubtable mother. 'Maybe. But she sounds a lot more like my grandmother. At least, they're more of an age.'

She told him then of what she knew about her grand-mother's lifestyle in Cork, how, when she was sure her family was reared, she had moved back to the city from the fastnesses of West Cork. How, at the age of sixty-two, she went to college and graduated with a degree in music, how she was now one of the leading lights in local music circles. 'Come to think of it, she does sound a lot like your mother.'

196

'It's odd she's never been out here, isn't it?' he asked. 'After all, three of her family are here, and crossing the Atlantic is only a matter of a few hours, these days.'

'She just never got around to it, I suppose. As my mother told you last night, ours, unlike yours, is not a close family.'

The rodeo ground was buzzing. As they threaded their way through the horseboxes, steer trucks, feed and veterinary wagons, pickups containing harness and blacksmith equipment, she could hear the amplified voice of the announcer urging on the barrel-racers inside the arena.

The only thing Sky liked about rodeos was the smell of the air: horseflesh, fresh sweat and dung, earth, leather, barbecue smoke, the scent of canvas, warm metal and frying onions, fresh coffee and beer. In a way, she thought as she showed her press card and ID at the entrance, the cocktail epitomized Montana. 'I have a guest,' she told the man scrutinizing her passes.

'I can pay,' Lynskey protested.

'Not when you're with me, you don't.' Sky waved to a colleague from a Great Falls radio station as the man allowed them to pass through. 'This is work.'

'Nice work if you can get it. I can't believe I'm here.' Lynskey snapped a couple of drovers leading one of the bulls towards the arena.

'Believe it,' Sky waved at another acquaintance, 'you'll be sick of cowboys before the day is over.' She left him briefly to go and talk to a woman she recognized from Butte. To her exasperation, when she went back she found he had joined a line in front of a hot-dog stand. 'I don't know what it is about American food,' he was unabashed at her obvious disapproval, 'it just doesn't fill you up. Want something? Come on, it smells delicious.'

Sky held firm and walked a little way off to wait for him and take colour notes. She was leaning against the tailgate of a station wagon and trying to summon up enough enthusi-

197

asm to walk across to an old-timer for a quote, when all heads around her turned in response to a helicopter slowly descending at the far side of the showgrounds.

Choppers were not unusual in Montana but this one was big enough to transport a modest glee club and obviously heralded the arrival of a VIP. She hurried back to Lynskey, who had not yet reached the head of the hot-dog line, and told him to meet her at the announcer's stand in fifteen minutes.

She arrived at the fringe of the landing site just as the pilot switched off the rotors. The reporter from the radio station in Great Falls was ahead of her, standing a little in front of the curious onlookers, recorder held protectively to his breast.

The buzz of the crowd stilled as she moved up to join him, and she was amused to see, as from the arena the amplified voice of a young girl sounded the first notes, of the 'Stars and Stripes', that he straightened his shoulders and laid his free hand under his recorder in the approved hand-over-heart position. Patriotism alive and well in Great Falls. As for herself she concentrated on the throp-throp of the slowing rotors.

When the door of the aircraft opened, she recognized the elderly man who alighted first; she had seen him here in previous years and had even interviewed him briefly, but his name escaped her. 'Remind me who that is?' she muttered out of the side of her mouth to the radio reporter.

'Name's Jerry Flynn.' He was checking his tape. 'He's a Canadian. Logging, minerals, that kind of thing. He also runs stock in Alberta on one of those million-acre spreads.'

Flynn, whose hair was longish, was wearing full Western gear, a huge cream-coloured Stetson, hide boots, check shirt under fringed jacket and a thong tie clasped with the silver and turquoise head of a bronco. 'Talk about cheesy! He'd

198

make a good Buffalo Bill, whaddya think?' the radio reporter gibed under his breath.

Sky did not altogether agree.

Although to judge by the wrinkled skin on his face, white moustache and liver-spotted hands the guy must have been at least in his sixties, his body was in good shape and she thought that the outfit did not look any more incongruous on him than it would have on Jimmy Stewart, who was one of her mother's favourite stars. Cheesy, though, was an apt description of his smile. The guy had two gold teeth on one side of his mouth.

The clothes of the much younger man who followed him out were similar but horribly inappropriate because of his weight. 'He could eat for the Olympics.' The radio man looked worried. 'Never saw him before – you know him, Sky?'

'Uh-uhhh.' Sky was staring at the third passenger just now getting out. Conservatively dressed in dark jeans and plain shirt, and looking around the ground as he descended, was Daniel Treacy. She had barely time to register her surprise before she was walking alongside the radio reporter towards the chopper to do her job. 'This is a first. Never saw Treacy here before either,' the reporter hissed. 'Let me talk to him first, OK?'

'Sure.'

While Treacy and the fat man stood a little apart, Jerry Flynn continued to stand at the door of the helicopter, talking to the pilot who had remained inside. Of course, Sky thought, Flynn had to be the 'colleague' of whom Treacy had spoken that morning. So far he had not seen either her or the radio reporter – or if he had, he was ignoring them. She had little time for further speculation because Treacy spotted her. 'We meet again, Miss MacPherson,' he said, as she and her colleague reached him.

199

'We do indeed.' Sky introduced the radio man, who immediately asked for an interview.

'No thank you.' As though willing Flynn to hurry, Treacy looked over his shoulder at his host, who was still talking to the pilot. Sky realized that, apart from the few seconds during which she had seen him walk from the door of the funeral parlour to his limousine, this was the first time she had seen him outdoors. In this bright sunlight, he looked tired: his complexion was grey and, standing so close to him, she could see deep, violet-shaded rings around his eyes.

'Nothing serious, sir,' the reporter persisted. 'Our listeners would just like to know how you're enjoying yourself today, that sort of thing . . .'

Treacy glanced at Sky then, not waiting for the reporter's cue or question, raised his voice to a commanding monotone and spoke into the microphone, congratulating the American Legion on another successfully organized event and assuring everyone that this would prove to be the best ever. Then he turned to the fat man. 'I'll go ahead, see you at the booth.' He smiled his cold smile at Sky. 'Perhaps we shall run into one another again during the course of the afternoon.' He walked off towards the arena.

'How about you, sir, what do you hope for today? I'm sorry, may I have your name?' The radio reporter immediately switched the microphone to the other man but Sky watched Treacy's retreating back.

The fat man was also a Canadian but had nothing to do with farms and stock. 'Unless I'm foreclosing!' His belly heaved over a bronchial laugh. 'I'm Mr Flynn's banker, just along for the ride. Rodeo's the only place I see creatures bigger than myself.' Again he laughed as Sky half listened, scribbling as fast as she could.

While she wrote, she continued to watch Treacy's progress and saw him pause once or twice to speak to people before he was swallowed up in the crowd. Then her eye was caught by Lynskey. Her companion for the afternoon was standing not in front of the announcer's booth, as they had arranged, but at a corner of the stand. She was too far away to discern his expression but, as she watched, she saw him take his little camera out of his back pocket and take a one-handed photograph of Daniel Treacy. She almost dropped her notebook. Then, as the fat man beside her was joined by Jerry Flynn, and the radio reporter switched the interview to him, she saw Lynskey turn, point the camera at the stand behind him and snap again, then turn back towards Treacy.

She had not imagined it. Fergus Lynskey was deliberately photographing Daniel Treacy.

Or was he? With the camera still to his eye he was now aiming at her, waving his other arm over his head to attract her attention as he did so.

Slowly, she waved back and, half listening as Flynn answered the radio reporter's questions, continued to watch Lynskey's activities. He was photographing all round him, the perfect tourist.

Sky forced herself to pay attention to her job. Although Daniel Treacy and Jerry Flynn were probably of an age, their appearances were entirely different. Whereas Treacy's closely cropped hair, lean face and thin, slightly stooped body lent him an autocratic, tired, somewhat ascetic air, Flynn's more flamboyant presentation sparkled with energy and vigour. This was an elderly man, sure, but one with drive. And unlike Treacy who did not flaunt his money, Flynn had no objection to flashing his: on his pinky he sported a ring, the diamond in which had to be, to Sky's inexperienced eye, at least two or three carats.

She decided that she had plenty of material, and thanked the two Canadians, told the radio reporter she would see him around, and walked towards the stand. Lynskey saw her coming and, as she watched him surge towards her, long legs covering the ground so they would meet half-way, Sky remembered that it had been his idea to come here.

'Isn't this great?' He beamed as he reached her, the little camera now dangling from a wrist strap.

Chapter Seventeen

The meeting at Gárda headquarters was coming to a close. It was taking place with much reduced numbers: the chief superintendent and Rupert de Burgh were in Killybegs and a detective inspector was temporarily in charge. The meeting had taken longer than planned – it was almost midnight – and the blond wood table was littered with coffee-stained Styrofoam cups and with the balled-up Cellophane wrappers and Sunday-stale crusts from bought-in sandwiches.

Word had been issued to the press office that the accident at Killybegs was to be downplayed, except for the normal expressions of regret about the tragic loss of life of the retired chemist, so popular in the area, and of the three fishermen, all of whom had left young families. Gárda presence at the funerals was to be minimal. It was agreed that not a word of admonishment was to be spoken to the young officer who had inadvertently precipitated the crisis in case he began to make the wrong noises.

There was still no word on the whereabouts of the missing *Agnes Monica*.

Sky stared at Lynskey's camera. Then, looking directly at him and giving him no time to dissemble: 'Why are you photographing Daniel Treacy?'

'What? Where?' Lynskey wheeled around and scanned the crowd in the stand. 'Is he here?'

'Gimme a break. I saw you, Lynskey.'

'Saw me what?' He looked down at her, his long face creased and frowning.

'Saw you deliberately taking photographs of Daniel Treacy.' Sky searched his expression and could see nothing but genuine puzzlement. 'You took two photographs of him.'

'I'm glad I did – if I did – but how would I know what he looked like? Not that it matters a damn, Sky, I swear to God I was just taking everything in. But if he's here, I'd love to see him. Will you point him out to me? Better still, will you introduce me?'

'He's vanished into a hospitality booth.' Sky was still not convinced. 'You sure you didn't recognize him coming out of that helicopter?'

'Why would I?' He chuckled. 'For God's sake, MacPee, would you ever lighten up? What's the big deal, anyway?'

Sky had no answer to that. She was unsure what concerned her. In the brief pause, Lynskey's eyes grew mocking. 'Look at us,' he flapped a limp wrist and flounced a hip, 'we're having our first row. Shall I storm away and insist on getting a taxi home? Blow all my traveller's cheques but keep my dignity at all costs?'

Despite herself, Sky laughed. 'That's better.' Lynskey hugged her shoulders. 'We're not going to let old mystery man come between us, now, are we? I'd still like to see him, though.'

Sky, telling herself she was a suspicious bitch, promised she would point him out.

She was so busy during the next hour or so, however, that she almost forgot about Treacy. And, intent on her story, she also failed to notice anything unusual about the two men in Stetsons, who sat munching Fritos high in the stand towards the back row. These two, although they consulted their programmes and seemed to be enjoying themselves as much as anyone else, did not seem to be talking to one another. Another odd factor in their behaviour: instead of watching the action, they spent most of their time scanning the crowd.

Sky could not be blamed for failing to register the jarring presence of the two men. Her hands were full: the name of every human and animal competitor in the rodeo was listed in the official programme so, although she had no difficulty with that part of her assignment, she also had to direct her photographer and engage in tedious gathering of the names of every spectator of note, along with homey little anecdotes about them:

> The Willard F. Keyneses barely made it on time for the barrel-racing, nearly missing the fine showing by their daughter, Sara, who turned in her best ever time and came fourth. They told this reporter that their pedigree Jerseys are producing record numbers of calves on their spread up by Opportunity . . .
> In the stands, Maynard and Peggy Olsen from Wisdom showed off their first grandchild, Otley, to their friends and rivals the Chuck Fenweigs, who are busy rebuilding since their barn burned down this spring . . . The William Harringtons were expecting great things of their Palomino, Misty. Misty's beaten every cowboy so far this season . . .

Finally, she located the proprietor of the *Courier* and did the obligatory interview. The old man, to whom the Butte paper was just one more page in a balance sheet, gave the same answers to her questions as he had the year before, and the year before that again.

'Yuck! I hate doing this . . .' The bulk of her work done, she rejoined Lynskey in the stands: in her absence he had been adopted by every family near him. Long legs spread wide, he was surrounded by drinks cans and plastic sacks and was chewing something. 'You're just a snob.' He rummaged in one of the sacks. 'You can't cover Watergate every day.'

'You can't cover Watergate *any* day in Montana.'

'Rubbish. There are no small stories, only small reporters. Here, cheer up and have one of Mrs Krabb's homemade oatmeal cookies, they're delicious.' He beamed at a woman behind him.

'No thank you.' She turned her attention to the arena, watching with gloomy satisfaction as one of the huge cross-bred Brahmas strolled out of his chute and refused to buck off his rider – or even to run – acknowledging the ribald groans of the spectators with a surprised look on his jowly face. 'You wanted to see Treacy?' Sky dug Lynskey in the ribs. 'There he is.'

'Where?' Instantly, he sat up straight.

'Down there, in front of the bull.' She pointed to where, backs to the stand, Treacy and the fat man were standing near the recalcitrant animal, which continued to resist all attempts of its rider and a posse of drovers to prod him into being a good sport.

'So that's him.' Lynskey leaned forward to get a better look. 'I wish he'd turn around so we could see his face.'

'I still can't work out why you want to meet him so much.'

'You've been talking about nothing else, MacPee. I told you, I love a good story.' He had to raise his voice to be heard above the crowd, which was in full cry at the bull, which had now spread its legs like a dog balking at being dragged along on a lead.

The rider was furious. He raked the bull's sides with his spurs, but all in vain. The beast simply eyeballed the crowd, swinging its massive head in a slow arc from side to side.

Knowing she was probably in a minority of one, Sky was delighted with the performance. 'Come on, bull,' she encouraged it silently. 'Don't give in now. Stand your ground.' As though it had heard her, the bull slowly turned its head towards the stand just as a sudden gust of wind whirled an empty popcorn sack a foot across its snout. Startled, it drew back a little and pawed the ground. Encouraged that this was some sort of progress, the rider once again dug in his spurs and the drovers redoubled their prodding.

The announcer's booming chuckles on the crackling PA system rose to a sudden shout as, without warning, the bull sprang four-legged into the air, twisting viciously to unseat its rider who tumbled to the ground. Then the animal charged the fence, scattering its tormentors and embedding one of its horns in the wood.

Sky and Lynskey sprang to their feet, along with everyone else in the stands, and for a few seconds, all that could be heard, besides the cracking of the fence, which seemed in imminent danger of collapse, was the shouting of the clown who was trying to draw away the maddened animal. Sky could see neither Daniel Treacy nor his fat companion, who had been standing directly where the bull had struck. 'Are they all right?' she shouted to Lynskey, who had leaped up on to his seat for a better look. 'Can you see them? Are they hurt?'

'Naw.' He helped her up beside him. 'From what I could see, Treacy pulled the big fella back just in time.'

Sky caught a glimpse of Treacy. He was helping his friend to his feet but seemed to be doing it one-handed; his left arm was hanging loosely from his shoulder. 'He *is* hurt.' Before Lynskey could respond, she was skipping down the steps of the stand to get to Treacy and the story.

By the time she got to the ground, the clown and the wranglers had detached the bull from the fence and were leading it, docile as a sloth, back to the pens.

'Bad luck for young Tuff Wexler,' the announcer opined

from the safety of his box, 'but that's rodeo, folks,' and went on to call the name of the next rider.

A few spectators were crowding around Daniel Treacy when Sky got to him. 'You've hurt your arm, Mr Treacy? Were you frightened?'

He looked coldly into her eyes. 'Of course I was frightened, Miss MacPherson, and you may quote me on that. Now, if you'll excuse me, I must have this shoulder seen to.' He turned to his companion, who was puffing visibly and as pale as mist. 'You're sure you're all right? Come with me to the medics, you've had a shock.'

The incident was already yesterday's news, and in the chute the next rider was aboard his bull. The gate crashed open and animal and rider erupted into the arena. The man was off within five seconds and as the clown distracted the animal, the announcer cut in: 'If Sky MacPherson from the *Butte Courier* is in the ground would she come to the front of the announcer's booth please. R. Sky MacPherson.'

The Oriental woman looked through one of the waterside windows of her Vancouver apartment. Outside it was drizzling and the stippled surface of the water between where she sat and Vancouver Island was as grey and lifeless as she felt.

No deal was ever snag-free, but this little trial run in Ireland was far more trouble than it was worth. She was as confident as anyone could ever be that she had not attracted the attention of the Mounties – her reclusivity and elaborate precautions with all communications saw to that – and, because of her FBI mole who was indebted to her in ways that he would never like his wife or his boss to find out, never worried about the Americans. However, the Irish police were an unknown quantity. She did not like dealing in the dark and the quality of the information her people were receiving from Ireland was not good; she was irritated that her money had perhaps been squandered. Perhaps she had become too greedy. Perhaps she was being given a sign.

Still at the window, she tapped out the numbers to call her man in Helena but, despite standing instructions to him and to all her lieutenants that while an operation was under way they should never be out of contact, she received only the automatic answering service and instantly pressed the 'end' button. Her first reaction was of fury but it was followed instantly by worry. The Helena man was one of her most long-standing and trusted: something must be wrong.

In downtown Vancouver, a detective who specialized in staying one step ahead of the latest communications technology, readjusted the faders on his equipment. And in Helena, the FBI agent assigned to decode the scrambled signals to and from his target's telephone sat on patiently.

'I'll kill her. I'll kill her . . .' Sky, strapped into her seat, did not know she had spoken aloud.

'I beg your pardon?' Daniel Treacy, his face strained and even greyer than before – presumably, Sky thought, with pain from his injured shoulder   looked across the narrow aisle.

'Nothing.' Sky glanced at him. 'Are you in a lot of discomfort?'

'A little.' They were having to shout over the din of the helicopter rotors. The message, relayed at the showgrounds to Sky via Jimbo Larsen, had been that her mother had had an accident and was in hospital. Apparently, one of the cats, lying in wait on the duplex roof, had snatched a humming-bird from a feeder attached to the eaves. Johanna had fetched the kitchen step-stool but in climbing on to it, in an effort to rescue the bird, had overbalanced and fallen off. Jimbo had not known to what extent she had been injured; all he knew was that she had been conscious when taken to hospital.

'Who's with your mother now?' Treacy yelled.

'A friend who found her.' Sky thanked the fates that Hermana had called in unexpectedly that morning. She had called the ambulance and had had the presence of mind to contact the *Courier*'s editor at home. 'She'll stay with her until I get there.'

'I hope your Irish friend will find his way safely.'

Sky had no doubt that Lynskey, who was driving the Nissan back to Butte, would have little difficulty. 'He's meeting me at the hospital later.'

'It'll be quite a gathering.' Treacy's wan smile lightened his austere features.

'Yeah,' Sky agreed, 'lucky for me you had the use of the helicopter. Are you sure your friends don't mind you taking me with you?'

'They're not going back to Canada until tonight and they don't need the aircraft until then. And to call them friends is a little overstated.' He leaned forward to look through his window. 'They're business acquaintances.' Sky was so consumed with worry about her mother that she did not care a fig about the relationship between Treacy and his colleagues.

It had been Lynskey who had suggested she go back to Butte in the chopper with the businessman. He had taken charge, overseeing the telephone calls Sky had made to Jimbo and the hospital, liaising with the paramedics who were strapping up Treacy's shoulder. To give the latter his due, Sky thought now, he had offered instant co-operation.

Through the window on her own side of the aircraft, she could already see Butte. The pilot was taking them low, skimming over the flat mountain-top ridge above the city where the Class of '92 had staked its claim to immortality in symmetrical rows of white-painted boulders, spelling out its identity. An image of Johanna's proud, tearful face at Sky's own graduation was almost too much to bear; she closed her eyes and, although she had not prayed since grade school, begged for mercy for her mother. *Please, God, please . . .* Then, hating this hypocrisy, she opened them and engaged her host. 'Are you going to sue the rodeo, Mr Treacy? You certainly have a case.'

'If anyone should be sued,' again a ghost of a smile, 'it should be our fat friend. It wasn't the bull, it was him. He fell on me.' If she had not been so concerned about her mother – and so careful about protecting the big story she was sure lay at the heart of this man's conduct – at that moment she might have liked him.

The hospital was quiet; even the gingham-clad volunteers with their wicker baskets full of books and goodies did not do their rounds on Sunday afternoons.

Sky's mother had been formally admitted from the emergency room. 'She's comfortable.' The youthful Asian intern scanned the clipboard in his hand. 'We've given her something for the pain and we're waiting for the specialist to view her X-rays. But I think he will confirm what we already suspect, Mizz MacPherson, your mother has broken two vertebrae.' Sky's heart lurched. A broken back could mean paralysis. She could not bring herself to ask but mumbled that she wanted to see her mother right away.

As she followed the intern towards the room, she tried to prepare herself to deal with this unthinkable situation. In all of her thirty-four years, she could not recall Johanna's having to spend a single day in bed, even for a summer cold. Her mother's robust health, which she herself attributed to her holistic lifestyle, had always been a matter of pride to her. To think of her helpless – perhaps for ever – was inconceivable.

Johanna was conscious but her neck and head were so rigidly confined in a brace that she could not see her daughter until she was standing right over the bed. When she recognized Sky, her face brightened. 'Hello, darling.

Here's a nice pickle we've got ourselves into!' Her speech was a little slurred from the medication but otherwise she was as calm as though she was receiving Buffy and Hermana in her own kitchen for a cup of tea. Gently, Sky picked up one of the inert hands, noticing as she did so that the pins which held her mother's long hair had come loose; one was dangerously close to an eye. She removed it, careful not to jog the metal clamps which framed Johanna's head and neck. Then outrage, relief, anger, fear all conspired together. 'What the hell were you doing, Mom? Where's Hermana?'

'Take it easy, Mizz MacPherson.' The doctor placed a soothing hand on her arm. 'Your mother's had quite a shock. There'll be plenty of time for explanations later. What we have to do now is rest.' His face split in a dazzling, professional smile as he turned from Sky to his patient. 'Isn't that right, Mom?'

'Moondancer had a little bird,' Johanna had difficulty getting her tongue around the words, 'a litt-le *bird* and I had to rescue it, Sky.'

As quickly as it had arisen, Sky's anger died away. 'Of course you did, Mom.' She sat abruptly on a chair beside the bed.

'Hermana's gone to get me a few things from the house. I'll be here a few – a few days, I guess.'

'I guess you will.'

'It was good of you to come home from work, darling. Thank you.'

'I told you I was at the ro—' Sky began the automatic correction then bit her lip. 'You're welcome. Are you feeling much pain?'

'Nothing.' Johanna's forehead creased with the effort to remember something. 'There was a me – message for you, Sky – oh, darn it, I can't – I can't—'

'Hush, Mom, it doesn't matter. You rest. The surgeon will be here soon.'

Johanna smiled beatifically at the intern. 'This young man is my angel. And, of course, my own dear guardian angel saved me. It could've – I could've – ' Here the words deserted her and, drifting away, she closed her eyes in sleep.

Bathed in a rush of love and recognizing that, guardian angel or no, she had a lot for which to be grateful, Sky leaned forward and kissed her mother's still, pale face. 'Don't worry, I'll look after you.' Then, remembering that the intern was still with her, she straightened up. 'Tell me the worst. Will she walk again?'

'It's too early to say, Mizz MacPherson.'

The doctor's expression closed in and she remembered she should have known better than to ask. So jumpy was the medical profession in the US about malpractice suits, concealment of information, misleading information, that she knew that no one below the rank of a fully insured specialist would venture an opinion. 'Thank you, doctor, we'll be fine here. Would you mind leaving the door open?' She dismissed the intern as politely as she could and settled down to await the specialist's arrival.

As the minutes ticked by, she heard, from other rooms along the corridor, the muffled sounds of visitors, TVs, doors opening and closing with small thuds. With none of her belongings lying about, no flowers or cards, Johanna's room, with its grey steel furniture, unnaturally tidy bed and plain sateen drapes in a nondescript shade somewhere between peach and pink, seemed too quiet and antiseptic. Like the anteroom to a morgue.

As she went to the window to distract herself, Sky heard the muffled throb of the helicopter rotors and wondered whether Treacy, too, would be admitted. When she knew more about her mother's injuries, and no matter what the outcome, she must remember to ask after him. The very least she could do would be to thank him.

Chapter Eighteen

Sky was able to thank Daniel Treacy sooner than she had imagined. A few minutes later, left arm secured across his chest in a sling, he arrived in Johanna's room a second or two in advance of the specialist, the young intern and a nurse. 'Oh!' Sky, who had risen when he came in, hesitated on seeing the medical entourage behind him.

'Mizz MacPherson?' The specialist, whose jaw was as well manicured as his hair and who was still wearing his golf shoes, shook hands with her. Then, hand still outstretched, he turned to Treacy. 'You're the patient's husband?'

When the confusion was cleared up he asked that both visitors step outside the room while he went about his work. 'I'll wait with you.' Daniel Treacy sat on the bench seat in the corridor and indicated that Sky should sit beside him. 'A broken neck, is it?'

'Back.'

'That can be bad but not necessarily so these days. No matter what this initial prognosis turns out to be, however, I give you my personal guarantee that everything possible will be done for your mother.'

'Thank you, Mr Treacy, but I'm sure we'll be able to manage. What about your shoulder? Is it broken?'

'No, it's just a dislocation. They've fixed it, more or less, and now it's just a matter of letting nature take its course. But to get back to your mother, I hope you don't think I'm stepping out of bounds here but I insist you let me help. If

214

you're not satisfied with what's going on here, you might consider the Mayo Clinic.'

Sky was not sure if she welcomed this intervention, no matter how well-meaning. She demurred tactfully but he seemed not to hear her reservations and said he would make a few calls when he got home. 'And, of course, your mother's accident alters the complexion of your grandmother's proposed visit.'

'I beg your pardon?' Sky could not comprehend what he was saying.

'Elizabeth.' He stared at the wall opposite where they sat. 'Your grandmother. Her visit.'

'Well, obviously we can't look after her now. My mother will be in no—'

'On the contrary. I'm sure that now that this has happened she will want to come as soon as possible to see her daughter. And, of course, your mother must be given time to rest and recuperate without the added burden of worrying about guests.' At last he turned to look at her. 'I'll see that she's looked after, Miss MacPherson.'

'But you can't—'

'It's the least I owe your family.' His eyes were so intense in his pale face they seemed almost black. 'You said this morning that your mother was going to call Ireland tonight. If it would not be too much trouble, could you make that telephone call? I know you'll want to give your grandmother the distressing news, but could you let her know that I shall be calling to issue an invitation to her? And please assure her that if she is worried about the propriety of staying in my house, I shall be happy to arrange a suite for her in the hotel of her own choice or yours.'

In other circumstances the notion of a seventy-five-year-old woman being worried about propriety might have struck Sky as funny but now it did not seem so. 'I'll do it and I'll call you when it's done.'

There was no sound from her mother's room. Sky hoped hard that Johanna was not in any pain, as she tried to imagine what was going on. She forced herself to remember her mother not as she was now, trussed up like a torture-ready victim, but as the mom who, when Sky was growing up, had sat for hour after hour on the side of her bed reading aloud from books thought unsuitable by other moms: Johanna had included authors like H. G. Wells, Orwell and Kerouac as well as Anna Sewell and Louisa M. Alcott. The downside of Sky's childhood had been the endless, unsuccessful struggle for ordinary friendships with her peers. In the places where she and her mother had paused long enough to constitute a home, other kids' mothers allowed visits to the MacPhersons only as a last resort and sleepovers were never authorized. They knew that Johanna was likely to distribute tales of star-crossed lovers along with the sunflower seeds and popcorn.

Yet, in retrospect, Sky's eclectic early upbringing had been mainly beneficial: long before she hit second grade she had known where Saigon was and what it signified, could recognize not only Bob Dylan but Che Guevara and the Berrigans. For one glorious summer, she played unfamiliar games with hordes of ragged, dark-skinned children in the dust of California while her mother strove to help Cesar Chávez better the lot of immigrant Mexican fruit-pickers.

'You're smiling.'

Startled from her reverie, Sky muttered something about being lost in a daydream. 'Look,' she stood up, 'I appreciate all your kindness, Mr Treacy, but you should go home and rest that arm.'

'It is a little uncomfortable, I guess those bloody pain-killers aren't all they're cracked up to be.' He levered himself to his feet as Sky reiterated her promise to call him when she had spoken to her grandmother.

'Are you sure you'll be all right here?' He glanced at the closed door. 'They're taking a helluva time . . .'

'That's probably a good sign.' She felt if she said it firmly enough it would make it true.

Treacy had been gone a good ten minutes before the door opened and the specialist came out. Sky, who had fetched herself a soda from the Coke machine at the end of the corridor, was on her way back to her station but she stopped dead on seeing the gravity of the man's expression. 'Sit down, Mizz MacPherson.' The specialist subsided on the bench. 'We need to talk.'

Dumb with apprehension, Sky came to sit beside him.

'There's good and bad news,' he began. 'The bad news is that we'll have to operate on those vertebrae,' seeing Sky's blanching face he put out a hand to comfort her, 'but the good news is that I have every reason to believe that the operation will be successful and that, apart from a bit of arthritis, maybe, in later life, she can make a full recovery. She was lucky. We'll take her to theatre in the morning. Have you Blue Cross?'

Sky shook her head and, although she tried to control them by squeezing her eyes tightly shut, the tears burst forth. 'Don't distress yourself.' The specialist misconstrued her emotion. 'It'll be expensive but I'm sure we'll find a way round it.'

'It's not that—' Sky could not continue. Her tears were of relief. It was only now that she realized how convinced she had become that her mother had been destined for permanent paraplegia. 'Can I see her?'

'Of course. But she's heavily sedated. We had to pull her around a little, I'm afraid. She won't know you're there.'

Behind her, Sky heard a familiar heavy footfall and looked up to see Hermana trudging round the corner of the corridor. 'Oh, Hermana, she's probably going to be all right.' She ran down the corridor and, like a child, flung herself against the older woman's bulk.

'Of course she is.' Hermana, laden down with paper sacks,

217

tried to return the hug with her forearms. 'She's well protected, someone like your mother. We all know that.'

Normally, Sky would have skirmished around this terminology but right now she could not have cared if the Bliss Sisters had carted in the entire staff of the Maharishi to pelt her mother with lotus blossoms. She disentangled herself and scrubbed at her eyes. 'I'm being silly. I'm not going to help her if I go on behaving like this.'

The specialist had come up behind: 'I'll be on my way.' He consulted his watch. 'We'll need your mother's details, and you'll have to sign consent forms for tomorrow and so forth. Try not to worry.' He patted Sky's arm. 'It'll take a bit of time but I've dealt with a lot worse.'

'It's going to cost a fortune, apparently.' Sky took some of Hermana's load as the specialist went off, and the two walked into Johanna's room. 'I suppose you know we don't have Blue Cross?'

'We're well protected,' Hermana repeated. 'I've called Buffy and she should be here in the next half-hour.'

They unpacked the sacks and stowed the contents, most of which were superfluous as Johanna would be wearing nothing but hospital gowns for the next few days at least. She continued to sleep although Sky was sure that the frame in which she was confined must be uncomfortable.

She and Hermana were seated by the bedside, reminiscing in low tones about Johanna's eventful life, when the door opened again and a dishevelled Lynskey appeared. 'I drove like the clappers,' he announced without introduction. 'How is she?'

They filled him in and Hermana urged Sky to let him take her home for a break. 'Buffy will be here in a few minutes and we can call you if there is the slightest development. Go on, Sky, you've had a terrible shock.'

'I could do with a shower.' To Sky, who felt she must

have aged ten years in the past hour, the prospect of clean water and fresh clothes was all too appealing.

She allowed Lynskey to drive her back to the duplex. He said nothing during the short trip and she appreciated his tact. Except for a few young couples who strolled hand in hand along the deserted streets, and a gang of kids who had set up an impromptu baseball diamond at the top of a hill, they might have had Butte to themselves. She found it difficult to keep tabs on reality; so much had happened that it was weird to find that it was still daytime and that this was an ordinary Sunday.

She realized that she had a thumping headache – sure sign of caffeine deprivation. The Coke had helped but her only other fix that day had been with Lynskey in McDonald's, so long ago now that it felt like yesterday. No wonder she had made an exhibition of herself in the hospital corridor, that her moods had been bumping up and down as though riding a child's teeter-totter.

'Will you come in?' Even the duplex seemed unfamiliar when Lynskey let the Nissan coast to a halt in the driveway.

'Are you sure?' He did not immediately turn off the ignition. 'I can easily wait out here.'

'Don't be silly.' Sky pushed open the door and got out.

He offered to make coffee while she had her shower, and she accepted with alacrity. Then, remembering his voracious appetite, 'And there should be some home-made muffins in the freezer.' On her way down the corridor towards her bedroom, Sky remembered she had had nothing to eat since getting out of bed that morning. Was it only this morning that she had gone to interview Daniel Treacy in his echoing office?

She peeled off her clothes and tied on her bathrobe. Towel in hand, she was going towards the bathroom when she heard the telephone and stopped, staring at the instrument on Johanna's little half-moon table beside the front door. It could be the hospital. She willed Lynskey to pick up the extension in the kitchen but the shrilling continued and she snatched up the receiver. 'Hello?'

'Miss MacPherson? R. Sky MacPherson?'

She did not recognize the voice and her panic grew. 'Yes, this is Sky MacPherson, who's this, please?'

'This is Bill Collins, the funeral director. We spoke before. I've left several messages for you, Miss MacPherson.'

Sky collapsed against the door. 'Yes, I'm sorry, Mr Collins. I was going to return your calls tomorrow.'

'I think it is very important that we speak.'

She could have strangled him. 'I'm sorry if you were dissatisfied with your coverage in the community notes, Mr Collins, but—'

'It's on another matter entirely,' he cut across her. 'When would you be free? Now if you like?'

'I'm sorry, but that's out of the question. My mother—' To her annoyance, Sky's voice unexpectedly wobbled. She cleared her throat. 'My mother's in hospital. I've come home just for a few minutes to collect some of her things.'

'Oh!' Instantly his voice changed, became professionally solicitous. 'Nothing too serious, I hope?'

'Serious enough, Mr Collins. My mother has broken her back. I'm very worried about her. Now I'm sure you'll understand . . .'

'Of course, Miss MacPherson. But I would still like to speak to you about something at your earliest convenience. Perhaps I could call again tomorrow. Depending on how your mother is getting on, of course.'

'I'll call you. Goodbye, Mr Collins.'

Odious man. Knowing she was overreacting, she flung the receiver back into its cradle. How on earth could Teddy and Melinda Morzsansky continue to work for him?

'Everything all right?' Looking around, she saw Lynskey standing in the kitchen doorway.

'Goddamn shamrock lot!' She made a sweeping gesture with the back of her hand, swiping at the telephone.

'That's our lot, I take it?'

She saw his expression and was contrite. 'Oh, Fergus, I'm sorry. I didn't mean you, of course it's not you.' She moved towards him but stopped when she saw his expression. 'What is it? I said I'm sorry . . .'

'I'd close that dressing-gown if I were you.' His voice was low and controlled.

Sky glanced down and saw that the belt of her robe had untied itself and her nakedness was exposed. 'Sorry.' Embarrassed, she reached for it but when she looked up again he was coming towards her.

'Don't close it, don't—' He grabbed her shoulders, his fingers biting so hard they hurt. 'I know it's probably inappropriate now—'

'It's not.' She was whispering.

'But your mother . . .'

'I know.' *Forgive me, Mom* . . . Sky closed her eyes as he scooped her into his arms and carried her like a baby towards the open door of her bedroom.

As they tumbled together on to the bed, her fingers got in the way of Lynskey's as she helped him tear at his zippers and buttons. 'I'm terribly afraid this won't take too long.' Lynskey's breath was sounding hard in his throat.

'I know.'

The car park beside Killybegs Gárda station doubles as a temporary morgue for written-off vehicles. Although the rain had moved off, the gale was, if anything, stronger than before and the sky remained overcast, permitting no moon-

221

light to penetrate. Conditions were ideal for the man lurking across the street.

It was coming up to three in the morning and, although he knew he was pretty safe Rupert de Burgh listened intently. From where he stood the remains of the Hiace and the Starlet were illuminated only by an overspill from the two lit windows in the station.

As satisfied as he could be, above the howling of the wind and the banging of a loose slate on a house nearby, that no one but himself was around, he broke cover and ran across the empty road.

As he crept across the car park, he kept well away from the elongated rectangles of light cast from the station windows but the light sparked briefly from the metal can he was carrying. Out of the corner of his eye saw the flash and froze, caught like a discus thrower poised on one foot. He waited until he was certain he had not been seen, then moved in a tight circle behind the two crashed vehicles, keeping them between him and the station.

As he sprinkled the petrol, taking care not to make any sudden movements that might attract attention, the fumes tickled his nostrils and he felt a sneeze coming on. Quickly he placed the can into the gaping hole where the Hiace's bonnet had been, balancing it on the engine block. The sneeze erupted as he lit the first match. Its force extinguished the flame.

Keeping his nerve, he lit a second and held the little flame to the muslin bag that contained the firelighters. When he was sure it had taken, he placed the bag at the start of the petrol trail he had laid.

Then he ran. He was out of range, but only just, when the Hiace blew, taking with it the Starlet, a squad car and two of the Gárdaí's private vehicles.

Chapter Nineteen

In Sky's bedroom, she and Lynskey lay like spoons. With one finger, he traced the hollow between her right shoulder and earlobe. 'I wanted you so much. From the first second I saw you getting out of your car. And then, when I saw you lurking in the shadows of that schoolyard my God!' He pulled her round and kissed her gently, first one eye, then the other.

'M-mmm.' Sky threw her arms around his neck and gripped hard. 'Shut up, Lynskey. Stop talking for once. Don't say anything, not one thing more.' He smelled of aftershave and sweat and sex, a potent, intoxicating cocktail which had invaded her body. She now wanted him so badly it hurt. It *had* been too quick, she thought, but he had buried her in the strength of his own passion.

Belatedly she brought her mother back into the frame. 'I should be getting back to the hospital.'

'Of course.' Lynskey nuzzled her cheek and then was still. 'Your mother was right. Did anyone ever tell you you have the most beautiful voice on earth?'

'I'm not actually thinking of my voice just at the moment . . .'

Neither of them moved for several charged seconds. Then, quick as a flame, he crushed her lips under his. She felt him come alive again and moved to accommodate him but he stopped. 'Will you trust us?' he whispered into her open mouth.

'Trust us? Trust us to do what?' Sky, so full of heat and desire she felt she could not wait another moment, would have agreed to anything.

'Let me take charge, Sky, just for five minutes. See if you like it. I promise you, you will.'

'Yes, anything, just hurry—'

'That's exactly what I'm not going to do this time.' Lynskey stopped kissing her and looked down at her, his expression tender. 'Trust me,' he repeated.

He pulled himself up, straddling her pelvis. When she attempted to raise herself to kiss him, he pushed her gently back on the pillows and extended her arms wide, away from her body. 'You said you'd trust me. Don't touch. Don't do anything at all, leave it to me.'

Trembling, ultra-conscious of his weight on her hipbones, she tried to keep still as, slowly, he tightened his grip on her with his legs and then leaned forward to run the outside of his joined hands between her breasts. 'Lie back, close your eyes, just *feel*, Sky . . .'

She surrendered as he opened his hands and spread them so he was massaging her stomach with the palms while the thumbs tickled the undersides of her breasts, releasing rivulets of sensation. 'Come on, feel me, feel it, Sky.' He tightened his thighs and, although she tried to resist, she could not avoid raising her own in response. Again he spread his hands over her abdomen, his thumbs continuing to caress her breasts. 'Feel what your body is saying to you. You're gorgeous, gorgeous—'

He bent forwards again and encircled one of her breasts with his lips. He did not bite, and the pressure was minimal, but whatever he was doing with his fluttering lips and the flat of his tongue against her nipple caused her to cry aloud.

He did the same to the other and, as his mouth connected with her, Sky seemed to split into two. Despite her best efforts to keep still, her top half writhed as he continued the

224

rhythm of the titillating massage, using his hands, fingers, lips and tongue as before, while her lower half, clamped into immobility, seemed virtually weightless and not to belong to her at all.

He took her right to the edge until she was moaning and crying, begging for release then, abruptly, he eased off her pelvis. She grabbed for him, expecting him to enter her. 'I told you I didn't want you to do anything,' he insisted, fobbing off her hands then sliding his own smoothly under her. 'Over now, come on, flip over for me.'

'I hope I can last—' Sky did not think she was capable of making such a sound in her throat.

'Ssh.' He pushed her head down into the pillow and again she surrendered as he began with joined hands at the top of her spine, spreading them only when he got to the swell of her hips.

She gasped. He was using his thumbs to tease the cleft between her buttocks in the same way he had used them on the tender skin under her breasts. Of their own accord, her legs drew up as, deep within, the orgasm began to ripple.

'Not yet, not yet . . .' He pushed her straight again, pulling her thighs apart a little. Then he repeated the action, slowly, tantalizing her by not using his thumbs until the last minute although she bucked and reared and begged. 'You've skin as white as the feathers of a swan . . .' he brushed his fingers across her buttocks, 'you're the most perfect, beautiful woman, you're an egret, a white dolphin—'

Sky knew it was the end. 'I can't wait—'

Instantly, he pushed up her thighs and entered her from behind, cradling her breasts and stomach in his big hands, kissing the skin between her shoulder blades and at the back of her waist as she shuddered and cried on a long, sustained note, which seemed to come from someone else's throat. From far away, she heard him join in.

He was the first to get his breath back. 'Jesus! What a

225

racket. Just as well we didn't wait until the War Bonnet – someone might have called the management.'

Sky never wanted to open her eyes ever again in her whole life. The pillow against her cheek was as soft as the water in a warm swimming pool. 'You're good at this, Lynskey,' she breathed. 'You should patent yourself – the world would beat a path to your door.'

'Thank you,' he rolled off her, 'but somehow the world's a bit shy, these days.'

'Just one thing.' Sky turned on her back. An insect walked across the ceiling and, as she watched, it seemed to stagger in conjunction with the blood behind her eyes, bigger and smaller, bigger and smaller . . .

'What?' Tenderly, he stroked the hair out of his eyes.

'Egrets?' She looked across at him. 'Swans – *dolphins*?'

He had the grace to look sheepish. 'I didn't think you were in any state to hear.'

'Think again, Lynskey.' Sky reached behind her to the bedhead and pulled so that her body tautened to its full length. She felt she had been transported to another medium, where human skin and bone could stretch like elastic. Then the vision of her mother swam in and she sat up. 'My mother. We have to go back – at least *I* have to go back to the hospital. I'll drop you somewhere.'

'You'll drop me nowhere. Of course I'm going back with you.' Lynskey planted a lazy kiss on her nose and then tumbled off the bed. 'Come on.'

They took a shower together, and when they were drying off she noticed a little circular welt, about the size of a dime, just below his hip. 'What's that?' she touched it. 'It looks like a scar.'

'It's a birthmark.' His tone was offhand. 'Great conversation starter, women love it.'

She was about to give him a playful slap when she heard the telephone. 'Damn.' Again fearful it was the hospital –

and with a resurgence of guilt that she should already be there – she reached for a towel, wrapped it around herself, and plunged out. She got to it at the third ring.

'I'm glad I reached you.' Jimbo's dry voice reassured her immediately. 'I tried the hospital but they said you'd gone home for a spell.'

'I'm on my way back, as it happens.' Sky scrubbed at her shoulder with a corner of the towel. 'I was just collecting a few things.'

'How is your mother? They wouldn't tell me anything.'

She filled him in as succinctly as she could. When she was finished, he cleared his throat. 'Look, Sky, take as much time off as you like. Don't even think about the office. We'll manage – and I know you're probably worried about the expense but come and see me and we'll discuss it.'

'Thank you.' Sky was touched. Maybe Butte wasn't such a bad place, after all. Then she thought of all those cheques in her mother's low-boy. She would contact her uncle Francey. 'Thanks a million, Jim, but I hope that won't be necessary. What about the rodeo copy?'

'Could you drop in your notes some time tomorrow? I'll get the kid to write them up.'

'I hope she can decipher them.' She pictured the hiero-glyphics in her notebook.

'Time she learned, isn't it?' Jimbo dismissed this, then, with uncharacteristic hesitancy: 'Er, there's one other thing.' He cleared his throat again. 'Is that Irish teacher with you?'

'No.' The lie was instantaneous. 'Why?'

'Now is not the time but I want to talk to you about him, Sky. Look, I know this is a bit delicate . . .' Conscious that the shower had been turned off and that Lynskey could probably hear her, Sky was silent. 'Are you there?'

'Yes.' She turned her back on the bathroom door.

'Don't get a fright,' his voice became crisp, 'and I hope

227

you don't think I'm interfering, but there is something you should know about him.'

'Not now.' Behind her, Sky heard Lynskey emerge from the bathroom and pad quietly towards the bedroom.

'Of course.' Jimbo's tone became even more impersonal. 'Just call me any time you feel you can. In the meantime, take care of yourself. Give my regards to your mother. Sam sends her love too – she says I'm to invite you to dinner anytime or just to talk, OK? I won't badger you with calls, I'll leave it up to you to get in touch.'

'Thanks. And tell Sam thanks too.'

'You bet.' He hung up before she could say goodbye.

Slowly, Sky replaced the receiver. The euphoria of just a few minutes before had drained away so completely that she felt as thin and as flat as a dollar bill. She knew Jimbo Larsen: he would never dream of indulging in petty gossip or interfere in someone's private life. There had to be some good reason for him to have said what he had. She glanced towards the bedroom. The corridor in which she stood benefited from no natural light and the sunlight flooding into it through the open door of her room seemed unusually bright. She could not hear anything from inside: Lynskey was a quiet dresser.

He sensed her behind him as she padded through the door. 'Is there news?' Clad only in a towel, he looked around from the mirror at which he was using one of her hairbrushes. 'I hope you don't mind?' He held it up questioningly.

'M-mmm.' She shook her head. 'That wasn't the hospital, it was just my editor enquiring about Mom. Look, I'm getting nervous, I've been away an awfully long time, could we hurry?' He looked hard at her and she was afraid she might have betrayed herself but he said nothing and they completed dressing in silence.

She tried to behave naturally with him in the car, even holding his hand. All the time, however, Jimbo's warning

228

sounded like a siren in her ears: *There's something about him you should know.*

'Are you all right? You're very quiet.' He raised the back of her hand to his lips and kissed it as they neared the hospital.

'I'm fine.' She shot him a quick smile. 'I think it's just all hitting me now. I feel awful that we were – you know – with my poor mother lying there in that state . . .'

'Try not to worry, sweetheart. They can do great things now. Are you sure that's all that's on your mind? You're not regretting what we did, are you?'

When Sky responded to this by glancing across at him, she saw watchfulness. 'Of course not.' She gave his hand what could pass for a happy squeeze.

'Good.' He seemed to relax as he squeezed back. 'Because I sure amn't. I can't wait for a return match.' Sky smiled back but knew, from those alert eyes, that he had not believed her.

Johanna, her two faithful companions in attendance at her bedside, was still sleeping when they got to her room. 'At least she's in no pain.' Buffy was stroking her friend's inert forearm. 'You poor thing, Sky. You must have gotten a dreadful shock.'

The guilt about her romp with Lynskey while her mother lay here like this smote Sky with such intensity that her stomach constricted. 'She's not gone into a coma or anything?' she gazed down at her mother's caged white face.

'No.' Hermana lumbered to her feet and stretched her big body. 'The doc says she's in great shape. It's just all the painkillers and sedation. They want to keep her quiet until they do the operation in the morning – oh, hello again!' She had caught sight of Lynskey, hovering in the doorway.

For the next hour or so, the four of them came and went in and out of Sky's mother's room, conferring in low voices with the medical personnel, who were doing little except monitoring Johanna's vital signs. Lynskey organized coffee and sandwiches, fetched and carried, made himself indispensable, so much so that, gradually, he seemed to be taking charge. Even the intern began deferring to him, addressing him first when he had anything to say.

Sky began to feel ever more helpless and guilty and – because of her unease about Jimbo's warning – increasingly irritable. She tried not to let this show but when, for the second or third time, the intern, having rechecked her mother's blood pressure, turned his back on her to talk to Lynskey, the room, which was spacious as hospital rooms go, suddenly felt claustrophobic and overcrowded. 'I'm sorry, doctor,' she did not care that she sounded petty, 'but I'm the patient's relative. I'd appreciate it if you would consult with me.' Both Lynskey and the doctor turned to her with surprise. 'I'm the daughter,' she repeated.

'I'll leave.' Lynskey grasped what was going on. 'No, it's all right,' he brushed aside Hermana's putative protest. 'She's under a lot of pressure. I understand completely.' Then he was gone, leaving Sky with a sense of anticlimax. This was not what she had wanted – or was it?

She was leaving the hospital a little later, acceding to the Bliss Sisters' urgings that she get some rest, when she just avoided bumping into a man carrying a bunch of flowers. 'Greg!' she tried to sound matter-of-fact. 'I was going to call your house to talk, I really was, but then—'

'I'm real sorry about your mom,' he interrupted, holding out the flowers. 'Is there anything I can do?'

'Thanks, but there's nothing anyone can do except wait.' She did not bother to ask how he had found out. 'But I sure appreciate the thought. Look,' she added impulsively, 'I *would* like us to talk.'

After a pause, 'When?' Then he became defensive. 'But don't give me any more shit about wanting us to be friends.'

'You calling like this already tells me that we are.'

Another pause. Then: 'Could you use some company? Will I come home with you?' Sky could see no reason why she should refuse him. She owed him a lot and, despite the serious thinking she had to do about Lynskey, she was not all that sure she wanted to face whatever truth lay in wait for her. In any event, she knew the next few hours would pass like years in the empty house. 'I'll tell you what.' On impulse, she took his arm. 'Why don't we go for a walk?' She looked at her watch. 'It's such a warm evening and I could do with some air.' Then, fearing Greg's propensity for hiking, 'A *short* walk, maybe in the forest.'

As they left the city behind and Montana's immense skies and open spaces unrolled above and around the pickup, Sky's spirits lifted. On such a lovely evening, the travel writers' excesses about the Rockies – snowy peaks now tinged with gold under the sinking sun – were justified; the antiquity of those jagged, thrusting contours dwarfed everything around them, including the concerns of R. Sky MacPherson.

They drove in silence until Greg turned off the highway on to a secondary route into the forest. 'I know I said we'd talk,' she turned to him, 'but I don't really know what to say. All I can come up with at the moment is "thanks".'

He went to take her hand but stopped himself, tipping his hat back on his head as though this was what he had planned all along. He smiled at her. 'Sorry it couldn't work out. Don't forget,' he stared ahead again, 'if you ever change your mind . . .'

Sky felt like a grub, but she knew that the unkindest response of all would have been to say anything that would give him even a smidgen of hope.

He wheeled on to one of the narrow forest trails, running through a tunnel of cool green between the trunks of lodge pole pine, quite bare at this level: there were so many that they had been forced to race upwards in competition for available light.

As the pickup, its springs fashioned for this kind of road, bounced joyfully along, the temperature plunged. Sky held the sides of her seat, and watched the way random handfuls of light lanced off the hood in front of her. Despite her feelings of being taken for a patsy by Lynskey, of her dejection at an inability to bid a graceful farewell to the man beside her, she could not help but be affected by her surroundings. The feeling was of exhilarating isolation and, although she had never scuba-dived, she knew this was what it must be like to sink downwards into a new world.

Greg pulled the vehicle into the side and they got out.

After the noise in the truck, the hush as they walked along under the high green canopy seemed at first absolute. Then the forest asserted itself, a sort of folded silence in which myriad sounds – a faint twitter, a flutter, rustlings, a little crash, a hum, a few clicks – swarmed through the furrows. She felt eyes all around as she walked a little ahead of her companion, endeavouring to put everything out of her mind except the sharp scent of the pine and the thicker, slighty musty smells of bark and forest floor.

Progressively, however, her awareness of Greg's tacit presence padding behind her became overpowering. Just ahead, a pale butterfly fluttered upwards from a black-eyed Susan and danced off along a boulevard of light between two trees; she followed its progress until it slipped off into the shadows and then became aware of how the light had diminished. The evening was shrinking. It was now or never. 'Greg?' She stopped and turned round to face him.

He stopped too.

'Words are easy, I know, but I'm really sorry, more than I can say.'

He looked so stricken that if she could have taken his suffering into her own heart she would have had done so. She wanted to kiss him but that was impossible. 'I know I said we'd talk, but there isn't much to say, really, is there?'

'Guess not.' He shrugged. 'I do – sorry – did love you, Sky.'

'I know you did.' Helplessly, she touched his hand.

He did not react.

Defeated – he was not going to help her out and she did not blame him – she stepped back a little. 'Well . . .' she hesitated, 'I guess I'd better be getting home.'

'You bet.' He turned, too quickly, and walked ahead of her back towards the pickup.

At least she had tried. Greg needed a cheerleader and she was not it. Yet the more Sky tried to convince herself she had done the right thing and with every step she took after his straight, rigid body, the more guilty she felt.

On the trip back to the duplex he continued to be stiff and formal, so much so that she was astonished when he accepted her invitation, issued as a semi-automatic reflex, to come in. It was what she always said when he drove her home.

Yet she had so much to do that once inside, her brain fell into its busy mode and she was able to instal him in the kitchen while – with only limited success – she made the calls to her aunts and her uncle Francey to let them know what had happened. Francey was at a county show – he was heavily into Shire horses – and his wife was out too. Sky left a message with the butler that he telephone her urgently. Constance's husband said she, too, was away, but Sky reached the two aunts in the States, and Margaret, who continued to live on the farm in West Cork.

There was no reply from her grandmother's telephone but she felt she could assume that now the bush telegraph had been set in motion, one of the others would reach her. Margaret had been of the opinion that Sky's grandmother would make the trip but that she would insist on paying for it herself. 'We're not the poor relations, you know.' Her tone had been acerbic.

Sky looked at her watch as she replaced the receiver and walked back in to Greg; she was regretting her invitation to him. Events were piling up so fast around her, she thought. She must try to stay calm, make a priority list. Her mother came first, before her grandmother, before Jimbo's puzzling call about Lynskey, before Greg, before the story she was pursuing on Treacy. Before anything. 'Sorry about that.' She plastered a smile on her face as he looked up.

She sat at the table opposite him. The doorbell rang. 'Oh, God, it's like Grand Central Station.' Heaving herself to her feet she went out to answer it.

It was Lynskey. Behind him, a cab was leaving the driveway.

'I kept trying to ring.' The Irishman had changed his clothes and now looked relatively dapper in a sports jacket and slacks. He spread his hands in apology. 'You were engaged all the time. I couldn't stay away. Look, before you say anything,' he seemed almost shy, 'I know I was too bossy back there at the hospital. Will you forgive me? I get carried away sometimes, comes of being a teacher, I suppose. I was only trying to help.'

That treacherous giggle bubbled to the surface. 'This is my worst nightmare . . .'

'What's wrong, will I go? Tell me what you want me to do, Sky. Stop laughing.' He grabbed her wrist. 'Are you hysterical? Sky, for God's sake, I don't want to make things any the worse for you—'

'Do you think you could?' Sky could not control the laughter now. 'Come on in! Greg's inside – oh, my God!' She doubled over as tears of mirth rolled down her face. 'Come on in, all of you.'

He looked blankly at her. 'Greg?'

'Come in.' She pulled him in and closed the door behind him.

She had herself under some semblance of control as she

234

ushered him into the kitchen. 'This is Greg. Greg, this is Fergus. Coffee, Fergus? Oh, sorry, it's tea, isn't it?'

Silence burned between the two men, then Greg rose. 'I'd better be gettin' going.'

'Are you sure you won't have more coffee?' Sky still felt giddy.

'No, thank you.' Greg pushed his Stetson to the back of his head. 'You know where I am if you need me. Give my love to your mom. Don't bother seein' me out, I know the way.' He left the kitchen. A second or two later, the slam of the front door reverberated through the house.

'Sorry about that. I didn't know . . .' Lynskey hung back, leaning against the door jamb.

Sky picked up Greg's mug and took it to the sink. She squeezed Lux from the squeegee bottle on to it, more than enough to wash the dinner dishes of the Sixth Fleet. As she ran water from the faucet and scrubbed with the dishmop, as though to remove without trace the mug's inoffensive pattern of daisies and sunflowers, he came over to stand beside her, staring at her with knitted brows. 'What's the matter, Sky?' His voice was soft. 'What have I done?'

'Nothing.' She scrubbed harder then ran more water over the mug to rinse it.

'I know it's not nothing.'

'Somebody told me that there was something about you I should know.' She put down the mug and picked at the grease congealed in the crack where the formica on the worktop joined with the metal surround of the sink.

'Who? What did they say?' Another man might have sounded indignant, or furious, or hurt. Lynskey did not even sound inquisitive.

She locked eyes with him. 'That's all. That there's something about you I should know. What should I know about you, Lynskey?'

'Maybe it's that—' Whatever he had been about to say he

235

bit back. 'My life's an open book!' he substituted, attempting a smile.

'I don't believe you.' She turned back to the sink and scrubbed again at the already squeaking mug.

Lynskey came behind her and put his arms round her. 'You can trust me, R. Sky MacPherson.' He hugged her close, a non-sexual embrace that was full of consolation.

'Don't patronize me.' She heard the echo of Greg's cry but did not care. She struggled for a second or two and then yielded to the warmth and ease. She felt very, very tired and no longer cared who was trustworthy and who was not. As Lynskey stroked her hair, she found she could not give two hoots even about stories or deadlines or the *Butte Courier*.

Or even if he was with someone else. If he was lying to her, so what? Now was what mattered, and right now she felt safe and comforted.

He took her chin in one of his hands and tilted back her head. 'I promise you,' his voice deepened, 'I promise you that you can trust me.'

Over Sky's head, however, Lynskey's eyes were dark and full of doubt. He had almost revealed the truth. That he had fallen in love.

Chapter Twenty

Sky was happy to accept Lynskey's offer to drive her back to the hospital. Left alone she might have fallen asleep at the wheel.

He had tried to dissuade her from going – there was little she could do. But her guilt was insistent and he gave in. 'I have to call in at the hotel first, though,' he said as he helped her into the passenger seat. 'I'm expecting a message. A friend of one of my sisters lives in Seattle and she's half expecting me to show up some time this week. I rang earlier to tell her my plans have changed – my plans *have* changed, haven't they?' He took her silence for assent. 'She wasn't in. I'm expecting her to call me back.'

Sky waited in the car when they got to the hotel. Her limbs felt like Jell-O and she wondered how she was going to get through the night, not to mention facing the world tomorrow. Apart from her concern for her mother, she did not want to hear Jimbo's bad news about the Irishman: although she was cagey about making too much of this new relationship – formed, after all, on the rebound from Greg – Lynskey's plea to trust him had found receptive ears. She wanted to trust him.

He had parked in the drop-off point in front of the hotel's entrance rather than in the lot, and each time the glass doors opened, she could see little clusters of conventioneers standing around in the lobby. Once, when she caught a glimpse of Lynskey, he was frowning, reading a note on white paper, holding something brown in his other hand. Next time the door opened, he was coming through. She wound down the passenger window as he bounded towards her. 'Everything OK?'

'There was a message all right.' He hunkered down to talk to her. 'I'll have to go up to my room to make a call. Do you mind waiting? Or would you like to come in and have a drink in the bar?'

'I'll wait here.' Sky could not have faced the hubbub she knew would attach to the conventioneering crowd.

'All right, so. I won't be long.' He loped away and she could see that the brown object, now sticking out of the pocket of his jacket, was a small padded envelope. What kind of hotel left telephone messages for its guests in brown padded envelopes?

Lynskey walked straight up to the reception desk in the lobby and placed the envelope on the surface between himself and the young clerk. 'Excuse me. Do you remember who left this in for me? If you didn't recognize him, a description would do.'

'I don't know, sir.' The boy went to pick it up but Lynskey was too quick for him, pulling it out of his reach with a fingernail.

'Could it have been a courier?'

'I'm afraid I can't help you, I've just come on shift.' The clerk plucked a clipboard from under the counter and scrutinized it. 'I could try to find out for you, if you like, but I think my predecessor has already left.'

'It's all right. It'll do tomorrow, but it's important to me to find out. What's the name of the clerk who was on duty earlier?' He took a courtesy note from the pad on the counter and scribbled the name the boy gave him. 'You're sure there was only this envelope and the one telephone message?'

The clerk checked the pigeon-hole again. 'That's all sir, just two for you this evening.' Lynskey thanked him and hurried to the elevator.

In his room, he tapped in the combination to unlock his briefcase. Before he made the call to the chief superintendent, however, he took a clear plastic bag from one of the pockets of the case and carefully placed the brown envelope inside. He fished out a second one and, holding it open with his left hand, turned a small object out of his jacket pocket so that it dropped straight into the bag. The object was a bullet.

He called the chief's number. He was not perturbed by the warning in the brown padded envelope, had expected it sooner or later. In many ways it gave him satisfaction: it meant he was getting somewhere.

At first the chief superintendent was irritable at being woken but thawed after a bit and told him what had happened in Killybegs, including the demolition job on the vehicles. Lynskey listened in silence but, entirely concentrated on his own side of the operation, had few suggestions to offer. Daly was less sanguine about the bullet than his subordinate. 'It's not only you, you clot, you've involved that reporter. I hope you haven't given her any idea of the scope of this thing?'

'Naw.' Lynskey was glad his friend could not see the grin on his face, 'She believes it's all to do with Treacy and his wife. But don't worry, she'll be all right. I'll make sure of that.'

'Speaking of Treacy, is he involved or not?'

'So far I've no proof either way and the feds have got nothing, for all their watching. Could be he's just an unfortunate citizen. We'll see. Look, there's something else

239

you should be exercised about. I think these beauties know where to find me a little too easily and I don't think the leak's over here, unless I'm being watched by people I can't see. I think you'd better step up the navel-gazing at home.'

'We're running checks but so far everyone has come up clean. And as for Operation Omega, no one knows except yourself, the Commissioner, meself and the three politicos about your man maybe coming over here. Unless those last three are blabbing. I doubt it.'

'Yeah, well, nothing would surprise me. Keep trying.' Conscious of Sky waiting in the parking lot, Lynskey looked at his watch. 'I'll courier the two baggies and the film to the feds. You should have results by Tuesday at the latest. That camera'd better be as good as Technical Branch says it is. I was quite far away. You'll know our Irish friend' – even though he had been assured that his satellite phone was secure, and although he rarely tooks risks with names, he did now – 'but the other two, the Canadians, should be new to you. Flynn's the one looks like Hopalong Cassidy.'

'Speaking of the feds,' the chief asked, 'see them around?'

'Oh, here and there. They wouldn't last a minute in certain parts of Dublin, they stick out a mile – even when they try to blend into the landscape. And you should see the cars.'

'Well, use them if necessary.'

'Yeah, yeah – look, I have to go.' He explained then where he was bound and about Johanna's accident.

'The mother too? Sounds like you're in over your head,' his friend drawled laconically.

'Yeah, yeah.'

'Be careful out there!'

Lynskey smiled as he punched the 'end' button on the phone. Like a good proportion of their colleagues, they both adored *Hill Street Blues*, missing the reruns only when matters of life or death – or newer episodes of *L.A. Law* – intervened.

When Sky and Lynskey got to the hospital, Johanna was alone except for the nurse on duty, who was taking her pulse. 'I sent the other ladies away, but they said be sure and call them if there was the slightest change. There's no need for you to be here either – she's going to sleep all night.'

'I'd prefer to stay.' Sky sank lower in the chair, testing its long-term comfort.

'Feel free.' The nurse checked the level of the drip running into Johanna's arm.

'What's in it?' Lynskey asked.

'Saline, mostly.' The nurse wrapped a blood-pressure cuff around Johanna's arm and pumped it up. 'There's really no need to whisper. Her sedation and analgesic medication is in here too and you won't wake her. We don't want her to move around too much.'

She checked the meter in her hand as she released the pressure, then, 'That's fine.' Making a note on the chart at the foot of the bed, she smiled across at Sky. 'Try not to worry, your mom's doing great. I'll be in and out during the night but if you or your husband need me any time, Mizz MacPherson, you just holler. I'll be at the station just down the hall.' She clipped the pen back into her breast pocket. 'Love your work, by the way. My daughter's at journalism school in Northwestern, Illinois.'

'Great. Good luck to her – and thanks.' Sky was still reacting to the connubial assumption about herself and Lynskey, and did not dare meet his eyes as the nurse left.

She dozed a little over the next few hours, barely rousing during the night nurse's periodic visits. At some point in the early morning, she came to, to find herself covered in a light,

241

woven blanket. For a few moments, she had no idea where she was. The only light in the room came from a green bulb recessed into the ceiling; under its dim wattage, the objects in her direct line of vision – the knobs at the end of her mother's bed, which were used to raise and lower it, the drip stand, even the slats of the closed venetian blinds between the sateen drapes – glowed outlandishly. Then she smelt the hospital smell and remembered.

Shaking her head to clear it, she struggled upright to see that Lynskey was sitting, Buddha-like, on the floor opposite the end of the bed, his back supported by the wall. 'Do you want anything?' he whispered, not moving a muscle. 'I can go for coffee, if you like.'

'What time is it?' The inside of Sky's mouth felt like a brush. She glanced across at her mother. Johanna was sleeping as before. 'Just after three.' Lynskey uncoiled himself and stood up. 'Coffee, then? Black?'

'Sure.'

After he padded out, Sky rubbed her gritty eyes then did a few stretching exercises to restore her circulation. When it came, the coffee was watery and weak, tasting of plastic. 'Yeuch,' she grimaced.

'I know.' Lynskey used his fingers to unknot the tension in her shoulders. 'If it tastes anything like the tea, it tastes like donkey's pi– I mean urine. Sorry.' He grinned. 'Don't finish it. Would you like me to get you a few pillows? You could lie down on the floor. I'm fine, not a bit sleepy. I'll keep watch.'

'I think I'll call my grandmother. I promised Treacy I would and it's eleven o'clock in the morning over there.'

She used the booth beside the drinks vending-machine in the hall, charging the call to her home number. When the operator put her through, the line to Cork, for once, was as clear as though it stretched only between the duplex and the next-door neighbours'. Not for the first time, Sky was struck

242

by how young her grandmother sounded. She already knew about Johanna's accident, Sky's aunt Margaret had reached her in the interim and although she sounded concerned, she did not seem panicked by the news. 'Of all the things to happen. Still, they can do wonderful things with surgery nowadays.'

'Daniel Treacy – I mean, McCarthy – continues to insist on being involved.' Sky took a deep breath. 'He assumes that because of the accident you'll want to come over right away, like tomorrow. He's offered to put you up.'

'Hmmm.' Her grandmother was noncommittal.

'Look, Grandma,' Sky did not feel up to pleading Treacy's case, 'he says he'll call you himself. I'm to break the ice, so to speak.'

'I'm still in shock that he has surfaced after all these years. I knew he was in Montana, of course . . .' her grandmother hesitated, 'but it is a bit silly, this, isn't it? At our age. I haven't seen Daniel for nearly half a century. I don't know how much you know, Sky.'

'He's told me everything.'

'Everything?' Her grandmother chuckled. 'How indiscreet.'

'Of course not everything. Look, Grandma, I'll leave it to the two of you to work things out. I'll call him now and tell him you're expecting to hear from him.'

The old lady's voice grew firmer. 'One way or another, I will come over to see Johanna. It's about time I went to the States anyway. It's a place we should all see at least once before we die. And I can't wait to see you again, Sky. I had hoped it would be here in Ireland, of course.'

'Don't talk about dying, Grandma. You've years yet.'

They arranged to speak again that night, when Johanna's operation was over and when the flight schedule was firm. Then Sky called Treacy, figuring meanly that since everyone else was awake he might at well be too.

'Is she very upset about your mother?' He did not appear to have been asleep.

'I think you'll be surprised at the way she sounds,' she did not want to engage in this, 'and she's quite philosophical about Mom. She's worried, of course—'

'That's only natural.' The Irish traces in Treacy's accent had intensified.

'I'll leave you to it. I hope you didn't mind my calling at this hour but I figured you'd want me to.'

'Of course.'

She told him her grandmother was at home and expecting his call and, although he seemed inclined to ask more questions, cut him off as politely as she could.

For once Lynskey did not pound her with questions when she went back to the room. Instead, he settled her down in the chair, covering her tenderly with the blanket. It felt wonderful to have someone else take charge. 'I'm not usually such a wimp.'

'It's three o'clock in the morning.' He crouched down before her to tuck in the ends of the blanket and his voice softened. 'And, little girl, you've had a busy day. Now go back to sleep.'

She woke again some time later to find he was no longer there. Assuming that he had gone to the bathroom, she held up her watch to catch the green overhead light and, seeing it was now only five after four, although it felt as though she had been alseep for a lot longer, snuggled the blanket over her shoulders.

But, as sometimes happens at that time in the morning, even in the teeth of extreme fatigue – or perhaps because of it – her mind sharpened and began to race, skittering around and across the surface of her impressions of the last few days. So much had happened, both personally and professionally, that it was difficult to organize the mish-mash into a coherent sequence. She began to make one of her mental lists, enumerating in order of priority what had to be done later that day.

Before anything, of course, came Johanna's operation, but Sky decided that while her mother was in the theatre she would slip home to shower and change. She could call her grandmother and then, on her way back to the hospital, drop in the rodeo notes for the kid to decipher. And it was then that she could find out from Jimbo what it was he wanted her to know about Lynskey. Or did she want to know at all? Her gadfly mind shied away immediately

Where was the man? She checked her watch again – he had been gone longer then ten minutes. Too restless now to sit and wait, she shook off the blanket and went to find out what was keeping him.

She saw him straight away: he was side-on to the corridor, using the public telephone. Sky wondered to whom he could be talking at this time in the morning – it was certainly not his sister's friend in Seattle.

Then, as she noted the set of his shoulders, the intense, almost covert way he held the mouthpiece close to his lips, a set of tumblers clicked into place in her brain. Everything fitted. Everything that had puzzled her about him and his behaviour, the locked briefcase, his persistent interest in Daniel Treacy – even taking photographs of him – Jimbo's warning.

This was no teacher.

Her sense of betrayal was balanced by chagrin at her own stupidity. She had fallen for the oldest trick in the book: a tumble in the hay and the pillow talk was his.

Sky could have cheerfully slit her throat: she had handed him everything she knew. She had been too trusting, or besotted, to follow up on her suspicions.

Keeping her eyes on him, prepared to walk forward if he turned round, she backed carefully into her mother's room, sat in the chair, pulled up the blanket and closed her eyes.

Her heart seemed to have enlarged with anger and she fought to control its beating, taking long, deep breaths.

When she heard him come back into the room, she stirred as though just waking up. 'Mmmm, what time is it?'

'It's about quarter past four.' He came over to stand beside her. 'Anything I can get you?'

How about an AK47 to shoot yourself? But Sky cuddled down under her blanket. 'Nothing, Fergus.' Her voice was dreamy. 'Well, maybe a cup of that awful coffee. It's a very long night, isn't it?'

'Yeah, not too long now, though. If this hospital is anything like home, they'll be around in a couple of hours waking everyone up. Coffee it is.'

When she knew she was alone, Sky, her temper barely contained, threw off the blanket and sat upright. The goddamned nerve of the guy. The knowledge that, just a few hours before, she had been rolling around in ecstasy under this traitor served only to double her fury. Dolphins and egrets, indeed. Her face burned. She'd show him egrets.

It took every iota of willpower and self-discipline to smile when he came back with the coffee. It helped a little that the night nurse came in with him to change Johanna's drip and catheter bags, and to monitor her blood pressure. This process took a few minutes, and by the time it was finished Sky had her anger somewhat in check. She could no longer sit in the chair, however, but paced the room like a hungry cat. 'You're very agitated.' Lynskey was leaning against the wall, arms folded across his chest. 'It's awful but there's nothing we can do except wait. I don't want to sound like a stuck record, but you know I think you shouldn't be here at all. You'd be much better off having a good sleep in your own bed.'

'I wouldn't have been able to sleep.'

'I suppose not.' Lynskey was watching her carefully now,

nothing showing except the compassion of a lover, and she had to remind herself how smart he was.

She smiled at him, even managing to drop a light kiss on his cheek. 'I can't tell you how much I appreciate all you're doing for us, Fergus. You're being marvellous.'

'You're welcome.' He went to hug her but she evaded his arms, pretending to be engrossed in thought.

'It's stifling in here.' She went to the window and parted two of the slats in the venetian blinds. 'It's a lovely night. Would you hold the fort while I go out for a bit?'

'Sure.'

Out in the parking lot she searched for something distracting on the Nissan's radio but could find only Jesus slots, lonelyhearts, wailing country, hard rock, or sad souls pouring their hearts down the phone lines to the night-time jocks. She killed them all, wound down the window and wallowed in the silence.

The bright security lights stained the empty lot with hard-edged shadows and, in front of where she sat, the hospital's bulk seemed unfriendly and alien. She felt lonely. Despite her mother's surface flakiness, and Sky's own attitude to her, Johanna, now lying pinioned and vulnerable only a hundred yards away, had always been a constant in her life and she knew she had been careless with this privilege. Suppose her mother were to die in the operating theatre? 'Oh, Mom,' she whispered to the blank windows of the hospital, 'you do know I love you, don't you?'

Unable to bear just sitting there, but unwilling to return to the room, she rummaged in the glove compartment and retrieved the notebook and pen she kept there. Turning on the map light, she made a list of every niggle about Lynskey and about Treacy.

She could come to only three possible conclusions about the former: the Irishman was either a private detective, an undercover cop, or, worst of all from her point of view, an investigative reporter.

The consolation was that at least the story itself was now in much sharper focus. She was no longer in any doubt that she had stumbled on something far larger than she had ever handled before: the fact that Lynskey had come – or been sent – all the way from Ireland meant it was big-time stuff. Treacy was the crux.

Back in the hospital corridor, Lynskey was again on to the chief superintendent in Dublin. 'She's twigged me. I don't know how – maybe she overheard something on the telephone when I was on to you a few minutes ago – but she's definitely twigged me.'

Chapter Twenty-One

The captain and crew of the *Agnes Monica* were weary. They had heard about the crash between the Hiace and the Starlet and, fearing increased police activity, were running for cover into a cave, the mouth of which was accessible to a vessel of the size of the *Agnes Monica* only at low tide.

They had lain low for twenty-four hours. A fishery patrol boat had passed twice, once in each direction and although they had not been detected, the captain was jumpy. Next time he got involved in something like this he would insist on better radio equipment: his stuff was not modern enough to intercept and decode signals from other vessels. But he reassured himself that this was only a fishing patrol, for God's sake, not a nuclear submarine.

It was again low tide and the captain was preparing to come out into the open. Conditions had improved: after a dry spell in the early morning it was raining again, but the gale had lessened.

The crew had been primed to tell their colleagues back at Killybegs that they been forced to take shelter in an isolated bay along the exposed northwestern coast. They would even have a few white fish to show for their pains: they planned to trawl on the way home.

Before they ventured into the open, however, the captain sent out the dinghy to check that their way was clear. But the water level was rising fast and, with the considerable swell, the exit would soon be impassable. The men in the dinghy reported nothing untoward and the captain decided to risk it.

As he emerged into the open, the ship-to-shore link, silenced by the depth of the cave, crackled into life. The news was not good: Killybegs was crawling with cops. Some dunderhead had decided to destroy the evidence but, in blowing up the Hiace, had taken half the parking lot of the Gárda station and three Gárda cars. What was more worrying was that the Guards were saying they suspected a Loyalist attack in retaliation for one launched by the IRA on an RUC station in Strabane.

That meant they wanted to put the press off the scent. To the captain, who was a seasoned campaigner in many areas that had little to do with fishing, it also meant the authorities knew what they were looking for. Or thought they knew.

He was told to go back to base and face down the action there in case it was thought he was running. He knew better than to argue, especially on an open channel, even though he was using a well-tested code, but he did question the order, indicating the presence of the patrol vessel, before setting a southeasterly course. Half an hour after he left the cave, he saw a vessel of about their own size ploughing through the brisk seas about a mile offshore. He recognized her as the *Slua Cailíní* from Burtonport and, to avoid attracting interest, slowed and ordered that his own nets be put out.

Five minutes earlier the fishing patrol vessel, now more than twenty miles away, had pinpointed his location.

In northwest Montana, the sheriff of Mayville was also becoming impatient. He wanted his money and, with the trip to Ireland imminent, he wanted it now.

With expertise born of long practice, he opened a pistachio nut and scooped out the flesh. 'Now, you listen,' he said softly into the telephone receiver. 'I've tried to scare the guy off the best way I know how. It's not my fault he's still snooping around. When am I going to get my fee, buddy?' He listened again, then, 'Very well, but this is the last. I'll be in touch.'

He broke the connection and considered, then punched out another number and stared into space for a couple of seconds. Then: 'It's O'Connor. That errand you ran? We need more of the same. And it needs to be done now.' He listened for a few seconds. 'I don't care. The slate is clean when I say it is. And before you show me any more slices of your bleeding heart, that file is still in my drawer here. Right here,' his eyes flicked downwards, 'locked, of course, but the key's on my ring. I could put my hand on that file right now. Cat got your tongue, O'Shaughnessy?' Then: 'Good, here's the address . . .'

Nothing much happens in Choteau if you discount its annual events: the Dinosaur Celebrations, its own Fourth of July rodeo, steak fry and parade, the 4-H Fair or Antique Steam Engine Threshing Bee. Apart from its pretty, wide-open scenery, the nearby Egg Mountain – where a nest of fossilized dinosaur eggs was discovered virtually intact – is its main claim to fame. Yet Choteau's cottonwood-lined streets are wider than many a Paris boulevard and its well-kept green in front of the old quarrystone courthouse is so well trimmed it invites pause. Out-of-staters are seduced into stopping here sometimes, while motor-homing between the National Parks of Glacier and Yellowstone, to admire the dinosaur eggs and bone exhibits in the small privately owned museum. Some dawdle, spending a few days at the dude ranches which supplement their owners' farming activities, but most visitors, if they stay, overnight in one of the four reasonably priced motels or two bed-and-breakfast houses.

Choteau folks mind their own business; but like all Montanans, who tend to be open-hearted and hospitable to a fault, they are not reticent about giving information. They would tell anyone who wanted to know that the beautifully presented ranch-style building a few miles outside town was one of those classy joints for rich nuts.

Right now one or two in the town were inclined to go further, muttering about the place being a waste-disposal unit for those elderly or awkward – but inconveniently strapping – relatives who stood in the way of some daughter's or son's rightful inheritance. And that its discreet but power-ful security arrangements were not for the protection of the rich nuts' money but to keep them from escaping. Further, these cynics knew that many patients were checked in by their status-conscious families under assumed names.

The Teton sanatarium, as its medical personnel preferred to call it, housed no long-stay patients but was used purely for assessment purposes. With the exception of one or two miracle cases, or where the relatives had a change of heart, the inmates invariably moved on to permanent-stay asylums. While they were here, however, they were accommodated in suites akin to those of a five-star hotel.

Luxury notwithstanding, Sunday was always a tedious day with a smaller than usual staff. Analytic and therapeutic activities were suspended, and the dull-eyed patients, never more than a dozen, lay around with little to do. For those *compos mentis* enough to realize where they were, the day must have been endless.

As it was to the staff – most of the nurses welcomed the dawn of Monday morning. The place hopped with cheerful queries about weekend activities as everyone buckled down to a fresh week.

'Good morning!' The smile on the face of the trainee died away as she came into the room and looked at the silent woman in the high, cot-sided bed. She came across and tweaked the already immaculate bedcovers. 'Did you have a good weekend, Peggy?'

She was not expecting an answer, of course. At least, she thought, this one was not abandoned like many of the facility's inmates: in the short time Peggy McGovern had spent in the place, she had suffered a surfeit of visits. Her husband attended regularly at her bedside and had spent almost a full day of the previous weekend with her, although she had been too sedated to know, and he had hired a companion for her, a gimlet-eyed young woman, who was staying in Choteau but who drove out to the complex every morning and stayed until nightfall. Peggy was bound ultimately for a facility in Oregon but while she was here, like all the other patients, she enjoyed – if that was the word – round-the-clock attention from the three nurses and the trainee dedicated to her care.

This trainee was as yet too green to have assumed the emotional armour-plating of the fledged professional. Now, as she gave her charge a bed-bath, she sang softly, hoping to penetrate the grey fog in which the woman seemed permanently wreathed. 'Attagirl, Peggy,' she cooed, when she was finished, 'you take it easy,' plumping up the pillows and then moistening a washrag to clean a speck of food from a corner of the woman's mouth. 'All nice and cosy? Would you like me to let your friend back in?'

She searched her patient's face for any sign of recognition or animation but saw nothing beyond the flickering eyelids which denoted disturbed or disturbing dreams. She knew she would have to toughen up: each case here was a hard case and she could not take them all to heart. She sighed and turned to leave. 'See you later at lunch, Peggy, OK?'

But as she opened the door to admit the paid companion, who was seated on a chair reading a novel, the young nurse missed something. The eyes of the woman in the bed opened momentarily and swivelled after her but the tiny squeak of the door hinges masked her weak whisper. Then it was too late. The girl was gone and in her place entered the silent companion.

The effort to speak had exhausted Mrs McGovern and her eyes had again filmed over. But she was not sleeping. Her brain felt like porridge. She could almost see it now: it looked like a porridgy flying saucer balanced on the tufts of a soft, soggy cloud. Holding on to the image with difficulty, she imagined her brain bubbling, hillocks of air bursting sluggishly – *pop! pop!* – just under the inner surface of the bone. Then she became aware of a noise beside her bed. Making a huge effort she half-opened her eyes.

That woman was there again: her face, a whitish blur, was wavering over an object. A book. The woman was reading.

Peggy allowed her eyes to close again and, for a second, her thoughts crystallized abruptly. She realized that she longed to die.

But, more than that, she desperately needed a drink.

Waves of half consciousness came and went and it was during one of the peaks that she became aware that the woman was no longer there. She forced her eyes open again. She was coming back in. She was leaning over the bed, saying something: Peggy tried to push back the fog in her brain and let the woman's words through. Something about her husband. He couldn't come today. What husband?

This was too difficult. Peggy's eyes closed of their own volition.

The paid companion sat back in her chair and reopened her book. She saw no point in repeating herself.

In the master bedroom of his pristine house, Daniel Treacy pulled aside the drapes, wincing at the brightness of the morning. Turning away from the glare, he stared at the

254

phone beside the bed he had shared for so long with his wife, and wondered if she had understood the message.

The first call Sky made when she got back to the house was to her editor.

The time between her return to her mother's room from the parking lot and Johanna's being wheeled off for her operation had not been as difficult as she had foreseen. Saying that he, too, could do with some fresh air and a change of clothes, Lynskey had borrowed her car and gone back to the hotel, returning only minutes before the transfer to theatre. He offered to drive her home then and she could see no way out of agreeing without making him suspicious. She had her own plan as to how he should receive his comeuppance and had no intention of tipping him off that he had been rumbled. 'Thanks, but do you mind if we don't talk?' She pretended to be taking something out of her eye so she would not have to look at him. 'I'm exhausted and I'm worried about Mom.'

'Of course.' He had taken her arm as they walked down the corridor and she had managed not to shy away. He was now safely back at the War Bonnet and she did not plan to see him again until after the operation. Now, as she waited for Jimbo's wife to fetch him to the phone, she was congratulating herself on the way she had played it; smugly, she felt that Lynskey could have no idea of her suspicions.

'Hello?' Jimbo sounded concerned. 'How's your mom?'

'She's in theatre. It'll be about three or four hours before there's any news. I'll drop in the rodeo notes before I go back to the hospital but I wanted to talk to you about that Irish teacher. I think I know what you were going to tell me about him.'

'Go on.' The editor's tone was cautious.

'He's not a teacher, is he? He's a reporter. Or a cop.'

'The latter, I believe. How did you find out?'

'Who told you?' Sky found little satisfaction in being proven right. She was having to fight waves of nausea. To think she had considered this might be a long-term relationship.

'Did Bill Collins get you?' Jimbo's multi-layered mind led him to answer questions with more questions.

'Well, yes and no . . .' Sky stared at the pad beside the telephone. The funeral director's name had been written on it several times. 'Not in the sense you mean. I'm afraid I was quite rude to him. He caught me at a bad time.'

'Maybe you should talk to him as soon as your mom's sorted out. Not that he has all that much information. But someone tipped him off.'

'Look, Jim,' Sky's nausea and tiredness fell away, 'I'm mad at that guy, Lynskey. Let me at the story, will you? I mean, don't give it to anyone else.' Once before when a mine disaster had threatened to overwhelm the meagre resources of the newspaper, Jimbo had hired a young male freelancer. 'I promise I won't let you down.'

'You sure you can be objective? You even have a family connection . . .'

'Trust me, please?'

'The story's not going to go away.' He remained circumspect. 'Just concentrate on your mother for today, OK? One thing to our benefit, at least if he's a cop he's not going to blow whatever it is all over the *Washington Post*. He might even turn out to be useful.'

Sky's febrile thoughts revolved at top speed while she was having her shower. She knew she was on the threshold of a bigger league than any in which she had played in her entire career: her day-to-day coverage of rodeos, community notes, obituaries, agriculture, zoning violations and local politics had not prepared her for this. Crime stories in Montana were largely to do with the relatively straightforward reporting of court cases relating to drunk and disorderly charges and the occasional murder or rape.

She knew her skill was perceived as being vested in the writing rather than the ferreting out of stories; even in Chicago, she had never been marked to cover any felony bigger than a mugging or petty theft. 'Get going and *do* it!' She turned off the water and addressed the chrome-plated shower head. 'Just *do* it.'

'Mr Collins?' She was businesslike when she got through to the funeral home. 'I'm very sorry we couldn't talk when you called yesterday.'

In response to his enquiries, she brought the funeral director up to date on her mother's condition. She even managed a joke: 'I'm afraid you'll have to wait a little longer, Mr Collins, to look after my mother in a professional capacity.' She waited while he chuckled at this and then asked him why he had wanted to talk to her.

'I have a little bit of news which might interest you, Miss MacPherson.' Collins's voice sank to a murmur. 'I've spoken to your editor.'

'Indeed I know you have.' Sky was too wound up for subterfuge. 'You think Fergus Lynskey is a policeman. Why, may I ask?'

'I can't tell you that.' He seemed miffed that Jimbo had stolen his thunder. 'But I thought you ought to know he's not what he seems. You seemed pretty friendly together . . .' He paused, then, in a different tone, 'You don't sound all that surprised, Miss MacPherson.'

'I'd be interested to know why this man is here in Butte, pretending to be a schoolteacher.' Sky hoped she sounded merely professional. 'Is he on duty? Is something going on here that might interest him?' She held her breath.

'Let's just say that Mr Lynskey *thinks* he knows something about something here in our city. But I would appreciate it,

257

Miss MacPherson, if you would get it across to him that he is wasting his time. That everyone knows who he is and that there is nothing for him. That there never was. That he would be much better off enjoying his holiday or going back to Ireland. Much better off. I think too,' his voice hardened, 'that this man may have turned your head with some nonsense about Daniel Treacy and his deceased wife. It appears that you've been asking a lot of questions and it can only be as a result of what you've heard from him. But of course *I* know, and I've reassured others, that you are much too experienced to fall for libellous lies. I'm sure you know that Mr Treacy has friends in high places, Miss MacPherson.'

Sky half smiled at the ridiculous terminology. Friends in high places, indeed. But the threats, not only to Lynskey but to herself, were clear. It was one thing to be used by Fergus Lynskey, she thought indignantly – at least she had enjoyed herself with him while it had lasted – it was another to be told how to conduct her work. 'Thanks for the tip, Mr Collins.' Her voice was now as hard as his. 'I'll certainly watch my step. I have to run now – thanks again.' She hung up before he could say anything more.

Then she called her grandmother and ascertained that the old lady would be arriving the following evening via Billings. After she made arrangements she checked her watch: she had plenty of time to pay another visit, a surprise one this time, to Daniel Treacy.

Chapter Twenty-Two

The area between the ornamental iron gates and the façade of Government Buildings, 'Versailles' to its Dublin critics because of its expensive restoration and fancy floodlighting, was as busy as a bus station on the night before a public holiday. Ministerial and Special Branch cars came and went while here and there earnest groups of lobbyists and public officials conferred. On the plinth in front of the entrance doors, an RTE television news crew was grouped around the Minister for Justice. Éamonn Vaughan, a reporter with large, sad eyes had just concluded an interview with the minister on a running story about Gárda recruitment, pay and overtime. Vaughan was loved and hated in equal measure by the present government because of his professional but tenacious, in-your-face style.

'That it, lads? I'm late – thanks . . .' But as the minister walked towards the front doors of the building, the reporter was still at his heels. 'Minister, off the record.' Vaughan's tone had sunk to a conspiratorial murmur. 'Any further developments on the Killybegs bombing? Is it true there's a big operation going on?'

'No news yet, Éamonn.' The minister waved to a party of schoolchildren being shepherded in crocodile formation past the ornamental fountain. 'You'll be the first to know, of course.'

'Minister—' The reporter tried again but the minister quickened his step and got into the building and out of reach.

The reporter had touched a nerve: the minister was on his way to a meeting to discuss the Killybegs episode prior to briefing the Taoiseach and the deputy prime minister, the Tánaiste, both of whose offices were in the building. He was being kept abreast of the developing situation in Donegal by the Gárdaí and, in deference to the involvement of the Navy, had invited the Minister for Defence to join with him in hearing what the Gárda Commissioner had to say.

The Defence Minister was in the room before him and so was the Commissioner. The latter had fresh news. 'Nothing found on our trawler, Minister, but, then, that doesn't surprise us all that much. Our Mountie friends warned us that this would be slick and although we've been shadowing the stuff from the beginning, our manpower problem—'

'I hope the search hasn't alerted them?' the Minister for Justice interrupted. He and the Commissioner had never hit it off.

The Commissioner's lips pursed. 'As far as the crew were concerned we were looking for illegal nets—'

'You think they bought it?' The minister again cut across, giving the Commissioner his most penetrating stare. 'I have to tell you that that shyster Vaughan from RTE asked me out there about some big operation he'd heard about.'

'He couldn't have missed it, Minister. As a cover we searched everything in the port. We gave it out that this was a new EC directive. The chief superintendent in charge of the operation travelled to Donegal but he stayed in the barracks. And the captain and crew of the boat were not brought in. We think we handled it.'

'But you haven't found anything, have you?' The Minister for Justice had thundered from the podium, in a powerful, passionate speech at his party's last annual rally, the Ard Fheis, that, subject only to his prime consideration which, 'first, last and always', was the protection of cherished family values, his ministry was laying heavy emphasis on ridding

Ireland of the scourge of illegal drugs, 'from crack to cocaine, from heroin to hash, until not a grain or a trace of it is left in Ireland. Until our cities can once again flourish and the streets and even the laneways are safe again for the little children.' Indeed, *Safe for the Little Children* was the catch-phrase in the current poster and television campaign.

'We're really concerned about this, Commissioner.' To compensate for her feelings of inadequacy, the Defence Minister spoke loudly. Both men ignored her. The Minister for Justice put his fingers to his temples, as though asking God to give him patience. 'Do we have any idea where it is now, Commissioner?'

'I'm afraid we have temporarily lost sight of it, Minister.' The Commissioner, who had seen out at least five governments of all political hues and many more cabinet reshuffles, was not in the least rattled. 'We followed the consignment from the time it was picked up and we know it was put aboard the *Agnes Monica* so, therefore, her captain either hid it somewhere along the coast during the twenty-four hours we lost her, or put it overboard to be retrieved later. Our lads will check every marker buoy and lobster pot along that coast. We've pinpointed to within a mile the place where she went out of contact. At the time, we thought she must have sophisticated jamming equipment but the search of her proved otherwise.'

'So the solution is obvious, man.' The minister's brows knitted incredulously at the obtuseness of all policemen. 'She hid somewhere, in some small cove. Find that and you'll find what you're looking for.'

'It's not quite that simple, Minister.' The Commissioner stretched his legs comfortably under the desk. 'Our American and Canadian colleagues tell us our fellas might have something new to this part of the Atlantic. At least, it's new to us. Apparently they can sink the goods in weighted waterproof containers with an electronic tag attached and recover it any time. All they have to do is activate this tag which releases the weights and the stuff comes back to the surface.'

The minister sighed heavily. 'So lean on the crew.'

'The recovery ship is rarely the one that dumps the stuff in the first place. It's almost certain this crew don't know who's involved at the top and possible they don't even know who would effect the recovery. We don't want to tip them off.' The Commissioner cleared his throat ostentatiously as though he hated having to repeat himself. 'As you know, the motivation of some of the creeps tied in with this is pretty mixed – and we'll be watching as many of the usual haunts as we can, not to speak of as many coves and inlets as we can manage in the circumstances.' He let it hang.

'I have to tell you, Commissioner, that I'm very concerned and so are my colleagues in Cabinet.' The Minister for Justice ignored the barbed reference to the recruitment and overtime dispute. 'How do you think it appears internationally? After all, both the Mounties and the FBI were spot on. It is a little humiliating to admit, don't you think, that we lose it as soon as it goes on to a two-bit inshore coaster?'

'Yes,' the Defence Minister chimed in. 'My department's been co-operating fully, Commissioner, but this has been going on for some time and our resources are scarce. We don't like them tied up like this at the height of the fishing season. It's time we saw some results.'

'This is one of the biggest operations we've ever mounted. If more overtime for the Gárdaí could be authorized . . .' The Commissioner raised his eyebrows.

'You know damned well what your budgets are,' the Justice Minister snapped.

'I'll have the costings of the overtime on your desk by close of business today.' The Commissioner remained calm and stared into his minister's eyes. He not only knew damned well what his budgets were, he knew damned well that cracks were showing in the glue that held the coalition parties together and that drug-related crime was one of the issues exercising the minds of the electorate.

'Incidentally, while we're on the subject of budgets,' the Justice Minister pushed his glasses up on his nose and stared back, 'I'd like to know how much that one-man expeditionary force you sent to America has cost.'

'I'll find out, Minister.'

'Get a move on, Commissioner, and sort this whole thing out.' The Justice Minister pulled towards him an unopened file as if he had better things to do. He glanced at his Defence colleague, then glared at the Commissioner. 'Time is not on our side.'

The Amnesty meeting was scheduled a few days' hence.

'Now,' he said brusquely, 'I have a constituency group in. And then I have to see the Taoiseach, brief him about this mess. He's taking a personal interest, as you know. I'm not looking forward to that meeting, Commissioner. I promised him we would have something positive at this stage. Anything else on your mind?'

'Nothing else to report at present, and the Taoiseach can hardly blame the force for a car crash, which seems to have put a spanner temporarily in the works. But it has not affected our morale and you can assure him that we have things under control. I'll telephone you this evening, Minister.'

As the Commissioner picked up his hat and gloves, he smiled and inclined his head towards the Defence Minister in a courteous bow. Poor woman: she had no idea what was going on. He knew that no one had briefed her about the possibility of a subversive strike from outside the state's borders. And as for the separate headache of a proposed royal visit, he doubted if she even knew there was an Amnesty conference in the offing, let alone who'd been invited.

The door closed behind him with a soft click as the Commissioner put on his hat. In the struggle between himself and his political masters over resources he held all the aces. A lot of unwelcome media attention had been paid lately to the fact that Ireland was being used as a clearing house not only for drugs but for all sorts of criminal deals. So with the bush telegraph positing an election sooner rather than later, this ailing coalition needed a big international press conference.

Sky telephoned Daniel Treacy's office to make sure he was in and was surprised to learn that he had not yet arrived. 'I'll call him at home.' She brushed off the secretary with a brusque guarantee that she was a personal friend. Then she grabbed her tape-recorder, notebook and purse and ran to the Nissan.

She had no difficulty in finding the house; although no one she knew had seen inside it, everyone in the city knew its location. What she was not prepared for was the view from the terrace at the end of the driveway. 'Jeez,' she gasped audibly as she let the Nissan coast to a halt before a spectacular Rocky Mountain panorama. The circular parking lot was large enough for at least eight automobiles, but only Treacy's Saab convertible was in evidence.

She heard the doorbell chime as she pressed the brass button, and then leaned towards the speaker grille set beside it. She waited at least ninety seconds, but when nothing sounded through the speaker, she reached for the bell again and was caught off balance as the door was opened. 'Miss MacPherson – Sky – what a pleasant surprise!'

Without a jacket, the grey hospital-issue sling cutting into the flesh of his neck, Treacy looked thin and far older than she had seen him before. 'Sorry to bother you at home so early.' She stepped over the threshold in response to his silent invitation. 'I did call your office. And I'm sorry about calling so late last night too. Did you get back to sleep?'

'Don't worry. I don't need much sleep these days.' He sidestepped the question. 'Have you had breakfast?' The soul of courtesy, he closed the door behind her. The reporter in Sky began to feel less intrepid than intrusive and shabby.

'As a matter of fact, I haven't.' She remembered she had not eaten for more than twenty-four hours. No wonder she was suffering from mood swings: it was all that caffeine on an empty stomach.

'This way.' He stood back and indicated that she should go through one of the doorways off the thickly carpeted lobby. 'Make yourself at home, I'll get a fresh pot of coffee.' The telephone on a console table rang as he passed it on his way to what Sky presumed was the kitchen. 'I'll let it be.' He smiled at her over his shoulder. 'A great invention, the answering machine . . .'

The electronically distorted voice of the secretary to whom Sky had spoken earlier rang through the lobby as she walked into the room to which he had pointed. Small and elegant, it was decorated entirely in tones of primrose and sparkling white, and contained the minimum of furniture: a glass-topped marble table, on which breakfast had been laid, six graceful chairs, a matching sideboard, over which hung an Impressionist watercolour of a spring garden, and two upholstered rattan chairs in front of south-facing full-length bay windows, which obviously allowed in maximum light from dawn to sunset.

The windows faced on to a sunlit Italianate terrace outside, and if the forest canopy beyond and below had been blue instead of green, Sky thought she could have been standing in a villa in Capri or the South of France. 'My wife and I did not entertain,' the carpet was so thick that she had not heard Treacy come back, 'so we didn't need a big formal dining-room.' He placed the coffee pot on a ceramic trivet in the centre of the table.

'It's beautiful.' Sky meant it: the room exuded a sense of peace and ease.

'Thank you.' He waited politely until she was seated

265

before he sat down. 'I like it too. Rather fancifully, I suppose, we referred to it as the garden room.' He waved his uninjured arm towards the painting above the sideboard.

'We'll talk about my grandmother in a moment, Mr Treacy . . .' But then Sky hesitated: she was suddenly unwilling to use her grandmother as a cover for her real purpose in being here. Treacy's courtesy made it difficult to beard him about why he was attracting the attentions of an undercover Irish policeman. Especially here in his own home. The blast of light from the windows revealed a network of fine lines all over his face, but it was the grey pallor of his skin and the tiredness in his eyes that were most striking. She bought time. 'How's your shoulder, Mr Treacy? Are you in pain?'

'Not really. Now, tell me about your mother. I hope you have not forgotten my offer of assistance – please help yourself to some croissants and fruit.' He gestured towards the baskets on the table.

As she told him about Johanna, Sky thought that this was not the stiff tycoon she had met before. 'I'm sorry I'm interrupting your own breakfast.' She looked at the untouched roll on the plate in front of him.

'I'm afraid I'm not hungry.' He pushed away the plate. 'Please don't keep me in suspense any longer, Sky. What's the news?'

The effect of her telling him that her grandmother was arriving in Billings the following day was shocking. Treacy put his good hand over his face and she was afraid he might even cry. 'Mr Treacy . . .' she half rose.

'I'm all right. I'm sorry.' He lowered his head and the words were muffled by his hand.

Sky was disconcerted: how on earth was she going to confront him?

As she dithered over what to say next, he coughed and lowered his hand. 'Do you think she'll stay here?'

'One step at a time, Mr Treacy.' She was relieved that,

although his eyes were brimming, he seemed to have regained his composure. Then, before she could stop herself, 'You're very different here at home from what you are in public, do you know that?' Immediately furious with herself, she thought that if someone were to institute an academic course in how to control an unruly tongue she would have to be the first in line for registration.

'Am I?' The unshed tears still stood in his eyes but he smiled a little. 'Who isn't different in his own home?' He seemed to come to a decision. 'I'm going to tell you something I've never admitted to anyone before.'

Suddenly, against all her training and reporter's instincts, Sky felt she did not want to hear. 'Are you sure I'm the right person?'

'Yes. Midge hates – hated – this house. It was far too open – I guess it made her feel exposed. It was one of the reasons she preferred the lodge, small windows, thick dark wooden walls. I chose this site, built this house, with your grandmother in mind. She always loved light and air. I knew she would probably never come here, but I lived in hope. Does that shock you?'

Sky was out of her depth, and she felt that to probe further would be voyeuristic. 'Do you live alone?' She knew it was inadequate. 'Does no one look after you?'

'You mean servants?' He seemed unruffled by the lack of a suitable response and smiled again. 'My needs are few. A woman comes in to clean three times a week, and I send out my laundry. I don't like being fussed over. Any servants we had were in the lodge. Midge   ' He stopped.

'What about Midge, Mr Treacy?' Remembering why she was here and glad to be on safer ground, Sky kicked at her resolve.

'I beg your pardon?' He looked almost startled.

'Midge,' she insisted. 'You were going to say something about your wife.'

'Yes.' He paused a little and, again, the transformation was stunning: the softness and openness had vanished, replaced by wary reserve. 'My wife was the one who had to have servants.'

'I came here not solely because of my grandmother, Mr Treacy. Or perhaps you might have guessed that.'

'Oh?' He retreated further.

'Do you remember my Irish friend from yesterday's rodeo? The one who drove my car home?' His eyes did not blink or flicker but seemed to darken as, staring at her, he let the silence develop between them. For once, she chose her next words carefully. 'I just found out he is not an Irish teacher at all, Mr Treacy, but an Irish policeman. A policeman with a particular interest in you and in your wife's death.' She looked at him as boldly as she dared. 'Would you have any idea why?'

His reply was so unexpected it left her almost winded. 'It is not news to me that he is a policeman. To answer your question, I have no idea what his agenda is. And I don't care, Miss MacPherson.'

Something about his demeanour puzzled Sky. His words rang true and yet she knew he was lying. If, as he had said, he knew Lynskey's identity, he had to know why the Irishman was going to so much trouble. What was it the funeral director had said? '. . . *He may have turned your head . . . nonsense about Daniel Treacy. I've reassured others . . . libellous lies . . .*'

'The guy tricked me, Mr Treacy.' She decided she had nothing to lose by being honest. 'I'm very angry. I wish you'd tell me what's going on.'

She felt him weigh up the situation.

'You're the press, Miss MacPherson.'

He was no longer as cold, however, so she pushed home her advantage. 'I'm also Elizabeth Sullivan's granddaughter. Could you talk to me on that basis?'

He looked sceptical. 'Come now! You're not expecting me to believe you wouldn't publish anything I might tell you?'

'Of course I can't guarantee that, but what I could do is make it so you'll suffer no damage.' Sensing she was gaining ground, she pulled her chair closer to the table. 'Somehow I cannot believe you're involved in anything illegal. You don't strike me as the type.'

A ghost of a smile. 'Is there a type?'

She cast around for something that would not pull down the shutters again. 'Well,' she grinned at him, 'are you?'

Treacy had another shock in store. 'I'm rather afraid I am.'

As she goggled at him, he reached for the coffee pot and refilled his cup. 'Mr Lynskey has competition. If you look carefully and quickly when you drive out again through the front entrance you will probably see a diligent member of the FBI or it could be the CIA or even a private investigator – it's a matter of complete indifference to me – in a cream-coloured Chevrolet making notes in a little notebook.'

'You're being watched?'

'Round the clock.' Treacy paused. 'I can tell you it's rather an odd feeling. I would have thought it might be irritating but in a way it's a privilege. One feels a little like a celebrity.'

'But what have you done, Mr Treacy?' Again Sky forgot to behave like a reporter.

He let another silence descend, stroking the shiny fabric of the sling over his injured shoulder. 'I'll tell you what,' his accent sounded very Irish now, 'I'll make a deal with you, Sky. I'll tell you what's going on – or as much as I know about what's going on – provided you agree to certain conditions.'

'Depends on what they are.' Sky tried to suppress her jubilation. She was there. She was sure of it.

'The first condition,' he was weighing his words, 'is that we work together, that I see what you're writing. If you agree, I think I do have a story for you, one that might even make you famous, R. Sky MacPherson . . .' Again that trace of a smile.

Sky wondered how Jimbo would react to deal-making. She had never before agreed to show copy in advance but, then, she had never dealt in this kind of stuff. 'What's your second condition?' To help her think, she took a mouthful of coffee. Too much, too fast. She almost choked, just managing to swallow without spluttering it all over the immaculate glass table-top. She was furious with herself for blowing the sophisticated, on-top-of-it-all Woodwards-and-Bernstein image she knew she should be trying to convey.

He waited until she had recovered, then went on, 'The second condition is that the name of one person involved in the story is for your ears only and is to be kept out of it. The name is integral, I'm afraid, but together we'll work out a way to do this.

'The third condition,' he looked so intently at her that she knew this was going to be the most significant of the three, 'is that is you must put a moratorium on publishing your story.'

Sky considered. 'Until when?'

'Until after my death.'

She was about to protest when he held up his hand. 'You won't have to hold the front page all that long. I have cancer.'

Chapter Twenty-Three

'So now maybe you can figure out why I'm so anxious to see your grandmother just one more time.' Treacy was matter-of-fact.

'How long?' Sky knew there was no point in being coy.

'I don't know. It may be weeks, a couple of months at the outside. It has spread to my liver. That will make it mercifully fast, apparently. Now,' he became brisk, 'perhaps since you know this, it makes it a little easier to hold off on publishing?'

Knowing full well that she should not take such decisions without consulting Jimbo, Sky agreed. She took out her tape-recorder and switched it on. 'No.' Treacy now reverted to his businessman persona. 'No tape.'

She tried to get him to change his mind but he was adamant. 'I think you'll have no difficulty in remembering what I'm going to tell you, R. Sky MacPherson.' That off-putting cold smile sent shivers of anticipation down her back; this man seemed able to switch at will between personalities. One second he was the perfect, considerate host, the next, a frosty, impermeable enigma. 'Listen, Sky,' he softened again, 'when you hear what I have to tell you you'll see for yourself why I wouldn't want myself quoted verbatim. Even after my death.'

She pressed the 'off' button on the recorder.

As Sky listened to his low, intense speech for the next five minutes, she began to feel as though she was sitting in the back row of a movie theatre. The scale of the revelations was so outlandish that she lost her sense of excitement about the scoop. She registered what he said but was unable to put it in context.

How could it be true, in pedestrian, nineteen nineties Montana, that Midge Treacy had not died – had not even been in that accident – but was in some upstate institution? That her husband had participated in the arrangements of her so-called death, had allowed the charade of her funeral to proceed – had even stood by a casket which did not contain her body. That he could stand there and accept the sympathy of Sky herself and every businessman in town. That some organization, for which the St Patrick's Brigade was just a local front, had such power it could arrange this bizarre scheme, which obviously included police forces, medical examiners and maybe even the judiciary.

'So there were three accidents.' Sky tried to collect her scattered wits. 'The one where your wife hit Sheriff O'Connor's Buick, the one where she hit the hobo – but didn't run away as you told me last time . . .' She allowed herself an accusing look to which he did not respond.

'Well, two really,' she amended, 'the third one being the staged one when your wife was already in Choteau . . .' It was so extraordinary that she could not sit still but stood to pace the room. 'If it happened as you say, if the sheriff organized that her automobile went off the highway like that and caught fire, how did he square the hospital? Even with a phoney accident someone must have called an ambulance. And with no body . . .'

'I left that to O'Connor. I wasn't there at the time.' His tone had become conversational. They might have been talking about Ross Perot's chances in November. 'Funny, when your life shrinks to a day-by-day affair, how little revelance that sort of thing seems to have. And my main concern was getting Midge settled. You haven't touched your coffee. Shall I fetch some more?'

'It's like something out of a thriller.'

'It may well read like a thriller by the time you've finished with it.' This time his smile was genuinely amused. 'But I'm afraid it's all too true. What about the coffee?'

'I mustn't have any more coffee or I'll go into orbit. Look, what was involved here?' Sky remembered her remark to Teddy Morzsansky about the oversized casket. 'That casket was very big. Was it drugs?'

'I don't know. I didn't ask. I resented it, of course, and after Midge is finally secure I will go to the police, but, for reasons I've already explained, I did not – do not care what they did with the coffin. With Midge's condition and my own death imminent, I felt I had no option but to agree. And, of course, if I die before I go to the police, you will be free to tell whomever you choose. I'm being frank with you now so you will have the truth.'

Sky's impression that she was caught somewhere in the middle of a thriller-writer's fantasy was reaching new heights. 'How did they organize the funeral on the other side? I mean, I know it's not unusual for Irish Americans to want to be buried in Ireland but were there no formalities? What about your wife's family? Who was there to greet the casket? And if there was no one at the airport, would that not have looked a bit suspicious? And presumably you didn't go?'

'Hold on!' Treacy held up his hand. 'You're going too quickly. To answer the last question first, I did not go to Ireland – for many reasons, not only the obvious one. You see, although the killing of your grandfather was an accident I had a manslaughter charge against me and I should not have been admitted to the United States all those years ago. I got in only through the good offices of the friend of an uncle in New York. This man's name was Treacy. He had political and union connections. It was he who sponsored me and it was his name I took.' He held up his hand again. 'Don't ask how he swung it, I don't know. I've always understood it to be what we called in Ireland "nod-and-wink" politics. He's long dead now and so is my uncle, so I'll never find out, and anyhow, it's irrelevant. But you understand now why I've never gone back – for fear I would be stopped coming back in again.

'I boarded the aircraft with the coffin and they put me off in Minneapolis. From there I went straight to Choteau to visit my wife. Before you ask,' he had seen that she was preparing to launch another barrage, 'I assume they have influence in airports too. As to what arrangements they made on the other side, I have no idea. And I don't *care*, Sky, I told you!' His voice rose momentarily. This was the first real evidence she had seen of the emotional stress he must be suffering, and she was tempted to back off.

Yet she had the nub of the story in her sights: having read and seen as much foreign current-affairs coverage as anyone in her line of business, she was well aware of the allegations as to what some of the Irish-American organizations were up to. Gun-running, for instance, fund-raising for weapons for the IRA and INLA, for the Loyalist paramilitaries. 'What about relatives in Ireland? You told me you'd put death notices in the Irish papers.'

'And you believed me, Miss MacPherson.' Again, he smiled, this time with something approaching affection. He might have been patronizing her, but she decided to give him the benefit of the doubt and smiled back. 'I'm glad you're not cynical,' he had meant no offence, 'and I hope you stay that way, notwithstanding that what I am telling you might move you away from our own cosy little corner and out into the piranha pool of the national press.'

'I doubt it, I'm afraid I'm a bit green at this, but – if I may ask you another question, Mr Treacy, a crucial one.'

She took a deep breath. 'Are you not concerned about what the contents of that coffin might have been? If it was drugs, for instance.'

'I thought I'd already made my position clear to you, Sky.' His eyes registered appeal. 'Having heard what I've told you about my wife, do you think I was in any position to make conditions? You must understand, you *must*, that I could not allow Midge to stand trial, maybe go to prison. Can you not try to understand? This was my wife, Sky, someone I'd vowed to protect.' He stared at her for a long time while, unusually, she schooled her tongue.

He seemed not to find comfort in her expression and looked away. 'If it makes you feel any better, although I don't suppose it will, I was assured that any money raised as a result of my "co-operation", as they so kindly put it, would be going solely to fund legitimate businesses in the north of Ireland and for relief of hardship caused to prisoners' families.'

She had little choice but to accept his *bona fides* and, in any event, saw the moral dilemma in which he had been placed. She went on to ask him for the names of the people involved in the deceit but he knew little. The only person who had spoken to him in any detail had been the sheriff, 'And he gave me hardly any information, said the less I knew the better. It was he who arranged Midge's admission to the sanatarium up by Choteau. And he is also arranging for her transfer to Oregon. I'll go with her, of course. So the only names I can give you are those of the Mayville sheriff and the funeral director, Bill Collins.'

Sky remembered the call to Collins's mobile telephone the night she was killing time in the car park of the War Bonnet before going in to cover the Brigade's monthly meeting. 'It was Bill Collins warned me about Fergus Lynskey. The man who's here from the Irish police. Collins tried to make me tell Lynskey to back off. What's more, it was he who called my editor to tell him too. In fact,' she saw the irony, 'I'd say he's the one who blew it because he actually tipped us all off, therefore *making* a story out of this whole thing.'

'Bill Collins is a fool. He probably panicked. I may be wrong,' Treacy spoke slowly as though working it out for himself, 'but I think he's only small fry.' He played with a piece of thread hanging from the sling. 'I would say that the St Patrick's Brigade are probably being used by a heavier crowd. The members of the Brigade believe they're helping what they like to call the Cause.

'You remember Jerry Flynn?' he asked slowly. 'The Canadian in whose helicopter we travelled? You might check him out, although maybe I'm not being fair. I've never liked the guy—'

'If you don't like him,' she interrupted, 'why were you his guest at the rodeo that day?'

Treacy raised his eyebrows. 'It's clear you don't know the way business works. Far more deals are made on golf courses and at lunch tables than in the boardroom.'

'Sorry, stupid question. So what makes you think he's involved in something illegal?'

'Oh,' Treacy looked off into the middle distance, 'just some things he said, nothing I could put my finger on and it was more the way he said them than anything else. We were discussing something we had both seen on CBS the night before, a small news item about the Irish Prime Minister going to see the British Prime Minister and the two of them standing pleased as punch for a photo-call. Flynn is third or fourth generation Irish and I can't even remember what it was he said. It was more a tone of voice, really, but I remember thinking at the time that there was a lot going on underneath.'

The telephone rang in the hallway, again picked up by the machine. The door was open and Treacy cocked an ear:

it was his secretary with changes to his appointments schedule.

While he listened, Sky checked the time. Although her brain felt sharp and she could think of nothing she wanted to do more than bite into this huge plum that had landed in her lap, she must not forget her mother. 'I'm keeping you from work, Mr Treacy,' she drained her coffee when the bleep on the machine ended the message, 'but you asked that a name be kept out of it. I assume you mean your wife's. I know I agreed in principle, but I'm sure you can see it would be difficult to run this story without referring to her.'

'I mean me, Sky. This is why I would not allow you to tape our conversation. By quoting me directly, there are those who might recognize figures of speech, vocabulary.'

'But why? And how can I—'

'You have all the information,' he interrupted. 'It's up to you to find a way to write your article. You could find another – ah – source. Of course I'm central, I know that. All I'm asking is that I'm not quoted. No one must know that it was I who divulged all of this.'

'But why?' she repeated. 'What would it matter to you? You'll be—' She stopped.

'Yes, I will be.' He interpreted correctly what she had been about to say. 'But medical science is, as you pointed out earlier, making great strides. Too late for me, alas, but where my wife is concerned, although the alcohol has damaged her brain, she might recover some day. If she does, I won't be around to protect her from knowing what happened. But I can protect her from knowing that her husband was the prime source of her public humiliation.'

Sky put her tape-recorder back into her purse, preparatory to leaving. 'One thing's puzzling me, Mr Treacy. It's obvious, after what you've told me about your wife, why you didn't go to the police, but why, having covered up for so long, have you decided to tell me all this?'

'The truth is . . .' he shifted in his chair and she felt his discomfort in her own body. '. . . I don't take kindly to being blackmailed or treated like a simpleton, a blind, brainless pawn in someone else's game. Anything I can do to make life awkward for the good sheriff and his merry men I'll do. At the time I felt I had no choice but to go along with them because of Midge and I still feel that, because the arrangements concerning her are not yet complete. But that doesn't mean I'm going to lie down with my paws up in the air like some dumb lapdog. For a while I considered going to the police, despite the dangers, but I knew if I did that it would be likely that the charges against Midge would be reinstituted by O'Connor's successor. I've no idea how he managed to stop them in the first place. But he was right about the effect on her. I dread to think what she might have done. Even had you and I not spoken together because of your grandmother, I would have come to you, some time before the end and when I was sure no one could touch Midge. I'm determined those crooks will not get away with it. I meant it when I said before that I admire your work, Sky. You're wasted in Butte.'

'Thank you.' Sky had received compliments before but knew that none had been so sincerely meant.

Treacy gazed away from her. The sun was still low enough in the sky to paint long shadows in the valleys between the mountain peaks to the west and under its fresh benediction, the green ocean that stretched to the foothills was full of light and shade. Yet despite all the architect's efforts to embrace the beauty outside, this ultra-silent, plush room remained isolated from it by the suffering of its owner. For the first time Sky understood Daniel Treacy's loneliness. 'It seems the authorities have now come to me,' he said, almost to himself, 'saving me the bother of making all these decisions. I don't underestimate those men outside. I wouldn't be surprised if they're also watching our sheriff and, with all my soul-searching, it may prove unnecessary in the end for me to give myself up and make my big confession.' When he smiled his teeth seemed too big for his mouth. 'You should ask your Irish policeman friend's opinion about how good he thinks they are.' He winced, then made an effort to turn his head back towards her. 'Would you mind if I asked you to leave now? I find I'm already very tired and I still have a long day ahead of me.'

'Of course.' Sky reached for her purse.

'That's wonderful news about your grandmother.' His eyes slid away from hers so he looked almost shy. 'I'd appreciate it if you wouldn't tell her what I told you about the house.'

'I won't.' It was such a private, intimate confession that Sky knew there was little danger of that.

'Did you extend my invitation to her?' He was still diffident. 'Do you think she might agree to stay here?'

'Did you not ask her that yourself?' Sky paused in the act of closing the zipper on her purse.

Treacy swallowed. 'I'm afraid I didn't have the courage to call her last night. It's been a very long time since we spoke. Look, Sky,' he winced again and she felt sure this time it was not from physical pain, 'I'm afraid I'll blow it.'

'I'm sure she's looking forward to seeing you.'

'Do you really think so?' His face lit up from within and, his present appearance notwithstanding, she could see how handsome he must have been in his youth.

'I do.' The hell with objectivity. Somewhere, during the course of this interview, Sky had definitely changed sides. Instead of a professional journalist on the verge of her breakthrough story, she felt like a mother encouraging a son to ask his favourite girl to Homecoming.

'There's just one more thing. I have no right to ask this, of course but in return for what I have told you exclusively I wonder would you do me one more favour?'

'That depends.'

'It would make me very happy if you did not allude to any of this in your grandmother's presence. If I get the chance, I'll tell her about Midge. And about myself. But I don't think she needs to know the ins and outs of what's been going on.'

With the story on hold anyway, Sky felt there was little to be gained by making the poor guy's last few days more upsetting than they were already. She relaxed. 'Done.' She was shocked then to see his face contort.

'I'm sorry to be so rude,' he gasped, struggling for control, 'but you really will have to leave. I need to go upstairs – I'm afraid my medication is overdue.'

The spasm passed and he made two more requests. He would be at the airport that evening in time for her grandmother's arrival but would hang back out of sight. Sky had gone so far down the road with him that she had no difficulty in agreeing to act as go-between and, if her grandmother was amenable, to take her to where he was.

She also agreed to keep the news of his cancer to herself. According to Treacy, the only people who knew were his doctor, his private secretary and his attorney. He had not yet told members of his various boards.

She took her time passing through the gate at the end of his driveway. The sedan he had talked about was there, parked on a strip of grass beside the highway. As Sky went by, the driver started up his engine and pretended to consult a map.

Chapter Twenty-Four

Five thousand miles and several time-zones away, the *L.E. Aideen* was steaming slowly through moderate seas, captained by an ambitious young officer whose first command she was. He was proud of his ship, and her state-of-the-art communications and detection equipment were having no difficulty in tracking the *Agnes Monica*: his instructions were simply to continue to relay her exact whereabouts, heading and speed.

The fishing vessel was making headway; she had trawled for a while, then hauled in her nets and was now, the *Aideen*'s commander ascertained, travelling at full throttle.

He instructed his radio officer to report that the craft would be off Killybegs in approximately one hour and twenty minutes.

As she drove to the *Courier* offices from Treacy's mansion, Sky struggled to come to terms with her conflicting feelings. She knew her mother's condition should still be her prime concern but it was hard to contain her sense of exultation at the story she had been handed. 'Get a grip,' she said aloud to the dashboard of the Nissan, reminding herself she had gone to see Treacy not only in pursuit of the story but on a personal mission of revenge. To blow Lynskey's cover. Some hotshot she was. She had not yet decided how to handle the Irishman but on the journalistic side, she would let Jimbo dictate.

But, for once, he was not in his paper-dominated office. 'Said he had a breakfast meeting but he's not back yet.' The junior's languid hands were fluttering over an open filing cabinet in the main office. 'Oh, and you had two calls, One was some man from the American Legion. I wrote down his name, Sky, it's on your desk. He wanted to know how you were going to handle the accident to Mr Treacy.'

Sky reached for the pad on her desk then changed her mind. 'I've got to get to the hospital. Call him back for me, will you? Tell him to mind his own business.'

'Really?' The junior's eyes widened.

'For goodness sake, no.' Sky sighed. 'Don't put it like that, use your judgement. Was the second call important?'

'He didn't say. I wrote down the number.'

Unable to curb her curiosity about this one, Sky picked up the pad. The number meant nothing to her. And then she saw the name. After a second or two, she remembered: it was the driver of the logging truck who was alleged to have driven Midge Treacy off the road north of Mayville. 'May I speak to Martin O'Shaughnessy, please?' As she waited for him to come on the line, she flipped through her notebook in an effort to find the entry she had made about the logger during the trip to Libby.

She had not yet found it when he spoke: 'Yes?'

'Thank you for returning my call, Mr O'Shaughnessy.' She stopped, realizing she should be cautious: the guy had to be involved in the fraud.

Something about his name, and not just that he was the logger she had been looking for, buzzed inside her brain. What was it?'

'The reason for my original call no longer applies,' she hoped she sounded convincing, 'because I was doing a story on road fatalities in the state and your name arose in connection with an accident near Mayville. But since you were on vacation I went ahead and wrote the piece without

282

you. It's finished now and unless you have anything new to add, I don't think I need any longer to talk to you.'

He did not immediately reply. Then: 'I had no chance that night. You sure you have all the details right? When's your story appearing?'

His response confirmed that her instinct to be careful was correct. She told him she had no definite date for publication, that it was not a huge story – 'just one of those perennials we do from time to time, you know?' She attempted to laugh.

'You sure I can't help you? Maybe if you could tell me what you're saying about that night?'

'I couldn't do that, Mr O'Shaughnessy. I gather you weren't injured in any way?'

'I had a very lucky escape. She was driving like a crazy woman.' He hesitated just a fraction. 'I had no chance to avoid her.'

'So I've heard.'

Sky waited but he said nothing more. 'Thank you for calling,' she said forcefully, 'but I'm afraid I have to go to the hospital, my mother's quite ill.'

The logger made ritual noises of concern and then: 'That woman was a soak, Miss MacPherson. You'd be better off not bothering about her.'

Echoes of Bill Collins's advice – or warning – to Lynskey.

'I appreciate the call.' Sky wanted him off. 'Now I have to go. Thank you.' She hung up.

She discovered her hands were trembling. The logger was taking instructions from the sheriff of Mayville; yet Sky felt that he, like Collins, was just a minor player. What was it about that name? She said it aloud, 'Martin O'Shaughnessy . . .'

'Yes? You want something, Sky?' The junior looked up, her bright vacant face enquiring.

'It's nothing.' She proceeded to explain the cryptic notes

283

she had made at the rodeo. 'Just type them up first, that'll give you a sense of the story, but all you really need to get right is the spelling of everyone's name. OK? Just do your best, it'll be fine. Tell Jimbo – Mr Larsen – that I'll call him as soon as I can.'

Johanna was still in theatre when Sky got to the hospital and she installed herself in the empty room to wait.

She had been there only ten minutes when Fergus Lynskey put his head around the door. 'Good morning, sleep well?' His expression was pleasant yet bland.

'Fine, thank you.' Sky forced herself to reciprocate. 'And you?' They might have been guests at a cocktail party.

'Is there any word?' He came into the room and sat down. Sky related what she knew about her mother's operation, which was precious little, and they lapsed into silence.

'I'm still half asleep.' Lynskey yawned noisily. He stretched his legs, folded his hands across his stomach and let his eyes close.

Given his perfidy, Sky was outraged at his air of relaxation. Yet, as she glared at his prone body, she knew that, without Jimbo's input, she should not show her hand. 'It may be hours yet, Fergus,' she said, as sweetly as she could, 'and you're so tired. Why don't you go back to bed and I'll contact you as soon as there's news?'

'Ah, no.' He did not open his eyes. 'I don't want to leave you on your own and I couldn't sleep anyway, during the day. I've hired a car, a Chrysler Topaz – if me ma could see me now! And it's the first time in my life I've ever had cruise control. Wonderful invention.'

'I don't mind waiting by myself.' Her exasperation was growing. 'If you're not tired, why don't you go somewhere? You said you'd like to see the Custer Battlefield, didn't you, that day we went to the rodeo?' It was a shock to Sky to realize that "that day" had been only yesterday. Lynskey's eyelids fluttered a little but he said nothing. 'So why not?' she went on. 'You're on vacation, after all. There's little you can do here and it's a pity to waste a pretty day like this stuck in a hospital room.'

'Maybe.' Still he did not open his eyes. 'By the way, how was Treacy this morning?'

Furious, she sprang to her feet. 'Were you following me?'

At last he responded, shaking his head as though to clear it. He pulled himself into a more upright position and looked directly at her. 'You're much too forthright for this game, MacPee. What's eating you?'

'I don't know what you mean—'

'Oh yes you do.' His intelligent eyes were still. 'One minute we're having the most fantastic time of our lives and the next it's igloo time. And you're too straight to carry it off. I wish you'd come clean.'

'Why don't *you* come clean?'

'Ahh.' His knowing tone inflamed her further.

She was trying to think of a riposte when he got up and went to the window. 'How did you find out?'

At least, she thought, looking at his back, he had the grace not to treat her like an idiot. Damned if she was going to let him run the show, she held out against him, letting the question hang. 'Well?' He turned back from the window.

'Does it matter?'

'I don't suppose, it does, really.' He walked back to his chair and turned it backwards, straddling it. 'So what are we going to do now? Are we going to help each other or what?'

Sky heard an echo of Jimbo's words . . . *he might even turn out to be useful* . . . 'No, we are not.'

Two simultaneous calls, both heated, were taking place on different sides of the world. The logger, Martin O'Shaughnessy, was reporting to Sheriff O'Connor, while the captain of the *Agnes Monica* was standing in a draughty public phone box in Killybegs, talking urgently to someone in a Dublin hotel.

'No more, OK?' The logger was so angry he forgot caution. 'We're quits.'

'Is that so?' Sheriff O'Connor's voice was silky, 'I don't think so. We're quits when I say so.' He smiled as the line went dead.

The trawlerman's anger had clearly alarmed his contact, but he would not be calmed. 'I don't give a shite who's listening, I'm fed up with this. You should see this place. Every shagging boat in the harbour turned upside down and the *Aideen* prowling up and down outside like a shagging sheepdog. EC directives, marya, I'm not going to be able to keep a lid on the crew much longer. This was supposed to be simple. You promised it would lead to bigger things.' The captain listened. 'Me arse,' he expostulated. '*Five per cent?* You can stuff your extra five per cent. With the kind of hassle we're going through? I could lose my boat. *Stuff* your five per cent.'

Again he listened, then: 'I couldn't give a shite who's on the line. I'm in it for the money, mate. And the fee's gone up by fifteen.' He was so angry that it was only after he slammed down the receiver that he bothered to check again through the salt-roughened glass of the kiosk to see if anyone had been watching. The afternoon was bright and clear and, although the harbour area was busy with vehicles and boats, the cops seemed to have withdrawn to barracks.

Satisfied, he left the telephone box and walked away. He paid no attention to the yellow Electricity Supply Board carvan parked on the quayside near a public light standard.

The technician inside wound back the tape he had just recorded. Both he and the detective inspector sitting beside him knew it would not be very helpful as no names had been used. They knew that the telephone the captain had contacted was in the lobby of the Majestic Hotel but since it was in a public booth, the knowledge was of little assistance. The only thing of any promise was the captain's implied threat that his crew was becoming hard to control.

The inspector picked up his handset and dialled Dublin.

To Sky's relief, Hermana arrived shortly after Lynskey left her mother's room. She and the Irishman had not rowed overtly, but she had refused to thaw and, seeing that in her present mood he would get nowhere with her, he had yielded.

As strongly as she felt she had done the right thing, his departure had left her feeling raw and doubting whether she had behaved any better than he. After all, her conscience prompted, look at what she had done to poor Greg the minute another man had showed up.

Still anaesthetized, the patient was wheeled back into the room a few minutes later. Although Sky was shocked by the body cast, neck collar, and the scaffolding of tubes and drips with which her mother was festooned, she was assured by the nurse that everything had gone routinely.

For the next hour or so, Johanna drifted in and out of consciousness. From time to time she moaned softly but, according to the nurse, the pain was being kept to a minimum. 'She'll be in and out of it all day,' Hermana offered, 'and tomorrow she won't even remember you were here. I'll be with her, in any case, so why don't you go home and get yourself some rest? After all, you have to be in form for your grandmother tonight.'

Sky gazed at the motionless form in the bed. The word 'sleep' conjured up a pleasurable feeling of longing and languor. And in anticipation that her grandmother would more likely choose to stay at the duplex than with Daniel

Treacy, she knew she would have to prepare Johanna's room for her. 'If you're sure,' she smiled gratefully at the big woman, then, 'See you later, Mom,' gently kissing her mother's damp cheek. Devoid of any makeup, her hair flattened to her head, Johanna looked older than she was but as vulnerable as a baby.

Seeing her like this was difficult. Sky had believed that they had plenty of time to improve their relationship but now she saw, with Johanna's mortality all too evident, that she could postpone it no longer. *I'm sorry . . . I'll try harder, I promise. Things will be different, Mom* . . . Conscious of Hermana's bulk behind her, she blinked away tears, which stung the back of her eyes. She must not get soppy, she had a great deal to do.

When she got home, the answering machine was flashing. The first message was from her uncle Francey who sounded concerned. He would wait in until he heard from her. Sky's grandmother was next: she was calling from Hubert H. Humphrey airport in Minneapolis. 'I just got in from London, Sky. I suppose you're at the hospital.' Her speech was hesitant, that of someone unused to speaking to machines. 'I won't ring again now, but I'm looking forward to seeing you both.' She paused and in the background Sky could hear the roar of the international terminal. 'Goodbye now.' A third message was from Jimbo Larsen's wife, asking after Johanna and repeating the invitation to come up 'any time'; and a fourth was from Buffy, who said she had been delayed but would be at the hospital by lunchtime. Sky rewound the tape and reset the machine. Fatigue weighed her down to such a degree that she could not face seeing to her grandmother's accommodation right away, nor even talk to Francey. He had the basic information, the money part could wait. The hospital was hardly going to throw Johanna out.

She fetched a camera and placed it on the telephone table

near the front door so that she would not forget to take it with her to the airport. Then, although she was not hungry but knowing she had to eat something, she fixed herself a large bowl of Cheerios and milk laden with extra sugar. She took this into her bedroom, set her alarm for four hours hence, and, too tired even to undress, climbed into bed and forced herself to eat. She had not quite finished, however, when tiredness overcame her and she put aside the bowl.

When the alarm penetrated her consciousness, she struggled to rise through successive layers of fuzz until she recognized where she was and turned it off. She felt as though a steamroller had flattened her body, reducing her dimensions from three to two.

Stumbling past the bedroom window towards the bathroom, she automatically looked out to see what kind of an afternoon it was. To her surprise, she noticed that the flag was raised on the mailbox at the end of the driveway. That was odd: with Johanna not here who could have put it up and why? It was not even windy . . . Unless some passerby had been lazy and had used the box as a convenience instead of going to the trouble of walking to the public mailbox on the corner of the street.

She went into the bathroom where she had a shower. Afterwards, feeling a little better, she belted on her robe and went outside to see what, if anything, the mailbox held. Perhaps it was a junk-mail drop and the company wanted to attract her attention. If so, it was all to the good; her mother had always been tempted by free offers. The gift of a gold watch with the purchase of seven gallons of cleaning fluid or a set of nesting suitcases always sent her racing for her pen.

A minute later Sky was standing, horror-struck, with a brown padded envelope in one hand and a small cylindrical object in the other. In all the time she had dated Greg, she had never accompanied him on a hunting trip and it was the first time in her life she had touched a bullet. She held it for only a few seconds, then, as though it were some slithering creature covered in slime, threw it from her, recoiling at the 'ping' it made as it landed on the tarmacadam of the driveway. From there it glinted malevolently up at her like the miniature rocket of death it was.

Chapter Twenty-Five

As Sky stared at the hateful little piece of metal, the afternoon sounds – a dog barking, the thock-thock of a basketball against a garage door – grew in volume until they seemed deafening. The sunshine which, only moments before, had seemed fresh and friendly, had become harsh and over-bright. She ran back to the house and straight to the telephone, instinctively punching out 911.

But, even before her finger had left the buttons, she slammed down the receiver. Panicked though she was, she realized that, as a reporter, the police should not be the first in line.

Jimbo Larsen remained composed. 'Go back out there and pick it up – use your sleeve or the hem of your skirt to cover your fingers so you won't leave more prints on it – put it carefully back in the envelope and wait until I get there. Where's your Irish friend?'

'I don't know – when can you be here? I have to get back to the hospital, the airport.'

'Calm down, Sky. Take a couple of breaths.' His unruffled tone got through to her but, as she obeyed, the trembling of her knees became too much and she slid down the wall until she was sitting on the floor. 'Are you there? Sky? Sky?' He at last betrayed concern.

'I'm fine,' she whispered. 'Come quickly.'

By the time she heard him pull into the driveway she was dressed in jeans and the last clean white shirt in her closet.

In deference to her grandmother's visit, she had tried to make herself look as attractive as she could, piling up her hair and knotting the tails of the shirt at her waist. She added some of her mother's chunky gold jewellery, and hoped the overall effect was sort of Côte d'Azur, an early Bardot look the junior had recently copied from an old edition of *Vogue* for the *Courier*'s fashion page.

She opened the door, and when she saw Jimbo's lugubrious but reassuring features emerge from underneath the roof of his car, she was tempted to throw herself into his arms. She held back, however, knowing that he would not welcome such a display.

'Where is it?' His expression was set and determined as he came up to her.

She handed him a bag, which he sealed into a *Courier* envelope he had brought with him. 'What are you going to do with it?'

'Don't know yet.' He put it in his jacket pocket.

'You look all right anyhow, nice outfit.' He stood back briefly, eyeing her.

'Thanks.' Coming from Jim Larsen, that had been a eulogy.

Knowing she could trust him with anything, as she made the coffee she gave him every detail. She even told him about Treacy's cancer because, in her book, the arrival of the bullet had called off all deals. He listened impassively but underneath she could feel the onset of journalistic excitement as fevered as her own.

She had finally remembered where she had seen an identical padded envelope to this one.

The editor seemed unsurprised that Lynskey had received a similar warning. He agreed that for the present they would keep the police out of the story. A discreet friend of his at the University of Missoula could type the bullet for them. 'What worries me most about it – thanks – ' he took the coffee from her and sat at the kitchen table ' – is not that it was sent and what it represents, although, of course, that's bad enough, but that they see a need to warn you off. They, whoever "they" are, know we're on to something. I wish I knew what, though. But who's watching and where? I'm sorry, now, that I got you mixed you in this.'

'You couldn't have known.' Despite his words, Sky felt he was not all that sorry. 'I still can't believe it's the shamrock lot.' She sat opposite him and bit into a rye bread and banana sandwich. 'I mean, look at them, Jim, median age sixty-something, those stuffy meetings, those formula notes?'

'I think they're mostly just a bunch of sad middle-aged people whose knowledge of Ireland and patriotism is hope-lessly out of date.' He stirred his coffee morosely. 'But I always suspected one or two of them would go further than that. I didn't think until yesterday that Collins was among them.'

'Well he must be. He made the call about Fergus Lynskey, didn't he? But Treacy reckons Collins is small potatoes, that all those shamrock lot are—'

'My guess is he's right. And we're not talking about any of the registered organizations we all know and love. This is something bigger and I'm even wondering if it has much to do with Irish republicanism. But that being said, Sky, I insist you take a break. You need a few days off – you've had enough excitement in the last week to last the lifetime of the average hack.'

When she objected he looked seriously at her. 'It's not only that, Sky. It's that much as I'd love to be able to run with this as quickly and as comprehensively as possible, I'm wondering if the *Courier* is up to this kind of story. I have a hunch that it's going to need a lot more resources than we have. I'll have a chat with our intellectual friend,' he used the disparaging epithet by which they referred to the paper's proprietor, 'but I'm not sure he'll authorize the kind of money I think we're going to need. How would you feel about sharing the legwork with a bigger newspaper, in Minneapolis, say, or Detroit? I have contacts—'

'Jim, that's not fair.' Every competitive instinct in Sky's body reared up against the notion. 'It's our story.'

'Yes, but when we started we had no idea how long its legs are. It seems they travel oceans and international borders. And not only that. Closer to home it's inconceivable that this story doesn't cross state lines. To my certain knowledge no organization in Montana is big enough to pull this off. Those watchers on Treacy? He's right, they have to be FBI. And there's the safety consideration. That bullet should have given you some idea of what we're up against, Sky.'

'I still think you should give us a chance. We can work together on it, maybe hire in a researcher.'

'Perhaps now's not the time to talk about this. We can discuss it again.' He finished his coffee in a long draught. 'One thing I can do is try to locate the guy who gave us the original tip-off on those coupons. Maybe I'll be able to shake a bit of information out of that airhead back at the office as to what he looked like. She's still typing up those notes you gave her, by the way.' He smiled and Sky saw that he thought he had gone too far. 'To be fair,' he admitted, 'I suppose she is making some sort of fist out of that fashion page. Now,' he patted himself down to find his automobile keys, 'as for you, young lady, I insist that you take that time off.'

When she objected again, he stood up. 'Look, the story's not going to go away. And Treacy's not going to die tonight, is he?'

'I'll take a day or two but I'll call you.' Sky recognized temporary defeat, and remembered simultaneously that her grandmother was probably even now boarding her commuter aircraft for the short flight from Billings to Butte.

'What about Lynskey?' Jimbo hesitated.

'What about him?' she frowned.

'Well, as far as I can see he knows as much as we do – probably more. I know you have your personal agenda with him, Sky, but I'd like to meet him.'

'Provided I'm there.' She had no intention of letting the story move on without her.

Sky had been expecting Elizabeth Sullivan to look well for her age but was unprepared for the tall, erect figure carrying a tote bag, who came through to the small airport concourse.

Her grandmother was dressed in a pencil-slim skirt and toning knee-length coat in shades of avocado. Her cream-coloured blouse draped softly from a cowl neck to a neat waist, her grey hair was sleeked like a ballet dancer's into a heavy bun at the nape of her neck and her pale shoes, far from being 'sensible', had court heels.

Sky was taken aback. She now realized that, photographic evidence to the contrary, she had spent a lifetime visualizing her 'Irish granny' as a cross between Maureen O'Hara in *The Quiet Man* and the mother from *The Waltons*, to neither of whom this smart sophisticate bore any relation.

'Grandmother?' she stepped forward.

'Sky!' Her grandmother's fine-boned face, set off by a pair of heavy gold earrings in the shape of Roman coins, lit up. 'At last! I've so wanted to meet you again. It's not the same in letters or on telephones, is it? Anyway, as you've probably noticed by now,' her smile broadened, 'I'm not the greatest writer in the world.'

'I've no excuse – I'm supposed to be the professional here.' They hugged, but to Sky's confusion she felt oddly shy. She put it down to fatigue.

'Let me look at you.' Her grandmother, who was suffer-ing no such qualms, stood back. 'You've grown up to be beautiful, Sky, everything I imagined and more. You were a lovely little girl but now . . .' Her accent, although soft and distinctly Irish, was nowhere near as thick or rapid as Fergus Lynskey's. As they smiled at one another, to add to her sense of unreality, Sky felt she was seeing into her own future. Those photographs again: she had never noticed before how much she and her grandmother resembled one another. They were even around the same height, with perhaps an inch or two favouring Elizabeth Sullivan. Given Sky's espadrilles, however, this could be put down to the older woman's high heels. 'You must be exhausted.' Sky recollected that she was supposed to be looking after her grandmother. She took the tote bag and the older woman's arm, and led her to where the bags were already arriving.

'I am a bit,' her grandmother admitted. 'A person really has to work very hard to get from Cork to Butte, Montana. Or from anywhere, I suspect.'

Echoes of what Daniel Treacy had said when he had offered the use of a private plane, Sky thought.

'Thank you, Sky, yes, that one there.' Her grandmother pointed to a neat tartan case, and her expression became serious. 'Now, tell me about poor Johanna. I tried to ring you but I got that awful machine.'

'I got the message.' Sky picked up the bag and, as they walked towards the exit, told her about her mother's operation. Then: 'There's something I have to prepare you for.'

'You haven't told me the truth about Johanna.' Her grandmother's face creased with alarm.

'No, nothing like that.' Sky pulled her aside a little so as not to block the entrance. 'It's Daniel Treacy, I mean McCarthy—' Her grandmother stiffened. 'He's waiting out in the lot.'

She had passed Treacy's parked Saab on her way into the airport lot, but, as she was running late, had not stopped to talk to him. 'He's hoping you will see him, Grandma. He's repeated his invitation to you to stay with him.' Somehow she avoided blurting out the story of Treacy's illness.

'I see.' From her grandmother's mask-like expression, Sky could not make out whether she was pleased or not at the news. 'I can go out ahead of you, if you like, and tell him you're too tired tonight,' she offered. 'After all, you've every reason. You've been flying for the best part of sixteen hours.'

The older woman's face cleared. 'To tell you the truth I'm dying of curiosity.' Her smile took thirty years off her.

As she accompanied her grandmother out into the warm evening air, Sky knew she would remember everything about this moment: the laughter and the serial explosions of car doors slamming throughout the small airport parking lot, the mackerel sky streaked with pale pink and primrose, the smell of warm tarmac and automobile metal overlaid with the sweetish odour of burnt aviation fuel.

Treacy was standing beside the Saab and straightened as he saw them. He touched the breast pocket of his dark jacket then checked the knot on his tie. His clothes stood out in exotic contrast with most of the other people in the lot, who were clad in cutoffs or denims.

The two old people came to within feet of one another and then stopped. They did not embrace or even shake hands but stared. At least, Treacy stared: Sky, who was behind her grandmother, could not see her expression. 'I'll wait in the car, Grandma.' She touched her elbow. 'Let me know what you decide.'

Her grandmother turned her head slowly and looked at her as though not seeing. 'Grandma?' Again Sky touched her arm. 'Are you OK?' The older woman's eyes swivelled back towards Treacy. 'After all these years. I wasn't prepared for how you look, Daniel.'

Sky thought it tactful to retreat immediately. 'I'll take your bags, Grandma.'

She threw them in the back seat, then got in behind the

wheel and wound down the window to watch them. Still they were not touching. All that restraint, she thought, even after all this time . . .

But although neither had moved, he was bent slightly forward at the waist and was making urgent gestures. He appeared to be pleading and Sky, trying to put herself in their shoes, wondered how she, or even her mother, would behave in such a situation. Johanna, no doubt, would handle it with circumspection: so her lover of five decades ago had resurfaced, that was lovely, and, of course, it had been pre-ordained. Sky, on the other hand, would no doubt be melting like an emotional grease-spot all over the parking lot. Or would she? Sky faced her sense of anti-climax on seeing her grandmother. Something was missing from this historic meeting: should she not be crying with joy – or, at least, with something? Was she just a cold fish? But she realized that her dominant feeling was of shock, as though she had stepped on what appeared to be rock only to discover it was cardboard.

Over the past few days, even when reading between the lines of Daniel Treacy's staggering revelations about the Elizabeth Sullivan he had known and continued to love, she had held on to her own storybook vision of her grandmother. Its dissolution was traumatic. This slender, elegant person, who would not have looked out of place in the more fashionable eateries of Manhattan, could never have been a real grandma, apple-cheeked dispenser of domestic ease and presider over sink, stove and knitting basket: a person who, even if physically absent, was always there in the background and could have provided alternative mothering. True mothering. As in *Little Women* and TV sitcoms. Sky had placed Elizabeth Sullivan at the opposite pole to that of her mother's fascinating yet self-absorbed free-spirit. Now no one would ever scold her for putting a dirty hand in the cookie jar.

For Christ's sake, she thought, recognizing the ignoble stab of self-pity, she was hardly a kid any more. And how could she be so disloyal to her mother? What sort of daughter – or granddaughter, if it came to that – was she? What kind of adult? Abruptly, for no apparent reason, Sky longed to see her father.

Moments later, she saw her grandmother touch Daniel Treacy's lapel, whereupon he seized her hand and raised it to his lips. Great, she thought, lighting on the distraction from her own maudlin thoughts, progress at last. But she was mistaken. Her grandmother extricated her hand, then they turned towards her and came across the lot. The old lady was walking briskly, a little ahead of Treacy. Sky could have wagered that his case had been unsuccessful.

She was right. 'She won't come home with me, Sky, in spite of all my blandishments.' Treacy attempted to smile as they came up to the car, and Sky felt so sorry for him that she was tempted to weigh in with her own advocacy. His dark eyes burned in their sockets and, despite the elegant clothes, or perhaps because of them, she believed that even since this morning she could see a deterioration in his condition: a yellowish tinge to his skin, the shrinking of his neck size so that his shirt collar looked too big. Then she chided herself for being dramatic: she saw this now, she thought, because she was aware of the true state of his health. She got out and went round to the other side of the car to open the passenger door for her grandmother, 'She's very tired,' offering this to him in an effort to make his rejection seem less severe.

'Sure won't we see each other tomorrow, Daniel?' Sky's grandmother hesitated before following her round the hood, then: 'You won't mind driving me over, Sky?'

Except for expressing a desire to go to the hospital immediately after depositing her bags and freshening up, the old lady was silent during the short trip to the duplex and

Sky let her be. But as they pulled up in front of the door, she turned to her granddaughter. 'It's been fifty years, Sky. Can you understand?'

'Yes, of course, Grandma,' Sky said, although she knew she could not.

It was not that she could not understand how a youthful romance had died a natural death in her grandmother's heart over the course of such a long period. It was that she could not conceive of the intensity of the passion Daniel Treacy had sustained over that time.

Chapter Twenty-Six

'It's a place called Killybegs.' The Helena lieutenant had more bad news for his boss in Vancouver and, for a woman who made a virtue out of staying calm in all circumstances, the degree of irritation she showed was remarkable.

In response to her anger, the lieutenant had to agree that perhaps the money so far committed to the test operation might prove to have been misplaced. In support of his own judgement, however, he explained that with Ireland being a new territory, he had had to rely on local sources to identify people who could help.

'I tried to call you,' the woman spoke even more softly than usual; 'but you were not available. This is bad.'

'There was a fault on my telephone. It's fixed now.'

The woman took a quick, deep breath to calm herself. 'Please continue.'

Irritation, however, was not what she felt about what she heard next. She was horrified that, on being instructed to deal with the setbacks in Montana, some subordinate, a sheriff, had threatened two people by sending bullets to them. That was crude – and stupid. One of the recipients had been a reporter for the meddling newspaper: no matter how insignificant this one was, all newspapers were bad karma.

Provided that meticulous precautions were taken against discovery of her own involvement, the woman had no objection to quick, clean violence. Indeed, this very lieutenant had been responsible for the disappearance of one or two people whom the police had never been able to trace. If people stepped out of line, violence, she felt, was justified. She treated people fairly; she expected fairness in return. But sending bullets to policemen and newspaper people would draw the authorities. 'Pay off that person. And if you think it necessary, please deal with those two people who are being inquisitive. Only, however, if you think it necessary. I'll let you know if we decide to go ahead. *If* we decide to go ahead. So far Ireland has not been what I hoped. And don't do anything else until you hear from me. I'll call you.'

The detective who had been monitoring the woman's calls since the raid in Ottawa conveyed the information to his superiors, who in turn passed it down the line to Lynskey.

As she helped her grandmother out of the car and pulled out the bags, Sky's eye was caught by a movement at the end of the driveway. She glanced over her shoulder to see Fergus Lynskey loping towards them.

Her grandmother followed her gaze. 'Someone you know, Sky?'

But, before she could explain, Lynskey was on top of them. 'Hello there.' His cheeriness did not seem in the least forced. 'I thought I'd drop in to see how things were going down at the hospital. This must be your grandmother, Sky.' He stuck out a hand and beamed. 'How do you do? I'm Fergus Lynskey. As a matter of fact, we're neighbours, I know your part of the country well. I'm from Kerry myself, just across the border. But, of course, you live in the big smoke now, don't you?'

'How do you do? I do. Live in Cork, I mean.'

'You must be exhausted,' he said, reaching for the suit-case. 'In fact you must be both be wrecked, here, let me,' and Sky knew it would seem churlish not to relinquish possession. He led the way towards the front door, as though he owned the place, and stood on the stoop, waiting for her to produce the key. As she opened the door, she thought she could murder him without a second thought.

When they got inside, he offered to make coffee, a proposition accepted with such alacrity by her grandmother it made Sky fume. Where women were concerned, did Fergus Lynskey's charms recognize no age boundaries? 'This way, Grandma.' She shot him a disdainful glance that he appeared not to see, and showed the older woman into Johanna's room. She left her to unpack, then telephoned the hospital. There was little change in her mother's condition: she was 'comfortable'.

Reluctant to go into the kitchen to face Lynskey alone, Sky went into the living room – little used by herself and her mother. Here, the landlord's taste in wallpaper, which was bad enough in the bedrooms, ran to oak leaves and unrelated berries in shades of tan and ochre, the furniture was early fifties leatherette and the room's single window faced north. Both Sky and her mother hated this room and rarely used it except at Christmas, when they made an effort to act like something resembling a normal family. The room had a real fireplace, however, and more to kill time than because it needed attention, Sky used a hearth brush to groom the wooden surround.

How was she going to get out of this situation? She could hardly be overtly rude to Lynskey in front of her grand-mother, who was buying his act as readily as had the Bliss Sisters and every other woman within a million-mile radius. He was a regular Don Juan, she thought, her sense of betrayal building towards white heat as she scrubbed at non-existent ash.

'I think your grandmother's gorgeous, a real lady.'

Hearing the stage-whisper behind her, she straightened and spun round, but Lynskey put a finger to his lips. 'Ssh, we don't want her to know we're talking about her.'

'We're not talking about her.' Sky lowered her own voice. 'I'm not talking to you about anything. Please go away.'

'Come on, MacPee, where's the harm in talking?' His expression belied his jocular tone and he came towards her. 'There's something I have to tell you and its going to be a bit of a shock. Don't say anything, please, until you hear me out. You have to get out of here temporarily.'

'*What?* You must be joking.'

'I mean it. You're in danger.'

'Even if I am I wouldn't take the word of anyone so – so – ' To her annoyance, she couldn't find a word to describe the depth of his duplicity.

'Tricky?' He was not being facetious. 'Yeah – fair point. But *think*, Sky.' He tried to take her wrist but she resisted violently and he let it drop. 'Put yourself in my shoes. At the beginning, all I was doing was sussing out my own line of enquiry. I had no idea I would . . .' He trailed off. 'This is a complicated situation,' he amended. 'You yourself told me so. Endlessly.'

'Sorry if I bored you,' but Sky hated petulance, even her own.

'Just as a matter of interest, purely academic, how did you find out?'

'I had a call from Bill Collins.' She watched him, then said, her voice laden with irony, 'I assume there's no need to explain who he is.'

'Ah . . .' Lynskey nodded as though he had guessed as much.

'Stop saying that!' Sky wanted to slap his face.

In lieu of reply, he stepped closer towards her and, although he did not touch her, when he looked down into her eyes, she felt his presence surround her like a cloak. 'I'm sorry.' He did touch her then, brushing one finger across her lips. 'But I'm deadly serious about this. You have to get away to somewhere you'll be safe. I can't tell you why just now. But I will. I promise.'

'Go away.' She batted off his touch. 'Can't you understand English? My grandmother's just arrived, my mother's in the hospital. I can't go anywhere. Please leave, Fergus, I don't want you in our house.' But she was uncertain now and she knew that he knew it.

'You understand why I couldn't tell you?' It was as though she had not spoken. 'I didn't know what I was going to be dealing with at first but then, when I met you—'

'I suppose that so-called novel in your briefcase is a heap of surveillance equipment and a transmitter?' Sky, unwilling to acknowledge the subtext of what he was saying, was stalling.

Lynskey did not flinch. 'Not quite, I'm not the KGB. But something like that. I'll show you, if you like.'

'I don't want to see it, Lynskey. I don't want to see *you* again. I don't think you know just how upset I am.'

'I can imagine. Normally I would say something stupid like all's fair in love and war. But, I wasn't expecting – well—' Before she had anticipated it, he had lowered his head and kissed her on the lips. For an instant her body responded but then her mind kicked in, and she broke away in fury.

'I can't believe you did that.' She took a step backwards away from temptation. 'Is this how you do all your police work? Make love to people to get information?'

'Never before, I promise.' He followed her.

'Go away, Fergus.' She stepped round him and made a run for the kitchen. He followed her again. Then, as she reached the kitchen and turned to face him, the picture of the bullet popped into her head. And, of course, her big mouth framed it and let it out.

His reaction was to throw his arms up in the air. 'Jesus!

305

Why the hell didn't you tell me straight away? Now will you believe that you have to leave here for a while?'

'I wasn't speaking to you, if you remember,' she stared him down, 'but while we're talking about warnings in brown padded envelopes, I know you got one too. Don't bother to deny it. And *you* didn't deem it necessary to tell *me*.'

His expression was so serious now that she began to run out of steam. She reminded herself she had done nothing of which she should be ashamed. 'And I might jog your memory about the small fact that you're standing in *my* house, and not at my invitation, so please don't treat me like I'm a – a – a *suspect*.' She sat down. Suddenly she felt woozy – too little food and sleep, too much caffeine and drama.

'You must see how important this is.' He pulled up a chair and sat beside her. 'Bullets are not playthings, Sky.' His speech became more deliberate. 'Where is it now?' He frowned when she told him. 'Look, I'll deal with it. Are you sure you didn't see anyone hanging around, get any odd phone calls? No one hung up when you answered?' It was only then she remembered the call from the logger. With all that had happened, it had slipped her mind.

'That's it, Sky.' When she had finished telling him as much as she remembered about it, he folded his arms. 'I'm instructing you not to follow this story any further. I'll tell your editor too.'

'You're *instructing* me?' She was too astonished to take immediate offence.

'I mean it,' she could see only too well that he did, 'and I'll have you stopped if necessary. You're out of your depth.'

'How dare you? How dare you dictate—'

'I dare because this is my line of work.' He cut her off. 'I know what I'm talking about. Think, Sky. *Think*. Do you want the next bullet turning up from the barrel of a gun?

Can you shoot? Have you got a gun? Do you know who your enemy *is*?'

'My editor will assign me to stories, not you,' she hissed.

Lynskey unexpectedly took both her hands in his. 'Your editor will be told to take you off this one. Please, Sky, listen to me.'

'Don't touch me! Take your hands *off* me!'

She attempted to pull away but he persisted. 'Listen, listen . . . sh-shhh, Sky, *listen* . . .' They tussled but as she had already found out, he was strong and within a minute or so, her forearms ached with strain.

She tried to intimidate him with her eyes while maintaining the haul. 'I won't be treated like a child, Fergus.'

'Are you listening?' He waited until she was still then, softly, 'If you won't listen to reason, listen to unreason. I love you. I don't know how it happened, I certainly didn't plan it and it's damned inconvenient, but I do. I don't want you putting yourself in danger.'

It seemed to Sky that a nuclear explosion had detonated somewhere near her solar plexus.

'Did you hear me? I love you.' He was as composed as if these were ordinary words.

'I heard you.' She heard someone else speak in her voice. Quite calmly too.

Then she heard a sound behind her. It could have been a sigh, or a gentle cough, and she looked round to see her grandmother framed in the doorway. 'Excuse me . . .' Lynskey let go of her hands.

'Sorry, Grandma.' Sky stood up and went to the stove to fetch the coffee-pot. She averted her face, which she knew must be as white as milk.

Behind her, she heard the chair scrape as Lynskey stood up. 'Come on in, ma'am.'

*

The sheriff of Mayville did not take kindly to criticism. 'Screw you,' he said softly into the receiver as his caller hung up.

As far as he was concerned, his end of the drugs deal had gone admirably, smooth as cream. Treacy had not kicked up and was unlikely to, seeing that he would be dead when that wife of his was out of harm's way. Because Brian O'Connor had no intention of drawing any attention to himself by leaving a single loose end. There remained a slight possibility that Midge Treacy, who was at present nothing but a vegetable, might resurface; and since he had more at stake than being middleman for some private profiteer he had identified someone at the Oregon facility to which she was to be moved who would ensure that she did not.

But now these suits were disposing of him. Who did they think they were? The sheriff had been absent-mindedly shelling a pistachio nut and crushed it in anger. It was hardly his fault if some loolas in Ireland messed up. And as for the bullets: he had been instructed to scare off the meddlers in Butte. It had been his experience ever since he had begun to walk on the shady side that one ballistic reminder was enough to scare off amateurs. Even professional amateurs like that Irish cop.

And now the Helena guy was losing his cool. Well, the telephone warnings from good old potato head Collins hadn't worked, had they? If these people wanted velvet gloves they should have said so.

He stood up and tossed the spoilt nut into the trash can. That done, he shook himself like a dog. He was going to be paid the full amount of what he had been promised and was not going to take shit from some jumped-up jerk in Helena.

*

'Well?' the chief superintendent snapped.

'Things are hotting up here,' Lynskey's voice was quiet on the phone. 'There's been a development in Vancouver.'

His superior hesitated, then spoke less belligerently. 'Is that all? I know that. Our friends there tell us the principals might pull out altogether. The natives here are more restless than they're used to coping with. I think our lady head honcho might be beginning to think she's bitten off more than she can chew in Ireland.'

'I think we should move in on them right now. We have enough on tape with all those monitored telephone calls, surely.'

'Not yet. She might go ahead – and why catch the sprat when you can have the mackerel? Everything's set, though.'

'Look, are we still keeping a tight grip on this other thing – Omega?' The word seemed to stick on Lynskey's tongue. 'And are we any way closer to finding out who's the villain on our side?'

'Only myself, yourself, the Commissioner and the two ministers, Justice and Foreign Affairs know about the first item so far, unless you've shot your big mouth off, to your – how did you put it? – your friend the reporter, for instance?'

Lynskey let that pass and his superior resumed: 'No, I haven't figured out who our canary it is yet. I'm getting jittery, Fergus, time's moving on.'

Down the hall from the chief superintendent's office, Rupert de Burgh worked busily at his desk, studying his notes. He had taken to wearing headphones connected to his Sony Walkman: he had told the others in the clattering room that to listen to music helped him concentrate while he was reading or writing reports.

Sky had no chance to react to Lynskey's declarations, of either love or danger, until much later that evening.

First came the trip to the hospital, during which he stuck to her like a parasite. She insisted on leaving him outside the room, however, and went in ahead of her grandmother in case the shock of seeing her mother after all these years might prove too severe for Johanna.

She was asleep, although her body was still punctured with the drips and drains. Standing beside the bed, Sky floundered. The last of the evening sun flooded through the west-facing window, highlighting the woven texture of the body cast and neck collar so that her mother looked like a sickly caterpillar, an impression reinforced by the pallor of her skin. 'Mom?' She touched the back of the hand which, curled like a child's, lay on the sheet.

Her mother's eyes opened. 'It's you, Sky!' Her voice was scarcely audible and, accustomed as Sky was to the lilts and musical swoops, it was terrible to hear. As though she were sweet-talking a baby, she squatted at the side of the bed to bring her head level with the pillow. 'Guess who's here, Mom?'

Making a great effort, Johanna focused glazed eyes.

'It's Grandma,' Sky swallowed hard. 'Grandma's here.'

Johanna's eyes moved slowly towards the doorway. Then her whispery voice cracked even more, 'Mammy?'

Sky's grandmother came forward slowly, her erect carriage faltering only as she reached the bedside. 'Hello, Johanna.' She clasped her hands in front of her as though touching might not be allowed – or in case touching her daughter might bring down some delicate edifice between them. 'I'm sorry – here's a thing – I never thought—'

'I'm sorry too, Mammy – I thought I'd never see you again—'

Johanna's hoarse croak and the emotional rigidity of both women finally pierced Sky's armour. She knew it was only a matter of seconds before all three would break down and, unable to bear the prospect, she fled.

Lynskey was coming back from the telephone booth and saw her agonized face. 'What's wrong?'

'Nothing.' Sky, reluctant to give in to her weakness, scrubbed at her eyes. 'She's fine, everything's fine, it's just that—' Only her pride saved her from caving in completely and weeping like a mermaid against his chest. 'I'll be all right in a minute.' She groped in her purse for a tissue and blew her nose. 'It's just that they haven't seen each other for such a long time.'

'Of course.' Lynskey had the wit not to embrace her and looked away to give her time. 'I feel like a cuppa, how about you? It must be at least ten minutes since you had your last caffeine fix.' She nodded gratefully and he loped off to the machine. She blew her nose again and gave herself a mental scolding for being such a weakling.

She had just managed to compose herself when one of the nurses sat beside her and engaged her in chat. This was followed shortly afterwards by the emergence from the room of her grandmother. 'She can't stay awake.' Her eyes were red-rimmed but the whites were shining. 'I told her I'd be back first thing in the morning – that will be all right, will it, nurse?'

'Of course.' The nurse stood up. 'Please don't worry, either of you. It'll take a few days but she's going to be fine. Here comes your coffee,' she smiled at Lynskey who was just arriving, 'hello again.'

Another conquest, Sky thought, seeing the way the nurse twinkled up at the Irishman, and her good humour reasserted itself. What was it about this man? This man who had told her he loved her.

All the way to the hospital that four-letter word had reverberated. While he, behaving as though he had lived here all his life, had cheerily drawn her grandmother's attention to the Butte landmarks, the statue, the High School, the Civic Center, the Court House, Sky let the words *I love you* roll around the perimeter of her consciousness, bouncing them away every time they came too close to her heart. Love with this man was not on her agenda.

Love with no man. No agenda.

Relationship, perhaps, that overused word, but not love. Greg had insisted he loved her, but, in Sky's opinion, he was far too macho to know what he meant when he said it.

Love with Lynskey? She had the feeling she was fencing with something very dangerous indeed. Sky had once fallen in love, with her feckless husband. That had been enough.

And yet the damburst of feelings Lynskey had released by the mere utterance of the word had shaken, no, had excited her in a way she found difficult to define.

For the second time in two hours, having thought little about him for months, maybe years, Sky longed for her father.

312

Chapter Twenty-Seven

Sky had to face the love conundrum head on when they got back to the duplex. Lynskey asked her for a quiet word outside as her grandmother went in and she could think of no excuse to refuse. As she trod beside him and trawled for something to say, the short driveway seemed to stretch into infinity.

It was a beautiful evening, with air as soft and warm as velvet: that time, just before dark, when every sound seems to spurt a little before muting for the night. Canned laughter rippled from the open window of the neighbour's house across the fence, to be subsumed by noise from the outside traffic – once by the cacophony from the faulty tailpipe on a pickup, once by the exuberant whoops of a crowd of boys on the prowl in a powerful convertible. And as they reached the sidewalk, sparrow wars exploded like firecrackers from a nearby tree.

She pretended to be fascinated by the overhead brawling and made as though to walk over to the tree, but Lynskey was having none of it. 'So what do you think?' He spun her round and took her hands in his, pulling her towards him.

'So what do I think about what?' She studied the gully between the wheels of the Topaz and the kerb and remembered the bag of marbles, perfect glass eyes with rainbow irises, sent to her from Ireland when she was a child. They were still pristine in her bureau because when they arrived she had found no one except Johanna who knew what to do with them. 'Look at me, Sky,' he tugged insistently at her hands, 'you know perfectly well. About where we were before we were interrupted in the kitchen.' He searched her face then said, gently: 'What is it? What are you afraid of?'

With these words, he had hit on the truth. 'I don't know.'

'It wasn't a declaration of hostilities, you know, or a request that you hang up your freedom shoes. It was, and is, quite simple. I love you. Simple.'

'It's not simple.' She felt her palms begin to tingle with perspiration and hoped he could not feel it. 'I mean it's not *that* simple—'

'It's very simple indeed. I love you. End of story, no demands, no nothing.'

'But I don't want you to love me, I didn't ask you to love me.' In spite of her best efforts her voice rose until it was almost a wail.

He regarded her for the longest five seconds of her life and for once his eyes were grave. 'Nobody but a fool asks for love.' He released her hands and kissed her softly on the forehead. 'Nobody deserves it or earns it or is owed it. At your age you should know that.'

'But we just met . . .' Sky, so self-contained, so worldly wise, felt lost.

As she vacillated, his mood changed and hardened. 'That's something for another day, perhaps, but don't worry, I won't mention it again for the foreseeable future. We have to talk now about your safety. If you won't co-operate, Sky, I'll have to take other measures, for your own good.'

The transformation was so sudden that she was taken by surprise. So much so that she could not resist when he informed her he was going to stay the night in the duplex. 'On the couch, so don't worry.' He got into his rental car and wound down the window. 'I have to go to the hotel and pick up a few things. Don't answer the door, don't answer the telephone. I won't be long.'

She watched his retreating tail-lights until he rounded a corner and all that was left of him was an echo of the engine note. As she turned to go back into the house she tried to make sense of what she felt. Or even to put a word on it. She almost settled on maelstrom but then discarded it as being too melodramatic. Yet maelstrom was the one word which exactly fitted.

As he drove away, Fergus Lynskey was attempting to sew up the wound in his heart. She was not interested. He had been a fool.

Super-conscious of Lynskey's presence in the living room, Sky slept badly, her dreams punctured with monstrous caterpillars, chases and falls, and vague, slithering fears. Several times, just as she felt she was about to be consumed, she awoke with a jump.

Heart hammering, she switched on the bedside radio and tuned to an all-news station, turning the volume low, reasoning that the murmur of human voices in the background might soothe her back to sleep.

It was not to be, however, and while it was still early she was delighted to hear her grandmother moving around.

She tiptoed towards the living room and, opening the door as quietly as she could, peeped round it. Lynskey's bag was in the middle of the room but the comforter she had given him was neatly folded and draped across the arm of the couch. Pinned to it was a note:

Sky: I'll be back in less than an hour. Please don't forget, don't answer the door, don't answer the telephone. I'll buzz the doorbell five times so you'll know it's me. F.

His handwriting was as neat and precise as the folds in the comforter.

After a quick shower, Sky dressed and went into the sunlit kitchen: the day promised renewed heat, and the brightness and kitsch normality of her surroundings seemed bizarre in the context of what was happening all around her. As she brewed her first pot of coffee, her grandmother appeared clad in one of Johanna's kaftans. When Sky's mother wore these relics of her hippie youth they inspired only ridicule, but somehow, she thought, the bright patterns and flowing lines gave her grandmother a regal air. 'Are you hungry, Grandma?' She opened a cupboard to see what – other than birdseed – she could muster. To her relief, she saw a carton of pancake mix, one of her own defiant purchases.

'I could eat something,' the old lady admitted. 'Airline food isn't wonderful, is it?'

'About ten minutes?'

The pancakes were ready when her grandmother reappeared. She had changed and looked cool and fresh in a dark blue linen dress with a white collar. Sky glanced disparagingly at her own outfit, the grey silk suit she had worn to dinner with Daniel Treacy in the Copper King Mansion. Although she had hung it up, it could have done with the touch of an iron.

'Thank you, dear. Grey suits you – it does wonders for your hair. It's a colour I used to wear myself.' They smiled almost shyly at one another.

'Oh, Grandma, it's great to have you here.' Sky reached out and hugged her, then realized this was the first spontaneous gesture of affection she had been able to make.

Her grandmother hugged her back and then stood away a little. 'We've got a lot to catch up on, you and I. I'm ashamed of myself I didn't come before now.'

'The onus wasn't on you,' Sky protested. 'Every college student I know has been to Europe at least once. But you do understand that I had had quite enough of going about when I was younger, don't you? It seemed like heaven just to stay in one place.'

'Of course.' Her grandmother laughed. 'But let's stop all this. At least we managed to connect again before I went down to start pushing up the daisies.'

'*Grandma!*'

'Oh, for goodness' sake, Sky, I'm seventy-whatever-age-I-am and I've had a full life,' the old lady's expression became wry, 'some of which has apparently come back to haunt me. What time are we going to meet my fate?'

'I'll call him after breakfast.'

They had been eating for less than five minutes when Lynskey's five-buzz signal sounded in the hallway. 'It's very early for callers, isn't it?' Her grandmother looked startled.

'It's Fergus. I'll explain later.' Sky went to open the door. With the old lady around, she knew she could not talk seriously to the Irishman but, without rancour, she made it clear to him as she let him in that she was going to go about her business as though he was not there.

'No problem.' He was freshly showered and shaved – he must have been back to the War Bonnet – and dressed in yet another faded T-shirt, this one advertising the rock group U2.

He chatted to her grandmother in the kitchen while she, reckoning seven thirty was not too early, telephoned Daniel Treacy's house to find that he, too, was up and about and anxious to see her grandmother. 'And Sky . . . ? He seemed about to broach something else but changed his mind. 'No, forget it.' She was too intent on ticking projects off her mental list to pursue it.

She got on to Francey, who offered money, access to medical expertise in Harley Street, anything that might help Johanna. When she told him about the pile of useless cheques, he laughed so hard she had no choice but to join

317

in. 'That's our Johanna, all right,' he spluttered. 'Hasn't changed a bit, has she?' Sobering, he outlined plans for himself and Sky's aunt Hazel to fly to the States within the next few days, but Sky, who felt she had enough to do with commuting to the hospital and looking after the guest already installed in the duplex, persuaded him to wait until her mother was stronger.

Lastly, she called Jimbo and found to her annoyance, that Fergus had already spoken to him and their meeting was set for nine o'clock. 'You have to come along too, Sky.' Jimbo's normal abruptness on the telephone had given way to gravity.

Half an hour later, Sky and her grandmother were in the Nissan: the nearer they got to Daniel Treacy's house, the greater the tension Sky sensed from the passenger seat where the old lady sat, erect as a queen. She chatted about her job, about the beauty of Montana, about anything that might put her companion at ease – and keep Sky herself from glancing in the rear-view mirror, which showed the ever-present hood of a Chrysler Topaz. At least Lynskey had the tact to pull into the verge and did not follow her up the driveway to Daniel Treacy's house.

Her grandmother's response to her first sight the view from Treacy's car park was similar to Sky's own. 'My God,' she breathed, her eyes widening, 'I thought the Béara Peninsula was lovely.' Then, virtually to herself, 'Hasn't he done well for himself?'

This morning, Daniel Treacy's panorama would have done justice to the ritziest Montana tourist brochure. Although the sky was limpid, the sun had not yet burned off the mist. Insubstantial as angel hair or a quilt crocheted from cobwebs, it drifted just yards above the deep green of the forest canopy and piled like sheared wool against the flanks of the Rockies so that the peaks appeared to float free. 'If you think this is good, wait till I take you up to Going-To-

The-Sun-Road in Glacier.' Sky, enjoying her grandmother's reaction, gave her a few moments to take it in, then. 'Shall we go in?'

'You don't have to come with me, you go off to your office.'

Recognizing that she wanted to be left alone, Sky did not insist. 'All right, see you later.' She could not resist delaying her departure, however, driving slowly enough away from the house to see, via the rear-view mirror, Treacy open the door within seconds of her grandmother's arrival on the stoop.

As she turned out of the gateway into the road, she looked for the plain sedan but although she continued to drive slowly, searching on both sides of the road and using all her mirrors, she saw nothing – except a blue Chrysler Topaz. She must not let him get to her. She gritted her teeth. She must not let him get to her.

The first thing Elizabeth Sullivan noticed when she stepped across Daniel Treacy's threshold that morning was the mass of flowers. All white. Banks of white roses – dozens, maybe hundreds – drifted out of vases and urns in every corner and on every surface of the lobby. There were more in the drawing room, augmented here by Casablanca lilies and baby's breath, still more in the garden room where she and Treacy settled to talk.

'All these flowers – they must have cost a fortune, Daniel.' She looked around.

He dismissed them with a wave of his hand. 'Are you sure it isn't too cold for you in here?' The windows along the terrace were all open so nothing stood between where they sat and the forest beyond the lawns. Butterflies skidded about on the warm up-draughts of air and the loudest sound was from a passing bee.

'It's beautiful.' Throughout the extensive tour of the house she had been sincere in her admiration. 'I feel like a princess in a fairy tale.'

'I hope so. Do you really like the house?'

'You know I do – what is it?' The fervour of the expression in his eyes alarmed her a little.

'I know nothing can ever happen between us again, Elizabeth, but having you here is a dream come true. I wanted to see you one more time. And I wanted to see you here in this house.'

'Why? Do you have a dungeon you can lock me up in, Daniel?' Afraid of his intensity, she endeavoured to make light of it.

'No,' he said softly, 'no dungeon. No tower either. This is your house, Elizabeth. I built it for you.'

It took a while for that to sink in. 'My house? What do you mean?'

'Every piece of wood and glass and every tile, every blade of grass outside was chosen with you in mind.'

She was so nonplussed that she sat further back in the cushions as though afraid he might physically try to bend her to his will.

He recognized the truth instantly, and sorrow enlarged his dark eyes. 'It doesn't matter now, Elizabeth, it's too late anyway. But having you here like this . . . Just once is enough.'

'What do you mean?'

He told her then about his illness, and while she struggled to take it in he came across and squatted in front of her, taking her hands. 'I said it doesn't matter now, Elizabeth, and I meant it. Now I've had everything I ever wanted, you here in your house with the flowers all around. I don't mind dying now. What I dreaded was that I would go to my grave thinking you hated me. I can see now that you don't – you wouldn't have agreed to come here otherwise.' The sadness in his eyes was replaced with tenderness. 'Please don't think I expect anything more. That you don't hate me is all I need to know.' Painfully, using the armrests of the chair for leverage, he stood up. 'There's just one thing I want you to do for me . . .'

He went out, leaving her stunned. Another woman would probably have cried. In her late years, however, Elizabeth's emotions, so unruly when she had been younger, had acquired a patina of rest, although not without a great deal of effort. Somehow she had achieved peace both inside and out.

'I want you to have this.' He was back, carrying a square jewellery case. 'I've kept it for you for many years.'

'I couldn't.' Her hard-won calm was threatened.

'Open it and look at it at least,' he insisted softly. 'If you don't like it, that's one thing, but I think you will. I was going to leave you this house I built for you, because even as they were putting the furniture in I knew that if Midge survived me she would sell it straight away. But then I thought such a bequest might be a terrible imposition, not to speak of an impertinence. This is an alternative.'

She stared helplessly at the case as though it were a lethal weapon and saw that he was holding it so tightly his hands shook a little. It was made from sumptuous black leather, tooled with gold, and she knew that whatever was inside must be valuable.

'Will you not just open it?' The shake became more pronounced. 'If you don't like it, you don't have to take it. But it would make me happy to see it on you, just once. And if it makes you feel any better, it's not the Koh-i-Noor diamond or anything like it.' A trace of a smile passed across his white face. 'It's not the value of it that's relevant, it's what it represents.'

Slowly she took the case and opened it, conscious of his scrutiny. 'I had it made for you, Elizabeth. I've never forgotten that blue dress you wore the night we danced. Do you remember?'

The Oriental woman had made up her mind. It was raining in Vancouver – probably an omen.

She had thought a great deal since talking to her lieutenant in Helena the previous evening and had reviewed her assets. Even with absorbing the loss on her investment in the trial run, she would have enough to be comfortable for the rest of her life. For two lifetimes in fact. The extra, which would have come had she continued the operation in and through Ireland, would have been the cream, but she had decided there was no point in tempting fate. She had had a smooth, uneventful career over the past ten years and so much had gone wrong recently that it would be wise to pay attention to the signals.

Perhaps she was losing her touch. Searching for new ways in which to run drugs into Europe, it was she who hit on the casket idea. And she had chosen Montana from which to originate the operation as it was hardly seen as the drugs capital of the world, or even of the US. In retrospect, neither the casket nor Ireland had been a good idea. Perhaps it was the combination of the two that had proved so disastrous. It was time to cut her losses and end it. She made the call to her man in Helena.

He was surprised, but accepted his orders to stand down the entire operation, even the test. The woman made her financial arrangements with him and, although she had no intention of talking to him again, told him she would be in touch the following day about something new, that she was running a little late now as she had an early appointment downtown.

She was careful to the last on the telephone: somehow the line was almost too clear. During her time in Ottawa, she had learned enough from certain former lovers to know that someone who has something to hide should be wary of a connection that never crackled. Even when it was made through supposedly secure cellphones. 'Have you dealt with those other matters? I don't like leaving loose ends.'

'They're in hand.'

'Thank you. Your consideration may be collected in the usual manner.'

After she rang off, the woman, who was dressed in a silk *cheong sam* and matching turban, as though she was going to see someone important, looked around her apartment for the last time. She would leave without regret. It had never become home. Vancouver, with its long winters, its damp and greyness, had never been anything but a staging post: she hated cold and rain and her eyes had always been firmly fixed on the blue and white world of the tropics.

She put on a voluminous cotton raincoat and placed her airline tickets, passports and the most personal of her financial documents into a largish leather purse, switched on her answering-machine and, having made sure the gas stove was off and the windows to her terrace secured, left the apartment, every inch the businesswoman on a mission.

'Have a pleasant day – thank you, ma'am,' the doorman responded as she handed him a tip while he held open the cab door.

'Thank you, Mel. You have a pleasant day too.' She smiled at him. 'See you later.'

As her cab moved into the rush-hour traffic, downtown, the detective was reporting to his superior on the call he had just monitored. The two men had a relatively brief discussion. The superior decided that, since the big deal they had been waiting for had now been aborted, they should reel her in. 'Where did she say she was going?' He walked ahead of the detective towards his own office.

'She didn't say, it could be anywhere. She has no regular haunts, as you know.'

'Put out an APB with her description,' the senior ordered. 'It shouldn't take too long. And put people on her apartment. If we miss her, we'll get her when she comes home.'

What the detective's superior did not know, of course, was that the woman's meticulous planning was paying off. She had given the doorman the name of a downtown restaurant to pass to the cab driver but, once inside the vehicle, seemed to change her mind and asked him to drive her instead to a shopping mall, which was just opening. She paid him off and walked purposefully inside, then seemed arrested by a window display of shoes. She used the glass as a mirror. No one seemed to be paying her any attention.

Moving away from the shoe store, she strolled along until, as if on impulse on passing a washroom, she went through the door marked *Women*. Once inside, she locked herself into a cubicle.

Underneath the coat she had concealed a lightweight nylon knapsack, the type children take to school. Unzipping it, she removed from it a boy-sized jacket and trousers in dark polyester, socks, soft boy's shoes and a wig.

When she emerged less than ninety seconds later, she was a small Oriental man with cropped grey hair.

The *cheong sam*, turban and clutch purse had been jammed into the sanitary can, the wide raincoat, with empty pockets and from which all labels had been removed, remained hanging on the purse hook behind the cubicle door.

The only point of danger was in leaving the washroom, but her luck held. No one was near the door from which she emerged except a bored cleaner pushing a floormop. And he had his back to her.

324

Chapter Twenty-Eight

It was when she – and the trailing Lynskey – were almost at the office that Sky remembered what it was about Martin O'Shaughnessy's name that had been bothering her. It was simply that it was Irish. Treacy, or McCarthy, Collins, O'Connor, O'Shaughnessy, Flynn. All Irish. And an Irish cop over here snooping around. It did not take a genius to work out the connections. No wonder the FBI was involved.

Jimbo and Lynskey greeted one another like cousins and settled in to talk. Since much of what was being discussed between them was familiar to her, Sky watched the Irishman. He was outwardly relaxed, although it was obvious he had decided that the editor of the *Butte Courier* was a man to be reckoned with. So far he had not mentioned his outlandish suggestion that she had to be taken off the story.

The editor was ultra-serious too, to a degree she had rarely seen. He kept darting glances at her, which was odd. 'Let's see where we are with this,' he said. He pushed his computer terminal to one side and reviewed the single sheet of foolscap in front of him. 'It's a pity you can't be more specific about certain aspects.'

Sky went over to the cooler to get a drink of water but then discovered it had run out of dixie cups. Even though she had not been listening closely, she had heard enough to know that Lynskey had not advanced the story one iota. All he had done was to acknowledge the accuracy of some of what Daniel Treacy had told her and what she and the editor had deduced between them. 'Could I say something?' Instead of resuming her seat, she leaned against the wall beside the cooler.

'Sure.' They turned to her expectantly.

She stared at the Irishman. 'Everyone we know so far to be involved is of Irish descent. I think we're talking about terrorists, isn't that right, Fergus?' To give Lynskey his due, he did not even blink.

'Why do you think that, Sky?' This was Jimbo.

Lynskey had still not reacted, but as she was watching him so closely she saw that his expression had become, if anything, even more bland. 'Why don't you ask Fergus, Jim?' She came back to the desk and sat down. 'I think he might know the answer. I'm only putting two and two together – and ask him, while you're at it, if this is the reason he wants me to hide.'

The editor looked from one to the other. He had not responded in a way she thought her statement warranted. 'Did you hear what I said, Jim?'

Lynskey splayed his hands on his knees. 'I'm sure you understand why I can't be specific – in fact, I shouldn't be talking to you at all, but believe me,' he looked across at Sky, 'I'm not exaggerating or being dramatic. On the assumption that everything said here is confidential and will remain unattributable – '

'Of course.' Jimbo put one foot up on his desk.

' – I will tell you that what you have discovered is only the tip of the iceberg. There are, we believe, two operations in tandem here. Whether they are deliberately linked or the linkage is just fortuitous, I don't know yet. My guess is the latter.'

It was beginning to dawn on Sky that somehow Jimbo already knew about Lynskey's proposal that she should make herself scarce. Disbelieving, she tuned in again to what the Irishman was saying. '. . . and I'd say motivations are mixed.

I would not be surprised if, to take Sky's point, a certain –
ah – national fellow-feeling binds the sheriff of Mayville, for
instance, to his Irish colleagues. I don't see him taking these
huge risks just for his own benefit. A nasty piece of goods,
sure, into anything he can get for himself, yes, but up to now
he was just a slimeball. What is going on now,' he was
picking his words again, 'in my opinion is beyond ordinary
villainy.'

'Excuse me?' Sky again, so incensed she wanted to give
both men enough rope to hang themselves – and to see how
far they would go without including her. 'If the FBI knows
all this, as you've admitted they do,' she asked conversationally, 'why don't they just pull in a few people?'

Lynskey hesitated, then: 'The FBI and ourselves are in
consultation. We want to wait a big longer to see what
exactly is happening but we can move at any time. I can't go
into any more detail, I'm afraid.'

So much for confidentiality. Sky saw then why the sedan
was missing from Treacy's house this morning: 'I suppose it
was you who pulled the watchers off Daniel Treacy after I
told you the story?'

'You did clear up a lot of things for us, thanks.'

For nothing, Sky thought. For being the patsy as usual.
Aloud, she asked who now had the privilege of being
watched.

'Yes, who? Bigger fish, perhaps?' This was Jimbo.

Lynskey clammed up further. 'You know I can't say.'

'Well, where, then?' Jimbo again. 'In Montana? I've made
a few enquiries of my own and the Montana state police
don't seem to be involved in any of this.'

'Perhaps,' Lynskey studied him, 'the state police are aware
of the Bureau's presence but are not playing any active role.
Not yet, at any rate. This, as you've already guessed and as is
self-evident from the involvement of both myself and the
FBI, is an international operation.'

'All this – you here, the FBI, police and the Navy all chasing their tails in Ireland – for one casket load?' The editor placed his pen at right angles to the margin of the foolscap, lining it up precisely with the point touching his pants leg. 'Hardly likely, is it?'

Lynskey did not move. 'No comment.'

'I see.' Jimbo picked up the pen again and began doodling an interlocking series of figures-of-eight. 'It was definitely drugs in that casket, was it?' He drew flower petals around his figures.

'No comment again.' Lynskey remained still. 'But if I could get to why I believe Sky here needs to make herself scarce for a little while?'

At last. Sky was so angry now she felt calm. 'I am *not* making myself scarce—'

'Let him talk, Sky.' Jimbo raised his eyebrows at her.

'All right, I'll let him talk, it's a free country, but I'm not going anywhere, not with my mother in hospital and my grandmother—'

'If I said that I'd take you with me to Ireland?' Lynskey glanced at the editor and then back to her.

Sky stared at them both.

'Don't fly off the handle, Sky.' Jimbo's expression was disingenuous. 'It was me who proposed it. This is a huge story. I've been on to our intellectual friend and, miracle of miracles, I've convinced him to authorize the expenditure.'

Sky sat back against the backrest. The arrogance of these two men having discussions behind her back on how she should or should not conduct her life and career was breathtaking. 'Good for you, Jim,' she said coldly. 'But you can unauthorize the money now. I'm not going anywhere.'

There was more to come as she discovered when, jointly, they set to work on her. Apparently not only was she being sent to Ireland, she was to be out of Butte 'for her own good' until her plane left. As soon as possible. Like tonight.

They had chosen a venue for her vacation: she was to visit her father for the night. They had even made travel arrangements. Apparently Daniel Treacy, who had been telephoned by Lynskey during his brief absence from the duplex earlier that morning, had agreed to lend one of the small company planes to fly Sky to Yaak, thus saving driving time. One of the summer airfields the company used was on a valley floor in the Purcell Range and was only ten miles from the town.

'Purely academically, of course,' Sky was having to work hard now to suppress excitement that at last she was getting the big break she had so long wanted, but she did not want them to have everything their own way right off, 'would I not be in as much so-called danger in Ireland as I would in Butte?'

'Definitely not.' Lynskey's statement was flat and brooked no rebuttal. 'I'll be able to look out for you better over there. It's my territory and I have a better chance of recognizing any strange villains. I'll have my colleagues to help too.'

'You really think my life is in danger?' Despite everything that had been said and the bullet in her mailbox, she found that difficult to credit. When he did not reply, she looked from him to her boss. 'Come on,' she appealed, 'you don't believe that, do you, Jim?'

'I'm not the expert here. He is. And I'm worried.' Jimbo looked it. She tried one last angle although her excitement was now growing apace. 'How are you going to get next week's edition of this rag out if I take off?'

'The same way we always do. I'll write most of it, we'll expand the advertorial, the kid can have the time of her life with a fashion spread and we'll lift stuff from the nationals. Piece of cake.'

Eventually she agreed, on condition that she could make adequate domestic arrangements.

Shortly afterwards, Lynskey departed. 'I've to see a few

people, make a few calls. I'll see you later, Sky. Stay here until I come back for you and then I'll take you to lunch.'

But she never got to eat lunch that day.

The moment the door closed behind their visitor, Jimbo shot to his feet. 'It's drugs all right. Ireland's currently fashionable in that line of trade.' He came out from behind the desk and began pacing the small acreage of floor space not taken up with piles of paper; she had not seen him so animated since she had joined the *Courier* eight years before. 'That would explain his agitation about your safety.' He cracked his knee against a corner of the desk and massaged it.'But there's definitely more. He wouldn't be here if it was just one casket load of drugs – or even guns.' He resumed pacing. 'There are easier ways to get guns into Ireland. Remember he talked about two intertwined operations? He's here because of the second part. Look,' he turned to her and she saw the lines of his face had lifted until he looked almost happy, 'I know you hate people making arrangements on your behalf, but think of the story, Sky. We could even *make* money with this story, syndicate it. For sure nobody else is on to it. Lynskey'd help us – you like him, don't you?' He was nearly shouting with joy. 'You get on with him OK?'

He was so excited he did not wait for her response which was just as well because she had been about to laugh. 'Aren't you getting a little ahead of yourself, Jim?' she asked, when he had calmed down a little. 'And I know I've provisionally agreed to this madness but a drugs story? Not to speak of the other unknown you both keep talking about. I wouldn't know how to start. I don't even have a passport. I've never done work like this, you know it—'

'He'll help you. I'll help you.' He went behind the desk, opened a drawer and rummaged through the hundreds of business-cards jumbled up inside. 'Remember that Salt Lake City seminar I went to on business investment in Ireland, the one that was addressed by their Taoiseach – I have the name of someone here from the Irish television station . . . Where is it? Never mind, I'll find it – and leave the passport situation to me. He said you weren't to be left on your own, although personally I think you're all right in daylight – '

'Well, that's nice—'

' – so I'll come downtown with you. You'll need to get photographs taken before you head up to the northwest and I'll have a passport for you by tomorrow morning. And while you're gone I'll be making a few enquiries so that I'll have more for you for when you fly out. You won't be on your own. Look, Sky,' he parked himself on the front of the desk, 'we all know there're huge drug deals going on all over the world, and if it was *only* that I wouldn't think twice about it. OK,' he shrugged, 'if Montana's become a centre for it that's news, but only within the state. No, I'd bet my bottom dollar it's something much bigger than routine passage of drugs. We have most of the bits, I know we do. We just need to find a few more and then tie them up. You have to go to Ireland.'

Sky forbore to remind him that only a matter of hours ago he had been insisting she take time off. 'You forget that I've no training as an investigative reporter,' she reiterated, thinking that he should be given the chance to pull her off in case she screwed up.

This energized Jimbo looked at her impatiently and said, 'For goodness' sake, just go and get the story.'

For the next while, he tried to teach her how to act on a foreign assignment. Then, just as she thought her head would burst with contact names and dates and historical detail, he gazed out at her from his tottering paper grotto. 'Now forget everything I said, OK? Use the contact numbers I gave you, get as much help as you can but, above all – I can't say this often enough – above *all*, keep your eyes and ears open. Trust yourself, Sky, I trust you. And if you can't think where to start, start with that casket. Find out who met it, where did it go. Your friend Teddy at the funeral parlour will probably be able to help you there – there must be *some* legitimate documentation stored over in Collins's. It's like nuclear fission, Sky. One item of information will lead to the next and there's no stopping it once it gets started. But *trust* yourself. Oh, and enjoy yourself too – I wish it was me.'

Reeling with plans, she went with him to get the photographs taken and then they drove to collect her grandmother from Treacy's house.

The old lady herself came to the door in response to the bell. 'I'm not ready to go, Sky,' she said simply. 'I can get a taxi or Daniel can drive me.'

'How are you getting on?' Standing there on the stoop and conscious of Jimbo waiting for her in the Nissan, Sky, feeling absurdly like an interfering mom, longed for details: what she really wanted to know was whether or not the two old people were renewing their love affair.

But her grandmother gave her no clue. 'We're getting on grand.' She was pale but composed: whatever was happening in there was restrained.

'That's good.' Sky hesitated and then, seeing she was not going to be invited in, cast around for a graceful way of making an exit. Her grandmother saved her. 'I've got to go in now, darling. Tell Johanna I'll be up to see her sometime this morning. See you later.'

As Sky and Jim Larsen descended again into the city, she was struck by how odd it was that just as her grandmother arrived in the States, she was going to Ireland. Maybe they were fated not to get to know one another.

And she found that Lynskey, with all his conspiracy theories and dire warnings, had gotten to her. For the first time she felt uneasy. With the sun shining gaily, the Rockies like sentinels on the horizon, the notion that someone was out there planning to kill her was preposterous . . . or was it?

It felt bizarre to have her editor babysitting her. 'Do you *really* believe that I'm in danger?' she asked him.

'He convinced me.' Jimbo's tone was sombre. Sky checked her rear-view mirror again. Nothing to be seen except the glittering, empty highway.

The controller of the Irish side of the drug-running operation now bitterly regretted ever having heard of this deal. He had been approached originally through an intermediary in the Department of Agriculture in Dublin who, over the years, had been dealt a proportion of the profits from the controller's agrarian activities: as a rule he dealt in pig-smuggling across the border, angel dust, fertilizer for the lads in the IRA. Nice, safe, traditional criminality. Although he had recognized the extent of the leap he was being asked to make, he had found the big money impossible to resist.

But now, having lost control of his troops, he was boarding the ferry at Dun Laoghaire to make a run for it to England.

The *Agnes Monica*, shadowed at a distance by the *L.E. Aideen*, was steaming slowly with nets out towards the cave and the heroin. The captain knew that he had attracted the attention of the patrol vessel but she was at least a mile and a half away and his plan was simple: the crew would take the *Agnes Monica* as close as they dared to the cave's mouth – the water was deep so they could get within twenty yards. He and another man would be in the dinghy, tied close to starboard and invisible from the open sea and to their stalker. At the last minute he would cut loose and dash into the cave. The *Agnes Monica* would continue on her way without pause, pulling the unsuspecting *Aideen* with her.

333

By the time the *Aideen* or anyone else suspected anything, the stash would be buried and the skipper and his mate a couple of miles further east towards Killybegs, calmly checking lobster pots.

And so it happened.

In Dublin, hours later, the chief superintendent looked slowly around his assembled troops over whom silence hung like a mushroom cloud.

'After X number of conferences,' he began, 'Y amount of resources, Z hours of missed sleep, we have no drugs, no big deal in the offing, no arrests. Just Gárdaí running in circles all over the effin' country, four corpses and a few innocent fishermen. And the humiliation of having to ask the Brits to watch out for our man on the ferry.' He glowered, leaving no one in any doubt that this last was the worst of the lot. 'Let's hope we get to him first. Oh, and I nearly forgot,' Daly's speech slowed further, 'we have an apoplectic Commissioner, not to speak of what's going on in the Department of Justice and beyond.' He paused, then: 'Would any of you geniuses have any ideas as to what we should do next?'

The telephone on his desk buzzed and he snatched up the receiver. 'What is it? I said no calls.'

Then: 'Wonderful. We might as well hear his great thoughts on the matter. Put him on conference.' He waited a few seconds. No one in the room dared move. Then, when Fergus Lynskey's amplified and distorted voice dropped like lead into the room, 'Hello, hello?', Daly inclined his head towards the small black box set in the centre of the table.

'How about you, Lynskey? You've heard what's been going on over here? Any brilliant ideas?'

'I heard, and I'm afraid I'm fresh out.' Lynskey sounded as brisk as always. 'But I want to talk to you privately after this conference.'

'Well, since this so-called conference has progressed precisely nowhere, I propose to dismiss it so you can talk now.' The chief studied his fingernails.

The others shuffled their notes together and as they filed out of the room, to the ominous crackle of static, the chief superintendent pulled so hard at his ear-lobe that anyone watching might have worried he would do it a permanent injury. 'This'd better be good,' he exploded, as the door closed behind the last of them. 'I greatly appreciate you returning all my calls – where the hell have you been? Apart from the circus here there's been another development in Vancouver.' He berated Lynskey for a full minute.

In his bedroom at the War Bonnet, Lynskey waited imperturbably for him to run out of steam and fiddled with the clutch of telephone messages from a 'Mr Harvey' in Dublin – Bill Daly's sense of humour was as transparent as Elwood P. Dowd's imaginary rabbit. But as the chief's funnybone was not much in evidence now he decided to keep quiet about his proposal to bring R. Sky MacPherson to Ireland with him. 'So, for Chrissakes, get a move on your end.'

The chief paused and Lynskey gathered that the wigging was coming to an end. 'The Commissioner is getting antsy about all of this,' Daly added, 'and guess whose turn is it to get it in the neck?'

Lynskey remained calm. 'What new development in Vancouver?' He listened as the chief filled him in, and then told him about his meeting with the editor of the *Courier*.

'Jesus, Mary and Joseph,' Daly roared. 'I don't bleddy believe it! Why don't you just put up a notice about our activities on the Great Wall of China? Then everyone'd know.'

'Keep your hair on. I had my reasons and it's to do with why you sent me over here in the first place. Now I'm ready to come home. I've been checking around with the men

335

who listened in to all the telephone calls and I'm as good as convinced now that these stupid buggers over here have no knowledge at all of what you persist in calling Operation Omega. You're probably in the clear to give the go-ahead for the visit. By the way, those bullets. The hotel porter who took delivery of mine remembers a man in the tractor of an articulated truck. If it's who I think it is there's no point in going after him. He's small fry. Anything from Ballistics yet on the one I gave the feds?'

'No,' the chief snapped. 'Get back to this newspaper guy.'

'Yeah, well, he's to be trusted.'

'I feckin' hope so, given people are about to be pulled in both here and over there. In Vancouver they're waiting for that woman to show up at her apartment any minute now and if the media gets hold of it—'

'The media won't. So it's all right if I come home tomorrow?'

'I'm sorry now we sent you over there in the first place.' The chief superintendent slammed down his receiver and Lynskey was left with an earful of static.

The Varig flight carrying the Oriental woman from Los Angeles to Rio de Janeiro was climbing out over the ocean. Naturally she was travelling economy, as befitted a dowdy peasant Filipina going for the first time to visit her servant daughter who worked for a rich family in Rio. Humbly, she accepted the tomato juice and peanuts offered by the stewardess, then glanced apologetically at her seat companions as she tore the top off the packet. It seemed she was worried about upsetting them with the noise. They were going to South America on the trip for which they had saved for decades. They felt sorry for the poor little woman. She seemed so frail and timid. 'You got family in Rio?' the man asked.

The Oriental woman looked terrified.

'Not to worry, ma'am,' the man smiled kindly at her, 'we won't bother you none. But if you need help with customs or immigration or anything, you just holler, OK?'

The Oriental woman's face broke into a shy smile of gratitude and the man exchanged compassionate glances with his wife.

Chapter Twenty-Nine

Breaking the news to Johanna about the possibility of Sky's trip to Ireland was not difficult. She was still drowsy from pain medication and accepted the notion with equanimity. 'Be sure to go and see everyone, tell everyone I said hello.'

Buffy did not balk when Sky asked if she and Hermana would step into the breach her departure would occasion, 'if I go at all.' There was still her grandmother to consider, but when the old lady arrived at the hospital, she would brook no argument. 'I live alone at home. For goodness' sake, don't you think I can look after myself?'

Sky's secret thrill that she was off on the story of a lifetime was tempered only then by the thought that if she was in danger in her own home so was her grandmother. She did not want to alarm either her or Buffy, however: she would discuss it later with Lynskey.

When Lynskey arrived to escort her on the short trip back to the duplex, she drew him aside and hissed, out of the hearing of the others, 'This has gone beyond a joke. It's broad daylight, the middle of the day. This is Butte, Montana, in 1992, not Chicago during Prohibition.'

'I'm driving behind you and there's an end to it.' She had no option but to agree.

When they got home, the digital display on the answering-machine showed two messages. The first was for Lynskey, asking him to telephone 'the usual number' in

Washington DC. Sky was outraged. 'You're giving out my home number?' She was so incensed that she let the second message proceed without listening to it. 'Well, that's the limit, Lynskey, it really is—'

'Ssh,' he put his finger to his lips, 'let's hear what this one is. Roll back the tape.' Furiously, she did so.

The second message deflated her. It was from a man who gave his name only as Matt. He asked Sky to meet him at nine o'clock that evening in a coffee shop on Highway 15, just beyond the outskirts of Butte. He had crucial information for her on a story. 'You're not going, I'll go,' Lynskey insisted. Which set her off again. They had another row – *sotto voce*, because she did not want to upset her grandmother.

Yet Lynskey held all the cards, would do as he saw fit, because the visit to her father had now become a reality. Sky was looking forward to it, not only for itself, but as a respite from the drama around her. The Treacy Resources plane would be ready for her in just over two hours' time.

'This suits us fine, Sky.' Lynskey loomed over her like a whispering angel – or devil, she could not decide which. 'If this guy's talking to me he can't be stalking you. Although I looked at all the angles and couldn't see how he could have found out where you'd be, I was worried about you going up to the backwoods. If they think you're here, you'll be fine.'

The implicit threat seemed outlandish in the context of her own home. Sky felt at a loss. She went into her room and took down a small bag and a suitcase: she might as well start getting ready for Ireland too.

'Can I use your telephone? I'll pay for the calls.' Lynksey was still standing in the hallway.

'Go ahead.' Stalking past him, Sky lugged her suitcase and the ironing basket into the kitchen and started the irritating business of packing. She closed the kitchen door ostentatiously, in case he thought she might be listening in.

The Prince of Wales's trip to Ireland was in danger of being aborted, partly from security considerations but also because the FBI, which was monitoring the calls and activities of the sheriff of Mayville, had discovered that O'Connor had suddenly decided to take the vacation he was owed. The Bureau passed this nugget of information to Lynskey when he called the number in Washington from Sky's duplex.

He immediately telephoned Dublin. 'I thought we'd heard the last of you. Aren't you on the way home?' The chief superintendent sounded unusually weary. 'The stuff just came in on those bullets, the one from that university with the name like cooking oil—'

'Missoula.'

'Whatever. And the one you gave the FBI. They match. Nothing remarkable about them. No prints, they hadn't been fired, could have been bought in any gunshop.'

'Surprise, surprise! I'm coming home tomorrow.' Lynskey was speaking as low as he could while remaining audible. 'I can't stay long because I'm on a private telephone, but our friend in Mayville is on the move. The day after tomorrow. I think we're on course. And although this is *not* a problem,' he hesitated a little, 'that Butte newspaper I told you about is sending a reporter over to Ireland. A Miss R. Sky Mac-Pherson if you remember.'

'What the—'

'Don't worry. They have no idea what they're looking for.' He lowered his voice still further. 'All they know is that it involves something big and probably subversive.'

'They could really make a mess—'

'Look, I told you, they don't know what they're looking for. And the newspaper's main contact in Ireland is Éamonn

340

Vaughan. He's too busy chasing day-to-day stuff for RTE's television bulletins to have any idea either. I think it's time we told the Brits about this group.'

'Would they tell us?'

Silence hung between them and Lynskey let it hang. Although, for public consumption, co-operation between the Special Branch of the Irish police force and Scotland Yard was superb and ongoing, in fact it was riddled with rivalries, xenophobia and post-colonial resentments on both sides.

'They're already laughing at the circus we're running here at the moment over that drugs bust,' the chief super's voice was tight, 'and for once I don't blame them. Leave it with me. On your side, I've already discussed it with the feds and they're ready to do a round-up over there. They're waiting until they're sure they have all the names and then they'll move on everyone simultaneously. After that, we'll make the decision about Operation Omega. If this group is out of action it'll be OK.'

'You're the boss.' Lynskey winced at the loud crack when the chief superintendent put down the phone.

Jim Larsen had decided to begin at the beginning, to look for whoever had started the ball rolling. It was clear that the black tramp, the guy who'd delivered the misspelt note, had known about Midge Treacy's hitting the hobo that night and might be able to put the sheriff of Mayville on the spot.

Firstly, however, in the vague hope that Mrs Treacy might be *compos mentis* enough to help, he tried the clinic in Choteau, where he ran into a blank wall of officialdom. 'No one of that name here, sir, who wants to know?' If he had had time to go up there he was sure he could have swung something, but time was in short supply.

'All right.' He called the kid into his office and spread out the coffee coupons on the desk in front of her. 'Now think hard, Lindy. You told us before all you knew about the guy's height and weight and so on, but we need more. You said the guy was black?'

'Yeah – well, I think he was black.'

'Coal black? Brown black or chocolate black or mahogany black?'

'Sort of brown black, I think. I'm sorry, Mr Larsen.' The junior picked nervously at the cuticle of her left thumbnail.

Jimbo gave her what he hoped was an encouraging smile. 'Now, could he have been Native American, do you think? What was he wearing?'

'Sort of a jogging suit, I think, no . . . yes . . . And he wasn't Native American. I'm absolutely sure of that. His cheekbones weren't anyway.'

'Do you remember the colour? Of the jogging suit?'

The junior's face cleared instantly: this was her territory. 'It was indigo – you know, that sort of very dark blue, not quite midnight blue but that's nearly black? It was quite new. And it had a very unusual boat neckline. To tell you the truth, Mr Larsen, it looked like quite an expensive garment for someone like him.'

'You mean, for a tramp?'

'Well, he wasn't a tramp, exactly. I mean, he didn't smell or anything like that. Well actually . . .' She reconsidered.

'Go on.'

'He didn't smell *bad* although I did think I caught a whiff of alcohol off his breath but there was another smell from him too. Kinda like burning? As if he'd been in a fire?'

It was not much to go on but it was something. 'Thanks, Lindy, that'll do for the moment, but if you think of anything else, anything at all . . .' He dismissed her and sat for a moment sunk in thought. Then he called the police station. His buddy there was out but before Larsen could leave a message he found himself switched to the desk sergeant. As

342

time was so short, he decided to take a risk. 'Jim Larsen, of the *Courier*.'

'How can I help you?' Although respectful, relations between the newspaper and the police had never been ultra-cordial. Larsen knew he was regarded as being far too independent. 'I'm trying to locate a black tramp, someone who might pick up a bit of work here and there, maybe at an incinerator, maybe a dump. Or someone who likes to hang around fires, even in summer. Anyone you know fit that description?'

'He done something?'

'Not that I'm aware of, but he gave us some information and I would like to trace him again.'

'Information concerning what, exactly, Jim?'

'Oh, just a story we're working on.'

'I see. Well, no one comes to mind right away. But if you come across a bit more information about the guy or what you're looking for, maybe we could help you out.'

The editor thought quickly. He didn't want to reveal too much but the death of old Leon was in the public domain anyway. 'The guy left a note in at the front office here. Apparently some friend of his called Leon died by the side of the road upstate and he wants us to commemorate him, write an obituary, that sort of thing. We'd like to facilitate him – it'll make good human interest copy – but we can find out very little about his friend. We need to talk to the black guy again to get a bit of material.'

'I'll ask around,' the sergeant was noncommittal, 'but I'm not all that hopeful. Haven't never seen a black hobo in Butte.'

With time ticking away towards her departure for Yaak and her suitcase for Ireland less than a quarter filled, Sky was becoming panicky. Her grandmother reappeared in the

343

kitchen. 'Sit down, Grandma.' She cleared a space on the table. 'Have you eaten?' At least her self-appointed body-guard had had the decency not to come into the kitchen. After his telephone call, she had heard him go towards the living room.

'I have.' Her grandmother sat in the chair indicated.

'I'm sorry, you don't mind if I continue with this?' Sky indicated her ironing. 'I don't have much time,' and when her grandmother shook her head, 'So come on, Grandma, tell me. I couldn't ask you at the hospital in front of the others but I'm dying to know what happened between you and Daniel.'

In response, Sky's grandmother drew a jewellery case out of her purse and placed it on the table. 'Have a look. It nearly finished me altogether.'

Sky placed the iron on its heel and opened the case. Spread out on the velvet was a necklace of emerald-cut gems of pale blue set in a flexible band of white gold. It was modern yet timeless, the most beautiful object she had ever seen. She picked it up and draped it across the back of her hand from which, catching the light, it poured like tassels chiselled from the blue-white core of an iceberg. 'It's very heavy.' She could think of nothing which would adequately describe such beauty.

'The stones are so pale I thought at first they were aquamarines,' her grandmother touched the necklace, 'but they're cornflower sapphires, apparently. He searched until he got the colour exactly right. They're yours, Sky. I can't wear them.'

'Why ever not?'

'Because of what he said but not what he meant. What that necklace represents. To him it's a talisman of something long gone. For me it's a reminder of too much pain, his – then and now – mine, everyone's, even his poor wife's. I

344

certainly remember that night and that blue dress.' Talking to herself now, she picked the necklace off Sky's hand and let it cascade through her fingers. 'It's uncanny how he matched the colour.' She looked back at her granddaughter. 'That dress was the one I was wearing at the dance the night he shot your grandfather. Daniel and I had danced together for the first time.'

'But that shooting was an accident, he told me – Mom told me—'

'Yes. But it's a chapter in a closed book. Take it, Sky.' Decisively, her grandmother put the necklace back in its case, snapped the box shut and pushed it across the table. 'I'll be leaving it to you in my will anyway. Just don't tell Daniel I've anticipated a little, will you? Anyway,' she brightened, 'white gold looks awful on old skin.'

Sky cradled the case in her hands. She would decide what to do with the jewels later. 'Tell me, Grandma, from the very beginning. I saw him answering the door when I was driving off . . .'

The story came out slowly and, while relating it, Sky's grandmother stared at the formica top on the kitchen table. She looked up now. 'What was I going to say when he gave me the necklace? Such dreams, such love. I felt unworthy but at the same time I didn't want all this, I'd put it behind me years and years ago.'

'Don't you think it's wonderful, though, Grandma, all this time he's kept this torch alive?'

'It's a responsibility I cannot accept. I feel awful about putting that so bluntly, but what can I do? The poor man is dying, I know that, and I'll do what I can for him but at my age, Sky, death is . . .' she searched for an analogy, 'not a friend exactly, more like a neighbour, liable to drop in at any stage of the day or night to borrow your remaining time. Although you don't think about it all the time, it's always

345

there, living right next door, in the next room. It's impossible to avoid because it's already called on other neighbours, good friends from school . . .' She trailed away.

'So if you couldn't tell him how you felt about this business with the house, are you able to tell me?'

'How did you think I felt? Moved and shocked and sad and yet flattered. All at the same time. I did love him, Sky, I was a foolish and headstrong young woman. He was gorgeous then – you should have seen him.'

Her grandmother smiled in a way that showed Sky how she had been as a young girl. She could see the two of them, in one another's arms. 'And now?' she breathed. 'Now that you've spent a morning with him?'

The smile died away. 'How could I not love Daniel McCarthy? But not the way he loves me. He saw it straight away. It was very sad. I could have pretended. After all,' she avoided Sky's gaze, 'what had I to lose? I could so easily have pretended for the few weeks he has left. But then I thought that would not be worthy of either of us. Or of his poor wife up there, wherever she is.'

Sky opened the jewellery case again, and examined the sapphires. 'When are you seeing him again?'

'Later today. He's taking me out to dinner. And tomorrow too, Sky. I'll see him as much as he likes until—' She stopped then went on, briskly, 'This is why, although I'll miss you, there's no problem at all with your going on your trip. It's funny, isn't it, that we'll have sort of swapped places again? Seems like we're forever destined to miss each other. Anyway, Johanna's going to be in hospital for a long time yet so apart from visiting her, I'll be available for Daniel. In fact, as it looks like your mother's lovely friends feel they have to baby me to extinction, it'll be nice to have a project of my own. He's going to take some time off. Apparently when he received the prognosis, he set up his work so it practically runs itself. He's going to bring me up to visit his wife.'

'I see.' Sky, who had not spent much time considering elderly people's motivations or their behaviour among themselves, wondered which of them had come up with such a bizarre idea but thought it better not to ask. Maybe when you got to be over seventy neither ordinary niceties nor taboos applied. 'So what happened after you took the necklace from him?'

'Nothing, we just talked. He offered me tea – can you imagine? After all these years, Daniel McCarthy offering me tea just like we gave our visitors in the old days. Twining's.' She smiled affectionately. 'Apparently that's the nearest thing to real Irish-style tea you can get over here. I was touched.'

In the absence of a mirror in the kitchen, Sky again held the sapphires against her forearm to see how they would look against her skin. 'They're beautiful on you, darling,' her grandmother said softly. 'Wear them, and remember I wasn't always so old.'

Chapter Thirty

After making his call to the reporter's home, the Helena lieutenant had set off quietly for Butte. He always worked alone. He had not yet decided what to do with this reporter woman: like his employer, he believed in violence only when it was necessary.

This appointment to meet her was really a reconnaissance mission. Or, at least, it would start out that way. If he managed to scare her into submission, well, everything was probably going to turn out all right.

He would know within minutes if she was prone to heroics. Most reporters had egos as big as redwood trees and were used to having things all their own way, imagined they were invincible: that their ability to place things in the public domain gave them power.

The Helena lieutenant knew all about power. Middle-aged, he had retired early from his post as an assistant district attorney at the DA's office. Ostensibly, his retirement had been because of an ailing heart, but in reality his work for the woman in Vancouver had started to make too many demands on his time. He still saw his former colleagues, however. It was how he continued to keep up with everything that moved in the state of Montana. How he knew where most of the bodies were buried.

He planned to confront this R. Sky MacPherson, not at the coffee shop, but on the pretext that it was too crowded – it always was – to take her somewhere a little more private.

He did not doubt that she would turn up. No reporter could resist the carrot of an anonymous tip-off.

Across the border in Canada, the elderly Jerry Flynn – the first of the plotters' group to start making the move to Ireland and the richest by millions – was walking to his limousine to be driven to the airport.

Unlike the rest of his co-conspirators, he was motivated less by the more recent events in Irish history than by vivid memories of stories told him by his Irish great-grandmother who, as a girl, had survived her trip to the Americas in one of the aptly named coffin ships that brought the starving and destitute across the Atlantic during the potato famine of 1847. Eight members of her family had started out from County Galway, but she was the only one who had arrived. To the end of her days at the age of ninety-four, through her late marriage to an Irish-American cop, through the move to Canada and the upbringing of her single son, the arrival of grandchildren and then great-grandchildren, she implanted in the minds of all around her tales of the heartless brutality of the English masters and the suffering of the Irish.

Jerry Flynn had polished those stories until they shone in his memory like jewels. He felt the hunger pangs of his great-grandmother and her neighbours, vomited with them the green slime of grass torn from the roadsides and stuffed into their mouths, watched sullenly as the carts laden with yellow grain harvests rumbled away from their homestead towards the ports and the tables of England and India in payment of English taxes.

For many of Flynn's co-conspirators, the crucible of the present impasse in Irish affairs was planted in the failure of the 1916 revolution and executions of Pearse and the other patriots. Their motives had been simple too: to get England out and let Ireland run her own affairs. For Flynn, however, everything that had happened in Ireland had flowed directly from the injustice of the famine. Now he was embarked on vengeance. For his great-grandmother, for all his ancestors. Those who now ran the Irish parliament, and bent the knee to loyalists and unionists, must be humiliated. Flynn's heart beat fast under his snappy business suit as he emphasized to his chauffeur that he would be in New York for about a week.

Three hours later, he took a cab into New York City and had his hair cut tight. 'And while you're at it, buddy,' he told the young barber, 'take off this moustache. I feel like giving myself a new image for the ladies.' The boy, hiding a snigger, shaved him so tightly his skin squeaked. Then Flynn went to a prearranged rendezvous on 42nd Street half a block from Times Square and had his photograph taken. He went for a short walk, enjoying his anonymity among the rubber-neckers, skateboarders and seedy lowlifes with whom the area was infested. Then he went back to the office where he had posed for the camera, and was handed his new passport.

When he got back out to Kennedy and presented his passport and ticket at the Aer Lingus Premier Class desk, he was John Mulqueen, American senior citizen. But he felt twenty years younger already.

'I'm glad you're taking this seriously at last, Sky.' Lynskey was driving her to the airport. 'I know you think I'm a nuisance but if you won't think about your own safety, someone has to. We have word back on those bullets but they were clean of clues as to who was behind the sending of them.'

'It's the sheriff, you know it is.'

'You're probably right but we've no proof. But whoever it was won't be shy. They mean business, Sky.'

'Talk to my editor about it.' She summoned as much hauteur as she could.

'You can bet I will,' Lynskey promised as he turned into the parking lot and stopped. He turned off the engine and shook his head. 'What am I going to do with you at all? You're a big eejit, do you know that, MacPee? Ah well,' changing tone and mood a full 180 degrees, he bent to kiss her cheek, 'go off and see your da and have a great time. I'll take care of things down here.'

She had stared at him. This man was a stranger of less than a week's acquaintance: what had happened that he was now 'taking care of things here'? He noted her expression, guessed the reason behind it. 'Sorry, I'm being a bossyboots again, right? Can't help it. I love you.'

Once again, she felt that flutter of terror. She fiddled with the shoulder-strap of her overnight bag, pretending to check that the buckle was secure. 'One thing I'm worried about. Will you make sure my grandmother's all right in the house? If I'm supposed to be in so much danger . . .'

'She'll be well protected. Have a good flight now.'

She raised her mouth for a kiss but he sideskipped and planted a second one on her cheek. 'See you soon, MacPee.'

'I'll see you when I get back.' Unreasonably, she felt a little piqued as she got out into the sunshine.

The single-engined Treacy Resources plane was already on the tarmac and the young pilot, whom she reckoned to be at least ten years younger than herself, took her on board.

As they banked after take-off, Sky tried to relax, yet she could not avoid facing the sludge of corrosive emotions which had been stirred up in the past week. She felt as raw as a scraped carrot: at heart, for the moment at least, she was a little girl who wanted her daddy.

The butterflies began to stir in her stomach as they crossed the wide flow of the Kootenai river, northwest of Libby, and then flew along the smaller and more tranquil Yaak. Northwest Montana unrolled beneath the wing like one of those bright relief maps she used to make from *papier mâché* for geography class in grade school: rivers glinting like threads of gold and copper between lush, steep banks of deciduous and coniferous trees; occasional, widely spaced glimpses of a cabin built from logs or a long, low, ranch-style house; a spooked horse galloping, tail up, across a bright green pasture, a brown clearing alive with loggers and their yellow, dinosaur-like machinery.

Parallel with and above the plane's wing, in a long lazy line, the frosted, dreaming heights of the Rockies.

They were making their final approach to the field. Now that she thought about it, Sky could not understand why she was taking this trip. Eight years was a long time, and now that she was faced with it, what was she going to say to her father? She could hardly throw herself into his arms – as she had earlier felt she would like to do – and ask him to fix everything: all her anxieties – about the trip, about Lynskey, about her mother. Larry MacPherson had never lived for a single day under the same roof as she and Johanna, much less had he had anything to do with their emotional well-being.

For the first time it occurred to Sky that not once had it crossed anyone's mind to let Larry know about her mother's accident. Least of all had she herself thought to tell him, although it was she who had spoken with him. She felt guilty about that: she had been bubbling over with the prospect of seeing him, of going to Ireland, and had forgotten.

Or could she have deliberately withheld the information for reasons she did not now care to analyse? As the aircraft flashed along the crushed-cinder runway past the Nissen hut that served as waiting room and service centre, she caught a glimpse of her father lounging in the doorway. The butterflies went crazy, although at least a few were dancing for joy. She would tell him now, first thing.

To banish the sensations in her stomach she bent double, leaning hard on her solar plexus and making heavy weather of retrieving her cabin bag from where she had stowed it between her feet. She regained control of herself as the aircraft swung around and began its short taxi run towards the hut. Reminding the pilot that he should pick her up again early the next morning, she jumped out and ran across the gate towards her father. 'Dad! Thanks for coming to meet me,' as she buried her face in the hug. The smell of him – tobacco, old leather, an overriding scent of the woodsy outdoors – soothed doubts about the reasons for this trip.

'Stand back there and let me see you.' He held her by the shoulders and looked her up and down.

'Will I pass?' She had to raise her voice to be heard over the pilot's take-off run behind them.

'Rainbow Sky MacPherson,' his voice was like pouring chocolate, 'you're a sight for my eyes.'

'You too, Dad. Let's see you, now.' He was dressed as she had always remembered him: chequered shirt, jeans faded to a whitish grey, boots of hide so scuffed it looked like ancient suede. 'You've cut your hair! Last time I was here you looked like Davy Crockett!'

'And didn't you just let me know it.' He grinned. The white tidemark around the sides and back of his neck under his baseball cap showed that the barbering was recent: she was touched he had had it cut just for her. 'Well, let it grow again, Dad. I take it all back, I preferred it long.'

'There's no pleasing women.' He threw his eyes to heaven in mock exasperation. 'Here, give me that, truck's just here.' He took the bag and threw it into the rear of a newish Daihatsu 4-track, which, with all four doors open, stood beside the hut.

'This new?' The last time she had been up he had been driving a pickup, held together by its own rust.

'Yep, business was good, last coupla years. How's your mom?' He closed the two rear doors of the vehicle and folded himself, lithe as a big cat, into the driver's seat.

Sky climbed in beside him: 'Mom's in the hospital. I should have told you, I know.'

'She all right?' Larry turned the key in the ignition.

'Well . . .' Sky was a little put out that he did not seem all that concerned.

'You would have told me if it were anything serious, yeah?' He engaged the gears and reversed away from the hut.

'It's serious enough, Dad. She's broken her back.'

Her father whistled, a long note, like a harmonica player's. 'She's going to be OK, though, ain't she?'

'What would you say if I were to tell you she won't?' It was out before she could contain it.

'Come on, hon, I know you'da told me.' Her father spun the steering wheel and took the Daihatsu out on to a wide track that seemed to lead directly into a forest. He glanced across at her. 'Hang on to your hat, it'll be a bit bumpy for a spell.'

Sky was silent. Wanting him to ask about her mother's operation. Wanting him to be frantic. Instead, he seemed content to concentrate on his driving as the wagon, engine roaring, jolted and juddered across the deep ruts in the track.

They came out on to the highway after about two miles which, to Sky, seemed more like forty. It was not the physical discomfort: rather, she felt almost in shock. She tried to put this in perspective as the vehicle picked up speed: her father and mother had never married – had never even lived together. Why shouldn't he take this news casually? What was Johanna to him now?

354

'You're very quiet, Dad.' She could not keep the provocation out of her voice.

'Up here you get used to silence and your own company,' he responded equably, 'you should know that, darlin'. It's you folks in the big cities make more noise than a posse of foxes.' She knew his penchant for silence: he was the type of man who would retreat to his own dreams at his own time.

They came to a T-junction and turned left into Yaak proper, which comprised a store, two telephone booths and the Dirty Shame Saloon. 'She'll be in for quite a while,' she said quietly. 'Mom,' she added as he looked across at her, incomprehension written all over his craggy, handsome face.

'Oh, yeah . . . She needs anything while you're gone on your trip, you just tell her to let me know, OK, hon?' With one hand, Sky's father extracted a spindly roll-up from a tin on the dashboard and put it in his mouth. 'Hey, there's a thing. My little girl's going to be a foreign correspondent – how 'bout that!' He grinned across at her while patting himself down in a search for matches. 'Hang on.' He came up empty, braked hard, then reversed to the front of the general store. 'I have to go in here for a second. My little girl a big newspaper star.' He chuckled, shaking his head. 'Who'da thought? Want a soda or something? They got ice.'

Sky did not trust herself to speak. After he had gone into the store, she got out of the 4-track to sit on the wooden glider set on the verandah under the eaves. It was the Yaak evening rush-hour: a pickup stopped in the middle of the street, its engine left idling as the man in the passenger seat went in for supplies; on the far side, with a hiss of air brakes, a huge articulated rig overshot the Dirty Shame and stopped opposite where she sat. The driver hopped down from the cab and stretched. 'Howdy,' he called across to Sky, 'how's your day goin' so far?'

'Fine,' she called back, and did her best to smile.

'You bet.' The driver shook himself like a bear coming out of a river and walked briskly towards the saloon.

'Here you go.' Her father was back with two Cokes and two dixie cups. 'Want to sit awhile?' Taking her silence for assent, he went to fetch a bag of ice, pulling it open with his teeth as he came back. He filled first her cup from the contents, then his own, before cracking the tops off both Coke bottles against the rim of the glider. 'Nice here,' he sat beside her, 'nice and cool.'

It was the last of evening and the trees at the forest's edge at the other side of the highway exhaled a quiet, green breath. It had been dry up here for weeks: the breeze stirred little eddies of dust around their feet and the two water-feeders slung from the rafter beside them were in constant use by humming-birds, their wings blurring as they sipped from the tiny pipes. 'I prefer it in winter,' her father's slow voice was reminiscent, 'never a breath of wind, two feet of powder. A blue and white world, so clear.

'Lovely little things, aren't they? Bet you don't see many in the city.' Hunched over, elbows on knees, the better to watch the activities of the humming-birds, he gazed at them with such tender pleasure she could not square it with his seeming callousness towards her mother's plight.

'It was because of a humming-bird that Mom's in the hospital.'

'Oh?' As she explained what had happened, Sky was trying to decide from his expression whether he was more interested in the fate of the bird caught in Moondancer's mouth than her mother's accident. She finished the story and pretended to bury herself in the delights of the Coke.

What had happened in eight years? She had been twenty-six when last she saw this man. An adult. Old enough, experienced enough, to see and hear the truth. Had he always had this *laissez-faire* attitude towards the mother of

356

his child – or was she just now seeing it because of her own reaction to Johanna's brush with death?

Even as they entered her head, Sky heard the pompousness of her thoughts and would have dismissed them if she had not been so taken aback. Because it was only then she realized she had been hoping that, somehow, Johanna's accident would have brought Larry MacPherson rushing to the hospital.

Happy ever after.

It was also why she had not told him on the telephone: she had needed to confront him about it. All these years she had held him in a web of dreams: her lovely, absent father, so beautiful, a Peter Pan in a fairy castle. Even at *her* age.

And now, dimly, she saw that the whole caboodle was tied in someways with goddamned Fergus Lynskey. 'I've met a man, Dad.'

'Oh?' At least that had got his attention. 'A better deal than that Randy, I hope?'

'Not much,' she admitted. 'Well, he's amazing, but he's a – a *trial* as well. I'm not sure I trust him, Dad – in fact, I know I don't. But he loves me,' she rose from the glider and wandered over to the water feeder, which was temporarily unattended. 'At least, he says he does, and I'm really worried about that.' She twanged at the pipe. 'I mean, what kind of a man says he loves a woman after only a few days? And just because he sleeps with her just *once* . . .'

'I see.' Her father's tone was wry. 'Sounds like an all together guy!'

'Oh, Dad, what'll I do?' She turned round to face him.

He was watching her, his eyes soft. 'You'll make the right decision, Rainbow Sky, you always do.'

'My life's a mess.'

'Of course it's not a mess. You're a big success, aren't you? And you left that Randy.'

'That's another thing. You didn't even come to the wedding.'

'Wise decision, as it turned out.'

'And you hate Mom.'

'But I don't hate your mother . . .' She could see he was genuinely mystified and something in her, perhaps her childhood, broke.

Chapter Thirty-One

Sheriff O'Connor, who was divorced and therefore free of busybodies who might question his comings and goings, told no one why he had decided to take off. Neither his deputy nor anyone else connected with his office even asked. On the contrary, they danced metaphorical jigs of delight. Brian O'Connor was not popular in Mayville. Anyone who talked about the snap vacation assumed that since his ex had moved to Florida some years ago, he was probably going down there to see his kids. Apart from himself and British Airways, the only people who knew he had bought a return ticket to London were federal agents. He planned to buy the Dublin ticket at Heathrow.

If his staff were delighted at his projected absence, the sheriff's own heart had expanded with fierce exultation. They were on the move at last. No more telephone calls, just action.

Now, on his final afternoon before the adventure began, he sat on the back porch of his clapboard house. The yard was dusty and overgrown; he had no interest in gardening or in tending to the shrubs and flowering trees planted so optimistically by his wife when they first moved here more than twenty years ago. He was brooding as he stared through the screen door but he neither saw nor thought about the tall weeds and rampant ivies. His excitement had been short-lived: payment for the part he had played in the casket deal had come through that morning, but when he had opened it

359

he saw he had received only a token amount, less than a third of what had been originally agreed. It was enough to fund his trip and his part of the ancillary expenses, but barely so.

The sheriff was sore: he had made plans for the rest of that money. He had been screwed around, something to which he had never taken kindly.

What was more, it appeared that the newspaper had ignored his warning to butt out: within the past hour he had gotten reports from people who owed him favours in both Helena and Butte that the *Courier* was still snooping around. He had to watch his back: the Lord only knew what damage they could do to him if they tried. Or got lucky.

He wished like hell he could think of some way to get back at the guy in Helena who had gotten him into this mess with the drugs. Not only at him but at the *Butte Courier*. Not only at them but at the whole world. The more the sheriff thought about the fix he had been put in, the madder he got.

He heard the metallic drone of a small aircraft overhead, a little to the west. He looked up: the plane, in the red Treacy Resources' livery, was travelling south. It was not all that odd to see the company's aircraft in these skies but, as far as he knew, Treacy's logging and mining activities in the northwest were dormant. The company operated a 'rolling' vacation system for its staff whereby instead of a few men on each side taking different times off, entire sites closed down and everyone went on vacation together.

Could Treacy himself have gone back up to his lodge? The sheriff hatched an idea. He would have plenty of time to go up there and get back – it was only a matter of fifty or sixty miles.

He put in a call to the company's headquarters in Butte and asked for Daniel Treacy. He was told that Mr Treacy was taking a little time off, but if it was urgent, messages could be gotten through. Declining to leave his name, the sheriff hung up and grabbed his hat and gun. He hurried around the police car and got into the little Hyundai loaner he still had from Deke and Skippy, whom he had caught fiddling mileage clocks on some of their used stock and who were therefore most amenable to giving him anything he wanted for free.

Maybe something could be salvaged from the wreckage. Geese could sometimes be induced to lay more than one golden egg.

The journey from Yaak to her father's cabin, about six miles to the west, passed silently for which Sky was grateful. Larry, humming quietly to himself as he drove, had no idea what had happened between them back there on the verandah of the store.

'Here we go.' He pulled the 4-track off the road through a rough, ranch-style entrance arch made from three lodge pole trunks lashed together. An ancient mongrel hound lolloped forward to sniff at Sky's hand as she got out.

'You have a new porch.' She was pleased to have some material for ordinary conversation, although the porch in question was a shiny aluminium excrescence on the lovely wood from which the house had been constructed.

'Yep.' Her father swung out of the driver's seat. 'Me and old dawg here decided we were fed up with the wind whistlin' through the cracks in our front door, weren't we, dawg?' He fondled the hound's ears and then took Sky's bag from the back seat. 'Would you like a beer?'

The interior of the cabin was exactly as she remembered it. Warm, although not too much so, from the big wood stove kept burning winter and summer, the living room bristled with hunting trophies and artefacts. The huge stuffed grizzly, more than eight feet tall, continued to snarl from one corner. Fixed to the log walls, heads of other animals, moose, deer, racoon, otter, beaver, even an ancient buffalo, still glared. Up here, there was no point in being a bleeding heart on behalf of all the creatures who had donated these trophies – her father would have looked at her with incomprehension. The display of Native American wall hangings, everyday and peace pipes, bear claw and shell necklaces, even a tomahawk, would have done justice to a small museum.

She kicked off her plimsolls and luxuriated in the feel of the soft fur rugs on her bare feet. 'Is that new?' She pointed at a beautiful rawhide shield, hung with eagle feathers and decorated with what looked like a brightly coloured pyramid.

'It was a big honour,' her father said, almost shyly. 'I was presented with it at a Crow gathering last year.'

'This new too?' Dwarfing the serving bowls and jugs on the table by the cabin's window was an enormous CB radio.

'Must keep up with the times.' He smiled his long, slow smile and headed towards the kitchen.

'Business must be really good – it must have cost you . . .' She followed him as he opened the refrigerator and removed two cans.

'Yep. All those city businessmen going native for two days once every three or four years. Some of 'em wait ten years for a licence for one moose, you know.' He shrugged. 'Can't see it myself. And then when they get one, all they want's the antlers to bring back with 'em to put on the roofs of their four-wheel drives. Me and my neighbours up here don't mind, though. We sure do love passing that meat counter in the store!' He opened the lid of a big chest freezer beside the fridge. 'Look here.' The cabinet was packed to the brim. 'All wild.'

They took the beers outside and sat at a picnic table set up in a little clearing he had cut into the dense forest. Out here among the trees the coolness had a sharp green edge to it and the quiet was unlike that in the national forest around

Butte. There it crackled and hopped busily; here, where the trees were virgin, the silence was stealthier by far, as though the creatures all around knew that they must be extra quiet or get killed.

Although their meetings had been so rare, Sky had never before felt like a stranger with her father. Some of the scales through which she had viewed him all her life had peeled off her eyes at the Yaak general store, and the rest had fallen away in the past five minutes. In noticing the big CB radio it had hit her for the first time that he had never even telephoned her. It was a phenomenon she had somehow overlooked. Sure, he had paid what he could towards her maintenance and had remembered birthdays and Christmases now and then, even her high school graduation. Sure, he said he loved her, said it in the same affectionate tone he used when talking to his coon dog. Sky wished she had not come. It would have been so much nicer to have kept him intact in the fairy castle of her memories. With her newly awakened sensibilities she saw that Larry MacPherson's self-sufficiency was so all-encompassing it excluded her. Not only her, but all human beings. He did not need anyone.

'I've been interviewing Daniel Treacy.' She was unable to let the silence go on. 'He says his lodge is near here.'

'Not far – want another one?' He held up his empty can.

'No thanks.' She had barely touched her own. 'How far is it?'

'Oh, 'bout ten, eleven miles, right on the Idaho border.'

'It's closed up now, yeah?'

'So folks say. Guess I'll have another myself.' He stood up.

'Are you not curious about *anything*, Dad?'

A small frown creased his otherwise unwrinkled forehead as he looked down at her. 'Not especially – maybe things like how fast the snow plough'll get here after the first fall, that sort of thing.'

'How about people? Aren't you interested in people at all, Dad?'

'Sure I am. But people always mess up, don't they?' He looked at the beer can in his hand – enlarged and cracked from manual work – and then went inside to get the next.

Because she could not bear to fret alongside him, locked into inactivity while he remained oblivious of her feelings, she asked him to take her to see Daniel Treacy's hunting lodge when he had finished his second beer. To justify it, she bent her mind to the expedition in a journalistic way rather than with any personal interest – although now, with her grandmother in the picture, she had every reason for the latter.

The trip to Treacy's lodge took less than a quarter of an hour. They came to a big wooden billboard welcoming them to Idaho. Her father veered off the highway and drove slowly towards what seemed to be a large, spreading bush. 'Want to go right in?'

'Sure.' She was surprised he had to ask but still could not see any road. 'Driveway's 'bout a mile.' At the last minute, the foliage gave way and she could see the dirt track winding uphill away into the distance. The camouflage was masterful: the track was hidden to any but the most knowledgeable. Expertly, her father drove through the leaves so that not one touched either side of the vehicle.

In the *Courier* office, the junior's brain was whistling at her: it had not worked so hard in years. Her job was to call every public building in Butte – schools, churches, utility offices, banks, office buildings and apartment blocks – every single place that might have given a job to a black guy, even for a few days, to tend their incinerators.

The editor was out walking the streets and back alleys. And although in the course of an hour and a half he did not

364

find the man for whom he was looking, he did find something.

He was walking down Dublin Gulch when, passing the liquor store, he saw Sky's boyfriend, Greg Landos. On impulse, remembering the junior's mention of drink on the messenger's breath, he went inside.

'Hi, Jim, what can I get you?' He was surprised at the guardedness of Greg's welcome but did not give the younger man's coolness more than a passing thought. 'I'm wondering if you can help me?' Briefly, he described this quarry.

To his delight, Greg did remember something. 'Black, you say?'

'I guess so.'

The tramp had been in only once but during the few minutes he had spent in the store, he had picked a verbal fight with another man, an elderly janitor, who was one of Greg's more frequent customers. 'I threw them both out,' it was in Greg's nature to be helpful, 'but about an hour afterwards, I saw them both, the best of buddies. They were sitting on a bench together over by the civic centre. The old guy works there.'

The janitor was not at work that day but finding him was easy. Armed with his address, the editor drove off to Walkerville, a straggling continuation of Butte. The house was a tiny ramshackle two-up two-down in the shadow of one of the defunct pithead cranes. Only the outline of a door bell remained and flakes of rotting paint and wood showered him when he knocked on the door.

It was opened by an elderly man, no bigger than a schoolboy and wearing an oil-stained coverall. His breath reeked when he spoke. 'Not buying nothing today.' He went to close the door but Larsen put a hand on it, introduced himself and explained why he had come. 'I ain't seen that guy but the once.' The janitor tried to close the door again but Larsen persisted.

365

'I have to find him, Mr Schindler, it's very important. Have you any idea at all where he was headed?'

'He said something about Anaconda.'

After about half a mile, the dirt track into Treacy's lodge ended in a little S-shaped bridge, which spanned two tumbling loops of a deep, brown stream. As the 4-track negotiated the second of the bends, the forest suddenly opened out in front of them and Sky saw the house.

In the sumptuousness of its design and the external appointments, Daniel Treacy's so-called lodge rivalled his elevated mansion outside Butte. It was dominated by the rounded spine of the mountains, which, like a cyclorama, defined it and gave it majesty. Her father engaged a lower gear as they began climbing an arrow-straight road between a pair of lawns. At the crest of this hill, the house was set into a semi-circle of ornamental trees. Long, low, and roughly crescent-shaped, it was constructed of the same wood as her father's house but Sky had lived long enough in Montana to know that the difference between the two log cabins was about a million dollars.

The windows were shuttered and blind, however, and the entire place had alrady taken on the forlorn look of a house abandoned. Not completely foresaken, however, as a little Hyundai was parked off to the side. 'I guess he's still having it maintained.' Larry let the 4-track coast to a halt. He got out and stretched. 'Want to see around the back?

'No.' Sky wanted, more than anything now, to be alone. 'I think I'll go for a little walk in the woods, Dad.'

Her father leaned into the wagon and unsnapped a lock box under the back seat. 'Take this.' Pulling out a rifle, he checked the breech. 'You know how to use it?'

'I couldn't possibly—' Sky recoiled.

'Then I'm comin' with ya.' He shouldered the gun.

366

'Bear,' he explained, as though to a two-year-old. Sky laughed, inappropriately as always.

Around the back, the sheriff was in a quandary.

He had arrived at the house only minutes before and had gone straight to the rear, but with no automobiles out front or in the garages the place was obviously unoccupied. Then he had heard the engine of the approaching vehicle and reckoned he had not come up here on a wild-goose chase, after all.

He had debated whether to reveal his presence right away – his auto out front was a give-away that someone was here – but, on instinct, he hung back. Better to wait until Treacy was inside. Slowly, he made his way to a corner of the house and listened for his target to go inside.

Instead, as the sound of the engine died away, he heard two voices. To his horror, one of them was that reporter from the *Butte Courier*'s. He recognized it instantly: outside of public-service TV, how many women talked in that fruity, lah-di-dah way?

He heard the unmistakable sound of a gun being breeched, the voices again and then her laugh. The unmistakable laugh of a bitch.

It was that laugh . . . The sheriff had to hold on to the side of the lodge to keep himself from running after them.

His rage had been bottled up for many, many years. After a few hothead explosions when he was young, he had recognized that rage made a person lose control and control was what success was all about.

Internally, though, the rage had continued to ferment. Rage against the crooks and conmen who got away, sometimes literally, with murder because of smartass lawyers. Rage against his dumb ass parents, who had beat him senseless, against his ex-wife who had turned his kids against him. Rage

367

against the federal government, which was restricting the rights of American citizens in favour of foreigners, spongers and left-wing agitators. Rage against the rich, against men better-looking than he. And against the bitches who laughed at his attempts to seduce them so that he was reduced to sleeping with whores.

He had been able to channel some of his rage against the Brits who would not get out of Ireland. But now, for the first time in decades, on hearing that laugh the rage boiled over.

The sheriff shook as he held on to a down-pipe at the corner of the house; he shook so hard that he was afraid the gutters might come down around him but he knew if he loosened his grip he would do something stupid. He struggled to control himself. After a minute or two, he loosened his hold. The pressure of the down-pipe had rubbed his hands raw and they started to throb. Walking stiffly, came around the side of the house.

The 4-track was carelessly parked behind the Hyundai, three of its four doors open. Unconcerned that he might be seen, the sheriff walked over to it and raised the hood. He identified the wires and cables and then, as though he had all the time in the world, joggled and pulled at the front brake cables. His hands and forearms were strong and it was only a matter of seconds before they snapped loose. The Daihatsu had a dual-line system so he had to perform the same operation with the second set of cables that ran to the rear wheels.

He closed the hood and checked to make sure that fluid had not leaked out conspicuously from under the jeep, but if it had the raked gravel had absorbed it.

The sheriff got into his loaner and drove away.

By the time he had crossed the little bridge half a mile from the house and the forest had closed round him, the rage had ebbed away. He felt empty. And puzzled. Why had he done that? They had obviously seen the Hyundai; it would not be difficult to trace him.

He did not know why he had done it. But, somehow, it had been cathartic.

When he reached the end of the dirt track and was turning on to the highway, he was calm. Even regretful. Now he would have to race back to Mayville to return the loaner and to lean some more on Skippy and Deke. The sheriff sighed. There was no accounting for human behaviour.

Chapter Thirty-Two

'It's getting dangerous.' It was almost midnight and Rupert de Burgh was speaking from a telephone box at the corner of his suburban road. 'From the way they're talking I think they know someone's leaking. I may have to take the – ah – you know, out.' Although he always called his brother from different telephone boxes and not at his London flat, he was never less than circumspect. 'But don't worry,' he rushed to reassure him, 'they haven't a clue who it is. Our little device has served its purpose and we're still on course. Anything your end?'

'I've been thinking about this.'

De Burgh, who knew his brother like he knew himself, heard the unease in Toby's voice. 'It's too late to back down now.' He concentrated on projecting energy and authority. 'We're dealing in cyphers here, not humans, remember? That man is honorary colonel of the Paras, Toby. Remember what the Paras did that day in Derry?'

'I remember.' His brother's tone had dulled again.

'Talk to you soon. At the club, lunchtime tomorrow. Not long now. Try to get me some more information your end, like times, routes. You're clear about what you've to do the moment he takes off?'

'Yes.'

'Three different telephone booths, the same code-word. You have the numbers I gave you? You remember what the code is?'

'I'm not a child.'

De Burgh sighed. He was glad it was coming to a head. 'Think of history, Toby.' He tried to sound bright. 'Our place in history.'

When Sky's father braked about fifty yards before reaching the little corkscrew bridge at the bottom of the hill that led away from Treacy's lodge, nothing happened. The 4-track was not in top gear but was gathering speed. He swore, jabbing at the useless pedal, then crashed into a lower gear and pulled at the parking brake.

The engine screamed but the gradient was too steep for the emergency brake. They had one second before they entered the bridge, wide enough for only one vehicle.

'Hang on,' he yelled letting go of the brake and directing all his concentration into steering.

As Sky, petrified, gripped the sides of her seat, her father accelerated and they successfully negotiated the first bend on the bridge. He accelerated harder, sending the rev counter way into the red, but on the second bend, the rear fender struck the wooden guardrail, splintering it. The smell of burning oil filled the cab as, ignoring the impact, Sky's father pushed the vehicle to its limit and soared off the bridge with the needle of the rev counter stuck at the top of the danger zone.

Once through, he took his foot off the accelerator and let the vehicle coast to a shuddering halt about a hundred yards or so into the bumpy dirt track where the engine cut out amid clouds of swirling brown dust. He looked across at his daughter. 'You OK, darlin'?'

'Yes.' She could only whisper it. After the screaming and the terror, the rustling trees and little breeze were as loud in her ears as a pounding ocean.

'I just don't understand it.' Larry, who seemed relatively

unshaken, jumped out. 'This baby was serviced only two weeks ago. She's never given me trouble, not since I bought her. I hope I ain't burned her out.' He raised the hood and looked inside.

Sky, whose legs felt like rubber, fell out of the Daihatsu. The full horror of what might have happened dawned on her now and she felt sick. She went to the side of the track and sat on a soft carpet of moss and pine needles, bending her head to her knees.

'Would you like a drink, honey?' Her father was standing over her, 'I got a little flask of bourbon. Always carry it.' He fetched it and sat beside her. 'Who do you know drives a Hyundai?'

As she looked at him with incomprehension, he expanded. 'Whoever drove it disabled my brakes. Cables are disconnected, front and back, all the fluid's gone.'

'Can it be fixed?' Sky took a mouthful of the whiskey; it burned her gullet but the effect on her stomach was miraculous, almost instant. It was hard to believe that someone had deliberately caused the crash.

'I carry most stuff,' her father did not even sound angry, 'but not enough brake fluid to be safe. And the cables are damaged. We'll finish our drink and I'll call someone. Guy that sold me that Daihatsu told me for sure that telephone'd come in handy someday.'

Sky's fright yielded to anger. Who would dare to do that to her – to them?

The same person who had dared to have a bullet delivered to her mailbox, of course.

By Montana standards this place was not far from Mayville and it should not be difficult to prove who was driving a Hyundai right now. She was so damned furious she could not even remember her fear. 'Dad, when you make your telephone call, tell whoever's going to fix the brakes to bring pliers, rubber gloves and *new* cables.'

'What?'

'Fingerprints. It's a long shot, I know, but maybe not so long. And may I use your telephone before you call anyone?'

When she reached the *Courier* offices, the breathless junior told her that the editor was out looking for the man who had delivered the Folger's coupons. 'I'm assisting, Sky, but I can't stop to chat. I'm only half-way through my list of calls.'

'Thanks, Lindy. Get him to call me at this number *immediately* you hear from him.' She gave the Daihatsu's telephone number and made the junior repeat it back to her. Next she tried the War Bonnet for Lynskey, but he, too, was out. She left the number there too, and tried to impress on the receptionist how urgent it was that he call her.

The approach to Anaconda is dominated by the huge smelter stack that towers over the town. Not only that but, on arriving from Butte the visitor sees first not the wonderfully wide parkways, and houses neat as buttons, but an enormous slag heap, almost big enough to be called a mountain. The city, proud of its illustrious mining past, had turned it into a tourist attraction, selling 'bags o' slag' in its visitors' centre.

Jim Larsen had passed the slag twice, first on driving into the city, then on foot as he searched for anyone who had seen or heard of a black hobo wearing an indigo jogging suit. He was on the point of giving up when he decided to try the shops and coffee bars one last time.

He got lucky. An old lady, walker by her side, was sipping iced tea at a table in Donovan's restaurant, a long, narrow room dominated by the buzz and ring of gaming machines near the bar. 'Excuse me, ma'am.' He waited while the woman lowered her newspaper, which featured a large photograph of Princess Di on the front page.

'Yes?' Her voice was slow and quavery, as though she had had a mild stroke, but behind the glasses, her eyes were sharp.

Larsen launched into his routine of questions but this time, instead of the blank stare he had received so far, the woman pursed her lips. 'Yeah, I know the guy. He ain't here, though – he's working at a little bar up by Georgetown.' Larsen could hardly believe what he was hearing. 'I don't know, do I,' the slow pace of her speech was infuriating, 'but he was there yesterday. My son took me up to the lake for my birthday and I saw a guy like that take out the trash. I remember because you don't often—'

'I know, I know.' Larsen just wanted to get going. 'You don't see that many black men in Montana. Thanks for your help, ma'am.'

He ran back to his automobile, passing a telephone booth on the way and wondering briefly if he should call in to the office to see how the young dipstick had got on. Maybe this black man was not the right one.

He decided not to call until he had checked it out.

By the time Larry MacPherson and his daughter were arriving back at the cabin in the repaired Daihatsu it was almost nine o'clock. Sky had supervised the removal of the damaged cables. Then she had used the pliers to place them on the back seat of the jeep and planned to put them in a freezer bag as soon as they got into the cabin.

Since leaving her messages, she had tried both the War Bonnet and Jim Larsen's home several times and was agitated at the lack of response. She considered calling a cop acquaintance of hers at the station in Butte, but reluctant to let go of the story without consulting Jimbo, she decided to hold off.

She was also aware that she could not expect Lynskey to

call, at least for a little while: at about this time he was due to keep the appointment with the man called Matt.

Lynskey had been in the parking lot of the coffee shop for half an hour. But this time he was not working alone. With the seriousness of what was at stake, and with no jurisdiction here, he had informed his FBI contacts of whom he was planning to meet and why. Four agents, two to a car, had turned up but they were so conspicuous in their clean-cut suits and conservative haircuts that Lynskey despaired. If 'Matt' recognized what was afoot he'd take off straight away. And Lynskey had no doubt that this man was for real. His federal contacts confirmed that no calls had been made to or from the Helena man since early that afternoon.

The agents wanted Lynskey to let them take it from here but he convinced them that he would learn more than they would and they agreed to hold off until he gave them a signal. Now they were seated inside and Lynskey hoped that in the bustle they might somehow blend in: it seemed to be a popular venue, not only for local teenagers but for adults as well. Tourists, bikers, and motor homers were attracted to its vast parking lot and the free showers offered along with the steak dinners.

Before taking up his position he had studied the restaurant both inside and out, the washrooms, all entrances and exits, and as much as he could see of the kitchen from the dining area.

Now, as he lurked outside in the shadow of a giant Winnebago, he saw it was five past nine and although three lone men had arrived in the past twenty minutes or so not one had aroused his suspicion. One arrived in a pickup so battered that Lynskey doubted it could have made it even from Helena, another in a brand new Porsche he dismissed as being too attention-grabbing. The third drove a huge twelve-wheeler loaded with candy bars. The graphic picture on its side of two children tucking into chocolate, made his mouth water; he had not eaten since lunchtime. But then another vehicle arrived and Lynskey's antennae twitched.

The automobile did a slow, three-sided tour of the lot. When it was temporarily out of sight, Lynskey flitted over to the candy carrier which he had seen the driver leave unlocked and hopped into the cab. It was dusk and from up here could see the faint sweep of the newcomer's lights along the perimeter of the lot until, at the far side, they went out. He shrank down in the seat but resurfaced to get a glimpse of the automobile driver just as he pushed open the door to the coffee shop: medium height, probably middle-aged, dressed in the Montana uniform of jeans, check shirt and boots. Then the restaurant swallowed him up.

Lynskey counted slowly to ten and followed. He spotted 'Matt' immediately he got to the glass door. The guy was parking himself on a stool at the counter and, with the plastic-coated menu in his hand, was perusing the crowd. Out of the corner of his eye, Lynskey saw one of the agents sit up a little straighter as he himself came in and paused, looking around expectantly as if searching for his date. The man at the counter registered his entrance and passed over him without interest.

All the stools but one along the counter were taken. The man in the check shirt had taken a stool between two pairs of teenaged girls.

Lynskey strolled over. 'Excuse me – Matt, isn't it?'

'No,' the man replied shortly. 'You got the wrong guy. My name's Pete.'

'Is it now?' Although every instinct was telling Lynskey he had guessed correctly, the man's demeanour was perfect. 'I could have sworn your name was Matt,' he continued pleasantly. 'The voice is right anyhow. Although you never can tell, I suppose, with those answering machines.'

The man slid off his stool. 'I said you got the wrong guy, and I don't want to talk with you, now or in the future.' He turned on his heel but Lynskey was too quick for him, catching his arm and squeezing hard. 'Sit down there now, like a good man, I want to talk to you. You don't want a scene here, do you? Bring the police maybe in on top of us?' He was much bigger and stronger, and the man yielded. 'That's better.' Lynskey sat in beside him. 'Would you like coffee or what?'

'Forget it.' The man was watching him closely.

'Very well, I'll have a cup of tea myself a bit later on. Now, Matt, or Pete, or whatever your name is—'

The man jumped and ran towards the door but, as he did so, all four federal agents leaped up to intercept him. Heavily outnumbered, the man did an about turn and ran back towards the kitchen. Finding Lynskey again blocking his way, he brought up a knee, jamming it hard into the Irishman's groin.

Gasping with pain, Lynskey doubled over, knocking a stool and its occupant to the ground. The man veered past, pulling a small handgun from an inside pocket as he ran.

The four girls at the counter began to scream, as the FBI agents upset everything in their path in their rush to the kitchen.

Brandishing his gun, the man was still ahead of his pursuers. As he raced through the metal swing door an elderly porter, lugging a tray loaded with crockery towards the wash-up area, skipped aside but the overladen tray crashed to the tiled floor. The gunman lost a precious second as, skidding on shards of broken crockery, he struggled to keep his balance.

Now the agents were through, their own guns out. The fugitive grabbed a young busboy and put the handgun to the boy's head. 'Stay back,' he shouted at the agents.

Everything stopped. The three chefs stood transfixed. A waitress who had been putting mash on to plates let the scoop fall.

The terrified busboy, who was only about fifteen, was too shocked to cry out as, breathing hard, his captor backed slowly towards the doorway away from the agents.

One of them, however, inched forward. Putting away his gun, he smiled. 'We can work this out. Let the boy go.'

'Stay away.' The man pressed the gun barrel tighter to the boy's temple and continued backing towards the door.

In the restaurant, Lynskey, although winded, nauseous and still in fierce pain, half ran, half limped towards the entrance, grabbing a handful of cutlery as he went.

Outside, he inhaled a lungful of fresh air, which, if anything, seemed to make the pain worse, but helped his nausea a little. He limped around the side of the restaurant towards the kitchen exit, praying he was not too late.

A refuse skip stood a few feet to the left of the kitchen door and Lynskey stepped behind it. Almost immediately the door was pulled open and the gunman, with the busboy held across him like a shield, backed through. He was followed by one of the agents who had both hands in the air to show he was not armed. 'Come on,' he was saying softly, 'we can talk about this. Let the boy go—'

'Back off, back *off.*' The gunman was in control but more jittery than Lynskey would have liked for the boy's safety. He tensed, ignoring the pain which still radiated from his groin.

As the agent stepped free of the door and continued to hold the gunman's attention, Lynskey came out from the shadows and moved swiftly up behind him, jamming the heel of a spoon into the man's neck as though it was a gun. 'Drop it!' Simultaneously, he grabbed the gunman's wrist, twisted it, and the weapon fell harmlessly to the ground.

With a sob, the busboy broke free and ran screaming around the side of the building.

Two seconds later 'Matt' was on the ground beneath Lynskey and the agent, just as the other three FBI men came rushing round from the front.

Chapter Thirty-Three

At last! Sky, who had telephoned the War Bonnet so often she knew she was wearing out her welcome at the front desk, rushed to grab the telephone beside her father's CB radio. The caller was not Lynskey, however, but Jim Larsen. He had located the originator of their anonymous message and, while the man's grasp of detail was hazy, he was willing to swear that Midge Treacy's Volvo had hit his friend that night.

He and his friend had both been drinking earlier in the afternoon but no way, the man insisted, had either of them been drunk. They had been heading up the highway towards a barn where they would spend the night. After the accident, the black man had made himself scarce – the law always made him nervous. But when he had heard on the grapevine that the woman who had hit him was not going to be charged and that his friend was supposed to have died, drunk, on the side of the road, it had been too much for him. In Butte for a spell, he'd decided to do something about it.

'I have news for you too . . .' She told him about the brake cables and the Hyundai.

'That's going to be real easy to check.' Jimbo was elated. 'We have him, Sky. Well done.'

'Shouldn't we tell the police?'

'I already have.'

'Well, I suppose that means I don't have to go to Ireland.'

Sky could not decide whether she was glad or sorry. She had begun to get used to the idea and the trip, with Lynskey along, meant she could postpone any definitive thinking about him. It would be a different matter if he were to vanish across the Atlantic alone.

'It's not over yet, Sky – I'd bet you a million dollars. I've been talking to Lynskey . . .' Jimbo hesitated.

'The rat. Why didn't he call me? I've left two thousand messages for him at his hotel.'

'He's not at the hotel. He's actually gone up to Helena with a few of the FBI men. Turns out his warnings to you were well founded. I think I should let him tell you, though.'

'*Tell me, Jim.*'

She listened, dumbstruck, to how Lynskey had probably saved her life.

Sky was unable to sleep during the night of distressing self-discovery she spent under Larry MacPherson's roof. It was bad enough to have found her relationship with her father so wanting, but to compound her confusion Lynskey's long face and merry eyes were floating above her every time she woke. The guy was a twenty-four carat hero.

But still he did not call . . .

As she tossed around under the tumbled bedclothes, she tried to find a way to categorize what was going on between them. The sex had been terrific, there was no doubt about that – her body burned with the memory of it. Good sex, however, was a long way from love; it had been wild with her ex-husband – and look where that had gotten her – and with Greg it had been good too, almost up to the end.

In the depths of that night, Sky's lifetime of sexual encounters paraded before her one by one, and pretty pathetic they had been, starting with the fumbles in the backs of T-Birds and beat-up Chevys during high school and college. The more sophisticated couplings during the early years of her career had been even emptier.

The greater proportion of those encounters had led to what she had thought then was falling in love. But her heart had been too quick and needy and the boys and young men to whom she exposed it had always been scared off. Until Randy came along. After him, she had put her wall of bricks in place.

She had gotten by perfectly well without love for most of her adult life and she had a lot for which to be grateful. She had her career which, although it had its downside, sure beat working in an office in Detroit or Chicago or, perhaps, as one of the army of women realtors who showed condos and split-level houses to couples who could not afford them; she lived in one of the most beautiful parts of planet Earth, with some of the best winter skiing on her doorstep, no pollution and a relaxed lifestyle. She did not need to be in love.

Fergus Lynskey, however, had made a mess of her carefully constructed defences. Extraordinarily she had not recognized this at the time: the progress of the realization had been like a slow burn, smouldering on even through her anger at his deception – not to speak of his bossiness. She ground her teeth with frustration: she was not mad at Lynskey any more but being in love with him was out of the question.

And yet, at three o'clock, four o'clock, five o'clock in the morning she did want to be in love with Lynskey. By six, though, when the alarm shrilled on the nightstand, she was afraid again. She looked at the grey-faced, tousle-haired wreck in her father's bathroom mirror and wanted to hide. From everything and everyone, from this editor who expected too much, from this father who expected nothing. Did she really want to run from Lynskey as well?

Suppose she did not run, her uncooperative reflection suggested. Suppose she trusted him and let him in? But suppose it did not work and he abandoned her? Anyhow he lived in Dublin, Ireland, she lived in Butte, Montana. Convenient that. Really nice. 'You're a goddamned mess, R. Sky Mac-Pherson,' she harangued the mirror, 'do you know that?'

The sheriff of Mayville was shaving. Although his feeder flight to Denver, via Billings was not due for take-off until early afternoon, he had always been an early riser because he slept badly.

As he regarded himself in the speckled mirror of his rundown bathroom, he was trying to retrieve the feelings of well-being he had enjoyed just twenty-four hours earlier. But that had been before his underpayment had arrived, before he had fixed the brakes of that 4-track. Idly, he wondered what had happened after he left. Had the vehicle gone into the little river? He must make enquiries. Then, he remembered that he would not have time for that today, and cheered up: only a few more hours and he would be off on the adventure of a lifetime.

The bell rang and he peered out through the bathroom doorway. Outlined against the glassed upper half of his front door, he recognized a colleague. What could he want at this hour of the morning? 'Just a minute, Ed,' he called.

Hastily wiping foam off his face with an old towel, the sheriff stepped into his pants, which were draped over the side of the tub and, still in his T-shirt, suspenders around his hips, went to answer the door. 'This is a fine time—' he began, before he was hustled out onto the porch by FBI agents, who read him his rights and handcuffed him. The sheriff knew enough not to bluster or to deny. Instead, he asked if he could be allowed to put on a sweater.

Minutes later, in the car, he offered to cut a deal.

*

Two hours after the sheriff had been driven away, in front of the splendid public library in Helena, another man, seatbelt on, direction light flashing – everything legal – was pulling out from the kerb into the flow of the morning traffic when two cop cars screeched up beside him. In Chicago, a third was apprehended as he walked towards his automobile in the driveway of his house in the suburb of Park Ridge; a fourth, waiting for his prescription dramamine, was taken out of the line in front of the pharmacist's high counter in a drug store in New York; a fifth was lifted as he answered the door of his house in Nashville, Tennessee; a sixth as he was dropping off his grandson at the local high school on his way to Dallas airport.

Three more members of the group named by the sheriff of Mayville were temporarily missing, although American agents called at both the homes and places of work of two: one, who was a cop in the LAPD, would be easy to trace, but in Santa Barbara, the plumber, Joe Mason, was not at home. Single with no dependants, no one kept tabs on him except for his answering service, which had recorded no callouts for him that day.

At Jerry Flynn's huge spread north of Calgary, Alberta, the Mounties came up empty too. Because, in the small Immigration area at Dublin airport, the Canadian was standing in the long line for people holding passports issued outside the European Community. Of course, he was no longer Jerry Flynn but the rather scalded-looking John Mulqueen.

He had arrived in Dublin four hours late. After check-in at New York the airline announced that the flight had been delayed due to technical problems and, although the lounge was comfortable and he had even dozed a little, he was tired. He had not been informed that there would be an hour's wait at Shannon before the twenty-minute flight to Dublin.

Momentarily forgetting that he should be blending into the background, Flynn reverted to type and became irked at the delays, and at having to stand in line for so long. And he was also irritated that there was no special treatment for first-class passengers in this dumb holding pen. He was fed up with having to listen to gabby Americans jingling coins in the pockets of their easywash pants and complaining about the way they did things in Europe.

Most of all, he was annoyed that his money and status seemed to count for nothing in the land of his ancestors.

He realized he was second next and snapped to. The American at the desk in front of him was still in full flow: 'Why don't you get more people on? Only two of you for two full 747s, for God's sake.'

The official was patient. 'It's beyond our control, sir. One of the flights was late.'

'Yeah, but Jiminy Christmas, look at this . . .' The American waved at the line snaking behind him.

'I apologize for the delay,' the immigration officer was unruffled, 'but I'm afraid we're short-staffed these days. Enjoy your stay in Ireland.'

Flynn's mouth dried as his own turn came at last. He touched his breast as though to reassure himself that the proclamation he would read for the world was still intact in his inside pocket then dropped his hand quickly in case anyone should notice. No one did, apparently. 'Good morning, sir,' the official opened the passport, 'and what is the purpose of your visit?'

'Just a va-vacation.' Flynn smothered his nervousness with a cough.

'Nice time of year for it. The weather's not too bad at the moment.' The official turned a page in his Suspect Index Book and ran an eye through it. Flynn's heart started to thump.

'How long are you planning to stay?'

'About three weeks, I reckon.' At least that had come out good and strong.

'That's grand.' The official closed both the book and the passport and handed back the latter. 'Have a pleasant holiday.'

He was in.

He took the public bus into the city centre and booked into a small hotel by the bus station in a rundown part of the town.

Half an hour later, which was much later than it should have been, because holiday time was aggravating the chronic staff shortage in the public service, several new names and passport numbers were inputted into the Suspect Index Book which was frequently updated by the Department of Justice. Flynn's name was on the list, along with that of a policeman and a plumber, both from California.

By that time, 'John Mulqueen', wearing beige polyester pants and a new windcheater in serviceable navy, middle-range Pentax hanging around his neck, had merged with the throngs in the streets of the capital and was strolling along Talbot Street towards O'Connell Street and the personal mecca he had heard and read about all his life: the GPO in Dublin, scene of the Easter Rising.

The only name not confirmed to the FBI by the sheriff of Mayville in his bid to save his own skin was that of Rupert de Burgh. The sheriff still nurtured hopes that, being on the spot as the Irishman was, if he could evade detection the plan could somehow go ahead. And, like the rest of his group, the sheriff refused point-blank to divulge any detail of the plan or the motivation behind it.

Because she was so tired and stressed, the parting of Sky and her father that morning was quick and without the resonance

386

she might have expected after the trauma of her disillusion-
ment. As he drove her back to the airstrip, he seemed again
to have little need to talk or to have the smallest inkling of
what had passed for ever out of the relationship between
them.

Sky could not imagine now why she had wanted to talk
to him about anything to do with her life. After she had
blurted out that she had 'met a man', he had not brought it
up again and neither had she. 'I'm sorry about your brakes,'
she said tentatively, when they were only a mile or so from
the airstrip. 'That was because of me.'

'Forget it.' He smiled his easy smile. 'But it looks like
reportin' is a much more dangerous game than I thought.
Be careful in Ireland, won't ya?' She could see, though, that
his mind was already miles away in his beloved wilderness.

The aircraft was on the runway when they pulled in
beside the Nissen hut. Larry put her bag in her hand and
hugged her. 'Bye now, sweetpea, have a great trip. Love
ya!'

'I love you too, Dad,' she replied automatically as she
hugged him back, then broke away to race to the waiting
plane. Looking through her porthole window as the little
craft took off, she saw that the Daihatsu had left.

She had no time to brood as the trip was short and, from
the moment she landed, the rest of the day took on a
kaleidoscopic quality.

She half-expected Lynskey to be at the airport to meet
her and felt vaguely disappointed when he was not. The hell
with him, she thought, and yet, perversely, she longed to
talk to him. Nevertheless, she put off calling and took a cab
home.

To her surprise, the duplex was empty although it was
not yet eight o'clock in the morning. She checked her
mother's room and the bathroom: both, although neatened,
showed evidence of having been used overnight. Sky decided

she could trust her grandmother's assurances that she could look after herself. She was probably at the hospital.

In fact Sky's grandmother and Daniel Treacy were in Choteau.

To Daniel's surprise, she had agreed with alacrity – 'Everyone should try everything at least once' – to his proposal that they should take a helicopter to save time.

'Maybe this was a mistake.' He watched her carefully as they walked from the lawn at the far edge of the grounds where the chopper had put down to the sanatarium building. The staff were expecting his visit so there had been no problem with the security, which was usually tight.

'Of course it's not a mistake. Daniel, only young people make mistakes. People like us just live what's left of our lives.'

'Afterwards, if you like, we can go down into Choteau itself. It's very pretty.'

'That'd be nice but this is pretty enough.' She looked around appreciatively and, seeing it through her eyes, he had to admit that the architects of the Teton sanatarium had chosen their site well: the single-storey complex was shingled with weathered cedar and blended seamlessly into the greens and golds of the prairie. This countryside was not spectacular like Yellowstone or Glacier: rather it was airy, rolling in wide swathes to the western foothills. It was the type of landscape that had lent Montana its affectionate nickname of Big Sky.

Daniel was nervous about seeing his wife. When he had tried to work out why he was bringing Elizabeth up here, he could come up with only a visual image: that with death imminent, it was necessary to bring ends together, or to close off a circle.

Although he was endeavouring to keep it from her, he was not feeling well this morning and, as they walked slowly

388

towards the facility, was having to struggle to breathe normally: perhaps the end was even closer than he had thought.

'Are you all right?' She stopped. 'Are you in pain? I can hear you wheezing.'

'I'm fine, never better.' He attempted to smile but the pain did threaten now: it rumbled like a gathering storm, and he could see he did not fool her.

'Let's sit for a moment.' She looked around for somewhere suitable. 'Over here.' She took his arm and led him towards a raised flowerbed, the front of which was grassed. 'Sit down, Daniel, we've all the time in the world.'

As he lowered himself gratefully on to the coarse, spongy material which passed for grass in this part of America, memories of the soft, velvety grasses of his childhood in Ireland swarmed unbearably into his mind. 'I know I promised I wouldn't be maudlin, but since you came here, Elizabeth, I can't stop thinking of all those years ago on Béara.' Even as he spoke he regretted the words. He was afraid he would scare her off.

But she came to sit beside him and folded her hands in her lap. He had remembered her as restless and always moving, but in the years since he had seen her she had learned the art of stillness. 'We can talk all you like, Daniel, and about anything you like. So long as you know that what was between us is long over. It's not gone, it's just locked away in time. Like those lovely sapphires you gave me: what was alive in them, what made them beautiful millions of years ago is now sealed in there and cannot change or grow any more. Do you understand? I hope I'm not hurting you.'

'You're not hurting me, Elizabeth.' He looked at her lovely, tranquil face and wanted to cry: 'You can't imagine how happy I am right now.'

But the gods caught him in hubris and the pain struck

like thunder. Although he strove hard not to grimace, she saw it. 'Have you your painkillers with you?'

'I'm afraid I've taken as many as I'm allowed,' he gasped. 'I probably need an injection—' He doubled over as the spasm ripped through again, so powerful and all-encompassing he could not have located its site.

Alarmed, she half rose. 'Daniel—'

'Hold on, it'll be over in a minute.'

A third one. But then the pain rampaged away, leaving him weak and bled of energy. 'I'll be fine now, honestly,' he panted as soon as he could find his voice. 'This is the way it is these days.'

'You should be in hospital, Daniel.'

'No.'

She saw there was no point in arguing and did not pursue it.

They were about two hundred yards from the parking lot beside the first building of the complex and, although they could see leisurely activity as people came and went, they could hear nothing except the swift hullabaloo of a bee, gone as quickly as it came, and the faraway, oddly muted twitterings of birds that served only to emphasize the delicate susurration peculiar to wide, quiet spaces.

Although he was weak after the battering from the pain, he found courage. 'Look, I've never apologized for your husband, Elizabeth.'

She would have none of it. 'It was all a long time ago. Please, Daniel, don't rake it up. We were all young and silly – at least, you and I were.'

'I have something for you.'

That upset her even more. 'You've given me enough. And I want nothing at all.'

'It's just something I'm giving back, really. It never belonged to me in the first place.' From the inside pocket of his jacket he extricated the silver case containing her family photograph. 'I've carried it with me everywhere but now I've no need to any more.'

'Where did you get this?' She had opened the case and was staring at the picture.

'I spent a fortune tracking down negatives through contacts in Ireland, but in the end, I did what I should have done right from the outset. I asked your daughter.'

'Johanna gave you this?'

'Don't be annoyed with her, Elizabeth. I'm afraid I put a lot of pressure on her, and she's a lovely, soft-hearted woman.'

When she asked, then, why he was giving it back, he told her that it should be obvious. 'I can't take it with me to the grave, can I? And, anyway, the real you is now stamped for ever in my heart – don't stop me talking like this, please.' He had seen she was about to try.

He gazed at the coarse grass, matted from too much care and feeding. He was not afraid to die, but the prospect of leaving her behind, now that he had found her, flooded him with almost unbearable sadness. 'Don't stop me saying what I feel, they're only words, Elizabeth. I don't have time now for anything but the truth.' He thought he might have gone a step too far and risked a glance at her, but she was staring away, towards the shimmering sea of automobile roofs in the parking lot. There was something else he had to say and now was as good a time as any. 'Did you mean it when you said we could talk about anything?'

'Yes.' It was as though she knew what was coming.

'I've made certain arrangements.' He gazed at her profile, acutely conscious of the overpowering, musky scent from the carpet of wallflowers in the bed behind them. If she gave the slightest sign of abhorrence or upset, he was ready to stop. 'I've a stock of certain drugs in my house.' As far as he could see, she betrayed no adverse reaction. 'When the time comes, will you be with me?'

'You're not asking me to . . .' Still she watched the cars.

'No. I just want you to be with me.'

She dropped her eyes to her hands, still folded calmly in her lap. 'What about the legalities?'

He had been expecting that. 'I'll make absolutely sure you're not implicated.'

'Can you?' She looked at him then, almost surprised. 'Is that within your power?'

'I've thought it out, and I've talked to an attorney who knows about these things. You won't be anywhere near when I actually take—'

'Please don't say any more.' She blinked hard. 'I'll do that for you, Daniel.'

'I think it will be soon.' When he felt strong enough, she helped him up and they continued towards the sanatarium.

Chapter Thirty-Four

Once unleashed, the full might of US authority swept through not only the sheriff's *ad hoc* group of conspirators but also the more formally organized and more mercenary band who worked for the Oriental woman, formerly of Vancouver.

Once he had been overpowered at the coffee shop, the woman's Montana lieutenant was driven from there to the FBI office in Helena. There, on being told his boss had taken flight, he had seen no reason any longer to be either secretive or chivalrous and gave enough information to engender pre-dawn swoops on previously unknown houses in Anchorage, Los Angeles and Orlando. The FBI's sister force in Mexico had organized a similar raid in Mexico City.

In Ireland, to the chief superintendent's relief, the cattle smuggler had been intercepted on the ferry by one of their own men before disembarkation on to British soil – thus avoiding the humiliation of having the Brits do it and having to go through the rigmarole of extradition.

After that small triumph, however, they were no nearer to finding the drugs. The controller steadfastly refused to reveal where they were hidden. He would neither confirm nor deny any of the names put to him. The skipper of the *Agnes Monica* and the funeral-home owner who had claimed the coffin had also been arrested but were playing similarly dumb.

*

As the demoralized Irish police demanded greater resources to handle their growing problems, a seaplane touched down on the shallow, cobalt-shaded sea which surrounded Santa Tomás, so named by its new owner.

Between the Dos Abrolhos archipelago and the Brazilian mainland, from which it was less than ten minutes' flying time, the island, which appeared on no international map, comprised only three hectares of trees and scrub. The small beach, however, which was shaped exactly like a cockleshell, boasted sand of the consistency and colour of talcum powder, while the artesian well, which the Oriental woman had had bored, offered reliable fresh water. Regular as a metronome, rain fell every afternoon in February, enough to ensure a year-round supply. Except for that one month, the island's climate offered nothing but sunshine, sunhsine and sunshine.

As the seaplane coasted to a halt, a powerboat set off from the shore and the pilot threw open the door to the warm, slightly sweet sea breeze.

As she waited for the launch to arrive, the woman could see her house. Of modest size, but constructed from the most durable and expensive materials available in Brasilia and Rio de Janeiro, it was set back a little from the edge of the beach and surrounded by shade palms. To the right and left of it were similar buildings. The first was the servants' quarters, the second the storehouse, which also housed the generator; the third and largest served as hangar and boathouse.

For the first time in her life, the woman felt she had a real home, somewhere she could spend the rest of her days in comfort and solitude, unharried. Especially by such bothersome documents as extradition warrants.

The visit by Daniel Treacy and Sky's grandmother to the former's wife was depressing. They found Midge alone in her room, and when Treacy made angry enquiries, he was told the paid companion had quit. At least, it was assumed she had quit: when she had not turned up for work and the manager of the facility had telephoned the motel in Choteau where she had been staying, he had been told she had left in a hurry and with no explanation.

Midge, who was still under heavy sedation, could not have cared less who was with her. Only semi-conscious, she showed no interest in either her husband or the woman he had brought along. Instead, she moaned incessantly while mouthing a litany of words which meant nothing: *egg salad, trees in the middle, total wipe-out, black without walls* . . .

'I'm sorry,' Treacy whispered. 'I'm truly sorry. I don't know, now, why I brought you here.'

'You brought me because you brought me.' Sky's grandmother took his arm. 'She must have been a beauty in her day.'

Treacy looked down at this raddle-faced woman with thinning hair and cracks at the side of her mouth. 'She was.'

The woman in the bed sighed noisily and rolled her head from side to side: *shame and the old stuff, millions, trillions, twenty-five and little bread and butter* . . .

'Don't upset yourself, Daniel.' She touched his arm.

'People liked her, you know.' The face he turned towards her, already ravaged from his illness, was tragic. 'She was gentle and kind underneath it all. Poor Midge.'

They walked back to the front door in silence but as they emerged once more into the sunshine, they saw a police car. A young officer, pink with embarrassment, got out. 'Mr Treacy?'

'Yes.'

'I'm afraid I have to ask you to come with us, sir. There are a few questions.'

'Am I being arrested?' Treacy looked from the youngster to his companion and back again.

'No, sir, it's just a few questions.'

The businessman slumped visibly, then, recovering some-what, 'If I give you my word that I will report to the Butte police station within one hour, may I take my friend back to the city? She's a visitor and – forgive me, Elizabeth – ' he smiled briefly at her ' – quite elderly. I have a helicopter.'

'I don't know, sir.' The young policeman glanced ner-vously towards his colleague who was standing by the automobile.

'Call in,' Daniel suggested. 'Ask your superior officer. I'll tell you what – here's my wallet as security.' He took it from his inside pocket. 'It contains not only cash but all my credit and charge cards.' He smiled a little. 'I won't get far without them.'

Both policemen visibly shrank from the proffered wallet. 'Do what he says,' the older one ordered. 'Call in.'

Treacy's word was accepted, without the security of his wallet, and he and Sky's grandmother walked slowly back to the helicopter.

Sky was trying to persuade Teddy Morzsansky to search the files – behind his employer's back – without telling him why. 'Trust me, Teddy. Remember we pledged each other, senior year?'

'That's below the belt, Sky.'

'Yeah. Come on, Teddy, just this once.'

He did what she asked, most unhappily, but when he called her he was reeling. Nothing remained of Midge Treacy's records in the files of Collins Brothers' Funeral Home. 'I can't understand it. Nothing like this has ever happened before and Melinda keeps *meticulous* files. I can't even find a copy of the invoice for the casket. This is extraordinary, Sky. What's going on?'

'Tell you later, Teddy.' Sky was not surprised he had come up blank.

This had made him more curious still and she had had to improvise. 'I thought, since I'm going to Ireland, I might do some research on a book I'm thinking of writing. You know, the Irish in Butte, that sort of thing? I have to dash, Teddy. Just remember not to tell Bill Collins I asked you to do this, OK? Or even Melinda. It doesn't seem proper, somehow, Mrs Treacy being so recently dead and all . . . But if you do come up with something, if you remember anything you might have seen or overlooked, will you let me know? Jimbo Larsen will have the number of the place I'll be staying at in Dublin.'

'You owe me a big one for this, Sky MacPherson. Have a good trip.'

Her grandmother arrived back at the duplex just as she hung up. Sky was struck by how subdued she seemed. 'You've been at the hospital, Grandma?'

'Not yet, dear. I was hoping you'd drive me.'

Sky changed her mind: She was more than subdued, she was sad. 'Sure I'll drive you, but are you OK? Where have you been?'

Sky listened as the old lady told her what she was sure were 'edited highlights' of her visit to the Choteau sanatarium, and was simultaneously getting on with her ironing, putting the folded clothes directly into the suitcase at her feet. Then something her grandmother said clicked into sharp focus. 'What was that, Grandma? Mom gave him a photograph?'

'This one.' From her purse, the older woman pulled out a flat silver box, like an old-fashioned cigarette case, opened it and passed it across the table.

Sky knew the photograph, but it was not that which made her purse her lips. She remembered Johanna's sudden flight to see Freda Little Calf when the subject of Daniel Treacy had first been mentioned. Her confusion when she returned. Now it was all clear as day.

When she and her grandmother got to the hospital later in the morning, however, she had not the heart to tax Johanna with it. Her mother, although still immobilized, proved fully alert and more cheerful than Sky could have thought possible.

Overnight, the room had been turned into what could only be described as a shrine: candles, their flames dim because it was full daylight outside, had sprouted like stalagmites from the windowsill and the bedside locker; favourite snapshots were grouped on top of the TV where she could see them easily, a huge pot of amaryllis scented the stuffy air, and over the bed, instead of the hospital-issue spread, was draped Hermana's fringed Indian shawl, which glowed with the colours of a peacock's tail. 'Isn't it wonderful, Sky? I'm so privileged.' In the middle of it all, Johanna, who could not turn her head, beamed like a lighthouse. 'No pain. Not a twinge.' Swivelling her eyes, she aimed a brilliant smile towards Buffy who was sitting beside the bed. 'My lovely friend here went all the way to the reservation to fetch a herbal infusion from Freda Little Calf and it has worked wonders. You're amazing, Buffy. Do you know how much I value you?'

'Oh, hush.' Buffy's pleasure showed through her embarrassment. 'You'd do the same for me.'

'Did you check with the doctor before you took it, Mom?' Sky had long suspected that Freda Little Calf's concoctions had less to do with medicine than with hallucinogens, an impression borne out now by the glitter in her mother's eyes.

'Oh, pooh! Of course we did, didn't we, Buffy?'

'They're quite understanding here,' the other woman reassured Sky. 'Your mom's specialist works up at the reservation hospital. He knows what's in most things and he says that as long as we tell the nurses so the conventional drugs can be adjusted, there's no problem.'

Sky let it be: Johanna was lucid and happy, so who was complaining? If Freda Little Calf's potion could make her smile like that while it took away the physical discomfort, why not let her have it? 'I don't want to change the subject, Mom, but Grandma has just gotten back a certain photograph . . .'

'What photograph?' Johanna looked genuinely puzzled and Sky suddenly had no desire to continue. Maybe she had grown up some in the last few days, but the emotional tension between her and her mother seemed to have evaporated. And she had a hunch it was not simply as a result of their separation since Johanna had been in hospital. She had no time to analyse it now, though. 'It doesn't matter. Grandma'll tell you.

'I'm sorry I can't stay long.' She placed a bunch of yellow roses on the bedspread; in the face of the Bliss Sisters' loving and opulent care, her contribution seemed inadequate. 'I'll put these in water before I go, but is there anything else you need?'

'Not a thing, dear. This accident has been such a blessing. I know now how loved I am. Just imagine, Buffy,' again she turned radiant eyes on her friend, 'my mother coming all the way over here. And we were just saying before you came in, darling, that I couldn't have a nicer daughter, isn't that true, Buffy?' Back to Sky: 'And guess what, Sky? Francey called the hospital. He's told them to send all the bills to him. And Buffy and Hermana say I should let him pay because he can afford it, so I'm going to. Can you believe it? Everything's perfect, I'm so happy.'

'Oh, Mom,' Sky could have wept with guilt, 'it shouldn't have taken an accident to make you feel loved.'

But of course it had. And that was what had changed between them.

Hermana came in then to relieve Buffy, and a little later, Sky kissed her mother and left the hospital with the *bon voyage* blessings of all three Bliss Sisters ringing in her ears. 'I'll see you later, Grandma – will you take a cab?'

'I will, yes.' There it was again, that note of ineffable sadness.

It was as she was getting into the Nissan that Sky realized she had not mentioned her visit to her father and not one of the women had asked.

On the way back to the duplex, she zipped into the office of the *Courier* to pick up the passport and new charge card Jimbo had had delivered. 'Oh, Sky,' the junior breathed, eyes like saucers, 'you're lucky you missed it here yesterday. It was incredible. You wouldn't believe the number of telephone calls I had to make – and isn't it wild about Daniel Treacy?'

'What about Mr Treacy?' Sky, who had been practically running down the room towards the editor's office, came to a swift halt.

'Didn't you know? He's been arrested. Oh, and there's a message for you from Mr Lynskey. I wrote down the number, he's in Helena.'

Arrested? Before she could consider this, Sky punched out Lynskey's number.

All he wanted, however, was to make sure they were on the same flight out of Minneapolis that evening. Hearing his voice, and with so much having happened since she last spoke to him face to face, Sky felt oddly shy. 'You heard about Treacy, I expect?' deliberately brisk.

'It's just a formality.' Lynskey was cheerful as always. 'The guy's not going to be charged with anything – despite what he thinks everyone knows his days are numbered. Anyway, he's a victim rather than a perpetrator. Take it from me, he's more than likely on his way home now.'

'That's good. Hey, Lynskey, I hear you're auditioning for Superman.'

'Perfect. You, of course, can be my Lois.'

'Seriously, congratulations. You were right and I was wrong about last night. I'm sorry.'

After a pause he was back. 'Come on, MacPee. Don't spoil it. I can't stand good losers.'

Behind the jocularity she could hear uncertainty. 'What's the matter?' Glancing at the junior, she lowered her voice. 'You can give it but you can't take it? I mean it. I'm sorry.'

'Apology accepted.' Again, that uncertain pause. 'I'll talk to you on the plane.'

'See you, then!' Smiling, she hung up and then collected the stuff from Jimbo. Then she was on her way.

Daniel Treacy went straight home from the police station. He was feeling vile: his medication was overdue. It had been humiliating to be confronted like that in front of Elizabeth – and it had brought back fears and memories he had thought long since banished. At least she had promised to come to the house for dinner. He felt so tired and low that he planned to take a long nap between now and the time he would have to shower. He would order in – he knew she would not mind. And food for him was academic now anyhow; the medication was so strong he found it difficult to differentiate between tastes, even the spiciest of foods. Everything tasted of metal.

He let himself into his chilly, beautiful house and climbed the stairs, each step of which felt like a mountain. At least he would be dead before he was reduced to the indignity of installing a stair elevator to reach his bedroom.

He sat on the side of his icy white bed, breathing heavily, feeling every insidious little cancer cell travelling and multiplying and eating into every part of him. He could visualize them chomping and masticating and spewing out bits of him and deciding which organ they would feast on next. Death would come as redemption. He had not been lying when he said he did not fear it.

He had been lying about something else, however, during that blessed time when Elizabeth sat in his garden room surrounded by flowers. He had told her that now he had found her again he did not mind dying. It had been the cliché of the century, prepared for the eventuality that she would not feel the same about him as he felt about her.

And so it had proved. But he could not be 'civilized' or 'mature' or 'adult' about this. The knowledge that she did not return his love caused him such keen agony it rivalled the pain of the cancer. He was not happy to die, to leave her. Now that he had found her again, he wanted to cleave to her, for her to cleave to him. At rock bottom he did not care whether she wanted him or not. Given time, he could probably have led her into seeing she did love him, after all.

But, of course, time was the one luxury he did not have.

His stomach contorted with such acute pain that he cried aloud. He had been taught to take fast, shallow breaths during these spasms, rather as a woman is taught to do in labour. He curled up on the bed and started to count the breaths – one – two – three – four – five – six – seven – eight – from experience he knew that by seventeen the spasm usually waned – fifteen – sixteen – seventeen –

He waited but, instead of abating, the pain intensified. He grabbed his bottle of pills from the night-stand and shook two into his mouth, swallowing them with a mouthful of saliva. The pain became worse. He forced himself to start panting again, to start over, almost hallucinating now: one – two – three – four – five – six – seven – eight – nine – ten – eleven – By twelve the agony was banding his chest with white-hot steel and sending a rippling sheet of it through his

402

upper arms and into his neck . . . his jaw . . . his head. Thirteen –

It was happening now. Please, not yet . . . It was happening too soon, too soon . . . She was coming to dinner. One – two – three – four –

He grabbed again for the pills but could not reach them.

In stretching, his entire body seemed to rip open. He curled up as tight as he could, trying to contain the pain but it was too late. The pain had won. One – two, one – two . . . He screamed aloud. One – two –

Then something, fireworks maybe, detonated all around his face and exploded through the back of his head.

Daniel Treacy died at one fifteen in the afternoon. His body, coiled in the foetal position on his blood-soaked bed, was found just after eight o'clock. His eyes were wild and staring; his mouth was wide open and contorted; both his fists were clenched. In each hand, like a fat white rose stained with red, bloomed a handful of the silk spread that covered his bed.

That night the paramedics, who lifted him off his bed and cut away the silk, opined to their wives that he must have had a most terrible death.

It was certainly the loneliest.

Sky's grandmother came home from the hospital to say goodbye and, at the last minute, on impulse and much to the old lady's delight, Sky clasped on the sapphire necklace, not caring if it looked incongruous worn with a white silk shirt and Levi's. 'I'll keep it on all the time I'm in Ireland. It'll be my good-luck charm.'

'Don't let Daniel see it,' her grandmother warned. 'I wouldn't like him to be hurt.'

Outside, Sky heard the honking of the cab horn and

threw her arms around her grandmother's neck. 'Goodbye, Grandma, wish me luck.'

'You know I do.' Her grandmother hugged her tightly. 'You're a lovely girl and I'm very proud of you.'

'Are you sure you'll be OK here without me?' Sky stood back.

'Your mother's friends will probably not let me alone for a second.' Her grandmother smiled. 'And I told you I'll be spending a lot of time with Daniel. I'm going up there for dinner tonight. To tell you a little secret, Sky, I might even stay over. Just one night. What harm can it do? I know I said I wouldn't but it would make him so happy. Don't tell your mother, though, will you? She mightn't approve.'

'Mom? Not approve?' Outside, the cab horn sounded again. 'I have to run. Enjoy the dinner – don't do anything you wouldn't want the baby Jesus to see!'

Her grandmother laughed. 'Get away out of that – you'll be late for your plane.'

Chapter Thirty-Five

Sky was half an hour out of Minneapolis that afternoon when she finally allowed herself to believe she was on her way to Ireland. She checked her watch: five o'clock.

Jimbo had been true to his word, utilizing his contacts to the fullest so that not only did she have a brand new passport and charge card, she had been upgraded from economy to business class. Now, as she sipped her drink in her wide, plushy seat in the upper deck of the 747, it was like a source of both guilt and satisfaction to her to know that, somewhere down the back, Fergus Lynskey was having to jam his knees under his chin.

She had no seat companion, which was just as well because it was a long flight and she could not have borne to have to talk to some stranger. She had forgotten to bring a book and, although she had been offered newspapers and magazines, had decided that for once she would relax and do nothing. She stared through the window, identifying shapes castles, a whale, a roller-coaster, a crouching rabbit – in the dense clouds below.

Thirty-six thousand feet above the ground, she was even more nervous than she had been when trying to assimilate all the information Jimbo had thrown at her. At long last she was getting the chance she had dreamed about, but now that she was staring down at it, it was terrifying. There was no going back – not after all the moaning about how frustrated she had been for the past eight years. She prayed that she wouldn't make a mess of the story – and waste all the *Courier*'s money into the bargain.

To reassure herself, she placed her drink in the little indentation on her seat tray and reopened the wallet containing all the contact numbers Jimbo had given her with a summary of what she was supposed to remember.

She still did not know, however, what she was to look for when she landed in Ireland. On the telephone, this Éamonn Vaughan character had been pleasant and sympathetic but more than a little baffled; although he knew about the drugs connection – he was working on it right at the minute – he seemed unaware of any other big story brewing in Ireland that might also involve players from Montana. It was clear that he was not aware of the FBI's second wave of arrests and she did not tell him.

Yet Jimbo, who had clearly been taken by the guy, had advised her to confide fully in him. 'You'll find you can trade with him what you know for his contacts. He'll have the best in the business and I'd be willing to bet he'll share with you. You'll be no threat, being foreign.'

Vaughan had been intrigued and had agreed to meet her. That was a start.

Lynskey held the key to the story, both she and Jimbo knew that. She was to stick to him like a leech. 'Use your feminine wiles,' he had been quite serious, 'after all, he used you.' Jimbo, great newspaperman and all round good egg, had never been insightful when it came to affairs of the human heart.

'You never told me how you got on with your father.' Sky, drowsy with the airline's alcohol, opened her eyes to find the Irish policeman plumping comfortably into the seat beside her. 'How did you get up here?' She did not know whether she was pleased or sorry to see him.

'The lovely Sherrilyn down the back in steerage said I

406

could come up to visit you.' He was again his cocky, flippant self. 'I told her you were my fiancée—'

'*What?*'

'—but that I was just a struggling musician and your lousy company wouldn't pay for me to go with you on your business trip. I told her we had only recently become engaged and that I couldn't bear to let you out of my sight even for a few hours.' He grinned. 'Want to join the mile-high club?'

'*Lynskey!*' Sky looked around involuntarily in case he had been overheard, but all the other passengers were either wired into their headsets or dozing. 'You'd no right,' she expostulated.

'I know. Ain't I the limit? That's lovely on you.' He became serious and touched her necklace. 'It goes really well with your eyes.'

'Thanks.' Sky stroked the sapphires: they felt as smooth as butter.

Lynskey activated the foot-rest on the seat and stretched his long legs with a contented sigh. 'This is sure the way to go.'

'You'll have to go back to your own seat now, sir. We're about to serve dinner.' The steward, who clearly didn't approve of social climbers, was standing in the aisle.

'In a minute.' Lynskey brushed him off.

'Now, sir,' the steward insisted.

'Listen, pal,' the Irishman's voice was low and intense, 'I shall go back to my seat in a minute.'

Something in his eye quelled the other man who, never-theless, leaned across him, 'Excuse me, ma'am,' and flour-ished a linen cloth over Sky's dinner tray. 'We're serving *right now*, sir.'

'I'll be back,' Lynskey whispered, 'or maybe you could slum it with me for a while?' Before he could say any more, the steward arrived with the hors d'oeuvres, serving fork and spoon raised above his tray. Lynskey stood up. 'I'll see you later.'

As Sky watched him lope towards the staircase that led to the lower deck, Jimbo's instructions returned to haunt her: 'Use your feminine wiles . . .' She knew it would be impossible.

The seventh co-conspirator in the Bodenstown plot, the man from the Los Angeles Police Department, was being hauled down to the station in LA just as the eighth, Joe Mason, was pulling himself together for disembarkation at Amsterdam. Like the ninth, Jerry Flynn, Mason was travelling under an assumed name and with a forged passport. Although his sight was perfect, the photograph showed him wearing glasses.

Now, as the captain of the KLM jet applied his brakes after landing, Mason scoured his eyes as though he was rubbing sleep from them and put on the glasses. The frames were of nondescript dark plastic and the lenses were a little scratched, as though well worn.

Of the ten originally involved in the plot, only three now remained operational: Mason, Flynn, who was safely ensconced in his seedy hotel, and Rupert de Burgh. And of these three, only the last knew what the prize really was.

The Taoiseach of Ireland, thinner than his love of good food and fine wine warranted, took a tissue and rubbed at a dried water-drop that had marred the gleaming surface of his desk. A man of fastidious personal habits, he worked until no trace of the stain remained and then, task completed, he folded the tissue in half before depositing it in the wastebasket beside him.

The others in the room, two civil servants and two advisers, a secretary and the Minister for Justice, waited for him to speak. He had less than two hours to decide whether or not to give the go-ahead for the republic's visit from the heir to the British throne. The previous night the visit was about to be declined on advice from the Department of Justice but then, at the Taoiseach's personal request, a stay had been put on the veto until lunchtime today.

It had been in Brussels, during an EC dinner, that the Irish Minister for Foreign Affairs had been sounded out informally by his British counterpart about the Prince of Wales's desire to pay a visit to Dublin for the Amnesty conference. The issue was so sensitive that the Irish minister, not telling even his most trusted advisers, had come straight to the Taoiseach's office on his return. Still only a few were aware of it – the two politicians present, the Gárda Commissioner and one or two others. Up to an hour ago even the civil servants in this room had not known. Now, with only twenty-four hours to go, the decision had to be made.

No member of the British Royal Family had made a formal visit to Ireland since independence in 1922, although some had slipped privately in and out of the republic, to attend horse shows or to visit distant relatives. An appearance by the heir to the throne, however, was a different matter. Although technically it would be a private visit, the conference was high profile, especially with Naboom Kebele coming, and there would be no question of the Prince's presence being unobtrusive.

The stakes were high: despite the IRA and Loyalist campaigns which continued to roil on in the North, behind the scenes relations between the British and Irish governments had improved steadily during the Thatcher years, a momentum which looked set to continue under John Major. This was a sensitive time: it was beginning to dawn on some leaders of the nationalist community in Northern Ireland that perhaps the way towards what they wanted lay not in violence, which, over nearly a quarter of a century, had produced nothing but more violence, but in democratic means. The Taoiseach had to weigh up whether the Prince's visit, even in a private capacity, would enrage Northern nationalists to the extent that this small opening in the blank wall of despair known for so long as 'The Troubles' could be closed over again.

Like most politicians, who would happily claim public credit for a week of sunny days, he was inclined to look favourably on the idea. Opinion poll after opinion poll had reaffirmed that the British Royal Family continued to be a source of fascination to many in the republic and there was no doubt that this visit would spawn acres of newsprint. Yet, the consequences of anything untoward happening to the Prince while he was in Ireland were unimaginable: the Taoiseach's party could probably wave goodbye to domestic power for a very long time, not to speak of the loss of international prestige.

He cleared his throat and looked round the room. He was kept informed about the progress of the investigation into the conspirators discovered in the United States. So far, those captured had not revealed anything much but, like his advisers, the Taoiseach tended to agree that whatever the plotters were about could have had nothing to do with the Prince.

In fact, the whole thing was a mystery: it seemed to make little sense for people with ultra-nationalistic leanings to want to harm the nationalist seat of power. Yet, in the Taoiseach's experience, no one ever went broke underestimating the cock-eyed fervour among certain far-out fringes of Irish-America. 'What do you think?' His eyes caught those of his Minister for Justice. 'I'd let it go ahead but I'll be guided by you. You say most of these so-called plotters have been rounded up?'

410

'Seven at last count.' The Minister for Justice lowered his voice as though they were being overheard. 'Two more probables have temporarily gone missing. Five so far, would you believe, are cops or ex-cops.'

'Doesn't surprise me.' The Taoiseach flicked at a speck on his Boss suit. 'With seven out of it I'd say they've collapsed. What's your best guess, Minister? Is it safe or is it not?'

'Well.' The minister hesitated and then cheered up. 'He's only going to be here for a couple of hours. We can fly him in and out of Baldonnel,' naming the military aerodrome twenty miles from Dublin, 'and sure didn't even His Holiness manage to get in and out of here without a problem, and millions around him all the time?' The Pope's visit to Ireland in 1979 had been the highlight of the minister's life. 'I mean, what can happen in a couple of hours?'

'Fantastic – *fan-fuckin'-tastic*.' Jill Tuffy, the organizer of the Amnesty seminar at which Naboom Kebele was to be the star speaker threw the telephone receiver back on its cradle. She was so excited that she got up and jigged around the floor.

Amnesty was in serious fund-raising mode. Her invitation to the Prince had been one of those four-in-the-morning inspirations which, in the cold light of day, had seemed so unlikely to bear fruit that she had not nurtured even the slightest hope of his acceptance. But as days and then weeks went by without rejection, she had let herself dare hope the tiniest bit. And then the barrel had started to roll.

She sat at her desk, making herself calm down. The instructions were specific. Only four named people were to know that the Prince was coming. If a single advance word appeared in the newspapers about it, the whole thing was off.

How to get around that one was the problem . . .

There had been considerable local interest in the confer-

411

ence from predictable sources: all the worthy Irish news-papers were sending representatives. But Ms Tuffy had a wider constituency in mind: she wanted a conference sexy enough to attract the world's media. She had been jubilant when Kebele had accepted, but then appalled that the international take up of press invitations was almost nil. Only *The Economist* was sending. Global media was looking to Eastern Europe and the election run-up in America. Africa, poor old starving, dying, warring Africa, was now old hat.

She thought hard. The only way to get them here without jeopardizing the Prince's appearance was to do a selective leak about a surprise guest. And if one bit, they would all bite – afraid to be scooped. She lifted the telephone. 'Hello, RTE? Newsroom please – Éamonn Vaughan . . . Thanks – I'll hold . . .'

At the Natural History Museum of Ireland, half a mile away, the reaction to the Taoiseach's call was more muted.

The awed man who took the call from Ireland's Prime Minister gathered his thoughts sufficiently to say that the museum's director was in Iceland, 'But I think I know where he's staying and I'll try to get him back.'

When he hung up, he stared at the old-fashioned black telephone on his desk as though it had rabies. Then he went to the door of his office and looked down at his two-hundred-year-old-domain, which slumbered quietly in a cramped narrow building between the Dáil and Government Buildings. Generations of schoolchildren and their parents had thundered and tramped along these tiled floors and wooden staircases, marvelling at the giant deer and the whale skeleton, suspended from the roof, horrified by the bullet hole in the skull of the polar bear, thumping the elephant and stroking the giraffe, or recoiling in disgust at the insects pinned to paper or the tentacles of the octopuses in glass jars. So old-fashioned and untouched was it that it was now world-famous as the best nineteenth-century cabinet museum extant: a large proportion of the collection, which had grown to encompass over four million specimens, had been donated in 1857 by Livingstone himself and was preserved intact. Naturalists and zoology students loved the place and, in the teeth of modern museum display science, begged that it be kept exactly as it was. Apart from a major clean-up and a yellow paint job on the walls a couple of years previously, they had been granted their wish.

In this man's lifetime the museum had never had a state visit from any important dignitary – none that made him or herself known, anyway. The problem with this one was that it was happening tomorrow and that the newspapers had been more than a little premature in touting the Eskimo curlew exhibit. With the cutbacks in public service biting hard, the staff, reduced now to four – which meant that the ratio of people to specimens was one to a million – were behind with everything: the top gallery, which housed the invertebrates and the priceless Blaschka Collection – hand-made glass reproductions of marine specimens – had had to be closed off to the public for lack of personnel.

Perhaps they might be able to rustle up a modest exhibit, he thought gloomily – a *very* modest exhibit: although the museum had the two birds, the documentation and habitat material was far from ready. All stops would have to be pulled out.

The man went back to his desk and reached for the telephone to begin the process of locating his director. He brightened a little: after years of neglect – it was all archae-ology these days – it was nice that someone was taking notice of the lovely old place.

*

Jill Tuffy was on her second call, to a reporter in the BBC television newsroom who had only recently moved there from RTE. 'No, I can't tell you, I really can't. The papers aren't to hear a word of this, do you understand? But, believe me, if you're not here you'll miss out on one of the stories of the century.' She listened, then, 'Have I ever given you a bum steer before?'

She sat back, satisfed. Whatever about Éamonn Vaughan, she knew the BBC reporter, who lived with a *Guardian* sub-editor, could not keep a secret to save her life. They'd all be here tomorrow evening.

Chapter Thirty-Six

Sky's mental image of Ireland, fed by the Irish Tourist Board and her mother's sepia-toned memories, had not prepared her for Dublin's modern, swarming airport. The culture shock was intensified as she and Lynskey made their way into the city by cab. This was not the city of posters, where tourists clopped through misty, elegant squares in horse-drawn carriages or strolled hand-in-hand across a graceful, lacy bridge. Instead, this was a city where gridlock threatened, which seethed with crowds, preponderantly young, and where people took unleashed dogs with them into the centre: the cab narrowly missed killing at least two which, kamikaze-like, darted across the street through the traffic.

Having come prepared with sweaters and raincoats, the bright sunshine, as hot as it was in Butte, was another revelation. Lynskey agreed the weather was uncharacteristic, which was confirmed by the number of sunburned shins and shoulders she saw under shorts and sleeveless dresses.

She sweltered in the back of the little Volkswagen cab, and debated crossly whether she would be better off with the window open or shut since each offered roughly equal horror. The outside air was choked with diesel fumes and the hot, acrid smell of melting tar, not to speak of dust from a plethora of roadworks and building sites. To add to the ambience, Gardiner Street, which seemed to be the main artery into the centre from the airport, was in the process either of being demolished or rebuilt along its entire length:

the thunder of pneumatic drills competed on par with roaring bus engines. When she closed the window, however, the heat became intense and she almost choked on the smoke from the front of the cab as the driver, despite a prominent notice on his dashboard thanking her for not smoking, puffed away like a crematorium chimney.

Sky knew she was tired – and irritable because of it – and decided to suspend judgement on Dublin until she was in a better mood. As they inched forward through a monumental traffic jam at a complex series of junctions and bus stops near the bottom of the street, she glanced across at Lynskey, who, head lolling, was dozing. Why should he sleep while she suffered? 'I could do with a shower. How about you?' She dug him in the ribs.

'Are we home?' He started awake and looked around, his eyes clouded with sleep, then: 'Ohh,' he jerked a finger over his shoulder, 'that *is* where I live. I've an apartment on the top floor.'

Sky looked across him at the five-storey, brick-built block, neat as a set of egg-boxes, on the other side of the street. 'Nice.'

'No need to be sarcastic.' He smiled and closed his eyes again. The plan was that he would drop her at her hotel and go on immediately to a briefing – or a debriefing – session at his office.

It was coming up to lunchtime and the newsroom at RTE was hopping. 'Hold on, I'll transfer you to his extension.' For the umpteenth time that morning, the secretary pressed four buttons and hung up.

'Yes?' Two desks away, Éamonn Vaughan, who had been battering his keyboard as though his life were at stake, snatched up the receiver as it rang. 'What?' He put his left hand over his ear, then, to the people nearest him, 'Would you keep it *down* there, please!' and into the mouthpiece, 'Sorry about that. What was that you said?' He listened, then, 'I see.' Thoughtfully, he replaced the receiver. It was the second so-called tip-off in as many minutes. And the subject matter of both could not have been more unconnected. He gave credence to anything that came from Jill Tuffy but the second caller had been anonymous.

On the previous night's *Nine O'clock News*, Vaughan had broken the story about the botched drugs operation and chaotic follow-up investigation. The morning papers had seized on it with glee as the Guards continued to chase their tails up and down the country. The anonymous informant had told him that the drugs could be found buried in the grounds of a Glengarriff hotel. Glengarriff was in the extreme southwest of Ireland: almost the full length of the country lay between it and Killybegs.

After a few seconds, Vaughan got up and trotted off down the length of the newsroom – he never walked anywhere – towards the security correspondent. 'Bella, who's the best person to talk to about a tip-off in this drugs affair?'

'Me.' She looked up, frowning.

'Yeah, you.' Vaughan did not smile. 'I know that but give me a name, not the Minister, not the Commissioner, certainly not the chief super in charge of the investigation. Someone who'll co-operate with us in return for information.'

'What information? You're encroaching on my territory, Éamonn.' He had gazumped her with the drugs story on last night's bulletin, and she glared at him. 'At the very least we should be sharing the information. At the last chapel meeting—'

'Sorry I asked.' Vaughan turned and hurried back to his desk. He thought again then, reluctantly, put a call through to RTE's Cork office. He was as ambitious as anyone but the story always came first. If the tip-off was accurate and the police were already on the way, he could not possibly get to Glengarriff in time to film. Better that a camera be there than not, even if he was not behind it. 'Be sure and call me back, even if there's no activity.' He said goodbye to the reporter in Cork and checked his watch. Now he regretted having to meet that woman from Montana. He had far too much to do.

Turning his thoughts back to Jill Tuffy, he pulled a piece of paper towards him and quickly, stream of consciousness, scribbled names of famous figures and world leaders who might pose a security headache. The more outlandish and the more unlikely to attend an Amnesty International conference in a little country like Ireland the better: Yasser Arafat, John Major, Mother Teresa, Saddam Hussein, Robert Mugabe, Nelson Mandela, the Queen of England, President Bush . . .

Vaughan was still adding and subtracting names as he and his crew travelled to the city centre hotel for a news conference. By the time he arrived, he had it down to three, John Major, Yasser Arafat, Moshe Dayan.

As he was walking into the Shelbourne, he reconsidered: John Major had been in Dublin for a European summit the year before so his presence here was no big deal. But this depended on what he was going to say – and a British leader on Irish soil was always a prime target for subversives. He put a question mark beside the Prime Minister's name and decided to begin his quest with the British embassy, if for no other reason than to eliminate him.

The conference was late starting and, taking advantage of the delay, he went to a quiet place in a corner of the foyer to begin making his calls.

The Prince of Wales was walking around a car-components factory, being shown a machine which was pressing little

418

discs out of a river of grey metal. He uttered appropriate words of fascination and was shepherded to the next stage of the process where the little discs were falling in a sort of waterfall and being lined up so that holes could be punched through them.

As the entourage moved along the production line, a palace functionary moved forward and murmured something in his ear. The Prince's expression did not change but at the end of the line, the managing director of the plant was told that, unfortunately, the Prince would not be able to stay for lunch. Within minutes, the directors and staff found themselves saying goodbye to their visitor on the helipad at the side of the plant.

The Prince's diary for tomorrow was blank. Officially he had a day off. In reality, it had been left clear for the possible trip to Ireland. Now that this was a going concern, the palace and Foreign Office officials were anxious to get working. Each syllable of each word – indeed, each emphasis on each syllable – uttered by His Royal Highness during the few hours he would spend in Ireland would be pulled apart and scrutinized by all sides. Although he would be speaking to the Amnesty constituency, the historical significance of his visit could not be ignored. It was still to be decided if he would say anything public during his courtesy visit to the Irish Dáil. And if so, what.

The officials, in both Britain and Ireland, did know that they had to build a visit to the Natural History Museum into the schedule. In the Prince's book, the attraction of seeing an Eskimo curlew was irresistible. Fortunately, the museum was right beside Irish Government Buildings.

Rupert de Burgh knew that the story would break sooner or later about the Prince's visit but it suited him for the moment to keep it from his co-conspirators. Given their depleted

419

numbers, the scale of what they were unwittingly planning might intimidate them. He wanted everything so far advanced that it would be impossible to pull out. His Semtex devices were ready and he knew where he was going to deploy them. The locations would be made secure in advance, like all areas the Prince was to pass through, but this was where he himself would come in. His operation hinged on whether he could get himself assigned to that security detail and, so far, he saw no reason why he should not be able to swing it.

Laying his hands on the explosive had been simple. Under the guise of police research he had sourced it through an ODC – Ordinary Decent Criminal – in one of the Dublin gangs which had contacts with the IRA and who, he knew of old, would keep his lip buttoned. Anyway, de Burgh knew the chances of himself surviving unscathed were not high. At the very least, he was sure of gaol so whether the ODC kept quiet about it or not, *after* the event, was irrelevant.

Never a great sleeper, the previous few nights had been so disturbed that he was having to resort to drinking copious quantities of coffee and eating lots of sugar to keep himself going. Yet this had its drawbacks since he could not appear jumpy or nervous with his colleagues. The effort to behave normally was a strain, and even his wife, who rarely noticed much and to whom he knew he was a puzzle, had asked him that morning if anything was wrong.

He had avoided any serious conjecturing about what it would be like to go to gaol, to leave his family. Whenever the prospect entered his head, as it had a moment ago, he forced it away. He did not want to weaken. The Cause that had obsessed him for so long was omnipresent, like his own shadow; it had taken over the places in his heart that he knew other men reserved for their wives and children. De Burgh's motivation was higher and finer than mere personal gratification. To him, the Damascus conversion he had undergone, when he went to Trinity and learned the truth about Irish history, was as profound as a vocation for the priesthood.

Although he was fond of his children, and the youngest boy in particular, he had long ago ceased to love his wife – if he had ever loved her in the first place. She was quiet, with a calm disposition which, he felt, had a great deal to do with lack of imagination. She had been a clerical assistant in a government department when he had met her at a Gárda Club dance at a time when almost everyone in his immediate circle was getting engaged. Hating her job, she was surrounded by friends showing off diamond solitaires and clusters on their ring fingers, was eager to marry – and happy to find someone interested in her. After marriage she settled into bringing up their three children efficiently and without complaint.

Wearing his Walkman, de Burgh wrote busily, stopping occasionally to chew the end of his pen, or to consider. What the others in the noisy room did not know, of course, was that his personal stereo was tuned to the tiny transmitter still stuck to the underside of the chief superintendent's desk. Bill Daly was in session with the Gárda Commissioner. He had asked Lynskey to be present.

Through his earpiece de Burgh heard the tinny ringing of Daly's telephone, and the chief answering. Then, 'Thanks for the call. No, no comment at present,' being across the desk from the bug, the chief's voice was a little indistinct, 'but we'll certainly follow it up.'

'That was RTE.' The chief spoke again. 'A reporter in Cork asking us about an anonymous tip-off Éamonn Vaughan got in Dublin. Same tip-off about the drugs being buried in Glengarriff which was telephoned anonymously to de Burgh – he's one of my men here.'

Down the hall, de Burgh bent his head as though he could not read what he had just written on his pad.

'Are you taking it seriously?' This was the Commissioner, who was positioned right over the device and whose voice boomed as if through the cello stops on an organ.

'Are you joking?' Lynskey, viola, quite clear too. 'The same anonymous tip-offs, one to us, one to the media? Glengarriff's the last place I'd be looking for those drugs. I'd be much more interested to know who's making those calls and why he wants us to go down there.'

De Burgh's knuckles whitened around his pen. It had been a misjudgement to ring Vaughan: the only mistake he'd made so far. But it was not insuperable. So they wouldn't go to Glengarriff. Although he did not have much time left, he would find another way to keep them thin on the ground in Dublin. The Gárda overtime ban still threatened and although it was not seriously affecting anything yet, with the swelling crowds in Dublin city, would be bound to within the next twenty-four hours.

'De Burgh, wake up!' To his intense irritation, Rupert saw rather than heard the other man standing in front of his desk. Pointing at the headphones, the detective mouthed, 'Take those things off,' as though facilitating a lip-reader.

'What is it? I'm busy.' De Burgh lifted off one of the earphones while trying to follow the conversation in the chief's office through the other.

'You're wanted on the downstairs public phone.' He was already walking away. 'The fella said it's important – he sounds American. And he's on a public phone himself so he can't hold on all that long.'

Rupert had no choice but to go. He took off the headphones and slipped them around his neck as he left his desk. It would be too much to walk through a nest of detectives and not expect them to wonder at why he needed to listen to music while walking down a corridor and into the front hall to take a telephone call. It had to be Flynn:

few people in Ireland could tell the difference between American and Canadian accents.

And it had to be an emergency. All of them had that number only for emergencies.

While he was on his call, the atmosphere in the chief superintendent's office had become leaden. 'You know as well as I do,' the Commissioner had put on his grave public voice, 'that we have to keep up the pressure.' All three men indeed knew it, and so did everyone in the country, because of the Justice Minister's personal crusade against drugs. 'With the amount of bad publicity we've had in the past few days,' he added, 'we've got to at least be *seen* to be doing something.'

'It is my considered opinion,' Lynskey butted in again, 'in fact I feel very strongly, that we should not take this tip seriously about a hotel in Glengarriff. Let RTE go off. If they find heroin buried under some fuchsia bush there, well, they'll have their scoop and it'll be a bonus for us. These tip-offs are either hoaxes or an orchestrated attempt to get resources as far away as possible from Dublin. I don't think it's a coincidence that someone is trying to move us just at this particular time.'

'For once I agree with this man here, but it's up to you, Commissioner.' Bill Daly folded his hands and waited.

The Commissioner thought for a minute or two, then picked up his gloves. 'On your head be it. If RTE finds the stuff we'll be made to look fools. About that other thing, at least make sure you've crossed every T. I know what they've rounded up in America and although my inclination is that they couldn't possibly know about yer man coming over here, I'm still uneasy.' He looked at a spot on the ceiling over his subordinates' heads. 'I'm long in the tooth and I

423

know when something feels wrong. Apparently this plumber fella has done this before – vanished, I mean. But the other one who's gone missing, Flynn, he has so far been a model Canadian citizen. I hate model citizens, you know. They're always the ones to watch. Going through the passport records for every departure from the United States to Europe – assuming he didn't necessarily fly directly in here – is taking a great deal of time.'

The Commissioner ceased his examination of the spot on the ceiling. 'If it was up to me this visit would *not* be going ahead and I've strongly advised against it. In the name of God,' he shook his head, 'how can we manage it all? Kebele, the Prince of Wales – and the town hopping with rogues, pickpockets, all these conventions and dancers and tourists? And Bodenstown in the morning as well. But, then again, I'm only a humble policeman.'

'Could we circulate a photograph of him, sir? Flynn, the one we know?' This was Lynskey. 'I took one of him.'

The Commissioner looked from one to the other. 'Do that, I suppose – not that it'll do much good. He's rich, apparently. He's probably had a face-lift.' He stood up, as did the others, then slapped the desk with his gloves. 'Between ourselves, gentlemen, your man's visit here is going to be a political three-ring circus. They want to parade him like a prize bull. Which I suppose he is.' He smiled for the first time since he had entered the office. 'Geddit? John – Charlie – Bull?'

'Very droll, Commissioner.' Lynskey did not dare look at Daly. 'Just one more thing, sir. What about our canary?' He stifled a yawn. 'With those two still not accounted for, and since all the raids took place at exactly the same time, is it possible they were warned? The only reason I bring it up is I'm wondering if the telephones here are bugged.'

'They couldn't be.' The chief superintendent involuntarily reached for the instrument on his desk and then withdrew his hand. 'Certainly impossible in here, no one has access to this office. I lock it every time I leave it.'

'Not even cleaners? The oldest gag in the book?' Lynskey raised a cynical eyebrow.

'Have the whole place checked,' the Commissioner interjected. 'Phones, computer terminals, everything, even the light-bulbs. And question all the cleaners, particularly part-timers. It's unlikely but taking the worst case scenario, if you *are* being listened to, have you said anything in here about . . .' He hesitated, then, 'Operation Omega . . . I damned well hate that. Sounds like a bad film.'

'The only time the name was ever used in here, Commissioner, was when you yourself used it not five minutes ago.'

The Commissioner stared at the chief superintendent as though trying to ascertain whether or not he was being subjected to insubordination. Then he drew on his gloves. 'Sweep the place and put off telling people for as long as possible. Just make your plans and put everyone on standby. No names until tomorrow morning. Until then they can be told it's John Major or someone – use your own judgement. What time is the strategy meeting?'

'Eight tonight.'

'I'll be there. Let's hope the press don't hear about it before tomorrow.'

Downstairs, it had turned out that Jerry Flynn wanted to tell Rupert de Burgh nothing he did not know already and the detective could have strangled him. This was what came of getting involved with geriatric idealists who had never before put a foot in the country. Constrained as he was by his surroundings, however, he had to watch not only his tone but his body language.

Jerry Flynn, or John Mulqueen, was calling from the bus

station. He was expecting Joe Mason, due in on a flight from Amsterdam, to arrive at the hotel any moment. 'Unless he's been arrested too. We can't do our work with only the two of us, Mr de Burgh.'

'We won't have to. I haven't heard that there has been any problem with that, but thanks for the call, Mr Mulqueen.' For the benefit of passers-by, he tried to sound cheerfully normal. 'Leave it with me.'

Flynn got the message. 'The reason I'm calling is to tell you that the flight was on schedule. And to check that the meeting is still as we arranged. Three o'clock?'

'As is. Don't worry. Thanks for letting me know, Mr Mulqueen, I'll be in touch as you say. Bye now.'

Before the Canadian could say anything more, de Burgh cut him off and raced back up the stairs. As he passed the chief superintendent's door, he nearly collided with the Commissioner who was just coming out of the office. 'More haste less speed, detective.' The Commissioner was not amused.

Chapter Thirty-Seven

Sky's initial impressions of Dublin city had changed already. Her hotel turned out to be a small private establishment located between two Georgian squares on the south side of the city where the traffic, although still heavy, was at least not intimidatingly so. Here, too, though, the pneumatic drills were hard at it: it seemed nowhere in the city was safe from them.

The receptionist in the little foyer was apologetic about the noise. 'It happens every summer.'

What was more upsetting was the reason for the drilling: apparently the water mains were being repaired and the hotel's supply was temporarily cut off. 'It couldn't be happening at a worse time for us.' The receptionist redoubled his apologies. 'All our rooms are full – the city is crammed to bursting point with visitors this weekend. But they promise we'll have normal service by six o'clock. In the meantime we've put a jug of water and a basin on your dressing table, madam, so you can at least have a wash after your long journey. And please take this with our compliments.' With her key he gave Sky a little card on which was written the name of a hairdresser's, just round the corner. 'They'll send the bill to us.'

The room was comfortable, if a little too lacy and flower-sprigged for Sky's taste, and it had a direct dial telephone and TV. She unpacked quickly and, as much as the limited water resources allowed, brushed her teeth and washed. Her appointment with Éamonn Vaughan was not for another two and a half hours and, too wound up for a nap, she decided to avail herself of the hotel's offer: with the long series of flights and the heat, her hair felt unpleasantly oily.

The hairdresser's, on the second floor of one of the tall Georgian houses, was small and busy, but they could take her if she was willing to wait for a few minutes. While she sat in the tiny, overheated reception area, Sky selected the only Irish magazine she could find from the publications on offer, although it was almost six months out of date. And she almost missed the fact that it was Irish because, oddly, the cover picture was a paste-up of Princess Diana and her husband who, superimposed on one another, were staring glumly in opposite directions. She was curious to see them used as a lead here: it had not occurred to her that, given the history of the two countries, the Irish would be interested. She opened the magazine but the article was standard stuff about marital difficulties, mostly speculation, and, to her experienced eye, compiled from features already published elsewhere: paragraphs about Diana's bulimia and lightweight tastes in music contrasted with Charles's more solitary pursuits of ornithology, an interest in nature and painting watercolours. Sky was turning to her horoscope to see if what it forecast six months ago might have been accurate when she was called to the washbasin.

She felt much better when she emerged again into the sunshine and, with ninety minutes still to go until her appointment with Éamonn Vaughan, she decided to take a walk.

She got no futher than a lovely little park, where among the flower beds, office workers in their lunch-break lounged around on emerald coloured grass to listen to a poetry reading. The atmosphere could not have been more different from that of the city centre during the cab-ride in from the airport. Although the top storeys of the terraced houses in the square were visible on all four sides outside the railings, and if she listened hard she could hear the muted sound of engines, the poet, who was standing on a grassy hillock which provided him with a natural platform, needed no amplification and had to compete only with birdsong.

A bearded man in his thirties, with large, hypnotic eyes, he read love poems that spoke of secrets and dark longings, which did not seem incongruous beside the brilliance of the sunshine and the holiday poses of his listeners. Gritty-eyed, disorientated from fatigue and jet-lag as she was, Sky was enchanted and almost forgot she was on assignment.

She left, reluctantly, about half an hour before her one thirty appointment with Vaughan. Along the way she called into a bank to change her dollars into Irish currency. The girl behind the counter was helpful and, in response to questions about the public telephone system, offered to give her a bag of the coins she would need but recommended the purchase of telephone cards, which were now in wide use.

When she got to the Conrad Hotel, situated across the road from a large concert hall advertising an Amnesty International rally for the following evening, she saw that it rivalled any such establishment she had encountered during her days in Chicago. Resplendent with modern plush, polish and glitter, it was far beyond anything she had expected in Dublin.

She was early so she went to the foyer shop and bought a fifty-unit telephone card, then sat in a squashy couch behind an enormous flower arrangement and began to search the face of every man who entered for a resemblance to the description Vaughan had given her over the telephone. She need not have worried. She would have known he was a reporter by the anxious way he came into the lobby, eyes searching before the door swung closed behind him. 'Mr Vaughan?' She stood up and was rewarded by a clearing in the thicket of lines along his forehead.

429

'You must be Miss MacPherson.'

'Sky, please.'

'Éamonn.' He headed up the stairs towards a mezzanine area, leaving her no choice but to follow. 'Sorry I'm late and I'm afraid I don't have much time. I was covering a news conference at the Shelbourne down the road. We should have met there, only I didn't know where to find you – Coca-Cola, please,' this to the girl behind the small bar at one end of the mezzanine, 'how about you, Sky?' He was dressed in a snappy suit and his shoes were polished; TV reporters here obviously dressed as formally as at home.

She was glad she had shed her jeans in favour of a crushproof summer dress. 'The same.' She nodded at the girl.

'How can I help you?' He obviously believed in wasting not a second.

'Are we on or off the record?'

'Whichever you want.' Vaughan shrugged.

'Off.' Sky took a deep breath. 'What I'm proposing to you is that we work together. I have some leads into two stories that connect Montana and Ireland.'

'We already know about the drugs connection.'

'Do you know about the second one?' Their Coca-Colas arrived and she insisted on paying.

'Try me.' He grimaced and took a slug from his glass. 'What is it about Montana, all of a sudden?'

'The deal is,' Sky did not want to let him think too much, 'I give you my leads in return for your help with local contacts. We progress the stories together and, if it works for us, we break them together, me in the States, you here.'

'That's the kind of offer I've never had before. I must admit it's original.'

'Well, have we a deal?'

'Is this something I couldn't find out by myself?'

'I don't know. But before I go any further, I need you to

430

agree – even if you're not interested – to keep this between us. That you will not run with it by yourself. If you pass on what I'm going to tell you, I'll have to start over with another reporter.' She dredged up what she hoped was a charming smile.

She had succeeded in making him curious. 'Give me a hint anyway.' He swizzled the ice around his glass with the tip of his finger. 'I give you my word that if I'm not interested I won't queer your pitch. But I must warn you that as I'm an employee I can't go haring off on my own.'

Sky decided she had no option but to trust him. As quickly as she could, she told him everything she knew about the conspirators.

'Any more?' He looked at his watch as though to remind her that his meter was running.

'We know that the police here are on to something,' she refused to rush, 'enough to send one of their detectives to Montana to snoop around. That's how I got involved. Something I'd written caught his eye.'

'Who'd they send?' He was definitely interested now.

'A man called Fergus Lynskey. You know him?'

'Not socially. I know of him – the names of all those Branch men pop up in court reports.'

'I mentioned terrorists to him and he didn't jump out the window denying it. All the people they've rounded up have Irish names, seven at last count from various states. But here's the interesting thing, Éamonn. Even *before* these guys get arrested, Lynskey suddenly decides to come back. He was on the same flight as me and he didn't even go home to change his clothes. He went straight into his office.'

'How well do you know him?'

'Fairly well.' Sky managed to keep a straight face. 'I'm meeting him again quite soon – apparently his office is near this hotel and he said if I waited for him here after our appointment, he'd come to collect me.'

'Don't tell him you're talking to me, all right? Not yet.' Vaughan pulled out a notebook. 'Have you got the names of these people who were picked up in the States?'

'Only one so far but my editor will have the others when I next call him.' Vaughan noted the sheriff's name and the states and cities where the other six were brought in.

'We have a starting point, I suppose.' He looked dubiously at the scribble in his notebook. 'Any idea if anyone's involved in this country?'

'Not yet but it would stand to reason, wouldn't it? Anyway, it's your turn now. Will you point me towards some people who might know something about the kind of area we might be talking about?'

'I will, but funny enough, your timing could be brilliant. I've just heard something else which might turn out to be interesting but it's my turn to insist that you keep it under your hat – not for long. If my hunch is correct it'll be all over the shop soon. I don't think it's connected with either of your stories. There's someone very big and hush-hush coming here for that Amnesty rally in the hall across the road. I've been ringing the embassies – the British embassy was so coy I'm beginning to believe I'm on the right track.'

'Who do you think it might be?' Sky stifled a sigh. If it turned out to be a story, she could cover it but the thought of all the work ahead was already overwhelming. He gave her his theoretical names and then the names of his contacts. 'I'll leave it to you to be discreet. You don't want to alert them by asking too many questions. If you get anything you'll ring me immediately? Here's my mobile number . . .'

He watched her write this, then cocked his head to one side. 'Maybe you could help me with your friend, Lynskey, on the identity of Mr Big at the Amnesty conference. Where can I find you later?'

She told him where she was staying.

They arranged that she should come out to RTE at

around seven that evening for them to compare notes and he hurried off.

Sky decided to call Jim Larsen collect while she waited for Lynskey to pick her up. It was just after six a.m. in Montana and she knew that he was an early riser. The hotel operator came back to her, however. 'It's an answering machine, madam, no one there to accept the charges.'

She should have remembered: both Jimbo and his wife always began their day with a run. 'Thank you. I'll call again later.'

She toyed with the idea of calling home but decided against it. It was far too early, and her grandmother, *if* she was there, might think she was checking up on her. Although Sky did not see herself as romantic or sentimental, she had to admit that the notion of the two old people getting together again after all these years was a blast. The only sad part was that, with Daniel Treacy's illness, they would not have much time.

She was about to return to the couch where she had waited for Éamonn Vaughan when she decided she might as well use the time until Lynskey came. It took her a while to master the intricacies of the Irish telephone directory – and then she ran up against the Irish lunch hour. It was now just after two o'clock but incredibly, after five calls, she had still not found anyone at a desk. The sixth switchboard operator who was a friendly soul, confided that with the sun splitting the stones, as it were, people were finding it hard to work. 'But he's not due back until two fifteen at the earliest anyway, love.'

'How long do people normally take for lunch?' Sky was bewildered.

'Well, *technically* we're all supposed to take an hour and a half, but no one really minds a few extra minutes, especially on a day like this. Will I give him a message for you?'

'No thank you. I'll call back later.' Sky hung up. An hour

433

and a half for lunch, never mind longer, was such a bizarre idea. She had never been very interested in food and would not have known what to do with all that time.

Still no sign of Lynskey. She looked up the Amnesty number in the directory and, ignoring the man in line behind her, who sighed ostentatiously, punched it out. Then she changed her mind, 'It's all yours, sir, sorry I've been so long,' and retrieved her card.

She would go across the street to the concert hall. If the rally was tomorrow evening, there would surely be someone around making last-minute arrangements.

Chapter Thirty-Eight

The foyer of the National Concert Hall was airy, lofty and virtually deserted, although a few people dawdled at tables in the little coffee shop. The girl at the box office pulled her longing gaze away from the sunshine outside when Sky approached.

As far as she knew, she said, none of the Amnesty organizers were around— 'No, wait, I tell a lie, there she is,' pointing across the foyer at a woman just leaving the coffee shop.

'Excuse me.' Sky hurried over to intercept her.

'Yes?' The woman, petite and curly-haired with merry black eyes, stopped on the steps in front of the doors.

Sky established she had the right person and introduced herself. She came straight to the point. 'I hear you're having some VIPs here tomorrow evening?'

'What paper did you say you represented?' The woman fiddled with one of her glass earings.

'The *Butte Courier* – you won't have heard of it, Miss Tuffy, it's in Montana, USA.'

'I can hardly believe it. That didn't take long.' The woman laughed. 'Well, you're right there – er . . .' she glanced down at Sky's business card '. . . Miss MacPherson. We do have an exciting evening ahead of us. Would you like some of our literature?'

'Could I ask you who is coming?' Sky took out her notebook.

'Naboom Kebele—' The woman stopped, looked side-long at Sky.

Pen poised, Sky looked politely interested. 'Yes, I saw his name on your poster – and anyone else?'

'You didn't come here especially for this, did you?' The woman's expression was sceptical.

'No, I'm afraid not.'

'Do you know any of our local hacks? Éamonn Vaughan, for instance? Or anyone at the BBC in London?'

'No. I was passing and saw your notice.'

'So where did you hear we had someone big coming? Apart from Naboom Kebele, I mean.'

'Oh, word travels,' Sky improvised. 'Let's just say that although you've never heard of my newspaper, many people have.' Inside her shoes, her toes squinched with embarrassment: she could not believe she was behaving like this.

'Let's put it this way, Miss MacPherson,' Jill Tuffy said slowly, 'if you're here tomorrow evening about fifteen minutes before our meeting begins, I'll personally give you a briefing. I'm *dying* to give you a briefing.' She dropped the façade of detachment. 'You won't be disappointed, honestly. He's really going to be big news—' She stopped, realizing she had just confirmed that it wasn't a woman.

Sky pretended she had not noticed. 'Montana is eight hours behind, and if this person is really as newsworthy as you say, we'll be scooped by the East Coast papers. You couldn't give me just the tiniest hint?'

'All I can say,' the Amensty woman hesitated again, 'is that this person has never been here before. And no one, in the republic of Ireland especially, ever thought they'd see the day when h – this person'd set foot here. I can't say any more – I've said too much already.'

Sky agreed to meet her before the conference, although she doubted that she would keep the appointment, depending on whether she found bigger fish in the meantime. As she stood on the kerb waiting for a gap in the traffic to cross back to the Conrad, she saw Lynskey. Her heart leapt. She quelled it instantly.

He spotted her and waved but as he got closer she saw that instead of the cocksure man-about-town image he normally projected, he looked harassed. 'Have you had your lunch?' He kissed her cheek.

'The whole of Ireland is having lunch as far as I can see.'

He did not respond but took her arm and propelled her, none too gently, along the street. 'We'll go to O'Dwyer's, they'll do us a decent sandwich.'

'Whoa.' She pulled her arm away. 'What's the rush? Maybe I don't want to go to O'Dwyer's. I've work to do.'

'Oh, yeah, sorry. Look, will you not come for just ten minutes, Sky? I could do with a bit of decent company.' He looked so dejected she capitulated.

The pub, which was done – or redone – in lots of shiny brown wood, was less than half full. Lynskey remembered to consult her before ordering and, on his advice, she decided to try a glass of Guinness. When it came, however, she found its unusual nutty taste and thick texture quite unnerving. 'Is this very strong?'

'One glass won't do you any harm.' He took a deep draught from his own pint glass. 'It's great for the old nerves. How did you get on with Vaughan?'

She told him, selectively, but realized he was not listening when he reached out and touched the sapphires. 'They really are beautiful.'

Her body, reacting to his touch, told her what was happening between them as now he stroked not only the sapphires but the skin underneath. Sky had noticed before that air travel always heightened her sexual desire and perhaps it was this, rather than his fingers, which sent all the old signals. Whatever the source, she wanted him badly right now. 'Stop it, please.' She put her glass of Guinness back on the counter.

'Stop what?' He ignored the plea and, leaning forward, kissed her.

'This isn't fair.' She glanced around but no one in the bar was paying them any attention. She looked him directly in the eye. 'You know we can't – we're both too busy.'

'Your hotel is only ten minutes away.'

'I have to *work*, Lynskey.'

'Do you think I don't?'

She could almost see the sparks in the air, could certainly feel them.

They sat facing one another. The barman came over, heel tips pounding on the wooden floor. 'Two ham and cheese?' He put the sandwiches on the counter.

'Thanks.' Lynskey did not remove his gaze from Sky. 'Just leave them there, we'll be back for them later.'

He put a handful of money on the counter and they slid off their stools in balletic unison. They did not speak again until they were in bed.

The young widow of the van driver killed in the crash in Killybegs was frantically weeding a flower bed in her front garden. She could not stand to stay in the house, was finding it increasingly difficult to deal with the well-meaning but upsetting and never-ending expressions of concern from everyone around her. She had no privacy: every member of her large extended family was inside, drinking tea and discussing her future. Tears – of grief and of anger against the world, her husband and God – dripped down her nose as she wrestled with a stubborn dandelion root, bigger than a carrot. It broke in two as she pulled and she cried aloud with frustration.

She straightened up to push the hair out of her eyes and saw, coming along the road towards her, the skipper of the *Agnes Monica*, who had just been released from the Gárda station for lack of hard evidence against him. Judging by his expression, he seemed to be coming to offer sympathy.

The heart of the driver's wife exploded with hatred and jealousy that he was alive and free and her darling husband was dead, imprisoned for ever in a wooden box.

She ran inside.

The hotel bar where Rupert de Burgh met his American and Canadian co-conspirators had been renovated recently and was too open for comfort: the hotel, booked by the Canadian, was also too close to Store Street Gárda station. It was one detail de Bugh had overlooked. He took the two men across the street into Connolly railway station. Here, the crowded platform café smelled like a cattery.

He ordered three coffees and brought them over to the table he had managed to secure. Flynn was carrying a brand new Adidas sports bag, which he clutched to him as though it contained pearls without price. Never having met the Canadian before but knowing him to be wealthy, de Burgh had been taken aback at the man's chicken neck, skinhead haircut and cheap clothes. His eyes were sharp and clear, however, and de Burgh knew that, appearances notwithstanding, this man had to be more formidable than he appeared and that it would be a mistake to underestimate him.

Joe Mason was almost exactly as he remembered, burly and pot-bellied, with a long, Connemara man's face, the genes of which always seem to survive from generation to generation. De Burgh's assessment of him, formed during that long night of talk in California, was that he was intelligent but pigheaded, always a dangerous combination.

'What's in the bag?' he asked Flynn.

'My wallet and stuff. I just thought it would look touristy.'

'It does that. We mustn't stay too long.' He passed out the coffee. 'I have the parcels for you.' He had brought with him a suitcase in which he had packed two pistols and two semi-automatic machine guns, together with ammunition. 'Both of you know how to use the hardware?'

'I got tutoring,' Flynn announced.

'I know them, no need to ask how.' Mason grimaced on tasting the coffee, grey and weak as dishwater.

'You're aware that these are back-ups.' De Burgh sized up a couple of new arrivals, who took the table next to then, then lowered his voice. 'They will be loaded, of course, but I hope you won't have to fire them.'

Of course you won't, he thought, lifting his coffee cup to his lips. *You won't know what you're going to do until I tell you tomorrow morning . . .*

He spoke then over the rim of the cup without moving his lips. 'The details of the Bodenstown timetable, who's going to be there, all the rest of it, are in the bag too. You've seen the place already?' He turned to Flynn.

'I was out there this morning and Mr Mason and I are going again later this evening. A lovely spot, I must say, with the hills in the background, although,' he frowned, 'my cab driver had difficulty finding it. Imagine! One of our national shrines and he'd never been there.'

He paused, then went on: 'Something is bothering me, Mr de Burgh. I'll be blunt. Bodenstown cemetery is quite an open venue, far more open that I had imagined. Are we engaged on a fool's errand? Can the three of us do what was planned for ten?'

De Burgh studied both men. Both pairs of eyes facing him had one thing in common: the subdued glitter of fanaticism. 'Let me be equally blunt.' He pushed away his cup. 'It's not going to be easy and the situation has drastically changed but if our plan is to make a point, a *strong* point, which will have serious impact, then yes, we can still do it. Although the police presence will be substantial, because of the presence of known subversives in the march, no one expects trouble at Bodenstown these days. We will be armed and we will have the element of surprise on our side.' He paused to let that sink in and, to his satisfaction, saw them exchange glances. 'But it's up to you,' he went on. 'You will be the ones in the front line. Please don't feel we have to continue. There'll be another day.'

They looked at one another. 'I believe someone has to do something. We have stood by long enough.' This was Flynn, his conviction absolute.

Mason was more circumspect. 'I suppose I've nothing to lose,' he muttered finally, 'and I agree that someone has to stand up and be counted. But I'm not so sure now that we'll succeed . . . With only three of us . . .'

De Burgh was alarmed. He needed both of them as diversion if his own scheme were to have any chance of success. 'Let's not make any decisions until I have the final list of who's going to be there.' He hoped he sounded soothing. 'And we needn't make our minds up tonight. Nothing is so far advanced that we can't pull back if you're too nervous to go ahead. I'll be in touch after a meeting I have to go to tonight at eight o'clock. And I'll come to see you tomorrow, early as we arranged. You found the pub all right?' Their final meeting was to be in an early house quite near their hotel which, given that it would be a Friday morning, was guaranteed to be swarming with customers.

'OK by me.' Flynn spoke again, but Rupert noticed that Mason said nothing. 'Right.' He stood up. 'We'll talk later.' He glanced at the tables around to double-check that no one was listening and raised his voice. 'Have a safe journey now . . .' Leaving the suitcase at Flynn's feet, he walked out of the café and down the steps into the echoing station.

He had waited too long to let the Prince slip through his fingers now, and it was far too late to recruit more help. He *had* to keep these two on-side – without them he had little chance of succeeding. From the outset he had never considered letting them go through with the original plan. They might have captured the Taoiseach for a few minutes, even have read their proclamation. But even if all ten were to have launched the Bodenstown operation, de Burgh knew far better than his transatlantic partners how their actions and declarations would be received by the rest of the world. Their notions of Ireland had been preserved in amber for generations whereas of course what he had planned for the Prince was in the realms of *realpolitik*.

He would reveal the role they were to play only at their final planning meeting tomorrow morning and was confident he could persuade them to stay with him. But before he did he needed to know exactly when the Prince would be visiting the Natural History Museum. It was there he planned to make his final move.

Perhaps part of what made their love-making so special was that it always took place in inappropriate circumstances. Sky rolled over and pushed her hair, damp and sticky again, out of her eyes. As she lifted her elbows, she loved the way the skin all along her flanks tightened, the way every inch of it felt as pliable as silk. Luxuriating in the sensation, she stretched up one arm until it was at right angles to the shoulder, then the other. Her thoughts drifted like straw on a quiet lake.

She should be getting dressed: she was due to meet Vaughan in less than an hour. Her clothes, Lynskey's too, lay scattered to the four corners of the room, which was dappled with lace-diffused light from the room's two sashed windows. She had packed only two summer dresses and hoped idly that the one lying crumpled on the floor was still wearable. Now, however, she did not care, wanting to float on and on like this into gentle, lengthy sleep.

Lynskey, lying on his back beside her with legs spread, was only now recovering his breath. 'Jesus, Mary and Joseph,' he breathed, 'I thought that would never stop, I thought I was dying . . . That was the best.' He levered himself up on one elbow and kissed her shoulder. 'You're amazing. *We're* amazing.'

'Mm.' She nuzzled his damp collarbone. 'By the way who's the mystery VIP coming to the Amnesty meeting?'

He looked at her in dawning horror and then recoiled as though he had been shot. 'This is not clever, Sky.'

She had not meant to say it, but now that she had let it out there was no going back. 'Just tell me, please, Fergus.' She attempted to stroke his back. 'Had it anything to do with why you were sent to the States?' She, too, got up on one elbow and cuddled in to him.

'This is not fair,' he cried passionately, shaking her off and sitting up. 'You know I can't tell you.' He reached for his shirt and started to put it on.

'Come on, Lynskey.' her sense of languor was fast evaporating and she was becoming annoyed. 'It's no big deal. You know you did the exact same thing to me in Butte. You milked me about Daniel Treacy.'

'Are you saying the only reason we did what we did just now is because you wanted to get information out of me?' He faced her, incredulity lengthening his already long face.

'Aha!' She sat up too. 'So now we're getting to the truth! Are you saying the same about what we did in my bed in Butte?' They glared at one another, recent intimacy banished – or too painfully bared, Sky could not tell the difference.

Lynskey looked away from her towards the window and sounded almost lonely. 'You've got it the wrong way round, Sky. The French have a saying about this kind of thing.

Something about the woman should ask for what she wants before, the man after . . .'

While he was going along the corridor to his desk at Gárda headquarters, Rupert de Burgh was appalled to see a man he recognized from outside his work environment. Just vanishing into the chief superintendent's office was a professional security expert whom he had seen at computer and electronics exhibitions. Rupert, in whose imagination that lethal piece of gum under the chief's desk now grew as big as a rhubarb crown, could think of only one explanation for his presence.

But having caught only a glimpse, he did not know if the expert had been carrying his equipment. Before he had thought out what he was going to say, he found himself knocking at the chief superintendent's door.

'Just a minute,' the chief called from inside. After a pause, the door opened. 'Oh, it's you, de Burgh,' he seemed hassled, 'what do you want?' Rupert took a lightning glance over the chief's shoulder, but could see no equipment. 'Sorry, sir,' he mumbled. 'I see you're busy, I'll come back.' He backed away and then half ran towards the office he shared with the others.

'Oh, hold on, he's just come in.' One of these others transferred the call.

'Who is it?' Rupert picked up the receiver and held it to his chest: he did not feel like dealing with anything other than his immediate problem.

'Someone in Killybegs, she says it's urgent.'

'Hello?' With a sinking feeling in his stomach, de Burgh listened as his informant told him where the missing drugs could be found in the cave. This was the last thing he needed today. He looked around but three of the other four men in the room were on calls and the fourth was writing. 'Thanks,' he said quietly. 'It's hectic here today but we'll get on to it straight away. Could I have your name – where I can get you later?' He was left holding the buzzing telephone.

He toyed with the idea of ignoring the call but the informant had asked for him by name. If she saw no police activity within the next couple of hours she might call again and go higher next time.

Then he saw how he could turn it to his advantage.

He raced out of the room and down the corridor. This time, when he knocked, it was with much more confidence. 'What is it?' The chief superintendent's roar could have been heard in the street.

Rupert opened the door and put his head round it. 'I know I said I'd wait, chief, but I'm afraid this is very urgent.' Then, to the electronics man, giving no indication he recognized him, 'I'm sorry to interrupt, sir, but it really is important.' He prayed that the chief would ask the intruder to leave rather than come to the door or out into the corridor. His prayers were answered.

'No problem.' The security man got to his feet. 'I'll go for a cup of coffee – I know where the canteen is.'

De Burgh smiled apologetically as the man passed him in the doorway, then went in and sat in front of the desk. He retrieved the gum within three seconds. What he had not bargained for was that he was now ordered to Killybegs.

'May I ask you a favour, sir?' His brain raced.

'What now? Just go, de Burgh, do it. This is not a good time.'

'May I speak in confidence?' He stared across the desk, willing his superior to listen.

The chief superintendent sighed. 'I'm very busy, de Burgh.'

'I appreciate that, sir, but I wonder if someone else could deal with Killybegs, at least until I get something personal sorted out.'

'This'd better be good.'

'My wife discovered this morning she was pregnant.'

The chief regarded him in silence, eyes narrowed. 'So?' he said at last. 'And, anyway, I thought it was your wife's sister who was pregnant.'

'She is, sir, she's about to pop any day now, but the news this morning has upset my wife very much. *Very* much.'

Two minutes later, reprieved and almost giddy with relief, he was back in the corridor.

Chapter Thirty-Nine

The crowds in the RTE canteen, a single-storey, open-plan building with floor-to-ceiling windows on three sides, clattered and chattered like a cageful of cockatoos as Éamonn Vaughan, with Sky in tow, searched for a free table. 'Over here.' He found one near a window. Sky, whose legs ached with fatigue, watched, bemused, as he shook little white showers all over his fried eggs and French fries. Shades of Lynskey: salt seemed to be an Irish obsession.

She and Lynskey had parted, if not as enemies, certainly not as lovers. He had continued to be upset at what he saw as her exploitation of him and the more she tried to point out that this was rich coming from him, the more he clammed up. She could barely believe they had known one another for such a short time: although the words 'days' and 'weeks' had ceased to mean much to her, she reckoned it must be only a week, maybe ten days. They fought not tentatively as new lovers do but as though they had known one another for years. She tried to shake him out of her mind and took a mouthful of her lasagne.

She and the Irish reporter had progressed their story not at all. Vaughan had been too busy all afternoon with routine work for his television bulletins; for her part she had shaded the truth a little to him, confessing that she had been so tired after the journey that she had gone to bed for a couple of hours.

'Never mind.' Vaughan larruped into his meal. 'I'll have

a bit of time now. You can come back up to the newsroom with me and we'll hit the telephones.' He seemed to be one of the stars of the station, and popular with it. Throughout the meal they were interrupted by a stream of people coming across to their table with titbits of gossip.

'Everyone's very nice here,' she said, when they were alone for a few moments. 'Must be a lovely place to work.'

'You're a stranger here, all right. Give yourself time.' Vaughan finished his tea. 'Shall we go?'

Before they could get up they were interrupted again by a man who could have been the model for the ubiquitous smiley face that had swept the world. Sky did not catch his name, but he was a children's TV presenter and wildlife artist. 'Butte, Montana?' he repeated. 'It's one of the places I've wanted to go all my life.' He went on to discuss a project in which he had been trying to interest the newsroom for a long time, a wildlife slot to be included once a week as a tailpiece – 'no pun intended, Sky' – to the bulletins.

'Or even once a month, people would be interested, Éamonn, I promise you. Even urban people. Magpies, foxes, mice, you should see my mailbag.'

'You're preaching to the converted here. I told you, I put it up and no one was interested.' Vaughan shook his head ruefully.

'Try again, please?'

'All right.' He rose and Sky followed suit.

The three walked together out of the canteen and across towards a colonnaded building where the newsroom and television studios were apparently housed. 'Saw an extraordinary thing today,' the wildlife man said as they approached the carousel doors. 'I had a group of kids in the Natural History Museum and for the first time in all the years I've been going there I saw what can only be described, in museum terms, mind you, as a frenzy of activity.' He laughed. 'That means, of course that there were at least three

448

people running around. That's the entire staff – the director's away. Could I interest you in doing a story there, Éamonn? They're shamefully neglected, you know.'

'What was going on?' Vaughan was waving at another colleague across the lawn.

'You may well ask. They wouldn't tell me, although they'd taken one of my little favourites out of his glass case – maybe it's something to do with the exhibit they've promised us. I don't suppose you saw anything about another little Eskimo curlew they found recently?'

'No.' Sky could see Vaughan was not in the least interested and was just being polite. By now they were at the doors and, as the wildlife man was not going inside, they stopped. 'It's a little bird which was thought to be extinct – oh, never mind.' He finally yielded to the fact that his enthusiasm was not being shared. 'It's of interest only to ornithologists.'

'Maybe I'll get along, bring my kids – see you around, kiddo . . .' Vaughan pushed the doors and then stood back to let Sky go first.

All the way up the handsome, cantilevered staircase, which led from the lobby to the second floor of the televison building, Sky was being bothered by the word 'ornithologist'. It had some resonance she could not grasp, but she had a feeling she had come across it somewhere recently and that it might be important.

The newsroom was busy but hushed, the clicking of keyboards being the predominant sound. Vaughan installed her in a small side office. 'Carry on here – no one will bother you. Dial nine for an outside line.'

When she reached him Jimbo had little to offer besides the names of those arrested, but as she wrote them to his dictation, Sky thought she detected an unusual undercurrent in his voice. When he had finished, she asked him if anything was wrong.

'Have you called home, Sky?'

'No.' It was as though something cold slithered down the back of her neck. 'Not yet. I was going to call after I spoke to you – why?'

He hesitated, then: 'I'm sorry to have to be the one to give you bad news, but Daniel Treacy died yesterday afternoon.'

'Oh, no.' Even as she reacted, Sky was relieved that it was not someone close to her. She had been afraid the news might have been about Johanna. Then she immediately thought of her grandmother. 'I've got to call home, Jim. My grandmother—'

'You won't find her there right now. It was she who found Treacy last night. She's taking it remarkably well. One of your mother's friends – I can't remember her name now.'

'Hermana? Buffy?'

'That's the one – your grandmother's at her home.'

Then, as quickly as she could, Sky gave him details – pitifully few – about progress in Dublin. 'But although I can't say too much about it right now, there's a possibility I – we – ' she glanced out at Éamonn Vaughan, who was whispering into his own telephone and paying no attention to her, 'we may be about to discover why Lynskey was sent to the States.'

'More than to do with why these guys have been arrested over here?'

'Maybe.' She lowered her voice. 'I'll know for sure tomorrow.'

She called Buffy's number, at which there was no reply, but just as she replaced the receiver, a wisp of memory floated to the surface, so weak and intangible that she almost let it go. Somehow she knew it was vitally important that she catch it and place it in focus.

Not caring who saw her or what they thought, Sky put her forehead against the cool wood of the desk and shut her eyes, squeezing tightly to force the memory higher into her consciousness. Something really significant . . . Something to do with that word 'ornithologist' . . . She pressed harder so the bones of her forehead hurt . . .

Then it burst through. Like tumblers in a combination lock, everything clicked into place: the out-of-date magazine article, the Amnesty woman's little hint about their VIP never having been here before and never expected to be here, Vaughan's comment about the coyness of the British embassy, the commotion at the Natural History Museum mentioned by the wildlife man who had linked it with birds, Eskimo birds.

'It's him!' she cried, so loudly that Vaughan stopped his whispering and looked across at her. 'I have it, Éamonn! I know who it is.'

'May I remind you there's an overtime ban due to start tomorrow, sir?' Unusually, the speaker was Rupert de Burgh, an officer not known for public contribution at meetings.

It was not going well for the planners. All Gárda leave had been cancelled for the weekend yet with the city stuffed to bursting point and the security risk at the Amnesty conference increased tenfold, the Commissioner still doubted that they had adequate cover.

'Can we not know who it is we're supposed to be protecting, sir?' This from a detective inspector well down the table.

'No!' The Commissioner's response had obviously been more violent than he intended. 'Not yet,' he said more quietly. 'We'll be letting you know, still on a confidential basis, of course, early tomorrow afternoon. In the meantime, just take my word for it, gentlemen – and ladies,' he nodded in the direction of the women in the room, 'this will be an unusual situation but one I'm sure we'll all rise to as we always do.' As he looked at the lines of serious faces, he was not half as confident as he appeared. He passed the chair to the chief superintendent.

After he had allocated the security personnel, and spelt out the plans for advance screening of the places through which their mystery guest was going to pass, the chief seemed to remember something. 'De Burgh,' he barked, 'keep in touch with Killybegs, keep it spinning. At least we'll have something good to report to the press for a change.'

'My fella's in at a meeting.' Éamonn Vaughan threw down the telephone. 'Why don't you try your friend?'

'Sure.' Sky steeled herself. Although she and Lynskey had parted with plans to meet the following day, it would not be easy to open the subject that had caused such dissension.

She was secretly relieved to discover that, like Vaughan's contact, Lynskey, too, was in a meeting.

'Must be the same one they're all at.' Vaughan drummed his fingers on the desk. 'The only thing to do is to ring the ambassador directly.'

The British ambassador to Ireland was at a function that night and was therefore unavailable to take Éamonn Vaughan's call. Lynskey had gone to ground and had not returned Sky's, and Vaughan's friend in the Branch was equally tacit.

Two hours had passed, they – or, rather, Vaughan – had telephoned everyone in his book and still they were no nearer confirmation. Buffy was not answering in Butte and Sky was reluctant to contact the hospital in case it disturbed her mother.

'We've got to pin it down, we've just got to.' Vaughan was pacing the small cubicle to which they had repaired after the return of the inhabitants of the office they had first occupied. Sky, sick with fatigue now, was concerned that

452

they were attracting too much attention. She saw how her scoop would grow wings and escape beyond capture, should any other reporter tumble to what she and Vaughan had been chasing: RTE ran radio bulletins through the night.

On the instant it rang, Vaughan snatched up the telephone in the little cubicle. 'Yes? All right, put her through. Oh, hello!' His voice dropped, sweetened. 'Talk about a blast from the past. What can I do for you?' Then: 'Funny enough, I heard the same thing. I wonder if we have the same source? No . . . you go first . . .' He pulled a face in Sky's direction. 'I see. Well, I was thinking along the same lines and I think you're right . . . Come on . . . You don't seriously expect me to tell you, now, do you?' He listened, then, 'Sure I'll see you when you come over then, all right? Come into the newsroom. Maybe we'll both have a bit more news to tell each other.'

He threw down the receiver. 'That was a BBC reporter, a girl who went over there from this place. She got the same tip-off I did but she has no clue. All she's found out so far is who it's definitely not. And it's definitely not John Major. But she did say something interesting. The British Foreign Office went ballistic when she rang them. Sky, I'm beginning to believe that you're a little genius.'

Sky summoned a smile. She certainly did not feel like a genius: she felt like a rabbit brought down with an elephant gun.

He saw it. 'You're dropping on your feet. Why don't you go and get a good night's sleep? I'll order a taxi. I promise I'll ring you straight away if I hear anything. Anyway, there's nothing we can do in the middle of the night – the ambassador certainly won't thank us for ringing him up at this hour. I'm going to call it a day, start again in the morning. But I think now you've got it right.'

*

'Spare me the details, Toby. Just ring as soon as you have anything concrete. So long as you know that, here, I won't be free to talk.' Rupert de Burgh was on his bedroom extension. His brother's Foreign Office friend was coming to his flat for a late supper after helping the Prince with his speech.

He put his head in his hands. Now that it was so close he had to keep his nerve even as all those around him – Toby, the plumber – were threatening to lose theirs. Even Jerry Flynn had been showing signs of softening when he had telephoned earlier.

At least he was on the security detail assigned to guard the mystery guest. Unfortunately, so was Fergus Lynskey. If de Burgh could have chosen any of his fellow officers to leave off that detail, it would have been Lynskey.

Ever since the tumultuous day in 1972 when Fergus Lynskey had set de Burgh on his present path with a single chance remark about joining the Gárdaí, the latter had lived in dread that the hawk-nosed Irishman would somehow remember the encounter and tumble to him. Their training days at Templemore had been tough on all recruits but de Burgh had had to take on the extra burden of watching Lynskey constantly, trying to determine whether that fateful meeting had registered. He played it over and over in his imagination, 'seeing' his own shadowed face from Lynskey's perspective.

As the days and weeks wore on, however, he began to relax a little. Although Lynskey made it obvious he would never court friendship, de Burgh divined that this had nothing to do with politics – he was very careful about that in public – but was a simple matter of personal dislike, or at best indifference. The Irishman gave no sign that he had ever seen de Burgh before.

In the intervening years, still ultra-cautious, de Burgh had continued to avoid overt contact with Lynskey. From

454

time to time – such as on the present assignment – when it had been unavoidable, he kept his head down and worked as efficiently as possible so as not to attract the other's attention.

It had to be said that even if the complication of de Burgh's political leanings had not existed, he would have hated Lynskey instinctively: the breezy ease with which he conducted his professional life, his detection rate, his enjoyment of the chief super's ear and personal intimacy. It was not surprising that de Burgh was chary of working so closely with Fergus Lynskey at the best of times. And this was not the best of times. But he was realistic enough to know that not everything would go his way and, when the crunch came, it would be just himself and the Prince anyway.

He opened his wallet and reread the letter he had written earlier that day to his family.

His wife was at the cinema with a friend, and his three children, who were all on holiday from school, were taking full advantage of her absence. Downstairs, the television blasted out some sitcom and, in the bedroom next door, the stereo was booming away: his elder son, a taciturn enigma to his father, played nothing but Metallica.

'Turn that down.' Rupert banged with his fist on the communicating wall. Nothing happened. In normal circumstances he would have stormed into his sons' room but tonight, most probably the last night he would spend here, he decided to leave it be. For a few seconds, struggling with feelings to which he was unaccustomed, he stroked the letter gently with one finger, then put it back in his wallet and went downstairs.

He walked through the kitchen and out into the back garden, down the path to his shed, always kept locked and to which he had the only key. His family knew that when he was in here, rebuilding hi-fi speakers from salvage stock, tinkering around with the model planes, boats and other electronic gizmos which were his only hobby, they were to leave him alone.

He let himself in, locked the door, and took a long, deep breath. He always felt calm in here, almost happy, although happiness was not something he could easily identify. The last time he could say he had been happy was in those heady, high days of his short Trinity career. He liked the smell in here, though – a combination of sweet, decaying wood, Airfix glue, and a sharp, fusty scent he associated with opening the packaging around new electronic components.

From a high shelf, he took down the Semtex devices, packed neatly in butter foil and, to all intents and purposes, if anyone saw inside his briefcase between now and when it was planted, just innocent packets of butter. If anyone asked, his wife had asked him to pick it up – she needed extra to seal her containers of home-made pâté. He had used enough of the explosive to cause damage and panic, but not enough for serious injury or death – unless he was very unlucky.

He also took down two other, more unusual and far smaller contrivances, packed into flat, teardrop shapes, each no longer than three inches and designed to self-combust at a pre-set time.

The detonator on the main bomb was activated by a TV remote control. At first he had toyed with a car-alarm remote, which he could have kept on his key-ring without arousing suspicion, but was unable to find components small and powerful enough to fit into the housing. He would carry the TV remote in his pocket and, if it came to light, act surprised – one of his children must have put it there during a game.

Someone knocked on the shed door. 'Dad?'

'What?' De Burgh paused in the act of putting the devices into his briefcase.

'I just want to say goodnight, Dad, I'm going to bed.' It was his younger son, thirteen years old and the only one of his three children who seemed now to have any time for him.

'I can't open the door,' he called gruffly. 'I'm in the middle of something – goodnight.'

'Night, Daddy.'

De Burgh listened at the door as the sound of his son's running footsteps faded on the concrete path.

No matter what disaster now befell him or his plan, he was determined to go through with it – alone if need be. If he had been asked to describe what it was that was pushing him, he would not have been able to put words on it. All he knew was that his concentration had been refined to focus only on that single point tomorrow when he would confront the Prince of Wales. It was as though his being had become as thin and elegant as a laser beam, which cut through his family and all personal considerations. Everything in its path was insubstantial.

Sky got back to the hotel ten minutes after leaving RTE and was paying off the cab when a figure emerged from an automobile a little way along towards the park. Lynskey.

'I'm sorry,' he said simply. 'Will you forgive me?'

'I shouldn't have said it. It was crass, you were right. But you should know by now that my tongue runs away with my brain.'

'You'd every right to say what you did, I was as bad as you. You were dead right, Sky.'

'No, I was the one—' Sky stopped. 'What does it matter? You're here now,' she said softly. 'Kiss me.'

He did, and for the first time it was as though they were kissing not as sexual partners or people mutually and over-whelmingly attracted but as a couple of human beings who needed one another. 'Maybe we shouldn't meet again until all this is over?'

457

Then he catapulted her right back into the problem between them. Holding her a little away, he looked down at her. 'It won't be long now, I promise. By this time tomorrow night we can be together without any hidden agendas or conflicts of interest.'

Final confirmation.

Chapter Forty

Sky looked at her wristwatch: although it was still only five thirty in the morning, the room was already suffused with quiet, milky light; she had not drawn the swagged curtains, preferring the more open look of the lace underneath.

She lay for a few moments in the deep comfort of the bed then, for the sixth time since coming to Ireland, reached for the telephone and called Buffy's number. This time it was answered.

'Oh, Sky.' The older woman was guarded. 'We're all fine. How are you, dear? How's Ireland?'

'Buffy, I know about Daniel Treacy. How's Grandma taking it?'

'She's here beside me.' Buffy's relief was unmistakable. 'I'll put her on to you.'

Sky's grandmother was calm and controlled. 'You're not to be worrying about me. Buffy here couldn't be nicer, neither could Hermana. The two of them are looking after me as though I was royalty.' Treacy's wake was to be held the following evening and she was not looking forward to it. 'I'm sad of course, and a little guilty.' The old lady's tone brooked no follow-on. 'What are you doing up so early? How are you getting on? Do you like Dublin?'

'Dublin's fine, I think, as much as I've seen of it.' Sky did not feel like going into everything that had happened – or had not happened – since her arrival. 'And as for being awake, I can't sleep any longer. The change in times I suppose. I'm going to call the hospital next. How's Mom?'

Johanna was well enough, her grandmother said, then: 'I'll let you go, dear, this telephone call must be costing you a fortune.'

'Not at all,' Sky protested. What was it about the Irish and telephone calls? 'The *Butte Courier* is paying.'

'Don't forget to ring your aunt Maggie in Lahersheen, will you?'

'I'll do better than that. I intend to go down there when I've filed my story. Ancestral pile and all that.'

After she hung up, Sky lay, staring at the snowflake patterns on the lace at the nearest window. Easy to reel off a few confident words about filing stories. Different when it came to the actuality.

Mentally, she listed what she knew: the drugs story, which was common knowledge and of little interest in Montana, except for a couple of paragraphs under a sub-heading: 'Helena and Mayville Men Implicated'; some plot involving terrorism and an Irish-American group in the States in which 'Mayville Man Implicated' also figured; the Prince of Wales arriving in Dublin today for an Amnesty conference and probably going to visit a bird show in a museum.

The more she thought it out, the more she saw the connection between the Prince and the putative terrorism: this was undoubtedly what had sent Lynskey to America.

She sat up, sleep forgotten. It had to be the story. Charles was the planned target.

And since the Amnesty conference was going to be so heavily guarded, that couldn't be the venue. She had to get the whole of the Prince's itinerary. She was reaching out to call Éamonn Vaughan's number when she remembered it was still not six o'clock.

*

Rupert de Burgh was also awake, going over and over in his mind what could and could not happen in the course of the day, and what would have happened to him by its end. He had covered every eventuality: his will was updated and his letter to his wife and family safely locked in his shed. It would be the first place his colleagues would pull apart for clues as to why he had acted as he did.

At six thirty, he stole out of bed and, taking his clothes with him, tiptoed towards the bedroom door. Behind him, his wife stirred and sighed. He froze: she was accustomed to his coming and going at odd hours but he did not want to answer any questions this morning.

It was nearly time to meet Flynn and Mason in one of the early houses where, among the tourists, nightworkers and alcoholics, their presence would be unremarkable. It would be a short encounter because he had to be home in time to drop his younger son to summer camp on his way in to work.

Bambi was a Rottweiler whose handler, or so his colleagues always said, had a sick sense of humour.

Not so, the handler would retort: Bambi, although vast and with a mouth like a bear-trap, was as gentle as his namesake and lived indoors with the family, frequently sleeping on the children's beds. Now, as the man stumbled into the kitchen, he wagged his stumpy tail and ran to the back door to be let out.

'Good morning, fella.' The handler plugged in the kettle, then padded across to stroke the dog's velvety head. 'Big day today.' Where explosives were concerned, Bambi's nose was infallible.

'I wonder how he'll react to all the bones. Anyway, there'll be no problem, I'm sure – I hear they're very well trained.'

461

The director of the Natural History Museum and one of his subordinates had had no sleep: it had taken all night to mount the Eskimo curlew exhibit. Now, as morning light flooded through the glass ceiling of the three-tiered exhibition space above the ground floor, the two stood back to admire their work.

'Have we ever had a dog in here before?' The director rubbed his tired eyes.

'Not that I can remember.' The other man yawned. 'Well, I'm going home for a bit of a kip. We've done all we can do, I think. How long'll yer man be looking at it, anyway? About a minute and a half?'

'I hope he'll spend longer than that.' The director frowned. He looked around his domain, the walls of which sprouted so many heads, horns and antlers that they might have been in the presence of a Rajah's trophy collection. 'The cleaners are due for a last go around.'

'Not to speak of the Branch and their bloody dog. I'll see you in a couple of hours.'

Jerry Flynn had slept well and felt buoyant, if a little tense. This was quite an adventure: he had stayed in five-star hotels and resorts all over the world but he was experiencing more true happiness in this little hotel in a run-down part of Dublin than ever he had in Toronto, New York or even Las Vegas. The shower might be a trickle, the noise from the bar downstairs might be disturbing but, by and large, he felt good.

Dublin itself had been somewhat of a disappointment to him, though: it was littered and the air was smoggy. To be fair he knew that the city was not Ireland and he also knew that this part of Dublin, rancid with trains and traffic and roadworks, was not the real city either. What was more disappointing was the flavour of the place: he had always felt

462

you could taste a town by walking around its streets and watching its TV. These streets were not relaxed and friendly as he had hoped. And as for the Irish TV, it showed a lot of British and American imports. Even the local news seemed to bend over backwards to be 'fair' to the Unionists and Loyalists and the British, while giving a disproportionate amount of air time to people who were condemning nationalist action. In fact nowhere – except on amateur posters affixed to lamp-posts and among the young people selling the nationalist newspaper, *An Phoblacht*, outside the General Post Office – could he find sentiments sympathetic to his own views. The Irish seemed to have obliterated the sins of the past from their collective memory. Nowhere, except among those young idealists, had he found an echo of his own burning sense of injustice. As far as Flynn was concerned, this collective amnesia and indifference were symptomatic of why he had had to come here. They were certainly justification for it.

Deeply religious, he had been disappointed to learn that no Masses were celebrated early in Dublin – or early enough that he would be finished and out in time to meet with Joe Mason and Rupert de Burgh. He had grown up with the image of the 1916 leaders attending the Sacraments on the eve of their own sacrifice and thought that hearing Mass this morning would have been a nice touch. Although he did not, deep down, think he was going to die, he felt that he had little left to detain him on this earth: he was a widower, he had lived a long, useful life, his children were grown and set up in their own lives. He was ready.

As he shaved, he admitted to himself that he was a little worried about the commitment of his colleague from Santa Barbara. Several times on the previous day the plumber had expressed reservations about the likelihood of their success.

Rupert de Burgh would sort it out. The Irish policeman

seemed to share his own passionate conviction that they were doing the right thing.

When the twin-belled alarm clock jangled beside his ear, Fergus Lynskey did not so much as flutter an eyelid. He continued to breathe deeply and evenly and, after a minute or so of vigorous effort, the bells ran down. As it was on the top floor, the one-bedroomed apartment was hushed; the bedroom window was open, but the early-morning traffic on Gardiner Street was light and the road gangs were not due to start work for another hour or so. The alarm, however, had goaded Lynskey into semi-consciousness and he felt as though he was caught weightlessly in a hammock slung between dreams and reality.

After a bit, the second clock started its intermittent, five-second on-off bleeping, which he knew would persist. He held out for a short while but the sound became so annoying that he had to get out of the bed to turn it off.

He hung over the dressing-table, both palms flat on its surface, while toying with the notion of resetting the clock for fifteen minutes hence. Then the realization of what day it was roared in like a tornado and he stumbled into the shower.

His private secretary brought the Prince of Wales a copy of his speech for the Amnesty seminar and left it with him so he could go over it. Of necessity it was short: as heir to the British throne, he would not refer openly to anything political. And as for the subject of the meeting, 'Political Repression, The New Global Holocaust', a future leader of the Commonwealth could reveal little of his true thoughts and feelings on that.

The Prince was being flown directly in an RAF plane to

an Irish military aerodrome and then helicoptered to the President's residence, which was apparently in the middle of a big park. Given the short time-scale, it appeared, unfortunately, he would not be able to see much of Dublin. Everywhere else he was to be taken – the Government Buildings, the Natural History Museum, the Amnesty meeting, the Department of Foreign Affairs – were all in the centre of the city and within half a mile of each other.

'Excuse me, sir,' it was the secretary again, 'Mr de Burgh is on the telephone. Shall I have him put through?'

The Prince took the call.

All Toby wanted was to wish him well for the trip.

Toby knew Dublin, and they chatted for a couple of minutes about the City's public buildings for which the Prince should keep an eye open if he had a chance. Then the heir to the throne said goodbye and turned his attention to his speech.

It was just after half past seven but the air in the early public house was already so blue, both metaphorically and literally – from cigarettes – that de Burgh, who detested smoking, felt it could have been cut with a machete. To the night workers this was tea-time and relaxation, to the revellers not yet gone home, it was just a continuation of the party. But at least the din was such that no one could follow anyone else's conversation.

He edged himself on to a bar stool between a bright-eyed Jerry Flynn and the Californian. Although a couple of other tourists were there, Dutch or German to Rupert's experienced eye, these two could not have been mistaken for anything else – at least, Flynn, who still clutched the Adidas sports bag, could not. Once he had established the normality of his presence and ordered a glass of Guinness, he dropped his voice a little. 'We need to talk.'

'Oh? Something wrong?' Joe Mason immediately picked it up.

Rupert adopted his most persuasive tone – the one he used to keep Toby in line. 'Nothing wrong. As a matter of a fact it's precisely the opposite. I've just learned that we've been presented with an opportunity beyond our wildest dreams.' Mason, he saw, was suspicious and Flynn simply startled.

'What is it, Mr de Burgh?' the Canadian asked.

'We won't need to go to Bodenstown.' He watched them carefully. 'I've just heard something which gives us the opportunity to make a greater impact. The Prince of Wales is making a surprise visit and I've amended our plans.'

'But I thought—'

Mason's lips were tight but Rupert immediately cut off any protest. 'Joe! Imagine the impact around the world if, instead of taking the Taoiseach hostage, we were to take the heir to the British throne. I've been working it out. It's eminently possible.' He held his breath.

'I'm not agreeing to anything I until I hear what you have in mind.' De Burgh could see that the plumber's resistance was growing.

'Just let me tell you what I've planned. At least listen.' He looked from one to the other, slowing his voice, hypnotizing them. 'I guarantee that if we do what I say, we will hit TV screens all around the world tonight, front pages tomorrow. No one will be able to ignore what we ask. Sometimes the most complex tasks can be solved with the simplest of plans.'

To her frustration, Sky found that the Natural History Museum, which was just a short walk from her hotel, did not open until ten o'clock. It was just before nine now and she was wound tighter than a new watch.

She had tried twice to contact Vaughan but his home number rang unanswered and both his office and his mobile numbers had taken messages. With nothing much to do until the museum opened, she wandered into the park where the poet had been reading the previous day. On this overcast morning, the atmosphere was different: the immaculate lawns were deserted except for people with briefcases hurrying through. When she emerged at the other side of the park, a double-decker bus was just pulling up at a nearby bus stop. Still with an hour to kill, she decided to hop on.

Ten minutes later she was standing by the brown river Liffey.

She walked towards what appeared to be the main bridge over the river. But when she got to it she saw that, across its six lanes, the Friday-morning rush-hour was in full, roaring disarray. To cross seemed like too severe a test of speed and nerve and she decided to turn left in the direction which should bring her back to the hotel and the museum.

As she walked by a long stone wall topped by railings, she was looking ahead towards a curved, stately building – and bumped straight into an elderly man standing stock-still in the middle of the pavement. 'I'm very sorry.' Flustered, she disentangled herself.

Another tourist, she thought, noticing the Pentax round his neck. He seemed about to smile but turned away. His bullet head was covered in white stubble and he was thin but, although his appearance was unremarkable, something about his near smile – perhaps it was the quick flash of gold teeth – got to her. 'Are you sure you're OK?' She touched his arm to detain him while trying to work out the connection.

He inclined his head to indicate he was fine then turned on his heel and walked away in the direction from which she had come. Still puzzling, she looked after him.

*

Flynn's heart was thumping as he hurried along by the wall, which he knew ran around the perimeter of the Trinity College campus. What was that girl doing here? Of all people to bump into in a city of a million! Had she recognized him?

He was distressed at his own reaction: if he got this nervous after such a simple accident, from which no harm could come, how was he going to deal with the big stuff later on today? He consoled himself with the thought that this evening he would be following instructions. What had shaken him was the unexpectedness of the encounter.

He looked around: in his panic he had walked blindly and, although he was not exactly lost – he could still see the first stones of Trinity's wall – he had to stop to get his bearings. He was standing opposite a public house on a corner of a side-street, which petered out to nothing: that had to be the river. From there, he knew how to get back to his hotel, which was on its north side.

Feeling a little better, he crossed and set off towards the water.

The traffic-clogged street was narrow, with tall apartment blocks on one side, a derelict garage and lock-ups scattered along it. He was standing at traffic lights at a cross street when he felt a sharp pain between his shoulder blades. Simultaneously, the shoulder strap of the Adidas bag was jerked, hard.

He tightened his grip and whirled around, finding himself instantly engaged in a tussle for the bag with two youngsters of ten or eleven. He kicked out, hard, and connected with the shins of one, but the boy came back, swinging a large stone in a length of nylon stocking. Flynn ducked and the other boys, chucked hard at the strap, pulling him off balance. As he fell, a motorist and a cab driver, both halted at the traffic lights, jumped out of their vehicles and ran towards the fracas.

The boy with the stone swung it so it cracked across the

back of Flynn's hand. He roared with pain and dropped the bag, whereupon the child snatched it and ran.

As the motorist reached him, Flynn looked up to see that the cab driver had taken off after the two boys. As all three vanished into a nearby entryway, the motorist helped him up off the ground. 'Little gurriers! Are you all right?'

'My bag – my bag—' Holding his injured hand with the other, Flynn started to follow the boys and their pursuer, only to see the cab driver emerging, shaking his head, from the entryway.

'Is your hand OK? I've the car here – would you like me to take you to a hospital Casualty?' The panting cab driver reached them.

'No, no, it's all right, really.' Flynn was frantic, not only at the loss of the bag and what it contained but at the attention the incident had drawn. The lights had turned and the air was full of the cacophony of horns from those stalled behind the two driverless vehicles.

'Did you have your money in the bag, Dad?' the cab driver persisted.

'Yes, but it's all right, really, it's all right.' Flynn tried to back away only to be stopped again by the cab driver.

'Wait a minute.'

'I'd better move my car.' The motorist who had helped glanced behind him at his fellow travellers.

'Yeah, you go on.' The cab driver dismissed him, then turned back to his captive. 'You should have that hand seen to.'

'I will.' Flynn, drawing on every ounce of the authority gained over years in management of a large staff, calmed himself. 'I'm really fine. I will go see a doctor.'

'And the Guards. They're only around the corner here in Pearse Street. You should ring the American embassy too – they're in Ballsbridge. Look, Dad . . .' As the Canadian moved off, the cab driver followed him. 'You've had a terrible shock. Why don't you just get in the car and I'll take you to—' he broke off. 'Oh, great! Thank God. Here's what we need.' Under Flynn's horrified gaze, he hailed a uniformed banghárda who was just turning into the street.

Chapter Forty-One

As Rupert met up with the dog handler and his charge, Bambi sniffed his hand but backed off, sneezing violently.

After packing the Semtex in the briefcase the previous night, the policeman had washed carefully in the juice of a dozen lemons. He had repeated the exercise this morning before his wife got up and this time added a dollop of pepper dust. 'What's on your hands?' the handler asked curiously.

Rupert explained that he had been working with creosote on his garden fence the previous evening and that some had got under his nails. The lemon juice had been his wife's suggestion. He looked at his hands. 'Nearly as good as Fairy Liquid.'

Before going to the museum, Sky called Lynskey at work from a telephone booth. He was guarded: 'I can't talk now.'

Indeed, Sky could hear the hubbub in the background. 'Could we meet for lunch?'

'I'll try, a quick one. Where can I contact you?'

'I'll be at the hotel at twelve thirty.'

He rang off without saying goodbye.

The sun came out as she walked to the museum, an oddly blinded building because of three unfilled niches and two blank window spaces above and on either side of the stone doorway.

Her initial impression of the place was of its singular lack of colour, or rather a play of darkness on light: dark wooden cabinets, dark bones, the fat dark body of a stuffed basking shark suspended from the ceiling. As she moved around, however, that somewhat doom-laden impression of suspended decay was dispelled by the coats of the creatures themselves: iridescent feathering of a kingfisher, the soft mottled honey of an exhibit of fox cubs in their den.

Upstairs was a series of the most extraordinary rooms she had ever seen. The creaking wooden staircase came out on a large gallery with two further minstrel's galleries overhead, dominated by the skeleton of a whale. The place was filled with bears, lions, a giraffe, a pygmy hippopotamus, monkeys, elephants, fish, birds. Then there were the invertebrates and octopuses, butterflies, beetles, spiders and flies, whitening in phials and jars or spreadeagled over black velvet display cases, while fixed to every vertical surface not made of glass were heads with or without horns or antlers.

'Excuse me.' She walked up to a man in his shirt-sleeves.

'Yes.' The man looked flustered.

Sky produced her most charming smile. 'I'm an American visitor. Could you direct me to whoever's in charge?'

'I'm afraid the director is not here at present.' The man adopted a hunted look. 'What can I help you with? You've come at a bad time.'

'I know I have.' Sky continued to smile. 'Perhaps if I told you why I'm here. I know you're receiving a very important visitor today.'

The man's eyes widened in horror. 'No one's supposed to know. We were told not even to tell our wives.'

'I know from my relatives in England.' She tried to adopt a simultaneously knowing and aristocratic expression. 'But don't worry, I just want to see the little Eskimo exhibit for myself.' She could not remember the precise name of the bird used by the wildlife man she had met in RTE, but

472

hoped that by tossing it off quickly it might sound like insider jargon.

The man looked hard at her, then, 'I suppose that's all right. First, though,' he recollected his security duties, 'could I see some form of identification, please?'

'Sure.' Sky rooted around in her purse. She was thinking fast. To know she was a reporter would send this functionary running for cover. 'Will these do?' She pulled out her brand-new charge card and her membership card for the camera circle, the latter of which showed her photograph.

He examined both cards closely then said, 'Follow me.' He led her to the back of the exhibition space on the first floor, where he showed her a largish glass case in which were two medium-sized birds. One appeared to be nesting in what looked like lichen or moss, the other was perched on a stone. As far as Sky could see they were unremarkable creatures, brownish beige with spindly blue-grey legs and beaks like miniature scythes. Certainly not worth creating a fuss about.

'What do you think?' They were joined by another, much younger man.

The first man's face cleared with relief. 'She said she knew who was coming.' He turned to Sky, 'This is our director.' Then, again to his boss: 'She's an American student, I checked.'

'Don't worry about it.' The younger man smiled. 'Not much anyone can do about it now, the word is probably out – this town is a village. You haven't been here long, obviously. After a few days you'll find yourself meeting the same people everywhere. We all meet each other all the time.' He held out his hand. 'I'm Declan Corkery, the director.'

'Sky MacPherson.' They shook hands.

He turned to his handiwork. 'Do you approve of our efforts? The case had to be specially made and we had the devil of a time getting the habitat material.'

'Very nice. Er – Declan.' She hesitated. 'Could we talk?'

'Sure, I've a few minutes, come on into my office.'

'I'll come straight to the point.' Sky took a deep breath after he closed the door behind them. 'I think you're wrong when you say that probably everyone knows about who's coming here today. The only people who know are the police and the authorities, yourselves, the Amnesty International people and me.'

The director was shrewd: 'So what are you asking me to do?'

Here it came. 'I'm not a student. I'm a reporter. I represent a small and impoverished newspaper in Butte, Montana. I would be no threat to any of your local reporters here, but it would be a lucrative coup for us if I had an exclusive – any exclusive – concerning the Prince of Wales.' On tenterhooks, she stopped. He had not reacted to the name. Further confirmation.

'Go on.'

'Could you arrange for me to be here when he comes? I will not approach him or speak to him unless he speaks to me and, even if he does, I'll not reveal I'm a reporter. I'll just write a colour piece about him being here, how he reacted to your Eskimo birds.'

'Eskimo curlews. If you're pretending to be interested in wildlife, at least get your names right.'

'Please, Mr Corkery, please.' She leaned forward, engaged him with Johanna's cornflower eyes. 'The rest of the press pack will have other opportunities – at the Amnesty conference, for instance. I'd be only one of many there. You've no idea how important this would be. It's a matter of life and death to our newspaper because we'll be able to syndicate it. I'll be out of a job if we don't get some money soon. But it's not my job, Mr Corkery, it's that our newspaper *needs* to be saved. We're one of the last independent voices in Montana,

474

in the whole United States, maybe. We represent small local and environmental interests against the big boys—' Thinking she might be gilding the lily she stopped.

Watching from under her lashes to see if he'd bought it, she was delighted to see him smile. 'I've got to admit it's a pretty impressive pitch. What would you say if I told you my wife's a reporter and I wouldn't let *her* in?'

Sky was crestfallen.

'I'm joking, Miss MacPherson, I'm not married.' But when she sat up eagerly he held up a restraining hand. 'I'm afraid it's out of the question. I'm a civil servant, I'm not my own boss.'

'Isn't there anything I could do around the museum? As a researcher? Even a typist? If there's any enquiry afterwards, I'll take full responsibility. You can say I deceived you and I'll back you up.'

'You clearly have no idea how the Irish civil service works.' He smiled wryly. 'To get in here – anywhere, really – requires the equivalent of an Act of the Oireachtas – in triplicate. I would like to help but I'm afraid I can't. Our orders are clear, I'm afraid, and the police are due here any minute to clear the place.'

Behind her, Sky heard a soft knock and then the door opening. She looked round as the older man she had met previously came half-way into the room. 'They're here with the dog, Declan.'

'Speak of the devil. Show them in.' He stood up.

Sky stood up also as two men, accompanied by a large dog, came in. The dog, panting a little, immediately lay down quietly beside its master's feet. And uncomfortably close to Sky's. The other man looked suspiciously at her: 'We've no woman on our list.' She hated the way his light-coloured eyes seemed to drill straight through her.

'This is Sky MacPherson, from America.' The director glanced at her and then back at the policeman. 'She's here purely by chance, I assure you.' Sky flashed him a grateful smile, but his expression was bland.

'I'm afraid I'll have to ask you to leave, miss,' the policeman with the light eyes said crisply. 'May I see some identification?'

She fished out the same two cards she had shown the attendant. Although both had photographs, neither showed her address. 'I'm on holiday. I was taking a walk in the park and just wandered in here. May I complete my conversation with the director?'

The cop handed back the cards, 'You can remain until we get as far as here. We'll be starting upstairs on the top floor and working downwards.'

The policeman seemed to lose interest in her, and asked the director if all the side offices and storerooms were open. When the director replied that they were, he said; 'They must be locked immediately they've been cleared. Will you come with us and bring the keys, please.'

The dog stood up as soon as the handler twitched the leash. 'Please stay here, Miss MacPherson. I'll be back as soon as I can.' The director took up the keys from the desk and all three men, with their four-legged companion, left the office.

Instantly, Sky picked up the telephone on the director's desk. 'Éamonn,' she whispered urgently when he answered his mobile, 'can you meet me? As soon as possible?'

'Jesus, Mary and Joseph! Oh shit, oh *shit* . . . I don't fuckin' *believe* it.' The two young thieves were safely tucked into a small rubbish-strewn space beside an electricity transformer and were rifling through the Adidas bag.

They had robbed more than they had bargained for. Not only had they bagged a wad of cash, but something else, too. Reverently, the bigger of the two pulled out a pistol, which was impressive enough, but the second item was really the business. Although he had never handled one before, the boy recognized a sub-machine-gun when he saw it. 'Are they real?' The smaller one's eyes were as round as plates.

'Of course they're real, dickhead.' The older boy put both weapons back in the bag and sat with his back snugly against the transformer to think.

'Would you like another cup of tea, sir?' In Pearse Street Gárda station, Jerry Flynn was being killed with kindness. At least the interfering cab driver had finally been inveigled into leaving but the policewoman who had walked him in here was still hovering solicitiously. She was buxom, with a fresh, country face and, in other circumstances, Flynn would have liked her.

He ached with anxiety to escape but as he was supposed to be an elderly tourist with time to spare, he had to play dumb. At least he had had the presence of mind to give no name and he had said he was staying at the hotel where he had had a cup of coffee the previous day which was in a much more salubrious area than his. 'I really must be getting along,' he stood up, 'and thank you kindly for all you've done. I truly appreciate it.'

'You're sure now you don't want me to ring Victim Support for you? They're very good. Would you like some-one to drive you back to your hotel?'

'I'll walk. Truly.'

As he left the police station he got an even worse shock than had been doled out by the two little muggers. Laid carelessly on top of a pile of ledgers was a glossy eight-by-ten photograph of himself in rodeo gear.

He was shaking when he got outside, so much so that he began to feel woozy. By a supreme act of will, he got himself across the road and to a little plaza in front of a cinema. He sat down on a parapet surrounding a flower bed but rather than lower his head, which was what his instinct told him to do, he pretended to be enjoying the sunshine. The last thing he needed was another bout of do-gooding from someone concerned that he might be ill.

Bit by bit, he began to feel more normal. He flexed his hand: it was sore and already swollen, but he was pretty sure nothing was broken.

His heart was, however. He had waited so long for this opportunity but now there was no avoiding the bitter fact that his dreams were in tatters around his feet. Jerry Flynn was an idealist and a patriot but not a fool: he knew his role in the mission was over.

At least he still had his air ticket and false passport back at the hotel.

He had to get out of Dublin.

Fergus Lynskey met the chief superintendent in the gents' lavatory at headquarters. 'How're we going to handle the press? As soon as they know who's here it'll be open season. I'm not worried about the print media – it'll be too late for them – but you can be sure it'll break on radio and that'll draw crowds.'

'I'm scheduling an impromptu press conference here about the drugs find in Killybegs at the same time as the Amnesty conference. That'll divert some of them, but not for long, I suspect.'

'Why here?' Lynskey, who was combing his thatch, looked disparagingly at his reflection in the mirror. 'We've no facilities – why not in town?'

'Because Harcourt Square is too close to the concert hall, dummy!' The chief ran water into the basin and soaped his hands. 'Where's de Burgh? He's the liaison man with Killybegs, he'll have to be there.'

'He's out with the dogs. He shouldn't be too long but I'm not his keeper.'

'You're not anyone's keeper. How's the little American?'

'No comment,' but Lynskey caught himself grinning into the mirror.

'Yeah, yeah, who do you think you're fooling, Fergus?' The chief dried his hands and came across to punch his friend affectionately in the ribs. 'If you see de Burgh before I do, tell him to come in to see me, time's getting on.'

Rupert de Burgh, Bambi and Bambi's master had finished their sweep of the museum, and had joined up with another dog unit to check out the Dáil.

They had put it about that the reason for the security activity was that Naboom Kebele was making a brief visit but the rumour wheel had already started to turn. During ten minutes in the kitchens, they had been asked several times who was really coming. Although a porter had the correct name and one of the commis chefs said he had heard it was the Duke of Edinburgh, most of the hot money seemed to be on the Duke of York. Having spent more than half his life here, Rupert de Burgh still marvelled at the way information spread in Ireland. It gave a new twist to what folklorists liked to call the Oral Tradition.

Chapter Forty-Two

When they had finished in the Dáil, Rupert walked with his colleague back towards their cars. He had taken his own under the pretext of having to register a letter for his wife at the GPO, and not having wanted to drag along his colleague and the dog. 'Damn,' he felt around in his pockets now, 'I can't find my car keys. There's a hole in my trousers' pocket – they must have fallen through. You go on, tell them I'll be along as quick as I can.'

'Sure,' his colleague patted Bambi, 'see you back at the salt mines.'

Under the pretext of searching the ground, de Burgh delayed until the handler's vehicle had gone and then walked quicky to his own, which he had parked far enough away so as not to attract the dog. From the boot, he removed the briefcase containing the Semtex and handcuffed it to his wrist.

'I thought we'd got rid of you.' The museum's door attendant was cheerful.

'Just one last check.' Now out of earshot of his colleagues, De Burgh's tone was equally light-hearted. 'Can't be too careful. You might have put a bomb in the elephant's trunk since we were here!'

He walked upstairs and tramped purposefully all around the upper galleries, looking up at the ceiling, gazing at light fittings. When he came to the director's office, he knocked once then opened the door. 'All seems in order.'

Declan Corkery looked up at him. 'I'm afraid I need to use your lavatory,' Rupert smiled apologetically, 'sorry, I know it's locked, but it's a bit urgent. Bit inconvenient too,' he added, 'with this attached to me,' indicating the briefcase.

The men's washroom was on the first floor, to the left of the staircase. The director unlocked it, handed the key to the door attendant, and went back towards his office.

Once inside it took only a minute to place the butter packs, strung together by detonator wire, behind the bowl in one of the two stalls. He locked the door from the inside, stood on the toilet seat and climbed out over the partition into the neighbouring cubicle.

He washed his hands then, employing generous streams of Jif lemon juice, as a precaution against running into Bambi or one of his mates.

The attendant was waiting when he came out. 'That's better.' He assumed a jocose smile. 'It's just as well I came back, we forgot these.' He locked the door, returned the key to the attendant and out of the briefcase took two pieces of yellow police ribbon, the type used to seal off crime scenes. He fixed lengths across the door frames of both the gents' and ladies' washrooms. 'Now don't forget not to let anyone, even the Pope, in there until after the famous visit.'

'The staff toilet is sealed off too – what happens if we want to go?' the attendant objected.

'There are plenty of hotels and restaurants around,' Rupert offered. 'Can I rely on you to tell your boss? I've somewhere else to go and I'm running late.' He had to assume that staff, even directors, of a place like this were unused to security alerts.

He was not wrong: 'Don't worry,' the attendant waved an airy hand, 'you can count on me.'

Rupert went downstairs and as he left, again checked quickly behind both the inner and outer entrance doors. He had previously noted that while the inner door closed with a

481

Yale lock, suitable to his purpose, the outer was secured with both bolt and turnkey. As before, there was no sign of the key. 'Pretty impressive.' He saluted the attendant and left.

As he got into his car he realized his palms were sweating and took a moment to compose himself.

He drove into town and down Abbey Street, turning right into Liffey Street and parked outside the back entrance of Arnott's department store. He switched on his revolving light as though answering an alarm call, locked up and walked quickly through the Friday shoppers into the store.

The menswear department of Arnott's had managed to retain the old-fashioned atmosphere of a country draper's and the staff, although attentive, were not pushy, allowing customers to browse unmolested. Rupert walked along the rails, pulling out here a suit, there a sports jacket, as he made his way towards the expensive raincoats and chose one at the end of the rail, size 54. He slipped it off the hanger, which was made from moulded plastic, each end spread like a pad to fill out the garment's shoulders.

He tried on the raincoat and moved to a mirror, carrying the hanger. This morning, the department was busy but not crowded, with older men predominating, and no one paid him any attention as he twisted and turned as though assessing the fit of the coat. As he did so he pressed one of the teardop-shaped packages into the hollow under one of the hanger's shoulders.

He checked the coat again from a different angle, then, 'No, I don't think so.'

'Excuse me, sir,' a salesman came towards him, 'that one's too big. Let me get you one in your size.'

Rupert had been prepared for this. 'It's for my father. Arnott's is one of the few places he can get decent coats in

482

this size. But I'm not sure about this colour. I'll have to bring him in, I'm afraid.'

'Do that.' The salesman lost interest and looked away for the next prospect.

Rupert took off the coat, replaced it on its hanger and put it back exactly where he had found it. In that size it was unlikely to be tried on again before the incendiary went off in just over four hours' time, unless he was very very unlucky.

He repeated the exercise two hundred yards away, in Clery's of O'Connell Street.

As he drove back to headquarters he felt relieved, almost jolly, now that the gears of the operation had engaged. Stuck in traffic in College Green, he called the office and was told that the chief superintendent wanted to see him urgently. 'On my way,' he said, 'had a bit of trouble with the car. Be there in about ten minutes.'

Sky was talking to Éamonn Vaughan in the latter's automobile, coincidentally a Nissan but far bigger than her own. 'So you think there's no point?' She was downcast. 'None of your contacts could help? He's a nice man, I think he'd let me stay if he got permission.'

He shook his head slowly. 'No one I know'd help me out for something like this. If they let just one journalist in they'd be in trouble with the rest.'

'How about a pool arrangement? I'd share my stuff with everyone.'

'That happened when Reagan was here but we all had to have security clearance in advance, stand behind ropes, all that sort of thing.' Vaughan twisted his lips in bitter recollection. 'We've got to think of some other way. He's definitely going there before the Amnesty meeting?'

'Definitely.' Sky had been able to garner that much from

483

the director. 'But please, Éamonn,' she sat up abruptly, 'I'm trusting you not to show up with all the TV paraphernalia. Whatever chance we have, we'll have none if you do that. If you help me get in, I promise I'll rush straight up to the meeting and I'll give you every single tittle-tattle, every wag of his head or his little finger.'

She was glad she had not told him her suspicion that there might be some incident involving the so-called plotters and the Prince.

'I could always send down another crew – I gave you this story in the first place—' he began.

'But I was the one who discovered the Prince's identity – and it's something I would have found out from my contact, Fergus Lynskey anyway.'

Seeing she was getting upset, he relented. 'You'll share everything with me? All Lynskey's information?'

'Everything I can legitimately find out.' She nodded.

'Give me a moment.' He stared through the baking windshield of the car and she could almost hear the clicking of his mind.

Then she had a brainwave. 'What's the name of that wildlife TV presenter you introduced me to last night? I never caught it.'

'Rory Traynor. Ye-es,' he looked at her with admiration, 'I see what you're at. And, by the way, it's not only the museum. Rory's very well got with the Taoiseach, who's given to making statements about our priceless natural environment.'

'Where can I find him? Can I use your telephone?'

'Try Directory Enquiries, 1190, he lives somewhere in Terenure, I think.' He switched on the mobile and handed it to her.

To her great joy, Traynor himself answered and remembered immediately who she was. 'Look, Rory,' she said quickly, 'you may or may not be able to help. But you did say Montana was one of the places you always wanted to visit. If you can help me with what I ask, when I get back home I will do my utmost to get the Montana Parks and Wildlife Service to sponsor you out to Yellowstone or Glacier National Park.' She was skating on thin ice, but all too aware of the smirk on Vaughan's face, she intended to honour the pledge.

Rory Traynor chuckled and said he wished he could be bribed every day.

Encouraged, she explained what she was asking him to do. 'I hear you keep exalted company sometimes. Could you ask the Taoiseach first? I'm sure he'd say yes to *you*, Rory!'

'Don't I bring you to nice places?' Lynskey grinned. He and Sky were eating in Abrakebabra. 'What's the matter? You're not with me.'

'Sorry, I was just thinking.' Sky, who had told Rory Traynor she would call back in an hour, was peppering for the hour to be up but there was still fifteen minutes to go. She attempted to concentrate on her food. 'Well, at least they give you lots of meat – ughhh.' Some of the kebab sauce oozed out of its wrapping and down the front of her dress. 'I'll have to go back to the hotel and change.'

'Want me to come with you?'

'I thought you were busy – hey! I've just remembered!' Sky put down the kebab.

'You've just remembered what?' Lynskey stopped mid-chew.

'The rodeo, you were eating fast food at the rodeo.'

'Yes?' He looked mystified.

'That's where I saw him.'

'Who, for God's sake?'

She glared at him. 'Forget it. If you can't be civil—'

'All right, I'm really sorry, but I'm under desperate pressure and you're behaving like a lunatic. Who did you see at the rodeo that I remind you of?'

'It's that Canadian, Jerry Flynn. I saw him today. He doesn't look at all like himself, Fergus, he's cut his hair and he's shaved off his moustache but it was definitely him. I *knew* I knew him from somewhere. It was the gold teeth that did it. Lynskey, he's in Dublin.'

Immediately he forgot the rest of his meal.

Gárda headquarters gave every appearance of being close to organizational meltdown: police vehicles shot off with tyres squealing and people ran, rather than walked, through the offices.

In the chief superintendent's office, the atmosphere was no better: Rupert de Burgh was being bawled out. Despite his quiet and steadfast insistence that he could not be blamed for a puncture, or that the tightness of the wheel nuts had defied all efforts to remove the wheel, the chief was not having any. 'You could have called in, you pillock. Today of all days! Four people already have not showed up for work—'

'It's the overtime ban, sir.'

'I know it's the bloody overtime ban.' The chief's tone contrasted with his subordinate's in much the same way as those of an elephant and a cat. 'Don't tell me what I know!'

'I'm sorry, sir, but I was so intent on changing the wheel.'

'Look,' the chief waved impatiently, 'forget it. What's happening with the drugs recovery in Killybegs? I want a detailed report on my desk in fifteen minutes. And I will also want to know what *exactly* we will be saying at that press conference in four hours' time.' The telephone on his desk buzzed and he picked it up. 'What is it now?'

As he listened, all the bombast left him. 'I don't bloody

believe it.' He collapsed against the back of his chair, 'When? How long ago?'

De Burgh started to back out of the office but his superior stopped him with a glance. 'Ring me back as soon as you have any more details,' he said quietly into the telephone. He hung up, looked up at the other man. 'That was the detective unit in Mountjoy. There's been a bungled supermarket robbery in Finglas. A Securicor van. The driver's injured and so is one of the villains. We know them, a father and nephew. But as if that wasn't enough, turns out this villain's gun is an AK47. And get this, the other one's got away on a mountain bike – a *mountain bike*! There go more of my resources . . . Apparently half of the northside squad cars are at present careering around Finglas.'

It was clearly the last straw and de Burgh almost felt sorry for him but this couldn't have come at a better time.

At first, he did not make the connection. When he did his heart jolted.

It settled down again. Although one of the weapons he had given the plumber and Jerry Flynn had been a Kalashnikov AK47 automatic rifle, 'borrowed' from the Gárda stores of gear confiscated from IRA weapons dumps, it could not possibly have been used to rob a supermarket in Finglas. AK47s were not thick on the ground but they could be found without too much difficulty.

'Go and do that report,' the chief superintendent said quietly. 'And then you and Lynskey go out to Baldonnel. You can peel off for the press conference after I find a replacement for you. But stay in touch!'

'Yes, sir.' As he left the office, de Burgh was fingering the comforting outline of the TV remote control in his jacket pocket. As soon as he got to his desk, he called the hotel. Neither Mr Mulqueen nor his friend were in. 'No message.' He hung up.

*

'It's like World War Three.' A woman pushing a supermarket trolley had stopped on the path at a safe distance from the action.

'It's a disgrace, with kids around and all,' her friend agreed. The two settled down to watch as, across the wide green in front of them, a mare galloped, closely followed by her terrified foal. They were bolting ahead of a desperate young man on a mountain bike. In pursuit and closing fast were three squad cars, sirens blaring, rooflights blinking in the bright sunlight.

Suddenly the youth bucked the bike into a wheelie and doubled back towards the main road. The pursuing squad cars skidded on the soft grass allowing the cyclist to gain precious seconds. Still paced by the frantic horses, he was now travelling so fast his feet were just a blur on the pedals. The traffic along the main road was brisk enough, with cars travelling in both directions on or just above the speed limit. The youth hesitated just long enough to judge an infinitesimal gap between a car and a lorry travelling in opposite directions, and shot across between them, reaching the other side of the road before either had a chance to brake.

The police drivers, seeing their quarry speeding downhill across a stretch of reclaimed land which led steeply to the Tolka river and Dublin industrial estate on the opposite bank, screamed to the roadway, which curved towards a bridge half a mile away. A Gárda motorcyclist, lights flashing and siren blasting, now joined the chase.

Sky could not believe her luck.

When she got back to Traynor, five minutes before her hour was up, he had good news. 'I was honest. I told the Taoiseach I wanted to be there too, and about your promise to get me to Montana. He knows how much I've wanted to go there all these years. I've to keep an eye on you. But

488

the deal is you're not to tell a single other reporter, all right?'

She felt like dancing. 'Oh, Mr Traynor, I could kiss you.'

He chuckled again. 'Is that another promise? Just get me to Glacier. That'll be plenty.'

As soon as she hung up she called Jimbo but his response deflated her. 'All right, it's a scoop of sorts, I suppose,' he acknowledged grudgingly, 'but come on, Sky, the British Royal Family? Who cares?'

'This will be a *world exclusive*, Jim. You'll find our readers care. You'll be able to syndicate it.'

'I suppose so.' He was still reluctant. 'Now what about the real story? Are you any closer?'

'Oh, sorry, I've run out of money, I'll call you back.' Sky was so angry she cut him off even though the visual display still showed twenty-three units left on her card.

The windy acreage of Baldonnel aerodrome was not Fergus Lynskey's favourite location. He was uneasy that Jerry Flynn was in town and wished he was nearer the city – in Government Buildings or Áras an Uachtaráin, the Irish President's residence in the Phoenix Park.

The airfield bristled with security. All roads leading to it were closed off and the fields around were being patrolled by the Ranger unit of the Irish army – a highly trained response group; a convoy of army helicopters was lined up on the tarmac, ready for the transfer to the park. That was another thing: Lynskey hated travelling in helicopters, hated their weightless, stomach-dropping manoeuvrability. Some private, low-key visitation this was. Again he scanned the crowded apron: although there was no honour guard or colour party, there had to be nearly fifty people there, from the British ambassador to the Ministers for Justice and

Defence, civil servants, a few supposed close associates of the Prince and a contingent of army and police brass with more stars and stripes on their uniforms than the American flag.

'Excuse me a minute,' he said, to no one in particular, and moved away a little to a spot where he would have space to call into headquarters.

To say that the chief superintendent was hassled was the understatement of the millennium. Every short-staffed police station in the city was filled to the gills with rogues and thieves. One lot, the chief said, had even employed a Kalashnikov in an attempted supermarket robbery. 'That's all we need, the IRA.'

'Did you say attempted?' Lynskey covered his free ear with his hand as a burst of raucous laughter erupted near him. 'Did you recover the gun?'

'Yeah. It's with Technical now but they won't do anything with it until next week.'

'Here we go, gentlemen.' The Gárda Commissioner and a chief superintendent from a division other than Lynskey's were standing nearby. Lynskey looked to the eastern sky: he could see the landing lights of the RAF plane. 'I've got to go. I'll call in again when I get to the park.'

'Let's try one more time. Where'd you get the gun?' The detective sergeant tried to intimidate his captive with sheer bulk. The youth, who looked as though he could do with a decent meal, stared up at a spot at the wall behind the detective's head. After the chase he had been found hiding in a car parked in one of the factory lots on the industrial estate. 'You uncle's in bad shape, son.' The other policeman tried a more confidential approach. 'It's all over. Why don't you tell us? You never know, if you do, it might even go a bit easier on you in court. "He gave us full co-operation, Judge," you know how it goes.'

The youth interrupted his contemplation of the wall and darted a look at his interrogators. 'Look, can I have a cigarette?'

'Here you are.' The sergeant shook one out of a packet of Benson and Hedges and passed it over. The youth took a deep drag and exhaled, filling the small interview room with fumes. Neither detective blinked.

He told them then where he and his uncle had hired the guns.

At about that time, a Gárda officer from the severely under-resourced Technical Branch had just labelled the AK47, wrapped it in a plastic bag, and was putting it away in the strongroom at the Gárda depot in the Phoenix Park. 'That's funny.' He looked at the metal shelving, then back at the package in his hand.

He went to check records.

Chapter Forty-Three

The tension in the museum had quickened. The unfortunate door attendant had so far had to deal with two disappointed parties of schoolchildren – and their teachers – who had booked a tour, as well as several academics and irate tourists who, brandishing information leaflets and printed guides showing the opening times, had demanded to go in.

Sitting with Rory Traynor and the director in the latter's office, Sky mentally reviewed her options. She was going to get something interesting, even if it had to be a bottom-line, first person, 'How I Talked My Way Into Seeing The Prince' piece, which was not the *Courier*'s style. Better that than nothing – she was already winning.

She quailed, however, at the task of pulling everything together for her main piece: leaving the Prince aside, an article spanning drugs and guns and conspiracies linking Montana and Ireland was not going to be easy to encapsulate. She would probably need a *New Yorker* word-count.

At least it was happening quite fast, so she would not be costing the *Courier*'s skinflint proprietor too much of a bundle. 'Not long now, eh?' The director had gone home at lunchtime to change and had returned dressed up like a haberdasher's window. They had been told to expect the Prince at three o'clock.

*

'Alone and palely loitering . . .'

'What?' Rupert de Burgh spun as though on ice skates.

'Relax, de Burgh.' Lynskey looked at the Englishman with surprise. 'I was being ironic.' He surveyed the ranks of Gárda and army outriders lined up outside the President's residence. 'I think this is a hoot, to tell you the truth. Here we are with a so-called anonymous visitor, who's supposed to remain that way, about to scream through the city with all the traffic lights turned off, the whole shootin' gallery. Sure half the press corps'll be after us before we hit Parkgate Street.'

To save himself the necessity of replying, de Burgh walked over to the car he and Lynskey were to share in the motorcade. He was aware that he was betraying how tightly strung were his nerves. As he reached for the radio handset, he forced himself to breathe deeply. Only another quarter of an hour or so . . .

Behind him he heard a shuffling on the gravel as approximately six dozen booted feet got ready to mount their bikes. He replaced the handset without using it and straightened up to look towards the door where the Irish President was coming out alongside her guest. Instead, he encountered the puzzled eyes of Fergus Lynskey.

The organizers of the Amnesty conference, due to start at five o'clock to facilitate the nine fifteen start of the *The Late Late Show*, whose only guest would be Kebele, were in a tizzy. Their chickens had come home to roost with a vengeance, not least because it was now widely known that a mystery guest had been flown into Baldonnel in the presence of the British ambassador and had been helicoptered to Áras an Uachtaráin in the Phoenix Park. It was also known that half the motorcycle policemen in the city had been diverted

493

to traffic duty. It did not take much of a leap of imagination to know who was in town.

And it was not only the newshounds who knew: the efficient, village-style grapevine in Dublin had ensured that a respectably-sized crowd was already present outside the concert hall. 'I hope they're not going to blame me for this.' Jill Tuffy looked with satisfaction at the film crews scrabbling for ladders and stools and tripping each other with lead wires and cables. 'I told no one.'

'It doesn't matter now how it got out.' Her colleague glanced sidelong at her. 'I only hope our other guests aren't going to feel left out.'

'Nonsense.' The woman checked a list on her clipboard. 'This conference is going to be the lead this evening on every bulletin in Europe. The world, in fact. What time is it now? I want to listen to the three o'clock headlines.'

Toby de Burgh was sweating. The three telephone boxes from which he was making his calls were in close proximity to one another near Leicester Square but he had to walk fast if he was to complete his task in the six minutes his brother had allowed.

Two down.

He had called the Dublin radio stations, using the recognized code word given to him by his brother. To the first, he had called in a bomb warning in McDonald's of O'Connell Street, to the second, McDonald's of Grafton Street.

Now, he moved as fast as he dared without breaking into a run, glancing fearfully over his shoulder as though people could read his mind. The sweat was stinging his eyes and, under his loose-fitting silk shirt, he could feel uncomfortably cold streamlets running from his armpits to his waist. It was one of those intensely hot London days when the air seemed thick as lint, when taxi drivers, resigned to the stifling traffic jams, hold conversations with one another through their open windows. 'Christ, Rupe,' he mouthed as he side-stepped around one of these conversations, 'why did I agree to this . . .?' Then he looked over his shoulder again, afraid someone might have heard him.

He reached the third box, one of a row of four at the top of an alleyway.

Inserted two pounds coins. They dropped.

The third radio station on his list, RTE, did not answer until the fourteenth ring and his heart felt as though it was exploding by the time he gave his message. This one located the bomb at Bewley's of George's Street.

All three restaurants were located in busy areas. All three were crammed to the doors and evacuation would be difficult.

Task completed, the adrenalin drained away like a falling tide and Toby felt so weak he thought he might faint. He looked at his watch. Right on the button. Ten minutes to three.

At ten minutes to three, a hunched old man wearing a woollen cap, gloves, and a scarf wound so tightly around his neck that it covered part of his chin, in spite of the glorious sunshine, got into a taxi beside the central bus station. He carried no luggage, yet he asked the driver to take him to the airport. 'Do you take credit cards?' When told this was out of the question, he reached into his pocket and took out a fifty-dollar bill. 'I always keep this for emergencies.'

'I can't change it. I'm not a foreign-exchange bureau.' The driver looked at him through his rear-view mirror.

'It doesn't matter.' The old man hunched deeper into his scarf. 'Would fifty dollars cover the fare to the airport?'

'I suppose so.' The driver shrugged and drove off.

Flynn relaxed a little. He would have moved earlier but,

fearful of discovery, had spent more than an hour sitting in his room trying to second-guess his decision to abandon the operation. But the more time ticked by, the more he saw that he was trapped. Each minute increased the chances of his being found. It was not only the unfortunate incident with the guns, he was sure that that reporter girl from the rodeo had recognized him.

If only he could have reached de Burgh: he had telephoned twice, but each time his office had said he was out. By the third call, Flynn had left a message: John Mulqueen and his friend had been urgently called away and would be in touch. It was the best he could manage in the circumstances.

The cab driver cursed the traffic in which he was stalled at the junction of Gardiner Street and the North Circular Road but Flynn cheered up somewhat: just because *this* adventure had not worked out did not mean there would not be another day. The Cause was still there, still waiting for someone to espouse it. He heard police sirens in the distance and tensed but then he realized they were receding. Only another hour or so and he should be in the clear.

Joe Mason, wearing his scratched glasses, was already at the airport, boarding a flight for Amsterdam. He had wasted no time in introspection but had left the hotel as soon as he had heard from Flynn what had happened to him.

Rupert de Burgh was now on his own.

In checking the records, the policeman who was logging in the AK47, confiscated after the supermarket robbery, had discovered that it had been logged in before – less than a month ago. He found no record of it having been removed.

And as he went on, he found something else peculiar:

496

three other guns were unaccounted for too, two pistols and a second assault rifle.

The Gárdaí had been recently successful in locating and raiding IRA arms and ammunitions dumps in the republic, and there were so many weapons in storage that it was not surprising that the absence of just four had been overlooked. Especially with the resources situation as it was.

He reported the discrepancy to his superior, who immediately passed it up the line.

The Prince's entourage was coming down the North Circular Road and crossing the big junction at Dorset Street, to the complete apathy of most of the pedestrians who were used to having their thoroughfare turned into a scene from *Starsky and Hutch*. Motorists stuck in the already heavy Friday afternoon traffic, who found themselves being waved peremptorily to the side by the advance riders, were not so sanguine and beat an angry tattoo on their horns.

De Burgh, with Lynskey beside him, was driving one of the lead cars. Such was the racket from the outriders behind them that the latter felt, rather than heard, his mobile ring against his thigh. He drew it out of his pocket and yanked up the tiny rubber aerial. 'Yes?'

All he got was static and interference. 'I can't hear you, whoever you are,' he yelled. 'Call back in a couple of minutes. We're just coming into Mountjoy Square.'

He switched the telephone to standby, looked across at de Burgh and shrugged.

Outside the concert hall, Éamonn Vaughan and the BBC reporter who had been the lucky recipient of Jill Tuffy's second telephone call the previous afternoon, were closeted in Vaughan's car. Their crews were part of the mêlée inside.

As they compared notes, a squad car, which had been passing at a sedate pace, suddenly spurted, tyres spinning. Then, lights flashing and siren blaring, it squealed around the corner out of view.

'What was that?' Vaughan jumped out of the car and listened. He heard another siren join the first. 'It's nearly three o'clock. Quick! Turn on the car radio!' He whipped out his personal stereo and put on his headphones.

'*Oh my God!*' The woman browsing through the men's raincoats in Arnott's department store jumped back and snatched her baby from his buggy as a tongue of flame shot through a coat at the end of the rail. She screamed as she pulled the buggy after her, cannoning into a display of Viyella shirts, which collapsed as staff and customers started to run. A quick-witted trainee manager grabbed an extinguisher and put out the small fire, but it was too late to avert chaos. The woman continued to scream, her baby, too, and a stampede began for the doors.

In Clery's, less than a quarter of a mile away, a middle-aged Texan tourist was not so lucky. Tall – he had been a basketball player in his youth – and broad now that muscle had turned to fat, he was just reaching for a coat when the incendiary went up, catching the side of his face and setting fire to his abundant snowy hair.

It happened so fast that his wife, browsing thirty feet away, did not know anything was amiss until she heard a girl scream. She turned round just in time to see someone throw a heavy wool shawl over her husband's head. One side of his face looked like a piece of grilled steak.

The information was coming in too fast: the chief superintendent put his head in his hands. The bomb scares had distracted him from a picture he saw hovering vaguely just outside his ken. He pulled a pad in front of him:

- AK 47 turns up at the supermarket robbery
- so does handgun
- handgun hired from kids who got it in mugging
- chances are AK47 part of same mugging
- Jerry Flynn recognized by Lynskey's girlfriend. Fits description of mugged tourist.

He picked up his telephone: 'Get me the names of everyone who signed in to that store-room at the depot in the last week. Everyone who doesn't work there. I want an answer NOW.' He flung the receiver back in its cradle whereupon the telephone rang again.

In the museum, Sky felt absurdly like a teenager. She had tried to persuade herself she was feeling this way because she was about to get a world exclusive – but if she was honest she had to admit the excitement was prompted by the prospect of meeting a real live prince.

'What is it about royalty?'

The director reacted as though she had struck one of his own specimen pins into him. 'What do you mean?'

'Oh, it doesn't matter. Are you sure you don't want us to be in the background?' She looked at Rory Traynor who seemed as calm as though he did this kind of thing every day.

'You're fine where you are.' The director glanced at his watch. 'Any minute now.'

As if on cue, Sky heard the bagpipe wailing of sirens.

'Jesus, he's here!' The director half ran towards the door and then back to the place he had allocated himself.

'Relax, Declan.' Oddly his agitation calmed Sky. 'It'll all be over in three or four minutes.'

'He'd better stay longer than that. After all we've been through . . .'

'Who?' The chief superintendent rose in his seat. 'Quickly! Are you sure he was the only one not actually working there?'

Whatever the person at the other end said caused him to drop the telephone and race out of the room. He was punching at his mobile as he ran towards the general office. 'Lynskey,' he hissed urgently into the mouthpiece, 'Are you alone?'

'No, chief,' Lynskey pulled a face, 'as you can hear we're surrounded by the third army. We're just pulling up now outside the museum.' The outriders came alongside and the rest of what the chief had to say was drowned in the thunder of motorcycle engines. 'What, chief?' Lynskey got out of the car as, behind him, the Prince and his entourage, to the heart-stopping amazement of the rapidly growing crowd, got out of theirs. All he could hear now was static. The chief was no longer on the line.

Rupert de Burgh looked towards where Jerry Flynn should have been. He was to have hijacked a bus and its passengers from outside Trinity College and have it at the intersection of Merrion Street and Merrion Square just before the Prince's party arrived and then drive it straight towards Government Buildings to distract the police from what he was about to do. But as he followed Lynskey towards the Prince's party, his heart pounded. There was no sign of any bus.

He saw that the Prince, instead of walking straight through the iron gate that led into the museum, had stopped just outside to shake hands and chat with Dublin citizens and thrilled tourists who were being corralled by a phalanx of policemen.

'He's got a gun.' Improvising wildly de Burgh ran after Lynskey and caught him by the sleeve.

'Who's got a gun?' Lynskey wheeled.

'That man over there!' He pointed up the street towards where an unkempt youth, curious about the commotion, was running towards them.

The mobile telephone in Lynskey's hand shrilled again. 'What?' he yelled into it, while keeping an eye on the fast approaching boy. He could see no gun.

More crackle, then, distinctly: 'Don't let de Burgh near the Prince.' The voice in his ear was low and commanding. 'He's our canary.'

The Prince and his bodyguards were now through the gate and walking up the path. Lynskey saw that de Burgh was now right behind them and closing fast. The youth indicated by de Burgh carried nothing in either hand. Lynskey started to run through the crowd.

He got to de Burgh just as the policeman reached the Prince and his group. They were only feet from the door now and the welcoming party which included – to Lynskey's horror – Sky MacPherson. Then he saw de Burgh's hand snake into his pocket.

Lynskey launched a flying tackle through the bodyguards, connecting with his colleague's back and knocking him off balance just as the Semtex erupted through the building. The bodyguards wrestled the Prince aside to safety but the momentum of Lynskey's tackle carried him and de Burgh through the doorway into the dust and debris flying through the gallery. Lynskey caught a brief glimpse of Sky's startled face before he and his colleague fell to the tiled floor.

*

De Burgh's plan had been to shove the Prince into the museum ahead of him as the bomb exploded and to slam and lock both the heavy outer door and the inner one. He would have about five minutes in which to force the Prince to sign a statement apologizing for British atrocities before he shot him. Just as his paratroopers had gunned down thirteen innocent civilians in Derry.

Instead, he found himself fighting for his own life.

Twenty years of planning and patient waiting all gone for nothing.

But twenty years of suppressed fury lent de Burgh a sudden spurt of strength and determination. He gouged at Lynskey's eyes and as his colleague instinctively arched his back, threw him off.

Lynskey spun through the inner doorway, giving de Burgh time to spring to his feet and bolt the outer door. In the split second before Lynskey came at him, he raised his gun.

Slowly, Lynskey lowered his and backed inside.

With a flick of his shoulder de Burgh closed the inner door.

Chapter Forty-Four

Everything had happened so fast that Sky did not even have a chance to scream. One moment she had been standing on tiptoe to see over the museum director's shoulder as the Prince approached, the next there had been a huge explosion, which had blown Lynskey and another man into the museum. The neon lights overhead had gone out and half of the ceiling had crashed down along with waterfalls of glass, while something huge and dark descended to fill her peripheral vision. Transfixed by the two men fighting on the floor, she was afraid to look away to see what it was.

The contest had lasted only seconds and then Lynskey's assailant had leaped to the door.

She could hardly breathe: the air was choked with fur, feathers, and ancient dust. She covered her mouth and nose with one hand and dared to look over it. Through the waning hailstorm of fragments she saw the second man standing against the closed door pointing a gun at them. The huge dark object was the skeleton of the whale from the gallery overhead. Most of it dangled by the tail bones through the destroyed ceiling.

Beside her, she could hear someone moaning. The director was on his knees, blood streaming from a gash at the temple, just under his hairline. Without thinking, she moved to help him, but the gunman roared at her: 'Stay where you are!'

'Let her be, de Burgh.' Shoes scrunching on shards of

glass, Lynskey pulled himself upright and came over to her. He, too, had a gun but it was held loosely by his side. Paradoxically, because his voice was so calm and matter-of-fact, Sky's heart lurched with fear. 'She's a civilian,' Lynskey said quietly, 'they're all civilians here except you and me. Let them out.'

'Stay where you are. *All of you, I'm warning you . . .*' The man called de Burgh bent his knees a little and pressed the small of his back harder against the door. He raised the gun, which he now held in both hands.

'How many rounds do you have, de Burgh? There're seven of us in here.' Lynskey stepped in front of Sky.

'Get back behind her *and drop your gun.*' His face contorted.

Lynskey extended his arm to its fullest extent and let the gun fall, theatrically, from between finger and thumb.

It occurred to Sky then that less than a minute could have passed since the door was shut. Dimly, she discerned that the attendant, the assistant director, Traynor and the other two men on the staff, were huddled together behind herself and Lynskey. Absurdly, the police ribbon taped across the door of the ladies' washroom was still intact, like a gay yellow flag. She remembered where she had seen this man before. He was the policeman who had questioned her about her ID.

Now only the director's harsh, half-sobbing breath could be heard. She did not dare move her head to look at him again. 'So now what, de Burgh?' Lynskey's voice was low, almost hypnotic. 'You can't kill us all, you know that. Why not just let them go? I'll stay in here with you. Just let them go. I've no gun now, even. There's no way out for you, you know that, so why not let them go?' He took a step forwards.

'Stay *back*! De Burgh lifted the gun higher, aiming at Lynskey's face. 'Back beside her.'

'Come on.' Lynskey took another step.

De Burgh lowered the gun and discharged it. Sky leaped

at the intolerable level of sound in the enclosed space and at the detonation of glass just in front of Lynskey's feet. This time she screamed and so did one of the men behind her.

'OK, OK.' Lynskey raised his hands and stepped back beside her.

The director collapsed into the glass under him.

'He's hurt, he needs help.' Sky's yell unnerved the gunman: 'Shut up, shut up, *shut up*!' He fired again, towards the ceiling this time, and hit the suspended whale skeleton. At such close quarters, the force of the bullet dislodged the remains and the giant cradle of bones cascaded to the floor, destroying what remained of the glass cases below it with earsplitting impact.

Sky closed her eyes and reached into her reserves of courage while the reverberations of the shot and the bursting glass continued. Beside her, the director whimpered softly.

'How many left now, de Burgh?' This was Lynskey, as the air gradually stilled.

His quiet tone seemed to calm the gunman. 'All right, you three,' his voice was decisive as he waved the gun at the staff members cowering behind their boss, 'pick up the injured man and take him outside. You, Lynskey, step over to the wall while they're doing it.' He hesitated, then: 'You can go with them,' pointing to Rory Traynor.

Then he motioned to Sky. 'You stay here, but first pick up that gun and hand it to me.'

From outside, Sky heard an amplified voice but it was too muffled for her to distinguish what it was saying. At least someone was thinking about their plight. Lynskey's gun felt like a lump of ice as she picked it up and, holding it in front of her like a votive offering, walked across the strewn no man's land to give it to the gunman.

He took it almost casually and placed it in his belt under his open jacket; he seemed to be regaining confidence with every second. 'Now,' he said to her, 'you stay here beside me. You three, pick up that injured man now and take him out. If there's any funny stuff while the door's open, I'm going to shoot this girl. And please don't think I'm not serious. I've nothing to lose.'

'Let her go too, de Burgh.' It was Lynskey again, from his position by the wall. 'Why are you involving her?'

'For the last time, Lynskey, will you shut up? I've been listening to your blather now for more years than I care to remember.' As she stood near him, penetrating Sky's senses was the surprising smell of lemons.

The three frightened men shuffled over to their director and picked him up, two at his shoulders, one at his feet. Blood had soaked into both sides of his shirt collar before spreading to the rest of his clothes and Sky had to avert her eyes: in the dim light, his mouth open and head dangling as though half-severed, he looked as though his throat had been cut.

'Now, here's what you're going to do.' The gunman's voice was right beside her ear. 'I'm going to open the door a little and you're going to appear in it. Not one step outside, understand? You're going to tell whoever's out there that an injured man is coming out. That's all. Then you're to step back inside. I'm going to be three inches behind you with a gun pointed at your head. Is that clear?'

'Yes.' From some reservoir she had not known she possessed, Sky found the courage to speak.

The gunman stepped sideways so he could cover not only her, but Lynskey at the far wall. He opened the inner door slowly and she felt his hand at her back, pushing her forward.

Slowly, with his back to the outer door, he reached up and pulled back the bolt. A crack of daylight appeared.

Then she could see, only feet away but to both sides of the door, several policemen all with guns drawn. About fifty feet away was a statue on a large stone plinth. Behind it were more policemen, and outside the railings she could see about twenty police cars. The man with the megaphone was in plain clothes, standing by the gate.

As the door opened wider, a number of armed policemen dropped to their knees and took aim. Birds sang in the branches of nearby trees as if nothing had happened, but everyone outside was as frozen as the bronze statue on the plinth.

She felt the pressure of the gunman's hand on her back. 'Excuse me,' she said, 'there's an injured man coming out.' The hand in her back pressed harder and, although for one blazing moment she considered making a dash for it, she reversed through the opening and back into the Museum. Just before the outside world vanished from her view she saw Éamonn Vaughan arrive at the railings.

Inside again, she was ordered to stand beside Lynskey while the three men, followed by Rory Traynor, left with their burden. Then de Burgh closed the door and she was marooned with him and Lynskey. She pressed close against Lynskey for reassurance and was conscious of something, a piece of paper, being crushed into her hand. 'Stand away from each other.' De Burgh waved the gun to emphasize his point.

'Now what?' As he stepped away from her, Lynskey was again speaking in that calm, mesmeric way. 'There's no way out.'

'Oh, yes, there is.' De Burgh smiled, 'I'm not stupid enough to think that it'll all work out happily ever after but at least I'm going to make my point.'

'What is your point?' Searching her palm with her curled fingers, Sky was now sure that Lynskey had passed her a note.

'You're not going to catch me as easily as that—' de Burgh began, when Lynskey's telephone rang.

De Burgh reacted to the shrilling as though shot by his own gun. 'Turn that thing *off*!'

'You're very jumpy.' Lynskey disabled the telephone and then, still holding it, leaned against the wall, crossing one foot over the other. 'Look, de Burgh, all your friends are rounded up, every last blessed one of them. There is nothing you can do by yourself. You know it, I know it, so why are we all wasting our time?'

Outside, the muffled instructions, or whatever they were, continued unabated.

While keeping her eyes fixed on the gunman, Sky was surreptitiously unravelling the balled note with her bent thumb and little finger. She was sure it contained instructions and, when the opportunity arose, she wanted to be able to read them at a glance. Her concentration on such a minor, but vital task, as well as Lynskey's close, warm proximity and calm demeanour, gave her some small sense of safety.

The world had shrunk to the dimensions of this murky room; and somehow it felt appropriate that the setting for such a bizarre act was in itself so fantastic: the gigantic whale pancaked like collapsed scaffolding on the floor, half of an antler at the gunman's foot, and beside her own, the small glass eye which stared at her from a nest of dust.

'All right.' De Burgh had recovered his composure. 'She's staying in here with me. Lynskey, you go outside and tell them that I want to see the Commissioner. In here. Unarmed and alone.'

'You're the boss.' Lynskey started to move forwards.

'Slowly, hands above your head where I can see them.' De Burgh raised his gun, covering every inch of the other policeman's movement.

Slowly, step by step, hands above his head – Sky noticed he still held the telephone – Lynskey advanced towards the door.

De Burgh never took his eyes off him. As Lynskey got closer, he circled away from his adversary, always keeping a distance of about six feet between them. Lynskey was almost at the door now, was reaching out to open it—

Sky screamed at the top of her lungs.

De Burgh glanced towards her.

Lynskey hurled the telephone into his adversary's face while unleashing a flying, two-footed tackle at the gun, which dropped to the floor and discharged, the bullet passing harmlessly through the open door of the men's washroom. Then he leapt on De Burgh in an assault so quick and professional that the gunman did not have a chance. He was brought down and flipped on to his stomach. Lynskey twisted his colleague's gun arm up behind his back while retrieving his own weapon from the waistband underneath.

The door crashed open from outside and dozens of armed men poured through.

It was dark but not quite night and, for several seconds, Sky had no idea where she was. Then she heard Lynskey's deep, even breathing beside her in the narrow bed. To judge by the quality of the light, they must have slept for hours.

She lay quietly, listening to the sounds of the city below. The events of the afternoon seemed like a dream. After the rescue, she had refused to go to hospital, or even to see a doctor, although she was familiar enough with psychobabble to expect some sort of physical or mental reaction to what had happened. At present, however, she felt nothing but a numbed peace.

In the immediate aftermath of the event she had insisted on filing verbatim copy immediately from the nearest telephone, which proved to be in the museum director's office. It was odd to do so in the presence of Lynskey, another policeman and Éamonn Vaughan, to whom she had honoured her promise. She had even been composed enough to give him a short interview on camera outside the museum. And to accept Jimbo's handsome apology for his earlier cynicism.

Then, she and Lynskey had come to his apartment directly from the museum: for once, he had been excused the briefing – or de-briefing or whatever it was he normally had to do.

At first she had been reluctant to accompany him, feeling she would be better to go back to her own hotel, have a shower and make the necessary telephone calls. But, even as she was insisting, she was overtaken by lamb-like languor, which allowed Lynskey to persuade her to go with him. Once inside his apartment he had undressed her, quickly and efficiently, given her one of his shirts to wear as a nightdress and ordered her to bed. She had fallen asleep – within seconds, it seemed.

By what little available light there was, she saw that his tiny apartment was Spartan. Apart from the bed, the room had a narrow floor-to-ceiling closet, a chest, which appeared to serve as a dressing-table, one chair, on which her clothes had been neatly folded, and a single night-stand on her side of the bed, with a lamp, a telephone and an old-fashioned alarm clock with two bright silvery bells.

She realized that her hand ached and discovered that it was clenched into a fist and that she could not relax it. Lynskey's note remained speared between her fingernails and her palm, welded there when she had screamed to divert de Burgh's attention. Was this the reaction she had been expecting? Did she now have a paralysed hand?

'Are you awake?' He did not move.

'Yes.'

'Would you like a cup of tea – sorry, coffee?'

'Sure.' She wondered why they were whispering.

Behind her, she felt him slide out of bed and heard him pad towards the door. She eased a little into the warm space he had left.

'Will I put on the light?' He was back after five minutes or so, carrying two mugs.

'No, it's nice like this.' She pushed her pillow up against the bedhead and leaned against it. He held out one of the mugs to her but as she tried to take it, she realized again that she could not open her hand.

'What's the matter with your hand, Sky?' He put down both mugs on the floor and got in beside her. 'Show me.' She let him take it and, after a brief examination, he leaned across her and switched on the bedside light. 'It's bleeding. Sky, what happened?'

'I don't know. I can't open it   your note's in there.'

He enclosed her hand in both of his and started to massage the inside of her wrist, just above the palm. Little by little, she sensed warmth, first in the heel, then creeping up her thumb. It was only when her nails finally unbedded that she felt the sting of the four small crescents of dried blood, like sickle moons, which lay along the centre of the palm. The note was crushed and stained beyond legibility. 'Don't worry about it.' Gently, Lynskey prised it off.

'What did it say?

'It was nothing, forget it. Try to forget everything about this afternoon.'

'I still have to write the piece. What I filed on the telephone was just a holding story.'

'Yeah. How could I have been so silly?' He grinned. 'Now do you want your coffee?'

They lay back together on their pillows. 'Please tell me what was on the note, Fergus.' Sky stared straight up at the ceiling.

She heard the smallest of hesitations, like a sigh on the intake then: 'The note would have said I love you.'

'Would have?'

'Yeah, it was just a piece of paper. I thought it would distract you.'

He loved her. Sky experienced no feeling of surprise, elation, or, for the first time when faced with this declaration, any panic or fear. 'I think I love you too.'

'You only think?' Another hesitation. Then he raised himself on an elbow.

'It doesn't come easy to me, you know.'

He smiled, closed his eyes and lay back again, which was exactly the correct reaction. If he had pressed her she might have fled. The acknowledgement was fragile. The warm air of the room crept around the narrow bed and isolating it it in a web of shared intimacy such as she had experienced only once or twice in her life, and not for years.

She had nearly finished her coffee when the practical problems of a relationship with Lynskey rose to the surface of her sluggish brain. They might yet prove insurmountable. 'What about the practical problems?'

'I love you, Sky.' He turned his head towards her, pulled back a little so their eyes could focus on one another.

Sky smiled at his certainty. She could feel the smile beginning at the soles of her feet and travelling up the length of her body until it reached her face, and she thought she could never, ever wipe it away. 'Would it be all right if I called the hospital?' She did not yet want to discuss the reasons for the smile. 'I don't want Mom to see me on the early evening news.'

'Go ahead.' He smiled too, resumed his contemplation of the ceiling.

When she got through to Johanna, her grandmother was there, and Hermana, 'and Buffy's coming in too for a spell. It's a real sorority dorm now, Sky, we're having a ball.' As soon as Sky began to prepare her for what she might see on the TV, however, she was immediately disabused of the notion that this was news. 'Fergus told us all about it. You're a heroine, Sky, we're really, really proud of you, all of us.'

As she heard the round robin of approval in the background, Sky looked over at Lynskey, who was calmly sipping his tea. 'When did he call you?'

'Oh, ages ago, he's very proud of you too, Sky. You give him a big hug from all of us.'

'When's Daniel Treacy's wake?' Sky thought it safer to change the subject. She had lost track of the days.

'Em . . .' her mother grew shifty.

'What's the matter, Mom? Is it over? Did something happen I should know about?'

'Look, Sky, your grandma would like to talk to you.'

Sky heard whispering and, after a short pause, her grandmother was on the line. 'What's all this about, Grandma?'

'Please don't take this amiss, Sky. We're just thinking about it and no decisions will be taken without your say-so. But your mother and I – that is all of us here, Buffy and Hermana too – had a thought. We were wondering how you would feel about all of us, not immediately, of course, for obvious reasons, temporarily taking on the care of Daniel's wife?'

The telephone was seized back before Sky could collect her wits. 'What do you think, Sky?' Johanna's voice was as fresh as though she had been out picking daisies instead of cemented into a body cast in a hospital. 'Sort of as a project. As your grandma says, not immediately, what with me in the hospital and poor Midge too. And you don't have to be involved, Sky. She has enough money coming to her that she could buy half of Butte. And your grandma says the house up in the foothills is lovely. Plenty of space up there – we can hire nurses until she gets on her feet again. But she has no one now, Sky. Only money. We'd all help. Freda Little Calf has a lot of experience in dealing with alcohol problems, you know she has—'

'Whoa, whoa, Mom.' For Sky it was like turning back the

clock. Nothing had happened in the last three weeks, no Lynskey, no Ireland, no guns or bullets or fantastical situations. She was back to square one with her mother.

And yet, suddenly, it was different. Suddenly she saw a gate opening on to a huge green field: she need not engage. 'I think it's a great idea.'

The astonished silence at the other end of the telephone bore testimony to what had occurred between them. 'Are you still there? Mom?'

'Are you sure you don't mind?'

'Why should I mind? Is Grandma going to stay there and help you?'

'No,' her mother chuckled, 'of course not, her life is in Ireland. But she'll stay long enough until we get the project up and running.'

'You're amazing, Mom do you know that? And I love you very, very much.'

She hung up abruptly. It was then that the tears came. And came.

Lynskey held her.